A

Philip E. Lilienthal

. ▪ . ▪ . ▪

B O O K

The Philip E. Lilienthal imprint
honors special books
in commemoration of a man whose work
at University of California Press from 1954 to 1979
was marked by dedication to young authors
and to high standards in the field of Asian Studies.
Friends, family, authors, and foundations have together
endowed the Lilienthal Fund, which enables UC Press
to publish under this imprint selected books
in a way that reflects the taste and judgment
of a great and beloved editor.

The publisher gratefully acknowledges the generous contribution to this book provided by the Philip E. Lilienthal Asian Studies Endowment Fund of the University of California Press Foundation, which is supported by a major gift from Sally Lilienthal. The publisher also gratefully acknowledges the generous contribution to this book provided by the Chiang Ching-Kuo Foundation for International Scholarly Exchange.

The Art of Doing Good

The Art of Doing Good

Charity in Late Ming China

Joanna Handlin Smith

UNIVERSITY OF CALIFORNIA PRESS

Berkeley   Los Angeles   London

University of California Press, one of the most distinguished
university presses in the United States, enriches lives around the
world by advancing scholarship in the humanities, social sciences,
and natural sciences. Its activities are supported by the UC Press
Foundation and by philanthropic contributions from individuals
and institutions. For more information, visit www.ucpress.edu.

University of California Press
Berkeley and Los Angeles, California

University of California Press, Ltd.
London, England

Library of Congress Cataloging-in-Publication Data

Smith, Joanna Handlin.
    The art of doing good : charity in late Ming China / Joanna
Handlin Smith.
        p.   cm.
    Includes bibliographical references and index.
    ISBN: 978-0-520-25363-6 (cloth : alk. paper)
    1. Charities—China—History.   2. Charity organization—
China—History.   3. China—History—Ming dynasty, 1368–1644.
I. Title.
HV418.S57   2009
361.70951'09032—dc22   2008040823

Manufactured in the United States of America

18   17   16   15   14   13   12   11   10   09
10   9   8   7   6   5   4   3   2   1

This book is printed on Natures Book, which contains 50%
post-consumer waste and meets the minimum requirements
of ANSI/NISO Z39.48–1992 (R 1997) (*Permanence of Paper*).

For Bob

CONTENTS

ACKNOWLEDGMENTS

If completing this book required considerable time, it was because the subject of charity baited my curiosity, drawing me deeper and deeper into the writings and worlds of late Ming benefactors, from the high-flown moral pronouncements of Yang Dongming and Gao Panlong to the absorbing, concrete details about activities in the medical dispensaries and rural soup kitchens reported by Qi Biaojia. My journey was greatly enriched by the scholarly contributions and the friendly support of Fuma Susumu and Angela Ki Che Leung (Liang Qizi), two historians who, though initiating their studies of charity at about the same time as I, published their studies first—in Japanese and Chinese, respectively. I not only have had the advantage of their books on Ming-Qing charity but also have benefited from their generosity in sharing documents with me. Also immensely helpful was Pierre-Étienne Will, pioneer in the study of Chinese famine relief. For his generosity in meticulously reading chapter 6, and making beneficial suggestions and some face-saving corrections, I am extremely grateful.

I have had the good fortune of access to the Harvard-Yenching Library for many decades—going back to the days of Chiu Kaiming. If I now occasionally shudder to recall that he kindly allowed me to take rare Ming editions home, I also appreciate that the intimate contact with those editions may have secured my fascination with Ming history. The Harvard-Yenching Library continues to be a wonderful resource, not only for its superb collection, which, under James Cheng's expert stewardship, has grown tremendously, but also for its staff, many of whom are themselves dedicated scholars. The entire staff has been extremely helpful, but I must especially single out the Curator of Rare Books, Chun Shum, for graciously helping me to decipher various problems in Chinese texts; Ellen McGill, for guiding me through ever-expanding electronic resources; and Horst Huber, for sharing his familiarity with recent European publications on China.

I have also greatly benefited from the remarkable collection of Ming-dynasty works in the Gest Collection at the East Asian Library, Princeton University, and particularly from the help of fellow Ming scholar, the Head of Public Services, Martin Heijdra.

For his extraordinary generosity in sharing information about publishing and in giving advice about my own work, I thank John Ziemer, masterly editor and friend. For help in preparing the two maps for this book, I thank Merrick Lex Berman of the China Historical Geographic Information System, Harvard University. Many other colleagues and friends have generously responded to my requests for information or for help in clarifying the meanings of difficult passages. I should like to thank in particular James Cahill, Katy Carlitz, Timothy Connor, Patrick Hanan, Haihong Li, Lillian M. Li, Nathan Sivin, Lynn Struve, Buzzy Teiser, Tu Weiming, Richard Von Glahn, Ann Waltner, Chün-fang Yü, and Judith Zeitlin. Sadly neither Frederic E. Wakeman, Jr., nor Frederick Mote, each of whom commented on early versions of portions of this book, are here to receive my thanks.

Early research for this book was generously funded by the American Council of Learned Societies and a Wang Institute Fellowship in Chinese Studies. I am extremely grateful to the Chiang Ching-Kuo Foundation for a grant subsidizing publication of this book, and to the Harvard-Yenching Institute for supporting the preparation of the index.

Parts of this book are drawn from material that was first published elsewhere. I thank the Association for Asian Studies, Inc., for permission to use material from: "Benevolent Societies: The Reshaping of Charity during the Late Ming and Early Ch'ing," *Journal of Asian Studies* 46.2 (1987): 309–37; "Gardens in Ch'i Piao-chia's Social World: Wealth and Values in Late-Ming Kiangnan," *Journal of Asian Studies* 51.1 (1992): 55–81; "Liberating Animals in Ming-Ch'ing China: Buddhist Inspiration and Elite Imagination," *Journal of Asian Studies* 58.1 (1999): 51–84. I thank Koninklijke Brill N.V. for permission to use material from: "Opening and Closing a Dispensary in Shanyin County: Some Thoughts about Charitable Associations, Organizations, and Institutions in Late Ming China," *Journal of the Economic and Social History of the Orient* 38.3 (August 1995): 371–92; "Social Hierarchy and Merchant Philanthropy as Perceived in Several Late-Ming and Early-Qing Texts," *Journal of the Economic and Social History of the Orient* 41.3 (1998): 417–51. I thank Indiana University Press for permission to use material from: "Chinese Philanthropy as Seen through a Case of Famine Relief in the 1640s," in *Philanthropy in the World's Traditions,* edited by Warren Ilchman, Stanley Katz, and Edward Queen (Bloomington: Indiana University Press, 1998), 133–68.

CONVENTIONS, MEASUREMENTS, AND DYNASTIES

CONVENTIONS

Late Ming writers customarily used courtesy names (*zi*) or pen names
(*hao*) when referring to their contemporaries, and posthumous
names for the deceased. Rather than burdening the reader with
a plethora of variant names for a given figure, I use, when known,
only the given name (*ming*), even when translating passages using
a variant. I have made an exception for Wang Shouren, who is now
best known by his pen name Yangming.

Qi Biaojia's diary uses informal terms for the titles of local officials. Where
I have been able to ascertain the actual position, I usually substitute
the actual title but occasionally, for variety's sake, retain such informal terms as "local authority" (*gongzu*) or the general term "official."

References to Lu Shiyi's diary, *Zhixue lu,* provide the month and day for
the daily entries, and page numbers for the ten-day summaries and
the editor's interlinear comments.

References to Qi Biaojia's diaries provide the year, month, and day for daily
entries, and page numbers for the prefaces.

If the referents are clearly stated in a Chinese passage from which I am
translating a short extract, I interpolate the clarifying words without
the conventional but clumsy use of brackets.

Occasionally I translate *juan* as "chapter," even though the term refers to
sections of a book that do not always coincide with thematic breaks.

The dates of all important Ming- and Qing-dynasty figures, when known,
are provided in the index.

When referring to places, Ming writers often used informal or ancient
names. I have standardized nomenclature, providing in parentheses
the name used in the text.

In reckoning age, the Chinese count the first year of life as year (*sui*) one.
I either retain the term *sui,* or speak of someone as being in his *n*th
year.

CURRENCY, WEIGHTS, AND MEASURES
Uncoined Silver

1 *liang* (tael) = 1 ounce of silver (not coin)
1 *qian* = 0.1 tael
1 *fen* = 0.01 tael

Coins

1,000 *wen* (bronze cash) = 1 string (*guan*)

The ratio of cash to silver fluctuated greatly during the late Ming, from
roughly 500:1 to 2,500:1. (See Von Glahn, *Fountain of Fortune,*
106–9.)

Capacity

1 *shi* = approximately 156 pounds of milled rice
1 *hu* = 5 *dou*
1 *dou* = 0.1 *shi*
1 *sheng* = 0.1 *dou*
1 *ge* = 0.1 *sheng*

Land Area

1 *mou* = 0.1647 acre
100 *mou* = 1 *qing*

Distance

1 *li* = 0.3 mile

DYNASTIES AND REIGN PERIODS MENTIONED IN THE TEXT

Qin dynasty (221–206 B.C.)
Han dynasty (202 B.C.–A.D.220)
Eastern Jin dynasty (317–420)
Liang dynasty (502–57)
Tang dynasty (618–907)
Song dynasty (960–1279)
Yuan dynasty (1279–1368)
Ming dynasty (1368–1644)
   Zhengde reign (1506–21)
   Jiajing reign (1522–66)
   Wanli reign (1573–1620)
   Tianqi reign (1621–27)
   Chongzhen reign (1628–44)
Qing dynasty (1644–1911)

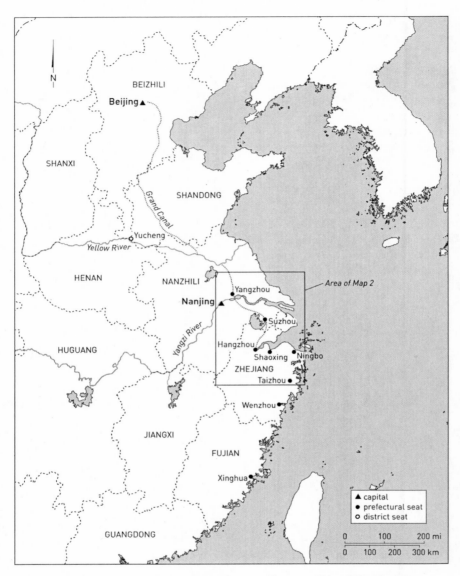

Map 1. Eastern China in the late Ming dynasty (Source: China Historical Geographic Information Service, Version 4. Cambridge, MA: Harvard-Yenching Institute, January 2007. Prepared by Merrick Lex Berman.)

Map 2. Detail (Source: China Historical Geographic Information Service, Version 4. Cambridge, MA: Harvard-Yenching Institute, January 2007. Prepared by Merrick Lex Berman.)

Introduction

This is the first full-length book on premodern Chinese charity to appear in English since 1912.[1] Until the 1980s, most scholars considered the subject of Chinese charity an anomaly pertaining only to a few towns and cities in a predominantly agrarian society.[2] If they noticed Chinese charitable activities at all, they dismissed their significance. The Chinese, it was commonly said, were charitable only to their kin; their benevolence lacked piety, was not altogether voluntary, and served the interests of the elite.[3]

Discouraging Western scholars from taking a good look at Chinese charitable traditions was the legacy of nineteenth-century Christian missionaries, who, though copiously documenting Chinese charity, marshaled their findings to spotlight deficiencies in Chinese practices, thereby to pave the way for their own, presumably worthier activities. When the direst famine of the Qing dynasty struck North China from 1876 to 1879, Chinese at many levels of society valiantly sought to aid the starving.[4] The emperor contributed funds; the governor of Shandong had grain imported for sale at reduced prices; local residents erected soup kitchens and orphanages; benevolent associations aided the needy and buried the dead; and gentry of other provinces, moved by the plight of victims in Shandong, reached across administrative boundaries to help.[5] Yet missionaries, who were then enjoying the strengths of a prosperous, progressive industrialized West, found fault in these efforts. The assistance from the imperial coffers was "a mere pittance,"[6] they claimed, observing that the careless distribution of grain had provoked food riots and invited false claims on resources.

The missionaries' criticisms appeared to be substantiated by overwhelming evidence: the famine of the late 1870s took between 9.5 and 13 million lives.[7] Surveying the disastrous outcome, the crusader Timothy Richard had grounds to conclude that the civilization of the West, with its science and

Christianity, surpassed that of China. The West, he explained, had discovered "the workings of God in Nature" and had, "in applying the laws of science to the needs of man, . . . [developed] marvelous inventions that were little less wonderful than miracles."[8] Fortified by the technological advancements of his own society, he intruded upon the Chinese scene to take over relief efforts. Confident in the superiority of his own civilization, he assumed a patronizing attitude toward the Chinese: he had those "dead idols" whom Chinese magistrates routinely supplicated for rain replaced with his own God. As he told it, he asked the Chinese to kneel so that he might "pray to God to look down in pity on them."[9]

The missionary Arthur Smith, writing around 1894, called attention to what he perceived to be a huge discrepancy between Chinese theories about benevolence and actual practice. The Chinese had "foundling hospitals, refuges for lepers and the aged, and free schools," observed Smith; nonetheless, surveying China's enormous population, he concluded that "such establishments must be relatively rare." At every turn, he saw inadequacies in Chinese "benevolence." He discounted "the provincial clubs" that cared for the destitute away from home as conducting "an ordinary business transaction of the nature of insurance."[10] He faulted the imperial government—which had, he acknowledged, responded with alacrity to famines and floods—for having nonetheless acted "in a makeshift way." He deprecated donors who distributed alms to beggars and migrants; they were, he claimed, essentially buying insurance against the possibility that marauders might raid their homes and warehouses, or they were encouraging migrants to be quickly on their way to other townships.[11] Even the Chinese practice of keeping accounts of their good and bad deeds was, Smith thought, motivated by a self-interested desire to make a good case to the judge of the underworld. Castigating the Chinese for seeking from benevolent acts what he called a "reflex benefit," Smith argued that the best palliative for their social ills was Christianity.[12]

Likewise did Gabriel Palatre of the Catholic mission in Shanghai use information about Chinese charity to build the case that Western beliefs and practices were superior to those of the Chinese. Noting in 1878 that many Western travelers to China denied having ever witnessed cases of infanticide and therefore refused to support his orphanage, Palatre collected for his French audience an abundance of information about infanticide—imperial proclamations, didactic tales, and woodblock illustrations. These materials all warned against the evils of infanticide, but Palatre drew from them another lesson: Chinese laws were ineffective—unlike Catholicism, which, "by simply proclaiming to the faithful the single statement 'God is the creator of human life and no one on earth has the right to take the life of his fellow creatures,' will work miracles."[13] Evidence that many Chinese opposed infanticide, though plentiful, did not shake his conceptual framework.

What Westerners saw of China in the twentieth century seemed to confirm the missionaries' grim assessments. The country, torn apart by civil war and foreign invasion, suffered overpopulation and food shortages with little sustained relief; moreover, by 1949 an authoritarian regime had arisen that would discourage individual, voluntary initiatives for the public good. China's deplorable conditions were vividly communicated to Westerners through photographs, one of which captured skeletal laborers harnessed like draft animals to a huge ship that they were tracking up the Yangzi River.[14] Who after seeing this could trust talk of Chinese benevolence? Who could see back to a time when Chinese society had been guided by—and at times even lived up to—a humane and life-nurturing rhetoric? That most twentieth-century Chinese themselves turned against their heritage as the creation of a self-serving elite further reinforced Western myopia. Thus in 1989 an op-ed piece in the *New York Times,* taking a cue from Deng Xiaoping's son, and sounding somewhat like Arthur Smith, made a statement that altogether ignored the centrality of the concept of humaneness (*ren*) in premodern Chinese thought: "The restraining philosophy of humanitarianism is absent or nearly absent in Chinese tradition." The journalist added, "China developed no great philosophy of charity, aid to the downtrodden or an obligation to help the less fortunate."[15]

Weighing against such skepticism are China's historical records, which employ a large vocabulary for charitable activities. They speak of "liking to be charitable" (*haoyi, leshan haoshi, haoshan leshi, haoxing shanshi,* and *cishan haoyi*), of "doing good" (*weishan, xingshan*), and of "good deeds" (*shanju* and *yixing*). They applaud "those who like to do good," or (without the pejorative and sarcastic overtones that the term has acquired in English) "do-gooders" (*haoshan zhe*). And they speak of "compassion" (*cishan*) for the poor, of "giving aid" (*shiji*), and, with a connotation of justice, of "aiding the weak and helping out in emergencies" (*yi*).[16] They tell of benefactors who financed the construction of bridges, maintained free ferry services, and sponsored community schools for indigent village boys; and of compassionate men who provided the poor and needy with food, shelter, burials, and medicines. The list of good deeds continues but in itself is nearly meaningless, composed as it is of disconnected items randomly displayed. How does one go about weighing their significance? How might one navigate between two temptations, either to collect facts endlessly (as though the longer the list the more incontrovertible would be the proof of China's charitableness) or to bring quick closure by organizing those facts according to some preconceived theory?

.   .   .

What prompted me to write this book was neither some conviction about the merits or flaws of Chinese charity in late imperial times, nor a fixed idea about what charity is or ought to be, but rather a chance encounter with a type of voluntary charitable organization that emerged in the late sixteenth century and was the forerunner of institutions that would in the nineteenth century acquire the English label "benevolent societies."[17] If, as has often been said, the Chinese focused charity on their kin, why, I wondered, did men who belonged to prominent lineages additionally establish these associations to serve the community at large?

The causes served by the benevolent societies had been encouraged by ancient Chinese texts and long pursued by various institutions whose main purpose was something other than charity. Emperors extended their governance to sponsor poorhouses (*yangji yuan*) and dispensaries for the "poor, sick, disabled, and lonely,"[18] thereby expressing their paternalistic care for the people. Buddhist monasteries, elaborating on their pious goals, provided shelters, medicines, and soup kitchens for the poor.[19] Lineages occasionally used income from land trusts, or "charitable estates"—whose main function was to foster lineage prosperity and longevity by relieving kin of burdensome ritual and educational expenses—to aid the poor and needy beyond their kin. Unlike these institutions, in which charity had an ancillary role, benevolent societies *appeared* to have charity as their primary, defining purpose. Given these alternative routes for aiding the poor, why did members of the local elite (which this study defines broadly to include former officials, educated men, and wealthy residents) voluntarily sponsor and manage benevolent societies, and why did these institutions first arise in the late sixteenth century?

When benevolent societies were making their appearance, the topic of charity became increasingly visible in the written record, thus inviting the historian's scrutiny. Ancient political texts had counseled rulers to employ, feed, and clothe the dumb, the deaf, the crippled, and the lame, and to aid those who were widowed, orphaned, and socially isolated.[20] Historical records had long spoken of rulers and officials who sponsored a host of welfare activities.[21] Before the late Ming, however, discussions of routine welfare were rare and generally unrevealing. State regulations (*huiyao*), administrative handbooks, and ethical guides underscored an ideal of caring for the needy and exhorted readers to share their wealth with others (*fencai, quanfen*), yet they tended to be terse, impersonal, and abstract, floating high above everyday particularities. Seldom did they document whether plans were actually implemented, let alone the names of individual benefactors.[22] Crises concerning food, especially from the Song dynasty on, were more likely to elicit comment than the routine needs of the poor. Still, with few exceptions—most notably, a Song-dynasty retired official who personally took responsibility for installing soup kitchens that enabled thousands of people to survive a famine—Song materials provide few links between abstract prescriptions and actual situations.[23]

Documents are invariably more readily available for recent periods than for earlier ones; such is the result of war, natural disasters, and changing values concerning what is worth preserving. Even for the late Ming, one reads of numerous books and essays, not to mention such ephemeral materials as account books, physician case books, population surveys, and proclamations to residents, that no longer survive. Accelerating the use and circulation of written information in the late Ming were twin developments: the spread of literacy and an explosion in publishing.[24] Yet, more important than the proliferation of written materials was the change in attitude that accompanied the expanded readership: before the late Ming, members of the literate elite had little interest in writing about charity and valued "hidden merit" (*yinde*)— that is, merit known to the self but not to others.[25] They feared that others might view any public display of philanthropy as harboring nefarious political ambitions. So it was with the eleventh-century poet-statesman Su Shi: when he raised funds for a public hospital, bridge construction, and a program to discourage infanticide, he credited religious figures and friends and begged intimates to keep his role secret. Already in political disgrace, he wished to escape suspicion that he was trying to build up his political reputation.[26] The record of Su Shi's good deeds has survived because he was a statesman and talented poet; the good deeds themselves did not bring him renown. The subject of philanthropy was peripheral to elite identity, and Su's philanthropy was unusual, according to a scholar writing a century later.[27] Men were reluctant to take credit for charitable acts because they lacked a consensus about what such acts meant.[28]

Late Ming benefactors, though they occasionally invoked the value of "hidden merit," more often strove to make their good deeds visible. They printed up pamphlets explaining the circumstances that had prompted their beneficence and listed the names of donors; they erected steles that explicated their fine goals and commemorated the sponsors. They wanted to be seen as do-gooders and were in full agreement that being so seen was respectable. The subject of charitable deeds thus gained a foothold in local gazetteers— records that districts (*xian*), subprefectures (*zhou*), and prefectures (*fu*) published once every few generations to preserve local lore and commemorate worthy residents. In contrast to earlier editions, district gazetteers that appeared soon after the Ming fall customarily reserved one section for biographies of men who had performed "charitable" or "just deeds" (*yixing*). (They relegated women to a separate section that celebrated chaste widowhood and filiality, commenting only incidentally on their charitable contributions.) There, under the rubric "charitable deeds," countless exemplars of beneficence parade by in cramped succession. One benefactor paid clergy to perform funeral rites for thousands of corpses that had washed ashore in a flood of 1628;[29] another burned the contract of a desperate debtor who was considering selling his son into servitude.[30] And so forth. Therefore, where previously records of charitable activities had been most likely to survive when pertaining to men of great political or literary stature, such as Su Shi, some late Ming men, even illiterate ones, gained stature and lasting reputations simply because they had performed good deeds.

· · ·

Pursuing questions about benevolent societies and the changes associated with their emergence, I researched late Ming documents. There, as though chasing after a runaway ball, I followed unfamiliar paths and bypaths, only gradually mastering the landmarks and making the acquaintance of the inhabitants—all far removed from Western charitable traditions. In contrast to early modern Europe, late Ming materials preserve only a few casual references to charitable women, no last wills and testaments such as those that have been housed by the thousands in European archives (and were written by women no less than by men), and certainly no records of confraternities of women or charitable homes for prostitutes.[31] From the start, my goal was not to evaluate Chinese charity against a Western standard, but rather to identify the principles that governed the late Ming terrain. Enabling this endeavor were five men whose writings stand out among all extant Ming sources for commenting not only on their charitable activities but also on the social environments that defined their choices: Yang Dongming, Gao Panlong, Chen Longzheng, Lu Shiyi, and Qi Biaojia.

Materials by and about the five men generally support broad assumptions about the late Ming: that it was a period of prosperity, when silver from abroad stimulated commerce and small market towns arose in the countryside; a period of intellectual innovation, when the pathbreaking ideas of Wang Yangming spurred the spread of literacy; and a period of governmental ineffectiveness and social unrest that would ultimately give way to dynastic collapse. Yet, just as a widely woven net cannot catch small fry, these assumptions proved too crude for explaining the specific features of late Ming charity.

Each of the five writers illuminates charity; each provides a distinct piece of the complicated puzzle that is late Ming charity, but none tells the whole story. Transcripts of multiple benevolent-society lectures survive only for Gao Panlong and Chen Longzheng. Diaries survive only for Lu Shiyi and Qi Biaojia. Accordingly, to fill in the picture of how charity was initiated and organized, this study delves into the lives of these five men and compares the approaches of each to the alternatives posed by his four counterparts. The study moves along several trajectories: from the moral mandates that high-minded leaders proclaimed in lectures and essays to the actual behavior as shaped by the personal, political, and social circumstances revealed through diaries; from the new, enduring routines for charitable giving that were institutionalized in benevolent societies to how those routines fared during a time of crisis; from abstract, idealized guidelines for conducting famine relief to actual performance; and from the highly audible voices of leading members of the elite down to scarcely visible players in the community—physicians, monks, students of meager means, and merchants—each of whose cooperation was vital to organized charity. The study thus progresses from the concrete experiences of the five men to generalizations about late Ming charity.

.   .   .

As any translator knows, Chinese and Western terms are only roughly comparable. Consider the distinction Westerners commonly make between "charity," defined as "love, kindness . . . with some notion of generous or spontaneous goodness," or "benevolence to one's neighbours, especially to the poor"; and "philanthropy," defined as "an inclination to promote the Publick Good."[32] Late Ming writers clustered both types of activities—food relief for the poor and bridge construction for the community—under two rubrics that have slightly different nuances but alike mean "good deeds" (*yixing, shanju*). Following Chinese usage and noting that the terms overlap even in the West, I use the terms *charity* and *philanthropy* interchangeably.

The type of voluntary association that arose in the late Ming went by a variety of names, which, translated literally into English, might be rendered as "Society for Sharing Humaneness" (Tongren hui), "Society for Spreading Humaneness" (Guangren hui), Humane Society" (Ren hui), and (for the term Tongshan hui) either "Society for Sharing Goodness" or "Society for the Common Good."[33] These associations often promoted a fellowship of goodness and conceptualized charity as a means to achieving a moral community that would embrace rich and poor. Therefore the term *benevolent society*, with its emphasis on the benevolence of rich to poor, is inappropriate. Nonetheless, having been introduced in the nineteenth century by missionaries, it is now well entrenched in the English vocabulary, and because it is terser than many alternatives, I often use it in this study.

Also slippery is the term *yi*. Sometimes it means "to aid the weak and help out in emergencies" and "giving something to be shared by everyone, such as charitable granaries, altars, and schools,"[34] and may rightly be translated as "charitable," as in "charitable deeds" (*yiju, yixing*), "charitable schools" (*yixue*), "charitable ferries" (*yidu*), "charitable burial grounds" (*yimeng*), and "charitable estates" (*yizhuang*). At other times, *yi* means "righteous," as in "righteous deeds" (*yixing*), embracing acts of filial piety as well. Thus seventeenth-century local gazetteers often lumped together into a single section the biographies of both "the filial" and "the charitable" (*xiao yi*). When commending several persons who had sponsored famine relief, canceled debts owed, and aided the poor, one editor explained: "The wealthy who like to put their virtue into effect" are also called *yi*, for they, like filial sons, "are also beneficial."[35] The term *yi* additionally intimates justice and signals the sense of equity felt by some late Ming benefactors, similar to the association between justice and charity elsewhere in the world: as Marcel Mauss observed,

"Originally the Arabic *sadak* meant, like the Hebrew *zedaqa,* exclusively justice, and it later came to mean alms."[36]

What ultimately defines the meanings of terms are not dictionaries but the social-political contexts in which the terms were used. The line between familial responsibility and charity that often figures in Western definitions of charity as giving that is "outside the family" was drawn differently by Ming-Qing writers,[37] whose relations included not only the family, or "household" (*jia*), but also countless relatives whose degrees of closeness were ritually defined. By no means did they count aiding members of their own households as charity, but they often praised as "charitable deeds" (*yixing*) those that aided maternal relatives or contributed to the well-being of one's patrilineal kinship group, the lineage (*zu*). A line dividing charity from other types of giving was drawn, redrawn, and occasionally contested, but not according to Western definitions.

Similarly problematic is the line between state welfare and nongovernmental charity. Though it is a common distinction in Western discussions of charity,[38] this line was blurred in late Ming times, in part as a consequence of how men were recruited into officialdom. The content of the civil service examination, which tested the candidates' knowledge of the Confucian classics as well as administrative lore, socialized officials to be far more than task-oriented bureaucrats; they were defined as men of moral judgment who were familiar with a tradition of humane governance and capable of taking the initiative in all sorts of contingencies.[39]

The fusion of bureaucratic competency and individual discernment is evident in the local officials, especially the district magistrates, whose paternalistic responsibilities were aptly conveyed by the informal title "father-and-mother officials" (*fumu guan*). One magistrate, facing an outbreak of disease in his district, explained: "The people are my children; I am the parent of the people. Where has there ever been an ailing child whom a parent has failed to nurture and cure?" Whereupon he commanded that medical clinics be set up and doctors be engaged night and day to look after the sick so as to reduce the number of untimely deaths among the destitute poor.[40] A counterexample is found in a cautionary account about how a local official's callousness precipitated a rebellion. Because he had failed to fulfill his parental responsibilities to the people, he lost legitimacy, prompting the editor to comment, "How could he be called a father-and-mother of the people?"[41] If these examples convey formal expectations that magistrates would care for the people, it was in their informal capacity as well-rounded leaders, and at their own discretion, that they initiated, organized, or sponsored philanthropic projects, invariably stressing that their contributions came not from the public coffers but out of their own salaries. Their financial contributions and those of the residents then combined in a common fund, which was often managed by local residents.

Further blurring the lines between governmental and nongovernmental realms was the very structure of the civil service examinations, which required that candidates take a sequence of examinations over many years, first qualifying at the district level and then seeking the licentiate (*shengyuan*), *juren,* and *jinshi* degrees, respectively, at the prefectural, provincial, and imperial capital levels.[42] Successful candidates were then assigned to posts throughout the empire, usually in accordance with the law of avoidance (that no official should serve in his own district) and with the rule of rotation (whereby an official was transferred to a new post at least once every three years), so as to discourage officials from forming lasting alliances with local elites, that is, men of wealth and informal influence. A consequence was that every district had not only a magistrate but also former officials who had returned to their native places, holders of lower examination degrees, and students aspiring to pass the examinations. Although social distinctions among these categories were made manifest by dress and privileges, these men shared an orientation of bureaucratic service that eroded the line between state welfare and nonofficial (or nongovernmental) charity.

Following late Ming prosperity and the spread of literacy, the ranks of men aspiring to enter officialdom greatly expanded. Yet, because the size of the bureaucracy remained fixed and the quotas for the higher degrees were kept low, the vast majority of students remained stuck at the licentiate level. Especially in the Yangzi delta area, where four of the five charitable men resided, the district capitals were well populated with highly educated men whose paths to officialdom had been blocked. The availability of such men, along with several other constituencies, such as literate physicians and monks, is one key to late Ming charity. Eager to affiliate both horizontally with their peers and vertically with their social superiors and inferiors, they readily formed organizations outside such existing institutions as the government, the lineage, and the monastery. Late Ming charity was a quasi-public affair. It not only displayed the participants' goodness; it also provided a medium through which men of varying social statuses could compete to stand out in their communities and to negotiate for rewards and favors from their communities and social superiors.

.   .   .

That social change affected late Ming charity is but part of the story. Inviting me into their world, and insistently speaking in their own terms, the five men featured in this study ultimately forced me to push to the side (but not completely out of sight) questions often asked about the functions of and motivations for charity. Late Ming benefactors worried that food shortages would spark riots. They understood that occupational instability—a problem that had worsened as commerce expanded the ranks of nonagricultural laborers and petty entrepreneurs—might provoke social unrest. Some even feared the possibility of political collapse. Yet none of these motivations explain why the benefactors chose charity over (or in addition to) other available means (both coercive and persuasive) for dealing with social tensions and maintaining social order; or why earlier periods of social instability had failed to produce benevolent societies.

Questions about motivation often (though not exclusively) involve the topic of class relations. Intrinsic to the recognition of poverty and need is an assumption of difference, of a gap between the haves and the have-nots. Hence some modern historians think of charitable giving as a means of negotiating class, of stabilizing society, or of asserting elite dominance over society. Such scholars are, as Gertrude Himmelfarb states, "in the habit of thinking of social reforms and private philanthropies as instruments of the status quo—as 'safety valves' to deflect popular discontent, or mechanisms of 'social control' to keep the lower classes passive and submissive."[43] Or, as Lewis Hyde eloquently declares (in reference to a nineteenth-century statement about charity "*promoting the happiness of our inferiors*"): "This 'charity' is a way of negotiating the boundary of class. . . . Charity treats the poor like the aliens of old; it is a form of foreign trade, a way of having some commerce without including the stranger in the group. At its worse, it is the 'tyranny of gift,' which uses the bonding power of generosity to manipulate people."[44] Even the word "benevolence," following Charles Dickens, now carries overtones of the assertion of power over dependent creatures—as when Dickens spoke of Mrs. Pardiggle "pouncing upon the poor, and applying benevolence to them like a strait-waistcoat."[45]

That the five charitable men in this study stood out from the common run of their peers redirected my thinking away from class tensions to the following question: what catapulted only a few members of the elite (and not necessarily the richest and most powerful ones) into leadership roles in charitable activities? In several cases, the sources reveal that childhood experiences, personal crises, and personality spurred a benefactor's charitableness; although these men were of the elite, in responding to the opportunities that social change had created they acted differently from their peers.

The exercise of power proved important but not as I had expected. Although some officials and members of the local elite attempted to control outcomes so as to serve their own interests, late Ming sources reveal that parties lower down on the social hierarchy exerted considerable influence as well. They initiated do-good programs and skillfully elicited sponsorship from their social superiors for programs they themselves chose. Even marginal figures who were of modest financial means and who lacked the degree-holding status that qualified one to start up the ladder toward officialdom could, and did, wield moral authority to win cooperation from their community for worthy goals.

Further compelling me to forgo easy generalizations about an elite class seeking to dominate and control local society were sharp disagreements that divided members of late Ming local elites when it came to deciding how to proceed in charitable activities. Social hierarchy was everywhere evident and important, but more to the point than the issue of class were the forces that moved late Ming benefactors of varying social strata to act collectively and the dynamics whereby multiple constituencies coalesced around leaders in charity. How was a consensus achieved that was viable enough for managing the large-scale cooperative efforts that treated the sick by the hundreds and fed the starving by the thousands? What endowed certain routines and institutions with the authority to inspire cooperation among donors whose motivations probably ran the full gamut from cynical displays of generosity to keep the peace to genuine compassion for the needy? How were men mobilized to support a common endeavor? And what sustained the charitable activities over time?

Our contemporary society, comments one American historian, tends to see benevolence as "the exercise of power in disguise" and regards with suspicion any notion that people might be genuinely moved by compassion.[46] Should one, then, pay no heed to the claims of the five men featured in this study that they were moved by feelings of compassion, or to reports that they wept for the poor at their communal meetings? What should one make of the fact that four of the five men (with the socially marginal Lu Shiyi being somewhat different) not only hastened to succor the needy but also labored hard, over days and months, on their behalf? More fruitful than questioning the genuineness of their feelings, I learned, is to examine how they defined themselves and how social, political, and cultural forces constrained and guided their compassionate impulses or feelings of responsibility. What, in other words, defined the scope of their compassion, both in terms of geographical reach and in terms of the kinds of needs they chose to address?

The five men further alerted me to the importance of their beliefs, but not quite in the manner that I had expected. Whereas the Judeo-Christian tradition suggests a close identification between charity and a specific religious tradition, the five men drew upon an amalgam of Buddhist, Confucian, and Daoist beliefs, and even strains of the behavioral conditioning through rewards and punishments that is espoused by Legalist texts. They were deeply concerned about their morality. Several of them vigilantly kept track of their good deeds and bad.[47] Each of the five struggled to practice what he preached, striving often to indoctrinate not just the masses but also fellow members of the elite. What these men believed served many functions, not least among them, to maintain order. Yet the beliefs also lifted them out of their ordinariness, equipped them to take the lead in charitable activities, and enlarged their own self-image as men who would do good. That they as a result wrote extensively about their charitable activities provides a rare opportunity to examine how late Ming charity worked.

PART ONE

New Routines

Associations for Doing Good

1

Societies for Liberating Animals

They scream like children.
YAO WENRAN

Shaping late Ming charitable organizations were forces other than poverty and need. So suggests the sequence of events: around the 1580s—before the first-known benevolent society—members of the educated elite took to recording how they, upon spotting a pig in the hands of a butcher or a chicken up for sale, hastily bought the hapless creatures and set them free. They were concerned, not only for oxen whose labors were so valued in tilling the fields, but for birds and fish, tortoises and tiny insects; not just for plump animals destined for the cooking pots, but for irksome flies and poisonous scorpions. The five men who play leading roles in this account of philanthropy—men who organized or participated in benevolent societies, distributed food and medicines to the poor, and promoted other charitable activities—either themselves physically engaged in liberating animals (*fangsheng*) or protested against it in favor of aiding human beings. Of the five, three (Yang Dongming, Gao Panlong, and Qi Biaojia) generously donated money both to liberate animals and to aid human beings; while two (Chen Longzheng and Lu Shiyi) outspokenly opposed spending money on saving animals. Yet, in making comparisons between the two types of activity—in arguing that benevolent societies were superior to societies for saving animals because human beings were more important than other creatures—even the naysayers acknowledged the two activities to be comparable at some level.

For proponents and detractors alike, the practice of liberating animals had become a common point of reference and provided much of the vocabulary that they would use when discussing aid for the poor and needy: compassion for fellow living beings; the importance of life; and the responsibility of large, powerful creatures for the small, needy, and feeble. That saving animal lives and aiding human beings were comparable was, moreover, a point implicitly made by several late Ming didactic books, which

15

lumped both activities under the one rubric "good deeds." Accordingly, it is with the practice of liberating animals that this account of late Ming philanthropy begins.

The Chinese term *fangsheng* literally means "releasing lives," but because it specifically referred to freeing animals from captivity or rescuing them from death, I variously translate it as "releasing," "liberating," or "saving" animals.[1] The term *fangsheng* has ancient roots. It is usually traced back to the fifth century, when it appeared in *The Book of Brahmā's Net (Fanwang jing)*;[2] and it can be traced forward to the present, where it is still used for practices observed in China, Taiwan, Hong Kong, Southeast Asia, and New York.[3] Understood to have originated in a Buddhist text and to have been in currency for at least fifteen hundred years, it signals the power and durability of a Buddhist belief and thus beguiles us to assume some immutable essence. But behind its lasting facade, the term *fangsheng* periodically acquired new contexts, attracted new associations, and thus its meaning continually transformed.

According to surviving accounts, for the period before the late Ming, the initiative for saving animals usually came from above—from monks, rulers, and the occasional official who wished to promote the interests of his ruler. The concept of *fangsheng* inspired the sixth-century Emperor Wu of the Liang dynasty to offer his ancestors noodles rather than meat; and it prompted the monk Zhiyi to set aside sixty-one ponds as havens for fish. It provided the Tang-dynasty emperor Suzong with a means whereby he could regain the goodwill of his people after the devastating An Lushan rebellion: to "spread feelings of kindness and . . . trust" throughout the empire, he had ponds for releasing fish set up in eighty-one locations. The idea of *fangsheng* also inspired a Song-dynasty official to propose to the emperor that the common masses assemble at West Lake once a year, on the eighth day of the fourth month, to pray for the emperor's good fortune by liberating fish and birds.[4] Before the late Ming, in other words, those acts of *fangsheng* that were noted for posterity took the form of grand public gestures.

If during this middle imperial period members of the scholarly elite did liberate animals in their daily lives—as occasional jottings and poems by Bai Juyi, Su Shi, and others suggest—they did so fleetingly and incidentally, without leaving behind much comment.[5] With the possible exception of Su Shi— who is said to have set up a meeting for liberating animals when serving as governor of Hangzhou[6]—the subject was peripheral to their consciousness; a matter of personal piety, perhaps, but neither a focus of routine social activities nor a subject deemed worth recording.

The concern for animals was by no means universal throughout late Ming society. Alongside displays of compassion toward animals are numerous examples of coldheartedness: young men took pleasure in bloody cockfights;[7] wealthy households feasted on choice birds; and butchers, though denigrated for their bloody trade, continued to attract plenty of customers. Brutality toward animals was often condoned or simply overlooked. Even so, that the concern for liberating animals should have surfaced in literati writings at all, and that it should, moreover, have become the basis of social organizations, marks a changed sensibility at least among some members of the society.

For the new sensibility explanations may be offered in terms of a growing social instability that arose from the following conditions: an expanding economy gave rise to merchants who occasionally wielded as much economic power as landed degree-holding literati; the spread of literacy produced far more highly educated men than positions in officialdom could accommodate; commerce infiltrated the rural areas, generating small market towns; and family fortunes quickly and often inexplicably changed. In addition, the teachings of Wang Yangming—that the authority for knowledge rests within the individual and that action and knowledge ought to be united—unleashed individual spiritual quests and activist initiatives.[8] Such monocausal explanations, though rhetorically powerful, fail to do justice to the complexity of the symbolic act of *fangsheng*, however. More than manifesting specific economic, social, or spiritual changes, the preoccupation with *fangsheng* during the late sixteenth and early seventeenth centuries points to attempts by literati to maneuver and redefine themselves in an increasingly complicated society. Like the charitable organizations that would quickly follow, the liberation of animals was a highly visible communal act that involved rich and poor, high and low.

This chapter focuses on the late Ming, but occasionally I cite writers who were born in the early Qing dynasty or straddled the two dynasties; for convenience, I occasionally use the term *Ming-Qing* when dealing with a cluster of writers, the bulk of whom were of the late Ming.

LATE MING DEPARTURES

Before the late Ming, written accounts of saving animal lives were scattered about and subordinated to other topics. In only two pre-Ming texts, to my knowledge, did the editors assemble materials about liberating animals as if to imply that the theme deserved focused attention; in both cases, the suggestion of focus has proved to be illusory. The first text in question is an enormous seventh-century Buddhist encyclopedia that includes a section on *fangsheng*.[9] Yet, when seen in the context of the entire work, this one section out of a hundred hardly stands out, for it occupies only a few pages, a tiny place among numerous more weighty issues. The second text is *Extensive Records from the Reign of Great Peace* (*Taiping guangji*), a tenth-century compendium of anecdotes that are mostly of the variety known as "accounts of the strange" (*zhiguai*).[10] Sixteen stories about saving animals are here collected into a single chapter.[11] Yet the main theme of that chapter, as announced by its title, is not "the release of animals," but "retribution" (*baoying*); and although the stories concern the rescuing of animals from the jaws of death, they do not use the term *fangsheng* but speak simply of *fang*, as in "let it go" (*fang zhi*). Only because these tales were later subsumed under the rubric *fangsheng* in Ming-Qing collections can they now be easily retrieved as illustrations of the liberating of animals.[12]

As the practice of liberating animals spread among the scholarly elite, editors of Ming-Qing morality books and compendia elaborated on the subject and built it up. To root contemporary practice in the venerable past, they incorporated into their own texts tales from *Extensive Records* as well as scattered notices from other early works about liberating animals and its companion theme, "nonkilling" (*jiesha*). Using old accounts, they legitimized new understandings. In the eighteenth century, the editors of the huge collectanea, the *Synthesis of Books and Illustrations Past and Present* (*Gujin tushu jicheng*), amassed materials from over a millennium into the category *fangsheng*. They had at their fingertips enough writings on the subject of releasing animals as to suggest that a tradition had been carried out for centuries, uninterrupted and unmodified.

That the term *fangsheng* was long-lasting and that new usages were repeatedly shored up by ancient lore make it difficult to identify shifts in meaning. The task of doing so is further complicated because the practice of liberating animals, like most symbolic acts, was far more often carried out than it was explicated, and was capable, therefore, of communicating numerous messages and inserting itself into a wide variety of situations. Consider the example of Qi Biaojia, who practiced *fangsheng* on several levels and whose charitable activities are the focus of part 2 of this study. Qi had an illustrious official career that took off immediately after he earned the *jinshi* degree in 1622, at the remarkably young age of twenty-one *sui*. By no measure might one judge him to have been a marginal, unorthodox, or idiosyncratic figure. Yet, throughout the 1630s and 1640s, he often took pains to note in his diary his practice of setting animals free. He wrote that, on a memorial day for his father, he was uncontrollably weepy, avoided guests, and then accompanied a certain Yan Maoyou and two other friends to a temple, where they were joined by a fourth acquaintance. There he used funds from his salary to buy a sparrow and let it free; Yan, too, as Qi put it, "bought a sparrow to make a prayer on my behalf, and the various friends did a 'liberating animals' chant."[13]

The memorial day of Qi's father had special significance independent of the act of liberating animals. Like making an offering, liberating the sparrows augmented but did not itself define the occasion. In spirit it thus resembled the releasing of animals that had accompanied the annual prayers at West Lake during Song times. Yet, it also differed from other acts of *fangsheng* recorded by Qi, acts that he did spontaneously and explicitly to save animals. When one of his bondservants just happened to have a goose tied up, Qi bought it to be released.[14] When he heard that someone was about to slaughter a pig, he purchased it to liberate it.[15]

Like many of his contemporaries, Qi Biaojia joined a small club, or association (*hui*), for liberating animals. Some clubs met at regular intervals, in Qi's case, on the eighth day of each month;[16] other clubs met irregularly, but nonetheless frequently.[17] Sometimes each club member individually purchased an animal beforehand to be released at the meeting. Sometimes the members pooled their donations to purchase animals collectively. The specific practices varied enormously, but two features stand out. First, where the few documented *fangsheng* meetings of earlier dynasties were on a massive scale and held to celebrate or enhance some special occasion, such as the Buddha's or emperor's birthday, the late Ming meetings were small, held frequently, and had as their main, articulated purpose the liberating of animals. Second, where early cases of saving animals had usually been initiated by rulers or officials and echoes in local society were faint, the spontaneous formation of Ming clubs shows that the interest in liberating animals was governed by conventions that were well understood and widely shared by members of Ming local elites. Thus Qi, who on one level perpetuated an expression of piety that had old roots, on another level was participating in something new.

The shift in the locus for the saving of animals is further evident in the matter of setting aside ponds and waterways for the protection of fish and other aquatic creatures. Before the late Ming, the designation of water bodies as animal preserves was invariably done under the auspices of officials and rulers—as when every circuit (*dao*) was mandated in 759 A.D. to set up a *fangsheng* pond.[18] During the late Ming, this practice spread to local society and became a matter of individual, nonofficial initiative. When Qi Biaojia constructed a large garden for himself at the top of a mountain, he also constructed a "pond for releasing lives" (*fangsheng chi*) below.[19]

DIDACTIC TALES

The theme of "liberating lives" loomed large in late Ming writings, sometimes dominating entire chapters of popular didactic works, a genre that was flourishing at that time.[20] These chapters collected, often from previous publications, colorful anecdotes based on history and hearsay to show that those who had been kind to animals became wealthy, lived long lives, and enjoyed successful careers—that they had, in other words, earned merit. One story tells of a wine brewer who was so compassionate that he took great care to keep flies from falling into his wine casks. Some time later, the brewer was wrongfully accused of a crime and found guilty. But just when the magistrate tried to draft the prison order, thousands of flies swarmed around the brush, preventing him from writing. The magistrate, recognizing that some divine power was at work, released the brewer.[21]

If such tales sound fanciful, they shaped how Ming literati understood and wrote about their experiences. They colored, for example, a record that the official (and son of a prosperous official) Feng Shike made in all seriousness about how a personal adventure converted one man to a vegetarian diet.[22] When a friend of Feng's had tried to persuade people to avoid slaughtering and eating beef, a certain Xie Shi persisted in "chewing away as he liked." Feng's friend later learned that Xie had reformed his ways after having witnessed a near escape from death: Xie was traveling on a boat, which docked alongside another vessel. Three strange-looking men suddenly appeared. Two of them boarded the other boat only to beat a hasty retreat. Xie overheard the two say to the third: "Some of the passengers don't eat meat. It will be difficult for us to work our stratagems." At the next stop, Xie learned that the other boat had scarcely survived its journey because of fierce winds. The reason it managed to survive at all, he further learned, was that three vegetarian passengers on board had in effect offset the malevolence of the wind demons. Thus enlightened, Xie, along with some sixty fellow passengers, burned incense and swore forever after to abstain from eating meat.[23]

This account, recorded around 1586, has certain characteristics of the tales from *Extensive Records:* a chance encounter, in this case, with another boat; the sudden appearance of men strangely dressed; the transformation of evil spirits into human forms; and heaven's recompense for deeds done. Yet here Feng Shike was recording an actual contemporary event as he understood it, an event whose lesson he himself put into practice. Out of regard for rats, he desisted from keeping a cat and once fervently beseeched a friend to spare a rat's life. When the friend asked, "Why does it deserve pity?" Feng explained that his own brother's hostile attitude toward rodents had been counterproductive.[24] Ever vigilant against rats, Feng's brother carefully placed his fine books in wrappers, yet whenever he checked the books he found that they had new tooth marks. He then bought a cat, but the rats chewed up the books as before. Feng Shike, in contrast, left his books scattered about, with the result that, though he found droppings, the books "remained unharmed." The key difference between the two brothers was not in practical strategy but in attitude. The brother "thought that rats were like bandits," whereas Feng Shike, by keeping no cat, inspired the rats to be so docile as to leave even goblets of wine and platters of food untouched.[25]

Feng concluded his plea for the rat's life by making a political-moral point: when compared to the lifting of grain by petty thieves or the "robbing of the state" by those big thieves, the ministers, the damage done by rats was insignificant. But Feng's defense of animals was more than a vehicle for political commentary. Out of regard for animals in general, Feng desisted from eating "beef, lamb, dogs, and pigs at home, consuming instead only the vegetables that serve as accompaniments to meat dishes." His family was strictest about keeping chickens out of the kitchen, rarely slaughtered ducks, restricted the consumption of fish, and refrained from eating seafood having claws.[26] Likewise out of regard for animals, he organized the dredging of a pond for liberating animals, and had shelters constructed to accommodate the crowds that would come to hear lectures on the saving of animal lives. By this time, he noted, societies for the liberating of animals had spread throughout the Southern Metropolitan area (Nanzhili) and the Zhejiang region (Wu and Yue).[27]

The didactic tales—and the practice of liberating animals that they endorsed—conveyed what many prominent literati themselves sincerely valued. Qi Biaojia recorded in his diary his acts of saving animals—a goose here, a pig there, four hundred aquatic creatures on one occasion, and countless fish on another.[28] He noted meetings for liberating animals, sometimes naming those who attended.[29] Clearly he took these matters seriously enough to make them part of his life record. Moreover, he wrote a preface to a morality book that contained a section of anecdotes about saving animals and the avoidance of killing, including several tales from *Extensive Records* and the story cited above about the wine brewer.[30] Commenting on these stories, the compiler of that work stated, among other points, that the killing of creatures results from crimes committed and enmities carried out in a previous life; and that, rather than repaying one killing with another, thus generating an endless chain of debt, it is best to repay resentment with virtue (*de*).[31] This editor was Yan Maoyou who, four years later, in 1635, would release a sparrow at the memorial service honoring Qi's father. Like Feng and Qi, Yan practiced what he taught.

ZHUHONG AND THE REVIVAL OF BUDDHISM

That the twin practices of liberating animals and nonkilling had long been defunct before the late Ming was the view of Zhuhong, the sixteenth-century monk of Yunqi Monastery who (among others) has been credited by historians for the late Ming revival of Buddhism. Zhuhong judged that habits inimical to animals had become deeply ingrained. He bemoaned that the wearing of silk—a material made by killing silkworms—had become a widespread custom, and he deplored "the human consumption of meat," which, as he put it, "has been customary for so long, that people are unaware that is it wrong."[32] To jolt people out of their complacency, Zhuhong wrote a substantial two-part essay, "On Nonkilling and Liberating Lives," which, as Chün-fang Yü has shown, formed Zhuhong's platform for proselytizing Buddhism.[33]

Zhuhong took advantage of a social environment conducive to the reprinting and circulation of information. Like those followers of Wang Yangming who urged each person to teach ten people, he built the very act of proselytizing into his program, prodding his readers "to pass the essays around in order to convert others."[34] As he explained: "Encouraging one person to avoid killing results in saving a million lives. If one encourages up to ten or a hundred persons, so as to reach trillions of persons, then one will gain enormous merit."[35] Inspired by Zhuhong, wealthy patrons and mainstream scholar-officials financed editions of his essays and elaborated on his ideas in prefaces and commentaries.[36] In one such preface, an official, echoing Zhuhong, declared: "If one person will avoid killing, then ten people will avoid killing. If we expand from this—gradually thousands and millions of people will avoid killing."[37] And so the word spread.

Zhuhong's teachings reached the top of society, penetrating the imperial court, where they touched the emperor's mother, who sent for instruction from Zhuhong. They also spread down to the villages, where officials and scholars used their authority and status to disseminate the ideas among the common people. One man instrumental in spreading Zhuhong's ideas was an official who had turned to Buddhism as a child of twelve *sui,* earned a *jinshi* degree in 1583, and then carried his religious beliefs to office. While serving as a prefect, he chanted the *Diamond Sutra* (*Jingang jing*) every day, restored a Buddhist shrine, and went so far as to forbid the people from killing animals for ancestral sacrifices. To defend his position, he took as his point of departure Confucius's teaching "to respect the spirits while keeping them at a distance,"[38] and then added: "It's not that I think there are no spirits, but spirits and human beings enjoy different things. Human beings like wine and meat, so they offer wine and meat to the spirits; this may be compared to maggots who, because they feed on manure, offer manure to people. How would they not thereby offend man? Now the spirits are pure; how can they not be endlessly disgusted by the filth of wine and meat among men? . . . Today I am telling the City God to forgive all your past wrongs, but hereafter you must not repeat the offense. If you continue as before to defile the spirits by killing animals, you will not only gain no benefit, but will also incur blame. These words are truly accurate, not lightly said."[39]

Falling in with the same trend was Qi Biaojia's senior fellow townsman Tao Wangling. Like Qi, Tao, who won first place in the *jinshi* examination of 1589, was of the elite mainstream. Tao joined friends to form a club for saving animals, and, lending his literary skills and high status to the cause, he wrote an essay to dispel the doubts raised by skeptics about Zhuhong's program for liberating animals. He further composed ten verses on Zhuhong's teachings—verses he hoped would be easy for others to memorize and circulate by word of mouth.[40] As Zhuhong's teachings spread, so did there take shape accounts of actual events that validated his message. It thus seeped into an early Qing popular didactic work, for example, that Tao's brother Shiling—who had lectured on the classics jointly with the formidable Confucian thinker Liu Zongzhou—reaped merit for his kindness to animals:[41]

because he and a friend had set ten thousand eels free, they passed the civil service examinations earlier than spirits had originally ordained.[42]

Among Tao Wangling's fellow officials was Huang Hui from Sichuan.[43] One night Huang dreamed that the bibliophile Jiao Hong gave him a book in one *juan*, which turned out to be Zhuhong's essay on nonkilling. When he awoke, he committed himself to lifelong nonkilling, using his salary to buy animals to be liberated. He also had Zhuhong's essay printed up for distribution to villages.[44] Thus did Zhuhong's teachings catch on, and so swiftly that, in his own lifetime, he could gratefully acknowledge the good fortune that there were "humane men in the world . . . who had reprinted the essays on nonkilling and releasing lives in no less than ten to twenty editions."[45]

Zhuhong's influence is indisputable. Many late Ming advocates of animals, including Qi Biaojia's father, had had some personal contact with Zhuhong or his followers; many of the animal liberators had strong Buddhist beliefs; and all the relevant Ming-dynasty essays I have collected were written by men who lived during or after Zhuhong's promotion of the twin precepts of *fangsheng* and *jiesha*.[46] Nonetheless, to explain the late Ming popularity of liberating animals simply as the result of Zhuhong's successful revival of Buddhism is to ignore several issues. It overlooks that, even in the Tang-dynasty heyday of Buddhism, the precepts of nonkilling and liberating lives had received scant attention in writing; and it overlooks that those precepts derived not from the most venerable of Buddhist sutras, but from the *Book of Brahmā's Net*, an apocryphal text that was composed in China.[47] It skirts the question: why did Zhuhong couple the Buddhist proscription against doing no harm with the act of "releasing animals," a practice for which no exact equivalent can be found in early Buddhism? Moreover it is based on the erroneous assumption that compassion for animals was an exclusively Buddhist notion.[48]

Keen to propagate Buddhism among educated officials no less than among the common people, Zhuhong sought to accommodate Confucianism.[49] He astutely identified, from the vast range of ideas represented in the enormous Buddhist canon, those issues that would appeal to his contemporaries and serve as vehicles for reviving Buddhism in his day: the dichotomy between saving and killing animals, the urgency of life, and the wrongful domination of the weak by the strong.[50]

Some late Ming and early Qing writers who stoutly opposed Buddhism nonetheless promoted the concern for animals. Some scholars in Zhuhong's wake struggled to give the ideas of saving animals and nonkilling a life of their own, apart from the Buddhist legacy. Wang Heng (the brother of the female religious visionary Tangyangzi) declared, "Being proper, I will not talk about Chan [Zen] Buddhism, but by nature I do hate killing."[51] Other scholars dredged the Confucian classics for antecedents for the view that animals should be rescued from death. They reminded their readers that, long before Buddhism reached China, Confucius had shown restraint by using a hook for fishing but never a net,[52] and Mencius had instructed that the superior man keeps away from the slaughterhouse and kitchen in order to avoid the unbearable sight of animals being prepared for dinner.[53]

Instead of dismissing the twin precepts as Buddhist perversions, some stalwart Confucians found justifications for embracing them. Qian Qianyi ingeniously argued that the terms *jiesha* and *fangsheng* could not be found in ancient texts simply because in that distant golden age, when all lives had been highly valued, the killing of animals for sacrifices, entertainment, and mourning rites was all carefully regulated and done according to life-preserving principles; the concept of *fangsheng* had therefore been unnecessary. "The ancient rulers," wrote Qian, "considered heaven and earth, mountains and forests, and rivers and marshes all as one family, and birds, beasts, fish, and the myriad living things all as one body; every place was a place for *fangsheng* and every living thing was a thing whose life had essentially been saved." It was not until the last kalpa (*mofa*), "when the Tang dynasty used eunuchs to murder throughout the world, and the Song dynasty used the New Policies (*xinfa*) to murder throughout the world," that ponds for releasing animals first appeared.[54] Gui Zhuang, the grandson of the renowned essayist Gui Youguang, conceded that the term *saving lives* did originally come from Buddhism; but he then argued that the Buddha promoted the idea in order to be in accord with the guidelines of the ancient Chinese kings.[55] Another noted essayist insisted: "The theory of nonkilling did not begin with the Buddhists."[56]

Efforts to wrest the concern for animals from Buddhist sources culminated in an eighteenth-century work devoted exclusively to the themes of saving animals and nonkilling, entitled *Records of Spreading Love* (*Guang'ai lu*). There Meng Chaoran—who had a reputation for disliking Buddhism—incorporated accounts of venerated Confucians to demonstrate that the concern for animals had untainted native origins.[57] He explained that Chen Di, though strongly abhorring Buddhism, likened eating beef to being unfilial and inhumane in that it showed ignorance of basic values.[58] Praising the eleventh-century brothers Cheng Yi and Cheng Hao (revered by the great Confucian thinker Zhu Xi) for their benevolence to birds and fish, Meng commented: "I often urge people to avoid killing, yet most of them consider it a Buddhist teaching; but how could the two Chengs have leaned toward Buddhism?"[59] Meng closed his *Records* with an entry about a contemporary, Mr. He, who, when asked why he bothered to avoid killing animals when he disliked Buddhism so much, replied in terms of the Confucian ideal of the "gentleman" (*junzi*), a man of supreme moral sensibility: "To hurt animals to please one's stomach is something that the gentleman will not do," and then added that, in the eyes of sages, nonkilling is not perverse, but a way of cultivating one's "benevolent heart-and-mind."[60]

As literati endorsed the practices of nonkilling and liberating animals, they also modified them. Using a hook but no net, they followed a vegetarian diet not as a matter of course but only on special occasions; or they avoided certain animal foods but not all; or they made fine distinctions between having animals killed for consumption and eating animals that had already been killed; or, like Yang Dongming, the founder of the first-known benevolent society, they followed Confucius's call for restraint (that is, for using "a hook but no net"), while defending the use of meats for ancestral sacrifices.[61]

At times Zhuhong allowed latitude in practice: if one must persist in eating meat, he instructed, then one should buy it rather than slaughtering animals oneself.[62] Generally, though, he upheld the strictest of guidelines. Of the passage about using a hook but no net, Zhuhong expressed incredulity that "Confucius could have been so insensitive to the feelings of living things" and suggested that "something had been dropped" inadvertently from the text.[63] He also argued that even the wearing of silk be abandoned out of consideration for silkworms. Many literati deviated far from Zhuhong's strictures—or they dissociated themselves from Buddhism altogether. Nonetheless, they—among them, staunch Confucians—found the idea of liberating animals so compelling as to make it the subject of their writings and the cause of their clubs.

LIBERATING ANIMALS ACQUIRES NEW MEANINGS

The animal-saving vogue can be loosely linked to numerous late Ming trends: political and social instability, the arrival of Jesuits armed with challenges to native Chinese traditions, literati enthusiasm for forming associations of all sorts (whether for poetry writing or mutual uplifting), and scholar-official commitment to educating the masses in ethical values (whether through lectures at community-compact meetings [xiangyue] or popular didactic works). Each of these currents may have contributed to the interest in fangsheng, yet the linkages are imprecise and inconsistent, with no one cause standing out.

The twin concepts of nonkilling and kindness to animals, according to one historian, may have appealed to men of the late Ming because theirs was an era of social turmoil, one marked by riots against landlords, pirate raids along the coast, and invasions along the borders.[64] Without doubt, the concern for animals was associated with the desire to put an end to strife and suffering, for as one animal-protector, citing a sutra, despaired: "Man eats lamb; and ram eats man: generation after generation they eat one another up—endlessly, through aeons and aeons."[65] Yet, explanations in terms of social instability fail to explain why literati preoccupation with saving animals persisted well into the relatively tranquil eighteenth century, or why earlier periods of disorder failed to stimulate a comparably strong concern for animals. Nor do they explain why the wish to end discord assumed the specific form of saving animals.

Challenging literati to crystallize their arguments for liberating animals were, moreover, the teachings of Jesuit missionaries who, having arrived in China in 1583, were frequenting elite circles and winning converts by the 1600s.[66] Zhuhong and a few of the animal protectors were familiar with and specifically opposed the Jesuit position that animals lacked immortal souls, that heaven produced animals for human beings to consume, and that the doctrine of transmigration was absurd.[67] It was probably in rebuttal to the second point that Zhuhong and Yang Dongming rhetorically asked: "If a tiger eats a person, would people say that men were raised for tigers?"[68] Jesuit proselytizing engaged and antagonized many literati. Still, the movement to liberate animals was in full swing by 1603, the year that Matteo Ricci launched his attack on the idea of reincarnation;[69] and the particular associations that Ming-Qing writers attached to the concepts of nonkilling and liberating extended far beyond Jesuit agendas. Though late Ming writers did touch on the issue of transmigration, they far more often dwelled on the themes of extravagance and frugality, cruelty and compassion, life and death, and oppression and liberation—in short, the very vocabulary with which they also discussed charitable activities.

Frugality and Extravagance

The precept of nonkilling indicated a vegetarian diet, which happened to be more economical than meat dishes, which were usually reserved for banquets. Thus accounts linking compassion for animals to the theme of frugality can be found from the earliest times. Consider the case of King Hui of Liang, who, being "unable to bear the frightened appearance" of an ox about to be slaughtered for a ceremony, substituted for the ox a lamb.[70] Mencius chose to construe the king's reaction as a sign of his capacity for compassion, and, for this reason, late Ming animal protectors often alluded to this passage. Yet Mencius also hinted that the king, in exchanging a large animal for a small one, may have been motivated by stinginess. Two themes, frugality and compassion, were thus confounded. Or consider the case of Emperor Renzong of the Song dynasty, who, when presented with clams, asked, "Where did these come from?" and then quickly followed with the question, "How much did they cost?" When told that each one cost a thousand coins and that there were twenty-eight clams in all, the emperor, displeased, said: "I have forbidden you to be extravagant. Today, to spend twenty-eight thousand for one meal—I cannot bear it"; he then refused to eat them.[71] Although this account is later cited by Meng Chaoran as an example of compassion, what the emperor found most intolerable was not the deaths of the clams but their price.

The theme of frugality similarly mingled with discussions of compassion during the late Ming. To encourage "frugality and simplicity" Zhou Rudeng (a native of Qi Biaojia's hometown) promoted two "Confucian teachings that one should not neglect": "Do not kill dogs or pigs without reason" and "Keep a distance from the kitchen."[72] "Affected by the extravagant banqueting of his village," Wang Heng wrote three verses to encourage nonkilling among the residents.[73] Feng Shike was concerned not just about protecting animal lives but about restraint in general. Regarding a compact he made with friends to keep entertainment modest, he explained: "I normally do not have extravagant tastes"; he then listed among the foods to be avoided not just animals, but certain expensive fruits.[74]

Feng Shike made a principle of moderate living. On the grounds that his home prefecture Songjiang was too luxurious, he chose to retire to Suzhou.[75] Thus he distanced and differentiated himself from his eight affluent brothers, who had maneuvered him out of much of his inheritance—just as he had, through his permissiveness toward rats, differentiated himself from the brother who vigilantly guarded books against rodents. By living more temperately than his siblings, Shike, the only one of nine brothers to earn a *jinshi* degree, occupied the high moral ground. Even Zhuhong associated a vegetarian diet with restraint: heaven and earth had produced grain, fruits, and vegetables for man to consume, and man moreover had acquired the know-how to prepare these foods in many different ways—they could wrap them into dumplings, make them into cakes, pickle and boil them. "That should," he proclaimed, "be enough."[76]

Betraying the close association between vegetarian fare and frugality, one Ming writer condemned some animal protectors for being miserly. Though endorsing nonkilling as a "beautiful deed," he also ascribed a range of motives to vegetarians—including that of stinginess: "There are some fellows in grand households who, when mourning for relatives, drink wine and eat meat as they please; but on sacrificial days, they, being tightfisted, put out only fruits and vegetables on the table of offerings." In his judgment: "The ancients forbade killing out of benevolence; the Buddhists forbade killing out of fear. Today people forbid killing out of stinginess, and that they avoid themselves killing the animals but eat what others have killed is even more laughable."[77]

Yet the prohibition against consuming meat was not necessarily part of a general program of frugality, for many of the late Ming animal protectors did not live parsimoniously. If they followed vegetarian diets, they, like Qi Biaojia, Wang Heng, and even the moderate Feng Shike, also maintained costly gardens, or they enjoyed private opera performances, vied with each other in collecting antiques, or dallied with courtesans.[78] It was roughly eight years after he first mentioned liberating animals in a diary that Qi, facing the food shortage of 1640, began in earnest a vegetarian diet.[79] Moreover, although some Ming-Qing literati formed bean-curd and no-meat societies, others seemed less interested in sticking to vegetarian fare than they were in liberating animals. In reference to an early Qing *fangsheng* society, a nineteenth-century commentator went so far as to suggest: "Today people do not believe in nonkilling but speak instead about saving animal lives."[80] And whereas a vegetarian diet required restraint and made frugality possible, forming clubs to release animals and erecting steles to mark fish preserves invariably involved the expenditure of money—expenditure that some critics, such as Chen Longzheng, denounced as decidedly wasteful.

Entertaining Guests

Far more often than had earlier accounts, late Ming texts placed the twin practices of nonkilling and liberating animals at the center of social interactions. Early accounts about compassion for animals touched on a broad range of situations: a lone hunter, deep in the woods, confronting the grief of his prey; the scheduling of construction work during seasons that would not upset the wildlife living in decaying walls and buildings;[81] random encounters with animals in distress; the benign disposal of live animals received as gifts.

While continuing to pay heed to these situations (often by retelling the old stories), Ming writings drew particular attention to the issue of feeding guests. As Zhuhong noted, all sorts of events—birthdays, funerals, weddings, and general hospitality—were occasions for consuming meat. Or, as the editor of one morality book tersely commented, "Most killing is done for entertaining guests." The editor appended this comment to a report about a certain *juren* (*xiaolian*) of the early sixteenth century. The graduate, who was from a wealthy Nanjing family, killed three to four pigs whenever he entertained. After he died, a sound came from his coffin. When the mourners looked inside, they found that the deceased had turned into a pig.[82] The tale thus cautions against the killing of animals; it illustrates the principle of transmigration; it points to the excess of killing three to four pigs at a time— an excess underscored by the type of retribution, transformation into an animal known for its gluttony; but it also makes clear that the occasion for malevolence was the feasting of guests.

A record about a Lin Jun around the mid-sixteenth century likewise placed individual behavior toward animals in a social setting. During a banquet he was hosting, Lin had a revelation about the urgency of nonkilling. Surrounded by his numerous invited guests, he fell into a deep slumber. When he came to, he announced that he had just visited the underworld, where he was the guest of an illustrious ancestor. The ancestor explained that Lin was being punished (with an early death, one presumes) because, when serving as a magistrate, he had failed to ban the slaughter of oxen. Lin protested that the accusation was false; and, upon investigation, it was found that he had truly posted a placard forbidding the slaughter of oxen. In the end, Lin's merit earned him longevity—he lived to the age of one hundred. But the main point for our purposes is a less explicit message, namely, that he let his merit be known in order to communicate a moral lesson. Shifting between the roles of host in this world and guest in the underworld—a shift that identified him with his guests and implied that they, too, might be suspect—Lin Jun told his company about the dream. Aroused by his account, they then "together swore an oath that they would not again eat meat."[83] Thus did Lin turn his personal confrontation with the underworld into a collective matter.

In still another way Lin's dream episode asserted a link between nonkilling and social action. It invoked the authority of a historical figure who, though he had been touched by Buddhism, was revered above all as a Confucian scholar exemplary in serving the social good: the king of the underworld happened to be the eleventh-century Fan Zhongyan, a man who will occasionally appear in this book because late Ming do-gooders admired him greatly, to the point of saying he was so charitable that he died penniless.[84] Through the connection to Fan, the dream associated nonkilling with broad social responsibility.

The taboo against consuming meat had become a group affair. Wang Heng—who was appalled to witness ordinary banquets serving up the sort of delicacies that had formerly been reserved for emperors and lords— formed a pact with his village to follow a vegetarian diet.[85] Qian Sule, an official whose household had avoided meat for ten years, had a few words printed up about man and animals being alike in their desire for life; he ostensibly did this to forewarn his guests not to expect meat dishes, but undoubtedly with the effect of publicizing his good example.[86] For Feng Shike and his friends, avoiding meat was also a collective enterprise. They formed a club (*she*) and made a compact to limit the number and type of dishes when entertaining guests.[87] Similarly, a seventeenth-century official integrated his concern for animals into daily social transactions: he entrusted to a temple any gifts he received of live animals; and each day he set aside thirty coins of "the money designated for buying vegetables" to spend on purchasing— at the market, in the public eye—fish and fowl to be set free.[88]

The social implications of nonkilling are further evident in Feng Shike's account of the people who escaped a shipwreck because some members of the traveling party had avoided meat. Feng's account resembles tales in *Extensive Records,* but only superficially, for in molding what he had heard, Feng accommodated late Ming concerns. As he perceived it, the virtue of the vegetarian passengers was not a private affair but had ramifications for the society at large. The three vegetarians who avoided beef brought benefit not only to themselves but also to their fellow passengers—both parties were saved from shipwreck. Their escape from disaster in turn moved some sixty passengers from the other boat to swear off beef, and those sixty travelers made their decision not individually, but as a group, in a pact. What enabled one event to have such wide-reaching consequences was the mediation of a witness (who saw the three "strange-looking men," that is, the wind demons) and a reporter (who explained to the witness how the other boat happened to avoid being wrecked). Though not present at the event, Feng participated in the process: having heard about this from a friend, he recorded it for posterity.[89]

Thus an individual's practice of nonkilling and of liberating animals simultaneously brought merit to the actor and spread throughout society, not according to hierarchical lines of authority (as when a ruler or official issued a policy or orchestrated a mass prayer in one of those annual ceremonies celebrating the Buddha's birthday), but in a helter-skelter way, through informal friendships, accidental encounters, word of mouth, and the witness of strangers.

The concern for animals became coupled with late Ming definitions of courtesy toward guests, who might be made to feel uncomfortable by the serving of delicacies. Disagreeing with Zhou Rudeng, who explained the discomfort in terms of regard for the host, Qi Biaojia's brother justified the vegetarian food in terms of Confucius's attitudes: the majority of delicacies came from killing animals, whereas Confucius took pity on animals; and extravagant delicacies were, as Confucius himself had observed, harmful to customs.[90] Yet both men assumed that the avoidance of meat (or kindness to animals) affected social relations. Making this linkage explicit, a Qing-dynasty household manual (cited by Meng Chaoran, who disliked Buddhism) instructed, "In treating guests with respect one must also maintain thoughts of love for animals (*aiwu*)."[91]

One model of compassion for animals was offered by the tenth-century *Extensive Records:* a lone person individually responded, without witnesses, to the plight of animals and kept his virtue secret (*yinde*). Late Ming practice additionally followed another model, in which the releasing of animals was often done in public places, in front of witnesses (who retold what they heard and saw), and by small groups whose solidarity lent legitimacy to their actions. The liberating of animals had assumed a place in social interactions. This was true even for Zhuhong, who, as Chün-fang Yü has pointed out, was wary about forming societies (since voluntary associations were at that time politically suspect) and therefore once advised that everyone should buy and release animals whenever they saw them rather than in group meetings. Nonetheless Zhuhong sustained the social dimension of liberating animals, encouraging everyone periodically (whether once a season or at the end of each year) to assemble in one place, where, he explained, "the number he has released can be tabulated, and his merit can be assigned."[92] As perceived and executed by Ming literati, the twin practices extended beyond matters of personal conduct and fortune. Literati had incorporated them into their social relations and integrated them into their social personas, to be displayed and shared with other people.

For the Sake of One's Stomach

What many Ming-Qing animal protectors reacted against was not spending per se, but, more precisely, indulging one's taste buds at the expense of other creatures. This sentiment, to be sure, had early precedents, as in a case that Yan Maoyou anthologized in his popular morality book, *Records of Right Behavior and Good Fortune* (*Diji lu*) concerning a Song-dynasty scholar who was fond of quail.[93] The scholar was moved to reform his ways (and to liberate several dozen quails from his kitchen—a gesture others might have judged prodigal) after he had a dream in which a quail, appearing in the guise of a shabbily dressed old man, chanted:

> Your stocks of millet and rice I eat
> That I may supply your soup with meat
> One soup takes several lives
> Though your chopsticks dig in, you remain unsated.[94]

Indulging the appetite at the expense of others similarly aroused Su Shi's abhorrence for killing—even though he recognized that liberating animals had wasteful consequences. He explained: "When young, I disliked killing, and recently I put a stop to it. When someone gave me a gift of crabs and oysters, I released them in the river. Most of the crabs and oysters lacked the wherewithal to live and not one would survive; nonetheless, liberating them was better than boiling them alive. How can one allow thousands of creatures to suffer limitlessly just for the sake of one's stomach?"[95]

Questions of moderation and waste were, in fact, tangential concerns for the animal protectors. Rather, it was this repulsion, voiced by Su Shi, for satisfying the self at the expense of others that Ming-Qing literati elaborated upon as a reason for *fangsheng* and *jiesha*. Observing that "ordinary people also say that vegetarians are skinny and those who eat meat are plump," Zhuhong opined: "To fatten one's own body without thinking of the misery of others—where, then, is the human heart?"[96] Expanding on this sentiment, the prominent statesman and philosopher Gao Panlong stated: "Flavorful foods enter our mouths, pass along our three-inch tongues, and descend our throats. But whether our food is delicate or coarse will make no difference when we enter the afterlife; so how is it that, to gratify three inches of tongue, we think so lightly of slaughtering animals?"[97] And likewise did the famous playwright Tang Xianzu capture the picture of self-indulgence when stating: "In this age of decline, the last kalpa, gentlemen consume meat to the point of being so fat that they cannot budge."[98] Benefiting the self at the expense of others spelled doom for a restaurateur in Suzhou, whose choice of fare had broad social implications because it promised to affect not only his own reincarnation but that of his clients. According to what the eighteenth-century Meng Chaoran had heard from an acquaintance, that shop specialized in noodles with eels and "was several times more profitable than other shops. It used some sort of basket-contraption that made the eels curl around and strangle each other, letting out their juices, which then beautifully blended in with the flavor of the noodles. A few years later, the shop owner suddenly disappeared. His son found him along the river bank, dead with thousands of eels wrapped around his stomach." Commented Meng, "This is a most extraordinary instance of retribution,"—and so we might agree. But if an account about eels wreaking revenge on a proprietor's stomach stretches our credulity, it illustrates a real sentiment: that killing animals to satisfy appetites—or worse, to make a profit—was despicable.[99]

Same and Different

Compassion for animals was advocated in the most ancient texts—and indeed may be a universal phenomenon—but the precise grounds for identifying with and representing the animals changed with time and place.[100] Before the arrival of Buddhism in China, a few rulers were so attached to their domestic animals that they provided them with funerals—the lavishness of which elicited criticism.[101] During the Tang dynasty, under Buddhist influence, people, moved by the service and loyalty that their domestic animals had rendered, offered prayers for their smooth passage into the next life. Yet, after making such supplications for the animal's benefit, the participants, at least in the case of one wedding celebration, had no compunction about consuming the carcasses.[102]

While retaining old wisdom about benevolence toward animals, late Ming literati represented animals in fresh ways. Without entirely losing sight of the hard-working domestic beasts to whom loyalty was due, they shifted their attention to the smallest and least serviceable creatures; thoughts of gratitude for service done by the animals gave way to talk of their subservience and dependence.

Some early tales illustrated that animals, no less than human beings, had the capacity to understand the messages of the Buddhist scriptures. In one account, someone who overheard the chanting of sutras traced the sounds to fish stored on a boat; this revealed the presence of Buddhahood in all living things and moved the eavesdropper to gain the release of the captured fish.[103] Late Ming texts preserved and reproduced such anecdotes pointing to the universality of Buddhahood among all creatures. The mother of a talented trio, the Yuan brothers (Zongdao, Hongdao, and Zhongdao), verified that even a spider was capable of understanding Buddhist teachings. When reciting a sutra, she spotted a large spider. "So you have come to hear the sutra?" she asked, and then continued reading. When she came to a certain phrase, the spider moved a bit as though making an obeisance, thus showing that it comprehended the recitation.[104] As Yan Maoyou put it (in another context): "Every living thing can recite the Buddha's name and beg for mercy"; and, as Yan commented on the flies who, though individually lacking strength, joined forces to save the wine brewer from an unfair sentence: "Everything in this world has human nature, and every creature has Buddha nature."[105]

But to tales underscoring the universality of Buddhahood, late Ming writers added other perceptions. Zhuhong argued that one should not kill animals because they, "like human beings, have blood and breath, mothers and children, knowledge and feelings, and can feel pain and itch, and life and death."[106] Heightening a sense of urgency about life and death, Zhuhong stated: "When they are about to be captured, lice will flee—even they know enough to avoid death; and when it is about to rain, ants will disperse—even they desire life."[107] Or, as the Buddhist-influenced Confucian scholar Hu Zhi observed, "When an archer . . . carries his bow into the forest, all the birds of the forest will screech out; and when a butcher . . . takes a rope to the market place, all the dogs in the market will howl; so, how can it be said that these animals are willing to die?"[108] Or as a *jinshi* degree-holder, Zhi Dalun, explained: "People who go fishing do not see that it suits the true natures of fish to form schools and ride the waves in contentment. They see a fish only when it falls into a person's hand: it jumps about and is frightened, and when it is choked so that its guts split open and when its stomach is gashed so that blood pours out, soaking the knife, then it is a lamentable sight; or they see the fish when it is tossed into the cooking pots, . . . into the bubbling broth . . . and then strains to jump out." Zhi Dalun wished to make the basic point that, for one chopstickful of food, people will subject fish to unlimited suffering, but he did so by elaborating on the fish's love of life (riding the waves contentedly) and by highlighting the cruelty of the slaughter. Along the way he also reminded his readers that fish are just like human beings in having a social capacity for forming groups, or schools.[109]

Likewise stressing that animals and humans are identical in their social relations, the early Qing-dynasty Zhou Mengyan explained that, although men and beasts differ in their shapes and bodies, when it comes to feelings, they are alike: "Watch how animals behave when about to be caught: they squeal and screech, jump over walls, and climb up buildings—just as we do during political chaos. The parents are at a loss as to what to do, and the wives and children have no escape from death. Are they different or not? Watch how when one decapitates chickens, if one chicken is killed, then all the chickens will shriek in fear, and when one slaughters one pig, then all the other pigs will refuse to eat—just like us."[110]

In tales in *Extensive Records* about recompensing animal rescuers, the suffering of the animals was implied or assumed, but without elaboration. With the exception of one fish, who "shrieked out its last breath,"[111] other animals, whether appearing through dreams or other devices, simply "begged for their lives" (*qiuming, qingming, qiming*).[112] Not so subdued were the Ming-Qing accounts, which dwelled on the suffering of the animals, emphasizing the instruments of capture and death (ropes, bows, knives, cooking pots, bubbling broths), and the signs of pain (screams and screeches, blood gushing out, desperate attempts at escape). As Zhuhong succinctly put it: "That thing in your plate came from screaming animals."[113] Ming texts stressed that animals were like human beings in having love for their children. Selecting from a vast literature those few pieces that suited his preoccupations, Zhuhong retold an ancient story about a deer who fell into deep mourning when a hunter struck down her child. The mother licked the doe's wound, but after a while, both doe and mother died. When the hunter cut the mother open, he found that her guts had burst into fragments, so strong had been her sorrow. The hunter was remorseful, destroyed his bow and arrow, and withdrew into the hills as a hermit. The point on which this story turns, that is, the element that moved the hunter to change his ways, was that animal mothers, just like human mothers, care deeply for their children.[114]

Ming tales about saving animals also emphasized that all creatures have feelings, or emotions (*qing*), a theme that preoccupied many sixteenth- and seventeenth-century writers.[115] Consider the account of a monkey who wept. This monkey was usually agile enough to catch all the arrows hunters aimed at him; one day, however, he found cause to burst into sobs: having just spotted a certain hunter who had a reputation for being a crack shot, the monkey recognized that he was doomed to die.[116] Likewise did Tang Xianzu recognize that animals had feelings—as when he described what he had witnessed when an animal was being prepared for a sacrifice: for several days before the event, the animal wept and would not eat; when men tried to lead him away, he refused to budge. Thus he avoided death several times. Finally, several men carried the animal to the kitchen, but the animal sobbed and kicked so hard that he died.[117] This echoes that account from *The Book of Mencius* where King Hui of Liang "could not bear the frightened appearance" of an ox about to be slaughtered for a ceremony.[118] But, in sharp contrast to the mute and passive ox in *The Book of Mencius*, the ox that Tang watched was spirited and vociferous.

Even the monk Zhuhong, who surely was familiar with the Buddhist ideal of detachment from all desires, had introduced the element of emotion into his discussions. It was on the basis of feelings that he posed the question, "How would we *feel* if the consumption of human flesh was so customary that chefs had no inkling that cooking it up was wrong?"[119] And it was on the basis of feelings that he appealed to his readers when ticking off the various situations where man habitually slaughters and consumes animals. With each of seven items, Zhuhong repeated the refrain, "This could make one weep endlessly with grief."

Without abandoning talk of retribution and merit, late Ming accounts altered the basis for understanding why one should be kind to animals. When anthologists retold the story about the mother deer who wept for her child, they aimed to move readers to identify with the mother. What moved Tang Xianzu to sympathize with the sacrificial animal was seeing it kicking in agony. And what had moved him to heed Zhuhong's teachings in the first place was that Zhuhong had expressed his feelings for animals. As Tang Xianzu put it, "How good was Zhuhong, who wept for insects."[120]

Late Ming texts thus drifted far from the arguments of the *Book of Brahmā's Net,* which had been the locus classicus for Zhuhong's program. That book had declared: "All sons are my fathers; all daughters are my mothers; . . . and all living things in the six stages of transmigration are my parents; to kill and eat them is to kill and eat one's parents and to kill one's own person in a previous existence."[121] Supplementing—or circumventing altogether—the issue of transmigration, late Ming writers argued for the liberation of animals primarily by appealing to the emotions, to one's capacity to sympathize with others, and by focusing on parent-child relations, not across the ages, but within the contemporary world. The difference was clear even to the early seventeenth-century Xie Zhaozhe, who declared: "The Buddhists oppose killing for the purposes of transmigration; our opposition to killing is because we cannot bear untimely deaths."[122]

Smaller and Weaker

Late Ming texts further differed from earlier writings in their portrayal of relations between animals and men. In the tales of retribution in *Extensive Records,* animals and men had near-equal footing: the animals seeking survival frequently appeared *as men* in the dreams of their potential benefactors; they were fluidly transformed into human beings and back again into their animal shapes. In some of these tales, moreover, the animals displayed humanlike, or even superhuman, physical strengths—as when a tortoise saved his benefactor from a shipwreck by carrying him ashore, or when a horse who had been well cared for by his owner saved that owner from a capsized boat, or when fifty tortoises who had been redeemed by a fisherman appeared as men to reward their benefactor's parents with five thousand coins.[123] Although these animals were portrayed as having been stuck in situations where they had to beg for their lives, once saved, they in turn were seen as taking the initiative in repaying the kindness.

To such portrayals of animals, Ming writers added new descriptions: they frequently saw animals as smaller and weaker than human beings, as the objects of trickery and deceit, of manipulation and, yes, of consumption. As Zhi Dalun stated, "Now, when people want to raise chickens, pigs, dogs, and horses, they feed and comfort them—and they are even more nurturing with the animals than they are with people; then, one morning, they kill and eat the animals, saying, 'This is how it should be.' But the livestock are unaware that they are going to be killed; and when they are about to be slaughtered, how can they not resent that they have been deceived? How much more true this is for fish, who hide in the deep and are not habitually reared by man. Yet man uses a hundred strategies to capture them, deceiving them when they are unaware and taking advantage of their unsuspecting natures. . . . This is a case of crafty deception filling the universe." As Zhi saw it, human beings carry out parental functions in nurturing the animals only to betray their charges; animals, lacking in awareness, fall victim to human stratagems.[124]

The practice of liberating animals was not mandated by the Buddhist legacy.[125] The Chinese accounts told in support of the precepts of nonkilling and saving animals stand in sharp contrast to animal tales in one of the earliest sources of Buddhist lore, the *Jātaka* stories of the Buddha's former births. Few *Jātaka* tales concern the smallest animals; Chinese tales and practice were especially preoccupied with tiny creatures—the flies who repaid the wine brewer; eels, centipedes, ants, and lice, all of which, according to Zhuhong, strongly "desire life."[126] Many *Jātaka* tales draw comparisons between animals of the same species: between one stupid and one successful stag; between wise and foolish birds; and among three fish, who are, respectively, overly thoughtful, thoughtful, and thoughtless.[127] The Chinese tales about the twin precepts make no such comparisons between individual members of a given species.[128]

Other genres of Chinese literature construe animal types allegorically to represent human traits; well-known examples are the pig in *Journey to the West* (*Xiyou ji*), who represents earthy appetites, and the rat in *The Book of Poetry* (*Shi jing*), who represents rapacious officials. But the tales illustrating nonkilling and liberating animals rarely concern themselves with the characteristics distinguishing various species, except in reference to size. The *Jātaka* tales tell of good and bad animals alike: a man rears a viper, which in turn kills its benefactor; a crab has the wisdom to bite off the head of a crane who is devouring fish.[129] The Chinese *fangsheng* tales tell mainly of innocent and helpless creatures whose chances for survival rest with man. Even rats, as construed by Feng Shike, are vulnerable beings in need of human considerateness.[130] The focus on man as the strong and animals as defenseless beings flattens out all contrasts—other than that of size—among the animals.

ANALOGUES

In Ming-Qing texts, animals had become analogues for those weaker members of the community who needed protection.[131] For this analogy, early writings may seem to offer a few, faint precedents. A Song text declared: "If one avoids the kitchen . . . then few will be the instances where living things are cruelly oppressed for the sake of filling one's own stomach and where the people are fleeced for the sake of fattening up one's own powers."[132] Yet, this passage, which Meng Chaoran included in his *Records of Spreading Love,* speaks only of avoiding the kitchen (borrowing from *The Book of Mencius*), not of nonkilling and liberating animals, and it comes to us not as a part of a Song-period program to liberate animals but because the eighteenth-century Meng appropriated the passage to build his case for kindness to animals.

The analogy between animals and weak members of society was well understood by Zhuhong—and was central to his conception of *fangsheng*. When skeptics pointed out that the ponds for saving fish were so small that it would be better to toss the fish into rivers and lakes, Zhuhong engaged the skeptics in the following dialogue: "Is it better," he asked, "to have the common people live in the cramped city, or in the countryside?" The skeptics responded that in the countryside would be better; but then Zhuhong persisted: "If there were bandits . . . approaching, which place would be better?" To which the skeptics replied, "The city." Zhuhong then drove his point home: "Is not the fear that fish have of nets like the fear that people have of bandits? And is not placing the fish in ponds . . . like putting the common people inside city walls to protect them against bandits?"[133] From Zhuhong's point of view, people who say that birds and animals are meant to be eaten "do not understand that it's just a matter of the strong oppressing the weak."[134]

The analogy between animals and the weaker members of society was also understood by Gui Zhuang. Gui expressed reservations about the practice of saving animals, arguing that the Song-dynasty designation of West Lake as a preserve for fish was less worthy than a famine-relief program that saved several million people. "Animals," he claimed, "are lowly, and human beings great." Nonetheless, he recognized the symbolic value of releasing animals, for he then went on to state: "From the concept of saving animals one can deduce the following: Young men should not oppress the weak or maltreat those who have no relatives, and servants should not lean on their privileges to lord it over others."[135] The same analogy had been made by Feng Shike. After rescuing a fly from a spider's web, Feng explained that he hated cases where the strong eat the weak.[136] And when urging people to cough up funds for the purchase of animals to be released, Feng stated that hoarding money is tantamount to "locking people up in cages and slaughtering them."[137] The analogy was also drawn by Yan Maoyou: "Everyone hates to see large animals swallow up small ones; how can heaven not feel the same when watching people? . . . Place yourself among the animals and think about it." And again: "The rich and high must think of when they were poor; prosecutors must think of the day when they might themselves be prosecuted. Our lives and animal lives are the same. Try putting yourself in their place, and compassion will suddenly arise."[138] Because the analogy was compelling, many writers saw in man's kindness for tiny creatures a test of concern for needy people. As Lu Longqi remarked: "If I am compassionate like this toward fish, how much more so will I be toward people, my own species? . . . If one widow, orphan, indigent person, or person without anyone to rely on does not have a place in society, can we bear it?"[139]

Animals were metaphors for piteous and powerless human beings. "Loving animals may be compared to loving children," stated Minister of Justice Yao Wenran,[140] thus connecting up with the paternalistic rhetoric so often used in describing local magistrates—those "father-and-mother officials" who carried most responsibility for the lives of the common people. The metaphor was made clear in a song warning market people against catching frogs. The author first accentuated the desperate pain and childlike features of the victims:

> When skinned, they die not
> With legs chopped off, they still leap about
> Holding two hands to their heads
> They scream like children,

and then, shifting attention from the measly children-like frogs to human beings in need, the songwriter spelled out his point for men in leadership positions:

> How much more so because their bodies are tiny
> We cannot bear to munch on them
> In governing and spreading benevolence
> One must give top priority to helpless creatures.[141]

The analogy between animals and weak members of society was implicitly made by some morality books, which arranged sections on the liberating of animals right alongside materials on such other good deeds as providing food and shelter for the poor.[142] The analogy was further implied by the actions of so many benefactors, who, like Qi Biaojia, easily alternated between saving animals and aiding the poor—all the while applying the same rhetoric and the same feelings of compassion to both activities. Thus it was out of one meeting of the Society for Liberating Animals (Fangsheng she), in 1636, that Qi and his comrades touched upon the subject of an epidemic then raging through their community and decided to establish a dispensary for the distribution of free medicines.[143] As Qi put it, liberating lives "also has the meaning of treating people humanely and loving all things."[144] Just as they could not bear to see animals slaughtered, so the supporters of the medical bureau "could not bear to see living men die."[145]

But why was it necessary to make that analogy at all? Why was it necessary to think about kindness to the poor in terms of kindness toward animals? Why did late Ming writers—especially those who opposed Buddhism—not dispense with the analogy altogether and simply teach the rich and powerful to aid the poor and weak? Why spend money on animals, ponds, and steles by those ponds when there were plenty of beggars around waiting for handouts? Why add animals to the list of the needy? Such questions were put to late Ming literati, some of whom in turn steadfastly defended, point by point, the practice of liberating animals.[146]

Even opponents of the practice accepted that aiding people and aiding animals were somehow comparable. Yang Tingyun of Hangzhou, whose father had joined a society for liberating animals, set up a humane, or benevolent, society (*ren hui*) in reaction—and as an alternative—to the wasteful spending of money on birds and fish.[147] Chen Longzheng argued that benevolent societies were better than societies for liberating animals because "they aided and supported good, living people"; he supposed that the two institutions were analogous, different only in merit.[148] When Lu Shiyi sponsored a benevolent society, he must have had the societies for releasing lives on his mind as well, for he criticized monks who "everywhere were setting up shelters (*fangsheng an*) and ponds to protect chickens, fish, pigs, and cattle, while neglecting people who were crippled or had no relatives to whom they might turn."[149]

That the practice of saving animals stuck is all the more puzzling, because, for all their talk of the value of life and the urgency of liberating animals, do-gooders recognized that many of the animals they tried to save would die anyhow, or would, upon being liberated, be instantly captured by vendors and riffraff for resale.[150] One early Qing organizer of a society for liberating animals admonished members to be neither stingy, for fear of appearing unwilling to buy the animals, nor liberal, for fear that high demand for animals would stimulate vendors to capture more creatures to cash in.[151] The societies for liberating animals were seen by some detractors as fundamentally futile, since "for every animal saved, ten thousand were missed."[152]

Despite all these drawbacks—that liberating animals was costly, siphoned off funds that might have been used to help the poor, and was, in any case, a dubious method of preserving life—do-gooders persisted in the practice. For them it expressed certain concerns that charity for the poor could not. By focusing on saving lives when purchasing the animals, the animal liberators were masking the fact that they were donating money to the poor vendors. This was clearly understood by Qi Biaojia. When one of his bondservants came by with a goose tied up, Qi bought it to be released, and then recorded in his diary that not only was the animal saved but "the seller got a good price."[153] Qi also assumed as a matter of course that sellers (of shellfish) would flock thither whenever they got wind of a *fangsheng* meeting.[154] The amounts of cash and grain Qi distributed in this fashion were substantial; in 1640 he entered in his *Diary* that, during the previous fortnight, he had spent one hundred and some *shi* of grain a day for saving snails and the like.[155]

By saving animals, members of the local elite could, moreover, communicate to the downtrodden certain messages for which other forms of charity were inadequate. By purchasing animals from some poor vendor or vagrant only to let the acquisition vanish into air or water, benefactors demonstrated—and communicated—their readiness to part with money in the name of a good cause. But more than displaying financial sacrifice, the act of saving animals established a particular kind of social relationship. Where most forms of charity to the poor involved a dyadic relationship between benefactor and recipient, the act of *fangsheng* involved a triangular exchange: the benefactor released the animal, the vendor watched the benefactor, and the animal was ostensibly the desperately needy one. With both benefactor and vendor thus sharing in the good deed of seeing the animal liberated, the distinction between the haves and the have-nots was temporarily transcended. In the minds of the animal benefactors, at least, rich and poor were momentarily united in a common purpose, namely, saving the lives of creatures who were more pitiable than even the most wretched of human beings.

The practitioners of liberating animals at once identified with the animals *and* set them apart. They both expanded their definition of the needy to include animals *and* construed animals as the "other," a point of reference to be shared by rich and poor. For all their declarations that animals and human beings were alike in their love of life, the benefactors understood well that animals (*wu*) and humans (*ren*) were different, and everything they wrote about saving animals turned on this grasp of an essential difference. Although Yan Maoyou declared that "human beings (*ren*) are one of the creatures (*wu*) in the world," he promptly proceeded to assert that those who are unable to love life are no different from "squirming insects."[156] Though exhortations to be compassionate toward animals dwelled on the humanlike features of the animals (parental love of children, sensitivity to pain, the capacity to form social groups), those same accounts reported instances where punishment for brutality toward animals (and for other offenses) was degradation to an animal state, as in the case of the glutton who, upon death, turned into a pig. So too did late Ming charity simultaneously affirm a united community of all humankind, who were on some level alike, and uphold a social hierarchy.

If liberating animals allowed benefactors to bond, ceremonially at least, with the most common of people, it also allowed them to display their own moral superiority. As Yu Zhi declared, "The petty man catches and sells; the gentleman buys and releases."[157] It was, after all, the benefactor who had taken the initiative in saving the animal; it was he who made the sacrifice of letting his money, as it were, vanish into thin air; and it was he who essentially showed the vendor what goodness is. As for the vendor who had sold the animal: well, he was left holding the coins.

Into the midst of this complicated three-way relationship stepped Qi Biaojia, Feng Shike, Tao Wangling, and other animal-liberating literati. They incorporated animals into their vision of all beings united but dealt with them as a contrasting "other." They simultaneously shared an object of compassion—the animals—with the poor *and* retained an edge as moral leaders; affirmed the sameness of all creatures *and* recognized basic differences between animal and man and between rich and poor. The triangular donor-seller-animal (rich, poor, and piteous other) relationship affirmed the literati vision of social unity while adjusting to new social dynamics. In portraying animals as a contrasting "other," writers on *fangsheng* tended to disregard character differences among the animals, each of which deserved liberation equally; rather they emphasized differences in size or strength. Given that they were projecting onto animals those humanlike features they saw and valued in themselves, their portrayals of animals suggest that at least some literati were beginning to perceive the social hierarchy, not exclusively in terms of moral standing and education (the good and the wise), but also in terms of power and wealth (that is, size).

CONCLUSION

The late Ming practice of releasing animals thus evolved far from its early sources, acquiring layers of meanings, many of which were not essentially Buddhist. Where *The Book of Brahmā's Net* had given equal emphasis to the two precepts of nonkilling and liberating animals, late Ming literati emphasized the latter. Where Buddhist discussions tied the two precepts to concepts of transmigration and retribution, late Ming and early Qing discussions made it possible to understand those precepts in terms independent of Buddhism.

If some Song-dynasty literati had liberated animals, they did so individually and in conformance with the value of secret merit (*yinde*)—the notion that good deeds should be known only to heaven. Consequently documentation of early animal saving is scant. For late Ming literati, in contrast, saving animals was a social affair to be shared with the community, whether by recording the deeds in diaries, insisting on having witnesses, or setting up steles by the fish ponds to advertise the names of sponsors. As a result late Ming materials on the subject abound.

The late Ming practice of releasing animals bears on the subject of charity not only because the Chinese texts themselves counted both activities as "good deeds." It also brings to light a cluster of ideas—in particular a heightened concern for human life—and modes of operation that characterize many activities that the Western tradition conventionally considers charitable, such as the distribution of food, money, medicine, and clothes to the poor, and the provision of shelter for foundlings and the homeless. At the same time, the practice of releasing animals shows that in addition to human poverty and need one must consider the preoccupation of the do-gooders themselves: an interest in displaying meritorious deeds; an emphasis on witnessing and spreading the word about charitable deeds; an impulse to form voluntary associations; and a concern about consumption at the expense of others. It further exposes a tension that the do-gooders felt between, on the one hand, recognizing a fundamental commonality among all creatures, large and small, and high and low; and, on the other hand, an anxiety about preserving a social hierarchy. These preoccupations all became manifest in the practice of saving animals, which predated the first-known benevolent society. Finally, the case of liberating animals raises a theme with which this book will end: the malleability of ancient beliefs, the latitude for reinterpreting revered texts, and the capacity for creating new texts to accommodate the fresh concerns of contemporary society.

2

Early Benevolent Societies
and Their Visionary Leaders

*There are two roads: to be humane, which is the road to life;
and to be inhumane, which is the road to death.*
GAO PANLONG

Hardly a decade after the practice of liberating animals caught the imaginations of the educated elite, one advocate of animals, Yang Dongming, founded the first documented benevolent society.[1] Echoing the rhetoric of the societies for saving animals, his and subsequent Ming benevolent societies placed a high value on life and promoted the harmonious unity of all humankind. Like the societies for saving animals, they defined new arenas for association and displayed good deeds out in the open, with no clear connections to religious or lineage institutions. Just as steles appeared at ponds to announce that the water was reserved for the liberating of animals, so too did halls spring up at urban centers to host benevolent-society affairs. The literary landscape also changed, with educated benefactors recording their charitable activities for public dissemination and eternal preservation.

Late Ming benevolent societies mark a turning point. The term Yang used for his society, *tongshan*, literally meaning "sharing goodness," has, according to exhaustive dictionaries, no pre-Ming sources. It appears to have been coined by Yang's close friend Lü Kun as the name of a community granary he founded; warning that hoarding grain would invite disaster, Lü advised that one could, through fair redistribution of resources, accumulate merit.[2] Following Yang Dongming, the concept of a benevolent society spread. By the fall of the Ming dynasty in 1644, over ten known benevolent societies had emerged;[3] and during the Qing dynasty, many urban centers of China—in Henan and Guangdong as well as in the prosperous regions of Nanzhili and Zhejiang—supported benevolent societies. However scant and obscure late Ming benevolent societies are in the surviving historical record, they signify new social arrangements that deserve attention.

Once introduced, benevolent societies, though adjusting their characteristics to the circumstances of each place and time and though occasionally going by names other than *tongshan,* remained visible into the twentieth century. One reads of a Tongshan Society, established in the early twentieth century, that had, by 1923, acquired over a thousand branches; its program combined worship and charity, and it included among its activities "self-sacrifice to help the poor, . . . setting living beings free and planting trees, . . . [and] building roads and digging wells."[4] The term *tongshan* was also appropriated by secret societies, whose character and goals differed from the late Ming charitable institutions: they demanded membership fees and sought the patronage of deities.[5] Yet, for all their differences, these organizations had something in common with the late Ming societies, namely, that they performed charitable deeds outside the institutions of the state, lineage, and Buddhist monasteries. They secured a firm place in society, harnessed members to an institutional structure, and, unlike some religious associations that also had the welfare of the common people in mind, they generally won legitimacy in the eyes of officialdom.

Benevolent-society sponsors kept numerous documents of their activities—so they attest. Among extant sources, however, one now finds only half a dozen or so late Ming literati who commented at any length on benevolent societies; and among these, Yang Dongming, Gao Panlong, Chen Longzheng, and Lu Shiyi are the most illuminating, not because they wrote so much on the subject per se, but because the concrete details of their other writings provide a context for their charitable activities. How the benevolent society, a new type of organization, could have inserted itself into local society, gaining legitimacy in the eyes of the local community and officialdom alike, and how it could have elicited voluntary cooperation, can be best understood through the writings of the early sponsors Yang, Gao, and Chen. Their observations indicate the social changes that welcomed the new type of fellowship and the sequence of events whereby the benevolent society established its authority independent of officialdom. Their writings further reveal that their exceptional personalities were key to their effective leadership.

Yang, Gao, and Chen were extraordinary men, accomplished scholars whose lives and writings earned much admiration. That they, highly respected men in their day, chose to found, sponsor, or participate in a new type of institution, the benevolent society, in itself deserves note. All three were aware of opportunities for doing good through long-established channels—through Buddhist institutions, community granaries, charitable lineage estates, state-sponsored poorhouses (*yangji yuan*),[6] and the ad hoc collecting of funds to deal with emergencies. All three continued to use these channels (with three of the four giving substantially to their lineages, for example) even after establishing their benevolent societies. All three occasionally made charitable gifts independently of any group effort. Yet, moving beyond the status quo, they additionally gave charity through highly organized benevolent societies.

LEADING THE WAY

In 1590, Yang Dongming, literatus and midlevel official, took temporary leave of his post in the capital of Beijing to return to his home in Yucheng district, Henan. The province of Henan was tucked in the interior of China, some four hundred miles southwest of Beijing, midway up the Yellow River. Compared to the affluent southeastern counties from which many of Yang's fellow officials hailed, Yucheng was backward and sleepy. The spread of cotton growing had, it is true, recently brought Henan some prosperity, but it did so without stimulating the great cultural flowering for which the southeastern Yangzi delta region was known.[7] Although roads served Henan well, the Yellow River, clogged with heavy deposits of silt, was barely navigable, rendering trade in the region sluggish.[8] In contrast, the Yangzi delta area, often called Jiangnan, referring to the area south of the Yangzi River, was crisscrossed with river ways and canals, many of which connected to the southeastern coast; shipping was cheap and easy, and commerce thrived. Merchants and even literati (who discreetly invested in trade while maintaining their image as disinterested scholars) had silver in profusion to sponsor painters and opera performances, to build private libraries and gardens, and to support the printing of books. The Yangzi delta region, with its cultural abundance, lured talented men from all over China to retire there; the somnolent area of Henan at best attracted back those of its native men who, like Yang, were invested in its land and tied to large, land-based lineages.

Yang was a man of two worlds. As a government official he had joined the national elite; as an owner of land in Yucheng and a member of a lineage long rooted there, he was deeply committed to his hometown. After returning to Yucheng in 1590, he retained his urbane outlook. He looked over his shoulder toward the accomplished literati he had met while in office, and back toward the imperial court, the center of political power where he had served. His vision had, after all, been opened to the grandeur and viewpoints of other, more central places. At the same time, he fastened his attention on the inhabitants of his district, many of whom were in dire straits: just before his return, in the years 1588 and 1589, a disastrous drought had caused a food shortage so devastating that some people resorted to cannibalism. Yang explained the crisis simply: no one had taken the lead in organizing the storage of grain, a task that he, immediately upon his return in 1590, took upon himself.[9]

Informed by two worlds—the court with its political power and cultural achievements, and his peripheral town with its pressing needs—Yang created a special place for himself. To deal with the affairs of his town, he drew upon resources he had cultivated while in office. Rather than fading into the sleepy, faceless activities of Yucheng district, rather than sinking into political obscurity, Yang maintained a transdistrict vision. Reaching for something beyond the ordinariness of his town, he took the initiative to move his peers to abandon old ways and strive for something new.

It was almost by accident that Yang established the first known benevolent society. Upon returning to Yucheng in 1590, he contemplated the option of joining a poetry club. As he understood it, in ancient times men like him—men who had been highly educated for government service but found themselves out of office—would, under similar circumstances, have grouped together to imbibe wine and compose poetry, in the manner of those free spirits (*fengliu*) who had formed the Luoyang poetry society over a thousand years before, in the Eastern Jin dynasty.[10] So it was in his own town: two residents who had resigned from office had already organized the venerable men of Yucheng to meet monthly. As Yang tells it, he had "heard about it and admired them" and was happy that, on the basis of past ties, the members of that group accepted him into their fold; thus he got to hear their elegant rhymes and stories.[11]

Yang's pleasure soon turned into disappointment, however. The poetry group, he learned, did little other than drink wine; the meetings were boring. Restless and disinclined to be self-indulgent, he sought to set the club on a more meaningful course. Straddling two worlds—as an official residing at home—he advised the members: "When at court, the ancients carried out good government; when at home, they worked to perfect local behavior." Then, making the point that even people without official positions had responsibility for carrying out the Way, and that one should not squander time, he asked: "If we merely collect dues for banqueting, thereby wasting years and months, what's the benefit?" Upholding a high standard, Yang redirected the members of the society to contribute funds for repairing roads, fixing bridges, helping with marriage and funeral expenses, and aiding the poor and sick. To mark the overhaul, he changed the group's name, from "A Society for Sharing Pleasure" (Tongle hui) to "A Society for Sharing Goodness" (Tongshan hui). Explained Yang: "Only doing good can be called most pleasurable."[12]

Late Ming social conditions were ripe for this new type of charitable association. Other towns readily copied it and the concept of a benevolent society outlasted Yang, gaining a life of its own independent of his leadership. Subsequently there emerged numerous societies that bore the same—or similar—names: "Society for Spreading Humaneness" (Guangren hui), "Society for Sharing Humaneness" (Tongren hui), or (referring to where the members met) "Hall of Goodness" (Shan tang).[13] These terms basically point to one sort of organization: a fellowship whose primary, expressed goal was to do good, a society that functioned outside the formal government structure and outside religious institutions.

Of the poetry-chanting Society for Sharing Pleasure no traces remain beside the essay where Yang mentioned it, fleetingly and only so far as to highlight the superiority of the benevolent society. Conceivably, records for the poetry society had been compiled but were then destroyed or lost: some fifty years later, foreign invaders and Chinese turncoats tore Henan province apart, demolishing buildings, libraries, and bureaucratic archives, thus hastening the demise of the Ming dynasty, which fell in 1644, after nearly three hundred years of rule. More likely, though, the poetry group did not record its pleasure-making activities; closed off from the rest of society, it had no need to address the community at large.

Yang's benevolent society, in contrast, was a quasi-public organization. Though its membership remained exclusive, it inevitably interacted with the local community and had public exposure because one of its goals was to ameliorate poverty. Whereas the poetry society had met casually, the benevolent society was a formal organization. To routinize its activities, to harness its members to work together toward a purpose larger than immediate merrymaking, it needed written documents stipulating the responsibilities of membership. After hearing Yang's persuasive arguments for doing good, "the various elders" asked him to write up some regulations (*tiaoyue*) for the benevolent society. The term *tiaoyue*, commonly translated as "regulations," more literally means an itemized contract or agreement, with *yue* conveying the meaning of "to bind, to restrain": to collaborate in group endeavors, the members had to curb individual impulses; and to make the benevolent society work, they had to submit to a discipline of a sort that had been altogether unnecessary for the relaxed entertainment of poetry chanting.

The contract spelled out eight rules, which the members apparently agreed to follow when joining the association. They would meet once a month, on the fifteenth day. They would, for each meeting, make a monetary contribution of "two bits of silver and no less"; if they "missed the meeting or arrived late," they had to pay a fine; those who failed to complete a project or broke the rules were fined five taels. The money thus collected was earmarked for "public, or shared, use" (*gongyong*).[14]

In compiling the guidelines, Yang built on the conviviality and solidarity that the members of the banquet-and-poetry club had already cultivated, but, in transforming the club into a charitable organization, he additionally urged upon members a decorum befitting their serious purpose. He permitted the associates to continue the practice of sharing a meal at each meeting—a practice that surely reinforced group solidarity—but he stipulated that "only a few dishes and only two bowls of rice" should be served. He allowed that "the amount of wine should not be limited," but he warned against becoming "intoxicated or dissipated."[15] The rules endorsed conviviality, but they regulated and routinized it as well. Where the poetry society had depended on the spontaneous participation of like-minded men, the benevolent society depended on each member's considered agreement to pay dues, attend meetings, and abide by the rules. Rather than being drawn together by an informal oral consensus or tacit understanding (of the sort that had probably united the members of the poetry-chanting club), members of Yang's benevolent society joined forces through a common object—the written regulations—to which all the members could refer and through which they could hold one another accountable.

The regulations called for maintaining two records. One record undoubtedly had the aim of preserving for posterity the members' generosity. In it were entered the amounts of their contributions, ranked according to the seniority of the donors. This record was to be kept for the long term, to be annually passed down to the next secretary.[16] In the second record, the secretary was to register all payments made from society funds "to repair roads and bridges, to help out with marriage and funeral costs, and to aid the poor and sick"; this record aimed to make all transactions "crystal clear and ready for inspection."[17] Though intended for use by the members, it opened the way for publicizing benevolent-society activities to the Yucheng community at large.

In writing up the contract, Yang built on an existing solidarity among like-minded men, but to that solidarity he added a degree of formality, ensuring—through enforcement—cohesion for the future. The contract mandated behavior in areas that the poetry society had probably taken for granted. It made explicit that "at the meetings one should strive to be cordial all around, and that one should love [the other participants] as though they were one's flesh and blood; one should, moreover, hide enmities and praise goodness, and respond with compassion to people in crises. If anyone should harbor obstructive thoughts, stirring up enmities to the point of being unseemly, that person ought not be invited to the meetings."[18] The regulations, in short, attempted to govern even areas of affect.

Appended to the contract was a roster of the twelve members (in addition to Yang), who were listed, as the headnote clearly stated, not by bureaucratic status but by seniority. An assistant magistrate preceded a subprefectural vice magistrate, who had the higher bureaucratic rank; and a mere "tribute student" (who had not yet passed the triennial provincial examination) preceded a district magistrate (*zhixian*). In asserting a hierarchy of age, the roster defined members according to the social conventions of Yang's local community, thus situating the benevolent society outside formal government. Yang did not entirely obliterate traces of bureaucratic rank, however. He made sure to append to each name the member's bureaucratic status, specifying whether a person held office, had earned a degree in the civil service examination or special student status, or worked in the subbureaucracy.[19] Even in ranking the participants, Yang combined principles drawn from each of his two worlds.

Just as Yang continued to identify with far-flung officialdom while residing at home, so too did he give the benevolent society a dual identity. He both embraced members of the local elite according to their seniority and made good use of ties to the bureaucracy, indirectly drawing upon its authority to help the benevolent society function. To provide local residents with incentives to be charitable, he was prepared to call upon the support of officials, declaring in the contract: if, through their benevolent-society activities, "the gentlemen and humane people" should happen to stimulate good types of people to set up similar societies in the rural areas, "then it is fitting that good literati should report them to the magistrate so that he might bestow upon them tablets commemorating their public service."[20] Working within an ill-defined space outside the formal government but within its reach, Yang tried to extend good works even to the rural areas.

DRAWING STRENGTH FROM BELOW

While reaching the heights of the court, Yang's vision penetrated deep into his local community. Ready to draw upon official authority to commend do-gooders, he conceptualized his benevolent association in terms of practices that had long been established among the common people. He confined benevolent-society membership to men who had been associated with, or had aspirations to join, the civil service, but he drew inspiration for the association from the bottom reaches of society. As Yang explained to society members: "Peddlers and plowmen know how to form associations, contributing resources with the hope of doing good"; then, to challenge his audience of pleasure lovers, he asked rhetorically: "How much more so should gentry and official types do this? It is fitting that we conform to those 'common societies' (*suhui*) in which each person contributes some money, and whenever they encounter impoverished people deserving pity or situations calling for good deeds, they jointly give from the fund."[21]

In speaking of "common societies" Yang was referring to the sort of voluntary associations through which residents of a given locale pooled resources for a wide range of goals, including religious processions, funerals, and crisis intervention. These associations, mentioned in texts dating as far back as the late fifth century, went by a variety of names, usually incorporating a term indicating the inhabitants of a given locale (*yi*) or one suggesting "village assemblies around the God of the Soil" (*she*), and sometimes forming compounds with the term for "charitable" or "justice" (*yi*), as in "charitable community" (*yiyi*). But, whatever their labels, these associations had as their common purpose the "creation of blessings."[22] Yang may also have had in mind mutual-aid societies, which can be traced back at least to the Han dynasty.[23] The common people had over the centuries developed among themselves numerous strategies for collecting funds to deal with crises such as unanticipated funeral expenses and, less frequently, for aiding the poor.[24] What was new to the late Ming, then, was neither the concept of a voluntary association nor communal methods of managing risk, but that Yang, a member of the gentry, should have appropriated something he explicitly identified with the common people and resituated it in his own, elite milieu. The first benevolent society remained elitist in its membership, but it presented an elite project in a form that the common people would understand, thus enabling the benevolent society to communicate its purpose easily to the community at large.

In arguing that "even people without official positions should take responsibility for carrying out the Way," and in modeling the benevolent society after "common societies," Yang, in his status as a retired official, cleared a legitimate space for nonofficial associations, and into this space rushed the well-to-do townsmen of Yucheng. In 1591, one year after Yang formed the benevolent society, thirty-one residents of Yucheng, who had apparently been barred from it, hastened to form an alternative association.[25] Membership in the latter group appears to have been based primarily on wealth. It consisted of lower degree holders—including several members of the prosperous local Fan lineage—various types of clerks, and five persons who were simply labeled as "men of the area" (*xiangmin*) and who were undoubtedly distinguished only by their financial resources.[26] From this second group, wrote Yang, "almost no rich city resident was left out."[27] The two societies combined had forty-two members, who contributed a total of seventy ounces of silver.[28]

This second society (which later earned the name Society for Spreading Humaneness) may have outdone the first in aiding the poor. So suggests a brief account in which Yang illustrated this group's philanthropic achievements, as follows: There was at that time a recluse, Zhang Chang'an, a widower who was impoverished but knew something about medicine. The society spent some of its funds to get him remarried and set him up as a distributor of medical care. A member of the society, Fan Bing, who was familiar with medical arts, selected excellent prescriptions for Zhang; consequently the medical care was efficacious. Several hundred people turned up each day, to the point that it became impossible to serve everyone. Occasionally the persons who had been treated came to express their thanks.[29] The Society for Spreading Humaneness had essentially transformed one person, the recluse, into an instrument through which its members could, using prescriptions tested by one of their peers, spread medical assistance, thereby reaping the goodwill of multitudes.

Through the recluse-widower, the Society for Spreading Humaneness achieved several desirable goals. By providing him with a new wife and work, it made sure that he had a proper, productive place in society; by sponsoring one person as a medical practitioner, it benefited hundreds of sick people; and by thus aiding the general populace, it earned widespread gratitude and a good name. As presented by Yang, the case of the recluse indirectly made another point—one that Yang himself seems to have marveled at: Yang's small act, converting the poetry club to a benevolent society, started a chain of events, each juncture of which expanded beneficence, ultimately yielding enormous benefits. The society that Yang founded inspired wealthy members of the community to form a second society; in turn, that society's support of one person, the widower, resulted in curing hundreds of ailing people. Moral leadership had worked.

Boundlessly optimistic in the power of good deeds to lead the way, Yang frequently expressed hope that word of goodness would spread, thereby bringing harmony to the community and attracting donations as well. Occasionally word about good deeds spread through written records; most often Yang and later benevolent-society sponsors wrote of seeing and hearing about them. It was upon hearing of the Society for Spreading Humaneness, noted Yang, that three officials who were natives of a neighboring district had made monetary contributions.[30]

Confident that small acts of goodness would effect great moral reformation, Yang's benevolent society sponsored yet another philanthropic project. For three full years, a resident had devotedly observed mourning for his parents by staying in a hut by their grave; he had, moreover, returned some money he found to its rightful owner. Declaring his admiration for this filial and honest person, Yang joined society members in funding a ceremony celebrating the virtuous man. After having a thatched hut constructed for the event, they, with a dignified ritual and some fanfare of drums and fifes, presented congratulatory gifts—a scholar's gown and cap, some silk—to the exemplary figure. "The intention," Yang explained, "was that by treating one person liberally, one would spread word to ten thousand persons. In this case, the observers who had gathered around were all greatly moved, and those who customarily fought over petty profits in the villages and market places suddenly became docile and ceased to brawl."[31] The elevation of one filial son broadcast the lesson that goodness would earn rewards. The goal of this particular beneficence was not the alleviation of poverty—for Yang assumed that material well-being would naturally accompany good deeds. The goal was rather to meet another challenge, which Yang phrased as follows: "How might one manage to publicize this goodness throughout the world, in accordance with my wish for great unity (*datong*)?"[32]

Promoting moral edification just as much if not more than material aid, the benevolent society of Yucheng additionally sponsored a costly ceremony to honor elders—a ritual occasionally performed by officials to generate feelings of respect for hierarchy. In 1593, Yang and benevolent-society "friends" contributed funds to prepare wine and to construct a pavilion so as to entertain the senior men of his area, fourteen of whom were in their eighties and two in their nineties. It also financed the printing of "A Record of Honoring Elders," which provided thumbnail biographies of the sixteen men, highlighting each elder's virtues—acts of generosity, filiality, wise sayings, and the like—all "with the intention of instilling in the young a respect for the elderly and bringing harmony to the world."[33]

The cohesion and focus of each of Yucheng's two societies were maintained by a respect for social standing and political power, an awareness within the community of who held power and whose good graces should be sought. Although the two benevolent societies stood outside formal government, political power played a role in their formation and durability. The relatively high status of the members of the first benevolent society (local officials and degree holders, as well as a few men who, though occupying subbureaucratic positions, must have stood out among the general population in that poor district of Yucheng), along with the exclusivity of its membership, enhanced Yang's image as moral leader and validated the merit of his endeavor, setting a precedent for others to follow.

That the first benevolent society was led by a meritorious official on leave appears to have goaded—or licensed—other residents to form the second society. Competition—whether for prominence in the community or for social connections—drove the wealthy to participate. This Yang intuited in his conclusion to the account of recluse Zhang. The second society, Yang noted, "competed in charity with the Society for Sharing Goodness."[34] Unwittingly, Yang had paved the way for the participation of persons whose main qualification was wealth. That wealth was an important force in doing good was recognized by Yang in his instructions for a community granary: whoever gave first—whoever "led the way in giving"—was to be listed first "regardless of age."[35] So too could men of wealth use benevolent societies to compete with their seniors as well as with degree holders for social standing in their communities.

Yang had the qualities needed for effective leadership. Born into a prosperous lineage of Yucheng, he had the financial resources to sponsor projects and to set an example in making charitable contributions. As a landowner, he was strongly motivated to maintain harmony in his community. He understood that, in order to keep his holdings profitable, he must protect the well-being of and generate goodwill among the tenant farmers who tilled his fields and paid rents. Moreover, as an official on leave, he commanded the respect of his community. His sense of superiority vis-à-vis the wealthy townsmen became evident when the second group sought his advice on what to name their association. Pointing out that the first group already had the name *tongshan,* they asked: given that our own "expertise in benevolence" is not negligible, is it right that "our society alone should lack a name?"[36] Yang responded by implying that they were inferior in understanding: "You claim achievements in humaneness, but do you also understand the theories behind humaneness?" He then launched into a small lecture: that heaven and earth take living things as their core is the basis of their humaneness; humaneness is the key to preserving life; and only by spreading humaneness can one generate something that Yang, following his own mentors, called the "perpetual renewal of life" (*shengsheng*).[37]

Yang's high status as former official and prominent landowner cannot explain his successful leadership, however, for these qualities were shared by other residents of Yucheng, in particular the two former officials who had initiated the poetry society. Distinguishing Yang from the other former officials, and enabling him to goad his peers to renounce banqueting for a regimen of doing good, was that he himself reached for a cause that happened to be nobler than theirs. When defining the purpose of the "Society for Sharing Goodness," he drew an invidious contrast between himself and the pleasure-seeking association of elders: he would leave behind—that is, he would rise high above—wasteful poetry-chanting banquets. Similarly with the second group, Yang upheld a good cause. Noting that the members were inclined to use philanthropy as an excuse for entertainment, he admonished them: "You have come because you admire justice (*yi*); how can you let loose with the pleasures of banqueting and drifting about? The aim is none other than to do good." It was then that Yang suggested that they distribute medicines through the widower.[38] Taking the high road, he asserted his role as moral teacher.

To convince the elders of the first society that contributing money would be more pleasurable than poetry chanting, Yang mentioned neither the food shortage that had occurred two years earlier nor other disasters. Rather he emphasized individual moral responsibility. "If they should forget the proscription against seeking gain," he explained, then, through the workings of karma (whereby one's behavior in this life determines the form in which one will be reincarnated in the next life), "their sons and grandsons would become horses and cattle, forced to labor day and night without a moment's pleasure. People who are stingy and unwilling to help the poor are truly benighted."[39] Then, drawing upon popular rhetoric about storing up merit, he added: "Now, for people to accumulate goodness (*jishan*) is like farmers applying energy to plowing: the more they plant, the more will they harvest; the less they plant, the less will they harvest; and if they fail to plant, they will get nothing. Formerly someone saved the lives of one thousand people; a descendant of his became one of the highest ranking officials. And someone else ferried ten thousand ants across waters; he subsequently won eminence through the civil service examinations." To wrap up his statement, Yang borrowed an image from the world of commerce: "Heaven brings good fortune to the good person just as though he were holding a bill of credit."[40]

Yang authenticated his teachings by himself performing good deeds. Immediately upon his return home in 1590, and being mindful of a dire food shortage that had stricken Henan during the preceding two years (1588 and 1589), he joined wealthy residents of an adjacent district to organize a community granary. Bemoaning that no one had taken the lead in doing good—hereby identifying a need for his intervention—he expressed hope that word of grain-storing techniques would now spread.[41] In 1596, he established a school for the poor.[42] In 1601, after his area suffered heavy floods, he joined his brothers and several eminent men of the community in contributing over 170 ounces silver for a program to stabilize grain prices.[43] Through public displays of generosity, he periodically asserted his leadership.

Yang repeatedly poured his own funds into his community. When severe snowstorms struck Yucheng in 1602, he sought to aid the poor by organizing a soup kitchen.[44] In 1606, he sponsored a highly visible, large-scale program to distribute winter clothing to the poor. Six years after the event, in 1612, he finally got around to writing about the program, in "A Record of Distributing Padded Jackets" (Shi mianao ji):

> The sufferings of the poor are pitiable in every season but especially during the winter. The rich protect their bodies against the cold with padded clothing; as it grows colder, they add clothing; if it's severely cold, they add linings and furs; and they reside in warm quarters, with charcoal to burn and wine to drink, to the point of being comfortable. But if one's defenses are down somewhat, then one will suddenly feel cold and fall sick. Alas, all beings are physically the same, alike in their intolerance of cold. Those people with old, tattered clothes shot through with thousands of holes and knots all over: they go nearly naked in the dead of winter, their hair disheveled and feet bare and their teeth clattering; crying out and terrified, they are able only to cradle themselves in their arms and to squat to protect their midriffs. Being solitary, they have no place to go. When they have the misfortune of encountering the bitter cold, and snow and ice have been covering the roads day after day, they take refuge in some run-down kiln or rustic shrine, sleeping on icy ground, while the wind rushes through them like arrows and the falling snow covers their bodies. At this point, their organs freeze and their bodies stiffen like pieces of wood. At first they are still able to groan. Gradually they cough up phlegm. Then, their lives are extinguished. Misery![45]

Then, echoing the rhetoric of those animal liberators who stressed that even the tiniest creatures had parents, Yang asked: "Are they not all the children of other people? How have they reached such a miserable state? Those people who enjoy red-hot braziers and warm quarters could, with the smallest amount of generosity, temporarily save the poor people from dying." The hardships experienced by the poor filled Yang with great pain, "as though dust had filled his eyes," he noted, here alluding to the ancient statement, "The benevolent men of the present age look at the evils of the world, with eyes full of dust, and are filled with sorrow by them."[46]

Yang declared his wish to aid the poor, but, on the grounds that his resources were limited, he also explained that "he could not expand the side rooms by the thousand mats needed to accommodate these people and clothe them. He could only follow the strategy of distributing padded jack-ets."[47] Thus it was that Yang, in 1606, initiated the plan with a quota of one hundred jackets. A year later, he doubled the amount. After four or five years, the word spread even further abroad, so that everyone—the Liangs, Songs, Yans, and Zhaos—all filed in for jackets. Between the start of the program and 1612, five hundred persons came. Lacking the means to respond to everyone, Yang and his younger brother made the most of their resources by establishing procedures, which they clearly announced. They limited dis-tribution to certain days, and they excluded the able-bodied, giving cloth-ing only to the sick and crippled. At a scheduled time, they asked the benefi-ciaries to line up and squat down—no doubt a device to control mobbing, for Yang made it clear that anyone who was rowdy would be escorted out. The drum was sounded three times, and everyone was made to salute the Buddha. Again the drum was sounded, whereupon each person was given a bowl of beef soup and five rolls (*mantou*). After three additional drum beats, the padded clothing was distributed, this one time only. "The poor people were happy to receive the clothing, and I was pleased that the poor people were happy," wrote Yang, who then added that the recipients' exclamations amplified his empathetic feelings, filling him with happiness.[48]

The padded jackets kept the people alive, Yang noted, but he then pon-dered: the needy still suffer the discomfort of cold piercing their bodies; how much more miserable is it for all the persons whom we do not see or hear about, or who are beyond the reach of donations. "Those who cannot avoid death must be countless. Alas! For their survival, the poor must rely on the surplus of the rich." Then, putting aside the report of his own charity, Yang used the occasion to proselytize: rather than piling up wealth in useless places, is it not better to proffer aid to those who are in distress while perfecting one's own benevolence? By himself setting an example of generosity, Yang assumed moral leadership in his community.

His expanded vision and deep sense of responsibility differentiated Yang from fellow townsmen and enabled him to lift them out of their ordinari-ness. Having observed upon his returning home in 1590 that no one had taken the lead in organizing grain storage, he immediately stepped forward. Equipping Yang to assume leadership were his status as a former official and his connections to men of power and wealth. But also important were his genuine empathy with the common people and his strong moral convictions. These qualities motivated his own financial contributions to his community and informed his impassioned memorial that successfully goaded the court to donate money and grain for relief efforts in Henan.

Yang's founding of a benevolent society appears to have taken place ca-sually, almost incidentally, when, being restless and bored, he redirected an informal association to a more serious purpose. This took place during trou-bled times, right after the food shortage of 1588 and 1589 and shortly before the severe floods of 1594 that would spur Yang to send up a "Memorial on the Starving People, Illustrated and Explained" (*Jimin tu shuo*), imploring the emperor to aid the residents of Henan.[49] However, the conditions of Henan, though desperate, do not explain why Yang's response took the form of a benevolent society. Behind Yang's seemingly impulsive and idiosyncratic initiation of a benevolent society were established social patterns. When Yang searched for strategies that would enhance the well-being of his community, he had already spotted, out of the corner of his eye, a fresh opportunity: waiting in the wings were men who possessed wealth but who, being poorly educated, lacked guidance in putting those resources to beneficial use.

MORAL IMPERATIVES

During the two decades following Yang Dongming's return to Yucheng, the concept of a benevolent society spread to the prosperous Yangzi delta region. Surviving records say little about how it arrived there and who was responsible for it. One account mentions that a Zhang Shiyi introduced the idea to Jiangnan from Yang Dongming's Henan.[50] Another record further tells that Qian Yiben established a benevolent society in Wujin (Piling), Nanzhili.[51] Meeting once each season, the participants in Qian's group pooled their contributions and, according to Gao Panlong, made distributions whenever they saw someone suffering. "Thus persons who had no one to rely on received care: for those who were cold, there was clothing; for the hungry, food; for the ill, medicines; and for the deceased, modest coffins." Then, using the term by which the society was called, Gao added: "Everyone sharing in the goodness (*tongshan zhe*) got to do good."[52]

Gao also speaks of a Chen Youxue, a native of Wuxi, Nanzhili, who, after earning a *jinshi* degree in 1589, served in Queshan, Henan, which is roughly 120 miles from Yang Dongming's hometown. There Chen gained a reputation for compassionate, enlightened, and just administration. He distributed oxen to the poor and spinning wheels to women; he had accommodations built for the homeless and mulberry trees planted. By using public funds economically, he was able to initiate numerous beneficial projects.[53] Then, hearing of Qian Yiben's benevolent society, Chen Youxue was delighted. Buoyed by its potential, he declared: "Learning should not take the form of empty proposals but should be made manifest through deeds."[54] Just as Yang Dongming had imagined, word of goodness spread.

This, then, is what remains of the early benevolent societies immediately following the one Yang Dongming founded: scattered traces, but no obvious trail; brief vignettes, but no grand narrative explaining why the idea of a benevolent society should have suddenly taken hold among literati, why news about this novel institution, disseminated through word of mouth, should have found fertile soil. Not until the spring of 1614 did the concept of the benevolent society finally reach someone who gave the subject a solid place in the written record, namely, the upright official and contemplative scholar Gao Panlong. Acknowledging Qian Yiben and Chen Youxue as sources of inspiration, Gao—along with several other men who were prominent but about whose benevolent society activities little is known—sponsored a benevolent society in his own hometown, Wuxi.[55] Because he deemed the subject important, he left among his extant writings a brief introduction to the benevolent society, three lectures he addressed to its members, and, scattered among other pieces, a few incidental but relevant comments.[56]

Like Yang Dongming, Gao Panlong had special qualities that equipped him for leadership. An unusual predisposition and his childhood experiences set him apart from his peers and propelled him to seek a high moral ground. Already, at only five *sui*, he displayed exceptional precocity, "acting and speaking like an adult," avers his chronological biography.[57] Special circumstances would then further distinguish him, especially from his six brothers. His father was a prosperous landowner. Blessed with an abundance of male progeny, Gao's father gave up Panlong to a grand uncle, who was childless.[58] When his natural father died in 1596, Gao Panlong, then in his thirty-fifth year, carried out the mourning rites with due reverence.[59] Though utterly filial in this respect, he nonetheless refused to obey his father's last will and testament, his "bequeathed wish," that the family property be divided equally among all seven sons. Having already inherited an estate from his adoptive father in 1589, Gao urged his share upon his brothers, but they rejected his offer. Unable to prevail over his siblings, he found an alternative that apparently satisfied all parties involved, displaying along the way his magnanimity: he used his share to defray the father's burial expenses; then, in 1596, he used the remaining funds to set up a trust that would aid poor members of his lineage to pay their taxes as well as support those secondary wives in the lineage who had the misfortune of bearing no sons.[60]

In refusing his share of the family property, Gao called attention to the difference between himself (both son and adopted son) and his six brothers—just as the vegetarian Feng Shike had differentiated himself from his eight affluent brothers. In spending his share to bury his natural father and benefit his lineage, he demonstrated that he was strongly committed—perhaps even more so than his brothers—to the well-being of their kin. To finesse a difficult situation, he reached for a higher good. And, in being charitable, he essentially exchanged wealth—the seventh share of a legacy—for a position of moral superiority.

A man of high principles, Gao deliberately denied himself certain luxuries. Literati of his status often acquired secondary wives, but he made a point of sticking with one spouse for life.[61] His wealthy associates indulged in sumptuous banquets, but, in instructions to his household, he called for moderation, insisting that one should keep luxury dishes to a minimum and should, out of consideration for animals, serve vegetables instead of meat.[62] Putting into practice what he preached, he spent his surplus funds on aiding poor scholars.[63] Such was his charitableness that after his death he was said "to have left no surplus."[64]

Strong on self-discipline, Gao followed a strict daily regimen.[65] On constant guard against dissipation, he kept a journal. In "A Notebook as Daily Mirror" (Rijian pian), he charted whether he was serious or lax, and upright or lustful. Daily he examined himself; monthly he evaluated himself.[66] Regrettably neither the notebook nor another journal, "A Record of Daily Self-Examination" (Rixing bian ji), are extant, yet their titles proclaim earnest efforts at self-improvement.[67]

The case of Gao Panlong as an adoptee who turned especially upright and charitable brings to mind another philanthropic figure, Fan Zhongyan, who, though of the eleventh century, was a key point of reference for each of the five leading figures in this study. Fan had earned an enduring reputation for being charitable toward others while himself remaining frugal. Five and a half centuries after Fan's death, members of Gao Panlong's generation continued to express admiration for and find inspiration in Fan's benevolence. Like Gao, Fan had been put out for adoption, although under different circumstances. When Fan Zhongyan was in his second year, his father died. His mother remarried into another clan, the Zhus, and raised Fan under the name Zhu Yue. As told by Denis Twitchett, Fan "learned that he was not a true son of the Chu [Zhu] clan only when, having reprimanded his adoptive brothers for their immoderate behavior, he was told that it was no business of his since he was not a full member." Fan thereupon sought to resume using his original name, succeeding only after reassuring the Fans that he would make no claims on their property. When he became wealthy later in life, he extended some aid toward the Zhus, and, by instituting the first charitable estate, he heaped great benefit upon the Fan lineage.[68] In broad terms, Fan and Gao had similar childhood experiences: having been defined as outside their natal families and consequently challenged by their ambiguous place in society, both men learned that kin relationships were fragile and empathy important. Both men were motivated to prove themselves as exceptionally dedicated and generous toward their kin; they strove to demonstrate their moral worth and were relatively frugal and restrained. Personal experiences distinguished them from their fictive and real brothers, impelling them to do things differently from the general run of their peers. If the quest for distinction led them to achieve high bureaucratic positions, it also led, at least in Gao's case, to a program of self-improvement and self-restraint. They were of the elite, yet their charitable impulses derived from highly individualized experiences.

Following Fan Zhongyan's example, Gao made sizable charitable donations to his lineage. In 1596, nearly two decades before he would found a benevolent society in 1614, he endowed rent-free lands for the poor of his lineage and he set aside lands the proceeds of which were to be used to aid childless persons.[69] In 1608, he further endowed land to free draftees in his borough (*qu*) from corvée labor.[70] Yet the similarities between the two men point to an important difference: something about Gao's social environment prompted him additionally to transcend his lineage identity by sponsoring a benevolent society.

Living up to high principles, Gao stuck his neck out to defend like-minded colleagues: during a brief appointment at the capital, in 1593, upon learning that many of his respected friends had been dismissed from office, he wrote a memorial denouncing the official responsible for the purges. For his outspokenness, Gao was promptly demoted to a post (in Jieyang, Guangdong) remote from both the urbane capital and his cultured hometown. A few months later, on the grounds that his ailing parents required his care, he was allowed to return to his home in Wuxi.[71] There he remained nearly three decades, from 1595 until 1621, when he again took office.

While at home, Gao, like Yang Dongming in Yucheng, retained a vision that soared beyond the borders of his district and above the trivia of quotidian life. A *jinshi* degree holder poised for bureaucratic service, he had expected opportunities to prove himself in office. Having had this expectation thwarted and being aware, moreover, of the unhealthy atmosphere of the capital—where political intrigue and ruthless battles had brought much suffering and frustration to his colleagues and himself—Gao, always seeking higher things, found opportunities at home. He studied and meditated. He participated in "learned discussions" and lectured at private academies.[72] He assisted, in 1604, in the restoration of the Donglin Academy a place where like-minded scholars debated ancient texts and contemporary political issues.[73] If Gao sometimes went into retreat, refusing visitors, he also devoted himself to ameliorating local conditions. In 1614, the year he composed his deeply introspective "On the Toils of Learning" (Kunxue ji),[74] he also established the benevolent association—an activity that brought him much public exposure.

Fervently embracing the highest principles of goodness, Yang and Gao overlooked obstacles and social complications that stood in their way. From their steadfast focus on moral imperatives came the strength of their leadership, a characteristic that differentiated them from their peers. Doing good is morally imperative, declared Gao's "Introduction to the Benevolent Society"; it is something one has to do. Gao expatiated on this theme by answering questions that sound as though they were posed by ordinary, unenlightened persons but were actually attributed to fellow townsman and former official Chen Youxue. Predictably, Gao comes across as having the superior knowledge.[75]

When asked by Chen Youxue, "Where does goodness (*shan*) come from?"

Gao said, "Ah, that is a big question you have asked," and proceeded to define it by associating two words that are homophonous but differently written: "goodness" is "humaneness" (*ren*), which in turn means "man" (*ren*). "Man," Gao explained, is connected to everyone under heaven, just as limbs are part of the body. Then, elaborating on the theme of interconnectedness, Gao stated: "My body has a measure of skin. If a knife cuts me, will I, like a piece of wood, feel nothing? If someone in the world is down and out and suffering, will I, like a piece of wood in its midst, look on unmoved? It follows that to be good is to be humane and that humaneness is to love others; that is all there is to it."[76]

Gao envisioned that one purpose of benevolence is to ensure that each person has a place in society and that social order is thus maintained. To this, Gao's interlocutor objected: "The true gentleman wants each of the myriad things to have its place (*ge de qi suo*), but this cannot always be achieved. To give liberally to aid the masses—why, even the sage rulers Yao and Shun worried that funds for this would be insufficient." Sidestepping this obstacle, shifting the responsibility away from rulers to ordinary individuals, Gao replied roughly as follows: those who strive for widespread charity look to other people's donations for the solution; the humane person dips into his own resources; if everyone does what his resources will allow, donations will be liberal and aid broadly diffused.[77]

At this point, according to Gao's account, Chen Youxue raised a question about charitable giving that perplexed many late Ming writers: "I have heard that the good will be fortunate; why is this sometimes not the case?" Replied Gao: "When I act virtuously toward others, I do not expect rewards from them; nor do I expect rewards from heaven when people do not themselves repay me for my generosity. If you do good with the express purpose of seeking good fortune, the good deeds surely will not bring good fortune."[78]

Chen pressed Gao further about the widespread assumption that one's good deeds will earn good fortune from heaven. Gao simply reverted to his point that doing good is morally imperative: "This is because you fail to understand that one cannot *not* do good." Then, resorting to a graphic image, Gao proceeded to explain: "If I am stabbed with a knife yet remain wood-enlike, it must be because I am dead. So it is if people are dying from deprivation yet I just stand by like a block of wood. Doing good is like drinking when thirsty and eating when hungry. When we drink and eat, do we look for recompense (*bao*)?"[79] "Does goodness, then, entail no good fortune?" persisted Chen. Gao maintained his focus on humaneness, this time by dichotomizing one's choices: "There are two roads: to be humane, the road to life; and to be inhumane, the road to death. . . . Humaneness gives rise to goodness and hence good fortune, just as a form has its shadow." What is important is the spirit with which the good deed is done. "Performing a good deed with an ulterior motive is not humane; doing good by second nature brings good fortune."[80]

Gao portrayed his interlocutor as unenlightened. Yet Chen Youxue was no ordinary person. He had proven himself to be a worthy official, an able administrator who had initiated beneficent programs in Queshan, Henan; and he was acknowledged by Gao as an inspiration for the benevolent society in Wuxi. Moreover, the two men had together weathered the ordeal of the civil service examinations and earned the *jinshi* degree in the same year; typically candidates who passed in the same year felt a close bond. What gave Gao the leadership position, the power to deliver the more enduring message? His unusual integrity and his quest for distinction, evident vis-à-vis his brothers, had undoubtedly moved Gao to seize the high moral road. But details about Chen Youxue's life suggest other factors as well.

Chen Youxue, according to an epitaph Gao wrote for Chen's wife, had in his youth been "especially poor and lived in a desolate village." He had also been undisciplined, once running out of money for buying the wine he apparently enjoyed to excess. Thanks to his wife's commendable influence—she was stern but supportive—he gave up drink, applied himself to study, earned the *jinshi* degree in 1589, and had a sequence of official posts. What had spurred Chen to reform himself was, Gao tells us, a lesson his wife taught him early on, before he took (and passed) the palace examination. One day, to teach him what failure and poverty could bring, she served him a soup she had prepared from wild plants of the kind used as a last resort during severe food shortages, saying, "In the future do not forget this coarse taste." At this time, Chen was living precariously at the margins of elite society.[81]

In a piece celebrating Chen's eightieth birthday, Gao noted that Chen's beneficence had won the people's praise and might be compared to "the branches, leaves, and flowers of a tree—all of which are realized in springtime because of their roots." Summing up Chen's meritorious life, Gao stated: "While serving as an official, Chen brought good fortune to the people. While residing at home, he brought good fortune to his native area." Such was Chen's goodness that "the world could not for one day do without this person"; then, implying a connection between Chen's "daily accumulation of good deeds" and the reward of longevity, Gao concluded that consequently the world has "blessed this person with many years of life."[82]

For all his accomplishments as an energetic, innovative, and beneficent official, Chen Youxue was ultimately overshadowed by Gao and has faded into obscurity. None of his writings is known to have been published; he acquired no followers to disseminate his teachings and name. Certainly, as portrayed by Gao—as someone who had been disciplined by his wife and instructed on the meaning of goodness by Gao—Chen lacked the sort of self-assurance that had fortified Gao, even as a child, to "act and speak like an adult." Above all, Chen's moral position differed from Gao's: whereas he apparently thought in terms of reaping rewards, Gao upheld a moral imperative.

Distinguishing Gao from Chen Yuxue was not only personality but also personal wealth and the power it brought. Gao was an affluent owner of two hundred *mou* of land.[83] He had integrity and was compassionate, to be sure, but he also enjoyed special opportunities created by wealth: by forsaking his share of his father's estate he established himself as noble and upright; by using his vast resources, he established himself as a benefactor. What resources had Chen to compete with Gao in making grand gestures sponsoring good works? Had his less affluent background made Chen more cautious, more skeptical, than Gao about pouring his own funds into good works without considering the rewards to be reaped? Even as an official, Chen supported his beneficent projects, not by making contributions from his salary (as many officials did), but by ingeniously reorganizing how they were financed (the details of which are obscure). In reality, wealth, though little discussed by literati, who defined themselves as men of learning rather than as investors in land, was an important source of power. Gao's possession of wealth and his willingness to part with it to do good—to share it with others—lent authority and credibility to his teachings. In Gao, moral integrity and wealth found a potent combination.

BENEVOLENT SOCIETIES LEGITIMATED

The year Gao founded the benevolent society, 1614, happens to have been when "bad elements" at court crystallized their attack on Gao and his upright associates. The buildup of enmities at court, especially under the ruthless eunuch Wei Zhongxian, may have stimulated Gao to support the benevolent society.[84] Possibly he hoped that, by intensifying his benevolent activities at home, he might mend the damage being done to his reputation by detractors abroad; or that, by using the benevolent society to improve morality at home, he might ultimately transform the sort of bad characters who then held power at the court. At the least, small do-good efforts at home compensated for the apparent disarray in the government's high echelons.

Actively participating in Gao's benevolent society were four other affiliates of the Donglin Academy.[85] In an epitaph for one of them (Liu Yuanzhen), Gao incidentally mentioned that, when Qian Yiben set up the benevolent society in Wujin (Piling), associates of the Donglin Academy helped to proselytize charitableness, eliciting the response of one hundred residents who were "fond of justice/charity" (*haoyi*); their beneficiaries were "the loyal, filial, chaste, and righteous among the poor," as well as "the cripples and worthy people without social support."[86] The benevolent society and Donglin constituencies were not entirely congruent, however. As Gao observed, "some

Donglin types did not join in, thinking that doing so would be superfluous, like 'adding legs to a snake.'"[87]

Cutthroat factionalism within officialdom, as well as the court's inattentiveness to local conditions, had perturbed many earlier periods but did so without producing benevolent societies. Government malfunctioning had periodically spurred local elites to take action, but, for each era, the manner of their response differed. New to the late Ming, especially in those urban centers of the Yangzi delta region where Gao and subsequent benevolent-society sponsors resided, was that prosperity, commerce, and the spread of literacy opened up opportunities for new types of association.

Contributing to the lasting impact of Gao's benevolent society and the preservation of his writings in support of it was his moral authority, which was authenticated by an exceptionally courageous act. After Gao learned that six kindred spirits had been tortured to death in a political purge, and that he too would be arrested, he chose to commit suicide rather than fall into evil hands—once again distinguishing himself from the common herd of literati. Having already sacrificed a share of an inheritance, Gao now sacrificed his life. His martyrdom greatly enlarged his stature, securing for him lasting renown. A student and admirer, Chen Longzheng, made sure to edit, comment on, and publish Gao's work in 1632.[88] An eminent official-turned-teacher of the day, Liu Zongzhou, extolled Gao for having been "at one with the Way."[89] Liu had countless followers; thus did word of Gao's fine reputation spread.

Gao's suicide, an incontrovertible demonstration of integrity, altered conditions for founding a benevolent society—just when the formation of private societies was widely regarded by some officials with much suspicion. Two years before he would pass the *jinshi* examination (in 1634), and three before he would receive his first official appointment (in 1637), Chen Longzheng, as holder of the intermediate *juren* degree, was able to establish a benevolent society in his hometown, Jiashan, Zhejiang, in the prospering Jiangnan area. When convening the first benevolent-society meeting in Jiashan, he, unlike his predecessors Yang Dongming, Chen Youxue, and Gao Panlong, lacked the advanced *jinshi* degree and the status of a former official who had returned home. Nonetheless, without seeking the approval of local officials stationed in Jiashan, Chen was able to command cooperation from members of his community.

Catapulting Chen into the position of benevolent-society leader was not precocious learning or outstanding achievement, but a strong paternal influence and a notable family tradition of benevolence. As Chen tells it, he had been woefully slow to apply himself to study. When he was in his eleventh or twelfth year, he leaned toward Daoism and Buddhism, often expressing a desire to master the art of achieving longevity; occasionally he declared a wish to become a monk. His father, Chen Yuwang, who was then serving as an official in Jurong, Nanzhili, got wind of this and grew extremely angry. But rather than reprimanding Chen, the father reviled himself, conceding, "I have been lacking in virtue. As an official I have committed many faults. Consequently I have given birth to this child. What can I do about it?" Then, further reflecting, "My son speaks like this for no reason other than to avoid his studies," the father sighed.[90] The father's reaction alarmed Chen Longzheng, who dared not again speak of his deviant leanings. In his fourteenth year (*sui*), he began to study in earnest. At twenty-six and twenty-seven he showed an interest in statecraft (*jingji*) but, as he himself put it, he did so "without true understanding." After reaching thirty *sui*, in 1615, the year when his father died, he fiercely recriminated himself for having neglected his studies. Having taken the slow, uncertain road, he finally passed the *jinshi* examination in 1634, by which time he was in his forty-ninth year.[91]

Although dilatory in studying for officialdom, Chen absorbed much wisdom about practical administration from his father, who had, by the time of his death in 1615, achieved the position of surveillance commissioner, in Fujian. The father was a firm but humane official, as attested by directives that he composed and accounts about him that Longzheng assembled posthumously. These pieces show Yuwang curbing local strongmen, setting up granaries, and otherwise improving local conditions. Two pieces in particular note Chen Yuwang's balanced mix of strictness and compassion. One item tells of his forgiving treatment of the wards of state-sponsored poorhouses (*yangji yuan*): whenever making distributions of food, firewood, and clothing to them, he would say, "'Some of the inmates must be here on false pretenses and might later run into trouble. Yet, even though man can do nothing about their deception, heaven will disgrace them.'" Chen Longzheng commented: "These slippery fellows stirred compassion in my father; and in return they feared his stern justice."[92] In the second item of note, Chen told of his father's handling of prisoners: "Jails are set up to punish villains. My father, who was stern in outer appearance but compassionate at heart, regarded the prisoners somewhat kindheartedly. Occasionally he made inquiries so as to aid them. If they were sick, he summoned a doctor for a medical examination. In the winter months, he provided them with warmers and padded clothing. His overflowing humaneness went beyond what was required by law."[93]

Of his father's administrative accomplishments Chen wrote admiringly. When heavy rains damaged the harvests of Huguang province in 1607, Chen's father, then serving there as surveillance vice commissioner, issued one thousand taels for famine relief, with the result that "thousands of people were saved."[94] When serving in Jurong, Chen's father reformed corvée labor, the heavy demands of which had been reducing local households to ruins. For some tasks he used clerks instead of conscripted laborers, and he eliminated other duties entirely, thus lightening the burdens on the common people. He had dikes repaired and he initiated a program to stabilize grain prices. Through capable and humane administration, Chen Yuwang so completely won the hearts of the local people that they tried to detain him on the day of his departure, saying, "In a thousand years, when would we again see the likes of you?"[95]

Although Chen Longzheng's laudatory account of his father, echoing the wording of countless other tributes to worthy officials, sounds cliché, it should be taken seriously. Clichés, after all, are crystallizations of a society's preoccupations (a point that has itself become a cliché), in this case, the respect for beneficent and intelligent administration. Moreover, writers understood that praise, if used recklessly and without foundation, would destroy the credibility of their compositions. As Longzheng asserted in his preface to "Family Records": "One should not gloss over the failings of one's relatives; nor should one forget their virtues."[96] To corroborate that the residents of Jurong had deep affection for his father, Chen offered several facts that must have had some validity, for gross misrepresentation would have discredited the entire account in the eyes of his readers: the local people were upset to see his father leave Jurong; they subsequently had a shrine built to commemorate him; and when news of his death later reached them, they wept.[97]

The record of Chen Longzheng's father enhanced a family reputation that had already earned favor. As Chen Longzheng must have known, his grandfather had been commended in the local gazetteer for having made loans of grain during a food shortage without exacting repayment. As Longzheng's sons were later to report, it was widely believed that this generosity explained the prosperity that blessed later generations of Chens.[98] The good reputation for deeds past, the accumulated family lore that filled the Chens with pride, upheld a standard by which future generations had to live, placing upon the Chens a responsibility to sustain the family tradition of charity.

Chen Longzheng's upbringing was thus shaped by principles embodied in his father: on the one hand, he was allowed plenty of latitude to drift through his studies, to find his own way; on the other hand, he was exposed to—and he eventually internalized—the fine examples that his father and grandfather had set. After a period of straying, when he absorbed other influences as well, Chen returned full circle to his father's standard: upon finally passing the *jinshi* examination, in 1634, thereby fulfilling his father's expectations, Longzheng wept, regretting that his father had not lived to see his success.[99]

Chen's commitment to benevolent action was further affected by the views of Yuan Huang, whose ancestors haled from Chen's hometown, Jiashan, and who had, in 1585, passed the civil service examinations together with Chen's father, Yuwang.[100] When Chen Longzheng was a young boy, Yuan had predicted his success. "Both of your sons are worthy," he told Yuwang, "but the younger one [that is, Longzheng] is the deeper in filial spirit and is capable of unlimited achievements."[101] Gratifying praise. How could this pronouncement not have moved Longzheng to attach some special authority to the general sweep of Yuan Huang's views?

Yuan Huang had earned the *jinshi* degree against great odds. For three generations, his family had been barred from officialdom because his great-great-grandfather had been implicated in a political plot. By Yuan Huang's time, the ban had been lifted, but by then, too, there prevailed a family tradition of making a living through medicine—a tradition from which it was hard to extricate oneself. Furthermore, a fortune-teller had forecast that Yuan Huang's options would be severely limited: Yuan would pass an examination but not earn a high degree; he would sire no children; and he would die at the relatively young age of fifty-three. From a Chan Buddhist monk Yuan Huang learned that another scenario might be possible: by keeping track of his merits and demerits, he could take fate into his own hands, or "establish his own destiny" (*liming*). Pursuing the latter strategy, accumulating merit, Yuan Huang eventually earned the *jinshi* degree, had a son, and lived into his seventy-third year.[102] His outlook thus altered, he proselytized—as converts will—spreading word that one's actions shaped one's destiny. His message suited the late Ming, a time of seemingly erratic social mobility, for it explained, in terms of personal morality, why some people amassed great wealth while others fell upon hard times. Yuan's teachings deeply affected many of the charitable men featured in this study. The notion of personal responsibility for one's own fate had apparently been embraced by Chen's father as well: when Chen Longzheng was inattentive in studies and, worse, expressed an interest in becoming a monk, the father blamed not the son but his own lack of virtue and failings as an official.[103]

In support of his benevolent society, Chen involved the name of Ding Bin, a fellow townsman known for his extraordinary generosity. In his youth Chen had met Ding, who was the uncle of Chen's maternal uncle, Ding Xuan,[104] and, at fifteen *sui*, Chen was betrothed to a young woman of the Ding lineage. On that occasion he observed that Ding Bin came from "an outstanding lineage."[105] After earning the *jinshi* degree in 1571, Ding Bin served as a magistrate (in Jurong, the district where Chen's father would later also serve), but was dismissed for insubordination vis-à-vis the strong-minded, heavy-handed grand secretary Zhang Juzheng, who at that time was at the height of his power.[106] Eventually Ding was reinstated, and then—for thirty years—he served honorably and successfully in the Southern Capital (Nanjing). He died in 1631, in his ninetieth year. According to beliefs of the time, his extraordinary longevity signified outstanding merit.

Ding Bin's good character was celebrated in the local gazetteer of Jiashan, which incorporated an account composed by another native of Jiashan, Qian Shisheng.[107] Though aware that Ding had held office for sixty years, Qian expressed a wish to avoid repeating information that had already been recorded in the formal histories; he would instead concentrate on Ding's exercise of goodness at home. A prime example was Ding's generosity during the years 1588 and 1589, a time that Qian recalled with horror: "A succession of severe droughts and floods had caused grain prices to soar, driving the people to such desperate measures as eating crushed chaff and ground elm bark; because of the food shortage, corpses lined the roads." Generously responding to the plight of the hunger-stricken, Ding, according to Qian, "issued grain that members of his family had stored in previous years. Thereupon the people came from all over, near and far, propping up the elderly and carrying the young in their arms. Forming lines that wound in continuously for several *li,* they surrounded Mr. Ding's home. Ding Bin set up population registers and established procedures. . . . Thousands of people were saved."

Proceeding with his account, Qian further tells of food shortages that again inflicted suffering upon the area of Jiashan, in 1608 and 1624. As before, Ding provided relief. Four times during his lifetime he provided relief, without once begrudging the depletion of his family's resources. The people were at peace, and the city was spared anxieties over whether grain prices might be artificially lowered (thereby making grain affordable to the poor but devaluing the stocks) or whether there might be forced donations. Great were Ding's achievements on behalf of his native place, concluded Qian, who then went on to report Ding's other contributions to his community: Ding Bin had led the way in contributing his surplus salary to the repair of city walls and the defense against pirates; he visited rural areas to inquire after persons who were sick, suffering, or lacked friends and relatives; and so that he might assist them, he prepared to register them in the poorhouses. He also had the village elders report filial sons and virtuous women to the officials so that they might receive honorary placards.[108] Another entry in the same gazetteer further states that, in 1624, Ding Bin contributed one hundred *mou* of land for a Confucian school (*ruxue*), specifically to aid "poor students," and three thousand taels to relieve poor households from tax burdens.[109]

Though wholeheartedly commending Ding, Qian's skeletal biography inadvertently hints at knotty issues and politics outside our purview. Ding's community was confronted with a choice: the wealthy could face the prospect of being forced by officials to sell their grain at devalued prices, or they could take matters into their own hands by making voluntary donations. Did Ding have stocks of grain, the bulk of which he could protect by issuing a portion? Was he fearful that some policy, imposed by local officials, might lower grain prices, thereby diminishing the value of his stock? Or did he, scanning the available options, want to take the initiative in ameliorating the situation, thereby fulfilling his sense of responsibility to his community while earning a good reputation? Such questions of motivation are rarely answerable. What can be surely said is this: whatever the various motivations may have been, they alike reverted to—that is, were expressed in terms of—a common principle that ran through all available options that were openly discussed. This principle was that, by some means or other, grain should be distributed to alleviate the suffering of the poor. Wealthy residents may have campaigned for strategies that favored their own stocks, maneuvered to substitute loan arrangements for the outright donation of grain, contrived to postpone the day of distribution, or promoted rules that narrowed the pool of beneficiaries. But outweighing or masking such self-serving strategies were cultural norms or expectations mandating aid to the indigent during bad harvests.

Even before his death, Ding Bin had gained fame as an exemplar of generosity and compassion, a model benefactor to whom literati commonly referred. His fine deeds were known to Gao Panlong, who, having been distressed by the sight of naked and starving beggars milling around the capital in 1621, tried to shame the emperor into action by reminding him, in a memorial, of Ding Bin's generosity. Though a mere official serving in Nanjing, Ding had, Gao explained, himself managed "to defray the costs of a food hall and to register all the starving people of the city for aid, so that everyone received real charity *(shihui)*."[110] In short, a decade before Chen Longzheng sought Ding's support for instituting a benevolent society, Ding Bin's moral authority had already won wide acceptance. Chen, who availed himself of Ding's authority, in turn would shore up Ding's reputation: when editing Gao's work (which was published in 1632, right after Ding's death), Chen commented in the margin by Gao's memorial of 1621: "Minister of Justice Ding everywhere performed deeds of substance. This is one example."[111] In joining a chorus of praise for benefactors of the past, in making his admiration for beneficence widely known, Chen articulated a standard to which he too would have an obligation to comply.

Sponsorship from Ding, who had official status, helped Chen's benevolent society to ward off any stigma of being a "private society" and enabled Chen to mobilize fellow townsmen to cooperate. However, if Chen found authority for the idea of a benevolent society in specific individuals, he was also responding to examples set by other districts. According to his sons, the idea for a benevolent society came to Chen Longzheng when he learned from a paternal first cousin that the town of Wuxi (Xishan) had such an organization, in which the literati *(shidafu)* each season contributed toward expenses to aid the poor. Chen's sons reported, "As soon as our father read the record of it, he was delighted and discussed it with Ding Bin. It was arranged that Longzheng's comrades Zhou Pixian, Wei Xuelian (son of Wei Dazhong, who was executed in 1625), and several other gentlemen would put it into effect."[112]

Holding up the examples of other districts, Chen himself explained in a 1631 letter to Ding Bin: "Wujin (Piling) and Wuxi (Xishan) have benevolent societies. . . . Today the various gentlemen, wishing to imitate them in

establishing one, have asked me to inscribe a few words about the basic principles." Then Chen, using flattery to smooth the way, implored Ding to en-
dorse the society: "To work diligently on small good deeds, one relies on great
men. With your leadership, the number of people responding will be great
and their activities long-lasting. I am being so bold as to present my crude
plans for a society for your critical reading; your endorsement will mean good
fortune for the gentlemen involved in the matter; it will also be my good fortune and the great good fortune of the entire city."[113] Again linking a city-
wide view with Ding's authority, Chen commented in another letter, "The
benevolent society obtained Ding Bin's generous leadership, and the entire
city followed."[114]

Ding's endorsement helped Chen to launch the benevolent society and
win community support. Yet, as far as surviving sources tell, Chen acknowledged Ding Bin's sponsorship only incidentally, in pieces not specifically focusing on the topic of charity—one exception being Chen's brief mention,
in a benevolent-society lecture, of Ding's charitable activities.

To build a case for the benevolent society, Chen also leaned heavily on
his own past closeness to his widely revered (and by then deceased) mentor
Gao Panlong. He invoked Gao's authority when he reiterated, in his 1631
"Introduction to the Benevolent Society," the "excellent points" that Gao "had
made clear in his own preface." He again invoked Gao's authority when he
cited Gao's pointedly worded teaching that "doing good is like drinking when
one is thirsty and eating when one is hungry"—that is, it is something that
comes naturally and inevitably.[115] So strongly did Chen identify with Gao Panlong that confusion has arisen concerning which of the two men, Gao or
Chen, actually composed a set of guidelines for the benevolent society. The
guidelines appear in Chen's collected works as a product of Chen's hand,
yet a nineteenth-century compiler of a collection of writings on charity ascribed them to Gao Panlong.[116]

Long after his death, Gao continued to have a towering presence. News
of his suicide had circulated widely, sending shock waves through literati society and publicizing his moral integrity. His courageous choice to commit
suicide, a dramatic protest against evil, secured for good a fine reputation
that nothing could tarnish. Through its association with Gao, the benevolent society gained a legitimacy and authority independent of officialdom.
Later benevolent societies continued to benefit from official approval, but,
fortified by Gao's legacy, they needed it less than before.

In the generations that followed, sponsors of benevolent societies acknowledged inspiration from Gao and Chen but neglected to mention Yang
Dongming, the founder of the first known benevolent society. Chen acknowledged the benevolent-society activities of several predecessors: Zhang
Shiyi, Qian Yiben, and Chen Youxue, not to mention his mentor Gao Panlong.[117] He knew of Yang Dongming; and Chen's senior townsman Ding Bin

had met Yang and acknowledged receiving a volume of his collected writings. This volume, though bearing the title *Achievements While Living in Retirement* (*Xianju gongke*) was no doubt the same work as the extant *Achievements While Living in the Hills* (*Shanju gongke*), which was published in 1624 and included Yang's pieces about the two do-good societies of Yucheng.[118] Chen made no mention of Yang Dongming's charitable activities, however. He apparently made a conscious choice to associate his benevolent society mainly with the more august Gao Panlong.

Likewise did later generations overlook Yang's role in initiating the benevolent society. When, after recovering from the turmoil of dynastic change, the benevolent society of Kunshan resumed its activities in the early Qing, Gui Zhuang related in a capsule history that the society had been initiated by Gao Panlong and Qian Yiben, and that its methods had been clarified by Chen Longzheng.[119] When contributing a preface to writings on a benevolent society (which are now lost), Peng Dingqiu of Changzhou prefecture, expressed admiration specifically for Gao's lectures.[120] Reporting on his establishment of a benevolent society in 1736, Huang Yang noted that, for this and for composing his own pamphlet on the subject, he had derived inspiration from the writings of Gao Panlong and Chen Longzheng.[121] The nineteenth-century collection of moral tracts *Records of Having Obtained What Is Good* (*Deyi lu*) includes pieces by Gao and Chen—as well as numerous Qing-dynasty essays acknowledging their influence—but it too ignores Yang Dongming. Gao Panlong's martyrdom had made him indisputably the most heroic among all benevolent-society sponsors; by associating their benevolent societies with Gao, philanthropists could best legitimize and advance their causes.

Gao, Chen, and later benefactors may have ignored Yang's role as benevolent-society pioneer for another reason as well: Yang's conceptualization of his benevolent society in terms of a closed membership poorly suited their vision of a united community. In sponsoring two distinct benevolent societies in his town, Yang segregated the title holders of the first society from the rich and influential townsmen of the second society. Yang, to be sure, had cited informal organizations among the common people as an inspiration for his benevolent society, yet it was as though he had stepped only momentarily into the arena of the common people, snatched their idea, and then escaped back into the safety of his own, exclusive benevolent society, where he might protect his elite standing. In contrast, Gao and Chen opened their benevolent societies to "everyone" (a term that in this context took for granted the exclusion of women), whether, as Chen put it, he be "a farmer, merchant, or yamen personnel."[122] Correctly they perceived their benevolent societies to be a new type of organization, with a city-wide embrace, whose spirit is conveyed by Chen's proud declaration: "Our city (*wu yi*) has been one of the starting places" for the benevolent society.[123]

CONCLUSION

Yang Dongming, Gao Panlong, and Chen Longzheng were able to wield authority in their hometowns in part because they enjoyed substantial holdings of land and connections to political power. Yet the key to their leadership was their strong moral convictions, with which they tried hard to comply, as their generous charitable gifts and Gao's suicide attest. Reaching for moral perfection and standing apart from their peers, they accommodated new types of social relations, which were solidified in the form of the benevolent society. Suiting the need for associations outside the lineage, monastery, or official-run community meetings, Gao's benevolent society continued to meet, for a total of eighty-six times, at least until 1671—long after Gao's day.[124] Chen Longzheng meanwhile witnessed the spreading influence of his own benevolent society. As he proudly commented at its fortieth meeting, in 1641, "in such nearby places as Hangzhou and Su-Song [that is, Suzhou and Songjiang prefectures], even in the faraway city of Beijing, and in every province, worthy literati are all imitating this society."[125] By the time of his last lecture, in the autumn of 1644, the benevolent society had assembled fifty-one times. This was shortly before Chen, already ill, refused to take food, thereby hastening his end in his loyalty to the fallen Ming dynasty. Standing apart from their peers, Yang, Gao, and Chen led the way. The alternatives against which they weighed the benevolent society as a cure for social breakdown is the subject of the next chapter.

3

The Benevolent Society
among Its Alternatives

We people who are of the same district . . .
GAO PANLONG

On the eve of the benevolent societies' first appearance, members of the local elite had—in addition to relying on Buddhist institutions and the state—at least four readily available strategies for doing good: liberating animals; working through the community compact (*xiangyue*), an institution through which officials tried to socialize—or inspire proper conduct in—the common people; giving charity independently of a group; and giving through one's lineage organization. Yang Dongming, Gao Panlong, and Chen Longzheng, each to a varying degree, defined the benevolent society against these alternatives; yet, either in addition to or instead of these options, they chose to express their compassion through benevolent societies. By comparing the benevolent society to its alternatives, and by exploring questions about efficiency and the definition of responsibility, this chapter shows that the new institution was not just another instrument for addressing poverty or moral reform. Rather, being unlike the alternatives in its organization, reach, and locus of authority, it expressed the solidarity of a district-wide community. Moreover, once in place, it became an important point of reference for activities outside the benevolent society. Inevitably the discussion will focus on Chen, whose extant writings, being voluminous, reveal far better than Yang's and Gao's the social environment that defined the benefactors' choices.

In 1630—at age forty-six and two years before his first benevolent society meeting—Chen had a sudden epiphany: on hearing a cock crow on New Year's Day, and feeling expansive and untroubled, he suddenly grasped the concept of the perpetual renewal of life (*shengsheng*) as the key to understanding virtue and goodness.[1] His awakening resonated with something Gao Panlong had pronounced: "Get up when the cock crows. Work tirelessly to do good";[2] this in turn echoed a passage from *The Book of Mencius:* "He who rises at cock-crowing and addresses himself earnestly to the practice of virtue, is a disciple of [the sage king] Shun."[3] Chen's moment of enlightenment came some years after he, in his restless quest for life's meaning, had sought from Gao Panlong the instruction that would lead him to a life of activism and an exuberant "love for mankind" (*airen*).[4] Though their meetings were few and poorly chronicled, Chen admired his mentor and would later edit, add his own marginalia to, and learn from Gao's collected writings.

The concept of *shengsheng* harks back to the ancient *Book of Changes* (*Yi-jing*),[5] but it came into vogue in the sixteenth century, in part, through the teachings of Luo Rufang, who, following Wang Yangming, did much to spread literacy by popularizing the notion that anyone could become a sage.[6] Yang Dongming referred to Luo and, like Luo, celebrated "the perpetual renewal of life" as the essence of humaneness.[7] Chen, in contrast, distanced himself from the excesses of Luo Rufang's thought—he criticized Luo for mouthing the words of Confucius and Mencius while being at heart a Buddhist.[8] Nonetheless Chen embraced the concept of *shengsheng*, which had gained a life of its own, independent of any one proponent; as an optimistic alternative to death, it captured the great sense of urgency that some late Ming literati felt about nurturing and saving lives. Feeding that sense of urgency were crises erupting in quick succession: Gao Panlong's suicide, pirate raids along the coast, foreign incursions along the northern borders, inclement weather, bad harvests, and uprisings by starving people.

Feelings of anxiety and confusion made stark, dichotomous choices attractive. Images of life and death, defining two distinct, antithetical states, caught the imagination of late Ming literati; the choice to save or abandon creatures on the brink of death served as a metaphor epitomizing the "crossroads," or "critical juncture" (*guantou*), between good and bad. Thus, Chen defined the difference between grasping Gao Panlong's concept of "the utmost goodness" and being deluded about it as "the boundary between the sage and the savage, and the crossroads between life and death."[9] Through such rhetoric, he and his peers tried to jolt members of their community into action.

Chen was aware that the practice of saving animals held great symbolic power. In 1632, in the first of nine extant benevolent-society lectures spanning twelve years, he observed: "Recently monks have often joined together to form societies for liberating animals, and all those who are good-hearted happily fall in." Chen perceived that liberating animals was on some level analogous to saving people. But he then proceeded to disparage the practice as wasteful: "Now isn't this benevolent society better because it gives aid to save human lives and lends support to good people?" Chen went so far as to invert the order in which these institutions had emerged, claiming that the benevolent society was "the real basis for the societies for liberating animals."[10]

Not animals, but those other helpless creatures, babies, captured Chen's imagination. During a terrible food shortage that occurred two years before the first benevolent-society meeting, he was haunted by the sight of despairing parents tossing their infants over the Bridge of Scattered Stars into the rapids below.[11] A decade later, when making a long journey to Luoyang, Henan, far from home, Chen again lamented the plight of those powerless and tiny beings, abandoned children. So too did he, at the first benevolent-society meeting, lament the desperate, life-threatening straits of the downtrodden: "For example, when one or two people have collapsed in some old temple from hunger and fatigue and then some good-hearted person gives them food and medicine, enabling them to regain their strength and walk off, then those who witness it will certainly be overjoyed."[12] Like those compassionate animal liberators, good-hearted persons could give the poor and sick a second life. In both situations, witnessing the survival of a creature near death brought the savior a gratifying sense of accomplishment. Because they had personally chosen to make a charitable gift, the event authenticated their moral worth.

AN ALTERNATIVE TO COMMUNITY COMPACTS

Community compacts, though claiming a distant precedent dating to 1077, burst upon the sixteenth-century scene as something essentially new. In 1518 (or 1520, by some accounts), Wang Yangming, who was then enduring an exile to the backwater area of Ganzhou, Jiangxi, initiated this institution to pacify the unruly residents and demonstrated its efficacy as a tool for maintaining local order. Some fifty years later, the seeds sown by Wang found truly welcoming soil: in 1567, in response to an official's proposal, the emperor ordered that community compacts be established throughout the country.[13]

The efficacy and extent of community-compact meetings are difficult to evaluate. Rarely were such highly localized activities recorded in writings that later archivists would consider worth preserving. Moreover, community compacts varied from place to place, often blending in with other institutions for local governance, such as those for the storage of grain; tax collecting; and mutual surveillance (*baojia*), a policing system that held neighborhoods collectively responsible for the behavior of its inhabitants. Chameleon-like, the community compact adjusted its colors to local environments and the aspirations of presiding officials, sometimes taking on variant names, such as *xiangjia* (to indicate a fusing with the *baojia*), and thus losing its distinct identity. These complications notwithstanding, some evidence suggests that the community compact thrived in the late Ming: the transcripts of a few community-compact lectures survive, and both Lu Shiyi and Qi Biaojia testify that they themselves attended such meetings. Still, some late Ming literati bemoaned that the program had withered into a hollow theory.[14]

Among the latter group was Gao Panlong, who once expressed regret that the community-compact system had become defunct. It was, he maintained, "an important part of civilizing education (*jiaohua*). But," he ruefully added, "many district officials were insincere about installing this institution, rendering it to be but a paper plan; and community-compact chiefs and assistant chiefs often ended up harming the people." Consequently Gao counseled: "If one really wants to make it work, one must politely ask worthy former officials or men with junior examination degrees—men whom the people respect—to be in charge."[15] Gao stated this in a memorial he drafted but then, for reasons that are unclear, did not submit to the court.

Chen explicitly defined the benevolent society as a supplement to the community compact. Benevolent-society lectures, he told the audience at their first meeting, had "the same intention as the exhortations and warnings that officials delivered at community-compact meetings, namely, to transform an entire district (*xian*) to have good customs."[16] Or, as he wrote in a letter of 1638 to the regional inspector of Zhejiang: "My city has a benevolent society, which has been running for the past eight or nine years, meeting four times a year. The participants are noble and humble, high and low, their hearts tightly united. Ever since this society was established, there have been scarcely any deaths from starvation or corpses along the roadsides. Occasionally there are the didactic lectures to awaken their intuitive understanding of goodness (*liangxin*) and dissolve their depravities—in tacit support for community compacts and the mutual-surveillance system."[17]

Not once in their lectures did Gao and Chen cite the high-minded Confucian classics or use the elegant phrases characteristic of literati language. For their audiences, these were all too bookish. Rather, they adopted the easygoing, colloquial style used at community-compact meetings. Especially visible in Chen's lectures—which cover far more pages than Gao's—is the liberal use of bisyllabic forms of words that are rendered monosyllabic in literary prose, and his adoption of scores of colloquial mannerisms: the numerary adjunct *ge*, the particle *de*, and, to indicate changed situation, the perfective particle *le*. Avoiding classical allusions, Chen opted for down-to-earth homilies about crushed flowers and abandoned babies. The lectures must be easy to understand, mandated the guidelines: "Whether he is speaking on old works of previous generations or new regulations, the person in charge of the lecture should put everything in the vernacular so that everyone will easily understand and their good hearts will be stirred. If one is concerned that the audience has not understood, then write up the lecture in big characters on one sheet to hang up on the wall of the meeting place."[18]

Gao pursued a simple agenda, basing his lectures on the Six Imperial Maxims (variously termed *liuyu, liuju, huangdi liuyan,* and *liuju yanyu*) that the founder of the Ming dynasty (Taizu gao huangdi) had commanded be promulgated through the streets of every village, and which went as follows: "Be filial to your parents; respect your elders; be neighborly; educate your children and grandchildren; stay put in [or, rest content with] your occupations;

and do nothing wrong."[19] Totaling a mere twenty-four characters, in a rhythmic pattern of four syllables per item, the maxims were easy to remember; yet they provided an outline for comprehensive discussions of moral issues, allowing lecturers—at community-compact and benevolent-society meetings alike—to expand, as they saw fit, on the various points, often embroidering dry dicta with catchy phrases and anecdotes.

In promoting the Six Maxims, Gao associated himself with imperial authority—not the authority of the reigning emperor, whose rule was fraught with problems, but with that of the Ming founder, whose distance in time and removal from contemporary problems invited unmitigated glorification. As Gao proclaimed, "This Taizu gao huangdi was the founder and sage ruler of our dynasty, which up to now has lasted 250 years, bringing peace throughout the world. We who, in comfort and peace, consume our rice and tea, have clothes to wear, and sleep securely through the night do so all because of his gracious favor."[20]

"Just look at the Six Maxims written on the placard!" Gao directed his listeners at his third lecture (this being the only time he referred his audience to a text), adding that those maxims, alone and without "any fancy words," would serve for a lifetime.[21] Erected right before their eyes, the placard must have impressed upon his audience that the maxims—and hence Gao, who was expounding upon them—represented an authority higher than his own. Then, reaching for an authority even higher than the founding emperor, Gao connected the Six Maxims to heaven: "Gao huangdi is nothing other than heaven, and these words emanate from heaven. Heaven will naturally be pleased if you follow heaven's words and will naturally be angry if you contravene them. Can we face heaven's fury?" Having thus directed his audience's attention to heaven's authority to assign retribution and recompense, Gao proceeded to tie the Six Maxims back to the ordinary lives of his audience: "They are basically useful everyday household words," he pronounced.[22] Pegging his benevolent society to both everyday utility and august but distant authorities, Gao defined a place where residents in his community could legitimately assemble outside the realm of institutions customarily endorsed by local officials and remain free from bureaucratic intervention. How could the reigning emperor and officialdom possibly object to activities that sought to promulgate those edifying maxims that the dynasty's illustrious founder had sanctioned?

To arouse an anxious attentiveness in his listeners, Gao warned that they faced two roads: one path ascending to bliss, the other descending to utter disaster. Making the right choice, he added, depended on whether they would follow the Six Maxims or dismiss them as "unpalatable, not worth fulfilling." At the next two lectures, Gao continued to push the Six Maxims: that everyone should be filial toward and obey his parents, respect his elders, and so on.[23] Elaborating on the choice between good and bad, he reasoned: "If everyone is good, then the whole district will be united and harmonious, and this will elicit harmony from heaven and earth, so that it will rain when it ought to rain, and will be sunny when it ought to be sunny, and the harvest will be abundant and everyone will have enough. How would anyone then not enjoy the fortune of a great peace?"[24] Gao then presented a counterexample, roughly as follows: if, on the contrary, someone is bad at heart and so perverted as to call a good person useless and a bad person a proper good fellow, and then does what he will while disregarding the Six Maxims, that would spark a disastrous chain of events. "When one person does bad, ten people will see how it is, and this will lead to the most unsavory mores. The bad forces will elicit all the bad forces of heaven and earth, the periods of rain and shine will be unseasonable, and the five grains will fail to ripen. The people will fall ill, and contagion will spread. Extraordinary military violence and banditry will follow. Ignoramuses will say, 'This fate is inevitable,' without realizing that fate is not some abstract talk but something gradually developed through the accumulation of attitudes and customs."[25]

Moral choices were life-and-death matters. So instructed one Ming official, who, when lecturing on the Six Maxims, illustrated "Be filial" with the following homily: there was a son who fished for a living but always hid his catch, refusing to share it with his mother; for his unfilial behavior he was eventually punished: one fish, turning into a snake, killed him with its poisonous bite.[26] Likewise did Gao caution his listeners, reminding them of the havoc, "the inconceivable harm," wrought by Japanese pirates (*wokou*) who had plundered Xinghua prefecture in Fujian, slaughtering scholars and common people.[27] The massacre stemmed from the region's moral depravity, Gao argued, pointing out that men "with foresight" had warned that the city would be attacked. "If this was not the result of human attitudes and customs, how," he asked his audience, "was it that, even before the pirates came, perspicacious people predicted the disaster?" Then, he drove his lesson home: "From this one can see that if a household does good, then it will have good fortune, and if every household does good, then the whole district will have good fortune."[28] Whether one accepts Gao's reasoning or not, the purpose of his rhetoric is clear: moral reform was urgently needed if the people were to avoid disastrous consequences.

And yet, the two homilies, that of the community compact and that delivered by Gao, differed in their implications. Whereas the former emphasized personal conduct, Gao derived an additional lesson from the incident at Xinghua prefecture, namely, that scholars and common people—members of the community high and low—had alike suffered the pirate raid and ultimately shared a common fate.

In their use of the vernacular, the Six Maxims, and a cautionary rhetoric, the benevolent society and community compacts were similar. Nonetheless, they strained in different directions. Community-compact leaders were only rarely "town residents."[29] Most often they were officials, as Wang Yangming had been. As such, they not only claimed some moral authority but also wielded real political power to demand attendance, to make judgments, and then, as warranted, to deliver praise and blame, rewards and punishments. Even if village elders were placed in charge of the meetings, they could, as Wang Yangming had instructed them, "deliver [any wrongdoer] to the government so that he may be openly punished."[30] Benevolent-society leaders, though often enjoying indirect connections to political power—for surely everyone in their communities knew that Yang Dongming and Gao Panlong were officials on leave—managed their benevolent societies without the tools of office. As stipulated by the guidelines preserved among Chen Longzheng's collected writings, "anyone of good conduct, be he of official rank or not, may participate in making recommendations for the chairmanship and may take turns assuming responsibilities."[31] Yang and Gao substantiated their teachings less through a show of their high status as former officials than by practicing what they preached: they made monetary donations for the society's charitable activities. They thus paved the way for a nonofficial like Chen Longzheng to initiate and lead a benevolent society.

Late Ming community compacts generally had a two-part program: lectures and a review of the residents' behavior. For the latter, the presiding official would ceremoniously register names of the residents in two distinct ledgers—one designated "good," the other "bad"—with the separation of records clearly informing even illiterate attendees that paths of behavior diverged sharply.[32] The community-compact meetings thus underscored a chasm between the ordinary people, who were subjected to public review, and the officials or other holders of authority, who sat in judgment.

Gao was familiar with the registers of good deeds and bad, as well as a third type: a "record of reforming one's faults" (*gaiguo bu*), through which the community compact encouraged wrongdoers to reform themselves so as to avoid the stigma of being labeled bad.[33] None of these registers had a place in his benevolent society, however. Simply by virtue of having volunteered to attend the meeting, all benevolent-society participants, whether high or low, educated or illiterate, shared in the goodness. In an all-embracing spirit, Chen insisted that consideration of wealth should not divide his community: "Today, we who are at the meeting are generally charitable, which is certainly to do good. But we must not assume that *only* giving charitable donations of money counts as 'doing good.' Would you mean to say that, except for giving charity, there are no good deeds? Or that the beneficiaries are at fault?" He assumed that small amounts of help would inspire the beneficiaries to intensify their efforts in doing good. Closing the chasm between the haves and have-nots, he pronounced: "Only when both the benefactor and the recipient are good is it truly 'sharing goodness.'"[34]

The community compact had, from the start, a component of mutual aid:

"Offer assistance to each other in cases of illness and calamities," exhorted the "Lü Family's Community Compact" (Lüshi xiangyue) of 1077.[35] One should treat one's neighbors generously because, explained one Ming community-compact lecturer, "when you become poor, you will need to rely on your neighbors for help."[36] Nevertheless, charitable activities appear to have been incidental to most community compacts, whose main purpose was to maintain order by promoting moral conduct. Early benevolent societies had as their main goal moral reform, but the vehicle they used to achieve that goal was charitable deeds—and over time, the means became the end.

Benevolent societies, moreover, expanded the roles for participants who lacked the status, authority, or voice to preach. In pooling the contributions from both leaders and followers, and in encouraging cooperation among all participants, they blurred the distinctions between educated and less educated associates. Although considerations of status continued to function in the benevolent society's day-to-day operations (as the case of Lu Shiyi, discussed in chapter 5, will illustrate), the benevolent society had made room for defining status in such nonbureaucratic terms as wealth and dedication.

The benevolent society further differed from the community compact in its reach. In Wang Yangming's vision of the community compact, each participant paid the small sum of three fen to defray the costs of such in-group functions as the consumption of wine (which was drunk, especially by the wrongdoers, during the review of the participants' behavior) and a communal meal. The purpose of the funds was to strengthen solidarity among participants in a community whose size was fixed. Benevolent-society membership was fluid, and its associates aggressively used funds to involve more residents. Through the act of giving, the society defined nonmembers as beneficiaries and bystanders as the witnesses of good deeds, thereby drawing outsiders into a project of "sharing goodness" (tongshan). The gifts, Gao assumed, would transform the once-indifferent beneficiaries. As he noted: "All the people who receive benefits through this society will naturally think that this money came from a good society."[37] Although Gao acknowledged (in the memorial he did not submit) that the community compact was "an important part of civilizing education (jiaohua)," he insisted that people were likely to improve their ways not because they are ordered to do so but because they had observed the good examples of their superiors.[38]

A proselytizing spirit—the desire to "spread exhortations" (guangquan), to quote Gao—infused the early benevolent societies. To draw outsiders into its fold, the benevolent society exposed its good deeds to the community at large. Or, as Yang Dongming had phrased the challenge: how can one spread this goodness throughout the entire world so as to accord with my aspirations for great unity?[39] The money coming from the benevolent society would, declared Gao, "produce good hearts; sons and younger brothers (would) be more filial toward their relatives and respectful of their elders."

Here he broke into a litany based on the Six Imperial Maxims, and then concluded: "Such is the intention of 'sharing goodness.' Although the aid is slight, the moral exhortation is great and this society will not be in vain."[40]

Gao's concept of "sharing goodness" was predicated upon his assumption that moral improvement "comes from within the self, not from ornate compositions,"[41] from which it followed that everyone in his benevolent-society audience would respond to the sight of suffering just as he did—that "upon seeing someone in the district who is old, poor, or sick, or a corpse that has not been buried, they would feel empathy and aid one another, just as though the person were of one's own family."[42]

When Gao returned to the capital in 1621 (after nearly three decades at home), the sight of poor, naked people milling about the streets overwhelmed him with the same feeling of interconnectedness that he had compared to the pain that shoots through one's entire body when a knife pierces a part of one's skin. Gao drafted a memorial imploring the emperor to undertake relief programs. To strengthen his case, he cited the successful recommendations of two late fifteenth-century officials: squatters should be given clothes and grain and lodged in poorhouses; when the warm spring weather arrives they should be supplied with travel expenses to return to their hometowns.[43] He further cited the precedent of Ding Bin, the resident of Chen Longzheng's town who had gained renown for generosity.[44] Reputedly Ding had set up dining halls in the Southern Capital, registered all starving persons of the area, and given them money and rice, so that everyone "received true charity." Holding up the exemplary kindness of an official, Gao essentially tried to shame the emperor into taking similar measures in the capital.[45] But what had thrown Gao into the role of urgent messenger in the first place was what he heard and saw. As he put it, "The vagrants' agonized cries and sorrowful appearances . . . were more than I could bear to hear or witness."[46]

Just as he had described, when addressing the emperor, what he saw and heard, Gao tried to engage the less educated of his benevolent-society audience by instructing them to look and listen: "Just look at the bandits in the world. Is any one of them not destroyed? Just look at the prostitutes, gamblers, bullies, litigators, and scoundrels: do any of them come to a good end? They end up being investigated at the official headquarters; and when they are locked up in prison and are thinking about those porters and peddlers out on the streets, each carrying on with his own business—that will all seem like heaven. Why are they suffering? Because they crave only momentary satisfaction, which instead creates endless suffering! Today, upon hearing these words, each of you should set your mind on being a good person."[47]

The faculties of seeing and hearing connected one to the conditions and cries of the suffering and allowed beneficial messages to sink in. In the dialogue Gao had with Chen Youxue, what ultimately proved the correctness of Gao's arguments was not Gao's reasoning, but that Chen heard and grasped his message. What clinched Gao's point was not some grand summation delivered by Gao but, rather, Chen Youxue's acknowledgment that he had understood Gao's message. As told by Gao on the occasion of Youxue's eightieth birthday, it was Chen who wrapped up the conversation, saying, "Now I know that what is called *tongshan* is to unify everything into one great body."[48]

Voluntary attendance—the will to listen—was itself testimony of man's inclination toward goodness. At the fourteenth meeting, when presenting the second of his three extant lectures, Gao appealed to what was before their eyes: Over a hundred people had assembled, each and every one there of his own volition; therefore "one can see that to be good is man's basic nature and that doing good is one's basic allotted business—like wearing clothes, eating food, which everyone likes to do."[49] Recognizing that his audience was the common sort—that "this benevolent society broadly encourages ordinary people to do good"—Gao dwelled on the efficacy of oral messages: "Everyone who has come to listen has the roots of goodness and consequently has good karma. Here, good words will enter your ears." Explained Gao: "When one sentence of good words awakens a speck of the goodness in your heart, you will become a good person for a whole lifetime." Then, reverting to the analogies between goodness and life, and between evil and death, Gao asked: "Is this not simply turning disaster into good fortune—just like bringing the dead to life?"[50]

Gao wrote in a colloquial, elementary style even when composing his piece "Household Instructions" (Jia xun) for his own family. That his choice of style was unconventional is implied by a comment that Chen Longzheng entered in the margins. Someone, wrote Chen, had asked: given that Gao's learning was refined, why did he write "Household Instructions" in unsophisticated language? Replied Chen: "Mr. Gao was concerned that, as the lineage branches out over the generations and its membership expands, not all members will necessarily be scholarly types; therefore citing rustic words and proverbs is at times perhaps useful, and literati will regard this as sufficient to rouse farmers, artisans, merchants; to hear these words will suffice to protect one's self and family."[51] His own kin, acknowledged Gao, was a heterogeneous lot.

Gao's instructions to his family, like his benevolent society lectures, stressed the Six Maxims. Addressing "even those persons who missed out on learning and are illiterate," he cautioned: "If they would simply stick to the Six Maxims of our august founding emperor—'Be filial . . .'—and if they would from time to time mull over or recite one's faults, why, that would be far superior to reciting Buddhist sutras." Gao continued: "Goodness would take root, wrongdoing would be eradicated, one would be a good person in one's village, and some of one's sons and grandsons would certainly rise."

Next, echoing the Six Maxims, he added: "Each person would then find an occupation [fifth maxim] and would stick to it; and when they encounter wrongdoing [sixth maxim], an internal conscience would still warn against whoring, gambling, and litigating—the three wrongs that illiterate people are particularly likely to commit, bringing destruction to their households and selves with exceptional speed."[52] To this extent Gao tried to maintain the status quo. Yet, while striving to stabilize society, he himself was being transformed. Making adjustments to a social environment where not all members of his own lineage were necessarily "scholarly types," he readily regarded the vernacular as a form of expression worthy of himself. He preserved the benevolent-society lectures among his papers, and his student Chen Longzheng chose to include them in Gao's collected writings.[53] The benevolent society thus blunted the sharp divide between the educators and the common herd that characterized the community compact.

AN ALTERNATIVE TO INFORMAL GIVING

After founding benevolent societies, Yang, Gao, and Chen continued to carry out some charitable activities either individually or through small, informal groups. In 1632, Chen, figuring that the benevolent society lacked sufficient funds, paid out of his own pocket for the burial of corpses that were piling up by the city wall.[54] During a food shortage in 1635, rather than working through the benevolent society, he devised a grain equalization system that, in his words, was "to supplement the benevolent society."[55] Again working outside the benevolent society in 1642, he sponsored a program of portable soup kitchens that his colleague the former official Qian Shisheng had initiated.[56]

The benevolent-society guidelines stipulated that one third of its funds go to coffins—a program that was apparently to serve only the city, for the guidelines further noted that the benevolent society was unable to provide coffins to the indigent of every rural neighborhood (*xiang*).[57] In 1642, taking inspiration from the precedent of a burial society (*yange hui*) that various "renowned gentlemen" had formed in the capital in 1637, Chen joined what he termed "worthies of my city" to organize a similar project in Jiashan. Prosperous years enabled the poor to scrape by, but disastrous harvests, he observed, left beggars dying in the streets. He proposed that each month a charitable person should make arrangements with the coroners of the urban wards (*fang*) to search streets and river coves for corpses, wrap them in straw, and dispatch them to the charitable graveyard. For each corpse, the coroners, who themselves were indigent, should be paid three *fen*—a sum that would allow them a small profit. From midspring through midsummer, Chen took responsibility for the project, which buried over 550 corpses.[58] Given the figures that he provided, this project cost sixteen and a half ounces of silver.

Chen subsequently encouraged town worthies to construct shelters for beggars outside the city walls. (Although Chen does not state it, providing these shelters offered the added benefit of removing potentially dangerous drifters from the city.) During one winter, according to an undated "Proposal for Lodgings for Beggars" (Jian gaifang yi), approximately five or six hundred persons had been wandering about his city begging; because they lacked protection against wind and rain from the second through the fifth months, over five hundred of them eventually had to be buried.[59] Chen pursued a dual strategy, sometimes affiliating with worthy residents and sometimes acting singly. Opportunities for doing good were numerous. What added value did the benevolent society offer?

By collecting numerous small donations, a benevolent society could fund activities too costly for a person of small means to handle alone. Chen made this clear to those naysayers who, themselves "being unwilling to do good, wished to obstruct others by declaring, 'Such small donations: What good can they accomplish, and how many persons can they help?'" Responded Chen: "They do not understand that, if one uses one's goodness to the utmost and according to one's means, then, although one's donation is small, when it is combined with the donations of all the others, the amount will be large."[60] In fact, maximizing donations to the benevolent society appears not to have been its goal. Recommended contributions ranged from nine *fen* to ten times that amount, or nine *qian*.[61] By naming upper and lower limits for donations, the benevolent society softened economic differences among donors. Fostering a united community among its members outweighed thoughts of maximizing the collection of funds.

From its inception in 1631 to the spring of 1640, the benevolent society of Jiashan distributed a total of fifteen hundred taels, according to a lecture given by resident and former official Qian Shisheng.[62] Whether one would judge that amount as large or small, certainly the sum of roughly 166 taels a year, or 41 taels per season, exceeded the individual donations (from nine *fen* to nine *qian*) recommended by the guidelines. The benevolent society was something more than an aggregate of individual donors, however. It expressed a moral vision. According to Gao's chronological biography, the fundamental purpose of his benevolent society was "to aid widows and orphans, while being especially kind to those among them who were filial or chaste."[63] Or, as put by another biography, which declared Gao's generosity to be "far and wide": Gao not only "set up charitable fields and charitable granaries in order to save lives through periods of food shortage; he also set up the benevolent society to provide charity to residents of the city who were orphaned, widowed, and lived alone. He was especially compassionate toward the worthy poor."[64] For Gao Panlong, aid to the poor was the means for achieving the goal of moral transformation, an endeavor for which expediency or efficiency was not a top priority. He made this point clear when greeting the attendees at the first benevolent-society meeting: "This benevolent society," he declared in no uncertain terms, "is solely for encouraging people to do good."[65] Then, alluding to the downtrodden only in passing, as a sign of the social disorder that inevitably follows moral degeneration, Gao lectured on the urgency of moral reform.

Echoing Gao's viewpoint, Chen wrote in a letter of 1631 seeking Ding Bin's endorsement: "In name, the benevolent society's purpose is to aid the poor; in reality, it is to exhort the multitudes. The activity seems small but has widespread implications."[66] Subsequently, upon noting that "the benevolent society had obtained Ding's generous leadership and the entire city has followed," Chen declared: "Human hearts-and-minds and customs will naturally be transformed and restored." He then hastened to add: "This is not simply a matter of aiding the hundred and some impoverished people."[67] It was with this aim of encouraging goodness that the benevolent-society guidelines stipulated that one should give precedence to those poor persons who are filial sons and chaste women, as well as to persons who have no one to rely on; next are the poor who are old, sick, and in misery, and who wish neither to enter the poorhouses in the public sphere nor to become beggars in the private sphere: their needs rest with "the friends of the society."[68] The benevolent society should investigate the circumstances; then, sparing the beneficiaries the trouble of additional formalities, it should dispense aid within five days after the meeting. By helping the genteel poor in this manner, the benevolent society upheld the notion of a well-ordered, stable society.

In support of its moral teachings, the benevolent-society guidelines ruled against helping "even the most impoverished" among those who are unfilial, who gamble and drink, and who, though young and robust, drift about; assisting such characters would "pervert the righteous cause of encouraging goodness."[69] Nor should one help four categories of people who might at first glance appear to be deserving: yamen personnel, who became impoverished in their later years for no reason other than that they had been rapacious and decadent in their youth; monks, who consumed food without themselves tilling fields; butchers who, though having had an occupation and a permanent residence, lacked humaneness; and dissipated sons, whose untrammeled extravagance—gambling and whoring—undermined their ancestors' accomplishments and ruined customs.[70] The benevolent society had specific, limited goals, so that attempting to satisfy all types of poverty and need would only undermine its moral purpose.

Gao Panlong, who had declared that everyone receiving benevolent-society aid would "naturally think that this money came from a good society,"[71] was concerned less about the amount of aid provided than about the message the monetary gifts signified. Moral uplift was the ultimate goal. Similarly, Chen recognized that money, even in small amounts, could have great exhortative power. In response to a rhetorical question he himself put—

namely, "Given that this society is for aiding the poor, why does it selectively help only good people?"—Chen explained: "Because resources are in short supply, this is how one exhorts people to reform. Those dissolute wastrels who day after day sink deeper into poverty and suffering can thereby be made to feel somewhat remorseful and consequently can change their ways. Moreover, one can induce people to observe: 'Originally he was not such a good person; that is why no one paid attention to him.'"[72]

Chen's benevolent society set its priorities according to two principles, need and moral standing. By categorizing levels of need on the basis of information carefully collected according to openly declared principles, and by justifying the selection of beneficiaries according to unquantifiable standards of morality, the friends of the benevolent society supported a notion of fairness in the distribution of aid and justified their allocations of scarce resources. "Need" could be quantified and, in theory, easily ranked; moral worth was difficult to measure exactly. Taken together, the two criteria, one subjective and the other elusive, allowed benefactors some flexibility in selecting beneficiaries and compensated for any erroneous assessments of need. In combination, the two complementary criteria sustained, among benefactors at least, a sense that justice was being done.

If Chen declared moral edification to be the goal and aid to be the means, the two ingredients were inseparable, each having important ramifications for the other. By defining a higher good that society patrons and participants alike might strive for, and by validating their message through their own gifts, benevolent society leaders aroused and mobilized followers to participate in organized good works. For a few cash, donors of modest means could buy into a sense of well-being, elevating their self-image. Moreover, the goal of moral transformation, always clearly articulated but never fully achievable, precluded any closure to benevolent society activities. Even when resources were limited or after a particular crisis or need had passed, it kept up the momentum for charity. The ever-elusive goal of moral transformation routinized charity, sustaining it as an activity independent of particular crises.

The benevolent-society lectures would, Chen imagined, inspire attendees to rise above self-interest. The show of numbers at the meetings in itself would verify the benevolent society's merit. "We can believe," Chen reasoned at the first session, "that doing good is most pleasurable because the society friends now number several tens."[73] The meetings would bolster each participant's resolve to do good. "It is only because one lacks enlightenment," he declaimed in his first lecture, "that, even though one wants to do good . . . one ends up thinking of oneself while ignoring other persons." But, he elaborated, "whether you are a farmer, tradesperson, or yamen personnel, listening to the lecture will awaken your hearts." Then, as though echoing a pronouncement that a community-compact lecturer once made ("Upon returning to your homes, act according to these words"),[74] he added: "so that, after going home, you will all resolutely try to avoid hurting other people."[75] Chen assumed that the meeting would invigorate his listeners, that the attendees would, "with each step on his way home, think to himself how happy he is. Henceforth, everywhere and always he would address beneficial words to kin and friends and, whenever encountering someone who is suffering, would do some good deed. Without attending society meetings every day, he will day after day retain the society's good intentions."[76]

Chen envisioned that the communal witnessing of goodness would rouse benevolent-society participants and that "those who witness" a benevolent person resuscitating "one or two hungry and sick people who have collapsed in an old temple" will be filled with joy. From such reactions he surmised that "no one can bear the thought of seeing others hungry or ill." Each seasonal meeting would thus renew the participants' determination to do good, spurring them to overcome selfishness. "A man of little virtue will," Chen promised at his second lecture, "become a man of great virtue, and a man of 'meager good fortune' will become a man of 'great fortune.'"[77] Asking, "What need is there to force oneself to learn this empathy for others who are suffering?" Chen encouraged his audience: "Everyone has it from the start; it's only that selfishness obscures it. After being aroused today, you will not again be so blinded."[78]

ORGANIZED CHARITABLE ACTIVITIES

Unlike the community compact, the benevolent society had an organization that engaged individuals to cooperate in charitable projects extending over time and space. The set of sixteen guidelines associated with Gao and Chen harnessed at least some benevolent-society members to a long-lasting group endeavor. It refers to members as "friends of the society," intimating a modicum of camaraderie, which—as in the case of Yang Dongming's "Society for Sharing Goodness"—was fostered by the sharing of food and drink. On the meeting day, the guidelines stated, "the various friends" would bow to one another and then consume tea (prepared by monks) and snacks (provided by the chair), paid for out of the society's common funds.[79] But in contrast to Yang's "contract," which had warned members against getting intoxicated, thus implying that socializing was extensive, these guidelines tempered conviviality with a strict protocol: no wine was to be served and bells were to be struck to signal the start of formal business.

To coordinate its affiliates to work for a common goal, the guidelines outlined various tasks as well as the procedures for registering and aiding needy cases. Yet, on the subjects of attendance and donations, they allowed much flexibility. Though they stipulated that the benevolent society should meet once each season—on the fifteenth day of the second, fifth, eighth, and eleventh months—they also permitted modification: to change the meeting date, the chair merely had to post a notice at the meeting place at least ten days before the event.[80] On the appointed day, the "friends of the society" should bring donations to the meeting, but here too allowances were made: participants "who do not have time to attend the meeting should in advance hand over their donations and what they have collected so as to facilitate the calculations of how much will be available for distributions."[81] Or, as the guidelines further stated, "Those who do not go to the meeting but wish to help anyhow should send in their contributions to be stored at the chair's place; those who have second thoughts after the meeting and wish to join the society after all may send in a payment to catch up."[82]

In contrast to the two benevolent societies that Yang Dongming had sponsored, which had mandated fixed dues for their members[83]—the guidelines associated with Chen and Gao made donations altogether voluntary and did not speak of fining members who failed to show up at scheduled meetings. Saving money for donations should be effortless, they advised: "Middle-income households need save no more than one *wen* a day. Those households with a small surplus need save no more than one *fen* a day; yet they still can help support the poor and suffering."[84] In any case, the guidelines declared: "There is no fixed quota. Some will give every season; some will give for one or two meetings. Each will act according to his own wishes. When the donors themselves take pleasure in giving, the recipients will be at peace."[85] Reiterating this principle, Chen instructed participants at the first meeting that they should express goodness and pity "according to their wishes and resources"; and they should do so, he emphasized, "without incurring for themselves the least bit of trouble."[86] Leaving ample room for individual initiative was utterly essential to the benevolent society's linked goals of "exhorting others to be good and taking pity on the poor";[87] only by parting with their money voluntarily—that is, by willfully sacrificing personal resources to help others—could benevolent-society participants affirm their merit, thereby both demonstrating to their community the power of goodness and enlarging their own sense of self. It was by "taking pleasure in doing good" (*leshan*) that they endowed charity with meaning.

The "society friends" busied themselves with paper work of all sorts, according to the guidelines. This inner circle presumably was literate. The chair, whose position rotated among participants, had to bring to the meeting his writing case, with paper and brush. One friend (whom Chen later referred to as "the registrar") collected the silver and entered the amounts into a record.[88] Other society friends assayed the donated silver, which was of uneven quality. The most degraded silver, explained the guidelines, was normally rejected by the poor people and was to be reserved for other uses. Silver of standard quality required compensatory adjustments so that "there would be no complaints about inequality."[89] A "reader," who was paid one tael for his services and may have been more hired hand than "friend," managed the lecture, although just what that entailed is unclear.[90] Each contributor was asked to "write down his studio name (*hao*) and the amount of silver contributed."[91]

Paper records joined donors of a mere nine *fen* (the sum accumulated by saving one cash [*wen*] a day over a period of ninety days) and those of much higher amounts, first in the logbook kept at the beginning of each session, and again in a final record of the meeting, which the chair, using funds from the common pool, was to have printed up and distributed to the "society friends."[92] Such records built up a solidarity among participants whose financial resources and social statuses varied; moreover they preserved a sense of connection to the benevolent society throughout the long hiatuses between meetings.

Having the society friends conduct case work was the first step in distributing aid. As the guidelines stipulated, whenever one hears about "extremely poor people, one should examine whether they have any faults. For those who are filial, friendly, honest, and chaste, or who are living alone with no one to rely on, one should list details and, pending verification, provide aid."[93] A month or so before the meeting the chair should distribute several dozen white sheets of paper to the "good friends," who should fill them out and hand them back five days before the meeting. The person in charge should then issue identification cards, to be distributed by the friends, instructing the designated beneficiaries to show up at the meeting at midmorning on such-and-such a day.[94] A sample form, which is appended to the extant guidelines, provides blanks for recording the beneficiary's residence and appearance (age, build, and hair), the name of the sponsor, and each dole that would be given over a ten-year period.[95]

The "friends of the society," instructed the guidelines, should also periodically check the facts about the poor households: "Only after investigating whether their address, age, and appearance match the records and are correct should you give them aid." As for "the virtuous women and poor scholars, the elderly and sick, who would find it inconvenient to go to receive the aid," the guidelines made allowances: the benevolent society "must issue a document, clearly filled out in conformity with the regulations, and send it to the person who originally made the recommendation; that person should then transmit the aid to the beneficiaries and seek an acknowledgment of delivery."[96] Such procedures had been common to food-relief programs.[97] In 1630, before organizing the Jiashan benevolent society, Chen had prescribed that the population of Xuwu borough (*qu*) be classified into rich and poor, with the latter category further broken down into "poorest and next poorest."[98] Yet here too moral considerations intruded, for Chen further instructed the persons carrying out the survey to consider not only the residence, clothes, and appearance of the poor but also "what the neighbors say."[99]

Maintaining rosters of the needy required vigilance. The names of those persons who had been "logged in long ago but have recently died" had to be reported so that their names would be removed from the lists.[100] It was, the guidelines explained, to deter swindlers from receiving aid under false pretenses "that the system of using identification cards has been set up."[101] Chen elaborated on this problem of fraud in 1635, in reference to a program, whereby the poor could buy grain at fair prices, that was designed to supplement the benevolent society: there is a kind of scheming person who, thinking only of the present, sells his tickets to other households, which in turn take the allotments under false names, causing onlookers to sigh over the muddling of rich and poor. Selling the tickets should be forbidden, Chen commanded, warning that wrongdoers would be excluded from the relief program the following autumn.[102]

The friends of the benevolent society were further responsible for managing the distribution of coffins to families too poor to bury their kin. The guidelines, which allocated two thirds of the funds for food relief and one third for coffins, specified the arrangements as follows: Before each meeting, the benevolent society should transfer funds to a carpenter who would make and store the coffins. Coffins acquired in this manner would, the guidelines promised, be of higher quality than those bought piecemeal. To expedite the delivery of the coffins, and to obviate the need to channel money through the kin of the deceased, coupons should be used. For each coffin produced, the carpenter should issue a small coupon to be kept at the chair's place. When someone was too poor to buy a coffin, the chair would, after verifying that no deception was involved, issue a coupon. The kin of the deceased would then hand the coupon over to the carpenter in lieu of payment. This method would deter cheating, for if someone tried to negotiate a rebate, the carpenter would simply take the coupon and return it to the chair. The top of the coffin, the guidelines further stipulated, should be stamped with the four characters "a benevolent-society gift" (*tongshan hui ji*), explaining: "Then we may rest assured that those who have falsely taken a coffin will find it difficult to pass it on"[103]

Thus the "society friends" did not simply drift in and out of meetings once a season while making occasional monetary contributions. As envisioned by the guidelines, they volunteered time for numerous and demanding chores—so much so that Chen drew an analogy between his exertions and the physical labors of ordinary folk.[104] In other contexts, concerning such community projects as building bridges and walls, Chen assumed a sharp division between ordinary persons who provide labor and the notables of the community who provide money—an assumption that harks back to the ancient thinker Mencius, who stated, "Those who labor with their minds govern others; those who labor with their strength are governed by others."[105] Without obscuring this distinction between mental and physical labor, Chen noted that "the accomplished man does not sit idle; he who sits idle is not accomplished" and then elaborated: "Even officials and lordly persons (*guiren*) must work with both mind and physical effort (*laoxin, laoli*). Although they do not use their own hands to do the dirty work, they do things beside establishing themselves through study: when seeing good people, they think of encouraging them through rewards; when seeing bad people, they think of transforming them; when facing cold and hunger, they think of relief; and when seeing exposed corpses, they think of burials. Even when their resources are insufficient, they use every possible strategy to make plans for, and share the worries of, ordinary people, never forgetting them for even a single day."[106] Although Chen took pains to distinguish these chores from what he called "dirty work," in asserting that even dignitaries must expend physical as well as mental effort, he entertained—at least momentarily—a close parallel between the exertions of the rich and the labors of the poor.

As they fanned out into communities to review cases, knocking at the doors of hovels to make inquiries, the "friends" inevitably broadcast their organization's far-reaching beneficence. Their efforts were made highly visible—through the advertised seasonal meetings, the posters outside the meeting place, the case work conducted by members, the distribution of coffins that clearly advertised "a benevolent-society gift," and the scattering of loose change to the riffraff who gathered outside the assembly place.[107] Under such circumstances, the notion of "good deeds done in secret" (*yinde*)—a virtue often celebrated in biographies of worthy persons—was unrealistic: "How," Chen asked, "can one exhaust one's energies (*li*) without other people seeing it? Being 'watchful over oneself when alone' (*shendu*) takes place within one's mind; helping other creatures is done in the world at large—how can the creatures not know about it?"[108] Chen expected his good deeds to reach the eyes and ears of society, yet he and other donors were shielded from accusations of buying fame by the corporate character of the benevolent society, an institution that generated a sense of local pride.

Running a benevolent organization had hidden costs: the case work, onsite inspections, record keeping, membership drives, and arrangements for the seasonal meetings required of its members—who had already made financial contributions—huge investments of time and energy. In light of these incalculable costs, there are no grounds for assuming that distributing funds through the benevolent society was more efficient than leaving it to compassionate individuals to make gifts on an ad hoc basis. Nor is there evidence for or against the case that net donations to the benevolent societies surpassed the aggregate of gifts that individuals independently made to charitable causes. Moreover, the benevolent society supplemented, without replacing, all sorts of other charitable activities that aimed to aid as expediently as possible, often with little or no moralizing whatsoever, the desperate poor.

If the benevolent society sanctioned the public display of doing good, it also offered participants protection against annoying and incessant demands for help. Adhering to the principle of aiding only the deserving poor, it curtailed spontaneity and established a strict routine for charitable giving. In one situation only did it allow the chair some latitude in giving. After contemplating all the indigent people who had failed to make it onto the society's roster of worthy beneficiaries but who would nonetheless amass outside the meeting place with high hopes of receiving some benefit—and after voicing the familiar lament "It is difficult for resources to extend everywhere"—the guidelines ruled: "Only on the day of the meeting, as the group is disbanding, may the chair distribute loose change in person as he wishes. On other days, do not give."[109] The guidelines thus compressed spontaneous giving into a brief moment during which the distribution of coins both advertised the society's responsiveness to solicitations and essentially curbed them. Similarly, in 1641, in his "Proclamation to the Poor People" (Shi pinmin yu), which was appended to the fortieth lecture, Chen spelled out the benevolent society's procedures for enrolling beneficiaries, adding: "As for all the other miscellaneous documents submitted and all those persons who come to the gate to plead their own cases: none of this should be allowed. You must not waste paper. In vain will they wait all day long."[110] The benevolent society and ancillary organized charity thus buffered their affiliates, enabling them swiftly and perfunctorily to dismiss all the miscellaneous, nagging demands for aid that flowed their way.

And yet, repeatedly throughout the duration of his town's benevolent society, Chen Longzheng's compassion readily spilled out beyond the bounds defined by the benevolent society; frequently he made the point that he was stepping in to cover the cost of projects the benevolent society could not manage. One such project was to bury the poor in 1632. By that time, Chen pointedly explained that "the humane and worthy people of the city had collectively set up a benevolent society." It was summer—a time when stenches surely were potent. A Jiashan resident, the Hanlin bachelor Cao Xun, felt profoundly aggrieved by the sight of corpses strewn along the city walls and wished to collect some funds from the society to buy some burial land.[111] "Hearing this, I was moved," recounted Chen. "I was pained that the corpses of innocent people should end up being tossed into the grasses, to be consumed by insects and dogs." After ascertaining that a certain area of wasteland was large enough to accommodate ten years' worth of graves and that labor costs would be thirteen or fourteen taels, Chen concluded: "Thinking that the benevolent society had little money left over, I thought that I myself ought to provide the funds."[112]

Surveying the perimeter of the city wall, Chen and two servants turned up 202 corpses with coffins, five corpses that had been recently exposed yet had no coffins, and countless old skeletons. They provided coffin lids and straw wrappings as needed. For the old skeletons that had been abandoned among the grasses, they dug out a large hole (four *zhang*, or forty feet square, and five feet deep) and leveled off the bottom. Using boats to transport the remains, they arranged the skeletons in rows in the hole, closed the hole up, and mounded the soil two feet high. At each of the four corners they erected a small stele, on which was engraved "The Collective Tomb of 1632" (Ren-shen gongzhong). In addition there was a charitable graveyard, which had accumulated over the years fifty-three exposed coffins, unclaimed by rela-tives or descendants and abandoned by neighboring villagers; and forty ex-posed skeletons, mostly of criminals, that had been dumped from prisons. Chen had these buried in a separate hole. The job required thirteen labor-ers working for fourteen days, and cost ten thousand *qian*. Having carefully recorded the amounts he spent, and taking no chance that his generosity would go unnoticed, he wrote about the project in a quatrain whose rhyme and rhythm would aid memorization, and sent it, along with a letter, to Han-lin bachelor Cao Xun—not for self-promotion, of course, but "so as to en-courage later generations."[113] By mentioning that this project was something the benevolent society could not afford to undertake, Chen highlighted his own voluntarism.

Similarly, in 1635 Chen placed a plan for the sale of grain at fair prices (*pingtiao*) in the context of what the benevolent could not accomplish. Ad-dressing the "poor households" of the city, he declared: "We have found that the number of poor in the fifteen wards is somewhat large. The charitable donations of the benevolent society are limited; to give everywhere would exhaust resources; to have omissions would be lamentable."[114] This was af-ter the magistrate, thinking the stores of grain insufficient, had proposed setting up community granaries and had notebooks distributed to the *bao-jia* chiefs of the fifteen wards so that they might compile registers ranking the resources of each resident. To kick off the campaign, the magistrate had donated fifty taels from his own salary and circulated a notice to the gentry throughout the city. Chen Longzheng thereupon took the lead by con-tributing three hundred taels, and each member of the gentry then gave in varying amounts; it was calculated that they could store one thousand *shi* of grain. The gentry would manage the intake and distribution, as well as the accounts—this, Chen noted, was to keep the program free from the cor-ruption of yamen personnel.[115]

After thus spelling out the terms for selling grain at fair prices and for us-ing tickets to track the transactions, Chen declared, "This method will sup-plement what the benevolent society cannot cover." Chen further instructed that those who were already registered with the benevolent society and were consequently "receiving kindness several times the amount being made avail-able through the grain program should not mix in the lines and compete with the numerous households for this small amount."[116] The sample card for entering the transactions that Chen appended to this proclamation stated "a ticket from the Chen establishment at East Pavilion Bridge" and reiterated that the program was undertaking what the benevolent society was unable to accomplish.

Likewise in 1642 did Chen discuss a proposal for a soup kitchen in reference to the benevolent society. His city, he wrote, had already set up a benevolent society to aid residents in good standing. The beneficiaries were all "poor people of the area" who, after having their cases examined, were given identification cards enabling them to receive some aid each season. They had "fixed residences and occupations." The soup kitchen was to serve the motley beggars who drifted about with no stability.[117] In recent years, Chen explained, floods and droughts had ruined harvests, and locusts and caterpillars had laid waste to an area extending over one thousand *li;* the upshot was that "90 percent of the people were digging for roots and scraping bark." Chen reckoned that the farmers could manage until the autumn wheat ripened, but that "50 percent of those who are not farmers will migrate as beggars." He further wondered how residents would find the resources to feed the starving people pouring in from other areas. "Though the transients scream out all day long, there is no way to fill their stomachs," he wrote. "Hunger and cold pierce their bones, silencing them. The neglected individuals dying under the crumbling walls of old temples are countless. Alas, their bare bones pile up. And it is not only in bad years that this happens."[118]

During the previous year, the "gentry and worthies" (*shenxian*) had deliberated running soup kitchens; but worrying that private stocks were limited and that hungry people would inundate them, "they debated the matter back and forth, most indecisively. They had good intentions but no plan." At this point Qian Shisheng initiated the "portable gruel" method, which, having no fixed quotas, times, or places, would deter mobbing. "Every morning they would have several *dou* of white rice boiled to make gruel that porters would transport on poles along thoroughfares or in the suburbs. Upon encountering poor beggars, each porter would have them sit in a row and would give each person a ladleful. Each porter would carry roughly five or six *sheng*, enough to prolong the lives of fifty or sixty persons a day. Ten porters would take care of five or six hundred persons. This arrangement would last three to five days, after which another benevolent person would continue the sponsorship; thus lives can be temporarily prolonged without the ill effects of having soup kitchens that gather crowds."[119]

Rather than cowering behind the benevolent society's facade to limit his responsibility for fellow creatures, Chen, and no doubt some of his peers, occasionally extended his generosity beyond the benevolent society's scope. Stopping short only at the custom of liberating animals, he found irresistible all sorts of opportunities to rescue people who appeared to be doomed to death. Now and then he contravened the very principle he espoused in his benevolent society lectures—that beggars, nonresident drifters, monks, and such inveterate losers as immoral, lazy, and dissolute persons who had themselves invited disaster were all unworthy of the benevolent society's aid. Acting independently of the benevolent society, Chen at times helped prisoners and beggars, two groups he perceived to be close to death. In 1642, he argued that the crimes of prisoners were but petty transgressions motivated by dire need. As though sensing his viewpoint to be controversial, he defended it by citing the precedent of the highly regarded Ding Bin. When Ding was providing prisoners with food during a severe shortage, someone asked him, "Why bother? Aren't they going to their death anyhow?" to which Ding replied: "Not so. Even though the prisoners must eventually be punished, they are still human beings, and each day preceding punishment is a day of life that heaven has granted."[120]

Chen's condemnation of beggars likewise dissolved when their lives were at risk. In his view, beggars had no place in the well-ordered society that the benevolent association aimed to sustain, but should, rather, be cared for by their chief. According to the rules, explained Chen, the beggar chief should be financially responsible for burying deceased beggars, should limit his cut to a fixed small amount, and should be prevented from "cleaning out the funds of the destitute." He acknowledged, nevertheless, that the chief often failed in his responsibilities: "He takes a great deal of the proceeds for himself. He has a wife, a residence, and fields, and he comfortably accepts tribute from the mass of beggars. But when they die, he tosses their corpses outside the city walls, without feeling the slightest bit of charity or compassion. What, then, has he done with the revenues he has habitually collected from them?"[121]

The real plight of beggars moved Chen to intervene. During the winter of 1641, upon learning that "approximately five or six hundred beggars have been roaming my city, and that over five hundred of them were buried between the second and fifth months," he provided them with shelter.[122] Called by a sense of urgency to save lives, and fortified by Ding Bin's example, Chen maintained that one should help even those beggars who would undoubtedly die soon.[123] In his zeal for saving the doomed, Chen resembled those same practitioners of animal liberation whom he criticized: uplifted by the symbolism of rescuing creatures from death, he sometimes ignored arguments and rules calling for a more judicious and sparing use of resources.

The presence of the benevolent society did not relieve Chen of a sense of individual responsibility for miscellaneous, unanticipated calls for help. On the contrary, once the benevolent society was established as a locus for sermonizing on doing good, it remained a public reminder of a charitable ideal. Chen repeatedly measured his own philanthropic activities—burying the poor, selling grain at price-stabilizing prices, and sponsoring portable soup kitchens—against what the benevolent society "could not cover." If he thereby highlighted his generosity, he was able to do so because the benevolent society provided his community with a common point of reference, a highly publicized standard for doing good.

AN ALTERNATIVE TO THE LINEAGE

The benevolent society simultaneously supplemented and competed with lineage-based charity—as Chen's donations in 1641 reveal. On the one hand he contributed five hundred *mou* of land to his lineage.[124] On that occasion, he noted that his father had cared deeply about their poor relatives—even distant ones whose kinship ties were not substantiated by genealogies or tombstones—and had frequently expressed a wish to set aside charitable land (*yitian*) to support both the close branches and the poor of distant branches.[125] The income from the estate would be used to aid the crippled, blind, and poor; to pay for lineage sacrifices, labor service levies, and famine relief; and, upholding the respect for the elderly, to provide meat for relatives over seventy years of age and clothes for those over eighty, regardless of whether they were rich or poor.[126]

On the other hand Chen that same year expressed a strong sense of regional community, extending to persons to whom he had no blood ties: he gave the benevolent society funds to build a meeting hall (*huiguan*).[127] Moreover, in his petition to set up a charitable estate (*yizhuang*), he argued that the estate would, among other things, pay for the commutation of labor services and that the "the entire city" (*tongyi*) would also benefit from a reduction in taxes in silver.[128] Whether his viewpoint was valid or not, he clearly was compelled to show that city-wide benefits offset partiality to his lineage. Also to counterbalance the aid that the charitable estate distributed to members of his lineage, and citing the precedent of Zhu Xi in the twelfth century, he set up a community granary to benefit the general population of Xuwu borough. This program would, he stated, "even out the differences between the haves and have-nots."[129] That many residents of Xuwu borough were his own tenants may have prompted his concern for residents outside his lineage.

Within the lineage context, too, Chen's sights extended to a broad local community. Once, after perfunctorily mentioning that a charitable estate had already been established for his lineage, he truncated further talk of that issue ("This need not be discussed again") and then hastened to explore channels for giving to nonkin. Declaring that "charity (*bushi*) must have its procedures," he instructed that one should annually exact a certain amount from the land rents for carrying out charity (*xingyi*) by helping, according to their needs, the following: poor maternal relatives and upright friends; distant relatives and nearby neighbors who have no one to support or bury them; and the descendants of longstanding acquaintances who are unable to manage on their own. Chen then added: "As for the great number of persons with whom one has no connection and who have been accidentally overlooked, one should occasionally help them, without a fixed quota. You should also make contributions as you wish for the repair of bridges and roads, which truly benefit mankind." He ruled out only "aid to itinerant monks," cautioning that contributing to Buddhist activities would ruin "the good name of charity."[130]

Like other late Ming figures, Chen referred to Fan Zhongyan as a worthy precedent for endowing lineage estates. Yet, with his own social horizons broadened, Chen questioned Fan's stipulation that his lineage aid only relatives whose kinship ties were clearly documented in the genealogy; and he also detected a shortcoming in Fan's plan: having branched out for six hundred years, Fan's lineage produced so many poor members that the aid per person was quite small.[131] Chen's solution was that the policy be flexible in response to his own lineage's fluctuating size. Recognizing that the close branches in his lineage had few members, he suggested that surplus funds be used to aid distant relatives even though their connections could not be authenticated; then, if future generations saw the number of close relatives grow, the lineage should revert to the more restrictive rules for distributing aid.[132] Contributing to his flexibility, and perhaps eroding his lineage identification, was Chen's awareness of the social diversity of its membership, which, "in addition to farmers and scholars, had artisans, merchants, and brokers."[133]

The strategy that Fan Zhongyan had initiated, to focus aid on lineage members, was obliquely criticized in an early Qing account of a mid-Ming figure, Gu Zhengxin. A native of Huating (in Songjiang prefecture, Nanzhili), Gu generously donated 14,700 taels to set up a charitable estate of 40,800 *mou*, the proceeds of which were to be used to defray the costs of corvée labor for two counties—another instance of going beyond the circle of kin. Later he was wrongly accused for someone else's offense and imprisoned. While incarcerated, Gu remained generous. Observing that inmates were freezing, he provided them with clothes and grain. For those who were eligible to redeem their crimes by paying fines, he provided the needed funds; his generosity nearly emptied the prison. Gu also donated money toward the repair of the prison buildings. Commented the editor of this account: "For a thousand years, Fan Zhongyan's charitable estate has had a fine reputation . . . but it was only for people of the same surname and not necessarily for nonkin. And the size of the fields was only one hundred *mou*, not as much as forty thousand. How much further did Mr. Gu go!"[134]

A tension between giving to strangers and giving to relatives is also evident in remarks that Chen Longzheng's contemporary Wen Huang recorded as his mother's.[135] Among her sage statements were two explanations for why men who generally like to be charitable (*haoshi*) often turn stingy when it comes to their relatives. First, relatives take the gifts for granted while nonrelatives will show gratitude for the slightest bit of charity (*menghui*), profusely proclaiming their thanks; second, nonkin find it difficult to broach the subject of help for a second or third time, while relatives assume that the giving is part of a lasting arrangement.[136] That the benevolent society could protect its members against their relatives' demands will be shown in chapter 5.

Yang Dongming, Gao Panlong, and Chen Longzheng venerated Fan Zhongyan and themselves lent generous financial support to their lineages; at the same time they strongly identified with—and contributed to building up—a community of residents that transcended lineage boundaries The same persons often established lineage estates while forging community-wide associations. Consider the case of Yang Dongming's hometown, some of whose residents claimed to be descendants of Fan Zhongyan.[137] Rising above lineage loyalties, Yang sponsored a charitable school (*yixue*);[138] and inspired by Fan's example, he set up a charitable trust that would, in addition to defraying taxes owed the government, assist poor villagers and neighbors.[139] The benevolent society that he formed and the Society for Spreading Humaneness (Guangren hui) that was inspired by it also crossed lineage boundaries. Yang Dongming was in the former group, while his two brothers were in the second.[140] Even the descendants of Fan Zhongyan were divided between the two societies, with two Fans in the first group and ten in the second. Gao Panlong likewise juggled two strategies. While using his legacy to establish a lineage trust, he energetically sponsored a benevolent society, declaring, "Seeing the elderly and sick, and the deceased who have had no proper burials in one's district, one sympathizes as though the suffering is within one's own household."[141] His goal was to instill feelings of kinship in a district-wide, nonlineage institution.[142]

THE SCOPE OF THE BENEVOLENT SOCIETY'S RESPONSIBILITY

Feelings of compassion led Chen to be charitable in numerous arenas, without prompting him to reformulate the benevolent society's purpose. When acting within the benevolent society, he stuck to its two interlocked goals, aid to the deserving poor and moral edification; only in the matter of scale did he think that the benevolent society might be elastic. As word of the society's activities went out and donations flowed in, the roster of beneficiaries grew, giving Chen cause to comment, in 1641, after the society's initial decade: "At first, only several tens received aid. Today, the number has already grown to three to four hundred." Then, in the same breath, he expressed regret that the society's aid had been limited: "If one talks of the poor of the entire district, then the number of persons who are kept alive or given burials is still less than 10 to 20 percent."[143] Despite the benevolent society's financial constraints, he wished to extend its territorial reach.

Of the criteria used for defining the pool of benevolent-society recipients, Chen readily accepted two, need and merit. He was, however, vexed by a third criterion, that of geographical proximity. Mandating this criterion were not indisputably worthy values but a mundane consideration: doing case work far afield was impractical. How, he once asked, were the literati, who customarily lived within the walls of the district capital, to "investigate the age, appearance, residence, and usual occupation" of the rural poor, who were scattered beyond easy reach?[144] The issue of distance also involved questions that had been percolating outside the benevolent society, about treating urban and rural residents equitably. During the autumn of 1640, farmers had complained: "The grain annually shipped by boats large and small into the city is the result of our hard labors, but in famine relief we are nonetheless placed last." Chen concurred, writing in 1641 to his colleague Qian Shisheng: "These are very moving words."[145]

Practical considerations favored concentrating resources on urban dwellers. Resources were limited, doing case work over long distances difficult, and distance attenuated feelings of connectedness. In a "Proclamation to the Poor" appended to his fortieth lecture, Chen noted: "In addition to the poorest of the urban wards—whom the chairman serving that season will, after investigating the details, add to the roster of persons to be taken into care—there are those from the rural boroughs who have of their own accord submitted requests." Leaving aside that "the old regulations of the society" had prohibited such requests, he identified the main problem: "They live scattered in distant places. To have people go out in boats to investigate them would involve every kind of difficulty, wasting resources and time."[146]

The policy for distributing coffins was similarly problematic. The benevolent-society guidelines promised that, as the participation of do-gooders expanded, it would be able to assist the rural as well as urban poor with funeral expenses.[147] At the same time, the guidelines declared that the benevolent society was unable to provide coffins to every rural neighborhood (*xiang*)[148]—a viewpoint that Chen himself endorsed in his "Proclamation to the Poor": "If one has not actually seen or heard about them firsthand, then circumstances make implementation difficult. Although goodwill is abundant, resources are limited. Therefore it is fitting to decline their requests."[149]

Maintaining the goodwill of city residents was of the utmost importance to members of the elite. The walled city, its gates nightly secured against marauders, protected stocks of grain, government buildings, the local officials who maintained order, and many of the district's wealthy households. The goodwill of the poor, who would man the ramparts, was essential to the survival of the urban elite. In 1633 Chen observed that the nearby town of Wenzhou had successfully fended off a pirate attack in 1632 in part because of its military strategy and chance, but also because rich and poor were united in sentiment. Each of the great households had supported one hundred soldiers (and the somewhat smaller households, sixty to seventy soldiers) and had supplied the poor residents with food. They even let the people from outside the walls seek refuge in the libraries and main halls of the great households—with the result, he explained, that "hearts were bound together, and no uprising occurred within the walls."[150] Chen subsequently opposed the view that the poor should, as a defense measure, be kicked out of his own town, Jiashan. Calculating that defending the city battlements in two shifts required 6,408 men, and that manpower was scarce, he argued that the poor from the surrounding villages should be allowed into the city to guard it in exchange for support from the rich.[151]

How one should apportion aid between urban and rural residents was debated by Chen's peers. In a piece on the distribution of gruel, Chen reported someone to have asked: "Why place the cities second?" Chen's reply ran as follows: "Farmers work the hardest, and they are the poorest. The majority of rural residents are farmers; the majority of urban residents are artisans and merchants, and another 30 percent of them are in the employ of officials and yamen personnel. Therefore those who end up in the ditches during bad years are mostly people from the countryside; one does not see more than one or two dying of starvation in the cities, and only those who sell produce lack steady employment."[152] Chen, who owned an estate in Xuwu borough, outside the city walls, but himself resided within them, was divided by competing loyalties and interests.[153]

Chen expanded the benevolent society's territorial scope in 1641, writing: "From today on, those rural people who are truly destitute ('orphaned, widowed, and having no one to rely upon') and who have never committed any wrong should each have the gentry and worthies in the neighboring boroughs and towns submit statements; and one should allow them personally to investigate the actualities, listing age, appearance, residence, and usual occupation. As soon as the recommendation card arrives, it will be exchanged for an identification card that will allow the person to be taken under the benevolent society's wing."[154]

All things were interconnected, according to Gao Panlong and Chen; personal behavior reverberated throughout the universe, eliciting responses from heaven and affecting the well-being of one's family. This thinking appears to conform to the spirit of *The Great Learning* (*Daxue*), which essentially envisioned the interdependence of three levels of activity: self-cultivation of the individual person, regulation of the family, and ordering of the state.[155] But the comparison serves only to highlight a huge difference. To the three nested entities that *The Great Learning* specified, Gao and Chen added a fourth: the district. Without altogether abandoning thoughts of the nesting units of individual, family, and state, they let questions about the state (or the imperial polity) recede into the background while they focused their benevolent societies' attention on achieving unity among the discrete households of the district. Addressing his first benevolent-society audience as "we people who are of the same district," Gao declared: "Complete harmony in the district will summon complete harmony from heaven"; and "When every household does good, it brings good fortune to the district."[156] In like spirit, Chen, though fully recognizing the heterogeneity of his audience—"Whether you are a farmer, tradesperson, or yamen personnel, the lectures will awaken your hearts"—urged his listeners "together to form good customs in the district," and expressed hope that "the entire district will be united into one heart."[157] The "benevolent estate" (*tongshan zhuang*), a trust fund that Chen established with his wife's dowry of one hundred *mou*, would, he asserted, benefit "the poor people of the entire city."[158] In contrast to their predecessor Yang Dong-ming (who had drawn clear boundaries between title holders of one associ-ation and the prominent and wealthy residents of a second), Gao and Chen envisioned their benevolent societies as embracing the district.

Chen was torn between his identification with his immediate neighbor-hood and a commitment to an ever-expanding community of indeterminate size; so suggests his response to a dire food shortage crisis in 1630—right before the idea of a benevolent society reached him.[159] After declaring that he "felt deep sympathy" for those poor people whom the dearth had driven "to buy bean sediment and wine dregs to mix in with grass in order to get by," he hastened to add, "My resources are meager and authority slight; I am unable to give universally." He defended his special concern for Xuwu bor-ough on the grounds of old ties: "Because my ancestors and parents were born and raised here, I cannot bear to neglect it. I figure that, not counting the grain that my household will consume this year, there will remain over six hundred *shi* of winter rice to be distributed, to carry them through the season . . . enough to last for thirty days per person while they await the next harvest."[160] (Given that he required that the poor register their surnames as well as given names in order to receive aid, one surmises that not all resi-dents of Xuwu were of his lineage.)

Chen's allocation of resources was challenged by someone who asked: "How, during a crop failure, can you aid only one borough and then sit and watch the others die?"[161] Chen replied roughly as follows: if one were to pro-vide help without making a distinction between "them" and "us"—between one's own locale and the next—then, given that the population of the twenty boroughs in his district totals sixty thousand, and allowing four *dou* per per-son, the vast amount of twenty-four thousand *shi* of grain would be needed for two months. "How could even the great households manage this?" Chen asked despairingly, and then elaborated: once word of relief gets out, crowds would pour in from other prefectures; then, finding that resources failed to meet the demand, "they would set back home wailing, collapsing along the roadside; one would thus essentially be hastening them to their deaths."[162] Unable alone to satisfy the gaping need, Chen tried to stimulate wealthy res-idents in neighboring boroughs to follow his lead—a goal that a proselytiz-ing benevolent society would help him achieve.

Even while defending his plan to concentrate his donations on the inhabitants of Xuwu borough, Chen perceived that markets tied the well-being of one neighborhood to that of another. He observed that the textile production that had enriched his area had also made residents vulnerable. Customarily households supplemented their income by spinning and weaving raw cotton into fabric, which they then took to the towns to exchange for grain; but "during bad years," noted Chen, "rice is expensive and cloth cheap. The merchants, taking advantage of the farmers' crisis, refuse to buy the cloth." Defenseless against market fluctuations and opportunistic merchants, petty entrepreneurs, whose ranks had grown in the early seventeenth century, lived precariously.[163]

Chen urged residents of other neighborhoods to be charitable, if not by making outright gifts, at least by facilitating exchanges that would effectively enable starving residents to eat. He called upon the help of "anyone in the rural areas who is charitable (*haoyi*), has some stored rice, and is willing to exchange it for cloth at its current price while waiting for silver to come by armed escort." The transaction, he promised, would "involve nothing more than a two- or three-month wait" and would ultimately bring them the original price, without reducing their wealth one iota. Declaring that "nothing is more meritorious than responding to the urgency of the farming households," he further advised rural gentry living in the city to enact this plan. "Then grain and cloth will be exchanged and circulated; and the farmers and the women working for wages will not be left starving and without resources." To add this expedient measure to donating relief is, Chen concluded, tantamount to "being benevolent at no cost."[164]

One year later, Chen initiated the benevolent society of Jiashan, which, though located in the city, theoretically involved the entire district, of which Xuwu borough was but a small part. It articulated principles, endorsed by its members, that justified how scarce resources should be allocated. At the same time, being armed with moral exhortations, a show of numbers, and an organization, the benevolent society could—far more effectively than a lone individual—mobilize wealthy households to undertake good works.

Looking beyond both his native Xuwu borough and his lineage, Chen often emphasized the welfare of his entire district, as when he declared that one aim of the benevolent society was that "the entire district do good."[165] Sometimes he spoke of "the city" (*cheng*),[166] using the term designating the area within the city walls. Frequently he spoke of "our city" (*wu yi*), in which *yi* more ambiguously may include the community outside the walls; in any case, the term "our" intimates his close identification with interests beyond his kin and his neighborhood.[167] It was to serve this city and district-wide community that the benevolent society emerged.

4

Lectures for the Poor—and the Rich

Why was I alone born rich and high, like an exotic fruit?
CHEN LONGZHENG

A phenomenon that Gao Panlong had scarcely heeded would in the next generation seize Chen Longzheng's attention: that sheer wealth—especially in the form of money—was a force in stratifying society, a source of influence independent of bureaucratic status, and a basis for social inequities. The difference between the two men is evident in their thinking about murderous bandit attacks on Xinghua prefecture, Fujian. To caution his benevolent society that moral reform was urgent, Gao claimed that social disunity had provided an opening for the incursions. This warning impressed Chen; in an afterword to Gao's lectures he flagged it and then echoed Gao's rhetoric, arguing: "If the entire district would learn goodness, then, even when facing a military conflagration, the people of this area might avoid a great calamity."[1] Yet, when addressing his own benevolent society in 1635, Chen elaborated upon the theme of moral reform in his own fashion. In addition to mentioning the Xinghua disaster, he contrasted how two other places had responded to bandit attacks. In Shucheng district, he observed, fifty or sixty bandits were successfully chased down and decapitated, whereupon the remaining bandits, seeing that their inside contacts had met with death, immediately vanished. In Cao district the disgruntled poor secretly joined the bandits and all havoc broke loose.[2] The lesson Chen drew from this in 1635 was: "If the poor people can anticipate having something to rely on, their rebellious thoughts will evaporate. Whenever military disasters unexpectedly break out, they will stick to thoughts of 'sharing goodness,' and order will be preserved." If, in contrast, one fails to share resources, and if each household thinks only of its own family, then protecting everyone will be impossible, and "those who delight in violence will conjure up visions of disaster." A well-ordered moral community depends on sharing wealth: "If one believes in the word 'sharing," then rich and poor,

102

and high and low, will be united in spirit. The large households will not place a high value on wealth. The little people will harbor thoughts of loyalty and love."[3] Nor did Chen confine this attitude to benevolent-society lectures. In an essay on recent banditry, also dated 1635, he reiterated: "When the rich give money and grain to aid the poor, everyone will, with united hearts, collectivize their energies"; whereas "when the grand households are stingy and unwilling to bring together the haves and the have-nots, each person will think of himself . . . and the evil among the poor will open the city gates to let in the bandits."[4]

Once Gao had mentioned the need that "the haves and have-nots aid one another,"[5] but he did so in abstract, sweeping terms, keeping his focus on broad moral goals. Chen explicitly linked moral reform, or the sharing of goodness, with the sharing of resources between rich and poor. In his first benevolent-society lecture (1632), he called for a just reciprocity between rich and poor: "The wealthy often wish to help the poor; and the poor will naturally rouse responses in the rich."[6] Focusing on the interplay between the two parties, he exposed the huge gap that had to be bridged.

Gao had expatiated upon each of the Six Imperial Maxims to promote an all-round program of moral self-improvement. Chen, being preoccupied with the relationships among the economic classes, invoked the Six Maxims selectively. Leaving aside questions of filiality and parental education of children, he dwelled instead on the fifth and sixth maxims, respectively: "Be content with one's lot" and "Do no wrong." By staying in their place and by being frugal and diligent, even the poor, he reasoned, would avoid hunger.[7] He commended the majority of the poor as "good people who keep to their lots and endure hardship," but he ruefully added: "There is also a minority who lack vision and rejoice in disaster. They think that it would be beneficial if those bandits roaming the north were to arrive on the scene."[8] Some nine years later, in the last of his lectures (1644), Chen persevered in fighting such desperate sentiments, arguing that the way to survival, to life, is "to stick to one's occupation" and "to avoid wrongdoing."[9] Chen likewise invoked the fifth and sixth maxims when addressing the middle social stratum. A sense of restlessness, he believed, prompted middle households to waste an enormous amount of money on religious pageants: "Clever people understand that they are using these events as a pretext to seek pleasure. Ignorant people think of these activities as a way of paying their respect to spirits." Then, alluding to the fifth and sixth maxims, Chen concluded: "They do not realize that this is an example of wrongdoing following from discontentment with their occupations."[10]

Gao once warned members of his family against overstepping the boundary of respectable behavior: they should avoid whoring, gambling, and litigation.[11] But his admonition was terse, and rarely did his purview extend beyond the realm of ordered society. Chen, in contrast, entertained at great length what was beyond the pale, recognizing all the complications that stood in the way of achieving social harmony. In theory he expelled from his vision "prostitutes, gamblers, litigation inciters, and wastrels," ruling that these groups "one need not discuss."[12] In actuality, he often allowed the images of deviant members of society to rush back into his view, as in the following: "There is a kind of good-for-nothing person who says, 'My poor fate; I have no capital.' If one looks closely, he in fact has some character flaw—a strong appetite, laziness, mental instability. A proverb says: 'One hundred social gatherings (*hui*) will bring poverty a hundredfold. What you eat and drink goes down and away without coming back.' Every day you want wine and meat. Where does so much of it come from? Strong appetites waste money."[13] Only after lingering in the position of the restless poor and imagining their mind-set, did Chen revert to the theme that one should rest content with one's lot.

In one benevolent-society lecture, Gao glanced briefly at ordered society from the viewpoint of the other side, that of prisoners; this was when he posed the rhetorical question: when you are incarcerated for wrongdoing, won't it then seem that those small tradespeople carrying their loads through the streets are, by contrast, in heaven?[14] Unlike his mentor, Chen took a hard, sympathetic look at the privation and injustices the poor endured. In an essay proposing that the number of prisons be reduced, he maintained that prisoners had been driven to petty crime, prison, and thence to their deaths not by serious wrongdoing but by dire necessity. Indeed, the cost of jailing such small-time delinquents far outweighed any benefit, according to his calculations: "If each district (*xian*) has one prisoner who dies from cold and hunger every five days, and given that the province of Zhejiang has seventy-six subprefectures (*zhou*) and districts, then it figures that fifteen prisoners die each day, which adds up to 450 deaths per month." Matters are even worse, he explained, "when pestilence strikes and three to four prisoners die each day in each district—how grievous!" Weighing the horrifying loss of life against the trivial crimes committed—crimes such as failure to repay debts during bad harvests—Chen concluded that the few pecks of grain or strings of cash that debtors owed hardly justified the waste of life.[15] He knew well that the large households had amassed the fields of countless families and that people who have been oppressed will turn hostile.[16]

Occasionally Chen condemned the downtrodden for their rebellious or anarchic spirit. Noting that "some people say that things will change for the better when bandits arrive," he adamantly lectured, "This sentiment is wrong."[17] Yet he also had a capacity for seeing matters from the downtrodden's point of view. Pleading their case, he argued that one ought to understand two reasons for their seditious thinking: "One, they are pressed by poverty and hunger; two, they have been oppressed by other people and hence speak out of bitterness."[18]

RICH, MIDDLE, AND POOR

Without completely abandoning high-flown talk of goodness, Chen repeatedly circled back to the themes of material aid and human survival, dwelling upon social and economic realities, and the tensions between rich and poor. Gao Panlong had lumped together everyone needing edification and spoke of "broadly proselytizing ordinary people to do good."[19] Chen too pursued the goal of district-wide harmonious solidarity, but he did so by offering a particular treatment for each economic stratum, somewhat in the manner of case workers triaging the population for food relief programs.[20] He divided his benevolent-society audience into "three classes of people: rich, poor, and the middle"; and, for each class, he tailored specific exhortations. "If one wants the entire district to do good," he instructed the benevolent society, "it seems not very difficult and can be roughly stated in three sentences: The wealthy should be somewhat liberal. The poor should be content with their lot. And the middle should neither curry favor with their superiors nor deceive their inferiors."[21] Or, as he elaborated in the same lecture, "The rich should be generous and accommodating, the middle group should neither oppress the poor nor fawn upon the rich, and the poor should avoid three faults—expensive tastes for wine and meat; laziness; and above all, the impatience in business ventures shown by petty entrepreneurs who restlessly shift from one line of work to another to increase their profits."[22] When lecturing exactly one year later, Chen resumed talking of three social tiers: "Last autumn I spoke about the three classes of people. For each there is a method of doing good; for each, I had a simply worded statement. . . . Now I shall again talk about the three categories of people and the reasons one must do good deeds."[23]

As Chen shifted his attention from one economic class to the next, he continued to use the first-person "we" (*wo*), thus revealing his strong identification with each stratum. Although he tried hard to socialize the poor, warning them not to "scheme for things beyond one's lot, hoping one morning to wake up rich,"[24] he sympathetically understood their situation. He perceived that most poor people were stretched to the limit, with few resources to waste: "As for the poor, who are completely luckless and are born to great hardship: most of these unfortunate people can not pare down their expenses any further." Then, slipping into the first person (*wo*), he acknowledged that their lives were often unfair: "When others do evil, recompense is slow. If we [the poor] do wrong, recompense is swift."[25] Shifting his attention to the "middle stratum"—still using the first person and thus showing that he identified with them as well—Chen chastised them for pouring money into religious activities and urged them to be charitable instead. "Doing good must benefit others," he instructed them, and then asked, "How does all that lighting of lanterns and burning of incense help anything?"[26]

Empathizing with the poor and the middle, Chen relaxed his hold on the fifth maxim: Be content with one's lot. With his mind open to the possibility that they might improve their standing, he exhorted the poor among his listeners to change their fate incrementally, through small expressions of filiality or genuine charitableness toward others, so as "to move heaven and earth, and ghosts and spirits, just as it is recorded in *Doing Good, Secretly Determined* (*Weishan yin zhi*), which provides much evidence for turning bad luck into good."[27] He further reminded his listeners of the message of *The Exalted One's Tract on Action and Response* (*Taishang ganying pian*), namely, that "it starts off by stating: 'Fortune and misfortune do not come through gates; man himself invites them'"; Chen then commented, "These words originally were not solely for the poor, yet they are especially pressing for the poor."[28]

For the middle stratum, Chen also offered specific prescriptions. reasoning with them at one benevolent-society meeting: "When compared to those above, the people in the middle do not have enough; when compared to those below, they have a surplus. Although we [the middle] lack the resources of the wealthy, every day we can save other people." He further counseled them that they could do good within the limits of their resources if they would simply not gouge and cheat the people with whom they daily interacted. "Most honest and public-spirited people will," he promised his listeners, "be protected by the spirits. Beds will be empty of the sick, rural neighborhoods will be happy, prisons will be vacant, and the years will go by peacefully." Then, rather than commanding the middle stratum to stay in their place, he informed them that literacy paves the route for advancement: "If you fear that your household will not gradually flourish, then do teach your sons to read so that they will aspire to advance."[29]

Chen's exhortations to the rich were nearly as extensive as those to the poor. At the benevolent-society meeting of 1632, he urged the rich to consider: "Others cultivate the fields, but it is I who eat the best white rice. Others weave, but it is I who wear the best silks. At home I enjoy heat in the winter and cool air in the summer; when I go out, if it is not by boat, then it's by sedan chair. Good luck comes to me easily. I already have a lot. How could I possibly take an additional share from others?"[30] He cautioned his listeners to take the "public-minded road" (*gongdao*). Noting that incessant talk about public-spiritedness sometimes masks a secret desire to gain some advantage, he asked: "If the goal is simply to come out ahead, how will others tolerate it?" and then added: "If good deeds are performed with the utmost sincerity, then one's mind will be at peace and one's descendants will enjoy prosperity."[31] In 1635, he again held the wealthy responsible for social harmony, insistently lecturing that to achieve a sense of unity "one must completely rely on the large households to treat their money (*qiancai*) lightly. If one avoids creating problems harming the people in normal times, then, during times of crisis, everyone will unite his strength and cooperate, and all minds will form a city-wide community."[32] Chen himself had set an example for the rich: it was as one of them that he initiated the benevolent society in 1631, and by the time he received the *jinshi* degree, in 1634, he had already delivered five lectures and had presumably backed his words with monetary donations.

Chen held the rich to a high standard of moral responsibility even outside the benevolent society. Upon learning of widespread starvation, during a journey in about 1640, he sent a colleague a letter condemning the "astounding habits" of the rich people in the north who selfishly enjoyed their wealth while disregarding their neighbors' plight. He found particularly offensive a report about a large household in Cao xian, Shandong, that owned an estate of one thousand *qing* (one hundred thousand *mou*)—in other words, two thousand times the fifty *mou* that Gao Panlong had inherited. The estate annually yielded rice, wheat, and vegetables in vast amounts ("forty to fifty thousand," stated Chen without specifying the unit), yet the owners would make no charitable gifts.[33] Cognizant of the sharp division between rich and poor, a break that needed mending, Chen warned his peers that they would have to rise above material self-interest if they were to preserve social order.

ON DISTRIBUTING WEALTH

Chen was troubled by social distinctions that were based on wealth alone. Once he came close to suggesting that the distribution of wealth was random and arbitrary: "The rich and high (*fugui*) should reflect: Why, of hundreds and thousands of persons, was I alone born rich and high, like a strange flower or an exotic fruit standing out among all the trees, or like a precious stone or a fresh spring standing out in all the scenery, or like bright haze or colored clouds in the sky—that is, like things everyone admires?" Then, finding a rationale for the apparent anomalies, he added: "That I today can save others by speaking out and doing good is clearly because heaven has given me a position whereby I can cultivate good fortune." Rather than bringing closure to moral responsibility, good fortune—the reward for good deeds—forced upon the wealthy a choice: to enjoy one's good fortune, gradually depleting it, or to cultivate it, thereby replenishing one's reservoir of blessings. Chen stated: "It all depends on whether one clearly understands this crossroads (*guantou*) or not."[34]

His concern about fairness in the allocation of goods infiltrated writings that Chen intended only his peers to read. In a journal of his studies, he divided society into economic strata—just as he had in his benevolent-society lectures. Observing that everywhere there are households rich and poor, he insisted: "The rich households of the rural areas should help the poor of the those areas," and then returned to the theme of fairness: "In good years, if one is not equitable, the poor will nonetheless avoid death; In bad years, if one is somewhat equitable, then one will rarely see the poor people in the ditches."[35] Resigned that one cannot institute "a method of small equities" by fiat, Chen settled for the hope that benevolent persons who manage the rural areas will express their compassion according to their resources.[36] Still, the point remains: what pressed the issue of equitableness—what served as Chen's standard for gauging justice—was the matter of survival, the preservation of life.

Thoughts about fairness took Chen back to the "equitable field system" (*juntian*)—a program for redistributing land among the people that rulers from roughly the third through ninth centuries had instituted with varying degrees of success. Overlooking the original intention of this institution, which was to remove land from magnates who had the power to resist taxation, Chen cherished instead the concept of "equitableness" therein embedded. He despaired of reviving the equitable field system in his time but proposed "a method of small equities," whereby "humane persons managing rural areas would naturally express their compassion according to their resources."[37] Though conceding that "the sages cannot equalize the fates of rich and poor," he hastened to add: "Nonetheless they can arrange that there be neither extremely rich nor extremely poor."[38]

Again when addressing an audience of his literate peers outside the benevolent society, Chen expressed sympathy for the poor at the expense of the rich. Of the practice of hiring wet nurses, he wrote: "The rich are spared the labor of nursing, the poor substitute for them." His own household, he noted, over the years had hired more than ten wet nurses, but, he explained, as he matured he had become increasingly concerned about the plight of wet nurses. To encourage poor mothers to abandon their own children in favor of nursing wealthy children was, he had realized, essentially "no different from killing other people's children to raise one's own." He reasoned that mothers who were forced by circumstances to neglect their own children so as to nurture wealthy babies might grow resentful; and that the wealthy children, having become the objects of resentment, would then cease to flourish.[39] As he saw it, the interests of the rich were inextricably bound up with the well-being of the poor.

In criticizing the injustices arising from the economic extremes of rich and poor, Chen had the company of a collection of didactic anecdotes, *The Complete Book of Good Fortune and Longevity* (*Fushou quanshu*). Published around the time of his benevolent society, this work devotes one section to "cherishing (or accumulating) good fortune" (*xifu*) and another to "spreading benevolence" (*guangci*). Resonating with Chen's concern for prisoners, one entry about the Song dynasty calls attention to the injustices that will lead to incarceration: when a rich person was about to donate the huge amount of five million *qian* for the repair of a temple, an official advised him to use the funds instead to redeem prisoners; the prisoners, explained the official, were guilty only of being unable to pay their taxes.[40] Another entry, about a Ms. Luo, chimes in with Chen's solicitude toward wet nurses. Even though Ms. Luo was over seventy years old, she insisted on rising at the crack of dawn during the cold months to prepare congee for her servants. Her sons said, "It's cold. Why make yourself suffer so?" She replied, "Female bondservants are also someone's children. It's cold at the crack of dawn; if one fills their stomachs with something warm, then they will tolerate following orders."[41] A few pages before this entry, the editor commented, "Female bondservants are also people; only money [*qian*] differentiates them from us."[42] *The Complete Book of Good Fortune and Longevity* and Chen alike viewed money as an unfairly arbitrary determinant of social status.

AFFLUENT LIVES

At a benevolent-society meeting during the food shortage of 1641, Chen raged against self-indulgent spenders of his district. He observed that, while people in the desolate villages and settlements were eating dregs and chaff, rich residents were frequenting markets and restaurants, buying, eating, and partying "as though they were unaware of a famine."[43] Hangzhou was the same, he told his audience: according to someone who had just been there, delicacies filled the streets and were being instantly bought up, and boats with wine and music were daily cruising West Lake. "Where is the appearance of famine?" he asked, adding: "Even if someone there did love the people, how would he be able to get a word in edgewise about the food shortage?"[44]

Just when benevolent societies and other charitable organizations were gathering momentum, irresponsible spending on gardens, operatic performances, and antiques was on the rise. Some thirty miles southeast of Hangzhou, in the prefectural city of Shaoxing, Zhejiang—the location for the numerous charitable activities discussed in part 2 of this book—Qi Biaojia, Zhang Dai, and many other wealthy residents simultaneously flouted the ideal of frugality and undertook charitable activities.[45] Their spending habits deserve note, for they set the scene for charitable activities, provide some specific numbers against which one might measure those charitable gifts for which amounts are known, and raise questions about the just use of surplus resources—questions that some late Ming literati themselves were asking.

Writing after the Ming dynasty fell, and after he himself had experienced severe losses—in short, writing with the perspective of a man disenfranchised—Zhang Dai took stock of five generations of his prominent lineage in a set of succinct but penetrating biographical sketches.[46] His great-great-grandfather and great-grandfather exemplified the virtues of frugality, simplicity, and modesty,[47] but, he reminisced, the more recent generations had built palatial homes, accumulated valuable art objects, entertained lavishly, and generally behaved in ways eccentric if not depraved.[48] One uncle spent thousands on carpentry projects; another drank wine from morning to night; and a third wasted his time with village wastrels, playing football, racing horses, and holding cock fights.[49] Among such crass spenders, there stood out his cousin Zhang E, a man so spoiled that he bought "whatever touched his fancy." He spent thirty taels on ten gold fish but, when they their color faded on the trip home, he flung them onto the road. He spent fifteen taels on a bronze mirror—nearly as much as Chen Longzheng donated for burying the poor—but, finding it to be rather dull, he tried to burnish it in a flame, inadvertently melting it down. He also ruined an antique ink slab costing thirty taels and discarded, after one night, a concubine who had cost him several hundred taels.[50]

Among Zhang Dai's friends was fellow townsman Qi Biaojia, whose wife's sister was married to the wasteful spender Zhang E.[51] Like members of the Zhang lineage, Qi too spent lavishly. He engaged troops to stage operatic performances in his home,[52] collected paintings and antiques, and purchased books for the renowned library of 31,500 volumes his father had assembled.[53] In 1635, after serving as an official for over a decade, Qi Biaojia took sick leave to return to his hometown, Shanyin, Shaoxing. Promptly he began construction of a garden for himself, a project that consumed five thousand taels, exhausted two years' of his energies both physical and spiritual, and obsessed him even in his dreams. Qi admitted that he was compulsive: "I again fell sick and recovered; and after recovering, I again fell sick. Such was my foolish obsession (*chipi*) to start a garden."[54] Nonetheless, Qi defended his actions: "Once I conjured up the idea of the project, I could not stop it."[55] The idea that obsessive cravings (*pi*), and the expenditures they incurred, were unstoppable had gained currency, even respectability. As Zhang Dai would note after the Ming collapse, *pi* had a social value: just as "flaws distinguish pieces of jade,"[56] so do the personal defects stemming from obsessions manifest the "deep feelings" necessary for "social intercourse."[57] Lavish spending on gardens, operas, and antiques—all conducive to successful entertainment—proved advantageous in forging social connections.

That garden ownership offered social advantages was well understood by one of Qi's acquaintances, the upwardly mobile salt merchant Wang Ruqian.[58] Over a decade before Qi returned to Shanyin, Wang was already lavishly entertaining "the famous and talented" in his *Unmoored Garden (Buxi yuan)*.[59] This was not a garden in the ordinary sense of being a place for cultivating flora or retreating from society; it was, rather, a large pleasure boat—of the same sort Chen Longzheng criticized.[60] Wang clearly perceived his boat to encompass the essential traits of gardens when he boasted, "My garden is everywhere and has no stopping place; the sounds of songs cover the water to the east and the west";[61] or when he asked, "What need is there to pile up rocks and dredge ponds, claiming them as one's own, saying, 'My garden, my garden'?"[62]

Wang Ruqian envisioned his "garden" as a social center for "famous scholars who came as guests."[63] Among these were the artist Dong Qichang, as well as the well-connected publisher Chen Jiru, who, after passing the licentiate degree abandoned the quest for office.[64] According to Chen Jiru, Wang had left Xin'an, Anhui, so as to have a multistoried boat at West Lake, because "he knew that where there was a West Lake there would be 'beautiful women and talented men' (*jiaren caizi*), and that where there were beautiful women and talented men, there would be drinking and literary exercises . . . and sojourners and men of letters. They would consort with courtesans who ply their seductive arts. Wang is such a person. Guests come from all over."[65] Also drawn to Wang's garden was Qi Biaojia, who visited Wang in 1635; mentioned (without providing any details) having rented *The Unmoored Garden*;[66] corresponded with Wang[67] (at least once on the subject of gardens);[68] and received Wang as a guest.[69] By offering lavish entertainment in scenic settings, Wang gained access to, perhaps even some influence over, literati circles—even though he was, it should be noted, but a prosperous salt merchant.[70]

Social pressures inexorably compelled Qi Biaojia and others to spend lavishly on entertainment—in sharp contrast to the Song-dynasty founder of the first lineage estate, Fan Zhongyan. When Fan left office to return to his hometown, Luoyang, he made a clear choice between building a garden for himself and establishing a charitable trust for his lineage. He reasoned: "At Luoyang, the estates of grand officials look out the one over the other. Those who own them can never go on enjoying them forever—should I alone be able to do so? And should I be able to enjoy such a life and feel happy about it afterward? No, my surplus salary and rewards should go to support my clan."[71] No such choice was made by Qi Biaojia and many of his peers, who generously contributed to their community's welfare while self-indulgently enjoying their wealth. Qi entirely bypassed the topic of frugality even when explaining why he appreciated Fan's decision to forgo a garden. He regretted, he said— perhaps with feigned frustration—that the countless visitors pouring into his garden had reduced him to being "merely one of the guests."[72] He thus used the reference to Fan to let it be known what an effective social magnet his own garden was.

It was in this social milieu of immense prosperity, evident throughout the Jiangnan region during the 1630s and 1640s, that Yang Dongming, Gao Panlong, and Chen Longzheng preached about moderation and charitableness in their respective communities. Likewise did Shaoxing resident Wang Chaoshi appeal to moral arguments to elicit socially responsible behavior from Qi Biaojia.[73] In 1637—before the severe food shortage—Wang wrote

Qi a remonstrative letter, which stated that when he saw Qi's garden he thought of four failings—three on Qi's part and one on his own. Foremost among the failings was that during two years at home, rather than assisting the community and nurturing the people, Qi had merely constructed the garden and ornamented its buildings. "If everyone were like this," Wang warned, "on whom would the state rely?" Wang further noted that Qi had failed his father, who had built up a collection of thousands of books for the benefit of his descendants; and had failed himself, for he was not effectively using his intelligence or his talent for aiding the world. As for the fourth failing, Wang himself took responsibility: in letting Qi move ahead with the garden, he had failed Qi as a friend.[74]

Appearing to be responsive to Wang's admonitions, Qi incorporated the rebuke into his essay on the garden, commenting as follows: "Alas! Such fine guidelines! How fortunate am I to hear these guidelines! Of all the warnings I have heard about my erroneous ways since starting construction on the garden, only Wang's words have touched me to the quick." But Qi then maintained that it was impossible to change his ways; in fact, because he had rejected Wang's advice, the fourth failing—the failure in friendship—was not Wang's but his. Consequently, Qi explained, "the determination that I will mend my ways" caused him to name one hall "Four Failings."[75]

Qi had many colleagues who sanctioned the enjoyment of wealth and urged him away from Wang's stern values.[76] The initial design for his garden project was modest, Qi insisted; only after much hesitation did he agree with the suggestions of guests that expansion "was indeed essential."[77] One friend "jokingly tried to make excuses" for Qi's disregard for Wang's advice.[78] Qi poked a hole in the friend's reasoning, but he also made sure to record in his diary what the friend had said, thereby preserving the friend's viewpoint for posterity. His behavior, moreover, implicitly mocked Wang's advice: frequently he invited friends for feasts, fireworks, and dramatic performances—extravagant entertainment held in, of all places, the Hall of Four Failings.[79] Within Qi's community as well as within his own mind, an emergent appreciation that the use of wealth could shore up power and social position battled with ideals of thrift and generosity.

The pattern of navigating between conspicuous, self-indulgent spending and serving the communal good had become evident in the early sixteenth century: when the merchant and art collector An Guo constructed his garden in Wuxi, Changzhou prefecture, he made a point of hiring famine refugees to do the work and generally strove to build up his reputation for good works.[80] The pattern continued into the Qing dynasty: when Feng Pu built a garden to host literary gatherings in Beijing, he purposely located it next to an orphanage that he had reestablished.[81] Likewise did the salt merchant Wang Ruqian balance entertaining scholars on his pleasure boat with establishing a reputation for responding charitably to all pleas for help.[82] As though to compensate for the conspicuous consumption of wealth, they let the public display of goodness eclipse the ideal of hidden virtue.

As conditions worsened during the late 1630s and early 1640s, Qi grew increasingly aware of and uneasy about imbalances between his enjoyment of prosperity and the needs of the destitute. Apparently heeding Wang Chaoshi's admonitions after all, he occasionally expressed misgivings about his ambition for a garden, describing his "fondness of natural scenery and garden building" as "a stupid addiction" (*zhuopi*);[83] or declaring, "What makes me happy is precisely what puts me to shame."[84] In 1639, when extending New Year's greetings to members of his lineage, he was so struck by their "poor appearance" as to write, "I sighed that we live in a garden with pavilion upon pavilion, and thought even more about relief measures, which I discussed with my brothers when I went home."[85] In the end, Qi proved to be socially responsible, organizing, with great dedication, numerous charitable activities. Nonetheless, right before dying, he had cause to confess to one of his sons: "Although your father did not fail in his family duties, I was however somewhat too addicted to the springs and the rocks. I was lavish in constructing my garden and this was my failing."[86] Chen Longzheng, in contrast, would posthumously earn his own son's applause for having been "frugal and charitable" and specifically for not having indulged in banquets, entertainment, and gardens.[87]

There were numerous social ties between moral, socially responsible men and recklessly wasteful ones. Through his wife's sister, née Shang, Qi Biaojia was connected to the prodigal and mercurial Zhang E. Thus, when Zhang E beat an innocent servant, creating a scandal that, in Zhang Dai's words, "almost ignited a popular rebellion (*minbian*)," Qi Biaojia had to intervene so as to protect the reputation of his father-in-law, Mr. Shang.[88] Wealth could serve for both good and ill: although his son-in-law Zhang E used money toward ruthless ends, Mr. Shang was known for being worthy and charitable.[89] At times, too, the fluid social relationships of the late Ming provided channels for influencing the rich. Wang Chaoshi, though critical of Qi, continued to consort and cooperate with him to distribute medical aid to the sick. Wang's mentor Liu Zongzhou joined forces with Qi and other garden owners (Jin Lan, Ni Yuanlu, and Zhang Dai, to name but a few) to carry out famine relief during the food shortages of 1640 and 1641. The visibility of such ostentatious expenditures as gardens—which enhanced the possibilities of social influence for the owner—provoked moralizing members of the community to exhort the wealthy to share their resources with the needy.

HOW MUCH SHOULD ONE GIVE?

As benefactors navigated between the call for charity and their self-interested impulses, what determined the amounts of their donations? By what standards did they make and judge contributions? How might they have weighed the 1,500 taels that members of Chen Longzheng's benevolent society collectively distributed to the needy over a ten-year period, against the 30 taels that Zhang E spent on gold fish? Or the 5,000 taels that Qi spent on his garden against those of his charitable donations for which figures are available: 10 taels for famine relief in 1637, 150 taels to aid his lineage, 100 taels for the village poor, and 80 and 300 taels, respectively, for famine relief in 1640 and 1641?[90]

Some late Ming texts implied that charitable gifts ought to be in proportion to one's means. Some texts defined the proportion precisely. Yang Dongming suggested in his record of a charitable estate that "it should not be difficult for those who are rich in resources to contribute 10 percent."[91] (By what principles he arrived at "10 percent" as an appropriate standard for giving, and whether he imagined the percentage to be based on annual income or the value of assets, is unclear.) So too did *The Complete Book of Good Fortune and Longevity* instruct the rich to donate one tenth of their expenditures to saving lives and forming small societies that would sponsor lodgings for the poor and ill.[92]

The figure of 10 percent resembled a tax, yet it differed from a tax because it was but a recommendation.[93] Charitable gifts were, by definition, expressions of compassion voluntarily made, something one gladly did, as conveyed by the oft-used term "taking pleasure in doing good" (*leshan*); and, because the gifts were voluntary, their amounts were left open-ended, up to the benefactor's discretion. Taken as a whole, late Ming texts conceived of donations as falling somewhere along a broad continuum. At one end was the option of depleting one's resources, and one occasionally reads of someone so deeply committed to aiding others that he did just that, living contentedly in radically reduced circumstances. At the other extreme was the option of doing good or providing gifts so minuscule that they essentially cost nothing.[94] Not only were the parameters for giving broad, they also cut two ways. The no-cost option, which benevolent-society leaders and popular-morality books insisted upon in order to engage men of meager means in the project of sharing goodness, enabled some donors to exploit small gestures for a big display of beneficence. The guideline of 10 percent, which aimed to remind potential donors how much they should give, also freed rich donors from pressures of giving even more.

The hoarding of surplus could be defended as the prudent preservation of resources. Working against the principle of being charitable, or "sharing one's wealth with others" (*fencai*), were not only greed and the pressure to shore up social networks, but also the worthy value of frugality, which aimed to conserve wealth for the benefit of one's household and future generations. Applauding his late mother as a model of frugality, Chen told his sons and grandsons that she had had but two small black horn combs in her cosmetic case, and that she never added fancy clothes or ornaments to her possessions. "You should not forget the meaning of this," he counseled them, "and you should, moreover, speak of this often to your wives."[95]

Gao Panlong circumvented the conflict between giving and keeping. In his household instructions, he advised family members that charity might be done inexpensively and conveniently by using leftovers, loose change, and unwanted scraps:

> As the ancient saying has it: "Among the best deeds in the world nothing is greater than rescuing people in distress and taking pity on the poor." Unless one has met with disaster, one should be able to spend several cash for charitable giving (*sheshi*). Indeed, aiding people does not lie in great expenditures of one's own wealth; just give whatever one feels is convenient and comfortable. Leftover soups and rice can save people from starvation. Tattered clothes and worn-out wadding can save people from cold. Save one or two dishes from a wine banquet; save one or two plates from ancestral offerings; use one or two fewer outfits of clothes; and do without one or two 'superfluous things' (*changwu*). Make urgent calculations on behalf of the poor, saving the surplus to aid people in distress. By dispensing with useless things, one can create things of great utility. By accumulating small kindnesses, one can achieve great virtue. Among "good deeds," these are the most meritorious accomplishments.[96]

Stressing that their gifts would leave no dent in their standard of living, Gao tread softly in placing sumptuary restrictions on members of his family.

Not so gentle was Chen Longzheng. Condemning waste to the point of challenging an established funerary custom, he asked, "What is the point of burning the clothes of the deceased?" and then suggested that the garments instead be given to descendants or poor friends.[97] Where Gao had gently encouraged generosity, Chen harshly attacked stinginess and hoarding, advising his benevolent society that its goal was not "hollow proselytizing" but "to get rid of greed and enhance the actual work of compassion."[98] He exhorted the rich to reduce expenditures so as to increase their charitable gifts: "Whenever I see the rich and high who will spare no expense on themselves but inevitably appear stingy when it comes to aiding others, I think: if they would only cut back on their extravagances and go without one or two sensual pleasures, they would then have enough to save the lives of countless poor people! If one would save item by item and day by day, reducing one's consumption somewhat, the assets thereby amassed would save an incredible number of people. Your household will, moreover, accumulate some blessings."[99]

Accordingly, Chen refashioned the image of Fan Zhongyan, transforming a man who was rich but both frugal and generous into someone who was so charitable as to have stockpiled no wealth whatsoever. Fan, according to Denis Twitchett, "amassed considerable wealth toward the end of his life, but continued to live in a frugal and restrained simplicity, while doing his utmost to assist not only his own Fan clan, but also his adoptive family."[100] Chen

Longzheng gave these facts a fresh twist, intimating that Fan's generosity resulted in his dying penniless. When someone suggested that being charitable would bring one a reputation for being wealthy, thus inviting annoying solicitations and entanglements, Chen talked past his interlocutor's concern and pointed to the case of Fan Zhongyan. Fan, he claimed, earned a salary of millions (Chen failed to specify the unit), but his donations for large-scale famine relief for the poor were such that, "when he died, nothing remained for his burial." Concluded Chen, "If one is somewhat generous, then one will not be rich; and the more generous one is, the poorer one will be. Charity does not allow for the accumulation of wealth (*cai*)."[101]

Where Gao spoke only about reducing the consumption of specific things—clothes, food, and "superfluous things"—Chen introduced into the discussion the topic of money (*qian*), whose use had greatly increased, at least in the Jiangnan region, with the influx of silver from the New World. Money, being merely a means of exchange, was in itself useless; it thus heightened Chen's awareness of the mean-spirited senselessness of hoarding.[102] In one lecture, after declaring that all people are essentially the same—"The rich and high have exactly the same bodies, guts, and skin as ordinary people"—and hence, by implication, that ordinary people deserve some equity, Chen challenged his audience: "In addition to living in peace and feasting on delicacies, what use is it to hoard more money and wealth (*qiancai*)?" Then, pointing to injustices, he added: "The ancients said, 'The accomplishments of one general derive from the bones of ten thousand troops.' Now to form one great household, who knows how many fields must be aggregated or how many residential lots must be emptied to complete the consolidation. Think about it carefully."[103] Money and wealth are corrupting, Chen warned: "In nine cases out of ten, the mind is damaged, the character is ruined, good feelings are destroyed, and the people's hatred is aroused, all because one has come in contact with money and wealth (*qiancai*)."[104] Chen's viewpoint continued to circulate in the Qing dynasty, when a didactic work cited him as having pronounced: "A proverb has it that 'the rich person is master of wealth,' which is to say, he can control his wealth. Although one should not deplete one's household resources, one must restrain oneself in order to aid others. The wealthy of today are all conscripted servants of wealth. . . . If one cherishes wealth without using it, one is nothing more than a slave to wealth."[105]

Chen declared money to be different in kind from other forms of wealth—food, clothing, and implements. It was a "natural principle," he believed, that "anything stored is unproductive, and anything that might be productive ought not to be hoarded." Elucidating the point, he noted that "given the right combination of rain, fertile soil, and human labor, one can produce clothes, food, and implements year after year," adding: "It is their characteristic to be valued for their newness, not oldness. When left for a long time, food will rot, clothes will disintegrate, and implements will break. Even people fond of stockpiling things will not collect these three items." Precious metal (*jin*) is different, he asserted. Unlike other kinds of goods, which rot, silver has three advantages: it is easy to store, it can be divided and recombined, and it does not decay. It also has three disadvantages: because it is easy to store, greedy people will accumulate it insatiably; because it can be divided and recombined, extravagant people will have beautiful ornaments created; and because it does not decay, stupid people will pile it up over long periods of time, forgetting to use it.[106] "Wealth," he insisted, "should be used, not stored away."[107]

Writers before the late Ming had condemned hoarding, especially during food shortages, when lives were at risk. When the object was grain, however, hoarders (perhaps deceiving even themselves) could mask greed on the grounds that preserving stocks was essential to their own families' survival. Moreover, because they understood that grain stored too long would rot, even the greediest of hoarders sought opportunities to turn over their stocks. During the late Ming, the increased circulation of silver, which Chen himself observed to be flowing in from overseas in exchange for silk textiles, put hoarding in a new light.[108] That silver could not be consumed, and that it could be stockpiled indefinitely, brought the senseless unproductiveness of hoarding into sharp focus.

Engaging the rhetoric of monetary exchanges, late Ming didactic works repeatedly warned their readers to pile up lasting virtue rather than ephemeral wealth, all the while providing cases to prove their point. One account tells, for example, of a household where four generations lived together, itself a sign of great concord: They "did not hoard"; rather they defrayed wedding and funeral expenses for relatives and friends while they themselves lived in such humble circumstances that they had to open up umbrellas whenever it rained; eventually the family produced five sons, "all of whom became officials."[109]

The rhetoric of monetary exchanges further articulated uncomfortable equations between rich and poor, pointing out that extravagant spending equals the oppression of the poor. When exhorting benevolent-society participants who were of middling wealth to spend their money on aiding the destitute rather than on throwing banquets to curry favor with the wealthy, Chen wrote that to host one such banquet required the oppression of ten small households.[110] Or, as Yan Maoyou, the editor of *Right Behavior and Good Fortune,* put it: "Ornamentations on one set of clothes cost what ten households produce; the bounty of single banquet is enough to keep several people alive."[111]

The patent discrepancy between the lavish banquets of the rich and the meager fare scratched out by the poor troubled Chen—so much so that he prefaced an account of his attempt to aid five abandoned children by citing

what an official had told the Tang-dynasty emperor Taizong: "The ban-
queters inside the capital are unaware of the famine outside." Only then
did Chen proceed with his own story: In 1640, while traveling by boat over
a thousand *li* to Luoyang, he had seen countless corpses piled up, as well
as abandoned children. So long as he was on the boat, and even if the boat
were to dock, Chen observed, nothing could be done. The party eventually
continued its journey by land, passing through a hamlet, where Chen es-
pied from his sedan chair a child of two or three *sui* sitting under a tree.
Not until the child, seeing the sedan chair, started to bawl "Daddy, Daddy,"
did Chen realize that the child had been abandoned. Though startled, he
again thought, "Nothing can be done." His party moved on. Tears blinded
his eyes, pain pierced his heart. A few *li* later, he had the sedan chair stop
and paid someone to fetch the child. Upon making some inquiries in the
village, he learned of a childless couple in their forties who had ten *mou* of
land. The couple happily came to take the stray. Chen wished to give them
one tael. They declined, insisting, "We wish to raise the child ourselves."
Commending their good hearts, he persuaded them that their acceptance
of the money "would also make his good intention visible." The child,
though appearing malnourished, was alert and able to digest noodles, and
was given the couple's surname. Chen concluded that the child would survive and might even carry on the couple's family line. As he continued on
his trip, he figured that he could spare an additional fifteen taels. Subsequently he attempted to rescue, with varying degrees of success, four other
children.[112]

Chen's account had something to teach both the high and the low. His
mention of the Tang emperor served as an oblique warning to the emperor
of his own day; his own actions demonstrated that small sums of money (relative to one's resources) could save lives. Above all, if these lessons had any
didactic power, it is because he had derived them from deeply felt personal
experience and displayed the process by which he himself found a way to
take action about a seemingly hopeless situation. Witnessing the corpses and
hearing the plaintive sound of "Daddy, Daddy" were keys to his awakening—
a point that Chen underscored by referring both to King Xuan of Qi, who
could not bear to see an ox sacrificed,[113] and to the horrifying image conjured up by Mencius, "seeing a child about to fall into a well."[114]

Weighing the cost of a banquet against the cost of doing good again figures
in an account of a sojourner who most likely was a merchant but who had
formed cozy relationships with the gentry (*shenshi*) of Kunshan, Suzhou prefecture. In 1699, the gentry wished to throw a party celebrating the sojourner's fiftieth birthday. The sojourner declined, opting instead to assemble his friends at a monastery and to use the funds they had collected to
distribute to widows, orphans, cripples, and the poor. He himself gave some
money, which was to be stored at a benevolent society—an indication that

by this time some benevolent societies had acquired the role of either a loan society or a bank. The editor of the account makes the point that the so-journer's rejection of a banquet spared animals from being slaughtered.[115] But the account itself explicitly mentions charity for the poor. Just as Yang Dongming had transformed a merry-making club into a benevolent society, so did the sojourner redirect the impulse to party into doing good—but with a difference. Unlike Yang, the sojourner lacked an official title and his influence was based on wealth alone. Nonetheless, for his initiative in doing good, he too earned some visibility in the written record. By 1699—a century after Yang had relegated the merely wealthy to a second benevolent society—the social milieu had changed to the point that the gentry of Kunshan made room for an untitled sojourner to lead the way. If he derived some interest from the money stored at the benevolent society, he, like other late seventeenth-century merchants, enjoyed, through his charitable activities, a public mask of respectability.

Just about the time when Chen was lecturing to his benevolent society that one banquet required the oppression of ten people, Yan Maoyou was making similar calculations to build the case for a charitable club, suggesting in passing the figure of 10 percent as a standard for donations:

> What a rich person spends for one night's sojourn is enough to save ten lives. The expense for hiring one priest or medium is enough to save two hundred lives. If one were to contribute 10 percent of grain valued at thousand taels and 10 percent of the clothes and food used for a year, the sum would suffice to save a thousand lives. The amounts put aside are inconsequential and the plan easy to execute. And if one could get several people to collaborate in forming a club that would make an empty room, with straw matting piled up in the middle, available for lodging the poor and sick so as to spare them the tribulations of feeding on wind and sleeping on the bare ground—then the down-and-out would recover. During the winter cold, doing this is even more urgent. But one must get a good person to manage the operation. If each of the four city gates were to have such a lodging, then untimely deaths would be rare.[116]

Yan founded the Yunqi Society in 1624, right between the starting dates of Gao's and Chen's benevolent societies in 1614 and 1632, respectively. Like these benevolent societies, the Yunqi Society combined moral reform and good works. Also like them, it welcomed a heterogeneous membership; as Yan put it, "May high and low, rich and poor, all enter."[117] Yet, differing from its benevolent-society counterparts, the Yunqi Society required wholehearted commitment from its members and established clear boundaries marking membership. Each prospective member had to confess and repent any major wrongdoings before entering the society; each member had to keep a ledger of merits and demerits with the goal of accumulating one hundred thousand good deeds; and members who committed serious misdeeds were to be expelled. Such differences notwithstanding, the Yunqi Society brings to mind Yang Dongming's allusion to the "common societies" (*suhui*) of "ped-dlers and plowmen" as an inspiration for his own benevolent society. Such was the social fluidity of this era that high and low converged in community welfare projects. Further indicating this convergence is that Yan founded the Yunqi Society two years before earning the *juren* degree; and that a decade later, after his good works had brought him into contact with high literati, he received, through a special recommendation, the *jinshi* degree and, sub-sequently, a bureaucratic position.

CONCLUSION

Sustaining Jiashan's benevolent society through the food shortage of 1641 proved difficult. Relying on irregular funding "could not go on," Chen noted. But rather than abandoning the institution, he resolved to shore up its foun-dation by contributing land to a trust, "the surplus rents of which would be used for benevolent-society affairs." (What counted as "surplus rents" and whether the arrangement brought Chen's family some material benefit are unclear.) Thinking that "there ought to be a record"—another gesture to-ward institutional longevity—he asked Qian Shisheng to oblige.[118]

At the same time, Chen had a Benevolent Society Hall (Tongshan guan) constructed upon the foundation of a defunct private academy. His choice of location is emblematic of a crossroads that many late Ming literati faced: rather than restoring an institution that had once supported scholarship, contemplation, and preparation for the civil service examinations, Chen used the academy grounds for a hall that would foster community activism. In pursuing the option of a charitable institution, he had the support of many contemporaries. This was when many other cities were imitating his benevolent society[119] and just a year after Qi Biaojia recorded that he had heard about and applauded the idea of a benevolent society.[120] Chen in turn drew inspiration from charitable strategies tested in other locations. From a friend who had traveled from Guiji, Shaoxing prefecture, Chen heard—so he stated in passing, in a letter of 1641—that Liu Zongzhou had recently put a plan for famine relief into effect and that Qi Biaojia had labored hard to manage it, with the result that the people enjoyed great harmony.[121] As news of good deeds circulated among the elite, benevolent societies won approval and legitimacy.

Benevolent societies would evolve into lasting institutions, with enormous buildings, large land endowments, and high visibility. They and other insti-tutions for routine philanthropy took hold not only because they nurtured the poor and responded to crises but because they satisfied the benefactors' needs as well. They provided legitimate grounds for association—just when academies and literary clubs of all sorts were under suspicion, especially after the political feuds associated with the Donglin Academy, with which

Gao Panlong and other benevolent-society sponsors had been affiliated.[122] That the political climate was inhibiting public associations is evident in the case of Lu Shiyi, who, expressing fear that it was "unfitting to have a private society (*sihui*)," urged the benevolent society of his town, Taicang, to seek the prefect's sponsorship.[123] Yet, stewards more confident than Lu—men such as Yang Dongming, Gao Panlong, and Chen Longzheng—were able, without official sponsorship, to organize benevolent societies free of the taint of private associations. Assemblies to save lives were less problematic than the gathering of learned minds.

Benevolent societies also provided arenas where a moneyed segment of society, though lacking literati status, could exercise influence at the district level—a point that Chen recognized in separating learning from "riches and high status" (*fugui*)—two components that many of his predecessors had seen as congruent, with the latter as a matter of course quietly following upon the heels of scholarly achievement. Once he declared, "Heaven would like everyone to be worthy, rich, and noble," only to back away immediately from this vision, stating, "but that is impossible," and then identified two sources of influence at the local level: "Heaven generates wisdom so as to enlighten people who are stupid, and it generates riches and status so as to aid the poor and lowly."[124] Each sphere, he assumed, had a complementary role in dealing with the problem of economic inequities: men of learning (whether they might be active officials, retired gentry, or nontitled scholars) would provide moral edification; men of wealth and honor would nurture and assist the needy. "By simply opening our mouths," Chen advised the rich and high, "we can aid others; by performing one deed, we can save others. Clearly Heaven has bestowed on us positions for cultivating our blessings."[125] The benevolent society institutionalized the message that men whose substance was solely material were just as capable as men of letters in serving noble causes. It conferred on money a meaning that proved acceptable to Confucian scholars, government officials, and merchants alike. Late Ming benevolent societies thus paved the way for the merchant leadership in charitable activities that would become highly visible in the next dynasty.

In deliberating upon the relative roles that learning and wealth played in ordering society, Chen wobbled uneasily. In theory he gave the edge to men of bureaucratic status (which, having been earned by passing the civil service examinations, was often conflated with learning). Officials should, he asserted in 1630, take the lead in caring for the poor: "To restore order, nothing is more important than uniting the hearts and minds of the people; and to do that, nothing is more important than saving human lives. Yet restoring equilibrium is not a task for the ignorant and lowly; it is completely dependent on persons of wealth and high status (*fugui*): *first*, the officials, then the rural gentry (*xiangshen*)."[126] Yet, in his benevolent-society lectures, Chen let talk of the literatus (*shidafu*) or the gentleman (*junzi*)—two terms that

referred to men who embodied Confucian ideals but also connoted achievement in the civil service examinations—yield to talk of large households or
the "rich and high." Thus, in one passage, Chen assumed that magistrates
(the "fathers and mothers of the people"), at the top of the local hierarchy,
should take the lead in good works, but he recognized that the bulk of contributions came from large, rich households: "Today fortunately there are
magistrates on high who will take the initiative in making donations, leading the rural bureaucrats (*xiangguan*) and wealthy households. Although the
amount of money thus accumulated will be small, with the mechanism having been set up, when there is a real emergency, every large household will
generously and naturally make donations."[127] Chen assigned the moral responsibility for good works to men of wealth no less then to men of intellectual achievement.

Chen's extant writings provide grounds for substantially modifying a
model proposed by some historians, namely, that, because the imperial court
was busy defending its borders and was low on funds, it neglected local communities, leaving a vacuum for activist residents.[128] To be sure, Chen, like
some of his contemporaries, promoted local control of resources, asking,
"How is contributing wealth to help the state (*guo*) as good as distributing
wealth to help the people through crises?"[129] He also insisted that grain storage should be managed by the people of the district rather than by the
state[130]—this at a time when border defense and internal uprisings were indeed absorbing much of the state's energies. Nevertheless, Chen's writings
also show that there had become available a compelling alternative to working through the imperial bureaucracy—an alternative in the form of the
"rich" whom Chen addressed in his lectures and the literate who managed
benevolent-society affairs; and this alternative enabled the shift of focus from
the state to the local community. Chen alleged that, to implement "the great
projects of the world," one must have high position. However, when prefacing a piece entitled "Strategic Planning for the Rural Areas" (Xiangchou xu)
he asserted that "at the local level (*xiangbang*), one might participate in making arrangements whether one has a post or not."[131] Rather than embody-
ing a coherent elite that would dominate local society, the benevolent society allowed men of wealth and holders of civil service examination status alike
to exert influence at the local level. Their charitable activities both exposed
tensions and conflicts among them and provided a forum for negotiation.
Highly visible, tolerated by the state, and sponsored by various constituencies of the local community, the benevolent society came to express a spirit
of district pride.

5

A Benevolent Society
Viewed from the Margins

*His family is lazy and brought the poverty on themselves. Especially
in this famine year, I could not go down a well to save a man.*
LU SHIYI

Among the surviving documents concerning late Ming benevolent societies,
only one conveys at any length the viewpoint, not of prestigious local leaders, but of a small player, a member of that middle economic stratum that
Chen Longzheng advised to participate in doing good at little or no cost.
The document is the diary of a young scholar, Lu Shiyi, who resided in
Taicang subprefecture, Nanzhili, some forty-five miles north of Chen's Jiashan, and it recounts events of 1641, the year that Chen Longzheng gave
the benevolent society of Jiashan funds to build a hall.[1] It displays Lu's
earnestness about moral self-cultivation and doing right and allows one to
infer why those other bit players who appear often but fleetingly in the
records, and who themselves left no statements, should have engaged in charitable activities. Lu's diary, moreover, is the only known extant late Ming
record that mentions beneficiaries by name and discusses their particular
hardships. It thus shows that the marginal participant, in addition to providing manpower for large-scale charitable projects, served as a conduit for
communication between poor and rich.

The celebratory accounts composed by prominent local leaders for posterity have glossy public facades. When writing about or lecturing to their
benevolent societies, Yang Dongming, Gao Panlong, and Chen Longzheng
neatly packaged their information to conform with generic expectations, or
unspoken rules, that they and their audiences alike understood. Focusing
fully on their goals, to promote a sense of united purpose and to elevate the
participants' self-esteem, they optimistically swept aside all complications that
stood in their way. In their motivational statements the exposure of behind-
the-scenes disagreements had no place. Generic conventions had condi-
tioned participants to take for granted that only favorable, uplifting infor-

mation would be preserved; accordingly, the formal records of benevolent societies create an illusion of harmonious completeness.

Recording only what impinged on his daily stocktaking, Lu Shiyi's diary is, in contrast, often elliptical in presentation and crude in content. Lu did not explain, for the benefit of future readers, how the benevolent society came to be organized or what rules of operation it followed. He did not properly introduce the various characters; his close friend Yuruo lives on in the diary but without a surname. Lu and his friends took these matters for granted. Rather than upholding an abstract ideal that would speak to a large constituency—articulating a general purpose to be shared by leaders and followers—Lu's diary discusses only what the benevolent society meant to him, exposing along the way untidy affairs behind the institution's public facade: heated, divisive debates among junior scholars over benevolent-society policy and procedures, and schemes by participants to use benevolent-society funds to help their relatives and acquaintances.

With its realistic revelations of daily difficulties and its lively particularities, Lu's diary promises to be more informative than his superiors' abstract, high-minded documents. The promise is illusory, however, for realism comes at the expense of coherence. Exactly where do Lu's fleeting half-glimpses of local life fit into the synoptic pictures of benevolent societies painted by august leaders? Do his revelations about benevolent-society troubles and self-centered participants outweigh, even negate, the slick records left by men at the top? To evaluate the diary's significance as a source about the benevolent society in his town, one must take stock of Lu's diary-keeping habits and purpose, as well as his place in Taicang society. Although Lu's reporting of events was forthright, his place at the periphery of elite society severely restricted his vision of the benevolent society's purpose and potential. Rather than contradicting the glowing reports of his superiors, his record complements them. The first task, then, is to determine precisely where and how the two types of records dovetail.

TRACKING PROGRESS

With two goals in mind—tracking his moral progress and advancing his scholarship—Lu fittingly entitled his diary *A Record of My Determination to Learn* (*Zhixue lu*). I shall simply call it his diary. By the time of the extant diary, 1641, anxiety about his moral self-cultivation had already made Lu a veteran journal keeper. To watch himself, he had kept logs of his activities, logs of his readings. Ever edgy about improving both habits and mind, he had shifted restlessly from one record-keeping strategy to another. Initially he followed a regimen for self-discipline that had been laid out in *The Ledger of Merit and Demerit* (*Gongguo ge*). This work dates back to around the twelfth century but gained a new life through its association with Yuan Huang, who has already appeared in chapter 2 as Chen Longzheng's fellow townsman, and who taught that, by accumulating merit, one could be master of one's own fate. Such was the popularity of Yuan's method that Lu Shiyi one day learned to his surprise that his friend Chen Hu had also adopted it.[2]

Lu quickly grew dissatisfied with Yuan Huang's technique, however. Like other serious moralists of his day, he found offense in Yuan's notion that moral self-cultivation could be mechanically achieved by stockpiling merit and then canceling out bad deeds with the good, like using cash to pay off a debt—an idea that Yang Dongming had articulated as follows: "Heaven brings good fortune to the good person just as though he were holding a bill of credit."[3] For many of Lu's contemporaries, Yuan's program evoked thoughts of profit making, reduced moral issues to cold calculations, and limited the understanding of ethical concepts. An especially outspoken critic was the scholar Liu Zongzhou, who had attracted a huge following among members of the elite, and whose lectures Lu Shiyi had attended. Liu fiercely attacked Yuan Huang's method for emphasizing so blatantly the goal of winning merit at the expense of inner spiritual self-cultivation. Echoing Liu's sentiment, Lu Shiyi cautioned a sororal nephew against Yuan's method because, he explained, "you forget the trap once you have caught the fish; you forget the snare once you have caught the hare."[4]

Lu subsequently started (in 1636) a different kind of record, *Investigating Things and Extending Knowledge* (*Gezhi pian*).[5] Inscribing the front page with the words "revere heaven" (*jingtian*), he committed himself to evaluating his morality daily; at the beginning of each entry he would announce "whether reverence or laxity had prevailed" that day. Around that time Lu also joined three friends for mutual reinforcement in self-cultivation, a group endeavor that would last several years. He further initiated a journal entitled *A Record of Examining One's Virtue and Studying toward a Career* (*Kaode keye lu*).[6] Every night he "wrote truthfully about what he had done and the books he had studied during that day." To evaluate his progress, he marked whether he had been "serious" or "not serious."[7] Or, to use Chen Hu's report: from 1637 on, the four friends (Lu Shiyi, Chen Hu, Sheng Jing, and Jiang Shishao) adopted a learning method through which they might "progress toward goodness and correct their faults."[8]

Soon after beginning his *Record of Examining One's Virtue,* Lu started yet another record, which he named *Reflection and Discrimination* (*Sibian lu*), this time drawing inspiration from a phrase in the classic *The Doctrine of the Mean* (*Zhongyong*): "careful reflection and clear discrimination."[9] When his father died, Lu also kept *A Diary of Mourning* (*Jusang riji*).[10] None of these methods satisfied Lu, however. Disparaging his stocktaking as sloppy, he again revised his approach, this time grading himself on a scale of ten, to produce the extant diary of 1641, *Zhixue lu.*[11]

Of the various journals Lu kept, only two are extant: *Reflection and Dis-*

crimination, which is a collection of thematically organized notebooks rather than an account of daily events; and the diary, which is preserved in a nineteenth-century collection of Lu's writings. The editor of the collection notes that this diary was more detailed than the journals for the previous three years, and that he had asked a friend to draft an abridgment; then, regretting that the result was overly condensed, whereas "every bit of the diary was beneficial to mind and body," he made a copy of the original, while shortening the friend's condensation further, to be used as the introductory note.[12] Having thus escaped bowdlerization, the diary provides, with the exception of one hiatus of twenty days,[13] a rare day-by-day view of ten months in the life of a late Ming literatus, months made stressful by the string of ominous events that were threatening the social and political order.

SELF-EVALUATION

Each day Lu assessed in his diary whether "laxity" or "seriousness" had gained the upper hand in his conduct. Every ten days, that is, three times each lunar month, he tallied his good and bad points in a grid chart that had twelve sections: two registers, upper and lower, running across six vertical columns. The columns represented categories of learning that were derived from *The Great Learning* and thus connected him to ancient wisdom: "investigating things and completing knowledge"; "thinking with sincerity"; "setting the heart-and-mind straight"; "cultivating the self"; "regulating the household"; and "governing states and bringing peace to the world."[14] Using this grid, Lu entered his positive deeds in the top register so that he might weigh them against the negative ones, which he recorded at the bottom.

Adding emotional intensity to all that Lu did and thought during the year of his diary was the loss of his father, who had died in 1638 and whom Shiyi had nursed, with much devotion, through five years of illness. During 1641, the third year of mourning, thoughts of his father still had the power to move Lu to grief. When he read the records of his various friends and saw that most of them wrote about family matters, he thought about his father and became very sad.[15] When he presented his birth mother (who had died when he was twelve days old; he was then nursed by his "beneficent mother") with some leftover sacrificial offerings (which were sparse because the harvest had been poor) and contemplated his own numerous children, he felt unhappy that his father "was unable to share the pleasure."[16] Of a time when he hung his father's portrait up in the ancestral hall, and bowed before it, he wrote, "Thinking back on days past, I could not stop weeping."[17]

After poring over manuals on mourning rituals, Lu decided to remain celibate throughout the three-year mourning period, a point he frequently noted in his diary with the phrase "I slept alone." Such abstinence, although ritually prescribed, probably was not widely practiced, for it became the subject of gossip: so suggests one diary entry, where Lu recorded that a servant must have leaked to a neighbor that "for three years I would not sleep with my wife," whereupon Lu had to explain to his wife: "This is because the ancients thought mourning important."[18]

Lu was a stickler for good form, for "what is fitting"—a phrase he often used. His penchant for propriety foreshadowed a trait that some historians have noted of his later life: a deep preoccupation with ritual.[19] At times, to be sure, his behavior conflicted with the social rules he had internalized. Though cleaving to a regimen of celibacy, he chastised himself for having deviated from some other mourning requirements and for having failed to keep to a vegetarian diet.[20] One purpose of his diary was to identify and deal with such discrepancies, to bring his behavior in line with what he thought proper.

Lu scrutinized even his dreams, noting in his diary whether they were "upright" or "improper," "pure" or "confused." "Improper dreams," he believed, "were the result of an improper mind," and any "little seeds of insincerity left to sprout during the day would reappear at night."[21] As he understood it: "It is not that the perfected man has no dreams, only that he has no reckless dreams. When dreams are scrambled, one's mind might nonetheless be much at ease."[22]

Burdened by a sense of loss, Lu dreamed of weeping for his father, and of "presenting sacrificial offerings to his deceased mother."[23] Of one dream about his father, he wrote, "I thought about him very desperately."[24] On another day his sense of personal loss converged with a premonition of dynastic decline to make him especially tearful. Noting recent disasters, including the obstruction of the Grand Canal—that is, the lifeline by which grain was transported from the fertile Yangzi delta region to the Northern Capital (Beijing)—and having just read some imperial edicts, he sharply blamed himself: "This truly makes one weep; it is especially lamentable that no statesmen have ability." Sobbing into the night, Lu remarked: "I slept alone and dreamed of my father's engraved portrait; I wept and bowed."[25]

As recorded and understood by Lu, his dreams were for the most part plain, offering neither revelations from heavenly spirits nor messages from the underworld. Once Lu did note prophetically: "I dreamed that I was watching fish; that must mean it will rain"; once he noted—this time without ascribing any special significance to it—a dream of "a large panther, divine goat, and black tiger"; and once, the night after taking the civil service examination, he dreamed of a demon.[26] But, with a rare exception or two, his dreams, unlike those of some other Ming literati, expressed neither high aspirations about examination success nor deep anxieties about failure. They reveal no sense of mission to save the world as had the dream of the unkempt, uncouth, and scarcely educated son of a salt merchant, Wang Gen—a dream that foreshadowed Wang's rise to some prominence. In 1511 Wang Gen dreamed that the heavens were collapsing, forcing panic-stricken multitudes to scramble to escape; singlehanded, he lifted up the skies, put the stars back in their proper place, and restored order, whereupon the crowds cheered him for his extraordinary heroism.[27] Called by a vision of serving the people, and confident that a deteriorating society needed his capabilities, he sought instruction from Wang Yangming and then devoted himself to teaching both literati and the masses—among the latter a woodcutter and a servant. Lu Shiyi had read Wang Gen's *Recorded Conversations* (*Xinzhai yulu*) but remained unimpressed, commenting that he found only roughly 10 to 20 percent of the text to be in accord with the Way.[28] Unlike Wang Gen, a man inspired by the teaching opportunities that prosperity had opened up, Lu remained cautious.

Lu's dreams neither expanded his horizons nor stretched his imagination. Narrow and flat, they operated on the same plane as his ordinary life. So reveals the following statement: "I slept alone. I dreamed that I was discussing with my brothers the method of recording facts—as clear as though it were daylight."[29] If Lu had dreams far more fantastic than those he set to paper, it remains the case that the dreams he thought worth recording had passed through the filter of his plain-mindedness. So too in life was Lu unmotivated to reach far and high. He lamented that statesmen had no ability,[30] yet himself lacked the personality, status, or prosperity to rise to the occasion. During the Qing dynasty, he would gain some distinction: in 1661, a magistrate whom he was serving as secretary sponsored the publication of some of his writings. But before the Ming dynasty's fall, Lu lacked the sure sense of authority enjoyed by Yang, Gao, and Chen, and even by the once marginal Wang Gen.

DIARY KEEPING AS A SOCIAL EVENT

Lu's penchant for record keeping was nearly manic. His logs proliferated. Cross-references among them abounded. In addition to keeping "a record of events" (*jishi lu*)—that is, his diary—Lu decided to compile his "Record of Gazing upon Others" (Xiangguan lu), where he would preserve the good words and deeds of his friends, his "brothers."[31] He noted this decision in his diary, and a month later he mentioned having just added five entries to the new "Record of Gazing."[32] An abundance of such cross-references added complexity to Lu's life, but within a narrowly circumscribed arena.

More than tools by which Lu and his comrades watched and disciplined themselves, the journals expressed the attitude that their words and deeds merited preservation. Lu and his friends therefore initiated yet another record, entitled "Proceedings of the Discussion Meetings" (Huijiang ji shuo). Its purpose was twofold: to preserve the fruits of their labors of the previous five years, and to inform future members of their group about past proceedings.[33] Thus did their reverently kept records pile up—and overly burden them, wholly absorbing them in microdealings within their tiny social circle.

Lu and his friends each kept his own record but did so in the context of social ties, consulting one another about diary-keeping strategies. When Lu and Chen Hu met, the two of them pulled out their diaries for comment and criticism, debating points until they reached a common understanding of general principles.[34] "It is fitting to record good points but not the bad," stated Lu, whereupon Chen Hu, according to Lu's diary, "disagreed." Only after visiting friend Qian Fanhou's library to check the general guidelines for recording events did they come around to Lu's viewpoint. Said Lu to Chen Hu: "My diary should record only faults; as for my family's hidden goodness (*yinwei zhi shan*), I ought not and need not record them."[35]

Roughly every ten days, judging from Lu's diary, the friends would convene to review their respective "records of examining one's virtue."[36] The expectation apparently was that they meet regularly, prompting Lu once to comment about a lapse: "From the beginning of the fifth month to today, the comrades have not read their records of examining one's virtue."[37] Attending these meetings was a serious obligation the friends owed one another: on one occasion, when Lu, who had the responsibility for taking notes, arrived late, he had to pay a fine.[38] The records of self-scrutiny were maintained in the context of social relationships and under the watchful eyes of one's peers. Lu was cognizant that friends would examine not only his *Record of Examining One's Virtue,* but—as five of them did one evening—also his diary.[39]

Lu and his comrades kept their journals in reference to a shared set of values, which they drew from the Confucian classics and used to reinforce their friendships. For his digest of readings, Lu chose the title "Sibian lu," an allusion to *The Doctrine of the Mean,* because it epitomized a trait he had admired in his friend Chen Hu's diary. Similarly inspired by Lu's *Gezhi bian,* Chen Hu started in 1647 to keep track in his own diary whether reverence or laziness prevailed.[40]

When Lu inscribed the frontispiece of *Gezhi pian* with the words "revere heaven," he situated his record in the context of heaven's workings and evoked a couplet from *The Book of Poetry:* "Revere the anger of Heaven, / And presume not to make sport or be idle."[41] When he labeled the sections of the ten-day charts for reviewing his behavior, he used key phrases from *The Great Learning.* When Chen Hu mentioned that Lu's selection of the title *Sibian lu* was influenced by Chen's own diary, he purposely deflected attention from his own writing, instead defining his journal keeping as an extension of an ancient, venerable practice: "I imitated the methods that the ancients used to study and read. Every once in a while, when I had understood something, I would jot it down. I called this *A Record of Seeking the Way (Qiudao lu).* Lu Shiyi saw and liked it, saying, 'This is what *The Doctrine of the Mean* called "careful reflection and clear discrimination"—*shen si ming bian*—and consequently there was his *Sibian lu.*'"[42] References to an ancient tradition of study sanctified and secured the two scholars' friendship.

Lu did not necessarily acquiesce to the judgments of his peers, but he had to contend with their views and establish enough common ground that his community of friends would deem his diary credible. His individual quest was in tension with—and informed by—their opinions. Though tugged in several directions, he found a modus vivendi for following the dictates of his conscience while remaining accountable to his peers. Within the conventions of his social milieu, his diary was earnest and forthright. His frankness is manifest especially when his diary contradicts accounts compiled posthumously by his admirers. Where Chen Hu commented that "Lu did not talk about sleeping apart from his wife . . . and members of his household were unaware of it," Lu had frequently made a point of noting in his diary (to be read by friends, including Chen) that he slept alone—and reported, furthermore, that word of his celibacy had leaked out of the household.[43] Where Lu's son Yunzheng commended his father for having secretly performed good deeds, mentioning specifically that he provided a coffin for someone who had failed to repay a loan,[44] Lu Shiyi left a different picture: in one episode, he both tried to shift the financing of the coffin onto the benevolent society and voiced his impatience with the dying person's wayward habits.

LU SHIYI'S DIARY AS A SOURCE

From extant materials there emerge two contrasting pictures of benevolent societies: one as an institution that is harmonious and effective and calls for joyous satisfaction on the part of its members; the other as an unstable arrangement fraught with tensions. The sharp divergence between the two images to some extent stems from the genres used: the formal, "public" documents composed by Yang Dongming, Gao Panlong, and Chen Longzheng on the one hand, and the personal daily record by Lu Shiyi on the other. Yet, the two perspectives of the benevolent society, idealistic and realistic, reflect as well the writer's character and social status. Self-confident and affluent, Yang, Gao, and Chen stepped surefootedly into their roles as moral leaders and were inclined to view with much optimism what their benevolent societies might accomplish. Prestige and wealth shored up their authority and equipped them to make public statements that would spur their listeners to act.

Lu Shiyi's background was far more humble. His ancestors had "hidden virtue but never held office," according to his intimate friend Chen Hu, who recounted how Lu's father had earned a position as a teacher. An official entourage, the story went, was rushing through their humble residential area and inadvertently splashed and dirtied Lu's father's clothes. The official immediately dismounted his carriage to extend an apology, but Lu's father had already disappeared. The official found out the man's identity and instructed a friend to invite him to teach at a family school. Thus did the father win a modicum of recognition for humility and his concern about offending others.[45]

When Lu's mother died twelve days after his birth, the family, being unable to afford a wet nurse, entrusted him to be raised by a woman of another lineage.[46] When Lu was in his thirteenth year, his father's patron observed Shiyi to be emaciated and weak.[47] As an adult Lu owned land, for in 1641 he expressed relief that locusts were no longer ravaging an area where he "too had fields."[48] His beneficent mother also owned land; so testifies Lu's casual reference to her collecting rents.[49] Lu was sufficiently well off to pursue an education, and during normal times, he never had to make do on "only two meals a day."[50] But compared with, say, Yang Dongming, who sponsored a program for distributing hundreds of padded jackets, Lu Shiyi had meager financial resources. In the autumn of 1641, finding that he had a balance of one and a half ounces of silver, scarcely enough to satisfy his household needs, he noted: "There is hardly any money this year, and I am anxious about losing it."[51] Two months later he described himself as "poor" (*pinjian*) and congratulated himself for having been parsimonious during his sojourn at the prefectural seat (Suzhou) while waiting to take the examinations.[52]

Lu had earned the licentiate degree in 1632, yet this achievement was but a preliminary step on an arduous climb through a sequence of civil service examinations that eventually might—against great odds—lead to official appointment. Presumably the degree brought him modest privileges—a stipend and exemption from certain taxes—but it gave him little authority. Lu essentially remained a mere student who had to retake the examinations every three years to renew his licentiate status and pursue the slim hope for a higher degree.

Still the student in 1641, Lu appears in his diary, here earnestly poring over a chapter of *The Book of Mencius*, there boning up on *The Book of Poetry*,[53] asking his peers to correct his draft essays, reading samples of "contemporary-style essays" required in the examinations,[54] attending study drills, and contemplating policy issues he might be asked to debate in the examinations. How could Lu, a mere licentiate so unsure of his learning, be a match for officials and holders of the higher degrees—men whose authority had already been legitimized by solid examination success?

Lu Shiyi lived in a congested neighborhood. When he tried to study, he was disturbed by the shouts of neighbors drilling with their weapons. When a runner came to summon him to serve as head of a community compact, Lu surmised, erroneously, that the runner had mistaken his door for a neighbor's. Although he stood among the literate elite of Taicang and had prospects for advancement, his living conditions were decidedly inferior to those enjoyed by the district's wealthy residents. When visiting one home, he marveled that his host "lived in a bamboo grove, where all around no sound of people could be heard and one could enjoy vegetation, fruit, fields, and ponds. This could be a place for learned discussions; moreover, it provides beautiful scenery."[55]

Hovering ambiguously at the fringes of official-gentry society, Lu responded to social opportunities with diffidence. Once he had a chance to curry favor with a highly placed out-of-town visitor. Many of his friends, Lu noted in his diary, "assembled to rush after the visitor." Among these was a certain Wang Chengzhao, who, wrote Lu, "paid respects as a follower and also put on an opera for him. He wanted me to join the banquet, saying that I too must copy out some poems and essays to send to the visitor with the hope of getting a recommendation." Lu had reservations, however, in part because he "did not know what kind of character the visitor had," but also because, as he put it: "To be placed among them would, I felt, be gauche and was not something I wanted. Certainly I would feel uneasy throughout the banquet; I therefore adamantly declined."[56]

Likewise had Lu Shiyi (along with his friend Chen Hu) in a previous instance "stubbornly refused to respond to all invitations" to an important gathering. This was in 1630, when famous scholars from all over China hastened to join the Restoration Society (Fu she). Under the leadership of Lu's townsmen Zhang Cai (a *jinshi*-degree holder and formerly a magistrate) and Zhang Pu (a *jinshi*-degree holder who declined to take office), this organization had grown from a small literary society into a vast network of scholars committed to moral and political reform, a network so vast, that the society's meeting of 1633 (in Suzhou) attracted over two thousand literati—all this, according to an account of the Restoration Society that Lu Shiyi himself would write some years later.[57] Though repeatedly urged to participate, and though surely aware that the Restoration Society provided invaluable networking opportunities (with the result that many of its members subsequently passed the higher-level examinations), Lu stayed at home.[58]

Some seven months before declining the banquet invitation, Lu Shiyi had learned just how shaky his social standing was. News came that he was to shoulder the burden of serving as head of the "community compact,"[59] the institution that was initially designed to assemble members of rural communities for lectures on morality but assumed the functions of policing and tax collecting. In Taicang, intimates one brief comment by Lu Shiyi, the community compact involved the collection of taxes and the drafting of laborers,[60] two tasks that burdened the organization's head with the responsibility of coercing an unwilling, indigent populace into compliance.

Word that he was to head the community compact arrived abruptly—and in a manner that resembled a bad dream of the sort recounted in short stories about strange events and anomalies. The summons came when Lu, having just heard rumors that the city of Yangzhou was under siege, and worrying about his younger brother being there, had returned home to sit for a while. Suddenly a man in black dress appeared. At first Lu thought the intruder was a neighbor's friend who had stumbled into the wrong house. He then realized that this was a geomancer serving as a messenger. As recounted by Lu: "From his sleeve he took out the subprefect's calling card ordering me to take the position of compact head (*yuezheng*). . . . I suddenly felt distraught, and I behaved and spoke with extreme rudeness. I neither bowed nor asked him to be seated; I only blurted out, 'I certainly cannot undertake this responsibility. I hope that you will decline on my behalf.'" Then, reflecting that it recently had been difficult to decline the obligation, Lu had his servant ask the messenger to enter, meanwhile having decided to discuss with his friend Chen Hu a plan to get out of it.[61]

Desperately Lu tried to escape the service obligation, pulling whatever strings possible. He drafted a letter appealing the assignment and asked a friend's father to review it; the father, judging the letter to be "overly blunt in spots," suggested changes.[62] Soon after, Lu heard that the subprefect was to leave town. "Fearing that the matter would not be solved in time," he hastened to send him a note, using "forceful words explaining that I could not undertake it"; but the subprefect would not grant him permission.[63] He then collected the support of several friends and hastened over to Zhang Cai's place, again to press his case for "declining the responsibility of compact head." This time Lu argued what promised to be a persuasive line: "It would interfere with my studies." Recounted Lu: "Zhang Cai assented and ordered me to select someone as a replacement. In the past, those whose names had been called to serve as compact heads in the city had found it extremely difficult to decline, and I had been very worried about it; now that Zhang Cai was being helpful, I suddenly became exceedingly happy."[64]

Lu was vulnerable to the whims and movements of men above him. When he heard at Zhang Cai's place that the subprefect was talking about quitting the area, he was "both anxious and happy." He elaborated: "I was happy because of the promise that I would get to decline the responsibility for being the compact head. I was worried because the subprefect might leave."[65] Lu then paid a visit to an acquaintance to ask "who might be able to take on the responsibility of compact head." He also met with Chen Hu to stop a certain Wang Han from registering Lu's name in the roster of community-compact heads.[66] Arising early the next morning, Lu went to the place of Wang Han's son-in-law He Xuxi to make an appointment to go together "to decline the position of compact head,"[67] only to learn from Wang Han that his name had already been entered in the subprefectural register. Recounted Lu: "He therefore wished that I go with his son-in-law to Zhang Cai's place to investigate what the real situation was. At that time, because of various affairs, Zhang Cai was not taking visitors; without knocking at his door, I returned home."[68] Lu Shiyi was powerless.

Reviewing his behavior of the previous ten stressful days, Lu found that on the positive side he had faced the ordeal with equanimity: "For ten days, matters were confused, but my mind was very clear. Even while I was running around dealing with various matters right before a large study session was to take place, and even while I was at a banquet, listening to the music, and then, at the appointed time, was running again to and from the public hall because of the matter of heading the community compact—through all this my mind was exceptionally calm." Concluded Lu stoically: "This is also a test." On the negative side, he faulted himself because, "On hearing about the matter of the compact head, I became rattled."[69]

Lu's diary is frustratingly inconclusive as to whether he finally had to serve as compact head. A month after his flurried efforts to extricate himself from the obligation, he still had the topic of community compacts much on his mind. He mentioned reading an essay by Wang Yangming on community-compact methods, which was undoubtedly the famous "Community Compact for South Ganzhou" (Nan Gan xiangyue), describing an organization Wang had improvised to maintain order among the rebellious backwater population of Ganzhou, in southern Jiangxi.[70] Some weeks later, while Lu and his comrades were chatting about various subjects—the exemption of literati from labor services, cloud formations forecasting rain, and the unfairness of the labor services—they touched also on "salaries for the compact head"; the conversation left Lu "feeling satisfied."[71] The following day finds Lu compiling a notebook entitled "Miscellaneous Sayings about the Community Compact" (Xiangyue za shuo).[72]

Well before the black-robed messenger arrived with the unwelcome summons, Lu had shown an interest in the community-compact institution. In the autumn of 1640, he had composed a long piece, "Three Covenants for Governing the Rural Districts" (Zhixiang sanyue). Envisioning that community schools, community granaries, and mutual surveillance should be wrapped together in the community compact,[73] he defined the compact head as a pivotal figure through whom officials and ordinary persons communicate: all official notices concerning public matters are to be passed down to the head, who then should discuss them with the three local elders; all matters concerning the people are to be referred to the head, who will then communicate them to the officials. Taking as his standard the institutions of the idealized "three dynasties," the golden age of ancient times, he criticized the practices of his day: posts are filled by wealthy, unreliable people; tasks, instead of being dignified with the term *duties,* are demeaned with the term *labor services.*[74] Also before the summons, Lu had read a piece entitled "Land and Population Registers for the Compact Head" and had remarked on its being fraught with errors.[75]

Ironically, then, Lu's "Three Covenants"—which extended to thirty thoughtful pages—may have drawn attention to Lu as a suitable candidate for the position of compact head. In 1638, the subprefect, along with Zhang Cai and Zhang Pu, had energetically promoted the community-compact system to deal with unrest in the vast area under his jurisdiction, which encompassed the neighboring district of Kunshan as well.[76] The major source of trouble was the Gang Stars Society (Gang hui or Tian Gang hui)—a band about which little is known other than that it pursued its nefarious goals with the cooperation of conniving bondservants. The subprefect determined that a compact head and assistant should be assigned to each of the established administrative divisions in the area: the twenty-four wards (*pu*) of the city and suburbs and the twenty-nine subdivisions (*du*) of the adjacent territory. The meetings would begin with a lecture on the Six Maxims, after which the heads would record the names of the good people and have evil doers put in cangues and beaten. In the cities and suburbs, the responsibility for lecturing on the Six Maxims would fall on members of the gentry; in the villages and towns, upon the compact head.[77]

Lu wrote his essay "Three Covenants" shortly after the subprefect had initiated the community compact. Having remained stuck in the status of licentiate for eight years, he may have done so to win recognition for his talents. Or, aware of the subprefect's new administration, he may have wished to ensure that the status of the compact head would be elevated. Whatever the case, his desperate efforts to extricate himself reveal his marginal status. Although he had some access to the men in authority, he was ultimately powerless to alter their decisions—so different from Chen Longzheng, who, even before earning the *jinshi* degree, was able to elicit from Ding Bin sanction for his benevolent society. Just as Lu's flat dreams failed to transport him to other realms, so too in real life did he remain mired in the ordinary, suspended uneasily between his respectable goals and humble reality, between a wish to belong and a state of marginality.[78] Self-doubtful and vacillating, he judged himself one day as "predominantly indolent" and another day as "predominantly serious." Though seeking self-improvement, he remained immobilized.

LU SHIYI THE BENEFACTOR

Hovering at the margins of the elite, his social status ambiguous, Lu was both beneficiary and benefactor. He was in a position of dependency when he asked a friend's father to edit a letter and generally tried to win support for avoiding the compact headship. But he also wished to cast himself as a benefactor who readily shouldered the cares of his community. One day he instructed his wife to discuss with an old woman living behind them that they should look after the well-being of "widowers, widows, orphans, and the childless"—that is, persons who lacked relations on whom they could rely for support.[79] On another day, which he graded "serious," he wrote: "I went toward the Pond for Releasing Animals. I saw the starving sleeping in the grass, almost beyond salvation. Whereupon I thought that the method of distributing gruel had two faults: the old and weak cannot survive on one meal a day, and the able-bodied youths mix in and get food, with the result that too much grain is wasted."[80] And when tallying up his deeds for the middle of the fourth month, he entered in the favorable "serious" column: "A day spent on benevolent society matters. . . . I showed compassion to the isolated and widowed."[81]

Lu's dual identity as benefactor and beneficiary again shows up in the seventh month of 1641—by which time it had become evident that the harvest would fail.[82] On the one hand, he was identified by other members of the local elite as a "poor scholar" in need of a stipend; on the other, he tried to assert himself as a man of noblesse oblige. As Lu told it: "The poor scholars of the subprefecture were being given monthly stipends of four and a half *dou* of rice. Wang Shangbin submitted my name as well.[83] I was about to decline. Chen Hu cited the precedent from *The Analects:* 'In villages and among neighbors, there is the benevolence of helping one another.'[84] Deeply agreeing with him, I then thought to divide the monthly allotments into three portions: one to be given to my younger brother Zhongyuan—he originally was not registered here, and because he has been abroad for a long time and has not returned, his family is in need; one to be given to Yuruo's orphan; and one to be distributed among poor households."[85] A man of limited means, Lu assumed the role of benefactor in a small way, redistributing funds not from his own pocket but from an unexpected windfall.

PLANS TO ESCAPE

In dealing with the impending threat of disorder, Lu characteristically followed a divided strategy. As a resident of Taicang, with landholdings to protect and obligations to his family and community, he prepared to fight the dangers straight on. At the same time, he made arrangements to escape to safer ground. As early as 1633, right after becoming a licentiate, he and his friend Chen Hu "both understood that before long there would be a great upheaval."[86] This was when pirates were escalating their raids along the coast[87]—the same year when a typhoon filled Chen Longzheng with premonitions of bandit raids. Lu practiced martial arts with a military man who had been invited to the area to train local troops in defense. He studied existing military manuals and, finding these too impractical, himself wrote *An Explanation of Eight Military Formations* (*Ba chenfa ming*), a work replete with illustrations on battle formations.[88] Presumably, he was well poised to meet attacks that might come his town's way.

Conditions during the autumn of 1638 strengthened Lu's conviction that the area of Jiangnan was headed for disaster. For months, no rain had fallen.

"The sprouts," he observed, "had all withered and the land was burnt so red and hard that it was impossible to insert wheat seedlings. The streams and wells in the cities and market places had all dried up. Shouldering buckets, the residents vied with one another to draw water from the rivers. But then the rivers also dried up, and so they dug wells over one *zhang* [roughly twelve feet] deep along the river beds to draw water." Water carried in cost fifteen *wen*"[89]—nearly as much, in other words, as a *sheng* of grain had in 1638.[90] Making matters worse were the changes in planting strategies that had temporarily generated prosperity in Lu's region: farmers had shifted from growing food crops to producing cotton and tobacco, "thus cutting off the source of life," grain.[91]

Aware that food shortages will usher in banditry, Lu composed a work entitled *A Complete Book on Defending City Walls* (*Chengshou quanshu*).[92] Yet, it did not escape his notice that conditions were nearly hopeless. In his essay "Three Strategies for Escaping the Area" (Bidi san ce), he recalled the red dust of the previous year: "People with foresight construed this dust as the harbinger of a drought. This year the red dust is even worse. Spreading across the skies, it looks like fire at dawn and dusk and brings disastrous drought and locusts that destroy the next generation of seeds. Thinking about next year chills my heart."[93] Throughout 1641 bad news poured in. One acquaintance spoke of cannibalism among people in the north.[94] An out-of-town visitor's talk of bandits attacking Yangzhou prompted Lu to imagine a descent into barbarism similar to one described in the ancient text *Zuo's Commentary* (*Zuo zhuan*): in the year 637 B.C., the sight of a man "sacrificing in the wilderness with disheveled hair" was interpreted to mean that the place would be occupied by the Rong tribes from the west.[95] Observed Lu: "Today the conditions of the Central Plain are also like this. I fear that behavior in future calamities will exceed even the barbaric." That day Lu noted that "his mind wandered" and that he "was unable to concentrate on composing essays." He then started to discuss with friends "the matter of escaping the turmoil."[96]

The next month, Xiangyang City (in Huguang, on the Han River) was flooded;[97] and the Grand Canal, which was crucial for shipping grain from Jiangnan to Beijing, was obstructed. Upon hearing this and that the wheat in his area had withered, Lu "went outside the city gates to take a look."[98] He then turned his thoughts to the timing of relief: "If one starts soup kitchens too early, then I fear that it would be difficult to sustain them when the seventh or eighth month comes around."[99] Inexorably the subject of soup kitchens now attracted attention. On a walk by a shrine that housed a soup kitchen, Lu's companion insisted on taking a look even though a placard firmly stated: "Loiterers stepping beyond this point will be fined some rice."[100]

The fifth month brought locusts. Wrote Lu: "They are covering the skies throughout Tanshan circuit. Everywhere appears to be endless fog. Jiangnan has never had this kind of disaster." Then, thinking back on recent years, he pondered: "This has happened every year from 1638 on, but this year is the worst. . . . I know not how to stop it."[101] The seventh month brought word that the bandit Gold Star was plotting rebellion; the eighth month news of pirate raids; and the ninth month delivered yet another blow: the ruin of the cotton crop.[102] "The footloose, unreliable men of the subprefecture have all lost their livelihood," noted Lu, adding: "Gambling has resurfaced. The subprefect is trying to curb this with strict laws, and imprisonments daily increase. I fear, however, that dealing with these unusually wild types who are bent on self-destruction—and to do so without nourishing and instructing them but only through prohibitions and arrests—is like dealing with uncontrollable river floods."[103]

Lu's interest in military techniques was briefly rekindled during the stressful late summer months of 1641. He practiced archery, which he had neglected during the three years' mourning for his father, and he ran through military drills, joining friends Wang Dengshan and Chen Hu to practice with spears, an exercise he declared "very beneficial for strengthening the shoulders and legs," adding that "if one shows fatigue, one must practice."[104] He devised plans to resist pirates, and he worried about defense even in his dreams. Once he dreamed of a certain kind of crossbow for shooting birds; four days later he made a drawing of it and commissioned someone to construct it.[105]

Nonetheless Lu also showed signs of losing interest in, or perceiving the futility of, military preparations. One day he expressed annoyance at neighbors who were creating a ruckus drilling with spears, noting: "Repeatedly I thought to chase them away. I could not concentrate and by evening, when they had finished, I had not yet completed work on a composition."[106] Even while planning for military defense, he was contemplating the alternative he had first envisioned in 1638: to escape.[107] In the fourth month of 1641, he discussed with several friends "the pleasure of escaping the territory in order to study," and came around to accepting the friends' choice of place for the planned retreat: "Today I see three advantages: to enjoy the scenery, to advance one's study of geography, and to avoid being conscripted as the compact's assistant head."[108]

Coalescing around the idea of escape were friends of similarly marginal status. While studying one day, Lu and fellow licentiate Gu Shilian were suddenly interrupted by another student, Zhou Jiaping, who, recounted Lu, "came bearing news that roving pirates had attacked Anqing prefecture (in Nanzhili); he wanted to form a covenant with the various friends about plans for leaving the area." Lu told him about the plans for going northwest. Zhou concurred, commenting on the availability of paddies there. Gu Shilian— about whom little is known other than that he was active in the Taicang benevolent society—"also gladly wished to participate," noted Lu. After discussing the matter for half a day the friends parted.[109]

Later that day, Lu browsed through the *Record of Military Preparedness* (*Wubei zhi*)—an enormous work in 140 chapters (*juan*), whose author, writing around 1620, had been much alarmed by the vulnerability of China's borders and deeply concerned about national defense.[110] Yet, a few days later, on a day he rated as "serious," he wrote, "I went everywhere making agreements with various friends about a hiding place, rushing about all day. Fortunately, the friends, who all concurred about the matter of a hiding place, assembled to formulate plans, to be undertaken five years hence. Although the matter has been settled today, precise details remain up in the air. Such is the difficulty of completing a project."[111]

Lu's thoughts of escape would eventually connect with images of an idyllic otherworld, particularly with a fantasy that the ancient poet Tao Yuanming had conjured up in his renowned essay "Peach Blossom Spring" (Taohua yuan ji). Tao tells of a fisherman who one day wandered behind a spring into a hillside cave, thence entering a hidden world. Residing there, peacefully and utterly carefree, were the descendants of refugees from the chaos following the collapse of the Qin dynasty. It was around 1644 or 1645, after Lu and his friends did in fact flee to a rural hideaway, that Lu reminisced about his longings, dating to his childhood, for such an "ideal territory" as that described by Tao. By then, the analogy between his own collapsed dynasty and a fallen dynasty of the past was painfully clear.[112]

COOPERATION AND COMPETITION

In the midst of this gathering storm, torn between wanting to solve his town's problems and wanting to escape them, Lu joined several friends in forming a benevolent society—the institution that Gao Panlong and Chen Longzheng had seen as an alternative to the community compact for ordering local society. According to his son's posthumous account, society members "daily collected money and rice to aid the starving people; consequently innumerable people survived."[113]

In managing the benevolent society, the various "brothers"—Lu Shiyi and his young student-friends—lacked ultimate authority over the funds and the lists of recipients. When fellow licentiate Gu Shilian went to discuss the benevolent society with the subprefect, Lu learned that the subprefect wished to "entrust the matter to Zhang Cai; it was as though," commented Lu in his diary, the subprefect "could not completely trust the various 'brothers.'"[114] The upshot was that the subprefect would take charge of the names recommended to receive society aid and that former official Zhang would manage the finances.[115]

Lu Shiyi initially appeared eager to involve himself in the benevolent society. When he sent in his monetary contribution, he tried to ascertain how the benevolent society was to be managed, prompting Gu Shilian to "take out the regulations." As told by Lu, the first item stipulated: "Before the meeting day, prepare a jointly signed petition inviting the subprefect, and also Zhang Cai, to take the seats of honor and lecture on the Way." The contract spurred Lu to be "very outspoken." Stressing the need for unity, he argued that the authority over the benevolent society ought to revert to the subprefect and that they ought not to have a "private society"—that is, a society run without official sanction. He further opined that "it is fitting" that the subprefect should himself formally invite Zhang Cai to lecture. Reported Lu in his diary: the various friends, "listening with trepidation to my forthright words, agreed. Consequently they wished that I write a letter to the subprefect. Without shirking, I took on the responsibility."[116]

Lu showed pride in his role, the next day reporting, "On behalf of the benevolent society, I have written a letter to the subprefect," then adding, somewhat self-importantly: "To write when able to do so is to be generous/righteous (*yi*). Not to give when unable to give is also to be generous/righteous. This time, I felt no obstacles in my heart. I slept alone and my dreams were upright."[117] In his summation for that ten-day period, under the rubric "Learning How to Govern and Bring Peace" (Zhiping zhi xue), Lu proudly reiterated: "Representing the benevolent society, I wrote a letter to the subprefect."[118] In the subsequent ten-day accounting, he again derived self-esteem from his participation: "I managed writing up the report on the benevolent society and got some private satisfaction from it."[119]

Such were the power relations in his town, however, that Lu was relegated to the role of letter writer and gofer and had little, if any, latitude for leadership. The ultimate authority for operating the benevolent society apparently belonged to the subprefect; the privilege of addressing the first assembly went to the retired official Zhang Cai; and nitty-gritty tasks—writing letters, making arrangements, and distributing the funds—went to the young licentiates, the stipended students Lu Shiyi, Gu Shilian, Chen Hu, and Zhou Jiaping. In return for their cooperation, the benevolent society provided the students with opportunities to demonstrate their talents and to gain some access to, even to form relationships with, men in power. Moreover, unlike the community compact, which promised to scatter students among the numerous administrative subdivisions within the district, the benevolent society brought them together, fostering camaraderie among them, all the while giving them an uplifting feeling of doing good.

The guidelines that Yang Dongming itemized for the benevolent society of his hometown, Yucheng, were tidy and authoritative, giving the impression that its members were in harmonious agreement. A similar set of guidelines, or contract, had also been composed for the benevolent society of Taicang. Lu obliquely mentioned it; and Chen Hu tried in the summer of 1641 to add two items to the "Regulations for the Benevolent Society" (Tongshan hui gui): to respect elders by making known their humaneness and longevity; and to practice archery so as to be militarily prepared. His suggestions, which he had to present to the official in charge, were not put into effect.[120] A contract, once committed to paper, held up the promise that an arrangement would be definite and above dispute. Yet, from the vantage point of Lu's diary, the actual situation is more visible than is the ideal: whenever fresh situations developed, the guidelines left plenty of room for interpretation—and debate.

The young scholars of Taicang were not only cooperative but also, inevitably, competitive. After Gu had the privilege of meeting with the subprefect about "the benevolent society matter" and brought back word that Zhang Cai should be in charge, Lu used his diary to set himself above Gu. He criticized Gu for failing to communicate the news effectively and labeled him "brash."[121] In another diary entry he explained that, "because the participants' names had already been registered, he did not wish the benevolent society to break up," even though Gu was not being compliant; after consulting with Chen Hu, he decided to let Gu do as he pleased.[122] One day, which he rated as "serious," Lu appeared to have reached a modus vivendi with Gu. "I was at the 'office' (quan) reading essays," he wrote, when "Gu Shilian came to confer about the benevolent society: he wished to swear an oath before the spirits. Chen Hu and I both praised him." An amicable and convivial mood had apparently been restored. They discussed methods for studying, and when Gu was taking his leave, "there was joking."[123]

The benevolent society of Taicang met twice a year, on the fifteenth day of the fourth and tenth months. The program had two parts: a moralizing lecture followed by the distribution of aid. At the first meeting noted by Lu, on a day he rated himself as "predominantly serious," Lu's sense of personal involvement in the program is evident. Immediately after he and his friend Chen Hu arrived at the Temple of the City God, where the meeting was to be held, they wanted to improve the arrangements. Explained Lu, "We saw that the lecture mat had been set up inside the hall; this would make it difficult for the masses to hear, so we conferred with the various brothers about moving it outside."[124] About the lecture itself, he excitedly wrote: "We heard Zhang Cai lecture to the benevolent society. His words were exciting, and the entire audience was filled with admiration. The subprefect looked pleased; I too was extremely pleased." Then, feeling the exhilaration of the moment, he loftily declared: "The subprefect likes worthiness (haoxian) and takes pleasure in doing good (leshan); we can look forward to peace in the region."[125]

Lu felt honored to have participated in the solemn and grand occasion but was less committed to the benevolent society than, say, Chen Longzheng, who envisioned the benevolent society of Jiashan enduring indefinitely and who would later that same year set up an endowment for a benevolent-society hall. In contrast, Lu was unconcerned about the benevolent society's future, wishing mainly that the organization would ensure peace so that, as he put it, "my kind may study in tranquility."[126]

Zhang Cai's motivational lecture gave the first meeting of the Taicang benevolent society an auspicious start. Right after the formal ceremony, however, tensions between Lu Shiyi and Gu Shilian were reignited, this time involving the business of distributing funds at an official building, to which the comrades proceeded. Lu "wanted to separate the men and women in two places, dividing them to the left and right." Grumbling that Gu Shilian "would not listen," Lu again settled scores in his diary: "Gu Shilian shouted out the names, issuing the money first to the men, very slowly. The old women who were waiting to receive handouts were suffering extreme hunger and fatigue. The various 'brothers' and myself all felt great pity for them, and we wished, moreover, to make the distributions to men and women separately. Gu Shilian monopolized the affair without heeding us. Chen Hu thought that this was simply because Gu Shilian lacked talent; and that we should conclude the proceedings nonetheless. I strongly agreed with Chen Hu but was deeply unhappy about Gu Shilian's obstinacy."[127]

Cohesion among the students was fragile. Two days after this flare-up, Lu and Chen Hu tried to extricate themselves from the benevolent society. That day, which he marked "serious," Lu wrote: "I discussed with Gu Shilian the matter of the autumn meeting of the benevolent society. Chen Hu and I wished to take our names off the list, but circumstances were such that it would not be permissible. It was feared that on the contrary it would wreck the matter. So we said that it would be unnecessary to remove our names, but that we would not be able to take responsibility for the labor. We wanted exceptions to be made for the two of us."[128]

When the time came round for the benevolent society's autumn meeting, on the fifteenth day of the tenth month, tensions again erupted, with worries about the failed grain and cotton crops no doubt aggravating the matter. Before the meeting, society members had sent in their contributions,[129] and made recommendations regarding who might be worthy recipients of aid. Lu attended the meeting at the Temple of the City God, where he listened to the subprefect lecture. As before, he sharply criticized how things were managed: "The distribution of benevolent-society money was poorly supervised, chaotic, and unregulated. One reason was that Zhou Jiaping did not firmly uphold the rules. Another reason was that He Xuxi [Wang Han's son-in-law] and Gu Shilian did not respect the rules. They were weak on fundamental issues and strong on trivial details. Truly unmanageable."[130] Lu then added: "In the temple were many poor people whose names had not been recommended. Zhou Jiaping stubbornly refused to give them money. I told him that everyone should receive a little charity. When the time came to issue money, the various friends again brawled, each with different opinion. I stuck to my view and would not listen. Had everything been done according to my regulations, the whole matter would have been orderly. Later I heard that some persons were blaming me, although their statements were groundless. Anyhow, who does not have some small character flaw? The main point is that, when something happens, one must keep the peace. Yet the various friends were extremely disorderly. If one speaks to them gently, they won't listen. What can one do about it?"[131] Who was the truly stubborn one is unclear. Yet, the lack of clarity itself conveys a message: the disagreements were among "brothers" who were much alike—Gu and Lu remained friends into the next dynasty. The lack of a policy for dealing with the unrecommended individuals who showed up destitute at the meeting paved the way for disputes among the licentiates in charge of distributing the funds. Each used strong words to forward his own view; none had authority enough to outweigh the others.

FIVE BENEVOLENT-SOCIETY BENEFICIARIES

How many men and women were recommended to the Taicang benevolent society as destitute, what procedures were followed for selecting beneficiaries, and what criteria were used to define need? Of these matters the surviving records say nothing. Yet Lu's diary illuminates, often with stunning clarity, six needy cases. These cases slipped haphazardly into Lu's consciousness, and hence into his diary, because their lives had somehow become intimately entangled with his own. Whether they are representative of the beneficiaries of Taicang's benevolent society is impossible to gauge. In several cases, Lu had long been cognizant of a particular person's impecuniousness; then, only after the benevolent society had been formed, was he awakened to offer assistance. He settled on these cases not by canvassing poor households (as Chen Longzheng's guidelines had advocated), but because they had come to his attention through accidental encounters or special occasions.

Consider an event that occurred on the fifth day of the fifth month, which, though not labeled as such by Lu, happens to have been the time of the Dragon Boat Festival. After performing rituals appropriate to that day, Lu Shiyi, bearing the gift of a fish he had just purchased, paid a visit to his beneficent mother's side of the family. There the sight of his "elderly distant relatives" moved him to such pity that he resolved: "In the autumn, I must recommend them to the benevolent society."[132] A meeting on a festival day thus stirred him spontaneously to respond to a situation about which he must have long been familiar.

The spirit of a special occasion, a break in routine, likewise prompted Lu to make recommendations in two other instances. The first was a joyful event. On hearing of the birth of Chen Hu's son, the elated Lu went to see his friend, later commenting in his diary: "Chen Hu has long wished to recommend his parent to the benevolent society. But because the autumn meeting had not yet been convened, this has not yet been done." Aware that "Chen Hu's father also seemed pleased by the idea," and that "the utmost filiality" was involved, Lu then pressed the old man's cause: "Do we friends dare not push strongly for it?"[133] Three days later, Lu drafted a "public recommendation" (*gongju*) that Chen Hu's father be entered into the benevolent society's roster.[134]

Lu had known all along that Chen Hu's family was extremely poor. Chen Hu owed his early education to the good fortune of having been invited to take lessons with the children of the Jiang household (the youngest of whom, Jiang Shishao, was to remain a lifelong friend).[135] Subsequently he was invited to teach Lu's beneficent mother's younger brother.[136] Toward the end of 1641, Lu Shiyi is found discussing Chen Hu's finances with an acquaintance who suggested that they ask "several of Chen Hu's top students to agree to pay a teacher's salary to help him through the present emergency."[137] Chen's father, Chaodian, had some pretensions to scholarship but never earned an examination degree; after the Ming fell, he followed Chen Hu into hiding in Wei Village, Kunshan, and to the end of his days remained dependent on his son.[138] But the most forceful testimony to the relative poverty of the Chen family is that Lu, nearly a full month before recommending Chen Hu's father to the benevolent society, had discussed with Chen Hu and Qian Fanhou the matter of forming a money-lending society (*jinhui*) because, explained Lu in his diary, "Chen Hu was cleaned out of funds."[139] What prompted Lu to move ahead with the recommendation was not new knowledge about the financial conditions of Chen Hu's family—although by this time, the seventh month, it must have been clear to everyone that the autumn harvest would be dismal. Rather, what prompted Lu to act was a break in routine, occasioned by news of the birth. Not only did the event open Lu's eyes to what had long been the case; it also generated good feelings within his social circle, giving him an opportunity to prevail upon his "friends" to help the Chen family.

In another case, that of a friend's uncle, the decision to make a recommendation to the benevolent society appears to have been entirely impulsive. In the eleventh month, when food supplies were rapidly declining, Lu and three friends (Zao Fen, Chen Hu, and Sheng Jing) went by boat to the prefectural city to take examinations. There they stayed with Zao Fen's uncle. Observing that his friend's "uncle was old, alone, and childless," Lu noted in his diary: "I had the thought that I should bring him to the attention of the benevolent society. Chen Hu had the same thought. I must make a point of remembering to do this."[140]

Lu also recommended that a great-uncle of the sixth branch of his own lineage receive benevolent-society aid. The uncle had been sojourning in Tongting, Hunan, where he taught in a village school. Being without family,

he had returned east to seek a livelihood, and had already solicited and received some beneficence (*hui*) from "various brothers." Thinking that the
great-uncle might receive additional benefits, thereby lightening the burden
on his kin, Lu mused in his diary: "Would this not also be fortunate for my
lineage?"[141]

Six weeks later, the great-uncle (whom Lu this time identified as having
the same great-grandfather as he) paid Lu a call. Lu reiterated in his diary
that the great-uncle had "returned home poor," this time elaborating: "His
brothers would not take him in; some of them leveled accusations at him,
stirring up resentments; they had neither food nor drink to give him. Destitute, he wanted to return home. He came to thank me for the benevolent
society's compassion of the other day. Pitying him, I had him stay for lunch."
Lu thought to discuss with a friend, Zhou Jiaping, the possibility of borrowing money to give him, but before he could make arrangements, the great-
uncle had left.[142]

Of the cases Lu noted as having conclusively recommended to the benevolent society, he spoke at greatest length about that of the widow of his
"brother" and close friend Yuruo, whose death, which occurred just before
the start of the extant diary, appears to have enlarged the void that had already been created by the loss of his father. Early in the diary, Lu commented
that he found Yuruo's son's refined behavior pleasing, "as though my friend
had not died."[143] Within a week, yearning to maintain a tie with his deceased
friend, Lu reasoned with his wife: "Yuruo's widow is chaste and extremely
poor, and her son is highly cultivated. I think we should betroth our daughter to him. Autumn would be a convenient time for completing the affair."
His wife, Lu noted, agreed to the proposal.[144] Subsequently he asked a mutual acquaintance for details about the chastity and family difficulties of Yuruo's widow after her husband's death, as well as about the horoscopes for
her son and Lu's daughter. Explained Lu, "Because I admired Yuruo's
widow's worthiness, I sympathized with her suffering."[145]

The friend's report was grim. "Such is her misfortune," he said, " that by
the fifth and sixth months, Yuruo's widow will have only one bowl of noodle
soup a day." Worse, he mentioned that "recently some monks and nuns have
moved into Yuruo's place." When the alarmed Lu asked for details, the friend
explained: "After Yuruo died, his widow's father, Li Huayu, moved in with
her. Huayu was also extremely poor and could not earn a living. Annexed
to the cottage was an empty room, which had, over time, fallen into disrepair. Huayu's nephew, who was escaping some sort of trouble, had come to
stay there, and he brought his wife's parents to live there as well. His wife
and her parents had already been putting up a monk and nun, which was
extremely improper. But because Huayu had made the repairs possible,
Yuruo's widow allowed it."[146] The defenseless widow had seen her home over-
taken by her father, her father's nephew, the nephew's wife's parents, and

monks and nuns, all of whom, with the possible exception of the nephew who funded the repairs, were desperately poor.

Lu inquired further about the "domestic situation," and the mutual friend reassured him, "'Yuruo's widow's motivations and behavior are extremely pure; this is beyond doubt.'" Lu then commissioned the friend "to go to the house and order Li Huayu to take his nephew and move out at once."[147] The next day, two friends and Chen Hu escorted Yuruo's son to Lu's house for a visit, after which they all proceeded to Yuruo's house to bow before Yuruo's coffin. When Chen Hu lifted the curtain, saw the coffin, and recalled the friendship of former days, he broke out into uncontrollable sobbing. Lu further recounted the episode as follows: "I told Li Huayu that it is unfitting to have monks and nuns running in and out of a widow's house, and that it would be best if he and his nephew would leave immediately." When Huayu seemed hesitant, Lu "told him straight out that his nephew, surnamed Li, could not reside in Ms. Zhang's house, and how much more so because he was sharing the place with a bunch of nuns and monks!"[148] Huayu finally acquiesced and, after taking a last look at the books and writing brushes left by "brother" Yuruo, he departed. Comforted that matters had been resolved, Lu wrapped up that day's diary entry: "My eyes hurt with dryness. I went to bed. I slept alone, and my dreams were upright."[149]

Five weeks later, Lu had cause to report: "We received the money from the benevolent society, which, together with contributions made by the various brothers, was sent over to Yuruo's widow's place."[150] Lu again tried to help Yuruo's widow some three months later, this time by writing a "public recommendation" that she—along with Chen Hu's father—be sponsored by the benevolent society.[151]

One needy case that Lu wanted to turn over to the benevolent society concerned a Fei Boyan, who had married into the Lu lineage, although his precise relationship to Shiyi is unclear. Boyan first appears late in Lu's diary, abruptly and with no introduction. Boyan was ill and needy. "After going to bed," reflected Lu in his diary, "I kept thinking of Fei Boyan. If he should die, he will still need burial clothes and a coffin. I have not inquired whether one can still get coffins from the benevolent society or not. Moreover, his children have no stability and would be unable to manage the funeral. I felt extremely anxious."[152] His social conscience aroused, Lu felt that he should aid this distant relation—though he really did not want to.

The next day Fei Boyan's son came to tell Lu of his father's illness, with the intention of borrowing money. Commented Lu: "To be sure, Boyan is a son-in-law in the Lu lineage. Formerly he borrowed five ounces of silver from my beneficent mother and two from me; and in three years he has repaid neither the principle nor the interest. Now he is critically ill, which grieves me even more. But because of the bad harvest, I gave him only one *sheng* of rice."[153] Lu's gift was measly, half the daily ration per soldier that he mentioned the previous year in reference to city defense.[154] Within the week Fei Boyan's son again visited Lu, this time carrying books he wished to exchange for money. "The books were almost useless," wrote Lu, "and I was short of money. Moreover, his family is lazy and brought the poverty on themselves. Especially in this famine year, I could not go down a well to save a man. I gave him one *sheng* of wheat."[155] Pondering that "Fei Boyan is ill and will surely die; and that even if he dies not of illness, he will die of starvation and after he dies there will surely be no coffin," Lu desperately ran around town to solicit support. "I went to Zhou Jiaping's place to ask about the benevolent society, but he was out. I visited He Xuxi and Gu Shilian; but they too were both out. I visited Xu Zijiu, who said that the benevolent society had long ago ceased to distribute coffins. Alas! This is Boyan's fate." He then tried to justify dismissing Fei as a lost cause. Availing himself of the rhetoric (so common to benevolent-society and community-compact lectures) about keeping a steady occupation, he concluded: "This can serve as a warning to those lazy drifters fond of leisure and eating."[156]

Whether these cases comprise all the recommendations for aid that Lu personally made to the benevolent society is unknown. His diary reveals neither how much the benefactors contributed nor how many beneficiaries the benevolent society aided. Nonetheless it shows that, for Lu Shiyi, the benevolent society compensated for where lineages failed. Though he lived in an area of prosperous lineages, his surviving corpus provides no evidence of an impulse toward lineage solidarity other than his brief mention that benevolent-society aid to his great-uncle would ultimately benefit his lineage.[157] Kinship ties in Lu's immediate social milieu appear to have been weak. His great-uncle was rejected by his own family; the hapless relative through marriage Fei Boyan was coldly regarded as an unwelcome burden by Lu; and the widow Yuruo received no aid from her relatives but was instead wrongly used by them. Lu's friend Chen Hu survived a deprived youth with no visible help from kin; what support he received came from patrons. Lu Shiyi and Chen Hu, the sons of mere school teachers, had few social connections, a lack for which they compensated by creating fictive kin: in 1650, on the occasion of Chen Hu's father's seventieth birthday, Lu declared: "Chen Hu regards me as an elder brother and I regard his father as my father."[158] The benevolent society lent assistance to those who lacked lineage support.

Lu's recounting of the benevolent society further proclaims another point, namely, that little separated Lu the benefactor from persons in desperate need. Little separated him from relatives such as his great-uncle and Fei Boyan's son, both of whom felt that they could justly make claims on his resources. Little separated him from his friend Zao Fen's uncle, with whom Lu lodged while waiting to take an examination, or from the father of his closest friend, Chen Hu. And little separated him from the widow of his dear friend Yuruo, to whose son Lu wished to betroth his daughter. Lu lived in proximity to, was related by blood or marriage to, and interacted socially with persons living on the remote fringes of elite society, the genteel poor.

Rather than making personal gifts to these acquaintances and relatives, Lu turned to the benevolent society. Possibly his own resources were truly inadequate to meet the demands that acquaintances and relatives made of him. So suggests the excuse he once offered for going out on a day when purification rituals required that he stay at home: "My household is poor and lacks servants."[159] So suggests his interest in a strategy that would enable rich and poor friends to form a corporation for buying land for their planned escape: after posing a rhetorical question—who among his comrades has surplus funds, the several hundred taels needed to buy land to which they might retreat?—Lu proposed that the comrades pool resources, each contributing according to his means and reaping profits proportionate to his share.[160] Lu's lack of resources is further documented by a diary entry right before the new year: "Because it is a year of dearth, I had little to offer the spirits. Never before have I been so shoddy, so crude."[161]

Though financially strapped, and certainly unable to match the grand gestures that Ding Bin and Chen Longzheng had made to save prisoners and other persons on the brink of death, Lu probably had some resources to spare. He had willingly distributed his scholarship stipend among persons more needy than himself, he had encouraged his wife to be charitable, and, in the end, he did provide a coffin for Fei Boyan. Lu had some latitude to act independently of the benevolent society, either by making small personal gifts or simply by flatly denying requests for aid. His choice to work through the benevolent society thus reintroduces a question that the case of Chen Longzheng has already posed, namely: how does giving through a group differ from giving directly to the needy? Materials unique to Lu Shiyi allow one to revisit this question in a new light.

Acting according to principles that its participants shared and openly declared to the entire community, the benevolent society reviewed and determined how to treat each case, thus removing the onus of decision making (whether to give and how much) from individual members. In putting a distance between donors and beneficiaries, the benevolent society buffered participants from the demands of persons like Fei Boyan—someone for whom Lu felt no sympathy, only burdensome responsibility. And yet, in three of six cases, Lu turned to (or thought of turning to) the benevolent society, not because he wished to shirk responsibility for others, but because he had been moved by compassion to take the initiative, volunteering aid even for persons (the friend's uncle, the beneficent mother's relatives) who had not asked for support. The benevolent society empowered participants to offer promises of help.

Regarding the cases for whom Lu did feel sympathy, the benevolent society put the beneficiaries at a *temporal* distance. Because the benevolent so-

ciety of Taicang met only twice yearly, a wait of many months often intervened between the moment when someone recognized a need and the time
when aid was given. When Lu thought to recommend that the poor members of his beneficent mother's family should receive benevolent-society aid,
the spring meeting had just passed and the autumn meeting was five months
away.[162] When Lu petitioned the society to help Chen Hu's father, the autumn meeting was three months off.[163] When he determined that he "must
make a point of remembering" to recommend the uncle of his friend Zao
Fen to the benevolent society, the autumn meeting had just taken place, so
Lu must have had in mind the distribution scheduled for spring, 1642, which
was five months away.[164] When intense special occasions—a birth, a trip to
take the examinations, and the loss of a friend—broke down his routine, Lu's
feelings of compassion for impoverished acquaintances and relatives welled
up. Moved to want to help yet aware that his own resources were limited, he
relied on the benevolent society's routine to temper his spontaneous feelings.

Lu's social world brought him into direct contact with ne'er-do-wells like
Fei Boyan as well as successful *jinshi*-degree holders like Zhang Cai, with victims of hard times and with men of ample means. Maneuvering his way between the extremes was challenging, arousing in him a sense of equity and
a desire for communion, that "oneness with all things" celebrated by many
thinkers. The longing for oneness is evident in a diary entry concerning his
sojourn in the prefectural capital to take a civil service examination, where
Lu explained why he gave up his habit of consuming three meals daily: "Although I am poor, in times of peace and prosperity, I never went by on just
two meals a day; or if on rare occasions I did, then after a while I was decidedly hungry. But because this year's harvest is bad and resources horribly
stressed, the various 'brothers' at the lodge are all eating only two meals a
day. I have joined them in this, without feeling hungry."[165] Not desperate in-
digence, but empathy, the desire to be like his comrades, prompted Lu to
tighten his belt.

The evening after he despaired about financing a coffin for the idler Fei
Boyan, Lu was invited to a banquet. Late that night, he uneasily recorded
that "the banquet was overly sumptuous" and then reasoned, somewhat de-
fensively: the host could well afford it; the banquet was not just for the two
of them; and, "moreover, it would also have been somewhat reprehensible
to eat with the same frugality and self-restraint as on ordinary days."[166] A single day juxtaposed lavish banqueting and Fei Boyan's needs; and the calculus that Chen Longzheng and others made explicit—that the cost of one
banquet could save hundreds of lives—was running through Lu's mind as
well. Knowing that he was participating in the benevolent society must have
allowed him to move, without feeling overly conscience-stricken, between
the realm of banquet hosts and that of students surviving on two meals a day.
The benevolent society not only offered the needy help; it also served as a

reminder—sustained over the months that intervened between the recommendation and the distribution—that the haves had the well-being of the have-nots in mind. In this connection one thinks of Chen Hu, who himself participated in the benevolent society while his own father was considered poor enough to qualify for benevolent-society aid: in claiming that the gifts represented a higher good, apart from need, the benevolent society must have also lightened the beneficiaries' feelings of personal indebtedness.

LOCAL SOCIETY VIEWED FROM ABOVE

Had Lu Shiyi's diary not survived, our picture of the Taicang benevolent society—indeed, of all late Ming benevolent societies—would be entirely from the viewpoint of power holders at the top of local society. Consider the formal account left by Zhang Cai, the retired official whose lecture Lu had heard at the benevolent society's spring meeting. Zhang placed his sponsorship of the benevolent society in the context of his peers' activities elsewhere: "Observing friends setting up such societies in Weitang (a town in Jiashan district, Zhejiang), I was moved; and seeing it subsequently established in Lucheng, I was even more deeply moved. Although I have been on the brink of death for two years, this idea would not recede from my mind, and while sick, I set up an agenda and rules, and had them printed to be promulgated."[167] Uplifted by the promise that the benevolent society will bring order, Zhang filled his essay with pious rhetoric, starting with, "Everyone is by nature good. . . . The ancients of former times had joined together to establish these 'compassionate societies (*cihui*),'" and ending with reassurances that the small good efforts of gentlemen will ultimately "bring harmony."[168] No less a leader than Yang Dongming, Gao Panlong, and Chen Longzheng, Zhang viewed the benevolent society as a vehicle for uniting the community. "Just as ditches will channel the water," he wrote, the regulations for a benevolent society will mobilize men to do good. Brief and platitudinous, Zhang's essay reduced to three pages an activity that occupied Lu Shiyi for many days. Without the complement of Lu's diary, with its details about Taicang, Zhang's account dangles, uncontextualized, in a vaguely defined past.

Nor does one learn much about the benevolent society of Taicang from the extant writings of the subprefect who lent his authority to the benevolent society, first by attending the spring meeting and then by lecturing at the autumn meeting. The subprefect was Qian Sule[169]—although Lu referred to him only by title, so deep and wide was the chasm between licentiate and high official. Immediately after earning the *jinshi* degree in 1637, Qian was assigned to Taicang, a place known to outsiders as a "difficult post."[170] He displayed compassion; placing a high value on all forms of life, he had for many years instructed his household to stick to a vegetarian diet.[171] He was also a strict and capable administrator.

It was Qian who, aided by Taicang townsmen Zhang Cai and Zhang Pu, had instituted in 1638 both the community-compact system to inculcate moral values and the mutual-surveillance system to enforce security. Additionally, he had the embankments along the lakes and rivers repaired.[172] In 1639, he assembled the local gentry and rural elders twice a month for lectures on the Six Maxims, chastising his listeners for "drinking and whoring with a handful of friends while allowing their elders to starve, and with no regard for their wives' suffering." Assuming that commercial enterprises gave rise to instability, he further chastised them for being so restless as to work as "farmers by day and merchants by night."[173]

To each of the subprefecture's twenty-nine divisions (*du*) Qian appointed a compact head and assistant head. The program for the community-compact meetings called for a lecture on the Six Maxims, after which the names and deeds of good persons were inscribed on a red placard. Music was played and honorary banners distributed. Wrongdoers were then registered on a white placard and brought before the authorities for a flogging.[174]

Qian's administrative abilities were put to the test by the food shortage of the summer of 1640. Driven by starvation, several thousand residents of neighboring Kunshan (which was also under Qian's jurisdiction) took to rioting. Among their targets over a two-day siege were the prefect's residence, a certain timber merchant, and merchants from Huizhou. Qian rushed out from Taicang to quell the uprising. He made arrests and had two of the perpetrators executed, whereupon the mobs disbanded. He had good and bad persons commended and chastised respectively on red and white placards. Order returned. Understanding the root of the problem to be not the rowdies but the households that were hoarding grain, Qian nudged residents to issue rice at fair prices. Consequently, "over ten thousand people survived and order was restored to Kunshan."[175]

Materials by and about Qian dovetail with one entry in Lu Shiyi's diary about a ceremony at which Qian prayed (with success) for rain and several entries about a scourge of locusts. Qian himself rode out to the fields to lead people of all social strata to capture the locusts. He also made it known that, for each *sheng* caught, he would pay one *sheng* of rice, a policy that resulted in locusts being "piled as high as mountains both inside and outside the official headquarters."[176] Though not identified by name, Qian must have been the official who, according to Lu's diary, held a meeting on the first day of the fourth month at a shrine for all the community-compact heads and assistant heads from the urban and the rural areas. (This was about three weeks before Lu would be summoned to serve as a compact head.) Lu accompanied friends Chen Hu and Wang Chengzhao to take a look. As reported by

Lu: "Almost the entire city (*cheng*) had poured out to observe the event, and it was the biggest meeting the city (*yi*) had in one hundred years."[177] No doubt this was the meeting described by Zhang Cai in which Qian's lecture on the Six Maxims roused everyone, moving some to tears.

If impressed by the size of the community-compact gathering, Lu did not feel uplifted. With cool, critical detachment he noted: "Unfortunately the rituals were incorrect and could not rouse feelings of reverence in the observers."[178] For Zhang Cai's benevolent-society lecture two weeks later, Lu would, in contrast, express enthusiasm and would specifically remark that Zhang's lecture also pleased the subprefect, that is, Qian.[179] Lu took pride in those benevolent-society proceedings in which he had a role as organizer. At the community-compact meeting, however, he was a mere observer, diminished by the enormous audience—knowledgeable enough to criticize the proceedings but without authority to act.

When the licentiates were quibbling over arrangements for the benevolent society in 1641, Qian the official was dealing with problems on a grand scale. He commanded the authority to convene the compact heads from all twenty-nine divisions and to attract virtually everyone from the city to hear him lecture; to him, addressing the benevolent society must have seemed a small affair. While Lu was dealing with problems immediately affecting his own family and friends, Qian focused on troubles looming on the horizon. He was concerned about the formation of dangerous bands and sects—such as the Gang Stars, the Rice Cake Society (Cituan), the Black Dragon (Wulong), and the Ten Dragons (Shilong); this is why, according to his own account, he urgently promulgated the Six Maxims.[180] These sects, explains the *Taicang Subprefectural Gazetteer* (*Taicang zhou zhi*) of 1678, were "private" associations that set up a communal treasury, to which members made contributions assessed on their wealth. Among the members were pettifoggers, guarantors, and yamen personnel. When facing some difficulty, a member could draw upon the treasury. The most visible such group in the subprefecture was the Black Dragon Society, which dissipated when confronted by subprefect Qian's punitive campaign.[181]

Qian worried, too, about the possibility of a future grain shortage. After confronting the food riots in Kunshan in 1640, he put in place mechanisms for maintaining the well-being of the local populace; and, when the food shortage hit in 1641, he had gruel kitchens installed at each of Taicang's four gates and supplied by the ever-normal granary. For the poorest there was rice; and for the next poorest, price reductions. As a result, the records insist, the subprefecture did not suffer from starvation.[182]

And yet, for all his energetic activism, Qian's extant writings make no mention of the benevolent society. One piece about Qian alludes to the Taicang benevolent society, but this is in a late nineteenth-century work whose compiler may have retrospectively deduced (from Lu's writings, for example), without direct evidence, that Qian was the benevolent society's founder. Most briefly the entry recounts Qian's accomplishments (praying for rain, waging battle against locusts, quelling grain riots, and encouraging the great households to make grain available for relief, thus lowering the prices); and then notes: "He established a procedure for preparing gruel, and, to show compassion for the good sorts of people, he started a benevolent society. Many lives were saved."[183] From the official Qian's point of view, large-scale programs for soup kitchens and the stabilization of grain prices were more urgent and more effective than anything the benevolent society could accomplish.

When Qian, having just been promoted to the Ministry of Justice, was about to depart the area in 1642, the residents of Taicang and Kunshan jointly celebrated his humane and effective governance, thus lending support to the glowing assessments of his administration and his relief efforts. His hagiographers completely gloss over gruesome conditions observed by Lu, who wrote: "An especially severe food shortage, coupled with freezing weather, caused an unknown number of people to die of starvation; in villages and alleyways, no sign of life could be found." Lu elaborated: "Moreover, faced with this food shortage, the men and women who had loafed about and been fond of food and drink without pursuing a livelihood were even more at loose ends than before. I have heard of many cases in which women let themselves be violated in order to survive. Customs have deteriorated to this extent. Those men who would nurture the people must blame themselves."[184]

Lu's worst forebodings were confirmed six weeks later, when, right in front of the subprefectural headquarters, he witnessed a woman eating her own child. Commenting that "the Way proper to the world has been altogether subverted," and observing that such behavior would be unspeakable even in the famine-stricken Central Plains, he expressed horror that it should have occurred in his own area and, worse, that the subprefect merely chastised the woman and evicted her from the territory.[185] Lu criticized "the worthy types who adamantly upheld the view that she ought not be killed." A stickler for good form, he concluded that human beings are more depraved than animals.[186] To avoid sinking to the level of the common lot, the marginalized Lu held tight to "what is fitting." Subprefect Qian Sule, his sights firmly set on maintaining order and minimizing hunger, no doubt grasped a message that the mother's horrendous deed, committed in front of his headquarters, conveyed: local officials had not done enough for the starving poor. Flexible and magnanimous in these extraordinarily difficult circumstances, he settled for expelling the blight from the district.

CONCLUSION

With its close-up view of local life and displays of sordid details—monks and nuns infiltrating a widow's household and squabbling students, not to mention matters extraneous to the benevolent society, such as a messy brawl at a friend's house and attempts to forestall seedy litigation—Lu's diary may seem to be more realistic, more accurate, than the formulaic accounts left by Yang Dongming, Chen Longzheng, and Gao Panlong. But to dismiss the platitudes in favor of Lu's intimate account is to miss an important point: optimistic visions of social harmony uplifted Yang, Chen, and Gao and gave them exceptional powers. Key to their successful leadership was their ability to move beyond all obstacles, to look past the wretched details of ordinary society. Rising above the mundane, they inspired followers such as Lu Shiyi, who was roused by Zhang Cai's benevolent-society lecture. Optimistic platitudes served a communal purpose. When Qian lightly let off the woman who had cannibalized her child, Lu Shiyi expressed moral indignation. But it was Qian who, focusing on such weighty issues as food distribution, successfully maintained order in a post that, even before the hard years of 1640 and 1641, had been labeled difficult; and it was Qian who, like Zhang Cai, articulated a benevolent-society program in terms that won broad appeal.

Though it exposes the underside of Taicang society, Lu Shiyi's diary does not discredit the accounts of visionary leaders. Rather, as a contrasting example it suggests that leadership went to those residents who held authority, had resources to preserve, and—for personality also played a role, as the case of Wang Gen illustrates—were optimistically self-confident.

PART TWO

Enacting Charitable Routines during a Crisis

6

Mobilizing Food Relief

*The various friends had some disagreements, probably because they could
not completely put aside all the thoughts of favors owed and grudges held.*

QI BIAOJIA

The severe food shortage that hit Shaoxing prefecture in 1641 stands out
among late Ming crises, not merely for involving, as crises will, persons up
and down the social hierarchy—from high officials and eminent members
of the local elite to aspiring students and obscure village headmen—but,
rather, for leaving behind a raft of documents about it. Representing several
perspectives—planning ahead, experiencing events day by day, and looking
back—these documents, placed side by side, allow one to see through the
conventions of each genre of reporting. They also display fissures within the
community and the process that ultimately mobilized local residents to cooperate; the qualities that distinguished a leader from his peers; and interactions between members of local communities and august imperial officials.

From on high came the report of Prefectural Judge Chen Zilong,[1] who,
early in 1641, after a brief sojourn in the capital paying respects to the court
for the New Year, was returning to his post. As he approached Shaoxing, he
sensed urgency in the air. Ten days of heavy snow had obstructed the mountain roads. In Zhuji, one of eight districts under the jurisdiction of Shaoxing
prefecture, the people were rioting. As Chen had noted in 1640, trouble had
been brewing there ever since the silver mines had been shut down during
the Wanli period, abandoning the hills to serve as bandit hideaways. Following the repeated floods of the previous five years, conditions had deteriorated
further. As Chen, who had been asked by the Censorate to manage Zhuji's
affairs, observed, "Like bristles on a hedgehog, up the bandits rose."[2]

Recounted Chen: "I hastened ahead. Along the roadside I saw thousands
of starving people forming mobs; with knives outstretched and sacks on their
backs, they crowded around, obstructing the carts. A report came in saying:
'The people are on the verge of dying; they must have gone to plunder so-
and-so's house.'" Having thus established the severity of the crisis that would

test and measure his talent for leadership, Chen described how he brought order to the area, incidentally mentioning his foresight of the previous year: anticipating a food shortage, he had prodded local residents to register their grain holdings in preparation for the eventuality that price-stabilizing sales would later be required; they recorded over ten thousand *shi* of grain.[3] Then, underscoring his willing endurance of hardship on the community's behalf, Chen wrote: "I walked through the snow to ask the wealthy households to issue grain, and they were all motivated. Some reduced prices by 30 percent out of kindness to the villagers; others contributed 20 percent for the formation of soup kitchens to save the poorest households. The urban wards (*fang*), market towns (*shi*), and rural areas (*xiang*) all commissioned the young graduates and various students to oversee the project. They also transferred several thousand taels of public funds to merchants . . . who were to go buy grain from the neighboring prefectures."[4]

Chen Zilong closed his account with the usual round of clichés: order was restored, thousands of lives were saved. Descending down the social hierarchy, he praised all those who had unhesitatingly responded to the emergency: the residing officials for upholding good governance, the former officials for taking saving lives to heart, and the graduates of the provincial and prefectural examinations (respectively, the *xiaolian* and the licentiates), many of whom, Chen noted, "had also been very worthy and helpful in managing the relief."[5]

In Chen's telling, the harrowing events surrounding the famine of 1641 assumed the shape of a good story. Writing with hindsight, he organized the elements to have a clear beginning, middle, and end: confronting the crisis, dealing with it, and celebrating the happy outcome. Smoothly and directly, his narrative progressed from the ominous encounter with the hungry mobs in the snow to the achievement of beneficence. What had meaning for Chen were those facts that fit into a comprehensible, familiar pattern—namely, the successful restitution of order.

For a stone inscription commemorating the donors, Chen again neatly arranged the material, according to the social hierarchy: officials took the lead in issuing grain, inspiring contributions from all levels of society—grain from the upper households, firewood and vegetables from the middle households, and labor from the lower households. The result was large-scale beneficence: "During the course of 120 days, 35,230 *shi* of grain were used, keeping 49,580 persons alive."[6] Complementing Chen's account, the Shaoxing prefectural gazetteer roughly states: the relief efforts were carried out through 276 soup kitchens and saved 19,600 lives (here, the replacement of Chen's "four" with a "one" suggests a scribal error in one of the two reports). Prefect Wang Sunlan drew up a document, with twenty-six headings, outlining procedures for distributing rice and money to the poor, controlling grain prices through the selling and stockpiling of grain by both officials and local people, and setting up soup kitchens mobile and stationary, medical dispensaries, and infirmaries. Nineteen districts in three prefectures subsequently put Wang's methods into effect.[7]

Likewise applauding the generosity of residents during the famine of 1641, the Shanyin-district gazetteers of 1724 and 1803 tell, with some variations in detail, of a Zhu Jiong whose donations sustained the victims of dearth; of a Ni Fu, who, when the price of rice reached three hundred *qian*, aided the starving with two hundred *shi* of grain;[8] and of a Shen Maojian whose unflagging generosity extended over many years. After a flood in 1628, Shen engaged Buddhist and Daoist priests to bury over several thousand cadavers; during the dearth of 1644, he provided food for an enormous number of people; he also prepared gruel for prisoners, buried abandoned corpses, and reunited husbands and wives. He "took pleasure in doing good," concludes the gazetteer, adding—as though to remind readers that good deeds will earn longevity—that Shen lived into his ninetieth year.[9] Another do-gooder, after returning to Shanyin from an official post in Shanxi, organized eminent residents into a Luo Society (Luo she) that helped relatives, provided relief to the poor, set up foundling homes, and liberated animals.[10] This man's initiatives bring to mind Yang Dongming's benevolent society, which also drew inspiration from the camaraderie of ancient Luoyang.

The gazetteer entries on charitable men signal an important point: numerous now obscure men of indeterminable status voluntarily contributed to the well-being of their communities. Yet the terseness of the documentation frustrates the historian. For data on the benefactors' social backgrounds and community standing, one might storm the pages with an arsenal of questions, but in vain. Between the statement "there was a great famine" and the resolution "ten thousand lives were saved," the biographies took the shortest route possible, admitting barely enough details to particularize each account. They aimed mainly to reward donors by securing their good reputations in print and to hold up exemplary behavior as an inspiration to future generations.

QI BIAOJIA'S DIARIES

Bridging two worlds, that of official Chen Zilong and that of now unknown residents, are the diaries of a member of the local gentry whom Chen Zilong singled out as having been particularly helpful in the relief efforts and who has already appeared in this book as a pious animal liberator and proud garden owner: Qi Biaojia. Qi resided in Shanyin district, which, along with seven other districts—Guiji, Xiaoshan, Zhuji, Yuyao, Shangyu, Sheng, and Xinchang—constituted Shaoxing. The administrative centers of Shanyin and Guiji stood, along with the prefectural headquarters, within the city walls of the prefectural city of Shaoxing, with Shanyin occupying the western half and Guiji the eastern half. Sometimes it is unclear whether Qi was referring to his own district or the entire city. Adding to the confusion is that he occasionally used the ancient place name Yue, which, depending on context, alternately referred to Zhejiang province, Shaoxing prefecture, and the prefectural city.

Qi, too, encountered the riots that Chen Zilong described. On visiting the city that fateful, snowy day, he learned that no fewer than ten (presumably rich) households had been raided and one household completely demolished. "Gentry households had decidedly not been spared," he observed, adding that when wealthy residents distributed rice and money, the troublemakers "grew even more arrogant and demanding." Businesses were shut down and scarcely anyone was to be seen. At this point, Qi diverged from Chen's narrative, capturing an intimate view of that day's events: "Just then," he wrote, "my wife and I were eating at my father-in-law's house; we threw down our chopsticks and set off for our lodging."[11]

Qi's diaries lay bare the randomness of events and openendedness of negotiations, the false starts and rude awakenings. They incidentally mention that someone in his lineage had used deception to take possession of a grain barge, that wrongdoers were smuggling rice out of the area to be sold elsewhere, and that some friends thought Qi self-serving.[12] When entering each installment into his journals, Qi could neither prejudge which matters would assume weight over the long run nor anticipate whether the squabbles of one day would boil over or cool down by the next. As he observed midway through the crisis, when incessant rain boded ill for the crops, "Everyone was anxious, truly not knowing how it would end."[13]

Chen Zilong's celebratory account praises Shaoxing residents Liu Zongzhou, Ni Yuanlu, Qi Biaojia, and Yu Huang for their labors but singles out Qi as the most energetic.[14] This chapter will ask: Given that many of Qi's and Liu's peers (Ni Yuanlu, Jiang Fengyuan, Yu Huang, Jin Lan, and Zhang Kunfang) were much like Qi, in that they, too, were former officials, came from eminent households, harbored images of themselves as generous, were eager to display their merit, worked hard on relief activities, commanded some wealth (though the exact amounts and rankings of their wealth are now unknown), and forged useful contacts with officials—given all these similarities, what differentiated Qi from the others?[15] Helpful here is that Qi's diaries, reaching back to 1631, illuminate how his personality and interests evolved before he confronted the crisis. His distinctiveness deserves note because it follows that, in discussing charity at least, one must be wary of making generalizations about Chinese local elites.

Chen's tidy, retrospective account collapses temporality, subordinating the sequence of events to the defining moment when riots spurred Shaoxing residents to work energetically and cooperatively in distributing relief. He refers to 1640 only to put on record his foresight in having planned ahead

for a time of scarcity. As the food shortage worsened, Qi's daily entries length-
ened; and his diaries for the period of severe dearth, from 1640 to 1642,
sprawl on for more than 150 folded pages, or approximately 55,600 characters. They show that, during the years running up to 1641, benefactors
were already forming opinions and forging alliances; they document numerous meetings and debates within the community, suggesting that the cooperation that Chen took for granted was achieved with great difficulty. Only
by resolving their differences did Shaoxing residents manage a large-scale
organization, which they sustained over several stressful months and extended from the prefectural city to the remote rural communities in the surrounding eight districts. Exposing the disagreements that divided his peers
on just about every issue imaginable concerning the form that famine relief
should take, Qi's diaries pose the question: Given the independent-mind-
edness of his fellow residents, and the multitude of strategies proposed, how
was cooperation achieved for the successful supervision of several hundred
soup kitchens?

Sailing smoothly from plans to implementation, Chen's account simply
declares that the relief programs worked. Qi's diaries stumble through the
messiness of putting relief programs into effect, the mishaps and changing
circumstances that repeatedly forced relief managers to renegotiate and read-
just their plans. Seizing the opportunity that Qi's diaries provide, this chapter will examine the process by which residents formulated relief plans and
then will compare those plans to actual performance.

SIGNS OF DYNASTIC DECLINE?

Historians have customarily explained the food shortages of the early 1640s
in terms of the dynastic cycle: as the Ming state declined, the infrastructure
crumbled; dikes decayed, leaving arable land defenseless against heavy
rains; organizations that had kept granaries stocked and society stable ceased
to function. According to this paradigm, what precipitated the decline was
moral decay, which, starting with such irresponsible and wasteful rulers as
the Wanli emperor, eventually contaminated the entire bureaucracy and society. Officials failed to act; the responsibility for social order and welfare
shifted from an imperial government that was ailing to members of the local elite, but they proved to be reluctant, rapacious, and self-serving. Thus
the dynasty's deterioration accelerated, and thus was justified the transfer of
power—of the "mandate of heaven"—from one dynasty to the next.[16]

Influenced by this moralizing paradigm, Chinese historians for centuries
preserved and emphasized information corroborating the correlation between political decline and human decadence, thus buttressing the paradigm
to the point that it now appears to have the accuracy of a natural law of
physics. Especially after the Ming fall, historians easily reverted to the the-

ory of the dynastic cycle, often failing to take note of facts that would undermine it.

Residents of Shaoxing were cognizant that China's borders were being besieged and that the court was both overburdened with difficulties and short on resources. Qi expressed anxiety about the fate of his dynasty and understood that famine inevitably sowed "the sprouts of disorder."[17] When he learned of disorder along the borders and the possible obstruction of waterways to the point that communications to the capital might be cut off, he wrote: "I was so deeply pained that I wanted to weep."[18] He understood that the food shortage of the rural area of Tianle was, "to be sure, the result of heavenly conditions," but he conceded that half of the problem came from man's failure to repair irrigation systems.[19] Still, his account of famine relief in Shaoxing negates the view that a declining polity had created a vacuum that members of the local elite had to fill. Rather, it shows that members of the local elite collaborated with officials to gain access to resources, maintain order, regulate grain prices, and ensure that grain be widely distributed among both urban wards and rural soup kitchens.

Like many diary keepers, Qi habitually noted weather conditions. No less true for him than for us, the weather that greeted him each morning immediately distinguished the new day. Occasionally in 1640, and then more markedly in 1641, his mechanical routine of observing the weather gave way to anxiety-ridden watchfulness. The Little Ice Age, which was then sweeping the globe, visited a succession of snowy days upon the Shaoxing area. His ink froze, Qi recorded early in 1640; snowflakes were the size of beans.[20]

Just one day before the rioting started, Qi took advantage of a letup in the snow to tour the scenery around a lake. A fierce wind forced his party to turn back, whereupon they found their docked boat buried in snow drifts. "The price of husked rice is rising daily; given this accumulation of snow, the people will surely be extremely anxious," Qi observed, the next day adding that the incessant snow worried him.[21] A week later, immediately upon stirring from sleep, he asked his servant girl to open the window "to see whether it was clear or raining," and then recorded, "It has been snowing or raining for the past nine days."[22] Remaining vigilant throughout the next month, Qi wrote: "Since the tenth day of the first month, there has been no more than three days of clear, calm weather; heaven is extremely angry."[23] Subsequently, upon consulting an old farmer about the incessant rains, he "was somewhat comforted when told that rain in the second month was not harmful."[24] Such reassurance notwithstanding, heavy rains, floods, snow, and locusts continued their merciless assault on Shaoxing.

Fearing the worst, Qi accepted at face value a book about the Song dynasty's final days, a book said to have been found in a well in 1638 and to have been written by a Song-dynasty patriot.[25] Whether the "book from the well" was genuine or, as some scholars have subsequently argued, a late Ming fabrication, its publisher astutely timed its appearance to tap into the pre-monitions of political decline harbored by Qi's peers. Yet, the message con-veyed by the "book from the well" was twofold. Though speaking about a dy-nastic collapse, it also celebrated a patriot's heroism. This message must have resonated with Qi and other leaders in late Ming relief activities; for, though they had forebodings about their dynasty, they believed they had the power and learning to arrest its decline.[26] They optimistically assumed that they had some control over their destiny—that, by doing good, they could elicit fa-vorable conditions from heaven. Though pondering the deleterious storms sent by heaven and the misdeeds committed by men,[27] Qi readily shouldered responsibility for relief efforts, hoping to reverse the course.

Once, when discussing famine relief in the abstract, Qi criticized officials for "sitting about ceremoniously, tending only to tax collection and crimi-nal investigations"[28]—behavior understood to presage dynastic collapse. Nonetheless Qi's diaries and other materials bearing on the famine relief in Shaoxing provide little evidence that local officials were lazy or that the au-thority they wielded on behalf of their emperor was deteriorating. Rather, the officials commanded the respect of and worked effectively with local com-munity leaders; and residents responded to the crisis with extraordinary re-siliency, dedication, and organizational know-how.

Ultimately Qi and likeminded contemporaries lost their struggle; the Ming dynasty fell, and with it—whether by suicide or illness—fell many of the men in this account. The outcome thus appears to validate the paradigm of dy-nastic decline. Yet if one loosens one's grip on that paradigm to reconstruct events from Qi's daily account, then another story emerges. Economic pros-perity, having endowed the Shaoxing area with a large number of literate men and plenty of surplus wealth, made available new courses of action for dealing with food shortages. What the residents of Shaoxing faced was not an absolute dearth created by a crumbling infrastructure but changing socio-economic conditions that rendered their region increasingly dependent on interregional trade, expanding their sense of responsibility and introducing fresh questions about the just distribution of resources.[29]

COMMUNAL ANXIETY, PERSONAL LOSS

Long before 1641, Qi Biaojia had already developed a habit of responding to needy cases on an ad hoc basis. Because his good deeds figured in his self-image, he made a point of recording at least some of them in his diaries: in 1631, when sojourning in the capital as a regional inspector, he gave five taels to enable someone from his native town to return home.[30] Occasion-ally he distributed alms to beggars congregating along Chang'an Street.[31] Once he observed that several dozen beggars, having learned his habitual route, "reckoned I would stop my sedan chair to distribute coins."[32]

After returning to Shaoxing, Qi gradually moved from small ad hoc acts of charity to long-term collaborative efforts. In 1636, he participated in a medical dispensary. Then, hints of impending dearth began to impinge on his consciousness, gradually involving him in large-scale collective activities. In 1637, when a food shortage hit the area of Guiji (Shanzhong), Wang Chaoshi and another person descended upon Qi to discuss a petition that the tax burden be lightened, a customary strategy helping people to weather difficult times. Joined by Ni Yuanlu, the group proceeded to meet with Prefect Wang and "made a strong case for famine relief for Guiji." Wang proved sympathetic and allowed leniency with taxes, Qi noted, adding (without elucidation), "but we still must procure two or three thousand silver coins." The subject of dearth resurfaced later that day, at a gathering of literati at White Horse Mountain. Following their study of philosophy, Wang Chaoshi broached the topic of relief, voicing his distress that no one was responding to the crisis. Reported Qi: "I again contributed ten taels to initiate the campaign, and I set up a plan for raising funds. On the boat ride home, I wrote a letter to Magistrate Liu Wangu about the plan to forgive taxes."[33] Three days later, Qi called upon the magistrate to thank him, on behalf of the people of Guiji, "for his compassion in bestowing charitable relief." After bending Magistrate Liu's ear about "three methods of relief," Qi proceeded to call upon a Magistrate Lu Guangxin to confer about imperial relief and leniency in taxation.[34] Qi responded readily to Wang's plea for help; but, if one takes his diaries as a guide, the subject of relief would not engross him until 1640.

Three years later, just when the food shortage was growing critical and an atmosphere of gloom was enveloping his community, Qi suffered the loss of two persons dear to him: in 1640, his mother;[35] and in 1641, Wang Chaoshi, the cherished and trusted friend who had counseled him against garden building and broached the subject of relief in 1637. His mother's death left Qi sobbing inconsolably. Some months later, when Qi had to bury her bones on a mountain, heavy rains discouraged relatives and friends from accompanying the coffin. Qi himself proceeded, weeping profusely. Observers were moved to tears.[36]

His mother's final, ailment-ridden months had set Qi on a course to save lives. To propitiate heaven to restore his mother's good health, he had taken to liberating animals.[37] When his mother showed some signs of recovery, he liberated water creatures, spending one hundred *hu*, explained his chronological biography, "so as to foster good fortune for his mother."[38] After his mother died, Qi's habit of liberating animals segued into one of saving human lives. On the boat ride back home from his mother's interment, according to one account, he "had a dream of people shouting for help"; the next day, he encountered a butcher who was about to slaughter a pig, whereupon Qi took pity on the pig, bought it, and set it free.[39] Qi's mother's sickness and death had left him emotionally fragile, sensitizing him to pleas for help and deepening his concern for others. Whatever self-interested goals Qi may have had in protecting his household, village, and lineage, the painful personal loss of 1640 moved him to identify his own interests with saving creatures at large.

Similarly moved by personal losses to participate in relief efforts was Qi's acquaintance Han Lun. At the age of four *sui,* Han lost his mother. Day and night, he wept, almost dying from grief. Some years later, a fortuneteller predicted that his father would die on a particular day, whereupon the shaken Han Lun determined to purify himself. He kept a vegetarian diet, bathed, and journeyed to the mountaintop Perfected Warrior Emperor Temple, respectfully kowtowing for forty *li* along the approach. That night he dreamed a spirit pronounced that if he was truly beneficent, his father would live an extra twelve years. To everyone in need Han was charitable. During the famine of 1641, he collaborated with Qi, who one night walked through the snow to Han's house to calculate what was needed for the relief efforts.[40] Having been similarly stirred by their losses to be charitable, these two men became fitting partners.

Shortly after his mother died, Qi received news of food shortages. A letter from fellow townsman Yu Huang told of a "worrisome rise in grain prices."[41] A visitor brought word of the dearth in Yuyao.[42] Friends and relatives came over to confer with Qi about "the relief matter."[43] A friend with a monk in tow informed Qi that funds had to be raised for a monastery that lacked food. For the record, Qi noted that news of the monks' suffering moved him to help them three times.[44]

FOOD SHORTAGES

In response to the shortage of 1640, Qi made plans to provide grain at reduced prices to his lineage and village; to publicize those plans he composed a statement entitled "A Method for Selling Grain at Below-Market Prices," to be distributed among the targeted recipients. Yet, at this juncture, eight months before the riots of early 1641, Qi appears not yet to have fully grasped the gravity of the looming dearth. He fretted about the style of calligraphy he should use for his public announcement, letting aesthetic concerns temporarily dominate other considerations. With the assistance of two companions, he settled on the style of renowned artist Dong Qichang,[45] disregarding the ill fortune that Dong's family had invited upon themselves: in 1616, their highhanded maltreatment of servants and social inferiors had infuriated thousands of townspeople high and low. Chanting, "If it's firewood and rice you want, first kill Dong Qichang!" they raided and destroyed his luxurious buildings and belongings.[46]

Murmurings about scarcity spread, apprising residents of the magnitude of the crisis, transforming their dim, amorphous apprehensions into urgently focused opinions and negotiations. Qi and his peers exchanged and forwarded letters among themselves, accelerating the circulation of information. When Liu Zongzhou, a moral conscience of the community, made an appointment to discuss relief matters with Qi, Qi attached to his reply a copy of a letter he had written to Yu Huang.[47] Six days later Qi rushed about the city—dropping in at a monastery and an acquaintance's library—and then received friends at his residence to discuss famine-relief policy.[48] Conferring in pairs and small groups, and on one day alone explaining to eight persons the urgency of collecting rice (*jiumi*) for selling it at below-market prices (*pingtiao*), Qi tested the climate of opinion and honed his views into a strategy that would win wide acceptance. He then prepared to draft a letter to Zheng Xuan, the circuit intendant in charge of Ningbo and Shaoxing prefectures, carefully laying out, "under three rubrics, with ten items in all," his case for controlling prices through the "harmonious purchasing of rice" (*hedi*)—that is, lowering the prices for buyers without harming the sellers—and importing grain to maintain a steady supply.[49]

Visiting Qi's home, and hence entering his diaries, was an enormous cast of characters, many now obscure. Right after one public meeting, there first came Jin Lan, who enjoyed a special "same year" relationship based on their shared experience of having together passed the *jinshi* examination. Jin Lan showed Qi a letter from a Li Weipan, which in turn conveyed someone else's intention. Li, the letter writer, was so removed from Qi Biaojia that he was, as Qi remarked, "unaware that I was in mourning." Nonetheless Li viewed Qi as a principal actor and urged him to join the relief efforts. Jin Lan additionally communicated to Qi the opinion of Magistrate Zhou, who apparently favored the strategy of giving out rice (rather than selling it at reduced prices). Having heard that this method had been used in Yuyao, Qi wrote a letter prompting Liu Zongzhou to approach two residents, "who," Qi reported in his diary, "then came around to discuss the matter of relief," apparently as Liu's emissaries. Toward the end of the day, after listening to yet another guest "speak about the difficulties of raising funds for aid," Qi noted of the negotiations: "Fortunately the various friends assumed responsibilities with true hearts; untiringly they encouraged one another."[50] As Qi's diaries of 1640 and 1641 amply document, the experience of this day was often replicated: information and viewpoints streamed toward Qi and then eddied out, often involving parties several times removed from him.

In addition to conversing informally and circulating letters, those residents who may be roughly defined as having some social standing frequently gathered throughout the crisis for formal meetings. For these large assemblies, Shaoxing provided plenty of venues: two City God Temples and one Prefectural City God Temple, whose deities mirrored the district magistrates and the prefect, respectively;[51] numerous monasteries, such as the Eternal Good

Fortune Monastery (Yongfu si) and the Bright Light Monastery (Rongguang si);[52] and a shrine dedicated to local hero Wang Yangming.

Word that a meeting was to be held typically went out several days in advance. During the food shortage of 1640, it was on the eighth day of the fifth month that a meeting was called for the eleventh. Early in 1641, Qi's maternal uncle and nephew came with an "official letter" (*gonghan*) stating that the gentry should meet the next day at the God of Literature Shrine.[53] Once the prefect made an appointment for a meeting three days later at the Wang Yangming Shrine.[54] Soon after, the friends were given a six-day notice to reconvene at that same shrine.[55] On another occasion, the "friends" from each ward had two days' notice that Prefect Wang would hold a meeting at the City God Temple.[56] Once Qi sent a bondservant to go around asking "the good and trustworthy residents of Ke Bridge" to meet at the Bright Light Monastery the next day, when, sure enough, over twenty students and elders assembled.[57]

Attendance at these caucuses was apparently voluntary. Occasionally Qi anticipated that certain key players would show up, for he mentioned that Liu Zongzhou, being unable to attend in person, had sent in a letter instead,[58] and that Prefect Wang managed after all to make a meeting (that he himself had arranged) even though he had sent Qi a note saying that unfavorable winds might delay his boat trip from Hangzhou (Wulin).[59] Still, Qi's diaries mention no fines of the sort demanded by Yang Dongming's benevolent society for failure to attend a meeting.[60] This fact, along with Qi's habit of counting the number of attendees or recording their names and his own refusal to attend one meeting,[61] suggests that the response to each meeting was unpredictable and membership fluid.

The attendees at the meetings ranged in status from officials and former officials to the various degree holders. Qi invariably listed them in hierarchical order, descending down the social scale.[62] At times he recorded the participants' names, among them small players about whose lives little if anything is now known. At times, too, he noted that the attendees were too numerous to list in full.[63] Qi referred to the many helpers often as "the various friends" and occasionally as "elder brothers,"[64] sometimes using the two terms alternately for the same person, leaving it unclear whether the two terms connoted different degrees of closeness. Nonetheless both terms intimate a camaraderie that softened status distinctions—even though occasionally an inner circle embracing both local leaders who held *jinshi* degrees and officials would deliberate before conveying the gist to "the various friends."[65]

Among those present at one meeting, at the Wang Yangming Shrine, were Qi Biaojia and five other members of the gentry (*xiangjin*)—Jiang Fengyuan, Yu Huang, Liu Zongzhou, Ni Yuanlu, and Zhang Dai's ninth uncle, Zhang Kunfang—and three provincial graduates (*xiaolian*). Qi proposed the harmonious purchase of rice from local households to stabilize prices fairly (*hedi*), and presented for their review a letter he had drafted. "Everyone," he wrote, "said it was acceptable, and the various students, who had assembled in great numbers, also said that it was acceptable, whereupon we entrusted to Jiang Fengyuan the task of informing the prefect. We also scheduled a meeting in three days, when the gentry should meet at a public place (*gong-suo*) to discuss the matter."[66]

The day before the scheduled meeting, rain poured upon the already sodden fields of Shaoxing. Qi, who had just finished drafting "A Proposal for Soup Kitchens, in Fifteen Items," was summoned into the city by the prefect and the two district magistrates. That day, he also received a letter from two townsmen who, Qi noted in his diary, were "placing the responsibility for relief on me."[67] At the City God Temple the following day, Qi found the various prefectural and district officials and gentry already assembled to make plans for "harmonious sales" (*hetiao*). The gentry had already written down how much they would sell. To underscore the prevailing mood of cooperation, Qi mentioned that, among those present, there was but one holdout.[68]

Another caucus, this time with two days' notice, was to be held on the eighteenth day of the fifth month, at Liu Zongzhou's place at Ji Hill.[69] Disagreements erupted. Liu Zongzhou initially proposed having "a private subscription pamphlet." Qi proposed that the subscription registers from all the locales be assembled in one place, with a general meeting; and that they should calculate the number of starving and collect from surpluses to distribute relief. "The various friends had some disagreements," recorded Qi, "probably because they could not completely put aside all the thoughts of favors owed and grudges held."[70] Qi's summary of the proceedings, though elliptical, reveals three points: the "friends" discussed and debated strategy; several "friends" ultimately abandoned their positions for a collective viewpoint; and Qi upheld a notion that one should rise above self-interest.

Concurrent with such debates was the gathering of data on the needy. Before launching the relief program in 1640, Qi had first ascertained from a letter from his nephew Yiyuan that there were "eight thousand starving persons in the city," and then calculated: "For each of the poorest, one should give one *dou* and two *sheng;* for the next poorest, one *dou*."[71] Then, turning his attention to the rural area roughly thirty-five *li* southwest of Shanyin to which he and his forebears had long been tied, Qi inspected the data for the two villages, Ke Mountain and Xizhe, and determined how much rice the affluent households there were willing to pledge.[72] Each household in his lineage would take responsibility for twenty-seven days; the surname groups Cheng and Wang were good for seventeen days, and the Kong branch in Lunan was good for one day.[73]

The next step was to establish procedures for distributing the grain. Qi prepared ration coupons for rice, checked the accuracy of the names on the list of starving people, and then issued the coupons at both the ancestral hall and the community shrine. Of that day, Qi reported: "In all, I had examined and reported 170 starving households, which I calculate to be 258 mouths."[74]

Thus, five days after Qi, acting on behalf of the magistrate, had posted "a signboard notice about giving out rice," the program was underway and Qi was fully prepared to receive a visit from Magistrate Wang Yuanzhao. Wang, recounted Qi, "descended upon the rural area to encourage relief at Mituo Monastery." This monastery was located in Meiye Village, where Qi was born and his father had resided. Qi went out to greet the magistrate, and "showed him the pledges of rice, the schedules for distribution, and the counts of the starving households."[75] Such copious records, kept for each stage of the relief effort, provided a common point of reference for all participants.

The meetings of 1641 followed a similar pattern: small consultations alternated with formal discussions. In the third month of 1641, thirty to forty "friends" assembled at the Heavenly King Monastery, in the northeast quadrant of the city, this time to thrash out their differences about the installation of soup kitchens in the rural areas. Reported Qi, "Some said that setting up soup kitchens in the city was inconvenient; some said that setting them in the rural areas was also inconvenient." But he added, "unfortunately there was no strategy for extending aid,[76] other than the method proposed by Lu Yongzhi, namely, to sell from the soup kitchens, to have the friends rotate daily in taking responsibility, to charge two *wen* for each bowl, and to allow anyone looking familiar to take the rice they purchased back to the starving." Eventually "the various friends" reached a consensus. One of them invited everyone taking responsibility to write down his name; moreover, each "friend" had like-minded men (*tongzhi*) join, so in all they got the cooperation of fifty to sixty people.[77]

The next day, Qi ran around town consulting with many of his prominent peers and making arrangements with Prefect Wang for a meeting, to be held three days later at the Wang Yangming Shrine.[78] On the appointed day, he accompanied three members of the prestigious Zhang family to the shrine, where already assembled were "all the friends who were taking responsibility for the wards in the city, and all the friends taking responsibility for the rural areas in the boroughs (*qu*)." Also attending this meeting were gentry members Yu Huang and Zhang Kunfang, two *xiaolian*, and numerous officials as well as the two district magistrates.[79]

While Qi and the friends were debating strategies for distributing grain in the urban ward of Xiahe, a letter arrived from a colleague stating that friends at the Heavenly King Monastery were awaiting his decision regarding his villages. Qi proceeded to the temple, where he found six individuals (who frequently appear in his diaries but are otherwise unknown), to whom he explained the tasks at hand: to identify locations for the kitchens, to select worthy, capable people to undertake the collection of subscriptions from the wealthy, and to investigate the hungry. One by one, each of the friends voiced his opinion.[80] On numerous occasions, members of the local elite ranking high and low met to debate policy among themselves and negotiate with the local officials. Each time, attendees voiced conflicting opinions but reached a consensus.

In connection with the meetings and deliberations about relief, Qi often uses the term *gong,* commonly translated into English as "public," as in "public place" (*gongsuo*) and "public letter" (*gonghan*). Once Qi described a meeting the prefect called at the City God Temple as a "public discussion" (*gong-yi*).[81] Yet, the term *gong* more precisely means "official," as opposed to "private"; and "open," not to the general public but only to men who by some ill-defined criteria felt that they belonged. Consensus was achieved through discussion, but with each voice weighing differently, depending on social status, connections both political and social, moral suasion, and a host of other factors. Qi's diaries allows one to reconstruct the forces that encouraged consensus and the characteristics that qualified him to become a leader in the process.

MASTER OF INFORMATION

In subtle ways Qi set himself apart from other former officials and appropriated for himself a special role. He arrived late to a meeting of mid-1640 at the City God Temple, as though he were above the wrangling typical of these gatherings; and after that meeting he lingered because, Qi took care to note: "The two magistrates asked to have a few words with Zhang Kunfang and myself." Then, thinking that the arrangements for relief remained somewhat unresolved, Qi asked "various friends" to stay a while, to settle such matters as when the account books should be presented under oath, where the price-controlled sales of rice should take place, and who would take responsibility for raising funds.[82] As told by Qi's chronological biography: "Heavy rains had ruined the wheat and rice, sending prices up. Qi composed 'A Strategy for Famine Relief,' in fifteen items. Officials and gentry, noting that Mr. Qi had already mourned his mother for over one hundred days, strongly urged him to come out to manage the matter. Whereupon he and Yu Huang put into effect the harmonious purchase of rice."[83] Qi alternately was chosen by others and himself assumed responsibility. At times he claimed that he had been called to the task, as when he noted: "Previously Liu Zongzhou had encouraged me to manage famine administration."[84] At times, he volunteered, once remarking: "Unfortunately there was no leader, so I resolutely took it on."[85]

A master of administrative lore, Qi was well equipped to lead the relief efforts. For information on food supply, he drew upon practical handbooks, repositories of past wisdom that scholars had assembled over the centuries, each one successively amending and elaborating upon previous publications to update discussions for his own time. A handbook of the early thirteenth century by Dong Wei—*A Book on Relieving Famine and Keeping the People Alive* (*Jiuhuang huomin shu*)—was supplemented in the fifteenth century by Zhu Xiong and subsequently consulted (along with many other writings) by Xu Guangqi, the compiler of a massive compendium in sixty chapters (*juan*), *The Complete Book of Agriculture* (*Nongzheng quanshu*).[86] A commodious store-house of information on husbandry, farming equipment, irrigation techniques, and sericulture, Xu's work also amassed materials on famine relief—the views of ancient political theorists and the proposals, memorials, and strategic plans of eminent predecessors. Xu died before finishing his masterpiece, but his manuscript was rescued from his grandson by none other than Chen Zilong. Collaborating with two colleagues, Chen edited Xu's work, added sections to fill in lacunae, and published it in 1639,[87] shortly before assuming the post of prefectural judge of Shaoxing.

In his youth, Qi must have had access to numerous such handbooks in his father's enormous library, where he had stored his own books.[88] After his father's death, he pored over *A Ferry for Shepherds of the People* (*Mujin*), a substantial collection, compiled by his father, of statements by past officials about administrative matters.[89] He also kept current with new publications. In 1639, he had a bondservant obtain from Hangzhou (Wu) a copy of the just-published *Writings on Statecraft from the Ming Dynasty* (*Huang Ming jingji wenbian*),[90] which I assume to be a variant title of (substituting *jingji* for *jingshi*) or an error for *Huang Ming jingshi wenbian,* the huge compendium in over five hundred chapters that Chen Zilong et alia had compiled and that Qi later often mentioned.[91] In 1641, he received from Chen Zilong a copy of Xu Guangqi's masterwork,[92] which he thereafter consulted, for example, on techniques for capturing locusts and for defending against drought through proper irrigation.[93] "No one has written more thoroughly than Xu about water control," declared Qi.[94]

The food shortage of 1641, along with the loss of his mother, sobered Qi. Setting aside lighthearted opera viewing and garden touring, he earnestly studied famine-relief strategies. He perused "Emergency Plans for Famine Relief," by a friend, and reviewed the previous year's relief accounts.[95] He perused the Metropolitan Gazette (*dibao*) of the previous year, painstakingly copying out whatever concerned famine; and—exposing his sense of self-importance—he assembled letters on relief that he had sent officials.[96] He consulted Chen Zilong's *Writings on Statecraft,* transcribing the sections on famine relief, bandit arrests, and city defense.[97] Even while traveling by a boat, he combed through old official memorials for passages on famine relief.[98] When a heavy downpour promised to ruin the sprouts, the alarmed Qi devoted several days to delving into Dong Wei's *Book on Relieving Famine and Keeping the People Alive.*[99]

Letters, proposals, and guidelines about famine relief flowed from Qi's brush.[100] These Qi often reworked in successive drafts, which he circulated among both "friends" and officials, soliciting their comments, as he did with a draft plan for his ward.[101] Once, during the course of six days, he discussed "a proposal for soup kitchens," finished drafting the proposal "in fifteen items," and sent a copy to a magistrate.[102] Also within the space of a few days, he composed: "A Proposal for the Inspection of Price-Stabilizing Sales of Grain, in Several Items"; "A Signboard Notice about Giving Out Rice"; "A Proposal for Giving out Rice"; and a piece entitled "An Ancillary Discussion of Famine Relief," which elicited positive feedback from a visitor.[103] By circulating proposals, engaging his peers in an exchange of views, and refining the plans, Qi built up a consensus among them.

Administrative handbooks, many now still extant, were widely available to men of Qi's social status.[104] Yet, their utility to historians has been limited, for rarely do they convincingly substantiate that the proposals were successfully executed. The actual situations that Qi's diaries track on a daily basis serve to anchor the administrative lore compiled by and about Qi Biaojia and fellow Shaoxing residents Liu Zongzhou, Ni Yuanlu, and Zhang Bi. These men were conversant with famine-relief tactics. They understood the strengths and weaknesses of the various types of granaries (charitable, community, and ever-normal); and the consequences of manipulating grain prices—that lowering prices, for example, simply encouraged merchants to hoard their stocks. They knew how to control crowds at soup kitchens and to triage the population according to levels of need so as to use limited resources fairly and effectively. They derived some authority and direction from past luminaries—even a brief essay by Zhang Bi displays knowledge of Song-dynasty precedents and policies[105]—but, understanding that the tradition must evolve to accommodate new circumstances, they continued to update and rewrite administrative guidelines.

Qi Biaojia's diaries help one to connect the grand, synthetic visions to actual famine-relief programs. They reveal a man too practical to follow past wisdom slavishly, who readily tested whether bookish advice suited current conditions. When locusts swept onto Yu Mountain, causing Qi to feel, as he put it, "extremely anxious," he promptly "read several books on famine relief, copying out anything regarding locusts that he might disseminate"; then, that afternoon, he "assembled the villagers to use firearms and the banging of gongs to drive the locusts away, and to strike and capture them in the south garden." Wrote Qi: "At night, with monk Wuji, we lit fires along the dikes, imitating what the books said: that the locusts, on seeing the flames, would fly into them." This tactic, he reported with resignation, "did not prove effective in the end."[106] The event nevertheless illustrates his openness to new ideas in an ever-changing environment.

Qi had an analytic grasp of the constituent parts and ramifications of each famine-relief strategy, as the plethora of itemized letters and proposals noted in his diaries suggest. His "Brief Discussions of Famine Administration" (Jiuhuang xiaoyi), drafted shortly before the riots, analyzes seventeen items under three general rubrics: (1) using merchants to bring in rice bought at a higher price and to be sold at below-market prices (*tongshang gaodi*), six items; (2) selling rice at below-market prices (*pingtiao*), five items, (3) soliciting aid in giving out rice, six items.[107] In a letter to Magistrate Wang, Qi "discussed seven matters concerning the present famine relief, which, among other things, dealt with the amounts to be borrowed as capital, the resolve to shoulder responsibility, and methods for exhorting hoarders"; and drew up two announcements for Wang, one encouraging the distribution of rice and the other discouraging selfish hoarding in the rural areas.[108] Repeatedly Qi introduced into the debates such fine-tuned analyses as "three guidelines in ten items" on the "harmonious purchasing of rice" (*hedi*)—that is, the purchase of rice at prices that would harm neither seller nor buyer;[109] ten items on the appropriateness of prohibiting private grain trafficking; and fifteen items on methods for enforcing this prohibition.[110] As he read and formulated opinions about famine relief, Qi distilled his knowledge and his readings into a work he hoped to leave for future generations, entitled *A Complete Book of Famine Relief* (*Jiuhuang quanshu*), an opus he appears to have nearly completed in 1642, when he noted having divided it into eighteen chapters (*juan*).[111]

Thus, when Qi found that the gentry attending the "public discussion" called by the prefect on the eve of the riots of early 1641 "were undecided in their various opinions," and that many, "having prepared their pledge slips, wanted to adjourn," he, who had arrived late, was fully armed with carefully itemized arguments: the basic method, he asserted, should be a three-step plan facilitating merchants to purchase rice that would then be sold at below-market prices (*tongshang gaodi*); auxiliary methods should be selling grain at reduced prices and giving out rice (*pingtiao jimi*). Upon returning to his residence, Qi composed a letter to Prefect Wang Sunlan, authoritatively ticking off the items of the program as follows: "(1) strictly enforce that pawnshops and grain shops remain open; (2) strictly forbid borrowing or purchasing grain by force; and (3) have the friends divide responsibility for the wards and immediately carry out inspections to determine the 'poorest' and 'next poorest.' If given the expectation of getting food, the people will feel somewhat reassured."[112]

PROCEDURES AND RECRUITMENT

Qi's community produced enough volunteers to supervise the distribution of relief throughout both the thirty-nine urban wards and the surrounding rural areas. So demonstrate the large numbers of students, "friends," and holders of degrees (ranging from the highly revered *jinshi* degree on down to inflated entry-level degrees) whose participation Qi records: thirty to forty at one meeting; around forty or fifty "friends" at another meeting, held with officials at the City God Temple;[113] visitors in groups of five and six; and lists of "friends" who "willingly shouldered responsibility." Further making it creditable that managers were plentiful is the device Qi mentioned of having each friend recruit other friends to help in the relief efforts, which in one case engaged the cooperation of fifty to sixty people.[114]

Not all literati residents readily volunteered, however. Qi had to expend considerable energy visiting and coaxing residents to collaborate in the relief efforts. Upon learning that a *xiaolian* whom he had recommended for relief work had failed to shoulder responsibility, Qi beseeched him to cooperate "on behalf of the starving people."[115] He also called upon, first, one acquaintance, "urging him to take responsibility for relief in Tianle," and then Liu Shikun, who was out, but who would later participate in the relief efforts.[116] Qi advised officials Chen Zilong and Bi Jiuchen to urge *jinshi*-degree holder Yu Huang to take responsibility for the soup kitchens. Chen wanted to visit Yu. Qi rushed ahead to Yu's house to await Chen's arrival. He discussed with Yu the importance of selecting "those large households in that village who were fond of charity" to take the responsibility for managing the soup kitchens. "In general he agreed with me," Qi noted in his diary, but then explained that Yu declined on the grounds that he was unacquainted with them.[117] Once, Qi also had to deal with a *xiaolian* who, though managing relief most energetically in the rural area of Tianle, refused to collaborate with other "friends."[118] Collaboration was desirable, one surmises, because it deterred corruption, limited the community's indebtedness to any one benefactor, and implied a consensus that legitimized the activity.

Such problems notwithstanding, the day after Yu Huang declined to serve, various friends, responding to notes Qi had circulated, streamed into Qi's urban residence. Partitioning each of the two districts (Guiji and Shanyin) into five boroughs, they divided among themselves the responsibilities for the soup kitchens, with each borough having at most five and at least four persons in charge. Just then, Circuit Intendant Zheng Xuan and other high local officials paid a visit, and Qi informed them of the plans. By sunset a list had been drawn up of the names of the friends who would be involved in the program.[119]

LACUNAE IN THE DOCUMENTS

Although Qi's diaries delineate the recruitment of managers, they give short shrift to all the laborers who must have transported the grain and prepared the gruel for the soup kitchens. These lowly underlings were negligible in Qi's vision of doing good. Once he expressed concern that conscripted village laborers—to whom, one surmises, the transportation of grain had been entrusted—were selling the grain, even to areas outside Shaoxing.[120] Once he learned, when investigating conditions in the rural area of Tianle, that village conscripts of one section (*du*) of the forty-eight sections into which the rural area surrounding the Shaoxing prefectural seat was divided had been encroaching upon relief supplies.[121] Another time, in a letter to Magistrate Wang, Qi, who was arguing for postponing the collection of taxes, incidentally mentioned conscripted village laborers in the relief efforts, roughly as follows: Although not everyone responsible for the relief or issuing the rice is a conscripted laborer, some are; given that it is impossible to be simultaneously in two places, one cannot expect them to run around managing both the collection of grain taxes and the relief efforts.[122]

Other lowly types important in distributing food likewise received scant notice from Qi. Among these were the monks who monitored the queues at the soup kitchens, carried gruel through the towns, and tended to the burials of the victims of starvation;[123] a bondservant who late into one night prepared strings of cash for distribution;[124] and the porters who managed the selling of gruel to people classified as "the next poorest"—a program designed to supplement the free soup kitchens. The sale of gruel would, according to Qi's general treatise on famine relief, benefit, not only those who were often unwilling to go out in public for the handouts, but the sellers as well: "Today's method of selling gruel, at two *wen* per bowl makes it possible to have one person go buy the food and take it back to feed a whole household. The head who manages the operation discounts the sales by 50 percent; still he earns the proceeds from the sale, which in turn will expand his trade."[125] The strategy of charging two *wen* per bowl was much debated, according to Qi's diary, and whether it was put into effect, and, if so, whether the program was effective, is beside the main point here: that Qi assumed a reserve of faceless laborers whose services might (either through coercion, as in the case of the conscripts, or through the promise of material benefits, as in the case of soup sellers) be harnessed to the famine-relief efforts.

Behind the surviving records much went on that is now outside our reach. Taking a lot of information for granted, Qi's diaries fail to specify how many households were in his lineage, who the other lineages residing in his rural area were, and how his beneficent peers compared in wealth with those many *jinshi*-degree holders who appear not to have participated in the relief efforts. Though Qi duly logged into his diaries numerous letters he received and sent throughout the period of dearth, rarely did he describe their contents. His diaries were to complement his personal archives, and either his descendants or students would posthumously assemble and publish his writings. Occasionally, a piece to which his diaries refer is extant.[126] More often the diaries signal that an incredible amount of material has been lost. One letter Qi sent during the food shortage of 1640 was to Wang Ruqian,[127] the rich merchant and the owner of the pleasure boat *The Unmoored Garden* that plied the waters of Hangzhou's West Lake. Two days after writing to Wang, Qi sent Chen Changyao—who appears to have been the manager for Qi's household affairs, supervising, for example, the bondservants in planting willows[128]—and bondservants to Hangzhou (Wulin). At the time, grain procurement was much on Qi's mind; the previous month, he had commissioned someone to go to Suzhou (Wuzhong) to buy rice;[129] but whether the errand to Hangzhou also concerned grain transactions, and whether it involved Wang, are left unclear in the diary.

PLANS

The relief plan devised by Shaoxing's local leaders in early 1641 was, first, to distribute rice to the urban wards; then, once the "middle" households had been appeased and order restored, to set up soup kitchens in the rural areas. Already in place were administrative divisions that provided the framework for each of these programs. The urban areas of the twin districts of Shanyin and Guiji, located inside Shaoxing's prefectural city, were collectively partitioned into thirty-nine urban wards. Resident Ni Yuanlu, according to his chronological biography, assumed that the rich of each ward should take care of its poor and that the poor households would—in a quid pro quo not made explicit in Qi's diaries—reciprocate the kindness by protecting the rich. Recounts Ni's biography: officials relaxed restrictions on trade and widened the channels for importing grain into the area from nearby prefectures Wenzhou and Taizhou. Officials and merchants provided the capital for purchasing grain at fair prices in order to sell it (*pingdi*). The starving people were classified into three categories: the "hungriest" (*shangji*) were to receive gruel; the "next hungry," grain; and the "least hungry" were to be given an opportunity to buy grain at reduced prices.[130]

For calculating grain allocations for the rural areas, the relief organizers had at their disposal not only the surveys of needy that they themselves compiled, but also existing population censuses taken in connection with the *baojia* system. Although varying in details from region to region, the *baojia* essentially organized households into nesting units—ten households into a *jia*, and ten *jia* into a *bao*—so as to facilitate tax collection and mutual surveillance in the rural areas.[131] Qi envisioned that the funds (sixty taels) the district magistrates had provided for the next planting would be distributed through the *baojia* (with the "*bao* controlling all the *jia*, and a *jia* chief controlling each *jia*"). The city manager stamped his seal on the printed forms to be used; and ten days later a colleague (Lu Yongzhi) returned from the rural area of Tianle, reporting that the distributions had been completed through the *baojia* "with everything in perfect order and pledged in contracts." They then compiled a record for the official.[132]

A day after the riots of early 1641, Qi Biaojia, acting on behalf of the prefect, sent around a circular to the friends responsible for each ward to arrange a small meeting about scheduling the grain distributions. In response there arrived at Qi's place "brothers" so numerous that, as Qi put it (while naming four of them), "I cannot count them all." Soon after, Han Lun—the resident who had undertaken charity in order to prolong his father's life—came by with a friend "to discuss relief for our ward."[133]

By the next morning the snow had stopped. Rising early, Qi wrote a letter making recommendations to Prefect Wang, this time analyzing the problem under four rubrics: issuing food from the granaries, promulgating announcements that the law would be strictly upheld, urging households with stored grain to share their supplies, and purchasing grain to control prices (*tongdi*). He drafted an announcement "strictly prohibiting both forced purchases and grain confiscation." In response, Wang visited Qi to discuss how the grain should be distributed so as to prevent mobbing. "If the hungry people come to the granaries to await the handouts," Qi explained, "they will certainly create a disturbance; it is best to distribute the grain in batches to those students taking responsibility for each ward and then have them distribute everything simultaneously, treating everyone equally."[134]

That day again brought more callers than Qi could count—he names but six of them. He had one person inspect those households within the ward that had not yet been visited. The "friends" responsible for Qi's ward then congregated at the Eternal Good Fortune Monastery, where, as Qi reported the event, "they took an oath before the spirits that they would assume responsibility for the matter. Each friend acknowledged the number of days for which he would give out rice." Underscoring his leadership role, Qi added: "I took the lead in accepting responsibility for more than six days; in succession, each of the friends then wrote down their amounts. Should there later be a shortfall, the friends would then raise funds to make up the amount." In addition to the six visitors Qi also named six "friends" who were accepting responsibility. These were small players in the community, about whom scarcely anything is known outside their rare appearances in Qi's diaries; yet Qi, valuing their contributions, took care to record their names, declaring, "With true hearts, they all took on the responsibility," and then added: "Han Lun rushed about, calculating and planning; he labored especially hard and, to the end of the relief project, showed not the slightest sign of fatigue." The arrangements having been settled, Qi initiated a register for the fund-raising, for which he drew strength from official authority: "Representing Magistrate Wang, I prefaced it with a few words of encouragement."[135]

Their caucus over, the friends of Qi's ward then joined the friends of all the other wards for a general meeting at the City God Temple. The assembly agreed to two principles, which would deter mobbing: decentralizing the distributions and distributing grain simultaneously so as to spare the starving any anxiety about who would receive rice first. In the presence of the two prefectural officials and the magistrates of Shanyin and Guiji districts, the friends responsible for each ward handed over their surveys of the starving population. Under the name of each ward was inscribed the name of the person responsible. Noting that about 80 or 90 percent of these records were in order, Qi deduced that lapses had occurred in only three or four wards. The students then dispersed, leaving Qi and the officials to explore strategies for acquiring grain at below-market prices.[136] The upshot, reported Qi, was that "we summoned ten or so grain brokers and negotiated with them, emphasizing the interdependence of officials and merchants."[137]

Interminable deliberations about relief consumed much of Qi's time. After taking leave of the officials, Qi further conferred with students. He then returned to his ward, whereupon "various friends" came to talk about raising funds. Wrote Qi: "Within the space of a few days, we had examined the starving of this ward and filled in the printed tickets for giving out rice. We have been extremely busy making all the arrangements. Now the friends and I went in person to the doors of the starving to distribute the tickets, once again making inspections to check whether anyone had gotten on the list through deception or had been overlooked."[138]

At another meeting two days later, Qi and the friends of his ward decided to distribute relief rice in six locations, one of which was identified simply as Jiuqu, where Qi had his city lodging, and five of which were buildings: the Eternal Good Fortune Monastery; Sea Goddess Hall; Wooden Ladle Monastery; Fire God Temple; and Great Emperor Temple.[139] If this ward may serve as a guide for the other thirty-eight wards, Shaoxing's city walls embraced numerous quasi-public structures for temporarily storing and distributing grain.

By dispersing the grain depots for his ward in six places, Qi explained in his diary, the relief organizers would enable women to obtain their allotted food easily (presumably by saving them the trouble of a long walk), and, moreover, would deter the hungry from massing together in one place. The depots of his ward would in total serve over 620 starving people, providing each person with three *ge*—a ration far smaller than the five *ge* estimated as the daily adult consumption in the eighteenth century.[140] The program was to end on the twenty-sixth day of the first month, but "friends" voiced different opinions. The prevailing view was, recounted Qi, that "the rice was in short supply and the period to be covered long, and that we should therefore be somewhat flexible about the days, writing down the tenth day for the eighth." Accordingly, Qi filled in the tickets to stop not on the twenty-sixth day but on the twenty-eighth of that month. He used twelve *shi* of rice, which he himself supplemented somewhat. That afternoon, he made distributions at the Sea Goddess Hall.[141] This appears to have been an interim measure, for on twenty-fifth day of the first month, funds were "raised through encouragement" in Qi's ward to provide for 622 persons over seventy days, until the wheat harvest at the end of the fourth month.[142]

A list of the "friends" responsible for the distribution had, Qi further noted, already been established, "so that there would be no backing out," and the households issuing relief had been so notified. Qi allocated money for getting grain out of the granary and called three shopkeepers. Each household of the ward that was entitled to buy grain at reduced prices would go to the shop specified on its certificate, and only after checking the name on the certificate would the shopkeeper dispense the rice.[143] On the twenty-seventh day of the first month, tickets were distributed at Jiuqu, and on the next day, Qi went to thank the friends of his ward; being the program's chief coordinator, he then roamed all over the city to thank those who had helped in other wards.[144]

POLICY DEBATES

First quietly in 1640 and then more heatedly throughout 1641, the friends repeatedly assembled in private homes and quasi-public buildings to deliberate strategies. In what form should relief be distributed? By selling rice relief at below-market prices, or, as one person insisted, only by giving "outright aid"?[145] By giving out grain or by setting up soup kitchens? And if the latter, should the soup kitchens be free of charge, or should persons in the category of "next poorest" be asked to pay a small amount per bowl? Some leaders maintained that the starving should travel to the depots for their handouts. Ni Yuanlu opposed this, arguing: "Because the territory is vast and the populace large, carrying out the inspections would be difficult and abuses would surface. Moreover, how can the starving bear to make the trip to wait for a paltry handout? The method of having each ward care for its own ward has been put into effect in the city; why should it not be so in the adjacent towns?" This strategy, Ni further argued, offered two advantages: with the beneficiaries being nearby, the program would be easy to manage; with no large crowds gathering, disease would not spread.[146]

How should grain be obtained? Should it be stored in local granaries, or imported from neighboring areas? Should one use force in purchasing grain (*qiangdi*) from households storing it, or simply encourage them to sell (*quantiao*) on terms that would help to stabilize prices?[147] How—if at all—should grain prices be regulated? When Liu Zongzhou "proposed that prices be lowered," Qi "forcefully argued that this could not be done."[148] Should charitable granaries be set up, and, if so, how should they be stocked? By taxing landowners according to the size of their landholdings or through loans?[149] Conversations are incompletely noted by Qi, agendas poorly explicated, and the debates that gripped his fellow residents throughout many months are recorded in fragments. Moreover, as events unfolded, opinions changed.

Each policy favored certain constituencies or locales; each participant had loyalties and interests. Qi was solicitous of his lineage and the rural area where his tenant farmers lived from hand to mouth. At each year's end, inspired by a paternalistic spirit, he would customarily bestow charitable gifts upon them. In late 1637 he and his wife went by boat to each village to give the poor households "relief rice."[150] In late 1639, after calculating how much money he had spent aiding his lineage, he "augmented the amount, bringing it to 150 taels";[151] he then engaged a teacher for the charitable school; and, after discussing aid for the villages with the neighboring elders, he brought the year to a felicitous close by contributing rice to be distributed, first to the poor households and then to members of his lineage.[152] Such were Qi's loyalties to his rural area that, immediately after the first meeting of 1641, he recorded: "I calculated that our villages could get over sixty *shi* of grain."[153]

Yet individual loyalties and personal inclinations often undermined or competed with lineage identity, sundering ties even between brothers, as is evident in the case of Zhang Kunfang, who often appears in Qi's diaries among the men particularly active in the relief efforts. When Kunfang received a congratulatory banner and placard for having earned the *jinshi* degree, his irascible, destructive younger brother exclaimed, "Your damn, trifling *jinshi* degree! How dare it insult my eyes!" He then ripped up the banner for trousers, sawed up the post for cooking fuel, and splintered the placard for railings.[154] From the same family emerged both an antisocial failure and a winner dedicated to his community's welfare.

So too did Qi's lineage harbor deviant members. People surnamed Xiao, Zhu, and Chen complained that members of his lineage had used false pretenses to deceive them. Wrote Qi: "My hair stood on end, and forthwith I wrote to the district magistrate, asking that he investigate."[155] Some months later, members of Qi's lineage formed a cabal to appropriate rice. Qi met with lineage and branch elders about punishing the perpetrators according to the lineage regulations. Hoping that they would reform, Qi passionately advocated that they simply be reprimanded.[156] Subsequently, Qi learned that a nephew had been misusing Qi's name to appropriate rice.[157]

Social relationships crisscrossed in highly unstable webs, where the pulling or loosening of any one strand unpredictably affected other strands. Qi's bonds with kin, village, and ward competed with, even undercut, his solidarity with members of his social class, each of whom likewise had numerous competing loyalties. At the same time, Qi's particularistic interests were themselves submerged by values professed by men of his social status and learning, men who not only aimed to maintain a moral order conducive to the productive cultivation of land and timely payment of rents and taxes, but who understood that, with examination success and high status, came a responsibility for the people's well-being. Thus, while protecting his village and ward, Qi acknowledged the needs of his neighbors and responded to pleas for help from acquaintances from districts outside his own. Caught up in a tangled social web, Qi throughout the crisis tuned into a wide range of opinions, voiced by participants at the formal meetings, visitors to his home, letter writers, and rumor; as well as by the lofty high circuit intendant, merchants, monks, and village headmen. So attests Qi's diary for the year 1641 and his frequent mention of who agreed or disagreed with him. At each turn, Qi vigorously advanced his own proposals, but not without granting some validity to opposing views. He fashioned himself as mediator: "Because the friends of the different wards had disagreements, they were backbiting and obstructionist. I tried to bring about peace."[158] Alert to the unstable climate of opinions, he took the trouble to log debate after debate into his diaries.

Though having similar educational backgrounds and occupying a narrow stratum at the top of Shaoxing society, Qi, his fellow degree holders, and the "friends" repeatedly articulated sharply conflicting views about relief strategies. On balance, no one policy consistently corresponded to a particular social status, or what may be called "elite interests" or "an elite point of view"; indeed, if one takes Qi's diaries as a guide, numerous Shanyin residents holding *jinshi* degrees (twenty-seven earned in 1629 alone) did not participate in the relief activities—and surely not all the nonparticipants were serving outside Shaoxing at the time. Rather than pursuing class interests or motivations to explain the choices Qi and his colleagues made, this study will address another issue posed by the debates: Given that members of the elite pursued a wide range of strategies with a wide variety of motivations, what forces pressed and enabled many of them, despite their disagreements, to participate in a large-scale cooperative program?

TO DO GOOD ALONE OR THROUGH A GROUP

From the arguments over relief strategies there emerge two general patterns of response: a few members of the community—including several of the charitable men commended by the local gazetteers—acted independently, sometimes with the support of a small coterie; other members strove to reach a viable consensus and gravitated toward cooperative endeavors, which invariably involved officials.

Exemplifying independent action was Zhang Bi, who, along with his uncle Zhang Kunfang and his first cousin Zhang Dai, was a scion of the prominent lineage descended from *jinshi*-degree holder Zhang Yuanbian.[159] During the food shortage of mid-1640, a difference in opinion prompted Zhang Bi to part ways with a core group of his peers. His "Directives for Famine Relief" (Jiuhuang shiyi) summarizes the circumstances roughly as follows: Liu Zongzhou emphasized soup kitchens, while Jin Lan, Yu Huang, and Qi Biaojia emphasized price-stabilizing sales of grain (*pingtiao*). Jin Lan "resolutely led the way, contributing funds for purchasing over seven hundred *shi* of grain for sale at fair prices (*pingdi*); for thirty days, the people have already been eating because of their kindness."[160] An undated memo by Qi states that Jin Lan made available three hundred taels for price-stabilizing sales; the goal was a revolving trade in grain, where the local gentry and rich households (*xiangshen fushi*) would issue their rice for below-market sales, causing rice prices to fall, while ensuring that subsidized grain will always be on the market. This, Qi declared, was far more efficacious than other strategies, which would last for only one round of aid.[161]

At that point, Zhang and friends had what he termed "private [or independent] discussions" (*si yi*). They diplomatically conceded that the "proposals of the other gentlemen were admirable" but opined that each strategy had shortcomings: soup kitchens would reach only beggars, not "poor scholars"; lowering grain prices would benefit middle households but not the dirt poor. "Poor scholars, widows, orphans, the elderly, and cripples who are suffering hunger but are housebound" would, they feared, be overlooked. Consequently Zhang turned to his maternal relatives for help in initiating his own program. He sold off two *qing* of poor land; and his maternal relatives assembled their friends to lay out several thousand taels, enough to buy over five hundred *shi* of rice.[162] "This," Zhang added, "was widely announced to the resident officials and gentry, all of whom encouraged and applauded the effort, with cries of pleasure as loud as thunder."[163] Zhang recognized that the grain he provided was a mere drop when compared to the needs of the entire prefecture; nonetheless, if the grain were properly distributed, innumerable residents of the two districts of Shanyin and Guiji would "eat the rice of my mother's lineage" for five days, thereby causing the price of rice to drop by 20 percent.[164]

Ni Yuanlu presented Zhang with a scroll stating, "He shares his wealth with others."[165] Liu Zongzhou, in a preface to Zhang's "Guidelines," praised Zhang by implicitly reproaching those residents who, as Liu put it, held back or "self-indulgently displayed their virtue." It was, Liu averred, only after Zhang distributed his family's grain that word of his deed spread, spurring anyone with the least bit of surplus to vie in providing relief—whether they did so through the price-stabilizing sales of grain (*pingtiao*), outright relief, or soup kitchens.[166] Zhang's initiative unleashed a competitive spirit and no one wished to be left behind.

From this distance in time it is impossible to judge whether Zhang was less selfish than his allegedly "self-indulgent" peers; and impossible to determine whether Zhang's relief program, which involved selling "poor land" to his in-laws, may have benefited him materially, or whether Zhang, through this one-time grand gesture, freed himself from charitable responsibilities on other occasions. Then, too, the concern to unload grain before prices might fall may have motivated not only Zhang Bi but also those who quickly followed his example. Whatever the motivations may have been, the point remains: Shaoxing had plenty of independent-minded residents, who, like Zhang Bi, provided charity on their own, or who both cooperated in the large-scale efforts while initiating independent projects. Even while assuming leadership responsibilities in the group efforts commended by Chen Zi-long, Ni Yuanlu organized his own relief efforts. He was concerned that the main program neglected the famine victims who dwelled in remote areas or who had been left off the "registers of hungry people." He therefore took it upon himself to set up a Life-Saving Pagoda Society (Yiming futu hui), which circulated subscription charts shaped like a pagoda, each floor of which represented one life to be saved.[167] According to his guidelines, donors could sign on individually or in groups for one floor (one life) and would then accept responsibility for making grain contributions every ten days, for roughly three and a half months, until the next harvest.[168]

Around such independent actors there gravitated small constituencies. Five or six in-laws assisted Zhang Bi in his relief endeavors.[169] A "famous licentiate," Shan Yiguan, joined Ni Yuanlu to set up the "Life-Saving Pagoda" and would, along with Ni, earn praise in the local gazetteer for having generously issued 150 *shi* of rice they had cooked, thereby saving the lives of over a thousand persons.[170] Other benefactors, cursorily noted in Qi's diaries, also acted singlehanded, among them one "friend," who, for repeatedly donating grain to aid his village, won Qi's praise as "truly charitable."[171]

The bifurcation between independent actors, working singly or in small groups, and large team efforts was not always clear-cut. Qi Biaojia, though leading the large-scale communal relief program that would enjoy official sanction and win loud applause, at times acted independently on behalf of causes he favored, as several journal entries about distributing cash in 1641, in the vicinity of his rural estate, attest. Thus, when he heard of a village widow who had fallen ill from undernourishment, and whose whole household was so sick that no one could manage the cooking, he gave them all money.[172]

Chen Zilong's glowing accounts pay no heed to dissension among members of Shaoxing's elite. Qi entirely ignored Zhang Bi's moment of glorious beneficence, and only once mentioned him in reference to the food shortage.[173] Yet, Zhang's "private discussions" with his friends, a counterexample to collaborative efforts, serve to highlight facts that Qi noted only in passing. For example, the one holdout at the meeting of mid-1640, where everyone else agreed to support the price-stabilizing sale of grain was Wang Siren, who favored outright relief (*zhen*).[174] Wang apparently sided with Zhang Bi; in a preface he contributed to Zhang's essay, he extolled both Zhang's generosity and the efficacy of his program, which had ensured that "every grain of rice went to the starving."[175]

Each policy favored a different category of need, as the benefactors of Shaoxing themselves recognized. Zhang and Ni expressed particular interest in aiding residents who might fall through the cracks; along with Wang Siren, they advocated "outright relief." Some relief sponsors were, like Zhang Bi, especially solicitous of the genteel poor, who wished to avoid being seen at the soup kitchens. As Lu Shiyi of Taicang wrote some time after 1638: "Unless they are crippled, widowed, and living alone, and unable to survive the day, they certainly would not wish to show their faces while sipping on other people's gruel."[176] But Zhang Bi expressed concern about the dirt poor as well, urging on their behalf that relief managers make personal inspections of their habitats. Dismissing the widespread assumption that population surveys had left no household or person out, Zhang asked rhetorically, "Who would have thought that, in the poor streets and humble alleys, there were houses not registered in the property tax rolls and persons not registered in the mutual-surveillance system (*baojia*), who lived in crowded conditions, like bees in their hives?"[177]

The categories of need that figured in the debates are at times themselves vague. The sponsors spoke often of the "next poorest" and "poorest," and designated for each of these categories a distinct treatment; yet their extant writings fail to define precisely the criteria for each category. Zhang Bi, for example, labels the dirt poor as those unable to light their own fires, and the next poorest as those somewhat able to feed themselves but with few resources.[178] Although some Qing-dynasty writers would define these categories with some precision, Ming-dynasty classifications were often based on such vague criteria as the famine victim's appearance.[179] And who exactly counted among the "next poorest," of whom Qi was so solicitous? Only in passing and as the opinion of one of his colleagues does Qi mention the possibility that, if the next poorest were not given access to subsidized grain sales (*pingtiao*), they would "create a disturbance."[180] His colleague Yu Huang more directly stated: "Not all the rioters were starving people; some were evildoers who used the food shortage as a pretext and whose faces seemed familiar to me."[181]

Qi's diary leaves many key points obscure. Amid some confusion, the division between small independent efforts and large collaborative ones unambiguously stands out as demanding explanation.

MODELS AND SCHEDULES

Qi envisioned relief activities as conforming to general models, or plans, which he laid out in written guidelines and directives. As he explained to magistrate Wang Yuanzhao, "The pledges of grain and surveys of the starving population could serve as a model for every rural area,"[182] a claim that the next generation would underscore in Qi's biography.[183] Such is the nature of diaries, to focus on the writer's experience, that Qi mentioned urban and rural areas outside his own only when news drifted his way. Yet the strategies for aiding Qi's district were widely replicated throughout Shao-xing prefecture. In Yuyao (Yaojiang) district, "friend" Wang Dahan (who appears often in Qi's diaries) assumed responsibility for managing relief.[184] In Xiaoshan, the magistrate donated grain from his salary, inspiring wealthy residents to follow suit, with the result that soup kitchens functioned for three weeks in each of the district's six boroughs.[185] An explicit model facilitated coordinating the large force of "friends" participating in the relief operations, ensuring that they make distributions simultaneously and somewhat equitably across a large region, thereby discouraging the indigent from roaming about in search of the best opportunities.

The projected models were enforced through several mechanisms. The swearing of oaths, witnessed by their peers, sealed the participants' commitment to the program. Records of pledges of grain and money held the pledgers to their promises. Announcements in public places—such as one Qi posted regarding the soup kitchens in the four suburbs—fixed the community's expectations while holding organizers to their obligations.[186] Moreover, as Qi frequently mentioned, the organizers kept records of every stage of the relief efforts: registers of needy households, lists of volunteers, and accounts verifying the collection or distribution of funds or grain. In early 1641, Qi consulted "relief registers" that had been compiled during the food shortage of the previous year.[187] When an official party inspected soup kitchens in the rural area near Xiaoshan, the district magistrate sent in registers for review.[188]

Armed with printed forms for gathering information according to a fixed protocol, a vast network of "friends" penetrated the rural areas. One day, the "friends" responsible for the western borough—whom Qi named in his diary, thus crediting each for his efforts—brought back reports about the people suffering in the rural area of Tianle; one friend "narrated a few sentences about each village."[189] Then returned a second batch of friends. "Everything," wrote Qi, "was in accord with the pamphlet my nephew Hongsun had compiled for the five boroughs of Shanyin. Prefacing each borough in the pamphlet was a detailed map, from which one could see how hard was the work of the various friends taking responsibility."[190] Again using forms, the men who had agreed to inspect the soup kitchens in the central borough "filled in information under the three categories: (1) whether the kitchen managers were earnest or lazy; (2) whether the gruel they provided was plentiful or scanty; and (3) the number of starving." These records then guided official Chen Zilong in issuing reprimands and commendations to the managers.[191]

Models for relief established a common understanding of procedures within the community, providing measures for accountability. Distributions of rice were made out in the open, readily observed by project leaders, "friends," and officials. Qi often checked up on the relief operations. He accompanied resident Han Lun into the city to watch rice being doled out at the home of a Mr. Hu.[192] He observed the third and fourth distributions in his rural area at the community and lineage shrines respectively.[193] He watched Han Lun dispense rice at the Eternal Good Fortune Monastery, in Xiahe ward.[194] He walked around with Chen Changyao to observe soup kitchens in Xiru and Xiahe wards; and months later he again observed a "friend" distribute gruel at Still Water Nunnery.[195] So too was Qi observed. Once, right after distributing ration tickets at the North Shrine on Heng Street, he proceeded to the Sun Zhonglie Shrine to distribute grain with various friends; someone surnamed Qin and his nephew came to watch.[196]

Observer and observed, Qi formulated plans and requests in broad terms that transcended particularistic interests. Though seeking to protect his lineage, village, and urban ward, he understood that "if relief matters are even slightly tainted by selfish interests, the people will thereafter distrust us."[197] In a letter requesting that Magistrate Wang postpone the collection of taxes for forty days, to the seventh month (when a new crop was expected), Qi argued, "The lives of thirty-six thousand residents of this city depend on the 120 food depots, each of which serves three hundred persons"; he then insisted: "This matter involves the entire city . . . and is not a matter of self-interest."[198]

IMPROVISING STRATEGIES AS EVENTS UNFOLD

Efforts by local leaders to standardize and coordinate the relief operations notwithstanding, lapses occurred, and not just because a few managers were derelict in their duties or downright corrupt. Occasionally benefactors chose to act expediently. One day Qi presented Magistrate Wang with a blueprint for aid for "every rural area."[199] A few days later, after having pledged to distribute rice to his "lineage and the nearby villages" over an eight-day period, he strayed from the agreement. He explained: "I gave out the grain all at once to save the trouble of storing it until later." Ignoring that the starving might barter their shares or consume them prematurely, Qi cut a corner to suit himself. Yet, that same day, finding the starving to be more numerous than he anticipated, he improvised to their benefit, using "almost seven *shi* of rice"—which presumably exceeded the original allocation.[200]

The calculus of need and resources was in perpetual motion. When Qi went to distribute grain at Stone Buddha Monastery in Ke Mountain, he learned that the initial population count had inadvertently overlooked "three loners." Because the amount of rice had already been fixed, he was unable to satisfy their need, Qi explained, hastening to add: "But, I couldn't bear it, so, in order to provide for them, I shortened the seventh period by three days' worth of rice."[201] When residents of Lunan Village came to ask Qi for an increase in the amount of rice, Qi "helped them somewhat, and also increased the amount to be given for each three-day period, so as to soothe their hunger pains."[202]

From the start an openendedness was built into the plans. Qi understood that, "in the event of a shortfall, the friends would raise funds to make up the amount."[203] For the southern borough, whose remoteness made managing soup kitchens inconvenient, the plan had been to distribute grain only once. But, after pressing District Magistrate Zhou to use rice garnered from penal fines to increase aid for that region, Qi reasoned: "Today we calculate that there is extra rice. Therefore we have set up three soup kitchens, in Huashan, Yunmen, and Pingshui [the last being twenty-five *li* east of the prefectural city], along the general route through which the mountain people go in and out."[204] Several weeks later, Qi's brother Junjia distributed leftover grain in front of a monastery and at three soup kitchens in Pingshui.[205]

Though plans, directives, and schedules for carrying out relief were firmly planted in their minds, Qi and his peers continually improvised and adjusted procedures, all the while mediating between the written guidelines and the parties involved. One day, Qi invited four friends of Xiahe ward to discuss the importance of distributing rice at the scheduled times. Then, after amending the amounts of rice and the days for distribution so as to give the people hope, he went out to meet "various friends" at the Supreme Ruler Temple; together they proceeded to the home of Guo Yingpeng, who, Qi explained, was late in fulfilling his pledge to give rice for two five-day periods. They persuaded Guo to make both distributions at once; "the starving people were pleased."[206]

Fluctuations in grain stocks likewise called for meetings and deliberations. In the fourth month Qi invited over to his place those friends who were responsible for Xiahe ward—he names Han Lun and three others—to discuss initiating another round of relief for that ward. Resources were running low. How could they last to autumn? asked Qi. Noting that "opinions varied," he proposed a fund drive. This would not necessarily bring in much revenue, he conceded, but would do much to "comfort the myriad hearts." He also argued against trying to stretch out supplies by substituting soup kitchens for grain distribution—a maneuver he likened to the underhanded technique of "three in the evening and four in the morning." Here he was alluding to an anecdote about a monkey keeper who, running out of food supplies, had to reduce rations. His first offer—three chestnuts in the morning and four in the evening—angered the monkeys. The keeper reversed the order; the monkeys were satisfied.[207] "The people are ignorant, but how can the gods be deceived?" Qi asked his listeners. "The friends," he noted in his diary, "were undecided."[208]

Plans were precise, but each sign of dearth or surplus, every unexpected problem, called for adjustments, generating fresh negotiations. Nonetheless, as told by Qi, each dispute dissolved into a working agreement. With a sure command of relief-administration lore, Qi diplomatically maneuvered his way between the conflicting viewpoints of his peers, the advice of power-holding officials, and the demands of rural and urban communities.

SCHEDULES UPSET

Qi's diary of 1641 displays the relief sponsors' efforts to follow set schedules and the circumstances that prompted deviations from their arrangements. The plan for feeding the 622 needy mouths in his ward was to make one distribution every five or six days, occasionally skipping a day, so that resources would last until the wheat harvest at the end of the fourth month.[209] Yet exigencies subsequently forced Qi and his peers to improvise ways to stretch resources. In the third month, Qi calculated that only forty *shi* of grain remained and that extending the program through the sixth month would require an additional fifteen *shi*. He therefore advised the "friends" responsible for Xiahe ward to reduce the number of allotted scoops (*ge*) from three to one; and, after informing Prefect Wang, as protocol required, he commissioned them again to raise funds.[210] Some weeks later, Qi spoke of stretching out rice relief in Xiahe, with one student managing the program every ten days; to those who still had received nothing, one should offer a little help, using five *shi* of rice.[211] Reassessing the situation some weeks later, Qi counseled the "friends" managing Xiahe ward concerning the distribution of auxiliary official rice: "Use three *sheng* to comfort the 'next poorest' while they are waiting to buy rice at below-market prices, and then, from what is left over, distribute one scoop to each person, to last until the tenth day of the seventh month. Use whatever still remains to augment aid for the starving." The friends "were all delighted and left," Qi noted.[212]

In what Qi called "my villages," the plan was to have seven distributions, one every five days, but that plan, too, was altered. After the second distribution, Qi reported: "Because the wheat harvest is still far off, my elder brother Feng jia will slightly postpone each of the next five distributions."[213] Accordingly, the third and fourth distributions were seven days apart; and the disbursement that Qi mentioned on the fifth day of the third month was probably the seventh.[214] At Ke Mountain, located near his rural estate, rice was to be issued six times, once every ten days.[215] Why it should have been treated differently is unclear; in any case, there too grain distributions were to follow a schedule.

Strive as they would to standardize operations, Qi and his peers repeatedly had to revise strategies to deal with the unexpected. Bad weather delayed crops. Locusts descended from the sky, first gradually, and then in such force as to blanket Qi's estate, prompting him to organize a defense.[216] He participated in prayers against the invaders, culled information on locust defense from famine-relief books, and had instructions for catching locusts carved onto woodblocks and printed up, to be disseminated by the friends, not just to his own village but to all the villages of the ten boroughs.[217] As a last-ditch effort, he offered first the incentive of food for each *sheng* of locusts caught, and then a bounty of fifty *wen* for each *dou* caught.[218]

Unanticipated, too, were the vagrants pouring into unwalled rural communities. Their care should rest with the monasteries, opined Prefectural Judge Chen Zilong. In a document one thousand characters long, Qi forcefully advocated soup kitchens instead.[219] The vagrant problem was discussed at a meeting that Qi, his elder brother Junjia, and colleague-manager Chen Changyao held with "over twenty students and elders" at the Bright Light Monastery, located at Ke Bridge.[220] After "singing praise of the worthy intentions of the local officials and magistrate"—thereby publicly establishing his connection to official authority—Qi mentioned the vagrants congregating at Ke Bridge, who, having neither food nor shelter, "were dying one after the other." Ten percent of those sleeping in front of the monastery will die, Qi estimated, adding that their grievous situation made him weep.[221] Six weeks later, when Qi went to Ke Bridge to distribute money, the vagrants numbered nearly one thousand and had more women than usual.[222]

The responsibility for the vagrants fell on local residents. As Qi explained to the head at Ke Bridge: "The prosperous shop owners in the market should provide rice for the soup kitchens; the less affluent shop owners, firewood and silver; and the monastery superiors should take turns (with six of them serving each day) in preparing the food and running about." The scholars and elders, Qi continued, "should unite to raise funds and should manage the gruel kitchens, with two of them serving each day." As for burying the corpses of those who had starved to death, Qi volunteered that his family would handle the expense, which he calculated would cost him one *qian* per body; this project would be managed by monks serving in rotation.[223]

Mindful of Liu Zongzhou's pronouncement that one should aid vagrants and the local population separately, Qi continued: "I feared that resources were inadequate for taking care of both." He figured that, if the residents who owned fields would give rice in proportion to their landholdings to help the local people, and if the shop owners would contribute aid for the vagrants, then both programs would be viable. Qi also feared that having only stationary soup kitchens, as the grand coordinator had strictly directed, would attract droves of riot-prone vagrants. Wondering, "Could Ke Market alone avoid this risk?" Qi endorsed monk Yuetang's proposal "to have monks carry gruel alongside the market, thereby keeping the vagrants scattered while feeding them."[224]

When he returned to Ke Bridge's monastery two days later to discuss the soup kitchens with the monks superior, a problem occurred to Qi: "Given that their lone operation would be limited, even if one were to segregate the vagrants from local people, the latter would, upon hearing about the soup kitchens, travel ten or twenty *li* and then, getting nothing to eat, they will die of exhaustion on the road back. The damage will have been our own doing."[225] At this point, a man surnamed Song, impatient with all the procrastinating, met up with two friends at a local pavilion. Reported Qi: "They decided to form a society to collect money. Without fixing a specific place or registering the names of the starving, they would distribute aid as circumstances demanded. But, fearing that people would come from all over and that resources would be insufficient to meet the demand, they thought it wise to place the money with some monk who had been a longtime resident and was trustworthy—and who would walk every day through the market and give something to anyone he encountered who was extremely hungry or sick." Qi debated options far into the night with his brother Junjia, monk Yuetang, and resident Shen Guomo. "While I was awaiting a decision," recounted Qi, "several people died; so I gave money to the monastery's superiors, asking that they make haste in aiding those in desperate need."[226]

Reconvening five days later at Ke Monastery, Qi, his brothers Junjia and Xiangjia, and Shen Guomo further deliberated aid for vagrants. "Most important is that money be distributed," recorded Qi, adding: "We wrote down the names of the friends who were taking responsibility for raising funds. I took the lead in distributing twelve hundred cash (*wen*) to set an example. One by one the vagrants were called into the God of Literature Temple, where they sat; then, as each received his share, they dispersed. There was no ruckus. As for those in front of the monastery who had been felled by fatigue, I had them sent to the infirmary." Upon returning to the infirmary by the dike later that day, Qi observed that the beggars who had received two bowls of gruel seemed to have recovered somewhat.[227]

Two weeks later Qi again joined others (his teacher Zou Rugong and Zou's brothers; his manager Chen Changyao and Chen's nephews; his elder brother Fengjia; and monk Wuliang),[228] in distributing money at Ke Bridge Monastery. Again the recipients were asked to sit down in the great hall, as well as in the God of Literature and Martial God Temples, and then, one by one, received a handout and left. Qi's group doled out "roughly seven thousand cash (*wen*) to over seven hundred persons."[229] Eight days later Qi asked Zou Ruhui and Chen Changyao to string cash—ten *wen* per string—to give to the poor, finishing in the middle of the night; and the next day they engaged monk Wuliang to go out to Ke Market to distribute eleven thousand cash. Several local "friends" who had been distributing relief in the western *qu* came by to observe the proceedings.[230]

In an essay, "Distributing Money" (Sanqian yi), Qi expressed "great pity" for the vagrants, who, "during the severe famine of 1641," had been dying at the rate of five or six a day in each village and town. He found two options to be problematic: if his colleagues were to set up soup kitchens in one place only, the mobs would be uncontrollable; if they were to collect rice to give them, the recipients had no place to cook. If they would instead rely on the bread peddlers who frequented the markets, his colleagues could help the starving people survive the day by providing them with four or five coins. Accordingly, Qi and local resident Wu Qisheng, along with their respective brothers, agreed to advertise that they would distribute money, roughly once every three days, for fifteen times, thus covering forty-five days.[231] Fearing that scheduled distributions would attract huge bands, for whom funds would be insufficient, and that store owners, anticipating mobbing, would close on the days of scheduled distributions, Qi's group "arranged to make distributions irregularly, sometimes a day early, sometimes a day late, but always within the three-day period." They "thereby reduced the crowds." According to this account, they gave each man ten *qian* as he exited the monastery grounds; for women and children, whom they segregated from the men, they followed the same procedure, but they gave the children somewhat less and the women somewhat more than the men. "At each distribution, one thousand people sought aid; sometimes there were more; absolutely never were there fewer."[232]

With the food shortage persisting into the summer months, Qi and his peers continued to improvise. Two "friends" returning from a tour of soup kitchens in the northern borough observed that the people would still be hungry after the beginning of the seventh month, when the gruel program was scheduled to end; they therefore proposed substituting wheat for rice, reserving the surplus rice for the seventh month.[233] Some ten days later, Qi, his brother Fengjia, who was managing the central borough, and Ni Yuanlu, whom Qi asked to participate in the discussion, decided that, when the official soup kitchens in the city stop on the tenth day of the seventh month, they should reinstate the private shops. They calculated that these would require roughly fifty *shi* of grain and entrusted the matter to Ni Yuanlu.[234] On the first day of the seventh month, Qi composed a letter about prolonging the distribution of gruel "to show the friends of all ten boroughs."[235]

The subject of extending relief resurfaced at a meeting at the Prefectural City God Temple, attended by the various "friends" representing each ward. Prefect Wang and the two district magistrates asked Ni and Qi to speak about prolonging the soup kitchens in the rural areas, something that the urban wards wished to imitate. Qi recounted: "We said that this time raising funds would be more difficult than before. If only one could, when the rice shipment arrives from Wenzhou, take some of the profits from it [probably here referring to the profits allowed the merchant importers] to provide two *shi* to each ward in order to lift their spirits." Other than that, not much could be done; Ni Yuanlu had already distributed three *shi* of official rice to each gruel shed.[236]

Another worry had dawned on Qi in the third month, when he witnessed, in the ill-fated rural area of Tianle, "women and children along the road picking grasses to eat and travelers looking cadaverous." Observing that village houses were all locked up, Qi made inquiries. Everyone had vacated the area, he learned. The embankments had burst, flooding the fields; consequently no grain had been harvested the previous year and the fields were overgrown with grass. When Qi further asked, "Why had they not plowed the fields for replanting?" remaining residents explained that they had sold all their belongings to pawnshops, adding: "Even if we were to sell our wives and children, we would get but a few coins, not enough to pay for the seeds."[237]

Thus among the challenges Qi had to face was that of financing loans for "seed and oxen" so as to restore agricultural productivity. In the fifth month, he calculated that the western borough still had over thirty *shi* of rice, for which they could get one hundred ounces of silver; that sum, combined with assistance from the circuit intendant, would provide over 220 ounces of silver— roughly two *qian* to lend out for each *mou* of land, for which they would exact 20 percent interest. After the autumn harvest, grain prices would be calculated and loans repaid in grain.[238]

CONCLUSION

Whenever fresh crises upset plans, disagreements erupted, threatening to drive Shaoxing's leading residents apart. Yet, rather than each going his own way, as Zhang Bi had done, a core of educated residents repeatedly reconvened to surmount fresh challenges, with Qi Biaojia emerging as chief coordinator of relief efforts. Qi's rise to a leadership position stemmed from his exceptional dedication to doing good, stirred by personal loss, his mastery of famine-relief information, and his enormous energy. Also important were Qi's broad horizons, which enabled him to reach for terms on which consensus might be built. In making that reach, he allied with official authority, which, no less than all the guidelines, oaths, and records, served to sustain cohesion among the participants through troubled and turbulent times. The centripetal forces that encouraged members of the local elite to collaborate is the subject of the next chapter.

7

Aligning with Officials

Use the ward to provide relief to the ward.
NI YUANLU

The two officials strongly agreed with me.
QI BIAOJIA

That official authority could be useful in maintaining order, coping with the swarms of vagrants on the move, and importing grain from abroad was well understood by Qi and his peers. Yet some residents resisted official interference in local affairs. Each had his neighborhood and lineage to protect, and even the most noble-minded were often bent on doing good in their own idiosyncratic ways. Though Qi, too, had special interests, he was cognizant that the fates of his urban ward, the rural area surrounding his estate, and his lineage were inextricably bound up with the well-being of neighboring areas. Viewing problems in transregional terms, seeking common grounds for supporting wide-scale relief programs over many months. he energetically forged alliances with officials.

MAINTAINING ORDER

Immediately after the riots of early 1641, Qi, with wife and two sons in tow, rushed from his rural estate for the prefectural city of Shaoxing. Not only did the robust city walls, whose gates shut tight at night, promise protection against desperate, marauding rural folk; city residence also offered advantageous proximity to local officials. En route, Qi composed a letter to Prefect Wang Sunlan about relief matters;[1] once in the city, dining at his father-in-law's home, upon hearing the mob's uproar, he abruptly departed for Wang's private office for a caucus. Also present were Vice-Prefect Bi Jiuchen and the magistrates of Shanyin and Guiji districts, Wang Yuanzhao and Zhou Can, respectively.[2]

One must, Qi told the officials, not only distribute grain to pacify the hungry, but also arrest and punish the culprits. By opening the granaries, he further advised, they would trick the culprits into letting down their guard. As for the calm areas, Qi recommended that they post announcements about food relief in each ward and dispatch runners to record the residents' names. Each official should supervise several wards. They should issue relief tickets as the residents' names are reported; by processing the starving people in small batches they would divide the mob's power. The people will receive grain; order will be restored. Qi further cautioned against letting the "literati and ordinary people" (*shimin*) distribute the grain. He feared that rogues would vie for control, that they would "use grain and money to entice the people and then, for no reason, grow even more evil." The officials, Qi noted in his diary, "agreed with what I said."[3]

The officials, recounted Qi, "called the roll of the yamen runners and is-sued sign-boards, and the unrest subsided somewhat." Instructions having been sent down through the mutual-surveillance organization (*baojia*), the *jia* chiefs held up the signboards and the members of each *jia* reported to their unit. That night "the snow turned heavy," wrote Qi, who then concluded the day's entry: "I printed up the tickets for dispensing rice, and, in the in-terests of uniformity, I had the entire city get them from me. I also pasted up announcements for the students who were taking responsibility for each ward and who had agreed to put a uniform program into effect. I had no sleep all night."[4]

The next day brought reassuring news: officials had captured and put nu-merous perpetrators in cangues. They ordered that grain and pawnshops stay open—a measure to forestall any panic-buying of grain. "The city ap-peared to have calmed down, with only one area, around West Suburb Gate, still harboring rowdies," reported Qi, adding, "Even if one were to arrest them, one still had to reckon with the mayhem that had just commenced in the rural areas and had not yet subsided. Everywhere were reports of agita-tion . . . even cases of raids."[5]

At that time bands from neighboring Zhuji (Jiyang) numbering in the hundreds and thousands were roving through the region, plundering villages. Having learned about this from his two elder brothers, and surmising that extreme violence would follow, Qi "hastened to pay a visit to Prefect Wang and Vice-Prefect Bi to tell them of the emergency." He also went to the gar-rison, beseeching that a military patrol accompany official Bi on his tour of the area. Once home, he wrote Bi a note about the urgency of pacifying the rural villages.[6] This is probably the letter preserved in Qi's collected writ-ings where Qi first commended Bi for having pacified the area through the mutual-surveillance system but then proceeded to comment, "One would not have guessed that the gang of the big bandit Gao Yuan, who had pillaged a nunnery only one *li* away from my village, would still be around." Gao, for-merly a bondservant in the household of Qi's relatives, had been expelled for breaking the law and had also wronged Qi's friend Wu Qisheng, but then managed to escape, emerging as a chief bandit. In nearby villages, men of this sort coalesced as the Ten Dragons, a band to which the recently captured Tao Three, Wang Five, Wang the Black, and Wang Nine all belonged. According to Tao Three's testimony, Gao Yuan had been raiding houses in the vicinity for food and now had ambitions to take to the sea to plunder coastal areas. Compounding Qi's apprehensions were his colleague Yu Huang's report of bandits using the waterways to plunder the coastal towns of Zheshan and Haining, in Shaoxing and Hangzhou prefectures. Furthermore, ensconced in the rural area of Tianle was the big bandit Yang Three, who possessed sharp weapons, commanded a following of over forty men, and, Qi feared, might grow violent in the future.[7]

Two days later Qi recorded (as would Chen Zilong's retrospective account) that vagrants from Zhuji were roaming the area in search of food and that "beggars north of the river were more numerous than before." At the meeting at the City God Temple that day, the friends who had taken responsibility for distributing grain to the various wards debated how to handle these menacing bands. Reported Qi: "Some said, 'Expel them.' But if one expels them from the city, they will infect the rural areas. Some said, 'Pacify them.' This would mean establishing soup kitchens for the residents of the prefectural city and giving travel money to those who had occupations to which they might return. These two matters rest with officials; they are difficult to manage." Qi himself acknowledged being "at a loss about what should be done." He had heard three dicta pronounced by Ni Yuanlu—"Use the ward to provide relief to the ward; use the ward to protect the ward; and use the ward to carry out arrests in the ward"—but Qi was skeptical: would this policy, he asked, "really deter the vagrants from making an uproar?"[8] A small militia was sent to protect Qi's city lodging,[9] but news soon had Qi "extremely worried": several thousand residents of the rural areas, hearing that relief was going to be issued in the city, were surrounding the city with the intention of using force to buy rice at below-market prices.[10]

Maintaining order remained problematic for several weeks. Unrest troubled the hills around Pingshui. In his own rural area, Qi selected, from among the starving, roughly one hundred stalwart men to form a militia, promising that rewards or punishments would depend on their performance.[11] He had recently learned that residents in Chang'an ward, in the northeast quadrant of the city, had used a similar strategy against looting: from the ranks of the poor who qualified for relief, they had selected the most robust men for defense, providing each with a daily food ration.[12]

Several dozen of Qi's recruits failed to show up at the community temple five days later. The dodgers were to be punished, Qi noted, without specifying how.[13] A week later, right after watching the distribution of rice at his lineage shrine, and as though he felt justified to demand service in return for gifts of grain, he selected thirty-two men from his lineage to form a night-watch corps. These measures did little to quell Qi's sense of unease, however. Later that day, news that a merchant had been killed, his body riddled with knives and arrows, reduced Qi to shivers and sobs.[14]

Small provocations easily ignited residents. One night, word reached Qi of a bandit alarm at his "elder brother" Ningfang's place.[15] He hastened over there, ascertained that over eighty men had rushed to the rescue, and wrote down their names so that they would be duly rewarded.[16] But, reported Qi the next day, "it turned out that someone had been leading an ox through our village. A member of our lineage mistook him for a thief, sounded the gong, and gathered the defense."[17]

While dispensing rice at the community altar three days later, Ningfang rewarded (with extra grain, one supposes) those who had responded to the alarm; then, Qi Biaojia, "hoping to rouse them to mend their ways," severely chastised those who were unfilial, prodigal, or prone to gamble.[18] A subsequent distribution of grain at Qi's lineage temple was likewise followed by a community-compact lecture.[19] Feeding the needy went hand in hand with co-opting and socializing them.

Qi's initiatives were highly localized, yet he understood that his interests, entangled as they were with several jurisdictions, could benefit from official intervention. To have the Three Rivers Locks reopened so as to protect the wheat fields from flooding—this was after the continuous rain and snow of early 1641—he had to ask Prefect Wang.[20] Understanding that victims of hunger would gravitate to wherever food is dispensed earliest, he counseled Prefectural Judge Chen Zilong to ensure that all the districts of Shaoxing prefecture initiate the soup kitchens simultaneously.[21]

Qi consistently pushed for comprehensive plans. Liu Zongzhou wanted to have subscription records compiled on a neighborhood-by-neighborhood basis. Qi insisted that the records be "united in one place."[22] Ni Yuanlu and other residents wished to have each ward and village take care of its own. Qi recognized that, if neglected, the needy of neighboring districts would surely rove into his own district, stirring up trouble.[23] When literati, gentry, and village elders of Tianle came to Qi's Yu Mountain residence to speak of the suffering in their nine villages, Qi raised the question, "Which is most convenient: having our rural area raise funds independently, or having the students in the city who are taking responsibility raise funds cooperatively?" "Everyone," noted Qi in his diary, "said that it was fitting to raise funds cooperatively."[24]

Official authority was invaluable in enforcing wide-based cooperation and performance in relief operations. Once, when someone had been hindering a soup kitchen operation (precisely how is unclear), Prefectural Judge Chen angrily fined that kitchen's head one hundred *shi* of fresh grain. "Various friends and other persons from Guiji" met with Qi at the City God Tem-

ple to ask him to defend the offender. Siding with official authority, Qi refused.[25] Once a party of five visitors informed Qi that "a bad type" was im-
peding a soup kitchen in the western borough; Qi promptly wrote a letter
asking Vice-Prefect Bi to punish the culprit as a warning to all.[26]

SHAPING POLICY

Though dependent on official authority, Qi was no lackey. Keeping his sense
of purpose and self-definition intact, he often countered official suggestions
with his own opinions and initiatives. The day after the riots, at a "public discussion" called by the prefect, just as the gentry were about to submit their
pledges, Qi arrived late and "could not help but disagree." They should, he
said, use merchants to bring grain to be sold at fair prices (*tongshang gaodi*),
and they should right away ensure that pawnshops remain open, that households not be forced to sell their stocks, and that the friends divide up responsibility for the wards. Qi thereupon wrote a letter to Prefect Wang, sum-
marizing this agenda for pacifying the region and distributing food relief.[27]
Some days later, he and other retired officials paid visits, first to one official
(Chen Huanzhou, prefect of Hangzhou), and then to Prefectural Judge Chen
Zilong, pressing them, among other things, to provide an armed escort for
the rice shipments and to tour the rural areas so as to bring the disorderly
people under control.[28] Day after day Qi wrote letters advising officials. When
Chen Zilong recommended that monasteries handle the vagrant problem,
Qi countered with an alternative plan. When Chen stated that he wished to
have the grain purchased from Jiangyou (Jiangxi); Qi declared that it would
be better to get it from Wenzhou.[29] When Chen advocated setting up soup
kitchens (with the intention of trusting the matter to Yu Huang), Qi insisted:
"No. At this time it is truly unfitting to set up soup kitchens," and recommended the fifth or sixth month instead, whereupon they argued about the
timing and the benefits and harms of each arrangement.[30] Moreover, Qi
placed numerous demands on officials; once, for example, after vouching
for the integrity of the various students who were taking responsibility for
the soup kitchens, he requested "four things" of Chen Zilong: that he deflect
slanders by deputing only trustworthy men; have the grain and money in
place early; prepare registers to be exhibited; and have each district syn-
chronize relief efforts.[31]

Qi respected official authority, but rather than passively capitulating to
it, he recognized it as a means for achieving his goals. He often took pains to
note in his diary that local officials had placed the responsibility for relief
on him, or that, when dealing with merchants or the young student managers, he was armed with the calling cards or letters of officials. He used official authority to bolster his own, especially in eliciting cooperation from the
numerous "friends"; they understood that he would commend them to offi-

cials for deeds done well, as when he wrote a letter to official Chen Zilong praising several students for their integrity in managing relief activities.[32]

When he held office, Qi demonstrated a talent for law enforcement. With no qualms about imposing severe punishments, he had once ordered that members of the Gang Stars be beaten to death and their corpses exposed in the market place.[33] At home, however, it suited Qi that officials would enforce the law and mete out corporal punishments while he and fellow high-status residents would focus their energies and resources on acts of kindness. Officials would move on to other posts; the prominent natives of Shaoxing would stay behind, to face for decades, even generations, the judgments of the area's inhabitants.

Once Qi heard that someone in Ke Market was smuggling Shaoxing rice out, and that his own brother Fengjia wished to issue a prohibition against it. Qi cautioned: "It is unfitting for those below to enforce the law." Noting in his diary that his "elder brother" (actually a cousin) Ningfang "strongly agreed with me," Qi accordingly wrote to the circuit intendant asking that he strictly forbid the smuggling.[34] When the official responded, requesting that "both officials and the people" forbid the smuggling of rice out of the area, Qi replied that he "would rather that the prohibition come from the officials," warning that it would be disastrous to allow the people themselves to prohibit such matters.[35] Qi protected the official authority he so effectively used.

Holding exalted positions and the power to dole out punishments, officials radiated their authority downward, but not without themselves being susceptible to pressures from below. Qi, who had himself served as an official, exerted an authority of his own that was based on his past official record, familiarity with local conditions, knowledge of relief matters, and responsiveness to the people's demands. When starving people were clamoring for food, it was not the officials but he who was able to calm them down by telling them about the relief plans "in their patois."[36]

When officials needed relief plans, Qi drafted and, in response to the officials' corrections, reworked drafts to produce "A Set of Regulations for Taking Responsibility of the Soup Kitchens" and "A Proposal for Soup Kitchens, in Fourteen Items."[37] The collaboration enabled him to forward his views, to bear official calling cards, and, along with other members of the local elite, to nudge and coax officials to work in ways that would complement their own, informal leadership. Equipped with a vision of what would best serve the community at large, Qi asserted a moral authority vis-à-vis officials. Not infrequently, he slipped into the role of praising and thanking officials, as when he "wrote a letter praising Vice-Prefect Bi Jiuchen for his labors in touring and boosting the morale of the southern borough and his achievement in catching bandits," or when he recorded in his diary, "I have the greatest respect for Bi's intelligence," intimating that Qi was the true arbiter regarding relief strategies.[38]

TOURING THE RURAL SOUP KITCHENS

Officials were indispensable for regulating the rural soup kitchens, and the need for inspection tours had been weighing on Qi's mind ever since the riots of early 1641.[39] During a dinner he was hosting, Qi opined that "the various elder brothers" ought to nudge Liu Zongzhou (Qi's senior by twenty-four years) to approach Chen Zilong about touring the soup kitchens as well as about importing grain for sale at below local-market prices.[40] Chen, recognizing that a tour would "encourage donations and pacify the people," proved amenable.[41] Weeks later Qi notified Chen that the villages were anticipating his visit and advised him that, even if he were unable to see every village, he should stop at the chief places throughout the ten boroughs.[42]

In preparation for the tour, the officials joined a meeting at the Wang Yangming Shrine. Qi examined the records borough by borough, expatiated upon the suffering of his own borough, and showed a plan for the inspection tour. "The friends not only got to express their views; they also carried out formalities with decorum," Qi observed, patronizing his social inferiors somewhat. The upshot of the meeting, Qi added, was that "Prefect Wang divided the task of touring the five boroughs among the officials, assigning the southern borough to the district jailor, the eastern borough to the irrigation intendant, the central borough to the prefectural judge [Chen Zilong], and the western and northern boroughs to the two district magistrates." The two district magistrates would each manage two hundred *shi* of rice, and the prefect one hundred *shi*. Thus each borough should get fifty *shi*—not counting any additional aid that might come from the offices of arrests and punishments or from contributions from the salt and circuit intendants.[43] The next day, Qi sent Chen Zilong an itinerary for touring the central borough and a copy to Bi Jiuchen.[44]

Plans appeared to be settled but were not. Immediately after returning to his lodging, Qi received five visitors who discussed "nothing but relief matters." Two of them expressed concern that the magistrate of Shanyin lacked the requisite authority for touring the western borough, which was under the jurisdiction of both Xiaoshan and Shanyin; they prodded Qi to ask Prefectural Judge Chen to take charge instead. Seizing upon the suggestion, Qi sent Chen a note.[45] It suited him that Chen, who ranked above a magistrate and commanded a militia, should tour the western borough, the location of his and several of his brothers' rural estates. Moreover, Chen, who had just published Xu Guangqi's *Complete Book of Agriculture* and was well known for poetic talent, promised to be a compatible companion.

Two days after learning that Vice-Prefect Bi would join the tour,[46] Qi forwarded "A Plan for the Inspection Tour of the Western Borough" and the itinerary to Chen. He then packed his things, noting: "Whenever I go out, I usually take along money for aiding the poor. Now, because the rural area to the west is extremely impoverished, I have prepared over one hundred extra envelopes of cash."[47]

On the appointed day, the party of two officials and Qi Biaojia set out, each on his own boat, and each undoubtedly with an entourage of aides and nameless servants. The journey was arduous, requiring frequent changes, from large boats to small and from water transportation to sedan chairs. They set up a soup depot in the village of Jiuyan, a backwater where, Qi once had noted, a studio once owned by a Mr. Zhou had long been in disrepair.[48] They then ate "a vegetarian meal"—Qi's oblique reminder that, in consideration of the scarcity all around them, they had to forgo their customary luxurious fare.[49] Changing to smaller boats, they proceeded to Xialü Bridge, fifty *li* southwest of the prefectural city,[50] and then went by land to a monastery, where they settled some disagreements among the residents. Shifting to sedan chairs, they traversed a mountain, "pausing briefly at the top," passed through remote hamlets, and, via Zhang Family Bridge, headed for Ge Family Hilltop, an area where, wrote Qi, "there should be abundant lakes, yet all around is wild, with almost no trace of cultivated fields. Because of the long drought there, the sands were blowing against our faces. The two officials looked ashen with anxiety."[51]

Equally demanding was the following day. Abandoning water routes for land, they traveled alongside "fields covered with wheat sprouts," at sunset reaching Linpu, thirty *li* south of Xiaoshan city.[52] Punning on the place name Tianle, which literally means "Heaven's Happiness," Qi observed that this particular spot was "the somewhat happier of the territories in the rural area of Tianle."[53] The drought had depleted the waterways, forcing the party to take sedan chairs through the fields, their way ever so slightly moonlit. They tried their best—Qi does not specify how—to mollify the chair bearers, who were suffering from hunger.[54]

As the group penetrated the hinterlands, inhabitants and "friends" surfaced. At one stop, a licentiate emerged to consult about the soup kitchen under his responsibility; starving residents of Shu Village registered complaints that they might get nothing to eat; and "friends" in charge of relief came forth to greet the touring party.[55] At another stop, three "friends" who were in a heated argument came forth; the two touring officials, recorded Qi, "settled the matter." Farther on, two students, Zhao and Chen, showed up to escort the party to a temple, there joined by another student and provincial graduate Wang. After calculating the amounts of grain for assisting that area, the inspection party learned that Wang and Zhao had had a disagreement, with the graduate proposing that the grain be distributed and the mere student pressing for soup kitchens. Chen Zilong loosened the gridlock by settling upon the latter option.[56]

The touring officials disciplined corruption and ensured that the kitchen managers stuck to prescribed guidelines. Upon reaching a monastery that was to be their lodging for the night, they investigated the misappropriation of funds that Magistrate Wang had provided as aid for each village, and then duly brought charges against the culprits.[57] At Linpu students brought word that it was "their private intention" to keep the soup kitchens of the two districts, Shanyin and Xiaoshan, separate even though the official plan was that they be jointly managed; the two officials chastised the students.[58] Upon reaching Yulin Pass, the inspection party learned that residents were not getting their allotted share of food. The managers made the lame excuse that the "hungry people were ashamed to eat gruel." Chen Zilong upbraided them.[59] Continuing the tour the following day, Chen fined someone who had been obstructing the relief efforts.[60]

Qi's firsthand account of the tour, with its mention of varied modes of transportation and the names of specific villages, restores weight to the time-worn cliché of Chinese officials enduring hardship (a vegetarian diet and long days) when they trekked to the rural areas to inspect conditions in person. In Shaoxing prefecture at least, the rural areas were populated with numerous "friends" of the cause—students and graduates—ready to manage the kitchens. Even those not motivated by compassion or a sense of noblesse oblige could, through charitable activities, forge advantageous social connections with men of high status. At the least, those who contributed labor and resources could anticipate a banquet or wine-drinking celebration following the successful completion of a philanthropic project; after the operation of the soup kitchen in Qi's village had ended, Qi's brother Fengjia invited all those who had issued rice, to drink wine together and participate in "the rituals of completion."[61]

Qi's account further shows that officials in Shaoxing, far from being impotent or lazy, as the paradigm of dynastic decline would have it, effectively used their authority to guarantee the soup kitchen program. Even in desolate areas, official presence, though transient, had a powerful effect, compelling local students eagerly to rush out to greet the entourage, to proffer reports on their performance, and to expose disputes among themselves in competitive bids for official attention.

Exposure to the suffering in turn affected members of the touring party. Of "Zhao Family Bridge, a thoroughfare to Zhuji," Qi observed: "Formerly it was a thriving market place. Now houses were locked up and empty. Along the roadside, we saw mostly emaciated, cadaverous shapes."[62] He then noted: "The suffering and misery I witnessed inspired me to offer some help, but I had brought little with me. So I borrowed from 'brother' Hua Mengcai and asked friends Ke Liangqi and Li Zhiyu to survey the starving and compile a report. Hua, Ke, and friends made up four hundred relief packets for me, working to the bitter end; that night, they also completed the register of the starving population. Extremely exhausted, I had gone to bed, but because the various friends had worked hard for me, I got up in the middle of the night to thank them."[63] At another stop, Vice-Prefect Bi likewise responded to the pleas of the starving by dispersing ten cash (*wen*) per person.[64]

As the inspection party wended its way through remote areas, inhabitants materialized with concerns other than food. Someone had been obstructing irrigation; the officials decreed that the practice stop.[65] A woman complained that she had been cheated by an uncle; Vice-Prefect Bi ordered the two overseers of the relevant lineage estate to set the matter straight.[66] Possibly wrongdoers reverted to their old ways once the touring party receded from the scene; still, the official rulings, broadcast throughout the community, must have empowered the victims somewhat. For a brief moment, the touring officials gave rural residents an opportunity to demand justice. Distributing food and restoring moral order went hand in hand. Qi himself finished the tour with a sense of balance regained; as though auspicious weather was reward for their efforts, he wrote: "Just when our tour was over, a timely downpour of rain arrived—truly a happy affair."[67]

Qi reported most fully on affairs in the western borough, to which he had a special allegiance. There, his brothers, lineage members, and tenants resided; his father had spent the salary earned as an official to build a garden; and Qi and his cousin ("elder brother" Xiong jia) had subsequently built gardens.[68] Nonetheless, he did occasionally remark on relief activities being carried out in other boroughs. When the "friends" who had taken responsibility for the five boroughs were about to leave for their posts, Qi gave them one tael for each borough's "public expenses" (*gong fei*).[69] When five "friends" finished accompanying Magistrate Wang on a tour of soup kitchens of Shanyin's northern borough, he received their visit.[70] Constantly he was in touch with the "friends" of the various boroughs.[71]

After touring the western borough, Qi urged Vice-Prefect Bi to visit the southern borough, providing him soon after with specific plans.[72] He was particularly concerned about the plight of Guiji district's Pingshui Village, which, alongside Tianle, ranked among the poorest rural areas.[73] Qi and Bi traveled by land to Pingshui, where, joined by Guo Erzhang, they offered sacrifices at a temple and then headed for a hamlet by a river crossing to distribute grain to the thirtieth *du*. With the heads of the tax collection divisions (*lijia*) "all standing at attention," Qi and Bi lectured about the community-compact and mutual-surveillance organizations. They then moved on to the twenty-ninth *du*, resting briefly at a hall, where they offered support to the licentiates and *li* heads. That evening, while Qi chatted with Bi about local affairs, Guo filled out the relief tickets for the twenty-eighth *du*—there were one hundred persons in all—and calculated the amounts, finishing his task at dawn.[74] The next day Bi chastised someone from a prosperous household in the twenty-eighth *du* who had been obstinate. Because the remote hamlets of this *du* harbored thieves, and perhaps to compensate for the paucity of student-managers in this area, Qi and Bi at one stop explained the mutual-surveillance method and at another stop, wrote Qi, their lectures on the imperial injunctions may have inspired members of the audience "to cleanse their hearts and reform their ways."[75]

For his independent relief program of 1640, benefactor Zhang Bi provided enough grain to sustain "ten thousand persons for five days" and yet, as he put it, "if calculated in terms of the entire prefecture, that was a mere drop."[76] In 1641, though some members of the community pledged grain from their own supplies, they had to turn to officials for help in procuring additional grain to supply large-scale relief over several months. Officials had more to gain (a good name, a promotion) from acts of generosity than from hoarded wealth. By donating their own salaries to relief programs, they would, Qi advised, move the common people.[77] Accordingly, Magistrate Wang contributed ninety taels, to be divided among the villages.[78] Officials also could exercise their authority for beneficial ends. They could seek imperial approval to postpone the collection of taxes. They could, as Qi once requested of Magistrate Zhou, use revenues from penal fines for relief.[79] Above all, they could lift costly tolls along the waterways, negotiate with officials elsewhere to permit interregional movements of grain, and provide the capital (by borrowing money from the treasury, for example) to initiate and guarantee financial arrangements. For facilitating the importation of grain into Shaoxing, officials were indispensable.

For importing grain, Shaoxing was ideally located, in the midst of a vast network of waterways conducive to rapid transportation, down the southern coast to Ningbo, Taizhou, and Wenzhou, respectively, or north to the cities of Hangzhou and Suzhou. Just before the grain riots of early 1641, Qi and his colleagues, anticipating hard times, deliberated using merchants to procure grain for stabilizing prices.[80] Right after the riots, Qi recorded in his diary: "By lamplight, I wrote an official letter to the two prefects [Chen Huanzhou of Hangzhou and Wang Sunlan] saying that Hangzhou (Wulin) was the channel for trade between Nanzhili and Guangdong (Jiang-Guang), and that it was unfitting to obstruct the passage of the rice boats." Qi further mentioned that official Chen Huanzhou had already given permission for ten thousand *shi* of grain to pass through.[81]

At the large meeting held the following day in reaction to the riots, it was right "after the students left" that prefectural and city officials "summoned ten or so grain brokers for a discussion, stressing that officials and merchants should work together for a shipment, with the officials providing the capital and the merchants supplying the goods." As Qi summed up the matter, "The officials rely on merchants to facilitate the shipment of the goods; merchants rely on officials to remove impediments." The upshot was that the officials provided between four and five thousand taels for capital.[82] Corroborating Qi's account, Chen reported that the merchants "were given documents verifying their purpose," adding: "In equal parts, the price manipulations brought charity/kindness (*hui*) to the people and benefited the merchants. Within ten days, the money reverted to the treasury."[83]

Qi then advised Prefect Wang: although Taizhou had already granted permission for the purchase of rice for sale at fair prices, one still ought to negotiate with Ningbo (Ning). By dealing with Ningbo, which was nearer than Taizhou, they would acquire "twice the amount with half the work."[84] Qi then paid visits to his father-in-law and Liu Zongzhou, making the case that a charitable food program was essential to restoring order, and that to supply such a program, "one absolutely must bring in rice to be sold at favorable prices." Aware that the quantity of rice from Taizhou and Ningbo would be limited, he concluded: "To sustain relief over a period of time, one must ultimately rely on the region around and north of Suzhou (Wu-Chu). Today Hangzhou rice is more expensive than Shaoxing rice, and not being able to pass through Hangzhou to Shaoxing poses difficulties." Liu, Qi declared in his diary, "strongly agreed with what I said."[85] Two months later, Qi calculated that the cost of rice imported from Taizhou would be about 1.5 to 1.6 taels per *shi;* even when sold at below-market prices, there would be a gain of 0.2 to 0.3 taels for every *shi* (or 200 to 300 taels per thousand *shi*).[86]

Using merchants by facilitating their activities (*tongshang*) was, Qi repeatedly asserted, the most suitable means for bringing down prices. Magistrate Wang wished to lower prices by fiat. Qi argued that doing so would prompt the closing of markets and precipitate looting. Upon hearing two officials say that Liu Zongzhou too had proposed that prices be lowered, Qi sent Liu a letter "stating emphatically that this would not do."[87] As Qi explained in his diary: "Since rice in the market was scarce, I definitely thought that one must import it from the Suzhou area (San Wu). In response to the circuit intendant's inquiry about lowering prices, I opined that sometimes market prices cannot be controlled by the men at the top. Only by purchasing through trade can one make the rice plentiful; when rice is plentiful, prices will naturally fall."[88]

Brokering arrangements between merchants and officials consumed much of Qi's time. Toward mid-1641, six or seven grain merchants, having encountered trouble bringing back rice they had purchased in Taizhou, complained to Qi about the extra profit (of two *dou* per *shi*) that the prefect wished to extract from the deal (to replenish the treasury, one assumes, for Qi makes no mention of private interests). Recounted Qi in his diary: "I believe that the only solution to the food shortage is to facilitate merchant trading; therefore one should generally encourage and sympathize with merchants." To reassure the merchants, Qi showed them a copy of a letter he had just sent the prefect proposing that levies be kept small.[89]

Merchants and brokers reiterated their complaints three days later.[90] Qi visited Yu Huang to discuss the policy of encouraging merchants; Yu Huang generally agreed with him, noted Qi in his diary. They proceeded to the garrison hall for a public meeting with the circuit intendant. Over forty members of the local literati had convened, whom Qi listed in rough hierarchical order: in addition to Yu and Qi were nine other residents claiming former-official status (*shen*), among them Qi's father-in-law, Ni Yuanlu, and Zhang Kunfang; over thirty licentiates; and a few graduates of the provincial examinations. They requested that the circuit intendant ask the two censors-in-chief to depute official Chen Zilong to go to buy rice from the Suzhou area to be sold at favorable prices.[91]

A letter from Chen Zilong informed Qi that the price of husked rice in Wenzhou was only 1.2 taels, that officials there had no strict prohibitions regarding its grain, and that Qi should discuss with the circuit administration about going there to purchase grain for sale at fair prices.[92] The price Chen quoted compared favorably with other prices mentioned by Qi: 1.5 taels for husked rice to the right of the river (Jiangyou); the 2.6 taels to which rice had risen in his own area.[93] A month later, Qi mentioned the possibility of getting one hundred ounces of silver for over thirty *shi* of rice that remained in four boroughs—something less than 3.33 taels per *shi;*[94] and five weeks later the price of rice in Hangzhou would be 4.3 taels.[95]

PERSPECTIVES EXPANDED BY OFFICIAL AUTHORITY

On the subject of relief strategy, the do-gooders of Shaoxing roughly fell into two groups. On the one hand were those residents (Zhang Bi, Wang Siren, Ni Yuanlu, and Liu Zongzhou) who favored narrowly localized relief efforts, funded by local resources and, ideally, through the maintenance of local granaries; these men generally resisted official interference. Epitomizing their viewpoint was Ni Yuanlu's statement, "Use the ward to provide relief to that ward,"[96] On the other hand were those (exemplified by Qi Biaojia) whose expanded horizons transcended lineage and administrative boundaries and embraced rural areas and urban wards alike. Sustaining this expansive view was the possibility of importing grain, for which official authority was essential. As Zhang Bi noted in 1640, Jin Lan, Yu Huang, and Qi Biaojia advocated that food prices be lowered by flooding the market with grain to be sold at fair prices (*pingtiao*); and Jin Lan resolutely took the lead in contributing seven hundred *shi* for the purchase of grain at fair prices (*pingdi*).[97]

Although Zhang Bi would live into the next dynasty, he rarely appears in Qi's diary and played no visible role in the community-wide relief efforts of 1641. Ni Yuanlu, who, like Zhang Bi, was inclined to distribute relief "privately," ended up cooperating with Qi Biaojia; he accepted that official help was needed for restoring order.[98] Liu Zongzhou, though he would acquiesce to having official participation during 1641, supported Zhang Bi's program in 1640 and persistently advocated community granaries (an institution associated with local control).

Ni Yuanlu and Qi Biaoji enjoyed a close friendship, cemented by their experience of having together taken and passed the *jinshi* examination in 1622. They socialized frequently over the years, testifies Qi's extant diary, which stretches back to 1631.[99] Yet, on the subject of famine relief, they disagreed. Ni generally favored the self-governance of discrete, localized communities, free from official intervention. He maintained that the prosperous members of each lineage ought to make contributions based on the amount of fields owned and then use the proceeds to aid its poor members. Although he allowed that the lineage might spend its surplus on helping non-kin residents, his aim was to keep the lineage self-contained: the program would, he reasoned, spare poor lineage members from accepting the charity of strangers while freeing well-to-do members from being accountable to government officials.[100]

Qi was skeptical of Ni's small-scale, piecemeal approach to need. He repeatedly maintained that relief efforts must be coordinated across administrative units; he perceived that residents of neglected wards would simply overrun those wards enjoying vigorous food distribution programs; and that not every rural subdivision (here using the term *tu,* to refer to subdivisions within each of the forty-eight *du*) had the resources for its own relief program.[101] When he visited the rural area of Tianle, he again countered Ni's strategy of having "each ward take care of that ward," stating: "Reporting what I had seen and heard, I wrote to Magistrate Wang, saying that that rural area had many poor people and few who were rich, so it is inappropriate exclusively to apply the policy of 'using the subdivision (*tu*) to save the subdivision, and the village to save the village.'" Qi then insisted that, even if they were unable to give to each *du* equally, it would be best to treat the villages collectively on a *du*-wide basis.[102]

Social realities eroded Ni's vision of self-contained territories. In 1642, ten natives of Ni Yuanlu's original home town, the district of Shangyu, complained that the rich residents of their section (*du*) had failed to provide aid. Ni turned to his mother to kick off a fund-raising campaign to benefit that community; she contributed ten ounces of silver and other families happily followed suit.[103] The program served a clearly defined community, in accord with Ni's beliefs. Yet his own far-flung social networks involved him in at least two communities.

Ni favored nongovernmental charitable granaries of the sort that Zhu Xi had initiated in the twelfth century. In a memorial to the emperor, he advocated that private community granaries replace government-operated ones, and shortly before being recalled to office in 1642, he formulated plans for what one modern scholar has termed a "grain-lending" or a "joint-stock company," in which five subscribing families would charge 20 percent annual interest on loans.[104] Informing these programs was Ni's distrust of officialdom: "Even the most worthy officials will move on after three years, whereas local people will be judged by descendants for a hundred years; thus, even if the local people in charge are not capable, they will do no harm."[105]

Charitable granaries, Ni asserted, should be distinguished from the usurious state-sponsored "Green Sprouts" loans to farmers, which had, ever since the eleventh-century Wang Anshi advocated it, suffered notoriety. As Ni put it, Green Sprouts loans essentially "used aid to extract a profit."[106] Qi, though invoking Zhu Xi's method at least once,[107] generally preferred to procure grain through markets rather than from local granaries. He felt no compunction about describing the "seed and oxen" loan program for funding the next harvest as "starting with the Green Sprouts method and ending with the community granary method." After assuring officials Bi and Chen that "the plan would serve Tianle for eternity and was not a bunch of useless words," he noted in his diary: "They were pleased and thought that this should certainly be put into effect."[108]

Conflicts over strategy simmered on, periodically boiling over. Prominent members of the gentry—no less than those humble students who asked the touring officials to arbitrate their disputes about managing the soup kitchens—took their quarrels up the political hierarchy. Even Ni, who wished to exclude officials from local arrangements for community granaries, attempted to win official backing. This Qi learned through the grapevine when his nephew Yiyuan relayed a message from Prefect Wang. Concerned that the official grain was insufficient to meet the demand of all the urban households wanting to buy, Ni argued for replacing the sale of grain at fair prices with another strategy: using the profits accrued from the capital provided by officials and merchants to assist the wards in installing soup kitchens; and including the "next poorest" in the program but charging them one *qian* for each bowl of gruel. Ni described the tactic of indefinitely replenishing the supply of grain as "the perpetual renewal of life" (*shengsheng bu duan*)— a phrase that had gained popularity, especially in reference to liberating animals. The details of his plan are vague but the gist is clear: the locus for managing the financial transactions for the soup kitchens should be shifted from officials (who import the grain) to those running the soup kitchens, who would collect and reinvest the payments.[109]

Long before his appointment to Shaoxing, Chen Zilong had been friends with Ni. Frequently he stayed at Ni's house, and, when their teacher Huang Daozhou was flogged in court in 1640, the two men "together wept all day long."[110] Yet, not to be outdone by Ni regarding relief policies, Qi pressed his opinion upon officials Chen and Bi, whom he was accompanying at that time on the inspection tour of the western borough. Rather than selling soup to the "next poorest," he favored selling them grain at favorable prices, thereby giving them some hope of surviving the next four months. "The two officials strongly agreed with me," noted Qi. Then, writing back to Prefect Wang, Qi contested the proposal made by the regional inspector (Yao Qinlü) that the city brokers should lean on the grain-storing households in the coun-tryside to sell grain at lower prices. "I emphatically stated that this was im-possible," wrote Qi, adding: "Today the basic strategy is to have merchants import grain from the outside."[111]

In response, Prefect Wang sent Qi a proposal by Ni, entitled "Eight Ad-vantages of Setting Up Soup Kitchens." No less skilled than Qi in marshal-ing arguments to defend his position, Ni insisted that the price-stabilizing sale of grain cease. Qi replied to Prefect Wang: "I have sought only to aid the starving; from the start, I have never held views for egotistical reasons." He also sent Ni a note making an appointment to meet the next day.[112] As soon as the tour of the western rural soup kitchens ended, and after taking leave of the two officials at Ke Bridge, Qi "assembled various friends" on his boat to confer about relief for the city; then, on his way home he dropped in on his two elder brothers, Junjia and Fengjia, no doubt to discuss the matter.[113]

The following day the City God Temple opened its gates to select residents. The circuit and prefectural officials, as well as the district magistrates, had already offered incense to the spirits. Qi addressed the assembly: "If they in-deed cannot sell grain at favorable prices, they ought to use the surplus profit toward comforting somewhat the 'next poorest' and use what then still re-mained to provide relief for each ward." Qi also arranged with Ni Yuanlu to meet at Prefect Wang's "public office" to finalize plans. There, Qi further pressed for having merchants buy rice for stabilizing prices, and he leaned on Chen Zilong to go in person to Suzhou (Wu). "Chen resolutely accepted the responsibility; he would go to receive the new crop of Jiang-Guang rice in order to aid our Shaoxing in the seventh month."[114]

Campaigning for his position, Qi discussed matters with Magistrate Zhou and then visited Yu Huang, who, recounted Qi, "agreed with what I had ini-tially said: that one must first institute the sale of favorably priced rice." Next Qi visited Ni, who by then had assembled three allies (two maternal uncles and another relative) who strongly endorsed soup kitchens because their wards had, as a matter of course, not surveyed the "next poorest" (for buy-ing rice at fair prices, one guesses) and everyone had been registered for re-lief. Remarking that other wards were already allowing the "next poorest" to buy from soup kitchens, they asked: "What difference is there between buy-ing from the soup kitchens and obtaining rice sold at favorably adjusted prices?" Replying that the low-priced sales had ended, Qi insisted that sta-tistics be compiled on the "next poorest" and "poorest" of the two cities (Shanyin and Guiji) and that the leftover rice be divided fairly—that is, proportionally—among the wards. Qi and Ni then agreed to compose a let-ter to be sent up to the authorities "to show that we were in agreement."[115]

The same pattern—two distinguished residents each trying to advance his point of view by seeking peer support and official sanction—holds for a disagreement between Qi Biaojia and his senior colleague Liu Zongzhou. Liu commanded a huge following, as amply displayed by the editors of his collected writings, who listed just over seventy "followers" (*dizi*), among them Qi Biaojia, as well as over sixty students.[116] Although Qi does not name Liu as a teacher,[117] he respected him, frequently pondering in his diaries what Liu might think. Moreover, he had to contend with Liu's viewpoints, for Liu, too, was effective in lobbying officials and mobilizing allies.

In the tenth month of 1640, Prefect Wang Sunlan had commanded each ward to stock two hundred *shi* of grain in preparation for stabilizing prices the following year. Liu wrote to the prefect, criticizing the plan as short-sighted. Rather, he suggested, the grain ought to be used as capital for a granary, which would charge 30 percent interest until it had accumulated four hundred *shi*. In the event of a large famine, the grain stocks would be distributed among the starving households, through either soup kitchens or fairly priced sales, depending on each household's classification. If the food shortage was small, 90 percent of the stocks would be made available for sale and the remaining 10 percent would be distributed as relief.[118]

Thus, right after receiving a letter from Magistrate Zhou outlining a plan for storing grain, Qi received a letter from Prefect Wang, to which was attached a missive from Liu Zongzhou pushing for community granaries. Again drawing upon his arsenal of arguments, Qi withstood the pressure: "Because we are now experiencing a disastrous harvest," he explained in his diary, "and because we have just raised funds for aid, there are six reasons why making these preparations would be difficult, which I recorded in a letter."[119] The next day, Qi derived some encouragement from several visitors, "who came particularly to discuss the matter of charitable granaries (*yicang*)." Declared Qi in his diary, "They too felt that it would be difficult to implement this in a hurry—which was roughly my view." Thus fortified by his friends, Qi replied to Magistrate Zhou, "reporting what had just been discussed."[120]

In a second letter to Prefect Wang, also dated the tenth month, Liu elaborated on his disagreement with Qi and Yu Huang: "They speak of temporary measures, where I speak of constant ones; they speak of selling at low prices, where I speak of saving." Liu then explained: "I worry that the sale at normal prices can take place once, not repeatedly."[121] Two months later, Liu, with endorsements from Prefect Wang, Vice-Prefect Bi, Prefectural Judge Chen, and Magistrate Wang, set up a granary in his ward, Chang'an.[122]

Pitting his proposal to import grain against the view that "the only long-lasting plan for the area was to have community granaries," Qi sought support from Circuit Intendant Zheng Xuan. Appealing to Zheng's wisdom ("Your vision is far-reaching and attentive, by far transcending the ordinary"), he asked him to alleviate the plight of his rural area by seeking to import grain so as to stabilize prices.[123] In his not-so-brief "Brief Prefaces to the Complete Book of Famine Relief," a work that covers numerous topics under eight rubrics, such as "Storing Grain" and "Expanding Aid," Qi allowed granaries some importance in preparedness. Yet, he saw a dilemma: storing too little grain would fail to meet the needs of a food shortage; storing too much would result in the grain rotting and going to waste.[124] Or, as Qi stated elsewhere: If one lets the people store their own grain and sell it at regulated prices, they will happily comply. If one tries to store it in a public place (*gongsuo*) but fails to find the right location, one will worry about rot. Moreover, if one fails to find the right managers, there will be misappropriations. Asserted Qi, "Most convenient is having the people themselves store the grain and themselves sell it at fair prices."[125]

The policy of relying on imported grain was certainly sound, for the warm climate of the Jiangnan area made successful grain storage difficult.[126] Nevertheless, Liu Zongzhou insisted on having community granaries. In his mind, these were emblematic of Zhu Xi, who had initiated the idea and whom Liu venerated as "a true Confucian literatus."[127] Zhu Xi's "learning of the Way," which had for centuries been central to the civil service examination curriculum, widely influenced moral reasoning and rhetoric; and through its association with master Zhu, the concept of community granaries had acquired a forceful sanctity. Actually, by Ming times Zhu Xi's exact vision of the community granary had been lost, but this fact, unknown to Liu's contemporaries, was irrelevant to his conviction.[128]

Liu revered the long-dead Zhu Xi. Qi warned against getting bogged down in ancient texts.[129] Ignoring contemporary conditions was, he argued, especially misguided in the matter of famine relief because soil types varied with place and crop yields depended on the times.[130] Questioning the feasibility of implementing Zhu Xi's community granary,[131] Qi opted instead for solving subsistence crises by supplementing household stocks, as needed, with imported grain. Thus, where Liu invoked Zhu Xi to defend the community-granary institution, Qi cited another fact about that past luminary, namely that, to alleviate a food shortage in Zhejiang (Eastern Zhe), Zhu Xi had used sea transport to import grain from Fujian and Guangdong.[132]

Using merchants to import rice would protect the grain stocks held by local households, including Qi's own. So Liu insinuated in his second letter to Prefect Wang: "Qi seems to feel that I wish to force scholars and gentry (*shishen*) to make rice available for setting up granaries for everyone's use. This displeases him."[133] Yet, leaving aside the question whether private stocks would have satisfied the gaping need, it is unclear that Liu's strategy, with its highly localized focus and its threat to charge interest at the rate of 30 percent, was the more beneficent or practical of the two. In 1643, Liu would retrospectively applaud equally each type of his community's efforts: storing grain, importing it, and favorably pricing it.[134]

More to the point than questions about what interests each policy protected is that there was a viable alternative, relying on merchants and officials for importing grain, and that that alternative empowered Qi to disagree
with Liu about community granaries. And pursuing that alternative while
aware that he had forsaken an option endorsed by Liu, who was known for
moral integrity, Qi understood that he must retain the trust of residents.[135]
He self-consciously recorded who agreed with him, and he worked hard to
gather support for his position and to make his choice succeed.

BOUNDARY-CROSSING NETWORKS

Ni Yuanlu cleaved to the principle that the rich of each ward and lineage
should take care of its own needy. Qi expansively involved himself in both
urban and rural relief, arguing that relief efforts be coordinated across administrative boundaries. Each man reflected his distinct situation in Shanyin
society. Ni was officially registered in neighboring Shangyu district; only after retiring from office, in 1637, did he take up residence in Shanyin in order to avail himself of its fine scenery. Moreover, he chose to build his garden home inside the city walls, within the "market gates."[136] A newcomer
and a city dweller, he had few ties to adjacent rural areas. Qi was rooted in
both town and country. His father had built, in addition to a rural estate, an
urban garden that he "intended as a lodging."[137] His elder brother Fengjia,
though residing in the rural area west of the city, had built a city resting-
place for "friends" of the Bearing Witness Society (Zhengren she).[138] Qi himself had a city residence, at Jiuqu, in Xiahe ward. Also residing in the city
were Jin Lan, a fellow graduand and owner of a half-*mou* garden; Zhang Dai;
and Qi's father-in-law.[139]

Running back and forth between "his ward" and "his village," Qi worried
about both. On the eve of the riots of 1641, he rushed from Yu Mountain
into the city to attend the meeting at the City God Temple. When the formal meeting was over, he lingered to discuss with two colleagues "the matter of the rural villages," for which, he asserted, the only appropriate relief
would be giving out rice. After conferring further with the prefect and the
two district magistrates, and having decided to move his family into the city,
Qi boarded his boat for Yu Mountain. Back home, he discussed "the method
of giving out rice" with his brothers, calculating that if grain were allotted
"according to the size of land, with each *mou* receiving one *sheng*," their villages would get over sixty *shi*.[140] The next day, he took his family back to the
relative safety of the city. His thoughts subsequently returned to his village:
"For half a month, from the fifteenth through the twenty-ninth, I have been
sojourning in the city, without bringing any benefit to my rural area."[141]

Qi gave high priority to what he repeatedly referred to as "my village, my
lineage." Once Magistrate Zhou proposed to Qi that, instead of spending sil-

ver from the grain tax, they should have a mandatory collection of rice. Qi granted that "this method is good, to be sure," but he expressed reservations: "It would be feasible only after the autumn harvest. Rice is scarce. The people would strongly oppose having it collected from the rural areas and townships to be purchased by the cities at favorable prices."[142]

Qi understood that levies on rural folk could ignite riots. Two months back he had written of Hangzhou: "The rural people had asked for tax leniency. Their request was not granted. Thereupon mobs plundered the market."[143] Yet, Qi and his colleagues acted not only to avert disorder. Such was their socioeconomic environment that they were also mindful that the interests of each village, and of Shaoxing prefecture as a whole, were inextricably linked to the well-being of other regions. With their social networks crisscrossing administrative boundaries, they genuinely cared about neighboring regions. Symptomatic of the networks of this time was the Restoration Society, the multiregional federation of scholars that fostered preparation for the civil service examinations and provided a forum for political discussion. Though its leaders resided in Lu Shiyi's hometown, Taicang, the Restoration Society penetrated all parts of China, attracting well over two thousand members, among them Chen Zilong.[144] Similarly transregional in character was the lodge that Qi's elder brother built for sojourning members of the Bearing Witness Society, one of several successive names for a study group led by the native Tao brothers and Liu Zongzhou.[145]

Thus Liu, though favoring local granaries, responded to the plight of neighboring areas, as became evident in 1637, during a "learned discussion" at White Horse Mountain Hut—where gatherings of over one hundred participants were not unusual.[146] In Sheng district, the poor harvest of the previous autumn had sent grain prices soaring (to one thousand *qian* per *shi*), forcing "the little people" to scratch the soil for food or feed on grasses and tree bark. The relief organized by the magistrate was, apparently, inadequate. After a long, deep sigh, Liu broached the subject with the students, according to one account, Or, as Liu told it, "The various attendees commiserated with one another as though they themselves felt the pain." The group commissioned Qi Biaojia to ask officials to contribute funds to purchase grain for resale at fair prices, but the official coffers were depleted. Fortunately a "friend" took the lead in donating money. Then, when they were about to launch grain sales, Wang Chaoshi, mindful of those people too poor to buy grain, proposed that funds be raised for soup kitchens, as had previously been done for the rural area of Tianle. This defender of the neediest was the Wang who had reprimanded Qi for building a garden[147] and whom Qi would commend, two years later, for having "taken the livelihood of the people as his responsibility."[148] Approving Wang's suggestion, Liu composed directives and distributed fund-raising pamphlets. They obtained over six hundred ounces of silver and 170 *shi* of grain. Liu then instructed Wang and others to go to

Sheng district to manage the relief. With help from a Sheng resident, they additionally raised over 890 *shi* of Sheng rice. Walking through mountains and valleys, and measuring the distances between places, they set up soup kitchens in 137 locations. For over one month, they distributed rice, daily feeding somewhere between forty thousand and fifty thousand people.

Two months later, the wheat supply was exhausted and the people were anxious. Again Wang Chaoshi solicited contributions for aid. Because the response was poor, he asked Qi Biaojia to seek help from the regional inspector. The inspector made available one hundred ounces of silver that had been collected from fines. Liu Zongzhou designated Wang and others to raise funds in Sheng. Obtaining over three thousand ounces of silver and reduced-price grain for relief, they aided over forty-two thousand starving people, sustaining the entire city until the autumn harvest.[149]

That neighboring districts should help one another was again advocated by Liu in the fourth month of 1640, this time on behalf of residents of Yuyao. Liu had just finished writing a piece praising Shaoxing residents for their relief program, when three unexpected callers informed him that Yuyao's conditions were even more lamentable than Shanyin's. Liu therefore appended to the piece he had just composed an appeal that his fellow townsmen consider the two regions as one family. "Without Yuyao, how would Shanyin and Guiji exist?" he asked.[150]

The theme of regional interdependence was reiterated by Liu in an essay of 1641 on administering famine relief.[151] Liu recalled the meeting of 1637, when attendees had wept over Sheng's desperate conditions and he had counseled them: "The starvation in Sheng is our starvation; some day in the future, the people of our Shaoxing (Yue) will survive a slow season by partaking of Sheng's harvest—like drawing funds from the Outer Treasury—and, then, how would our region survive without a Sheng district?"[152] Sure enough, Liu continued, when Shaoxing prefecture suffered a bad food shortage three years later, it beseeched to purchase grain at fair prices from the less severely hit Sheng district. The magistrate of Sheng led the way, depleting his entire salary; townsmen followed his example.[153]

Thus did beneficent gestures travel routes that social networks had paved. At convocations, such as that at White Horse Academy, attendees bore witness to the suffering of starving people, stirring the emotions of their comrades. Competing with Ni's vision of self-sufficient units, thinking transregionally gained validity, even among literati who would defend their own areas' interests. On the grounds that Shanyin had twice as many starving people as Guiji, Qi opposed giving each district sixty *shi* of grain, favoring instead allocating grain proportionately to population; he thus protected his native Shanyin, but not without high-mindedly capping his argument by saying, "Yet those in charge are still unable to avoid the 'boundary viewpoint.'"[154] As social networks widened, thinking beyond the "boundary viewpoint" increasingly challenged narrow interests; and securing the broad vision was access to official authority, both to mediate among regionally based interests and to import grain.

THE LAND AND POPULATION OF SHANYIN

Rice ought to be imported, Qi insisted, because his region produced far less grain than it consumed. Shortly after 1641, he asked how it was possible that Shanyin's population far exceeded what the land could support and explained the imbalance in terms of the region's geography: trapped between the mountains and the sea, Shanyin's territory was just over sixty-two thousand *mou*, while its population exceeded 1,240,000. Reasoned Qi: "The land is fertile, but, with each *mou* feeding two persons, the yield would last but half a year. Therefore, only by relying on imports can residents make it through the year. From the winter harvest of 1641 on, dearth was everywhere and outside shipments failed to arrive."[155]

Complicating Qi's neat calculations of the land-to-population ratio were other facts. Not all Shaoxing rice was reserved for local use. As Qi went on to state, "The neighboring areas continued to rely on us for imports"; and once he inquired of Vice-Prefect Bi whether Shaoxing rice was still being sent out to Hangzhou.[156] Or, as Liu Zongzhou stated: "Formerly, when our rural area had a good crop of early rice, I heard that we let merchants transport grain to Suzhou, day after day wrapping and taking the profits out. . . . Everywhere to the south of the Zhen River, people are daily eating Shaoxing rice."[157] Moreover, not all of Shaoxing's fertile land was planted for food crops. Some was used for growing glutinous rice, the raw ingredient for the wine for which Shaoxing would later become famous. One local official, observed Qi, had prohibited the planting of glutinous rice precisely "so that Shaoxing might accumulate edible rice."[158] Or, as Qi put it in his "Brief Prefaces": "Growing glutinous rice to ferment wine commandeers food from over 30 percent of the people. During bad years, a grain of rice is as valuable as a pearl. . . . One should therefore stop producing wine."[159]

Some of Qi's peers produced goods other than edible grains. In his Garden of Eternity, west of the city, one of Qi's elder brothers planted mulberries and created a pond for raising fish.[160] A resident of Ke Market farmed fish in the concavity left by the quarry that had long ago provided the stones for the city wall.[161] In light of his district's unfavorable land-to-population ratio, Qi thought it unrealistic that all residents should own or rent land for farming; making a living through handicraft industries was, he asserted, also an acceptable way of "averting famine."[162] Investing in silk production, as some Shaoxing residents did, brought in revenues that, he claimed, ultimately bolstered famine relief.[163]

Whether the fish were farmed for sale is unknown. How much of the economy of seventeenth-century Shaoxing depended on cottage industries is impossible to quantify. Nonetheless it appears that Shaoxing was well compensated for its overpopulation by revenues from the production of exportable products. When one friend proposed that the grain allocated for sale at reduced prices be apportioned according to the number of fields each household owned, Qi countered that many local landowners did not reap rice and many rice-cultivating households rented out their land.[164] Circumstantial evidence thus suggests two points: Shaoxing depended heavily on trade with surrounding areas, and much of its labor force became vulnerable whenever economic downturns curbed spending on anything other than food.

As residents of Shaoxing's rural areas abandoned food crops for commercially profitable ones, small market towns arose. One of these was in the rural area of Tianle, located roughly one third of the way to Xiaoshan district, which was right across the river from Hangzhou. Sections of Tianle being barren, its fields would support only one fifth of its population, wrote Liu Zongzhou, who, like Qi, punned: "In vain did heaven (*tian*) attach the word 'happy' (*le*) to the name."[165] And yet, in good times, the population of "Heaven's Happiness" apparently survived on brisk commerce.[166]

Even during the subsistence crisis some Tianle residents enjoyed a surplus, among them the three "brothers," each with a distinct surname, who told Qi that they wished to set up a "relief bureau" (*zhenju*) and a soup kitchen.[167] The one surnamed Sun possibly was the Sun Wenhuan whose great virtue the local gazetteer commemorated: he refused to remarry after his young wife died; remained filial long after his parents passed away; and cheerfully practiced charity (*haoshi leshan*) into old age, particularly during the "great famine" of 1641, when he "sold his property in order to provide relief." Concludes the gazetteer of 1724, "Down to the present day, the people of the rural area of Tianle continue to praise him."[168]

Also en route from Shaoxing through Xiaoshan and on to Hangzhou were Ke Market (forty *li* west of the prefectural city), Ke Bridge, and Ke Mountain—all in the vicinity of Qi's Yu Mountain estate. Though times were hard, the people of Ke Market leapt to the rescue of a woman who was about to drown herself because her husband planned to sell her: "Taking pity on her, they collected funds to redeem her to be returned to her husband."[169] Ke Market had timber yards, indicates the biography of Zhang Shaofang, a licentiate who was famous not only for his essays but also for such charitable deeds as aiding prisoners and repairing roads and bridges. (According to one edition of the Shanyin gazetteer, he was Zhang Bi's father.) When it came to light that a servant managing timber yards at Ke Market had been fleecing the people, stirring up resentment, Shaofang intervened. He remitted half of the capital to the rich creditors and burned the loan agreements of the poor, spending "fifteen hundred taels and then some."[170]

Ke Bridge accommodated brokers, supported prosperous shops, and maintained Bright Light Monastery, which eighty years later would be portrayed grandly dominating a hillside and was where Qi attended a large meeting to deliberate the vagrant problem, noting, "Few of Ke Market's local inhabitants were starving, for they had shops on which they could rely for survival."[171] And because Ke Bridge was more prosperous than surrounding rural areas yet unprotected by walls, it inexorably attracted vagrants—"nearly a thousand," reported Qi in the fourth month of 1641, "and with more women than before."[172]

CONCLUSION

Reviewing Shaoxing's relief efforts, Chen Zilong proclaimed success. In addition to the food relief, local benefactors established an infirmary (*bingfang*) for the sick, and a bureau (*ju*) that hired old widows and wet nurses to look after abandoned infants. "Sometimes," wrote Chen, "we tracked down their parents; sometimes people asked to raise them. In all, seventy-five thousand [no unit is specified] of grain from public funds and wealthy households were used, and all told over ten thousand people were saved. The infirmary used over ten thousand doses of medicine, keeping a thousand adults and over three hundred infants alive.[173]

Though confirming that Shaoxing residents worked tirelessly in charitable activities, Qi's writings indicate results less rosy: many residents took to the road in search of food, joining the ranks of vagrants. In an essay extolling the virtues of economizing, Qi noted an apparent contradiction, roughly as follows: from the winter harvest of 1641 on, dearth was everywhere; yet, though shipments failed to arrive, the markets were never depleted, and neighboring areas continued to import goods from Shaoxing. "Some people," he wrote, "explained this by saying that consumption had been cut by 30 percent because of the toll taken by disease and emigration from the area."[174] Likewise did Liu Zongzhou, who in 1643 applauded the residents' energetic response to the starving, acknowledge mixed results: "Death counts daily increased, but those who were kept alive numbered in the hundreds and thousands."[175]

Surviving sources, though copious, will not permit a quantitative evaluation of Shaoxing's late Ming relief efforts. They do, however, reveal two models for action: individual donors working alone or in small, self-sufficient groups; and large, highly coordinated organizations, working in alliance with officials. The former, whose projects were short-lived, localized, and engaged few participants, receive little attention in extant documents. Zhang Bi's name survives only because he produced a pamphlet about his relief efforts that, as someone in the next generation noted, "circulates today."[176] The three Tianle residents who sponsored a "relief bureau" are known to us only because Qi happened to have noted them in his diary.[177] Likewise preserved by slender odds is the name of Liu Kuangzhi, who founded a large do-good society (*shanhui*) that used monthly contributions to set up charitable granaries, save abandoned children, and buy back the freedom of women sold. Yet Liu is known only through a brief biography in the local gazetteer of 1724, which the edition of 1803 stripped of revealing information.[178] From such fragile and seemingly insignificant records does information about a few of possibly many independent actors emerge.

Undermining the impulse to act independently were strong centripetal forces exerted by official authority. Zhang Bi, who accepted that his aid would be but a "trickling stream in the great ocean," nonetheless petitioned for official sanction for selecting the worthies who would carry out the population census; official backing would, he recognized, deter corruption in his program.[179] Liu Zongzhou understood that to launch community granaries it was important to have officials "take the lead in encouraging the people."[180]

Qi, too, occasionally acted independently, distributing cash here and handouts there. More often he reached for (or tapped into) official authority to resolve conflicts and transcend narrowly defined interests and responsibilities. Official authority—especially the power to mete out punishments and distribute rewards—enabled Shaoxing's informal leaders to deal with vagrants crossing administrative boundaries, to achieve some equity in the distribution of resources among neighboring districts, and to ensure that relief programs were simultaneously established throughout the prefecture. Official support enabled Shaoxing residents to acquire grain from the outside, to prohibit the export of grain to other areas, and to enforce cooperation across administrative boundaries. Official authority, in short, sustained Qi's expansive, transregional view. When he reached for official authority, it was his good fortune that there just happened to be in place Zheng Xuan, Wang Sunlan, Bi Jiuchen, and Chen Zilong, worthy officials of like mind.

CODA: A CONTRASTING EXAMPLE

Shaoxing's constructive response to the food shortage of the 1640s represents but one of several scenarios played out during the late Ming. The residents themselves looked back with shame on a famine of 1588, when, as Liu Zongzhou put it, "The rich kept to themselves and many people died."[181] What distinguished the two responses? Was it a change in the residents' sense of responsibility for others, or a change in their view of what was worth recording?[182] Favoring this last possibility is that scholars residing in Shaoxing during the 1580s, though prolific, appear (on the basis of their extant writings) to have been relatively hushed on the topic of the 1588 crisis—except when addressing the court. The difference between the two periods stems not from some fluke in leadership or the accident of having in place several talented administrators who were informed about relief strategies; rather, the intervening sixty years had transformed the region's socioeconomic relations, providing the local manpower for running large-scale relief operations and embedding residents in a nexus of interregional trade upon which they could draw.

Other regions weathered the 1640s less well than Shaoxing. So suggests a deeply pessimistic and sensational account concerning the food shortage in Suzhou, roughly 180 miles north of Shaoxing prefecture. There, skyrocketing grain prices in 1637 brought trouble: a shipment of grain taxes was robbed, its commander subsequently ambushed; some tenants burned down the country residence of their landlord; townsmen rioted against a magistrate; grain transport soldiers mutinied, plundered, and murdered; and prisoners broke out of jail. In 1640, neighboring prefectures, having themselves suffered floods and drought, failed to export rice to Suzhou. Rice prices rose, first to 1.6 taels, and then to 1.8. Thousands of poor people, ridden with anxiety, rioted in the city center. In the eastern section of the city, residents, learning that a neighbor had sold grain at a good price to an Anhui merchant (despite a prohibition against selling to traders), forcibly relieved him of one thousand *dou* of his hoard. In the western section, someone known for his wealth and well-stocked granaries was also plundered—not only of grain, but also of ancestral treasures and thousands of ounces of silver.[183]

Rioting escalated. One official had the leaders beaten to death as a warning to the masses, but this failed to pacify the mobs. Other officials had tickets for purchasing rice at favorable prices distributed to poor households, but this measure was inadequate. In 1641—precisely when Shaoxing was trying to buy rice from Suzhou—grain prices rose further, whereupon officials, fearing that the poor people would instigate a rebellion, erected food kitchens at six locations. Some people thus "received kindness," yet many continued to go hungry. The older generation recalled the big famine of 1589, which back then they had thought to be an extraordinary event. But, asked author Ye Shaoyuan, "with the price of rice up to 2.5 taels . . . is this (famine) not more extraordinary?" He then lamented, "How can the people bear it?"[184]

Peppered with such phrases as "Is it not strange?" Ye's account emphasizes the sensational aspects of Suzhou's crisis. Completed after the fall of the Ming dynasty, his account conforms to the model of dynastic decline, with disorder spreading out formulaically from the center of the city to the eastern and western districts. Reporting on the last two reigns of the Ming dynasty, it draws attention to the inadequacies of government and the failure of a state that had callously insisted on raising taxes in the area precisely when local officials most urgently requested that taxes be remitted.[185] In light of the outcome, Ye saw no need to waste ink celebrating charitable deeds or to reserve space for commemorating do-gooders.[186]

Shaoxing prefecture was extraordinary in many respects. It enjoyed unusually high concentrations of officials, wealth, and residents with administrative know-how and connections to men with political authority. Above all, it enjoyed a high concentration of literate men—among them Qi Biaojia, whose firsthand account survived. Shaoxing's uniqueness does not, however, diminish its significance for understanding charitable activities for China as a whole. Rather, the case of Shaoxing demonstrates that, when given resources and a dedicated leadership, organizing vigorous charitable activities was possible within the framework of China's imperial political structure and cultural traditions.

8

Medical Relief and Other Good Deeds

*Mr. Wang went to announce the dispensary to the comrades, and
everyone enthusiastically jumped up and down, wanting to join in.*
QI BIAOJIA

Three times within the space of seven years—during the summers of 1636,
1641, and 1642—Qi Biaojia joined fellow residents of Shaoxing to set up
and operate medical dispensaries for the poor.[1] The idea that medical care
should be provided to the needy had a long if intermittently visible history.
Buddhist monasteries had sponsored medical infirmaries during much of
the Tang dynasty.[2] Then, the imperial state, after wiping out many of these
monasteries in 845, took over responsibility for the sick—at least in principle. Individual donors too occasionally stepped in. While serving as an official, in 1089, Su Shi dipped into his own pockets to establish the Peace and
Happiness Ward.[3] As far as one can tell from surviving documents, his example is nearly unique. Nonetheless it signaled the possibility of nonstate
individual initiatives of the sort that would gain widespread recognition in
late Ming writings. Yang Dongming directed a benevolent society to sponsor a doctor to heal the rural sick. His friend Lü Kun, noting the deplorable
condition of medical care in his own time, looked back with longing to the
beginning of the dynasty, when the imperial court had sponsored the training of medical officials and set up "medical bureaus for the compassionate
care of the people" (*huimin yaoju*) to distribute medicines to the poor.[4] Chen
Longzheng's father, Chen Yuwang, when serving as a magistrate in Jurong,
established a dispensary and, toward summer's end, organized thirty-two
doctors to tour the surrounding rural areas.[5]

Qi Biaojia was undoubtedly aware of these precedents. He had access to
his father's enormous library, one small portion of which had nearly two
hundred titles of medical books—so testifies the catalog, extant today, in
which Qi's father classified his medical books under such categories as pulse
taking, methods of treatment, prescriptions, pharmacopoeia, gynecology,
infant care, and external medicine.[6] Among these was Li Shizhen's *Materia*

medica (*Bencao gangmu*), an enormous, innovative survey of materials with pharmaceutical properties in fifty-two chapters (*juan*) that was first published in 1593. Such was the success of Li's work that, by the time of the first opening of the dispensary of Shaoxing, it had been republished four times in rapid succession (in 1603, 1606, 1620, and 1630), and it would then be reprinted in 1640 and 1655.[7] Medical knowledge was within easy reach of Qi Biaojia and his peers. However, the impetus for establishing Shaoxing's dispensaries of 1636, 1641, and 1642 came neither from the medical books at Qi's fingertips nor from the historical precedents for medical welfare preserved in these texts, but rather from social forces within Shaoxing that fostered affiliations between highly educated, title-bearing members of the elite and constituencies of small players—doctors, lesser literati, and Buddhist monks.

Information regarding the founding of the Shaoxing dispensaries is provided by several documents that Qi Biaojia composed—two short essays, two proposals, and a set of guidelines[8]—and by fragmentary comments in his diary, local gazetteers, and other materials. Though decidedly thin, the documentation suffices to suggest that sponsorship of dispensaries independent of the state was a relatively new phenomenon and to explain why it should have emerged in such late Ming urban centers as Shaoxing.

Not accidentally, the dispensaries of 1636, 1641, and 1642 were opened during the summer months, when dwindling food stocks left the people debilitated and anxious.[9] The dispensary of 1636, Qi explained, was set up after untimely storms portended "to those in the know" that the autumn harvests would again fail.[10] A sense of desperation was spreading among the poorer inhabitants; at any moment a riot might erupt. Wrote Qi, "Formerly one worried only about famine; now one worries about disorder."[11] Thus it became paramount for the wealthy to win goodwill through generosity. In the past, they had done this by lowering grain prices, reducing taxes, and holding uplifting community-compact meetings—options that Qi and his contemporaries pursued. Why, then, did Shaoxing's leaders additionally offer medical relief?

The grim conditions of 1636, the heaping cadavers, putrid and polluting, were in themselves enough to motivate action. "With the rapid spread of 'dysentery' [a generic term for a disease or diseases that elude precise definition], corpses were," Qi reported, "piling up everywhere. In some households, every member was out flat, with the result that no one was available to administer medications." Yet distributing medical relief was not the only option for responding to the scourge. Members of the local elite also dealt with deadly epidemics by providing coffins and endowing "charitable graveyards," sometimes raising funds through burial societies. Chen Longzheng sponsored burials for the poor, as did (for a short time, at least) the benevolent society of Lu Shiyi's Taicang county. Likewise did Qi Biaojia and fellow townsmen shoulder responsibility for interring the dead. In 1637, at White Horse Mountain Hut, Qi deliberated with three colleagues about burying abandoned corpses, and months later he composed a statement about raising funds for abandoned corpses.[12] In 1639, accompanied by his elder brother Junjia, he surveyed a mountain so as to identify a spot for a charitable graveyard; they then discussed with younger brother Xiangjia not only distributing medicine and giving relief to prisoners but also the topic of charitable burials.[13] Eventually Qi would summarize two strategies for charitable burials that he implemented in 1640 and 1642: he gave the head of each monastery money for handling burials for the area's households; and he equipped monks with boats on which they might eat and sleep while using the abundant waterways to ride out to villages to collect the corpses.[14] In 1641, shortly before Qi would sponsor an infirmary and a medical dispensary, his household assumed responsibility for providing one *qian* for the burial of each deceased person in Ke Bridge.[15] Already in place were routines for charitably burying the deceased indigent. What impelled Qi and his friends in 1636 to add to their repertoire of charitable activities yet another type of intervention, the distribution of medicines?

STIRRED BY A SON'S ILLNESS

The loss of life Qi witnessed all around him coincided with an intimate, painful experience: in 1636, his eldest son, Tong, who was then in his sixteenth year, died of smallpox. Upon hearing of Tong's illness, Qi stayed at home, worriedly administering his son's medicines. He consulted one doctor after another and engaged some of them to stay nights. During the course of eight suspenseful days, there streamed into the household Doctors Zhou Jinglan, Tao Dengsheng, Ling Shaoguang, and Zhu Qingyu, along with seven other persons who, though not specifically titled "doctor," claimed to have medical knowledge or who, in one case, was known to be "expert in pox diseases." The physicians debated the merits of "hot" and "cold" therapies, and Qi sought some agreement among them regarding the proper course of treatment. Medical expertise was plentiful, but to no avail. Within a few days the son's illness took a turn for the worse. "The doctors all left," recounted Qi; there remained only his friend Wang Chaoshi, who, having on a previous occasion taken Qi's pulse, apparently knew something about medicine. With Qi weeping imploringly, Wang tried to jolt Tong back to life with words. Tong appeared to understand them, but a day later he died. Sorrowfully, Qi commented in his diary on his son's magnanimous spirit: "Even when Tong's illness was deteriorating, he asked me, 'Have you eaten?'"[16] Nine days later, Qi founded the dispensary.

Personal loss of the sort Qi suffered was commonplace. What differentiated Qi's experience, what enabled his grief to find lasting expression in the form of a dispensary, were particular circumstances of his social milieu: the availability of physicians and the propensity of late Ming elites to form voluntary associations. Qi himself participated in at least two poetry clubs—one for linking verses (*lianling zhi hui*) and the Maple Society (Feng she) — as well as the Society for Liberating Animals.[17] He also mentioned, albeit briefly, three study societies: the Yuan, Restoration (Fu), and Ying Societies.[18] Many of Qi's peers likewise participated in multiple societies. Xia Yunyi (a native of Huating, Songjiang) was both an associate of the Society for Liberating Animals and had joined Chen Zilong in forming the Ji Society before Chen would become Shaoxing's prefectural judge. Yuan Liuqing was active not only in the dispensary, but also in the Society for Liberating Animals.[19] Other participants in the dispensary of 1636, many of whom were men of marginal social status, easily moved among these organizations. On the day the dispensary closed, they quit the premises and proceeded by boat to join Tao Shiling at a lake, there to liberate animals. "The participants were all friends who had put the dispensary in order and friends of the Bearing Witness Society," reported Qi, who then added that they shared a congenial feast, laughing and talking.[20] Not only did these clubs narrow the social gap between official and physician; their overlapping affiliations meant that participation in any one society afforded opportunities to tap into extraordinarily far-ranging networks.

The late Ming proclivity to form associations has often been explained by historians in terms of prosperity and the spread of literacy, phenomena that produced a pool of literati far greater than the civil service could absorb. Whether awaiting a chance to enter the bureaucracy, or whether, like Qi Biaojia, they were on leave from official service, many educated men of means resided at home with time on their hands and resources at their fingertips.[21] Qi's region was, moreover, amply populated with Chan Buddhist monks and marginal literati who willingly contributed their labor to running the dispensary. Still, it does not necessarily follow that men at loose ends should specifically sponsor a dispensary.

Nine days after illness had taken his own son, Qi attended a meeting held by the Society for Liberating Animals.[22] At the meeting, the members touched upon the subject of the epidemic. In Qi's words, they "commiserated together just as though the pestilence had stricken their own bodies."[23] The decision to distribute medicines to the poor thus emerged within the context of an existing association, the Society for Liberating Animals, to which Qi Biaojia belonged. Like their predecessor Yang Dongming, who had transformed a hedonistic society into a benevolent association, Qi's associates redefined an already existing society to take on a new and, by some measures, nobler purpose. Qi saw the two societies as having roughly the same function. When the participants wanted to close the first dispensary, they held a "meeting of the Society for Liberating Animals," which, explained Qi, "also had the intention of treating people with benevolence and of loving animals."[24]

Sickness among the poor, though inevitably extensive, was not in itself sufficient to summon into existence a program for medical relief. Sometime around 1629 and 1630, the well-known Doctor Dong Wulai and a Chan Buddhist master had proposed that a dispensary be set up but had met with resistance. The comrades, Qi recalled, had found difficulties with the plan and would not implement it. "It was as though," Qi added, "one had to wait for the opportune moment."[25] Yet, in the sixth month of 1636, these same comrades readily leapt into action. Qi's friend Wang Chaoshi calculated how they might meet the need for medical care, and that night, under lamplight, Qi drafted the regulations, itemizing ten points.[26] Recollected Qi: "The thought was that it just had to be done. Mr. Wang went to announce the dispensary to the comrades, and everyone enthusiastically jumped up and down, wanting to join in."[27]

Differentiating the second event from the first was the social status of the initiators. In 1629, the proposal came from a Chan Buddhist monk and a doctor. In 1636, the initiative came from Wang Chaoshi, who had been at Tong's deathbed. Timing mattered too. In 1636, a mounting sense of urgency galvanized Qi Biaojia and scholar Wang to act upon an idea first offered by men of inferior social status. That year rebels swept through Shenxi, Henan, and Nanzhili; worse, that summer the Manchus were encroaching upon China, and even upon the capital of Beijing.[28] Qi's double sense of crisis, personal and political, connected up with the then widespread fervor for saving lives.

Prompted by Wang, Qi Biaojia and his brother Junjia "took the lead by contributing some funds." Others quickly followed suit. The social hierarchy worked to encourage cooperation. In initiating the campaign, the brothers not only set a good example; they also created opportunities whereby fellow residents might, by supporting the cause, earn the favor and friendship of their social superiors. In the arena of doing good, officials and nonofficials mingled. As the official Chen Zilong would observe of the welfare activities of 1641: the contributions, totaling seventy-five thousand units of grain, that were made to finance famine relief, medical care, and a foundling home came from official coffers *and* wealthy households, and the merit belonged to "superior officials *and* worthies and elders."[29]

The dispensary sponsors structured the fund-raising to ensure thorough solicitation from the community: they made up ten subscription booklets to be distributed among "friends," who would then collect contributions. One associate moved that the daily cost for medicines should be four to five taels, whereupon the friends formed groups, each of which was to raise the amount needed for a day. The associates understood that, in the event of a shortfall, Qi Biaojia would again make a contribution;[30] group pressure nonetheless stimulated individual voluntarism. The regulations themselves stipulated that donors should contribute as they wished, that the amount did not matter. It was important, however, that they hand over the collected funds, to be stored at Qi's brother Junjia's place, and that they also return the pamphlets to the brother's house so as to facilitate the printing of a booklet that would, as the regulations put it, "broadcast the names of those who have faith in goodness (*shanxin*)."[31]

The Society for Liberating Animals, from which the dispensary emerged, was a loose association, its purpose unaffected by the variable attendance of its members. The dispensary, in contrast, had goals requiring a clear division of labor among comrades and doctors, each of whom, upon signing on, became essential to the operation. Ten doctors were engaged to work in pairs, from morning to noon in six-day shifts; these were joined by Palace Physician Yao Dongbo, whose presence ensured against interruptions in the dispensing of medicines, and two aides—bringing the total number of attendants to thirteen. The various comrades were responsible for managing the funds, medicines, records, patients, and accounts.[32]

Dispensary records were meticulously kept. The registrar, according to Qi's instructions, was to use a printed form to keep track of three categories: the treatments provided each day, the names and addresses of the doctors for that day, and the doctors' diagnoses and prescriptions. Buddhist monks took turns regulating the queues of patients. To each patient they gave a ticket that had a number determining the place in the queue and was colored either red or green, directing the patient to the east or west entrances respectively.[33] Anyone too ill to travel to the dispensary or wait in line was allowed to send in a proxy, who would "describe the symptoms in detail" so that the patient would receive an appropriate prescription.[34]

Qi Biaojia meanwhile did what he could to enhance the medical care. To contribute to the doctors' knowledge, he made abstracts of medical books, consulting, perhaps, his deceased father's library.[35] To solicit funds for medicines, he wrote letters.[36] Frequently he visited the dispensary, sometimes twice a day; and when Wang Chaoshi visited him, he discussed dispensary affairs.[37] He further composed both the guidelines that would harness loosely affiliated participants to dispensary goals, and, after the program ended, "A Record of Dispensing Medicines" that would fill them and their descendants with pride.[38]

Judging the efficacy of the medical care is impossible. Without information about the population of sick, one cannot weigh the significance of the "over 570 doses a day" of which Qi boasts.[39] Were those patients who had the strength to walk to the dispensary and line up for care truly so seriously ill that their lives depended on the handouts? Did the mere experience of receiving care from physicians whose diagnoses and prescriptions were reverently recorded have a placebo effect, spiritually healing the ailing? Alternatively, did amassing the sick at the dispensary have the unintended effect of spreading contagion? The paucity of information renders such epidemiological questions pointless.

Late Ming medical care nonetheless deserves respect. Around this time Europeans were showing a great interest in and learning from Chinese medicine, particularly from Li Shizhen's *Materia medica.* The doctors of Shaoxing prefecture were among the best in the land, trained to follow well-tried methods for ensuring that medical care be efficacious: as Qi's guidelines mandated, they kept meticulous records of the prescriptions—at the rate of one notebook a day—so that they might determine whether subsequent dosages should be increased or reduced.[40] They also had procedures for testing prescriptions. When fears of food shortages were mounting during the third month of 1641, Qi learned that a monk had a prescription "three pills of which, taken daily, would curb one's appetite." He instructed an associate—Zou Rugong, who was Qi's son's teacher and a participant in the Society for Liberating Animals—to compound the medicine and test it on several priests so that it "might then be widely distributed to the poor."[41] Although Qi does not report the results of this test in his diary, the experiment itself indicates his receptiveness to, and interest in testing, new pharmaceuticals.

Dispensary organizers expected that patients would be treated just as efficaciously as members of their own households; and Qi engaged for the dispensary the very physicians who treated his own illnesses—with one noticeable exception: those physicians who had attended to his son Tong were conspicuously absent in the lists of dispensary doctors. Whether this was because their specialties (say, in childhood diseases) served the dispensary poorly, or because they had been discredited by the son's death, is unclear.

The dispensary was sustained by the participants' commitment to doing good and compassion for the sick. When Qi commended the associates for having "personally performed their duties with the requisite care and reverence,"[42] he above all applauded their capacity for empathy. When asked whether "errors had been made in the medications," he responded with a sigh: "Alas, if those who govern the people today would only be like those who work in the dispensary—who treat others as though they were caring for themselves and managing their own homes—then all the concerns of the world would be cared for." Qi then remarked, "With hearts of bodhisattvas the famous doctors displayed the skills of the Buddha of Medicine."[43] A proposal he wrote, probably in 1641, appealed to the doctors' goodness in order to encourage them to arrive at the dispensary promptly in the morning and not to leave early. He impressed upon them that one does not want "the sick to lose hope" and that punctuality would display the doctors' "universal compassion."[44]

As portrayed by Qi, the associates of the dispensary were motivated by a philanthropic spirit. All the doctors went to the dispensary at their appointed times, he noted approvingly, and then singled out three of them for special mention: Doctors Dong Wulai, Fu Huiyu, and Yuan Liuqing occasionally went to the dispensary "out of their own compassion, even when it was not their turn; and although it was at the height of a broiling summer, they did not shy away from the strong stenches there."[45] As though to measure and certify the depth of his comrades' compassion, Qi reported that they willingly toiled in unpleasant conditions, sacrificing sleep and good food. Everyone labored strenuously (*lao*), according to Qi: "Mr. Wang [Chaoshi, the chief manager] fell sick from exhaustion. After recovering from his sickness, he again worked untiringly. Again he fell sick. To the end he showed not the slightest appearance of fatigue. The friends who were on duty had little sleep and mediocre food, with the result that they looked haggard."[46]

The onerous burden of diagnosing the patients streaming into the dispensary was the doctors' responsibility. The dispensary "friends" then issued the medicines according to the doctors' prescriptions. They also maintained records, particularly medical case books (*yian*), in which they registered, in the blank squares provided, the name and residence of each patient, and entered the medications and dosages; when patients returned, the doctors would consult the log in order to adjust dosages.[47] The responsibilities of the doctors and friends, though distinguishable from those most menial tasks performed by porters and servants, involved time-consuming, exhausting, and unpleasant labors.

INITIATIVES FROM BELOW

Much of the initiative and enthusiasm for the dispensary came from students and doctors. Initially the comrades had agreed that the dispensary of 1636 would stay open until three days after the middle of the seventh month. When closing day arrived, the dispensary had already saved three thousand people, and the general opinion was that the society should be disbanded.[48] Wang Chaoshi disagreed: "Not yet," he insisted, adding: "Given that not every sick person has been completely cured and that lives still hang in the balance, how could one bear to stop in midcourse?" At that time, Qi explained, the supplies for the dispensary had been depleted and the dispensary had no spare cash; indeed, it was short ten ounces of silver for medicines, and everyone raised objections to continuing. Mr. Wang nonetheless urged them not to be so fainthearted, insisting, "If one tries hard enough, anything can be accomplished." One comrade then took the lead by contributing an ounce of silver. Most of the friends joined in, and before long, they had collected ten ounces.[49] Roughly a month later, the associates again confronted the issue of shutting down the dispensary. They had assembled for a vegetarian banquet to toast Wang Chaoshi for his labors. As though not enough had been done, Wang diffidently asked, "How can we leave the people who are pouring in from the rural areas to weep at the street corners?" Physician Yao Dongbo was again retained. "Everyone," Qi reported, "said how convenient it was that the end was not really the end. Such are truly the sentiments of a Confucian scholar (*ru*)."[50]

As told by Qi, the physicians shared with members of the elite a genuine zeal for saving lives. When it was announced that the dispensary of 1636 would remain open, the doctors "again exerted themselves untiringly, taking pulses, issuing prescriptions, and proffering the concocted pills they themselves had brought in. They also took the lead in raising funds. [Doctor] Dong Wulai raised more than the various friends, with the result that for twenty-six days we had the 'Later Dispensary.'"[51] In addition to accumulating merit and reaping gratification from their calling, doctors who worked at the dispensary could garner material benefits—although rarely in the form of direct remuneration. In only one documented instance was a doctor given a stipend to cover daily necessities. This was the one who, after the program had been closed down and doctors had been given rewards, was kept on to distribute the leftover medicine.[52] Of course, during a food shortage, the meals the physicians received at the dispensary were a significant bonus— as were the stipends for meals that the managers were to be paid every three days, according to Qi's first proposal.[53] Yet the most substantial benefit was that, by doing good, by ingratiating themselves with members of the local elite, the physicians and managers could expect to be summoned to treat and interact with members of illustrious households.

The doctors serving the dispensary had busy private practices. Recognizing this, Qi stipulated in his "Guidelines for Dispensing Medicine," that the doctors should devote mornings to the dispensary but would then have afternoons free for their own patients—an arrangement that would, Qi noted, suit the dispensary patients as well, for they would avoid the afternoon sun.[54] By spending half a day at the dispensary displaying their beneficence and expertise under the scrutiny of members of the elite, the doctors could build up their private practices. They were aware that Qi frequently engaged physicians to treat members of his household. Before the dispensary was founded, Qi had already formed relationships with several of those who would later serve the dispensary. Among these were Doctor Wang Peiyuan, who had treated both Qi and his mother;[55] and Doctor Zhang Jiebin, who had come to take Qi's pulse several times in 1635.[56] After the dispensary was closed, Qi continued to engaged both of these doctors' services.[57]

DOCTORS AND DEGREE HOLDERS COMMINGLE

Working at the dispensary opened up opportunities for advantageous social interactions and convivial entertainment. The ten famous doctors who were invited to serve the dispensary in 1636 had the honor of attending a small dinner that Qi's brother Junjia put on so as to "secure the agreement" whereby they would serve on rotation.[58] Upon the closing of that dispensary, the participants again assembled to share a vegetarian feast and toast chief manager Wang Chaoshi for his labors. Once, after dining at the dispensary, Qi went out to thank various doctors and then went back to the dispensary, where he chatted with Wang Chaoshi and various friends, returning home only after the moon rose.[59] Another time he invited to his home Palace Physician Ling Yungu and eight gentlemen—to be accompanied by Zhang E, Wang Chaoshi, and Qi's elder brother Junjia.[60] That same evening, Qi then returned by moonlight to the dispensary, where, as Qi put it, "he had a pleasant chat with Wang Chaoshi, who most keenly inspired me." The dispensary doubled as a social center, where banter joined serious deeds.

Through the dispensary, doctors could build up their reputations, expand their practices, and gain entré into such prominent households as Qi's. After the first dispensary was launched, several doctors whom Qi had not previously mentioned are seen diagnosing and treating Qi's and his family's ailments—in one instance at the dispensary.[61] Dong Wulai—the doctor whose proposal to set up a dispensary had fallen on deaf ears about 1629 or 1630, and who then worked overtime and raised more funds than had the various friends for the dispensary of 1636—was asked by Qi to take his wife's pulse.[62] Doctor Yuan Liuqing, whom Qi praised for having worked enthusiastically on behalf of the dispensary of 1636, was some months later invited by Qi to treat his mother.[63] Through hard work for and dedication to the dispensary, each physician strove to establish and protect his name. Conversely, with rare exceptions, Qi meticulously identified by name each physician who treated members of his household or participated in the dispensary; he valued each name as a signifier of a particular skill and a distinct reputation.

Prominent among the dispensary doctors, and often mentioned in Qi's diary both before and after 1636, was Zhang Jiebin, for whom, among all the physicians, Qi apparently had a uniquely high regard. Whenever he or family members needed medical care, Qi invariably summoned doctors to his home or, if he was traveling about, to his boat. However, he could not always presume house calls from Zhang Jiebin; occasionally he troubled himself to go to Zhang Jiebin's place for treatment.[64] Once, rather than sending for Zhang, Qi even had someone else take his wife's pulse and then to go in her stead to ask Zhang Jiebin for medicine.[65] Zhang Jiebin was accustomed to circulating in high places. As a young man of fourteen *sui*, he had accompanied his father, who had been retained by a military commandant, to the capital, there to consort with the "talented and exceptional scholars" who frequented the commandant's place.[66] So recounted a resident of Yuyao district, Huang Zongxi, who himself had once attended a dinner party where Zhang Jiebin too was a guest.[67] The party in question took place at the home of Zhang Yi, who often appears in Qi's diary, often in the company of Zhang Dai,[68] and himself may well have been one of Dai's relatives.

Proud of his craft, Zhang Jiebin elaborated on the physician's role, the limits of medicine in the face of severe illness, and the distinctions between good physicians and bad. Medicine, he insisted, was in no way inferior to philosophy in "relating to life and nature" and should not be disparaged as a "lesser Way"[69]—by which he implied that a skilled physician was just as worthy as scholar-officials who claimed mastery of the Way. Over the course of several decades and with extreme thoroughness, Zhang wrote about diseases, anatomy, and pharmaceuticals, pouring his vast knowledge of medicine into two enormous compendia, which continued to circulate long after his death and are available today. One of these titles—published in 1624, shortly before the failed motion to set up a dispensary in 1629 or 1630—incorporated much material from earlier medical books but embraced fresh information as well. He experimented with new prescriptions and drugs, among them tobacco, which, he noted, had just been introduced, during the Wanli period, into the southern areas of Guangdong and Fujian, becoming widely cultivated in the Nanzhili-Zhejiang area (Wu and Chu). The spread of tobacco was a source of distress for Lu Shiyi, who in 1638 fretted that, along with cotton, it was displacing food crops.[70] Zhang Jiebin was not so condemnatory, noting that although tobacco had some pernicious intoxicating effects, it offered medicinal benefits as well.[71] Whether tobacco was ultimately for ill or good, Shaoxing had access to the most up-to-date medical information.

It was from Zhang Jiebin's writings that Shanyin resident Zhang Pei learned the skills of pulse taking. So we are told by Pei's elder cousin, Qi Biaojia's acquaintance Zhang Dai. Pei was blind. The malady stemmed from the overconsumption of sugar, according to Zhang Dai, an explanation that in turn suggests diabetes as a possible cause. Pei's nurturing grandmother spent one thousand ounces of silver on seeking a cure for his blindness— a testimony to the faith that people then had in medicine. When those efforts failed, Zhang Pei mastered the art of medicine by memorizing texts recited by hired readers. He then dedicated himself to treating the sick, "never accepting money" for his services. Shaoxing's social milieu and values had provided him with a calling that would earn him the community's respect.[72]

Likewise driven by a sense of mission was dispensary doctor Dong Wulai. Not only had he pressed—though in vain—to start a dispensary around 1629 or 1630; he was also an energetic fund raiser for the dispensary of 1636.[73] Likewise zealous was Ling Yungu, who was one of the ten dispensary doctors listed by Qi,[74] and whose generosity was commemorated in the local gazetteer as follows: "When young, he liked to study; as an adult he practiced medicine and was very skilled in curing 'typhoid.' To patients too poor to pay, he donated medicines; to those who were extremely poor, he gave money and rice. His family was not particularly prosperous, but throughout his life he was, spontaneously and unhesitatingly, most charitable." As though to underscore Ling's dedication, the gazetteer mentioned his asceticism: when he lost his wife in the prime of his life, he refused to remarry.[75] Physicians so dedicated to their art as Dong Wulai and Ling Yungu must have considered that one advantage of working at the dispensary was to have the opportunity of exchanging medical information with and learning from their peers, especially from the erudite physician Zhang Jiebin.[76]

Doctors and degree holders of Shaoxing commingled with relative ease, and all the while sons of some physicians were making their way up the social ladder. Wang Siren, who had earned a *jinshi* degree, served as an official, and socialized with Qi Biaojia, was the son of a poor herb doctor.[77] Jin Lan, who cooperated on famine relief with Qi Biaojia, was the son of "an expert in the art of treating mortal infant diseases who did not calculate profits, did not shirk the cold or the heat [presumably when making sick calls], and did not put the rich first and poor last. In his eightieth year, Jin Lan's father was still walking about, saying, 'I want the poor folk's infants to receive a modicum of kindness.'"[78] The charitable Ling Yungu had, by the time of the first dispensary, seen his son Yuanding earn a *juren* degree, in 1624.[79] What made the dispensary feasible at this time—what enabled members of the local elite to realize the ancient notion that those in power should care for the ill—was that waiting in the wings were numerous doctors, some of them genuinely dedicated to their calling, and some with aspirations for their sons' bureaucratic careers.

A RESERVE FORCE OF DO-GOODERS

Ready to cooperate in dispensary activities were also numerous scholars of modest means and accomplishment, among them Wang Chaoshi, the enthusiastic sponsor of the dispensary of 1636, who happened to be something of a healer as well. In 1635, shortly after Wang Peiyuan had treated Qi, Wang Chaoshi stepped in. He took Qi's pulse, wrote out a prescription, and, then, because Qi was feeling "sick at heart," counseled him on "methods for nurturing the mind."[80] Subsequently, it was Wang Chaoshi who, after all the doctors had left, tried to bring Qi's son back to life.[81] It was also Wang who seven months later would admonish Qi against excessive garden spending, compelling Qi to address (even if somewhat cavalierly) Wang's objections in his diary.[82] Although Wang Chaoshi the healer and counselor is now nearly unknown, his opinions deeply affected Qi.

Wang's life is summarized in the Shanyin gazetteer, roughly as follows. He studied with Shen Guomo. He moved to Sheng district, Shaoxing prefecture, and was active in famine relief, saving many lives. With Su Yuanpu and Zheng Xiyuan, he set up the Yaojiang Academy.[83] Wang, in short, had not earned even the lowest examination degree. His literary output was modest: "A Proposal for Setting Up a Community Granary"; a chronological biography (*nianpu*), which one presumes was about himself; a record of scholarly conversations; and a "Record of Relief for the Shan Area" (here using an alternative name for Sheng district)—none of which are extant.[84] Only a paltry piece nine lines long remains, buried in an obscure work—*The Record of the Yaojiang Academy* (*Yaojiang shuyuan*) and of interest to local residents alone. By conventional measures of literary output or bureaucratic advancement, Wang was a failure. Nonetheless, having won Qi's friendship and trust, he succeeded in pressing him to extend the duration of the dispensary of 1636. Whence came Wang's authority?

In 1631 Wang Chaoshi moved into Liu Zongzhou's house; and, together with Qi Biaojia and various scholars, he started the Bearing Witness study group, which was to hold meetings on the third day of every month. "With this," states Wang's biography, "study sessions began to flourish in the Shaoxing area."[85] Wang also aligned himself with good causes, at significant financial cost—so attests his sole surviving nine lines, entitled "On Contributing Fields." His family was poor, Wang declared. Yet, in 1639, he managed to scrape together three *mou* of land to donate as an endowment for the Banlin Community School. The land had originally been reserved for future use, as a source of income for offerings to his father's legal wife (Chaoshi's birth mother had died in 1630); but after a night of anxiety-ridden sleep, and with his "legal mother's" approval, Wang reached the conclusion that donating the land was the right thing to do. In wrapping up his essay, Wang extracted a general lesson from his experience: many households, though strapped for funds, are nonetheless in a position to scrimp for a good cause; anyone fond of being charitable (*haoyi*) might do as he had.[86]

The Bearing Witness Society brought residents on the margins of the elite in close proximity with former officials Liu Zongzhou and Tao Shiling. Although the society's main agenda was to study the classics, which obviously required some literacy, such was Shaoxing's abundance of educated men that its first meeting, according to one report, attracted over two hundred attendees.[87] Liu accepted that the attendees were a socially heterogeneous lot; in one version of a set of regulations he wrote for the society, he declared: "The gentry who join in should not flaunt their authority; even persons from diverse walks of life should not be barred."[88] By participating in such associations, low-status scholars like Wang Chaoshi gathered moral strength and wielded some moral authority in local affairs.

Among these small players was Wang Chaoshi's teacher Shen Guomo, who had once aspired to earn a *jinshi* degree, apparently without luck. Much taken with Wang Yangming's ideas, he sought instruction from one of Yangming's followers, local resident Zhou Rudeng. When Zhou declined on the grounds of being too old, Wang turned to Liu Zongzhou and Tao Shiling. In 1631, he joined Qi Biaojia and other residents in asking Liu and Tao to lead the learned discussions that would later become formalized as the Bearing Witness Society. As presented by Shen's biography, at this time—that is, just before Qi left home to assume an official post—Shen and Qi were on the same level in initiating the society. Nine years later, working within the framework of the Bearing Witness Society, Shen initiated another public-spirited project. Noting the irony that the country, all told, had seventy-two shrines and academies dedicated to Shanyin's native hero Wang Yangming, while the local shrine to Wang had ceased to function, Shen recommended that the site be used for a community school. Liu, Tao, and Qi, along with various fellows of the Bearing Witness Society and others, supported the project.[89]

Also contributing their time to worthy causes were several descendants of officials who were downwardly mobile, had rejected bureaucratic careers, or lacked the talent and luck to pass the civil service examinations. Highly visible in Qi's diaries was Guan Zongsheng, the great-grandson of an official. Though recommended by Qi to the court, Guan declined to go. Still, as an educated resident, he was active in the Bearing Witness Society and numerous local welfare projects.[90] Also appearing frequently in Qi's diaries were the Shi brothers Xiaoxian and Xiaofu, whose father had been an official.[91] Countless other small players, whose social backgrounds are unknown, and whom Qi's diaries identify merely by name, evidently had social connections that carried them into Qi's orbit. Though scarcely noticed by the local gazetteers and lacking biographies in the *Ming History* (*Ming shi*), Wang Chaoshi, Shen Guomo, and numerous other residents of modest accomplishments and marginal social status appear in such localized and intimate writings as Qi's diary and the *Record of the Yaojiang Academy* because they made substantial contributions of time and energy to local good works.

OFFICIAL INTERVENTIONS IN THE DISPENSARY OF 1641

When the dispensary was revived in 1641, conditions in Shaoxing had changed. The subsistence crisis had hit Shaoxing, and fears of social unrest had deepened. Also changed were members of the local elite themselves: even as their apprehensions of disorder grew, they could look back on, and draw strength and inspiration from, the success of the first dispensary. Firmly implanted in their minds was a glowing picture of the first dispensary and the gratification they had gained from it, all made permanent in print in Qi's testimony of 1636: "When the poor and sick heard the names of the doctors, they were happy; and when they found that the prescriptions worked, they were overjoyed. Their songs and praise have filled the streets;

and stooped gray-haired hags have composed poems to take note of the virtue."[92] In 1641, past precedent upheld a mandate that medicines be distributed to the sick; and the experience of 1636 taught that triumph was within the benefactors' reach.

The dispensary of 1641 appears to have been larger than that of 1636. It engaged not ten doctors but twelve. It was located not at the Guangxiang Chan Chapel, in the far northwest corner of the city, but at the large Monastery of Great Goodness, located almost at the city's dead center; and it stipulated that women were to have their illnesses diagnosed separately at the Hall of the Ten Kings.[93] Distinguishing the two dispensaries above all was the fact that the dispensary of 1641 involved local officials, whereas the one of 1636 appears to have been entirely in the hands of local residents. In 1636, it was the scholar without a degree Wang Chaoshi who insisted on extending the time for operating the dispensary. In 1641, a similar request was made by local authority Dao.[94] In 1636, the termination of the dispensary was announced only to the former official and local resident Tao Shiling.[95] The document drawn up to mark the closing had, Qi tells us, the names of the doctors, the amounts raised and spent, and the names of the various participating friends, as well as "this rough account of the dispensary from beginning to end";[96] no officials are in sight. In all of Qi's visits to the dispensary, his solicitations for donations for medicines, and his meetings with physicians, as recorded in his diary of 1636, and in all his extant compositions about and guidelines for the dispensary of 1636, Qi made no mention of officials.

The initiative to involve officials in 1641 came from Qi Biaojia himself; so indicates his diary. Qi initially broached the subject of the dispensary with Circuit Intendant Zheng Xuan, ever so obliquely in the context of ascertaining how much of his official salary the official might donate to local welfare. The contribution would not go wasted, Qi reassured Zheng, adding that, by providing funds for sowing the next crop, he would win the people's gratitude. At that point, Qi also touched upon the benefits of having both an infirmary (*bingfang*), which was already in operation, and a medical dispensary (*yaoju*).[97] Soon after, Qi wrote a letter to Zheng asking whether he would allow the dispensary.[98] Then, after receiving Zheng's endorsement, he proceeded to retain Doctor Yu Zhongfu and make an appointment with two colleagues to discuss the matter.[99]

With official involvement came financial support. The next day, Qi sent a letter of thanks to Zheng for his donation.[100] Magistrate Wang, acting on Circuit Intendant Zheng's orders, sent in over fifty ounces of silver for the medical dispensary, as would Magistrate Zhou two days later.[101] Immediately after receiving funds from Magistrate Wang, Qi invited Shen Guomo and seven other friends (whom he names in his diary) to discuss the dispensary at his place.[102] They asked Shen Guomo to take charge of the dispensary and unanimously recommended that Qi's elder brother Junjia be the general manager. They then proposed someone for each task—handling accounts, keeping records, supervising the medications, and marshaling the queues[103]— and designated twelve "famous doctors" (whom Qi does not name). Qi wrote a letter asking a friend to select a place for the pharmacy (*yaosuo*) and conferred with the temple monk about expenses for food as well as about organizing monks for such tasks as distributing numbered slips for assigning places in the queues and managing the utensils.[104] Three days later, he drafted "A Proposal on the Division of Responsibilities for the Dispensary," which is probably the piece preserved in his collected writings under a slightly different title ("A Proposal for the Dispensary").[105]

The extant "Proposal" spells out the tasks as follows. The general manager should calculate the dispensary's financial resources, judge the quality of the medicines, evaluate whether the supervisors have been lazy or diligent, and "motivate the physicians with heartfelt sincerity so that they will empathize with the ill. He should ensure that the prescriptions match the disease and the medicines ameliorate the conditions."[106] Under the general manager are four supervisors:

1. The supervisor of accounts oversees all the money issued; distributes money every five days to the dispensary and every three days to the supervisors for their food; and does accounts every five days according to the four-column method, noting the original amount, recent receipts, expenditures, and balance. Whether there is a surplus or shortfall will determine the duration of the dispensary.[107]

2. The supervisor of medicines estimates and reports to the general manager the amount of medicines needed. He, along with the accounts supervisor, distributes the money for medicines. Together they weigh the incoming medicines and issue a form, which they stamp with their personal seals. (At this point, the instructions further outline procedures for issuing tickets to procure medicines that are running low, examining the color and odor of the medicines, and keeping track of the prescriptions— procedures carefully designed so as to "prevent cheating and being sure that the medications reach the vital organs.")

3. The supervisor of records enters the date as well as the physician's name and address onto printed tickets.[108] While the physician is taking the pulse and writing out the prescription, this supervisor registers the information. At the end of each day he binds the sheets together as a "medical case book." For those who take only a prescription, he applies the seal that says "no medicine given." If the registrar fails to write clearly, hence causing errors in the prescription, or if he should fail to write fast enough, hence causing mobbing and outburst (among the patients)—this is entirely his responsibility.

4. The supervision of tallies is to be carried out by Chan monks, each of

whom will take a turn for a day. The monk distributes red and green tallies to the patients, instructs them to go to the east and west sides of the monastery, respectively, and has them proceed according to the numbers. Only when one person has finished going through should the next one be issued a slip; this will deter the sick from mobbing and will protect the physicians from the stench.[109]

FORMALITIES

As officials became involved, formality set in. The easy conviviality, the bantering and laughter under moonlight, of the earlier dispensary gave way to elaborate ceremony. So suggests one entry in Qi's diary: "I went early to the dispensary. The various friends and doctors had assembled in hierarchical order. They burned incense and prayed before the Buddha's image." Three of the associates "kneeled and prayed most reverently," remarked Qi, who then took care to list their names. Among these were Shen Guomo and Shi Xiaofu, participants in the Bearing Witness Society. After the ceremony, Qi continued, "we asked the palace physicians to enter the east and west wings of the dispensary to examine the sick, who numbered over one hundred." At noon, Qi, his colleagues, and the physicians fraternized, "sharing a vegetarian feast in the Chan Buddhist hall."[110] If such rituals had played a part in the dispensary of 1636 but without Qi bothering to mention them, the point remains: this time such matters did catch Qi's notice. Official involvement, their authorizations and contributions, elevated the event and increased Qi's consciousness of the formalities, giving them enough importance to deserve note in his diary.

The second dispensary ran into a problem not mentioned in 1636: how to balance expenditures for the meals shared by the friends of the dispensary against expenditures for medical supplies. The "Second Proposal" of 1641 stipulates that the physicians and managers should have meals and snacks every day, that this should be arranged by the monasteries, for which they would be paid, and that "in years of dearth, one must be parsimonious, with only three meals and two snacks."[111] At a meeting at the Deva Kings Monastery (in the northeast corner of the city), the friends deliberated how they might maintain frugality and simplicity in the operation. The accounting of days past had shown that two thirds of the funds had gone to food and only one-third to medicines. "How is this," asked Qi in his diary, "what we mean by 'saving the people'?" To correct matters, they eliminated the position of manager.[112] Explained Qi: "Hereafter the supervisors also would strive to follow the agreement; and the doctors suggested that the food they had been eating was too sumptuous and should be simplified."[113]

His awareness of formal arrangements having been heightened by official involvement, Qi duly noted in 1641 something he had ignored in 1636:

the posting of announcements. To launch the dispensary of 1641, he had an announcement put up at the Monastery of Great Goodness.[114] To prepare for its closing, notices were "pasted up at the crossroads."[115] Not until officials cast their authority over the dispensary of 1641 did Qi gain an outsider's perspective that brought into sharp focus such interfaces between the dispensary and the general public. Official sanction endowed announcements with power and introduced fresh options into Qi's purview: when he wished to warn patients against disorderly conduct at the dispensary, he thought to ask local authority Bi to post a sign to that effect.[116]

Recruiting doctors and managers, a task Qi scarcely noted in 1636, proved time-consuming and difficult in 1641. By then, several of the medical experts who had rallied around the dispensary of 1636 had faded from the scene. Wang Chaoshi, the dedicated champion of the first dispensary, had fallen ill and died in midsummer of 1640.[117] Another "friend," Qin Hongyou, participated in organizing the dispensary of 1641 but then himself fell ill; only after recovering, weeks after the program was well underway, did he go to the dispensary.[118] Nearly all the doctors who had been on the dispensary roster of 1636 failed to reappear in Qi's diaries of the 1640s.[119] Had they, through incessant exposure to the sick, succumbed to disease? Zhang Jiebin continued to treat Qi's family in 1641 but, if one accepts Qi's diaries as a guide, he played no role in the dispensary of 1641 and died in 1642. The upshot of all the attrition was that Qi had to expend effort, first writing letters to ascertain the names of additional physicians and then recruiting them.[120]

His colleague Yu Huang recommended to Qi "the famous doctor Sun Xiehe,"[121] who readily stepped in; such was Shaoxing's profusion of dedicated physicians. Sun, a local gazetteer remarks, had studied medical books with such concentration as to forget to eat and sleep and, once trained, treated patients regardless of their financial means. Then, as though to remind readers that Sun's merit was duly rewarded, the gazetteer appends a note about his sons' achievements: one became a licentiate (*zhusheng*); another earned the *jinshi* degree in 1667 and was assigned to a post as magistrate.[122] Here again the fluidity between the social realms of literate doctor and degree-holding literati is evident.

In 1641, Qi proved especially solicitous of physicians and those men he and his colleagues deemed fit to be managers. One day he traveled all around, crisscrossing the city, exiting first one gate and then another so as to make contact with physicians and colleagues on behalf of the dispensary. He wanted to pay his respects to various physicians, he explained, because, on the previous day he "had failed to visit them all." He went out the city to ask a Fu Yuliang to manage the dispensary, only to be disappointed that Fu "would not agree to it." He again left the city "to beseech" Physician Shen Jingchu, presumably for cooperation.[123] A few weeks later, Qi was still running around, one day begging residents Yan Yizhi and Jin Wulian to "manage the dispensary"; and another day paying sick calls to "friends" Yan Yizhi and Qin Hongyou, and then asking yet another resident to help manage the dispensary—meanwhile paying respects to officials and quelling slanders about the medical bureau.[124]

His schedule already crammed with famine-relief matters, Qi undertook numerous dispensary-related chores and busily drafted letters and documents, often for official eyes. In response to a donation sent in by Magistrate Wang, he had to compose a note of acknowledgment.[125] After selecting the twelve doctors who were to serve the dispensary, he had to forward their names, along with a revised proposal, to the circuit intendant.[126] Upon learning from a friend that Vice-Prefect Bi had favored the dispensary with a visit, he felt compelled to send Bi a letter of thanks.[127] He further composed at least three documents: "Directives for the Dispensary," which he drafted one day and finished the next;[128] "A Proposal for Dividing Responsibilities for the Dispensary";[129] and "A Record of the Dispensary."[130] The last item he showed to Circuit Intendant Zheng in response to a letter accompanying additional funds for the medical bureau.[131]

Adding stress to Qi's work was the requirement that he and his friends periodically review accounts and submit the results to the circuit intendant. The guidelines for the dispensary of 1641 stipulated that the person in charge of accounts would be responsible for providing a general tally every five days, and that the duration of the dispensary would depend on the amount left in reserve. Balancing the books proved frustrating. One day Qi and "various friends" tried to review the accounts at the Monastery of Great Goodness but were interrupted by a visitor; the next day they reviewed the accounts while traveling about by boat, but, repeatedly interrupted by visitors, they managed to come up with the gross figures only: with but four or five ounces of silver remaining, they would be ten taels in arrears by the scheduled end date. Thereupon Qi forwarded the gross figures and the medical records to the circuit intendant with a request for instructions on whether to continue or stop.[132] The number of patients getting medicine was daily expanding, Qi observed.[133]

After staying up late into the night to calculate the cost of the medicines,[134] Qi returned to the medical bureau, again to balance the books; the expenditures, he found, had exceeded reserves by forty taels. At home later that day, he resumed reviewing accounts and found an overrun of three taels; his brothers entered the calculations into a record.[135] Right before the closing of the dispensary, Qi had to send Zheng Xuan the account books along with a written report.[136]

The decision to end the dispensary program of 1641 appears to have belonged to officials. After sending in the accounts and medical records, Qi learned that the official Dao wished to continue,[137] and two days later, Qi received a formal letter from Dao to that effect. Having discussed the matter with "friends" (Qi provides no details), Qi sent Dao a reply and wrote to Magistrate Wang. He also wrote to his personal manager Chen Changyao.[138] Qi reentered the city the next day to discuss when the dispensary should stop; the closing date was set for the fourth day of the eighth month.[139] Three days prior to that date, he visited various "brothers," again to discuss the closing. Circuit Intendant Zheng again provided money. Officials Bi and Chen both provided rice in support of discounting prices at the pharmacy. Memos were sent to the various participating friends and physicians about a vegetarian banquet celebrating the dispensary's closing, and announcements about the closing were posted at the main thoroughfares.[140]

Officials exercised some authority over the dispensary of 1641 but did not necessarily stand to gain from the privilege. Undoubtedly they derived some sense of pride from sponsoring the good cause. Along the way they may have earned the gratitude of the local populace. Yet those officials who voiced opinions about how the dispensary should be run ended up themselves making financial contributions to the dispensary and assuming burdens. Like the "friends" of the dispensary, they added chores to their own busy dockets: reviewing proposals, checking account books, making occasional on-site visits, and officiating at reward ceremonies. Precisely when other problems—supplying and distributing food, policing vagrancy, fighting locusts, and providing farmers with seeds for the next crop—had become most urgent, officials had to bother with paying calls to the dispensary and generally apprising themselves of the affairs of this relatively small local operation. The challenge of balancing dispensary demands against other costly and time-consuming urgencies added tension to official routines.

If Circuit Intendant Zheng gained some authority over the dispensary, local leaders too won advantages. Their collaboration with the officials opened up opportunities for discussion and negotiation about matters other than medical relief. When Qi wrote thanking the magistrate and the circuit intendant for their monetary contributions to the dispensary, he seized the chance to speak "on behalf of the Taizhou merchants" about reductions in their profit margins.[141] When the circuit intendant went to the dispensary, Qi bent his ear about locust control and famine relief; when the two district magistrates Wang and Zhou visited the dispensary at the Monastery of Great Goodness, Qi again seized the opportunity to "talk with them exclusively about such matters as catching locusts and the price-stabilizing sale of grain."[142] Moreover, official involvement enabled Qi to borrow official authority to advance the dispensary program, as when he asked an official to post a sign prohibiting disorder at the dispensary or went in Circuit Intendant Zheng's stead to pay respects to the physicians.[143]

The dispensary likewise served as a meeting place where Qi's fellow literati might seek opportunities to broach matters with him. When Qi visited the Monastery of Great Goodness to discuss with the two magistrates such matters as controlling locusts and equilibrating grain prices, as well as to await an afternoon review of the medical accounts, word of his presence got out: "When the various friends heard I was at the dispensary, many came to visit—to the point that I could hardly catch my breath."[144] Within the context of a shared dedication to dispensary work, demands from below ran up the social hierarchy just as directives were sent down by men at the top. While officials claimed some authority over the operation, and while Qi Biaojia occasionally claimed to represent official authority, the lowest participants reaped benefits as well, piggybacking their own requests onto their service to the dispensary. When one resident pressed for setting up a dispensary and a burial ground, he simultaneously asked for a loan for preparing fields.[145] The negotiations, exchanges of benefits, and sharing of responsibilities were multilateral; the range of motivations broad. With no party gaining complete control over dispensary affairs, many types of players—officials and residents alike—were pulled into the vortex of dispensary activity.

Thus, when the time came for assigning credit midway through the program in 1641, the hardworking dispensary participants successfully insisted on receiving a share of the merit. The circuit intendant had wanted to single Qi out for praise, but, recounted Qi in his diary: "The various friends, thinking that I was making this my own private affair, were displeased." Accepting such input, Qi emended the draft document and explained to the circuit intendant why: "Because various gentry [*shen*] had cooperated in the event, it was inappropriate that I alone should take the praise."[146] About a week later Qi met with a friend (Wu Qisheng) at a monastery (to discuss trying to keep the circuit intendant on in his post). "Shortly later," wrote Qi, "In succession, the two magistrates and the circuit intendant arrived. The circuit intendant commended the doctors, rewarding them with goblets of crab-apple liquor and printed booklets [presumably to commemorate the dispensary]. Everything was done most heartily, and every one of the doctors was pleased."[147]

At the closing banquet roughly a month later, wrote Qi: "The physicians had all assembled. Wang Taihan and five or six 'friends' came. Together we ate in the Chan Hall. I bowed to them all around to thank them for their labors and presented gifts to the various friends who had managed the medicines; everyone on down to the runners got something and was pleased." That same day, local authorities Wang Sunlan and Chen Zilong dropped by to discuss with Qi such matters as "whether grain should be stored with the officials or the people, relief for the area of Shaoxing (Yue), and the distribution of rewards."[148] A couple of days later, Qi announced the end of the dispensary to local authority Zheng and then went around to thank the various doctors.[149] He spent the rest of the month tidying up dispensary affairs by writing up a record,[150] making arrangements for the distribution of rewards and honors, and poring over account books.[151]

The dispensary was revived in 1642 but received little attention in Qi's diary. The initiative this time came from Circuit Intendant Zheng, who urged the matter upon Qi. Qi had two of his bondservants accompany a Lu Jingquan to a monastery to distribute medicines.[152] Ten days later, he asked two physicians from the city for an account of the expenses for distributing medicines so that he could make a report to the circuit intendant.[153] By the first of the seventh month, the pestilence had spread throughout the area, whereupon Qi asked Buddhist monks to recite sutras to protect his home.[154] At the end of the summer, he handed over to Circuit Intendant Zheng the various records for the soup kitchens and dispensary.[155] This is the sum of what Qi wrote about the dispensary of 1642.

During the middle months of that year, one finds Qi instead performing, in the environs of his rural estate, small acts of kindness, which he took care to record in his diary. He walked around the Ke Bridge market, distributing coins to the poor; giving three *fen* each to villagers afflicted with hunger; observing the distribution of money to beggars at the soup kitchen at the monastery at Ke Bridge; receiving a starving visitor at his home, presumably for a meal; and visiting villages around the area of Ke Bridge and Ke Mountain to distribute relief.[156] Had opening and closing the dispensary, now a familiar routine under official supervision, ceased to interest him when it came to writing entries in his diary? Had Qi, who finally himself resorted to religious spells to vanquish pestilence from his home, lost his enthusiasm for and trust in medical treatments? Or had he retreated from the urban-based dispensary to protect his rural area? The surviving documents do not say.

One of Qi's protégés, Zhao Gongjian, would later comment that Qi, with doctors and servants in tow, went to the rural areas to distribute famine relief *and* medicines.[157] Judging from Qi's diary and essays, however, dispensary activities were confined to the city. Qi and his associates had discussed the problem of caring for those invalids too sick to travel in from the rural areas. They expressed the wish to distribute medicines to each urban ward and rural village, and to have "doctors take medicines right to the doors." But Qi also expressed his "fear that, without the manpower for inspecting scattered sites, the doctors would be but a fiction." Reasoning that having multiple dispensaries in city and country would require the accumulation of resources, Qi reached the conclusion that "this idea may be reserved for future sponsors."[158] While making hard choices in the distribution of care, Qi envisioned a model for a more equitable, universal distribution that future generations might attain.

SMALL CAUSES: A FOUNDLING HOME, AN INFIRMARY, AND AID TO VAGRANTS

Along with the provision of food, medicines, and charitable burials, Qi's diary affords glimpses of numerous other, lesser causes, among them a foundling home (*baoying ju*), whose rooms were filled with infants being suckled and fed, The sight, Qi commented in his diary, "made one sigh."[159] Qi elaborated on the care of foundlings in his draft manuscript of the *Complete Book of Famine Relief,* as follows:

> During the food shortage of 1641, Qian Yuandeng collected abandoned infants and raised them in a building. He assigned a place to each one, from the toddlers on down to those who were still nursing, and put them under the care of several old women. For infants needing to be nursed, he sought wet nurses. Overseeing the activity was a manager who got up several times a night and, shirking neither the stench nor the howling that filled the room, looked after the infants. If the person abandoning the infant had placed a name on the infant's chest, the manager assigned a number and made a tag, which he tied to the baby's wrist; then, he entered the number, along with the corresponding name, in a register, and noted where the baby had been abandoned and when found. News of the benevolence will spread, enabling those households who cannot raise their children to entrust them.

In some cases, Qi further mentioned, children from nearby ate and slept at the foundling home but frequently returned to the parents; or the parents sometimes went to see their children and, once times improved, reclaimed them.[160]

"The parents always wept when they took their leave," observed Qi, who then went on to explain the fates of those children who could not go home: "The manager would raise them, marrying off the girls and helping the boys get established. Countless survived."[161] The following year, Circuit Intendant Zheng proposed instituting a "bureau" in the city to which every ward and village would send any abandoned children they collected.[162] This account parallels a diary entry where Qi noted that he and Zheng inspected the foundling home. After reporting that Zheng was "very pleased" to find that regulations by a Qian Yuandeng were being followed, Qi made a point of noting: "I had also helped somewhat."[163]

Also surfacing in Qi's diary of 1641 are scattered and fragmentary references to an infirmary (*bingfang*) near his rural estate at Ke Market, the town that, being relatively prosperous, attracted numerous vagrants in search of food.[164] To accommodate those "who were so sick that they could not stand up," Qi proposed establishing an infirmary, stipulating that, as soon as the vagrants recovered their ability to walk and beg, they were to be expelled from Ke Market. Because no vacant buildings were available, Qi explained, they set up a sick ward by the village dike and had the vagrants transferred there to be nourished."[165] A few days later, Qi accompanied his brother to look at the infirmary, after which they met with their comrades to review various methods for aiding vagrants.

Assuming responsibility for managing the infirmary was Wuliang, a monk deeply ensconced in Shanyin society and well acquainted with Qi Biaojia.[166]

Wuliang was affiliated with the monk Mailang, who had, around 1629 or 1630, joined doctor Dong Wulai in proposing (albeit unsuccessfully) a dispensary. Mailang, himself a native of Shanyin, had taken his Buddhist vows from Zhuhong—the widely influential popularizer of the practice of liberating animals. Subsequently he followed another monk, Zhanran, who, after taking vows with Zhuhong, had settled in Shanyin and for thirty years had been a friend of Qi Biaojia's father.[167] In 1630, Qi Biaojia and several of his brothers asked Mailang to restore the Mita Monastery, which was located in Meiye, where Qi's father had resided and Qi was born. After consigning the project to Wuliang, Mailang unexpectedly died.[168] Likewise following Zhuhong and admiring Zhanran was another Shanyin native of Qi's father's generation: Tao Wangling. Even while fervently practicing Buddhism, Wangling, along with his younger brother Shiling, lectured together with Qi Biaojia's colleague, the staunch Confucian Liu Zongzhou.[169]

Sharing both a discourse and a social world with scholar-officials, the Buddhist monks of Shanyin in several respects resembled the lesser literati: they enjoyed easy access to members of the elite, a relationship conducive to the exchange of favors; they readily engaged in good works; and their contributions to causes earned some attention in the written record. Monks steadily streamed through Qi's house and on into his diaries. Frequently Qi summoned them to officiate at funerals, conduct masses, and guide him in reading sutras. Just as often, when Qi received casual visits from monks or invited them to share meals, they dealt with mundane concerns—as when he and monk Wuliang mulled over the bandit situation.[170] Dealings were mutually beneficial. When some monks felt that they had been wronged (precisely how is not made clear), Wuliang prevailed upon Qi to write up a complaint to the magistrate.[171] When a monk approached Qi for funds for a vegetarian meal for his fellow clergymen, and spoke of their hardship and rising grain prices, Qi helped them.[172] When their resources were running out, monks asked Qi to write a prayer in support of their fund drive for meals.[173] When monks from Roaring Tiger Monastery begged Qi for assistance during the food shortage of 1641, Qi obliged.[174] In several instances, he provided monks with lodgings.[175]

In return for such favors, Qi reaped some material benefits—most noticeable in his diary was the monks' assistance in importing lumber. Once Qi noted that his elder brother commissioned a monk to go to Fujian to buy wood expressly for the construction of a small Buddhist chapel.[176] But once, while still adding touches to his garden in 1638, he recorded that he commissioned monks to buy timber specifically "for me."[177] Several times, he did not mention the purpose of the wood-buying expeditions, leaving one to surmise that these too may have been for his own use.[178]

The long-standing symbiotic relationship between members of the local elite and Buddhist monks facilitated collaboration in charitable activities. It was in the context of a social occasion—a vegetarian dinner hosted by Qi's elder brother Junjia, during which the conversation turned to the topic of vagrants—that Wuliang happily agreed to manage the infirmary.[179] Three months later Wuliang reported to Qi that at least one hundred persons at the infirmary had recovered and been discharged, whereupon Qi noted, "I was extremely happy about this, and therefore helped out with expenses, urging that he bring the infirmary to a close."[180] As reported in Qi's diary, other Buddhist monks undertook numerous good deeds. They buried the dead, oversaw the infirmary, assisted in operating the dispensary, and distributed coins at Ke Market.[181] They also carried "portable kitchens" through Ke Market to distribute soup to vagrants.[182]

From men at the margins of the degree-holding elite thus came the impetus for many good works. The idea of a dispensary was initially proposed jointly by Wang Chaoshi, who had no examination degree, and monk Mailang. The idea that Qi "wanted to follow" for distributing food at Ke Market came from monk Yuetang.[183] The guidelines for and the management of the foundling home were the work of Qian Huanzhong, identified only as a resident of Shanyin. Although Qi "helped him somewhat," the key to the foundling home's success was Qian's dedication.[184] These initiatives from below bring to mind that Yang Dongming had drawn inspiration for his benevolent society from practices among the common people.

By riding good causes, literate monks, skilled physicians, and men who were literate but lacked civil service degrees could gain power in local affairs. Some used good works to ingratiate themselves with, and win favors from, members of the elite, and even to line their own pockets. Others had themselves been won over by a sense of moral obligation. A conspicuous example of the latter type is Wang Chaoshi, who resided in Liu Zongzhou's home. Though poor, Wang found the means to sponsor a school and, fortified by Liu Zongzhou's teachings, repeatedly cautioned Qi Biaojia against erring ways. In terms of family wealth or examination success, Wang could not compete with the prosperous degree holders of his community; his chief resource was, rather, his high-minded moral stance. Armed with moral integrity, and backed by Liu's moral authority, Wang eagerly joined—even led—members of the elite in good causes.

Though having held no official position, not even a degree, Shen Guomo, like his student Wang Chaoshi, had the temerity to admonish Qi Biaojia. In 1633, when Qi was serving as regional inspector in the lower Yangzi area, Shen chastised him for having ordered that some rogues be beaten to death.[185] Citing *The Analects,* he asked: "Have you not heard the statement, 'When you have found out the truth *of any accusation,* be grieved for and pity them [the people], and do not feel joy *at your own ability*'?" Qi would have readily recognized that the statement, by one of Confucius's followers, immediately followed an observation that could have applied equally well to late Ming times: "The rulers have failed in their duties and the people consequently have been disorganized for a long time."[186] In response, Qi reportedly bowed before Shen, saying, "I respectfully accept your instruction."[187] Empowered by the moral teachings of the highly educated elite, Shen Guomo, Wang Chaoshi, and other small players of the Shaoxing area developed voices sufficiently persuasive and authoritative to influence local affairs. Pressure for good causes and virtuous behavior thus ran up the social hierarchy as well as from top down. Just as Qi Biaojia had impressed upon his superiors, the officials, the importance of touring the soup kitchens, so did these lesser literati urge upon their social superiors various beneficent projects. Whatever the motivations of the instigators may have been, charitable projects proliferated, with Qi Biaojia's records alone identifying—in addition to famine-relief programs—an infirmary, a dispensary, a foundling home, programs for aiding vagrants, and the organized burial of the corpses of indigent families.

Setting priorities among the many worthy options, each of which competed for resources and patronage, was problematic, tempering, for example, Qi's enthusiasm for the infirmary. A few days prior to visiting it with his brother, Qi cautioned that everything had to be discussed in detail, that it was unfitting to initiate such a scheme lightly, even when one felt supportive. As he put it, "Some harm, I fear, might be embedded in the benefit."[188] The question of priorities and resources again weighed on Qi's mind in connection to sending to the infirmary those ailing beggars found prostrate in front of Ke Market's temple, prompting him carefully to explain that the funds raised in Ke Market would be reserved for the soup kitchen, and that two families (his and Wu Qisheng's) were sharing the responsibility for the beggars.[189]

As sponsors of good causes reached out for financial support, they inevitably also reached up the social hierarchy. Qian, the obscure foundling-home organizer, obtained assistance from Qi Biaojia. Monk Mailang and Doctor Dong Wulai, though they had failed in their first attempt to start a dispensary, found on a second try that they could succeed by forming an alliance with Qi Biaojia.

Sponsorship of large causes expanded opportunities to justify small, localized programs. The larger the program, the greater the latitude to improvise funding. Once, Circuit Intendant Zheng granted Qi permission to have some grain left over from the relief program exchanged for money for distributing medicines.[190] Another time, on a day when Qi several times discussed "the matter of burying corpses," and himself supervised the receipt and logging in of pharmaceuticals at the dispensary—in short, on a day of hard work for good causes—Qi "moved ten taels from the dispensary to respond to a monk in charge of the infirmary" that was near his rural residence.[191] Still another time, Qi dealt simultaneously with two urgent needs when requesting additional funds from Magistrate Wang: funding for the dispensary, which was located inside the city walls, and funding for a campaign against locusts that were scourging his rural area. Wang granted eighteen *shi* of leftover grain, whereupon Qi replied that exterminating the locusts at that time was of the utmost importance lest they return with increased vigor.[192] How the funds were finally allocated is unclear, yet the point remains: by expanding official involvement with community-led projects, Qi increased opportunities for discussing a whole host of relief activities.

The pattern of piggybacking small causes onto large not only reflects competition for limited resources; it also points to the effects of official presence radiating downward throughout Shaoxing society. As in their debates about famine relief, the residents of late Ming Shaoxing tried to resolve their differences of opinion about how charitable resources should be used, not through a simple vote, but through negotiations that left open the option that participants reach beyond their group, in quest for official sanction. To be sure, there were cases where small groups made decisions within the confines of a circumscribed membership. Examples are Zhang Bi's organization of famine relief, Ni Yuanlu's grain-loan societies of a fixed number of households, and Yang Dongming's first benevolent society. Far more visible, however, are the large, long-lasting organizations that inevitably became entangled with official authority—not just because they welcomed the substantial financial contributions of officials, but because they were structured in a particular manner from the start. The contracts or agreements (*yue*) that do-gooders swore to follow outlined roles and duties; they did not speak of the procedures whereby the circle of friends might resolve disputes through a vote. Discussions, debates, and disagreements were frequent. Participants voiced their opinions and could threaten to quit. They influenced operations because leaders understood that, to win cooperation, they must heed the climate of opinion. Yet the course of the decision making was ultimately shaped not by majority rule but by the workings of a sociopolitical hierarchy. Whether the leader of a good cause was a lesser literatus (like Wang Chaoshi) or an official on leave (like Qi Biaojia), that leader had the option of resolving disputes by seeking intervention from a superior.

CONCLUSION

Shaoxing's social networks were far-flung. In 1640, Qi received, from a friend (Xia Yunyi) a booklet on city governance that discussed, among other things, the idea of benevolent societies, which Qi extolled.[193] Before the year 1641 was out, word that Liu Zongzhou and Qi Biaojia had labored hard managing a relief program that brought the people great harmony reached the ears of benevolent-society lecturer Chen Longzheng.[194] Leaders in charity tailored their strategies for specific places and conditions, but not without thinking in terms that spoke to their peers elsewhere. In 1636 Qi "heard that the Hangzhou area (Wulin) would also like to put a dispensary into effect." Qi commented: "This is simply because our kind cannot bear to see others suffer. If we could expand the organization, then it would not be only for a particular time, but for all time; and it would not be for one place but also for other areas."[195] "For all time": enabling this option was a new social dynamism that arose from the region's prosperity and high rate of literacy, and hence from the numerous networks that interlaced horizontally through the social hierarchy. Small constituencies and parties today unknown could, by hitching onto good causes, negotiate with and influence men in power— even while the invisible hand of official authority and power remained omnipresent. These social conditions, new to the late Ming, sustained both numerous benevolent causes and a vision that such activities would endure well beyond the period of grave crisis.

At the level of local administration, one finds not a vacuum abandoned by a failed imperial bureaucracy (as the model of dynastic decline would suggest), but a strong official presence that made it attractive for men far down the social hierarchy to participate in philanthropic projects. These circumstances made charitable activities highly visible. As their numbers expanded, members of the local elite grew competitive, reaching upward for recognition and affirmation from men with political authority. In an increasingly cramped social space, doing good and saving lives offered opportunities to stand out in the community and to influence the course of local affairs. At the same time, it enlarged and elevated those men who would be benefactors.

9

Beliefs in Charity—and the Rhetoric of Beliefs

Today we get to dip into our money bags . . . to aid others; . . .
this certainly counts as a fortune-yielding deed.
QI BIAOJIA

Cooperation for the large-scale charitable projects of the late Ming was based on a shared rhetoric about the importance of doing good, the just distribution of resources, and the urgency of saving lives. This rhetoric was understood and used in many ways, by Gao Panlong to express ardent beliefs and by cynics to control the masses. In either case, the rhetoric had become a widely acceptable currency for social and political exchanges among parties high and relatively low, facilitating cooperation across the boundaries of class, kinship, and region. This shared understanding allowed charitable deeds their social significance.

One must, of course, abandon any quest for the viewpoints of the lowest social strata. The beneficiaries—those faceless and illiterate poor whom the texts of this period rarely mention by name—lacked means and voice to enter their opinions into the written record. How they responded to charity is known only through the eyes and imaginings of literate, socially prominent donors: the recipients were grateful, the genteel poor feared losing face in public, and some poor resented the rich, occasionally growing arrogant and more demanding after receiving handouts. With each charitable gift and every speech preceding a distribution, benefactors tried to indoctrinate the poor with their own values. Feeding the poor and socializing them went hand in hand. The benefactors were capable of acute observation; yet, as they sought words to describe what they saw, they inevitably fashioned their observations in terms of their own values and expectations. Whether they were imparting deeply felt beliefs or expediently mouthing a do-good rhetoric to achieve selfish ends, they declared that giving to the poor was a way to realize the interconnectedness of all living things, thus ensuring social order; or it was an attempt to achieve some equitableness or social justice; or it was a way to save lives and reduce suffering; and, because charity accomplished all these things, it also communicated the donors' goodness.

For someone who has been socialized to be charitable, compassionate, and just (whether socialized through parental models of caring, ethical teachings, the examples of ancient heroes, or peer pressure), charitable acts will carry meaning; to the untutored cynic, giving away money may seem reckless. Consider the account of a Fan Yuanzhi, who found money in a ditch. The rightful owner, it turned out, was a woman who had just sold land at great sacrifice in order to liberate her husband from prison. Fan returned the windfall to her, whereupon the villagers ridiculed him for lacking good business sense. This tale, whose aim was to edify its readers, then predictably unfolds to reveal the nay-saying villagers' shortsightedness: a year later Fan, who had responded to all the derision by "just smiling," ended up passing (along with his son, no less) the civil service examinations. Success rewarded benevolence and vindicated Fan.[1]

At times even the most dedicated late Ming philanthropists disagreed among themselves about what counted as good deeds. Some praised liberating animals, giving money to strangers, and extending charity to prisoners. Others condemned these particular activities as misdirected and wasteful. Nonetheless philanthropists generally agreed that good deeds deserved recognition. This chapter explores the sources of their shared understanding. It argues that, though informed somewhat by past traditions, late Ming charity cannot be traced to any one specific tradition or belief but rather emerged through the interplay between two forces: a moral imperative, the insistence that one simply must do good, about which Gao Panlong and Chen Longzheng lectured; and social realities that shaped how one realized that moral imperative. Though many of the charitable men covered in this study took seriously the Confucian classics on which their training for the civil service examination and office rested, they had no need to refer to those texts to understand and interpret the imperative to do good.

TRADITIONS OF THOUGHT

Leaders in late Ming charity inherited a legacy of ancient ideas about caring for the needy and nurturing the people, ideas associated with various systems of thought that historians through the centuries have labeled Confucian, Daoist, and Buddhist. Tracing late Ming charity specifically to any one of these is difficult, however. Over the centuries, the three traditions not only evolved; they also periodically overlapped and merged, with the result that many Ming writers (like their predecessors) spoke of the "unity of the three teachings" (*sanjiao heyi*). In this spirit of accommodation, one of Qi Biaojia's friends pronounced that a message of *The Doctrine of the Mean*—that is, of one of the Four Books associated with Confucius and central to the curriculum for the civil service examination—was essentially conveyed by the "unity of the three teachings."[2]

Confounding the problem of identifying ideational sources for late Ming charity is the legacy of Huang Zongxi—the Shaoxing resident who had dined with physician Zhang Jiebin. Huang's magisterial *Records of Ming Scholars* (*Ming-ru xue'an*) has greatly influenced modern scholarship on Ming thought but presents a distorted view of late Ming currents. Wishing to restore fundamental values after the catastrophic fall of the Ming dynasty, Huang asserted distinctions between the "correct" learning of the Way, derived from Confucius and his followers, and "heterodox" thinking, especially Buddhism. Accordingly, he cleansed some of his subjects of their Buddhist impurities and dropped from consideration anyone who did not fit his definition of correctness—the influential Buddhist monk Zhuhong and Qi Biaojia's acquaintance Yan Maoyou being two examples. He also climaxed his study in a celebration of his teacher Liu Zongzhou, defining him as protector, preserver, and amplifier of correct values against the corrosive and deviant ideas of late Ming times. Qi Biaojia, being more an activist than a thinker, had no place in Huang's survey. Although Huang lived in Shaoxing prefecture, it appears that he scarcely interacted with Qi. Once he visited Qi's library at Mei Market, only to put down Qi's collection, observing: despite their elegant ivory fasteners, the books could be readily found in the shops by anyone who had money; what made the library valuable, declared Huang—whose own father had been executed—was that it had been assembled by Qi's father.[3]

If one looks at late Ming texts directly, without Huang's mediation, the neat lines of intellectual affiliation drawn by Huang disintegrate and a complex picture emerges. In 1630 (that is, before the formal start of the Bearing Witness Society and before the start of Qi's extant diaries), Liu Zongzhou, Tao Shiling, and Qi Biaojia had carried on formal philosophical discussions, on such themes as "the study of substance and function" (*tiyong zhi xue*).[4] Though they by no means shared a unified vision, Liu and Tao lectured together and had many devotees in common. Differences between them were still inchoate in the 1630s and appeared inconsequential to Qi in 1637. Of a meeting at the White Horse Mountain Hut, he observed that Tao and Liu engaged in a lengthy debate about the study of the mind, with Liu favoring the slow method and Tao the fast. "Each method had its strength," was Qi's accommodative conclusion.[5] Later the two men drifted apart. Liu reacted against the populist concept of easy sagehood that Wang Yangming's thought had stimulated. Tao, who appears to have had more demagogic leanings than Liu, appropriated many Buddhist ideas.[6] Nonetheless, looking back across the dynastic divide, Huang Zongxi emphasized the differences. He complained that he "once heard Tao teach" but "did not like what Tao said" because his "disciples all studied Buddhism . . . and got into such topics as causation and retribution."[7]

Both Qi Biaojia and his elder brother Fengjia are recorded as having spoken at the second meeting of the Bearing Witness Society,[8] but Qi scarcely mentioned the society in his diaries. Once, without specifically naming the society, he noted that he joined Tao, Shen Guomo, and Guan Zongsheng at Jiuqu (the neighborhood where Qi had an urban lodging) for a formal discussion of "cause and response" (*yinguo*), after which they shared a meal.[9] Once he remarked that he had declined to attend a session of the Bearing Witness Society;[10] and once he accompanied Shen and Guan to attend a lecture at the White Horse Mountain Hut, which was where Liu Zongzhou and Tao Shiling customarily lectured.[11] The paucity of Qi's references to the Bearing Witness Society—even when one allows that he was away during much of its first two years—suggests lack of interest in its proceedings. While maintaining a cordial and accommodating relationship with his peers, he was drifting away from what he called "the empty words of sagely scholarship" to embrace instead learning that he could immediately apply to life-and-death problems.[12]

Men of Shaoxing shared ideas and socialized across the lines of intellectual affiliation that Huang Zongxi would later trace. Even Liu Zongzhou—the epitome of correct thinking in Huang's view—did not always repudiate Buddhism as decisively as Huang would later assert. Moreover, leaving aside the case of Lu Shiyi, who lived into the Qing dynasty and therefore under no circumstances would have been included in Huang's *Records,* three of the six men who figure prominently in this study of late Ming charity (Yang Dongming, Gao Panlong, and Chen Longzheng) have biographies in Huang's *Records,* while three (Ni Yuanlu, Zhang Bi, and Qi Biaojia) do not. Yet, on the subject of doing good, all six men shared a common discourse.

Prominent in that discourse are elements of Buddhism. Ni Yuanlu once dreamed of a monk who pronounced that chanting sutras was not as good as copying them; then, instructed by his grandmother to write out a sutra, he reverently worked all day to produce an error-free copy of one section of the *Diamond Sutra* (*Jingang jing*).[13] During the subsistence crisis, he started to keep a vegetarian diet and independently organized a Life-Saving Pagoda Society to raise funds for the needy.[14] To participate, men made vows to the Buddha; and to end the program, they held a Buddhist ceremony for the "transfer of merit" (*huixiang*): Buddhist monks chanted from the *Lotus Flower Sutra* (*Lianhua jing*), the names of benefactors and beneficiaries were listed, and everyone present burned incense. In concluding the guidelines for the society, Ni asked, "If anyone is not wholehearted in doing this, will the Buddha not know about it?"[15]

So too did Zhang Bi, organizer of an independent relief effort, refer to Buddhist beliefs, especially in connection to his efforts to persuade members of his mother's lineage to contribute funds. Wrote Zhang: "My mother worships the Buddha and has long kept a vegetarian diet; throughout her life, her charitable gifts have been as bountiful as the sands of the Ganges River, and she has long been concerned that we achieve enlightenment." Appealing to her Buddhist faith, Zhang argued that, by selling off a parcel of poor land to raise funds, he would "create merit for my mother"—that is, she would accumulate the good karma needed for a rebirth closer to Buddhahood.[16] Liu Zongzhou, though he would later be labeled by Huang Zongxi as a fierce opponent of Buddhism, praised Zhang Bi for having showered "the rains of Buddha truth."[17]

Qi Biaojia frequently consorted with and sponsored Chan monks, once crossing paths "with a priest from India," whom his friend Yan Maoyou had questioned about the principles of causation.[18] Like Ni Yuanlu, Qi once dreamed about Buddhism, in his case, about discussing Chan matters with an old monk.[19] During the vexatious famine years, especially in connection with memorializing his deceased mother, Qi pored over and recited the *Śūraṃgama sūtra* (*Lengyan jing*) and one day suddenly determined that every night he would bow to the Buddha and call out his name 150 times.[20]

The precise role of Buddhist concepts in motivating beneficence in these men is impossible to pin down, however. Little if any evidence suggests that Buddhist beliefs specifically inspired or shaped Qi's charitable activities. Notions associated with acts of charity—compassion and humaneness, good deeds and just acts, repayment (*bao*) or rewards and retribution according to the principle of "cause and effect" (*yinguo*)—appear in Confucian and Daoist works as well. Most philanthropists drew on the vocabulary of all three teachings. Many benefactors spoke of both "good deeds" (*shanju*), a term that may be traced to Buddhism, and "just acts" (*yixing*), which has Confucian associations.[21] Much lore about doing good accorded with the two key pillars in the edifice built by Confucius and his followers: the value of humaneness and the concern for the well-being of the common people. These notions hold nearly universal value, however, and do not distinguish late Ming charity as "Confucian."

The late Ming discourse about charity embodied as well concepts drawn from those so-called Legalist writers who had coldly striven to manipulate rewards and punishments so as to strengthen and enrich the state. Xu Guangqi, whose work Qi read and quoted, frequently cited both the writings of Xunzi—who, though a follower of Confucius, foreshadowed Legalist thinking—and the *Guanzi,* an eclectic text that incorporated Legalist ideas. In the spirit of the Legalists, Xu Guangqi declared, "Agriculture enriches the state; the military strengthens the state."[22] At times sharing the utilitarian outlook of the Legalists, Qi defended hydraulic projects of the sort advanced by Xu Guangqi as a way to "enrich the state and strengthen the borders."[23] But most germane to the study of charity (and to be explored later in this chapter) is that Qi, no less than the Legalists, understood rewards and punishments as tools for motivating men to cooperate in relief activities.

Efforts to isolate a particular strand of belief as responsible for late Ming philanthropy are complicated by another fact, which needs to be addressed here if only to discourage readers from themselves running into a wall: coinciding with the upsurge of literati interest in forming do-good voluntary associations was the arrival, in 1583, of the Jesuits. Gao's student Chen Longzheng knew that Matteo Ricci had come from the West to proselytize Christianity, with its devotional images and concept of substantiation. He marveled that Ricci "had learned to speak and read Chinese, and could even write a bit"; and he noted that Ricci possessed some "ingenious instruments"—referring to the clocks and astronomical tools imported by the Jesuits. Yet Chen faulted Ricci for failing to understand the ultimate importance of self-cultivation. Moreover, observed Chen, when Ricci died, so did many of his accomplishments; though his followers could still manipulate the clever instruments, they failed to match his cleverness. Christianity, Chen concluded, was inferior even to Buddhism.[24] Likewise did Gao Panlong, Yan Maoyou, Liu Zongzhou, and (though probably writing after the Ming dynasty's collapse) Lu Shiyi all criticize Christianity.[25]

Other literati welcomed Western learning. Xu Guangqi met Ricci in 1600, converted to Christianity in 1603, was baptized as Paul, and collaborated with Ricci in translating texts on mathematics, astronomy, hydraulics, and geography.[26] Yet Xu's great work, *The Complete Book of Agriculture,* which Chen Zilong edited and Qi Biaojia read and quoted, shows no signs of Christian teaching but frequently cites Chinese precedents. Qi's father, who had read the writings of Christian convert Yang Tingyun, perhaps knew of Yang's Humane Society (Ren hui) in Hangzhou—a cause to which Yang's wife donated part of her trousseau.[27] Yet Yang incorporated no identifiably Christian elements into his philanthropic program.[28] Qi Biaojia in passing mentions Wang Zheng but without noting that he was a Christian convert. Rather, he refers to Wang's idea of "shouldering of responsibility," alluding, perhaps to Wang's emphasis on exerting oneself.[29] In 1634, Wang Zheng drafted a set of guidelines for a Humane Society (Ren hui) in Xi'an. The guidelines referred to "the Lord," Jesus, and seven categories of Christian charity. Moreover, echoing Christian attitudes, and, in sharp contrast to the moralizing benevolent societies of the times, they insisted that the society ought not distinguish between deserving and undeserving poor.[30] Still, Wang's society did not require that its members believe in Christianity, and the Christian vocabulary appears simply to have glossed a traditional Chinese agenda.[31]

Such encounters between key Chinese benefactors and Jesuits notwithstanding, evidence that Jesuit presence shaped Chinese philanthropic activity is lacking. China already had a rich, long-established tradition of voluntary associations and mutual-aid societies.[32] By the time of Ricci's arrival, in 1583, the practice of liberating animals was already gaining momentum. By 1595, when Ricci published his first work in Chinese (on the topic of friendship), five years had passed since Yang Dongming's founding of a benevolent society.[33]

Also influential during the late Ming were the views of innovative thinker Wang Yangming, whose ideas were both within the Confucian tradition and colored by Buddhism. Most simply put, Wang taught that the key to enlightenment resides not in an external authority but within each person and can thus be intuitively attained; and that one's action should accompany and be aligned with one's thought. Wang's ideas quickly caught on, giving voice to two trends that were already underway: the spread of literacy and local activism. Wang's ideas appealed to men who had rudimentary literacy but no patience for rigorous, protracted training in the classics; they also emboldened less-educated persons—such as the numerous students and licentiates who appear in Qi's diaries—to take action in local affairs.

A native of Shaoxing, Wang Yangming had been registered in Yuyao district and for much of his life resided in Qi's district, Shanyin. Many were Shaoxing's inhabitants whose forebears had personally known Wang or his students. Qi Biaojia's father studied with Wang's second-generation follower Zhou Rudeng, and Qi himself studied under Zhou Rudeng's sons. Occasionally Qi cited statements by Wang, and, during the food scarcity of 1640, he mentioned poring over Wang's writings.[34] Despite all these connections to Wang, Qi's writings reveal that shaping his charitable activities were forces far stronger than Wang's thought per se. Neither the late Ming craze for liberating animals nor the heightened concern for life can be directly and uniquely traced back to Wang Yangming. Wang died in 1527, long before this account of late Ming charity begins, and by the 1580s, his followers had splintered into many competing "schools."

Following in Wang's wake were two men who, though ignored by Huang Zongxi's *Records of Ming Scholars,* deeply affected late Ming do-gooders: the Buddhist monk Zhuhong, who figures in chapter 1, and Zhuhong's exact contemporary, Yuan Huang, whose influence on Chen Longzheng is noted in chapter 2. Both men show traces of Wang's thought but each himself took off in a new direction, promoting a method of personal accounting—keeping track of merits and demerits—that was congenial with the genre of popular morality books. Fueling the dissemination of this genre was the growing belief that one could earn merit by publishing and distributing copies of the morality books. Zhuhong had one such didactic work reprinted and distributed free of charge.[35] In thinking about charitable activities, both Qi Biaojia and Chen Longzheng—the one excluded from and the other represented in Huang Zongxi's *Records*—alike reflected the rhetoric and thinking of the popular morality books.

THE POPULAR MORALITY BOOKS

Popular morality books can be traced back to the Song-dynasty *The Ledger of Merit and Demerit* and *The Exalted One's Tract on Action and Response,* both of which date to the twelfth century.[36] These books promoted the idea that, through a law of "cause and effect" (*yinguo*), or "stimulus and response" (*ganying*), a divine mechanism distributed rewards and retribution for good and bad deeds, respectively. The idea of cosmic retribution had become entangled with the Buddhist idea of karma by around the fourth century A.D. It is not exclusively Buddhist, however, for it can be traced back to ancient concepts, in particular, to the concept of "repayment" (*bao*), that predated the introduction of Buddhism to China.[37] During the late Ming, it became further entangled with Yuan Huang's teachings that placed the responsibility for one's own fortune (or the fortune of one's descendants) squarely on the individual. New editions, amplifying and updating their predecessors, appeared, with their distinct blend of Buddhist, Confucian, Daoist, and even Legalist ideas. In emphasizing personal responsibility for doing good, late Ming morality books offered a much needed moral explanation for sudden reversals in social status and wealth and gave men on the margins of the bureaucratic elite a sense of control over their destinies.[38]

Gao Panlong wrote prefaces for two new editions of *The Exalted One's Tract,*[39] and he counseled family members to acquire merit: "Goodness must be accumulated. Accumulate it today, accumulate it tomorrow. Accumulate little acts of goodness; accumulate great acts of goodness. One mistaken thought, word, or deed becomes the seed of self-destruction and family failure. . . . To seek good fortune, watch for error in yourself; to escape bad fortune, examine yourself."[40] Chen Longzhong, too, had read "books on cause and effect" (*yinguo shu*).[41] He frequently spoke of "retribution and response" (*baoying*) and referred his benevolent society audience to *The Exalted One's Tract* along with two other books on "action and response."[42] Lu Shiyi initially derived his own daily self-examination from *The Ledger of Merit and Demerit.*

One morality book to which both Chen Longzheng and Qi Biaojia referred was *Records of Right Behavior and Good Fortune (Diji lu),* by their contemporary Yan Maoyou. Yan created this text out of didactic anecdotes from earlier works, but rarely named his sources. Only by accident does one note that this work overlaps with the Song-dynasty collection *Records of Taking Pleasure in Goodness (Leshan lu).* One account appearing in both works tells of a scholar who, espying the shoes of his deceased father at a cobbler's, awaited the return of the shoes' owner. The owner turned out to be his father's ghost, who counseled the son to perform good deeds. The son obeyed and eventually rose to a high position.[43] Yan imbued such old material with a decidedly new flavor. He composed substantial prefaces to many sections of the book, and postscripts to some of the anecdotes: an official, Gu Xichou, then added marginal comments throughout the work and graced it with a preface.[44] Regarding the son's encounter with his father's ghost, commentator Gu wrote: "He wished to see his deceased father. The deceased father instructed the son. This was the root of the son's putting goodness into effect (*xingshan*)."[45] Gu thus articulated a phenomenon evident in the cases of several philanthropists, namely, the close linkage between grieving for a deceased parent and the internalization of that parent's benevolent values.

Taking Pleasure in Goodness simply divided the material into three sections (*juan*), according to thematic categories. Yan dichotomized the anecdotes, arranging them into paired sections that illustrated good and bad deeds respectively—thereby displaying, in reference to each topic, a choice of two routes, one leading to fortune and the other to disaster. Moreover, he devoted one of the eight volumes (*ce*) of *Right Behavior and Good Fortune* entirely to the topic charity; and while embracing all social groups within the one work, he also divided his book into sections, each tailored for a particular audience—officials, members of the gentry, ordinary people, women, and military men. As Yan explained in reference to the section "A Ledger for Merit and Demerit: A Mirror for All" (Gong jian): it was intended "for male and female, rich and poor."[46] In this respect, *Right Behavior and Good Fortune* resembled Chen Longzheng's benevolent-society lectures, which individually addressed the upper, middle, and lower strata of his benevolent society while embracing all three within one format.

Right Behavior and Good Fortune spoke to learned and elementary readers alike. In 1634, Chen Longzheng recommended the work to his two sons (Kui and Xiu), declaring it to be "a truly precious book for saving the world. One can buy one or two sets and browse through them in one's leisure time." For his sons' benefit, Chen marked with circles several dozen passages that he found to be "especially incisive for beginning students." Yan's work was "Marvelous, marvelous," concluded Chen.[47]

By relegating *Right Behavior and Good Fortune* to the status of leisure-time browsing for beginners like his sons, Chen the adult somewhat distanced himself from it. Yet Yan's work was no child's play. Yan, who, soon after the work was published, would receive a *jinshi* degree and serve as an official, incorporated much material specifically for officials. The opening section, "A Mirror for Officials" (Guan jian), instructed that officials who sent memorials up to the emperor to save lives would be recompensed.[48] Another section, entitled "For Those in Official Positions" (Dangguan gongguo ge), assigned to each type of good and bad deed a number of merits and demerits, respectively. An official who during a famine obtains tax relief for the people and saves many lives will receive one thousand merits.[49] Conversely, officials failing to provide relief will receive retribution; and those who have the resources to aid other people but are unwilling to do so will incur five demerits.[50] *Right*

Behavior and Good Fortune further encouraged officials to establish medical clinics during outbreaks of disease and specified one merit to be earned for each person treated and ten for resuscitating someone near death. It similarly assigned merits for such other good deeds as providing burials; taking in orphans, solitary people, and elderly folk; and prevailing upon people to support needy relatives.[51]

Tuning into late Ming insecurity about wealth and status, one passage in *Right Behavior and Good Fortune* warned of the impermanence of material goods, particularly of money, observing: "Many will not give one coin toward the future well-being of their sons and grandsons or toward the welfare of people right before their eyes; they fail to understand that floods, fires, banditry, illness, and disasters can all suddenly destroy their family resources; would it not be better to 'accumulate virtue' and seek the protection of a generous heaven?" Declaring the principle of accumulating virtue to be crystal clear, the essay then concluded: "Those who reek of bronze coins simply have not thought about this."[52] To invest in the future, accumulating virtue was far safer and wiser than amassing money.

In one passage, Yan Maoyou segued from an ancient tale to a fresh, timely topic that resonated with contemporary concerns. He first told of a Zhi Zishan, who had fled the turbulence at the end of the Han dynasty and who, joined by a companion, then turned to farming melons. The land they worked was owned by a member of a powerful lineage. Fearing harm from the landlord, they sent him a fine melon as a gift. The landlord summoned them and, while himself enjoying a huge banquet in the central hall, had them partake of humble vegetarian fare outside. Feeling humiliated, Zhi's companion would not eat; Zhi, in contrast, ate to his fill, explaining that, when poor, one ought not be ashamed of being so treated. Subsequently, he became a high official. At this point, Yan interjected a comment on the hardship of "beggars," who are cursed and abused but lack the means for fighting back. Then, simultaneously echoing both the imperial maxim that everyone should remain content with his or her lot and Yuan Huang's teaching that each person ought to establish his own destiny, Yan advised: those who are polite like scholars will not be limited by their circumstances.[53]

Qi first met Yan when serving in Xinghua prefecture, Fujian, in 1624[54] and again saw him in Beijing in 1631. Feeling unwell and anxious—this was three years after his father's death—Qi sought Yan's counsel, after which he remarked, "One evening of discussion with Yan is more beneficial than ten years of studying books."[55] Moments of uncertainty periodically opened Qi's mind to the influences and moral authority of socially inferior men. During several mental crises—labeled by Qi as "ailments of the heart"—he welcomed treatment from Yan Maoyou, Wang Chaoshi, and numerous Buddhist monks, spiritual healers who hovered nearby just when narrow and rigid interpretations of what might be termed the Confucian classical tradition were failing to serve him well. A few months after the evening discussion with Yan, Qi, like his contemporaries Lu Shiyi and Chen Hu, started a journal as a device for self-improvement.[56] His *Ledger for Merit and Demerit, under Eight Rubrics* (*Gongguo ge batiao*) is no longer extant, but a few days after starting it, he discussed it with Yan Maoyou (much as Lu Shiyi and Chen Hu had discussed their journals); and, perhaps mindful of the importance of earning merit, he also made a point of recording in his diary that he gave some beggars money.[57] Soon after, he endorsed Yan's *Right Behavior and Good Fortune* by gracing it with a preface, signing it as "a friend."[58] In 1634, Yan was granted a *jinshi* degree in recognition of his scholarship on the classics, and then briefly held office.[59] His thought was both sanctioned and co-opted by officialdom.

Right Behavior and Good Fortune exhorts readers to undertake just the sort of good deeds that Qi routinely performed: burying abandoned corpses, rescuing animals from slaughter, and the like. When reviewing Yan's work, Qi must have encountered the materials about relief strategies that Yan had organized under the paired rubrics "Recompenses for Providing Famine Relief" and "Recompenses for Failing to Provide Relief."[60] One entry recounted how the callousness of a magistrate (living toward the end of a declining dynasty) so angered the people that they killed him, broke into the granaries to make distributions to the poor, and let the city fall to rebel troops. Another told of a wealthy man who refused to make his grain available for price-stabilizing sales: just when he was discussing price fluctuations, lightning killed him and ignited his grain stocks.[61]

Qi no doubt read as well a passage in *Right Behavior and Good Fortune* that I have already cited at length in connection with Chen Longzheng, namely, Yan's exhortation that his readers form societies (*hui*) for providing shelter for the poor and donate a little grain from their huge granaries. "Elaborating on this point, Yan stated: "One never knows when fire, banditry, illness, and other disasters will clean out one's own family. . . . Would it not be best to accumulate merit, inviting protection from heaven?"[62] That actions in the world of man reverberated with heaven was well understood by Qi, who recounted: "I wrote a note to Wang Chaoshi, saying that our kind have the thought to love living beings. In response, rain then came. Who says that the way of heaven and affairs of man are far apart?"[63] To elicit heaven's response, Qi joined members of his lineage in offering charms and prayers against locusts. When a fierce wind, accompanied by light rain, greatly subdued the locusts' power, he observed, "That was the doing of the spirits"; then, not for public display but in the privacy of his Hall of Four Regrets, he burned incense and prayed.[64]

Chen Longzheng and Qi Biaojia each recorded personal experiences that resemble accounts in *Right Behavior and Good Fortune*. A year before that work was published and two years before he founded his benevolent society, Chen

Longzheng was deeply shaken by an event, which he recounted roughly as follows: thunder and lightning pierced the night; ghosts howled until dawn, their shrill sounds penetrating both outdoors and in. Every household heard it and thought it most uncanny. Chen soon linked heaven's thunderous communication to something he presently learned: poor people, carrying half-year-old infants in their arms, were going from door to door, wishing to hand them over but, failing to elicit responses, tossed their charges over the Bridge of Scattered Stars, into the rushing waters.[65] Fastening onto the specter of babies—the most defenseless and dependent of creatures—being thrown to their deaths, and letting out cries of woe ("Alas! How miserable!"), Chen extrapolated from the case of infants the plight of all poor people, reflecting: "What limit, then, is there to all those other persons whom one neither sees nor hears about but who also die of hunger and illness?" (Unlike Mencius, who had conjured up a vision of a baby dangerously about to fall into a well in order to arouse an obdurate listener to awareness of his innate compassion, Chen himself stood among those to whom heaven was signaling a sense of urgency.) Again asserting a connection between heaven's signals and earthly events, Chen observed: "When the people below have reached extremities, the ghosts above will scream out."[66] It was under these circumstances, when the howling of heaven was resonating with the desperate straits of the poor on earth, that Chen undertook famine relief in his native Xuwu borough.

Heavenly portents, Chen thought, were credible comments on human activities. In 1633, a farmer in the fields (in Yongba north borough) was struck dead by lightning. The disaster was witnessed by several hundred persons, who unanimously attested that the victim had done no great wrong. The conundrum "how could heaven have inadvertently killed someone?" so bothered Chen that, as he put it, he "commissioned someone to look into the matter." He learned that the tiller's wife, who was at home when the disaster struck, saw black smoke fill the house, while the houses of the neighbors remained bright and clear. Everyone, he noted, saw this happen. From these facts Chen deduced that heaven had specifically targeted the tiller, and that the victim must have secretly committed some great crime that had long gone undetected. Chen thus put his own mind at ease.[67] Whether readers today will find his inference persuasive is beside the point: Chen mounted an investigation because heaven had sent a message.

Also in 1633, when a typhoon hit his native district, Jiashan, Chen reasoned as follows: in 1631, Wenzhou suffered winds so fierce that houses the least bit flimsy were blasted away and innumerable people killed. According to Wenzhou's elders, never before had such an event occurred. But, a year later, "in the exact same month," wrote Chen—here underscoring that the winds of 1631 were a meaningful omen—pirates attacked Wenzhou. By analogy, the typhoon of 1633 was a heaven-sent harbinger of danger to man.[68]

Chen's report of the thunderbolt resembles the account in *Right Behavior and Good Fortune* about lightning killing a greedy man: in 1147, when people took to the roads in search of food, the man, who possessed several fully packed granaries, refused to sell his stock at reduced prices. Then, just as he was explaining price fluctuations to his family and rejoicing that grain prices were soaring, the sky darkened, fireballs filling the room. He and his hoard were destroyed.[69] Conversely, households with reputations for goodness were, in Chen's view, spared disasters. "I have heard," he wrote, "of fires ignited by lightning burning for several *li* but leaving one solitary house standing; of an epidemic spreading but sparing everyone in a particular household; and even of cases where bandits were wreaking havoc but said to one another: 'Mr. So-and-so lives here; one should not disturb him,' and, thus, because of one person, a whole rural area or city was protected. Alas! What kind of clever strategy or bravery will outweigh the disorder? Households that have accumulated goodness will move people's hearts and reclaim heaven's favor. Today it's grievous that people are in extremities, and worrisome that ghosts are screaming." With the reassurance that "these are not difficult matters," Chen advised: "One might empty out the grain stocks and make distributions; or one might, according to one's resources and heart, proffer one's surplus to others," and then warned: "If one actually sees calamities yet sticks to the position of the hedonist Yang Zhu that one should not pluck out one hair to help others, and if no one dares to reprimand this, then when disorder comes, where will you escape?"[70]

This declaration, which is dated 1630, four years before Chen presented his sons with copies of *Right Behavior and Good Fortune*, anticipated a passage in it that recounts that a certain Peng Zhu liked to do good. During food shortages he fed the hungry, and during cold spells he clothed those in need. He repaired bridges and roads and did everything his resources would allow, even preparing pharmaceuticals for the poor. When he was sojourning in Sichuan, riots broke out and 90 percent of the households died, but Peng's entire family was left unharmed. His family also survived a shipwreck. When another riot broke out, he escaped to a mountain refuge, but several hundred horsemen descended upon the area. They piled up the captives and set the mountain aflame. No one escaped—except Peng; for, just where he was hiding, the wind reversed its course, extinguishing the fire.[71]

Yan Maoyou taught what Chen Longzheng knew well: it is better to accumulate virtue than to amass material wealth. In an agrarian society, where, generation after generation, the vast majority of the population remained tied to their native places, a good reputation had real currency. Philanthropists earned trust and respect that enabled them to obtain credit for financial transactions.[72] Possibly, too, the posting of official banners by the entrances of beneficent households, manifested an association with official authority that intimidated bandits.

Chen and Yan were also alike in empathizing with the small entrepreneur. Chen argued in a benevolent-society lecture of 1632 that tiny handouts of one or two hundred bronze coins as capital could help those petty businesses to improve in the space of a few months.[73] Yan preached that tiny donations would enable people who were too hungry and sick even to beg to get back on their feet and resume their business ventures. It was with this aim that he exhorted his readers to form societies for providing the poor with lodging and food.[74]

Right Behavior and Good Fortune and other popular didactic works upheld the view that good deeds would earn merit only if performed with genuine feelings of goodness and without thought of rewards. To this extent, they concurred with Gao Panlong's insistence that doing good was something one just had to do. Yet, repeatedly and profusely, the morality books illustrated the principles of reward and retribution, and told how charitable men did in fact win long life, prosperity, male progeny, and success in the civil service examinations.[75] One account first dictated, "Instead of craving for your own good fortune, you should commiserate with the suffering of all living things," but it then concluded, "Then . . . your good fortune will of its own accord be doubled."[76] Another account, after applauding a benefactor for being so virtuous as to turn down a reward of a pearl, went on to say that his upstanding behavior in the end earned him two pearls.[77]

The crudest interpretation of the morality books' lesson—that one could earn merit points through good deeds and use them to cancel demerits—offended many scholars. Liu Zongzhou, in particular, abhorred such calculations; moral perfection, he believed, should be an end in itself.[78] Chen Longzheng in theory stuck to the idealistic view that one should preserve a "unrapacious state of mind";[79] in practice he had absorbed the reward-and-retribution rhetoric of the popular morality books. His ambivalence appears in his account of the dramatic recovery in 1630 of his son Kui, who for over two years had been desperately ill. A doctor had advised Kui to take a pill concocted from embryo bones. Kui refused. "How can one bear to eat of one's own kind in order to survive?" he asked. He then instructed that some rice he had accumulated be distributed among the poor residents of their borough, Xuwu.[80] In all, 635 *shi* of white rice were distributed to 1,923 poor households, or 2,979 persons. Then, one day, Kui suddenly got out of bed and started walking about, causing Longzheng to reflect: "If my son had ingested that bone medicine and had been tightfisted about famine relief, then ignoramuses would have assumed that the medicine had been efficacious."[81] Chen thus dissociates the outcome from his son's choice; at the same time he provided the information intimating that the convalescence was a reward for the son's humanity and charity.

Elsewhere Chen explicitly promised rewards for goodness. He advised the prosperous households attending a benevolent-society meeting: "I guarantee that you will have extraordinary rewards";[82] and, when asking his wife (in 1641) to donate one hundred *mou* of dowry land to endow an estate for the benevolent society (*tongshan zhuang*), he argued that her descendants would remember her not for "harvests from her land" but for "the harvest from her virtue," and that her charity would earn her a fine, lasting reputation.[83]

Qi Biaojia likewise expressed ambivalence about doing good with the goal of earning merit. Occasionally he referred to the subject of "cause and effect."[84] At times he distanced himself from the notion that good deeds will bring rewards. When composing a prayer to help monks raise funds for their meals in 1640, he set the record straight in his diary: "To exhort goodness, I did not talk about 'cause and effect' but just stated the following: Monks are people, like ourselves. The myriad things are all of one body. How is it fitting to dismiss them from our care and ignore providing them with relief?"[85] Nonetheless, Qi here also persisted in putting his good deeds on record, leaving open the possibility that he might reap as his reward the approval of posterity. Of his activities in distributing medical care, he calculated: "Today we get to dip into our money bags . . . to aid others; . . . this certainly counts as a fortune-yielding deed."[86]

In emphasizing rewards for good deeds, Qi and Chen had company. Prosyletizing the idea of earning merit was none other than Zheng Xuan, the circuit intendant who lent support to Shaoxing's relief operations. Like Yan Maoyou, he compiled a didactic work (with some prefaces dating to 1635), now best known not by its original title but as *The Complete Book of Good Fortune and Longevity* (*Fushou quanshu*), the name that Chen Jiru gave it when falsely publishing it as his own.[87] Calculating rewards for good deeds, a practice that Liu Zongzhou abhorred and his student Huang Zongxi dismissed, had entered mainstream thinking.

QI BIAOJIA'S PRAGMATISM

By giving men on the margins of the bureaucratic elite a sense of control over their destinies, late Ming morality books helped them to deal with the challenges of unpredictable social mobility, economic change, social unrest, and spiritual anxiety.[88] But more important is that the morality books' specific focus on merits and demerits, on rewards and punishments, boosted mobilizing men to do good. Liu Zongzhou's criticisms notwithstanding, the outlook prevailed because it served well the demands of organizing charitable activities, as the case of Qi Biaojia illustrates.

Qi had been thoroughly socialized in the Confucian classics, which placed a high value on humaneness, benevolent government, and the protection and nurturing of the populace, He accepted that self-cultivation—particularly, examining one's own faults—was essential to protecting society against natural disaster.[89] Nonetheless he appears to have been far less interested in self-cultivation than in taking action. This was observed by his friend Qian Qinzhi, who, several months into the relief efforts, wrote Qi a letter that exceeded a thousand characters in length to upbraid him for slighting moral self-cultivation. Qian, recounted Qi, "roughly said that my recent activities are visible and pleasing enough but my accomplishments in the area of 'perfecting knowledge and rectifying the heart' are nonetheless slight."[90] Taking Qian's admonishment "to heart," Qi immediately conferred with another friend about the "importance of eradicating selfishness in learning."[91] Yet, scarcely visible in Qi's diaries and his other extant writings is the sort of high-minded moralizing that characterized Gao Panlong's and Chen Longzheng's lectures, or the diffident soul-searching of Lu Shiyi's diary.

Qi had numerous opportunities to expatiate on moral issues or attend learned discussions such as those at the White Horse Academy. Once he mentioned going to the Heavenly King Monastery, where Shen Guomo had been holding a seven-day meeting for quiet contemplation, and Qi mentioned, too, that, after Liu Zongzhou arrived, Shen Guomo raised a question about "intuitive knowledge" (*liangzhi*)—an issue bearing on whether man was innately good.[92] Such comments on philosophical discussions are rare in Qi's diaries, however.

Rather than elaborating on the mandate to do good, as Gao Panlong had done, Qi simply followed lessons he absorbed from experience, responding flexibly to the exigencies of each day. In this, he was following advice his father had given when Qi, then twenty-three *sui,* was leaving for his first post. Eschewing pious moralizing, Qi Chenghan essentially stated: when trying to swim to safety, one should, instead of strapping on some prop like a jug, just plunge into the waters. One will float. One learns bit by bit. "We who are put in the sea of officialdom will, after some years, become capable administrators."[93] One lesson Qi would learn was that "if our discussions of relief are the least bit tainted by selfishness, the people will hereafter distrust us."[94] A sense of realism about what would work buttressed the ideal of generosity.

Without mouthing moral pieties, Qi assumed that doing good was uplifting. He observed that those who pledged to provide relief grain "all did this happily, without any sign of stinginess";[95] and he was optimistic that his relief efforts and acts of generosity would inspire others to follow. Thirteen months before the riots of early 1641, in reference to aiding his village, he explained in his diary: "I first gave one hundred silver pieces to aid the village poor in order to encourage a fondness for charity (*haoyi*) thereafter."[96] Goodness would spread by example; carefully designed plans would abet the process. A few days after declaring his relief plan to be a model, he, leader that he was by nature, encouraged several colleagues at Yu Mountain to distribute relief. When two visitors subsequently informed him that the nearby village of Hou Mei had also put a relief plan into effect, he deduced from this that "one could see the speed by which the fondness for doing good (*haoshan*) spreads by example."[97]

Qi occasionally referred to community compacts—the institution for socializing rural residents that had inspired Gao Panlong's and Chen Longzheng's benevolent-society lectures. Qi did not dwell on the contents of the lectures, however, and only once do his diaries describe a community-compact meeting in any detail: he named nine persons, some of them his relatives, who filled the various community-compact posts. He, a relative, and the two heads of the *bao* and *jia* units gathered and lectured on two of the Six Maxims: "Be filial" and "Respect one's elders." Interspersed with the lecture was singing—for which his own sons had rehearsed on the previous day. After the formal lecture, Shen Guomo elaborated on the main points. Qi Biaojia then wrote up a covenant that aimed to bring the wrongdoers in line.[98] Unlike Lu Shiyi, who felt uplifted by hearing a rural lecture, and unlike Yang, Gao, and Chen Longzheng, who took sufficient pride in the pieties they addressed to their benevolent societies as to leave behind transcripts, Qi passed over the topic of moral instruction. Instead he reinforced the community compact with rewards, especially food. Right before a lecture at one meeting, he noted, rice was distributed at the community altar. Gifts of food conveyed expectations that the hungry would heed the teachings.[99]

QI'S SELF-IMAGE TRANSFORMED

Qi Biaojia's charity was shaped by a general sense of justice, a sense of his responsibility for fellow humankind, and his firsthand experience of a food shortage. In the wake of the riots of early 1641, the fear of disorder goaded him and his peers to take action. Once relief activities were underway, other forces deepened his commitment and defined him as a charitable man.

Spanning fifteen years, Qi's diaries trace—as does no other extant source for any other late Ming figure—his transformation over time from lavish spender to dedicated, belt-tightening do-gooder; it further tracks changes in what he considered worth writing about. Illuminating Qi in the round, as a man of evolving parts, the diaries defy attempts to make easy generalizations about the self-indulgence, proclivities, and beliefs of late Ming literati. Before the early 1640s, charity was part of Qi's life but not prominent in his writings. Qi recorded that he distributed alms, ransomed someone's wife about to be sold as a prostitute, funded the burial of the poor,[100] and sponsored a medical dispensary. But he recorded these deeds sporadically and sparingly, all the while paying considerable attention to the construction of his garden at Yu Mountain and pursuing his passion for opera.

Opera performances were wasteful, Liu Zongzhou had declared in 1619. The problem, he explained, was especially acute in the densely populated city of Shaoxing, both in the pleasure quarters and at banquets, where residents caroused from dusk to dawn, wasting thousands of taels.[101] Through most of the 1630s, Qi paid no heed to such high-minded condemnations of pleasure. Routinely and unhesitatingly, he recorded in his diaries the titles of operas he saw and sponsored and his exchanges with fellow Shaoxing resident, the dramatist Meng Chengshun.[102] Then, late in 1639, after noting one last splurge on a performance that accompanied a five-course banquet for Ni Yuanlu,[103] Qi's diary abruptly turned silent on the subject of opera performances—and remained so for two and a half years. In a work he compiled during and after the food shortage, Qi spoke of theater's deleterious effects: actors consumed food they did not produce, and the performances themselves could be inflammatory, inciting people to riot. He further noted that, though Circuit Intendant Zheng Xuan had prohibited performances a few years before the food shortage, it was during the food shortage that the prohibition gained force.[104] As circumstances changed, so did Qi and his wealthy peers.

Qi, to be sure, had a strong sense of justice even before the food shortage. When launching the garden project in 1635, he made a point of setting aside a hundred *mou* of land, the proceeds of which were to be used to aid "his lineage and his neighbors."[105] Although he did not make it explicit, he was in effect balancing self-indulgence with a gift to his immediate community. In 1635, Qi additionally showed himself to be compassionate, according to his chronological biography, which recounted the following vignette. When Qi went in person to make customary year-end distributions to the poor members of his lineage, he encountered a rainstorm, which drenched his clothes. Someone urged him to postpone the event, but Qi replied: "Those people who are hungry and cold must be suffering a hundred more times than I. Helping them get food and clothing makes me happy. How could I be mindful of bitter wind and rain?"[106] Written retrospectively, the biography may have been portraying Qi's early years in light of the later man. Of this event, Qi himself simply recorded, without elaboration, that he distributed silver to the poor members of the lineage and "prepared food for them, to show respect and thanks."[107]

Of poor cave dwellers he saw on a trip in 1635, Qi remarked, "They filled one with pity" and expressed regret that he "unfortunately had nothing with which to help them."[108] A week later, after pondering, "What will the people eat?" he commented: "When I lift my chopsticks, I feel sad."[109] On New Year's day, 1639, months before completing the construction of his residence, which would cost some five thousand taels, Qi again mused in his diary: "Seeing the members of my lineage looking miserable and poor, I sighed that our house, garden, and everything else exceed what is our due. I therefore turned my thoughts to relief measures."[110] Up to this point, Qi bothered to record sighs of compassion, but he addressed his comments to no one in particular. Although he may have been writing for an imagined or future audience, as he told it, his sighs had no immediate witnesses. Earning merit remained a nearly hidden matter.

From 1639 through the food shortage of the early 1640s, his diaries reveal, it was increasingly in the context of social interactions that Qi aired his laments about the victims of hunger. One evening, about a fortnight before the riots broke out, sighing overtook Qi, who, having already discussed "relief matters" with a colleague (Qian Qinzhi), was entertaining several guests. While they were enjoying their ample fare, Qi raised the topic of "the misery of the food shortage" in their region. Recounted Qi: "Together we sighed that the extravagance of the Shaoxing region (Yue) was certainly enough to take care of the famine."[111] When a friend showed him the corpse of someone who had starved to death, Qi wrote, "The miserable sight made me sigh."[112] When he accompanied several friends to observe a foundling bureau, and its roomful of children being fed by wet nurses, it was enough, he noted, "to make one sigh."[113] Once, "the various friends responsible for the western borough [among whom was Liu Zongzhou's nephew Liu Beisheng] came from the rural area of Tianle to describe the sufferings of the starving, and one of them (Lu Yongzhi) spoke a few words about each village."[114] To communicate the scenes so described Qi reached not back to homilies from the Confucian classics, but to an evocative visual image: "It can," he said, "be likened to the painting about vagrants (*liumin tu*)"—here referring to the work of a Song-dynasty official who used illustrations to impress on the imperial court that Wang Anshi's policies were harming the people.[115]

The sheer presence of dearth, with its highly visible suffering and threat of disorder, spurred Qi Biaojia and some of his peers to abandon extravagant habits, at least temporarily. Growing self-conscious about consumption, Qi tempered his indulgences. One day, after he, along with elder brother Fengjia, cousin Ningfang, and another person, listed those households who had taken responsibility for providing gruel in their villages, Qi "proposed many methods whereby they might save in order to make up the amount needed." For the project, he would reallocate the resources that had been earmarked for aiding their villages and lineage during bad harvests; Fengjia would save on resources destined for the God of Literature, and another brother, Junjia, would save from noonday feasts and summer sacrificial offerings.[116] Around this time, too, Qi felt compelled to set the record straight: although once, on the inspection tour of the rural areas, he had accepted snacks from the local people, at all other times he had steadfastly refused "every bit of tea and fruit" offered him.[117]

Qi further determined that throughout the summer of 1641 he would reduce by half the sacrificial offerings to his deceased parents, reserving resources for the soup kitchen instead.[118] He took to a vegetarian diet. He had already been keeping it for ten days, he noted, and had offered a guest "only vegetables from the garden."[119] Three weeks later, he elaborated: "These days the whole household has been eating vegetarian fare, because, as a popular saying goes, 'The heavenly spirits will descend to investigate.'"[120] Then, roughly a year later, as the food shortage continued, and when Qi happened to be reviewing records from his former days of official service, he expressed regret that his consumption of food had once been excessive.[121]

Each act of communal sighing, each shared meal of vegetarian fare, rippled out, affecting how others would regard Qi. Each record of fine deeds publicized a concrete measure by which their fellow townsmen would hold benefactors accountable. Gradually the community's expectations solidified Qi's self-perception as a charitable man. Secured in diary entries that peers future and present might read, Qi's persona as a compassionate man acquired an authority of its own, which he himself then had to respect. One day, just after he reported feeling "uplifted and motivated" by dedicated and talented "friends," he expressed remorse about having lapsed that evening from his austere regimen: he had just attended a five-course dinner at Ni Yuanlu's garden that was followed by drinking and music late into the early morning, and regretted that he had not declined the invitation.[122] Ni Yuanlu, too, would eventually mend his ways. After seeing corpses along the roadside in 1642, he asked himself, "What heart have I to serve wine and meat?" and then proceeded to report that, from the third month to harvesttime, his entire household and even guests had kept to a vegetarian diet; and that they saved small morsels so as to aid the starving. As for guests receptive to the vegetarian meals, they too, he stated, will enjoy good fortune.[123]

MAN OF RESPONSIBILITY

The transformation of Qi (and his peers) into charitable men was effected by several other processes as well, among them the experience of shouldering responsibility, the swearing of oaths before one's peers, and the promise and distribution of rewards. Yang Dongming, Gao Panlong, and Chen Longzheng stressed the motivating power of humaneness, compassion, and the moral imperative to do good. Without abandoning these values, Qi Biaojia emphasized more than they the importance of what may be variously translated as "performing duties," "shouldering responsibility," or "managing affairs" (*renshi, danren*)—in short, the efforts through which one moved from feelings of compassion to saving lives.

Qi referred often to the "friends" of good causes as "those who are shouldering responsibility," as when he noted: "Fortunately the friends took responsibility with true hearts and were untiringly motivated."[124] He high-mindedly insisted: "Keeping thousands of people alive is based not on the money lent or grain relief doled out, but on the compassion and love filling the hearts of those shouldering responsibility"; but, whereas Gao Panlong had assumed that moral enlightenment would naturally stimulate good acts, Qi stressed finding "talented and perspicacious men to shoulder responsibility."[125] Although he insisted that "love of the people must be true," he explained this in terms of the functional utility of shared values: genuine feelings of compassion can be instrumental, inspiring others "happily to be at service" in undertaking relief activities.[126] And although he recognized that persons taking responsibility must have talent and wisdom, he asserted that it was "even more important that they be united in spirit," for, as he put it: "Famine relief is like fire fighting—not something that one person can do."[127] Values unite, but "in administration, nothing is more important than knowing who is good in taking responsibility."[128] What ultimately defined the benefactor's stature was the program's success. As Qi pronounced, "Thousands of lives depend on the one or two persons managing the operation."[129]

Soon after the riots of early 1641, Qi "took on the responsibility, because," he declared, "there was no leader." Then, as though to provide a measure by which his enormous responsibility might be gauged, he took to mentioning the adverse conditions that he experienced and witnessed. He recorded how he, accompanying two colleagues, "braved the snow, going all over the place to inspect the hungry households"; and then added: "We went from Han Family Bridge to the poor wicker-gated houses by Sifeng Gate north of Heng Street. The appearance of the destitute and downtrodden was unbearable to see."[130] A few days later, he wrote of one trip home: "I encountered a snowstorm. I walked and sighed. All night long I worried."[131] Difficult conditions proved the depth of his compassion.

The hard work demanded by the relief activities kept Qi up deep into nights, exhausted his energies, and shook his nerves. Yet, instead of skipping days in his diaries or perfunctorily jotting down something along the lines of "too busy to write anything today," he stayed up late night after night precisely so that he might record (and hence leave for posterity) just how enervating his labors had been. It was already "by candlelight," he wrote, when he "finished a draft of 'Arrangements for Giving out Rice.'"[132] He was kept up "halfway through the night" filling out ration tickets, he noted, and then added: "The cold wind pierced my bones; I was extremely tired and only then went to bed."[133] It was "under lamplight" that he "drafted some 'ten items on distributing gruel,'" with the result that by bedtime he was "extremely exhausted."[134] And, after one emotionally draining day that began with visiting soup kitchens and ended with consultations on how to quiet his broken nerves, Qi observed that, although it was "already dusk" when he reached his boat, he nonetheless used the time on the boat ride home to critique a book on city defense, "reaching home at night."[135]

Just when Qi was most harried and rundown, his diary entries stretched out explicitly to underscore his busyness, as when he described a day packed with such tasks as negotiating with grain brokers, filling out food vouchers,

visiting the homes of the starving to distribute those vouchers, and responding to letters that asked for loans or discussed relief. "All very busy" is how Qi
summarized that day, and then, so that no one would miss the point, he added,
"It was about the third watch [11 P.M. to 1 A.M.] when I went to bed."[136]

Taking pride in his hard work, Qi made sure to recount how he juggled
numerous conflicting demands, especially concerning problems with the
soup kitchens: "For the past ten days, . . . sometimes the starving complained
that they had nothing to eat; sometimes the prosperous households complained that the exactions were unfair; or the persons overseeing the collections said that the wealthy households refused to cough up their resources;
or the managers said that the starving were irascible. Some communicated
by letter; some visited in person. I estimate that there were at least five or six
crises a day. Today I again received various letters . . . and responded to them
all, with the result that I have had scarcely any rest."[137] In the final diary entry for 1641, still haunted by memories of the mob attacks with which the
year had begun, Qi reviewed the intervening months: "I thought of how in
the first month the people had been plundering, and how I went out to mediate the conflict. From that point on, with the relief efforts, soup kitchens,
the infirmary, and the dispensary, and with the recommending of rewards
and the completion of reports, I scarcely had any leisure."[138]

Hard work was Qi's measure of his commitment to doing good. With the
relief efforts of 1641 well underway, he self-consciously testified in his diary:
"On the boat ride home, I wrote up what I had done during the past five
days"; and then, giving away his intention to inform posterity of his merit,
he added: "The seven pages that I recorded about relief matters somewhat
displayed my labors (*laoku*)."[139] The term *laoku* brings to mind a passage in
The Book of Mencius: "Some labor with their minds [*laoxin zhe*], and some labor
with their strength [*laoku zhe*]. Those who labor with their minds govern
others; those who labor with their strength are governed by others"—a passage that appeals to and had been cited by historians accustomed to analyzing events in terms of class relations and the elite's exploitation of the lower
social strata.[140] Yet, blunting the sharpness of the dichotomy postulated by
Mencius, Qi applied the term for physical toil to members of the literate elite.
Moreover, he spoke both of the "friends" who labored for him—"Because
the friends had labored (*laoku*) on my behalf, I got up in the middle of the
night to thank them"[141]—and of his own labors.

As Qi Biaojia became caught up in the food-shortage emergency, he increasingly defined himself in terms of his economizing, hard work, and compassion. Collaborating with others on distributing food relief simultaneously
elicited his magnanimous spirit and expanded it. So suggests a diary entry
about a particularly busy day, when Qi ran all around to pay his respects to
the various students who had agreed to take responsibility for the five boroughs; visited someone at the Wang Yangming Shrine; returned home to

dine; again went out to meet, first, with several friends at one house, and then with another friend at another home; and then proceeded to a colleague's home, where he reviewed an "Announcement to Guiji District" that the colleague had written, presumably to publicize arrangements for food distribution. Of that day, Qi observed: "Among these friends, there certainly are many who are self-reflective and learned and who truly make it their business to save starving people"; and then added: "If one or two of them are talented, it would be fitting to rely on them. Being open-minded, I have joined forces with them; consequently I feel somewhat uplifted and motivated."[142] Although he was their leader—and in most cases, their social superior—Qi felt buoyed by the enthusiasm of those whom he led.

Likewise making a show of his hard work was Chen Zilong, who mentioned that he had "penetrated the poor rural areas and deep valleys" to inspect the rural soup kitchens and had "for months trod through brush by foot and raced through thickets by horse."[143] So too did Zhang Bi recount what he "had been through." One must, he stated, personally inspect "the poor streets and alleys, whose households were not on the real estate taxes rolls and whose residents were not registered for mutual surveillance (*baojia*)—their living quarters like beehives and ant hills."[144] He then commented on how he had "rushed about day and night, without acknowledging fatigue," to the point that he had become "emaciated and weak"; and how the "various friends" who had "from beginning to end . . . toiled and rushed about, . . . and who had gone from door to door making inquiries and not shirked work . . . and who had recorded information in their notebooks and filled out the printed ration tickets, to the point that their hands had almost dropped off."[145] The picture of the worthy official who endured hardship on behalf of the people was commonplace in Chinese writings.[146] Materials for late Ming Shaoxing embellish that picture. They verify that the cliché characterized actual experiences; and they show not only officials but also former officials and mere students participating in the endeavor.

With leadership came onerous burdens. Qi and some of his peers both worked hard on the relief efforts and had to answer to their community's sundry expectations. One day early in 1641, as soon as word that Qi was taking responsibility for the relief program went out, people eager for favors came rushing in. Qi claimed he had nothing to give them and could afford only a little aid for the poorest of his relatives. Nonetheless he felt compelled to record this apology in his diary, incidentally adding that, all day and without a break, he had to deal with requests that came to him by letter and in person.[147] Identified as a man of responsibility, he had to shoulder burdens that increased in weight as the succession of crises (food shortage, disease, and locusts) overtook Shaoxing. For any benefits that his leadership role might have brought him—opportunities to guide the decision making, earn a stellar reputation, preserve his community, lineage, and resources, or garner personal satisfaction from having done good—Qi paid a high price, in the form of incessant hard work. Thus the concepts about the quest for control and dominance, with which some historians have viewed the activities of the Chinese literate elite, fail to capture the nexus of considerations within which Qi Biaojia and his peers worked.[148] Qi took a leading role, to be sure, but he was also subject to numerous demands and ensnared by negotiations with resident officials, his peers, and his community.

Accepting responsibility for relief programs was not lightly done. To clinch their momentary impulses to participate, the friends of Qi's ward took a communal oath before the spirits.[149] As Qi explained: "For the students taking charge of fund-raising, shouldering responsibility is difficult while drawing hatred from others is extremely easy. The majority of wealthy households, regarding their 'superfluous things' (*changwu*) as their own flesh, will not heed discussions about crises. Some of them even vilify the students, motioning them to stay outside. Therefore taking on hard work always means taking on resentment." Oaths not only expressed a commitment to doing good; in Qi's view, they specifically fortified timid do-gooders to overcome obstacles.[150]

PUNISHMENTS AND REWARDS

Pressures to do good came from many directions other than moral teachings. From below came the threat that the rural residents, if desperate for food, would disrupt the social order. One riot, one raid against a wealthy household, or the sight of one thousand rural residents ominously circling the city often sufficed to spur grain hoarders to organize famine relief.[151] From above came harassment by officials, sometimes in the form of menacing rumors that wealthy households who failed to distribute grain would be forced to sell it at below-market prices. Such pressures could be coercive, intimating punishing consequences for those who would remain tightfisted, as when Vice-Prefect Bi Yutai chastised someone for refusing to share his grain.[152] Qi himself was well aware that officials might force prosperous households to sell their grain at reduced prices—a policy he opposed.[153] Under such circumstances, it was preferable to pursue an alternate route: by seizing the initiative in giving, by showing that they "liked to make donations" (*haoshi*), or "took pleasure in doing good" (*leshan*), they could at least earn merit, stand high in the community, and take some personal satisfaction in their own goodness.

Such pressures notwithstanding, the relief activities were largely voluntary. Only occasionally does one read of "friends" being fined for not living up to their commitments. "If someone who has been designated to manage the sale of gruel fails to show up, he should be fined five taels," instructed Qi, who then allowed, "If that person has been called away by a truly urgent matter, he may have a friend take his place," adding: "Those who arrive late should be fined one tael."[154] Yet, along with such penalties were numerous positive incentives to be charitable. The act of relieving the suffering of other creatures could in itself—with no clear reference to a specific belief system— suffice to reward benefactors with a gratifying sense of their goodness. As was the case with liberating animals, rescuing a human being from a state of near death affirmed the benefactor's power; and because the benefactor had willingly expended, or sacrificed, either labor or financial resources to effect the rescue, the goodness achieved was his to claim, his self-image thereby elevated. Amorphous feelings of compassion were articulated in many voices, each having a distinct timbre resonating with the speaker's educational background and beliefs, but each harmonizing with the others to sing out such general concepts as humaneness, the sanctity of life, and goodness.

Sustaining the impulse to save lives, motivating men to do good, were material and honorary rewards. Marking one far end of the spectrum were quid pro quo payments, such as those that Qi's brothers distributed to laborers who had responded to a bandit alarm;[155] these payments essentially brought the exchange to a close. The labors of various servants did not count in the reckoning of merit. "They simply carried loads and did nothing else," one of Qi's protégés dismissively insisted in a retrospective account—all the while making sure that he too would receive credit for his share in arduous expeditions to the rural poor.[156] At the other end of the spectrum was the satisfaction of having done something that, as Gao Panlong had put it, one just had to do. Between these two extremes was a vast range of rewards that, in varying proportions, simultaneously satisfied selfish desires for rewards and acknowledged genuine expressions of generosity and voluntarism.

Rewards to benefactors were sometimes substantial, as seen in a set of regulations for famine relief that Chen Jiru, a friend of Qi Biaojia's father, had appended to his own guidelines for soup kitchens, in 1609. The author of the regulations, Grand Coordinator Zhou Kongjiao, stipulated, among other things: "Those who contribute 150 *shi* of rice would avoid taxes on five hundred *mou* of land for three years, and those who contribute 300 *shi* of rice would avoid taxes on a thousand *mou*." Yet even Zhou assumed an element of voluntarism on the part of the donors, for he further stipulated that those who paid no attention to famine relief "should not be forced."[157]

Other rewards were honorary, deriving their meaning or prestige from official and imperial authority. Zhou envisioned, among other honors, a placard that he, as grand coordinator, would himself inscribe.[158] Qi recommended that officials should, after touring an area, issue a placard to the student managing the soup kitchen, commissioning him to hand in a report on who was diligent and who was lazy, as well as facts about the quality of the gruel; accordingly one or two men who worked the hardest or gave the most money should be given rewards, so as to serve as an incentive for others. Those who were delinquent in their duties should be reprimanded.[159] Qi further envisioned that benefactors would be commended to the emperor and receive inscribed tablets or banners for their front gates; they would be invited to special wine-drinking ceremonies; or they would receive a "cap and sash" with the insignia of low-ranking officials.[160] Qi's formulations corresponded to practices documented in his diaries. When touring the western borough, passing through Qianqing, fifty *li* west of the city center, the officials he was accompanying encountered one of those private, undesigning donors who might easily have slipped into obscurity: for three or four months, one Zhu Shengzheng had been voluntarily and singlehandedly providing relief. The two officials lavishly applauded him and posted his name on a public announcement.[161]

Like Zhou Kongjiao, Qi Biaojia wrote up schedules for rewarding contributors to the relief efforts. His diary of 1641 refers to a "Proposal for Recommending Rewards for Famine Relief" and alludes to "three grades for the category of 'venerable and righteous men' and two grades for the category of 'students' as the basis for calculating rewards."[162] This diary description roughly corresponds to the contents of an extant "Proposal for Giving out Rewards," in which Qi argued that punishments and rewards were essential to making a relief project work.[163] The threat of punishments (one supposes that Qi had in mind such punishments as fines exacted from "friends" who failed in their responsibilities) would ensure that "many people would be united in their resolve." The promise of rewards would arouse enthusiasm for the project. Qi then proceeded to outline two broad categories (which roughly correspond to those mentioned in the diary of 1641): outstanding, venerable residents; and men with lower degrees or scholarly status—licentiates, state students (*jiansheng*), and scholars (*rushi*). Further dividing each category into three grades, Qi spelled out equations whereby each grade would receive honors corresponding to the amounts of their donations. Accordingly, the top grade would be earned by outstanding residents who gave over twenty *shi* of husked grain *(mi)* or over fifty taels of silver, or who made available fifty *shi* for equitable sales (*pingtiao*) of grain or forty *shi* for grain sales at reduced prices (*jiantiao*).

Qi further factored into his reward schedule something that Zhou Kongjiao, who was of an earlier generation, had ignored: hard work on behalf of the relief effort. Thus residents who contributed but ten *shi* of unhusked grain (instead of twenty), could qualify for the top ranking if they also "took responsibility and worked hard" at the various soup kitchens. Those who provided little grain but who "were outstanding in working hard" qualified for the third grade. For lower degree holders and scholars, Qi gave top priority to hard work and weighed material contributions as insignificant; he thus made room for scholars who "had worked most energetically even though they were too poor to provide resources." Among the rewards that participants in this broad group might expect was permission to take the prefectural examination.[164] Given that record keeping, accounting, and general know-how were needed for running the relief efforts, rewarding service made sense. Moreover, giving even the poorest, most marginal "scholars" a valued role in the relief operations discouraged them from voicing discordant opinions, or worse, from fomenting disorder. Qi surely perceived what his local acquaintance Yu Huang explicitly stated: not all rioters were starving people; some were trouble makers whom starving people followed.[165]

Respect for the social hierarchy helped to endow rewards and honors with meaning and hence to make the relief programs work. Qi took care to notify officials of local good deeds. He urged Prefect Wang Sunlan to confer rewards upon those households who had provided relief in 1641 and 1640;[166] and he asked Prefectural Judge Chen Zilong to reward those students who had "taken on responsibility with sincerity and pure-heartedness."[167] Words coming from the mouths of august officials, even when benefiting his social inferiors, mattered to Qi, moving him to record, for example, that two local officials applauded a "friend" and several students for their satisfactory management of grain distribution at soup kitchens in Tianle.[168]

Qi understood that praise, especially from one of high standing in the community, had the power to encourage participation in the relief efforts. Before addressing a large gathering at the Wang Yangming Shrine about the task at hand, he made a point of first "calling out the 'friends' of each ward, commending them for their labors in shouldering responsibilities thus far."[169] Again, to hearten those who had joined the relief efforts, he one day "took a sedan chair everywhere to pay respects to those scholars who were taking responsibility for the five boroughs of the two cities."[170]

Praise traveled not only down the social hierarchy but up as well, from the nameless multitudes whose applause often resounded through the streets, and from identifiable members of the local elite. For the record, Qi mentioned in his diary those officials who deserved praise: Vice-Prefect Bi Yutai "for his accomplishment in catching bandits and his labors in encouraging the relief efforts in the southern borough;[171] and Magistrate Zhou for being "smart and extraordinarily talented."[172] Lower down the hierarchy was a protégé who would later praise Qi with the same sort of rhetoric about tolerating harsh conditions that Qi had used to applaud his comrades— and to describe himself. Reflecting on his mentor's labors in distributing food and medicines to the poor in 1641, the protégé wrote that Qi often trekked ten *li* a day to remote valleys and destitute rural areas; and, emphasized the protégé, when it came to providing coffins, Qi personally inspected the corpses "despite the filth and odor."[173] Further up the hierarchy were officials like Chen Zilong, who also conveyed praise on upward to the highest echelons. Chen's report resulted in having the names of charitable men recorded by imperial decree.[174]

The sheer presence of officials at times elevated Qi's sense of purpose and importance. He was acutely aware—for he took care to note this in his diary—that when he "called out the names" and distributed two *fen* to each starving person in one section of Tianle, "the two local officials sat and watched" him. As he performed his duties under the eyes of high-level officials, Qi's self-image as a compassionate man expanded. Observed by officials, he self-consciously observed himself within the surrounding scene. To capture this moment, a Buddhist image served him better than a Confucian text. The pitiable appearance of the starving was, he mused, "just like Wu Daozi's painting of hell."[175]

Qi appreciated as much as everyone else that doing good would bring him personal benefits. When he made the extended inspection tour of soup kitchens in Chen Zilong's company, it was with pride and a touch of exhilaration that he recorded in his diary how they had ridden around together, "laughing and talking," and how Chen had shared a vegetarian meal on Qi's boat, where they discussed not just the business at hand, but poetry and scenic splendors, topics conducive to a cultured friendship.[176] When it worked well, the system of rewards, linked with symbols of status, encouraged charitable behavior. This "system"—as envisioned by the writers discussed here—depended on a respect for the existing social hierarchy. Qi Biaojia and Chen Zilong assumed that students, aspiring to pass the civil service examinations and form ties with officialdom, would scramble to aid local officials or gentry who had access to those officials—just as Qi welcomed the opportunities created by the relief efforts to hobnob with the high-ranking, well-connected, and urbane Chen Zilong.

The communal oaths to shoulder responsibility, the promise of rewards, and the presence of official authority all helped to motivate the "friends." Consider a large gathering held at the Wang Yangming Shrine. After commending the friends for their labors thus far, Qi instructed them on additional measures for mitigating the crisis, only to learn that, contrary to his design, the friends "did not wish to do soup kitchens but wanted instead to prolong the period for giving out rice" while using portable soup kitchens to aid the indigent and the vagrants.[177] Rather than giving an inspirational lecture (as Gao Panlong might have done), Qi mobilized the friends through the above-mentioned means. He wrote up a proposal to show various officials, thereby associating his plan with their authority. He listed the names of "the friends" in a notebook to be presented to local authority Chen Zilong, who then, "calling them out borough by borough, spoke encouraging words and talked of rewards." Finally, recounted Qi, "using the pledge I had written out beforehand, we swore an oath in front of our former teacher" (that is, an image or tablet of Wang Yangming, in whose shrine the meeting was taking place). Thus it was settled that the friends would install soup kitchens and the officials would follow up with an inspection tour so as "to encourage" the project.[178]

With their eyes on rewards that might, at the least, take the form of public acclaim, late Ming do-gooders took it upon themselves to advertise their fine deeds. They published pamphlets, ostensibly to describe relief strategies for future reference but all the while displaying the importance of their own participation. As Zhang Bi stated of his various helpers, "I have here recorded their names to make their charitableness (*haoyi*) known."[179] Eventually word of Zhang Bi's generosity reached the court, and he was duly honored with a placard.[180] So too did Ni Yuanlu make sure that posterity would remember his leadership in the Life-Saving Pagoda campaign. The purpose of the campaign was, explained Ni, "to aid those left out of the relief efforts and to broaden the art of doing good"; but in recording the guidelines, he also established his merit in his community's eyes. Subsequently, the compilers of local gazetteers, Ni's chronological biography, and his collected works all mentioned his fund-raising efforts. Ni's account of his campaign secured his reputation for doing good.[181] Likewise did Chen Zilong consciously strive to leave a record of his good name, declaring in his self-narrated chronological biography: "The affair of the famine has been made clear in the *history of relief* (*zhenshi*)."[182]

And for whom if not for some imagined audience did Qi comment in his diary that, when he organized various friends to aid vagrants, he first distributed twelve hundred cash (*wen*) to set an example?[183] And to what end, if not to enhance his own image, did he state: "I sighed, 'Those who wish to take on responsibility for the world must certainly have talent and insight'"?[184] Occasionally he feigned modesty. When a friend came by with a poem celebrating him "for having worked so hard for famine relief," Qi commented, "Embarrassed, I dared not accept the praise,"[185] meanwhile taking care to record the incident in his diary. Six weeks later, when he learned from the Metropolitan Gazette "that my relief efforts of last year have been honored by a report from the board," he again protested, "I was deeply embarrassed," yet here, too, he made sure to log the information in his diary.[186] Thus did local participants in the Shaoxing relief operation of the early 1640s appropriate for themselves an image that earlier writings had most frequently associated with officials. Moreover, rather than entirely entrusting the painting of their portraits to later hagiographers, they often assumed the task themselves, taking no chance that their wish for a reputation of beneficence would go unfulfilled. The value of secret merit (*yinde*), deeply cherished in earlier dynasties, had given way to competition in publicly displaying one's dedication to doing good.

MORAL AUTHORITY RESIDING IN THE LIVING

Late Ming didactic tracts and morality books applauded not only the distant dead, but also contemporary benefactors whom local community members had known in person. Accordingly Chen's benevolent society lectures mentioned Confucius only once, and even then most perfunctorily, while honoring the local philanthropist Ding Bin as "a living ancient whom we have seen in person."[187] The practice of placing recent worthies among great sages of dynasties long gone is also evident in a work of the next generation, *On Spreading Kindness/Charity (Guanghui bian)*, compiled by Zhu Shi.[188] There, Zhu accorded first place to the great twelfth-century metaphysical philosopher Zhu Xi but placed close behind him, among others, both Yan Maoyou and Chen Longzheng.[189] Zhu Shi made the point that men who performed good deeds explicitly to reap rewards would go unrewarded. Nonetheless, by commemorating those who had recently contributed to their communities, he and other compilers of didactic works made credible the idea that good behavior would earn recognition, that the acquisition of merit and its rewards was realistically within the reach of all. Moreover *On Spreading Kindness* flattens distinctions among Zhu Xi, Yan Maoyou, and Chen Longzheng. Using the advocacy of doing good as the criterion for inclusion, it overlooks Zhu Xi's philosophical breakthroughs—his interpretations of the classics that the civil service examination system later took as its standard—and it overlooks, too, that Yan Maoyou and Chen Longzheng were not systematic, innovative thinkers. As popular didactic works preserved and circulated old exemplars, their rhetoric of do-good activism put doers and thinkers both contemporary and ancient on the same level. A version of *The Exalted One's Tract on Action and Response* published in 1880 applauds Yan Maoyou at length for having, among other good deeds, written *Right Behavior and Good Fortune,* a work, reports the editor, that has moved hundreds and thousands of people to change their ways, and that "today still circulates in Jiangnan and Jiangbei."[190] In the context of community activism, the rules for judging greatness were far different from those of Huang Zongxi's imagined intellectual world.

The late Ming environment called for renewing old terms with fresh meanings. Though occasionally drawing upon Buddhist, Confucian, Daoist, and even Legalist concepts, Qi Biaojia and his peers formed a fresh amalgam that had distinctively late Ming features—such as establishing a good name, shouldering responsibility, accumulating merit or material rewards, and avoiding retribution. Moral authority and beliefs about goodness and justice played an important role in the late Ming relief efforts, but they did so through routes other than specific textual traditions and often in unexpected ways. Appealing to the moral conscience of the rich and powerful was the weighty heritage of famine-relief knowledge and precedent (to which the Christian convert Xu Guangqi no less than many stalwart Confucians had contributed); this heritage stood as a constant reminder of what those men with power or influence might accomplish. Surely, too, there rang in Qi's ears the words of his friend Yan Maoyou: "The gentry are the hope of the state. The good they do while living at home can affect the prefecture and district and transform the customs of the subprefectures and villages."[191]

Within Qi's hearing were, moreover, several Shaoxing residents whose integrity and strong moral teachings continually grated on his conscience. Among them was Wang Chaoshi, whose repeated cautions against extravagant garden building Qi disobeyed but could not ignore. Above all, there was Wang Chaoshi's mentor Liu Zongzhou, whose friend and model Gao Panlong had insisted on the moral imperative to do good. Like Gao, Liu was uncompromising in his moral integrity—his courageous frankness angered but ultimately won the emperor's respect—and for his integrity, Liu won wide admiration, attracting an enormous following.[192] Although Qi showed little interest in Liu's "learned discussions" and strongly differed with Liu on many issues, he was susceptible to Liu's moral authority. Repeatedly he looked to Liu for approval or (on the subject of famine relief, at least) sought to bring him around to his own views.[193] Often in his diaries—as when he noted, "Formerly Mr. Liu had urged me to manage the administration of famine relief"[194]—Qi revealed his esteem for Liu's position and took pride in his connection to Liu. If Qi did not always follow Liu's and Wang's advice, he registered what they said, often feeling compelled to note their views in his diaries, as though he was dealing with his own conscience externalized.

The fear of disorder, the satisfaction of shouldering responsibility for benevolent projects, and the promise of rewards nudged residents toward doing good. But also decisive was the presence in the community of men like Gao Panlong, Liu Zongzhou, and Wang Chaoshi. Their insistence on the moral imperative to do good articulated for residents, each of whom had his own unspoken motives for participating in charitable activities, a reason to cooperate; and it mobilized the likes of Qi Biaojia to undertake arduous leadership responsibilities. The moral mandate to do good transformed charitable activities into an uplifting experience.

·   ·   ·

In 1645, Qi Biaojia, who was then in his forty-fourth year, chose, rather than accepting an invitation to serve the Manchus, to pursue the honorable alternative: after making deliberate preparations, he drowned himself in the pond at Yu Mountain. His only major wrongdoing, he had told his son before taking his leave, had been his addiction to garden building.[195] So, too, did Ni Yuanlu, Chen Zilong, and Liu Zongzhou, take their lives around this time. As they did during the food-shortage crisis, they thereby took control of their destinies, acting upon their beliefs.

Conclusion

From Moral Transformation
toward the Legitimation of Wealth

Two roads that initially promised answers about late Ming charity proved to be dead ends: the one in search of such crises as poverty, hunger, and dynastic decline that might have demanded charitable interventions; and the other in search of motivations for charity. Granted, each of these roads turned up some material relating to the subject of charity, which in this study I duly note. Yet, neither route yielded satisfactory explanations for the distinctiveness of late Ming charity, or for why the late Ming, in contrast to earlier periods that had also suffered dearth, destitution, and dynastic decline, produced an unprecedented number of highly visible charitable institutions and writings about charity. Moving away from the two cul-de-sacs and putting many preconceived notions about charity at a distance, this study has pursued a third course: to let five men, whose extant writings illuminate numerous connections between their charitable activities and late Ming society, be the guides. This procedure led to several unanticipated findings.

Materials by and about the five men revealed, above all, two interlocked social changes as key to the high visibility of late Ming charity. The first was the expansion of ranks hovering at the periphery of elite society: the well-to-do men of Yucheng who rushed to form a second benevolent society patterned after the one Yang Dongming had set up for men of bureaucratic status; Lu Shiyi and his fellow students who managed the benevolent society of Taicang; and those many physicians, monks, and students in Qi Biaojia's circle who carried out the tasks of distributing grain, organizing soup kitchens, and dispensing medicines. Already well established by historians of the late Ming is this: the spread of literacy generated a surplus of aspirants for the civil service examinations and bureaucratic service; and the fiercely competitive environment forced many literate men to apply their skills to such other pursuits as publishing, commerce, or writing. This study shows that the large reserve of literate men additionally played a critical role in late Ming charity. They surveyed and kept records of the population of needy, supervised soup kitchens, maintained records of medical prescriptions, kept account books, and themselves initiated do-good projects.

The second change was the growing salience, outside the lineage, of a social connectivity running vertically between the high and lower (if not the lowest) reaches of local society. This connectivity should not be confused with formal conceptions of a social hierarchy or the grandiose declarations by late Ming writers about the unity of all beings. Rather, the term here refers only to active relationships between men of different social strata—such as the relationship between the high-status official on leave, Qi Biaojia, and the relatively indigent student, Wang Chaoshi; or the ties between Qi Biaojia and the physicians and monks of Shaoxing. Such vertical relationships had undoubtedly always played a role in local society, but, during the late Ming, they gained enough strength to slip into the consciousness of men at the top of local society, and hence into their records. Accordingly, Yang Dongming acknowledged that the idea for a benevolent society came from the common people, and Qi Biaojia acknowledged that the program for distributing medicines in Shaoxing had first been suggested by a monk and a physician. The vertical associations are further evident in the societies for liberating animals and sharing goodness that embraced rich and poor, and degree holders as well as the semiliterate and illiterate; in Gao Panlong and Chen Longzheng, who, though standing among the elite, addressed their benevolent societies in an easygoing colloquial style suitable for uneducated listeners; and in the case of Lu Shiyi, who both consorted with members of the bureaucratic elite and counted among his friends and relatives persons who were desperately poor.

Contrary to the narrative of dynastic decline that dominates much writing about the late Ming, this study found that, even during the accelerated deterioration of the 1640s—a deterioration of which some of the leading figures were painfully aware—political authority, which was wielded by such officials as Chen Zilong in Shaoxing and invoked by former officials residing in their hometowns, continued to play a vital role in local politics, at least in the regions here studied. The presence of political authority, and the respect for the social hierarchy it protected, worked like lightning, igniting the vertical associations—but not in the ways that historians have customarily assumed. Replacing the picture of the local elite attaching themselves to imperial authority so as to dominate and control local society, this study exhibits a multitude of exchanges and negotiations that ran up from the lower reaches of the social hierarchy as well as down from the top. To be sure, members of the local elite exerted pressure on their social inferiors, and often they did this by invoking imperial authority—whether by citing the Six Imperial Maxims, as Gao Panlong did; or by seeking the approval of local officials, as Qi Biaojia did. Yet late Ming materials demand that the picture of domination and control from the top be modified. The diaries of Lu Shiyi and Qi Biaojia display sharp divisions among members of the local elite, who, competing among themselves, often sought to settle their differences regarding charitable strategies by individually seeking official approval. For them, dominance, or, more accurately, winning support for a strategy of one's choosing, came at the cost of having to subordinate oneself to a superior authority. Late Ming documents further display numerous cases where men lower down the social hierarchy—students, doctors, and monks—either themselves initiated charitable activities or successfully piggybacked their own interests on collective efforts to do good. Moreover, those men who sought leadership roles ended up shouldering burdensome, time-consuming, and exhausting responsibilities; for the opportunity to shape policy, they paid a high price.

Activism within local society was strong and talk of public-mindedness frequent. But just when the makings of a civil society or a public sphere seemed to be emerging—just when horizontal relationships among the small players at the margins of the local elites were becoming salient in the form of numerous voluntary associations, the vertical ties between local society and the imperial bureaucracy gathered strength, simultaneously facilitating initiatives from below and inviting official interventions from above. The findings for late Ming charitable associations thus affirm arguments that Frederic Wakeman and Susan Naquin have made in reference to the Qing dynasty: the concepts of a public sphere or a Harbermassian civil society do not fit the realities of social activism in late imperial China.[1]

If members of the local elite held those two tools for asserting some control over local affairs, wealth and access to political power, they were nonetheless constrained in many ways—by the pressures from constituencies below them, the threat of "forced sales" of their grain from officials above, and the demands of colleagues in neighboring districts. Moreover, even residents who lacked both substantial wealth and ties to officialdom had their own tools for backing demands: they could resort to violence (a point that historians have well documented), or they could make moral arguments. Whether they used moral arguments as mere rhetorical strategies, the means toward an end, or advanced them with the utmost sincerity is beside the point, which is this: during the late Ming, regardless of the motivations involved, the rhetoric of doing good, of undertaking the indisputably worthy and urgent goal of saving lives, had become the lingua franca for negotiations among various constituencies and between high and low.

By doing good, men at the margins of the local elite could enter the competition for resources, attention, and advancement. Marginal men—Lu Shiyi, Wang Chaoshi, and Shen Guomo—proved effective in wielding the only weapon (other than violence) they had for influencing local affairs: moral arguments. Their loud appeals to social conscience made an impression on their socioeconomic superiors. Chen Longzheng heard—to the point of recording them in his writings and engaging them in his thinking—the strident demands for fairness that came from the rural areas and the poor; and Qi Biaojia paid attention to, if he did not always heed, the moral arguments of Liu Zongzhou's humble protégé Wang Chaoshi no less than those made by former official Liu himself. To legitimize their choices and to win cooperation and approval from their communities, especially from those literate but lowly residents on whom their organized charity relied, leaders of local society had to speak a widely understood moral language. By the same token, it was those men who spoke that language comfortably and with conviction who were the ones most likely to float up into the role of leader in charity. Chen Longzheng and Qi Biaojia had been socialized to live up to their family reputations for doing good; whatever motives may have been driving them, they were persuasive leaders because they had become captives of their own do-good rhetoric.

For why the rhetoric of saving lives moved into the foreground of late Ming discussions, several explanations deserve consideration. One concerns the enormous anxiety that some late Ming men were, by many accounts, suffering. Extreme restlessness troubled Chen Longzheng before he settled down to serious study. Anxiety infused the diary-keeping mania of Lu Shiyi and his friends. Mental fatigue prompted Qi Biaojia to seek spiritual counseling from Yan Maoyou. The focus on the crossroads between life and death—a metaphor for making a critical choice—enabled them to identify something truly important and galvanized them to take action.

This sense of anxiety that perturbed late Ming literati was, some historians have suggested, stimulated by the rapid and capricious social mobility and by an examination system so competitive as to bar many qualified candidates from officialdom. By doing good, aspiring students proved their merit, and successful candidates and prominent households validated their social standing. Yet, if one further asks what transmuted that anxiety into charitable activities and, specifically, into a preoccupation with saving lives, another scenario comes to light. As the ranks of men at the margins of the elite expanded, so did the conduits between high and low proliferate, bringing the issues of poverty, suffering, and needless deaths into the homes and consciousness of the wealthy. Among this marginal population were the many visitors who streamed into Qi Biaojia's residence to make requests on behalf of friends and relatives. Also among them was Lu Shiyi himself, who counted among his relatives the truly down-and-out, and whose closest friend's father needed the benevolent society's help.

The value of life may have also been highlighted by changes in labor patterns and the resulting recognition, at least among the Jiangnan elite, that nonagrarian laborers were not only at once vulnerable and threatening but also valuable.[2] The spread of commercial crops, textile production, and commerce enriched some members of the late Ming elite while rendering the men and women engaged in producing and distributing these products especially susceptible to market fluctuations. This problem impressed some benefactors. Luckless sojourning merchants appear here and there in the records either asking for help (as did one of Lu Shiyi's uncles) or winning sympathy and funds (from Qi Biaojia, for example) to cover homeward travel. Although the Six Maxims instructed that each person should stay in his or her place, Chen Longzheng recognized that peddlers and laborers, through no fault of their own, frequently suffered unemployment. Moreover, he had heard that "all the silk-producing cities"—from Wuxi and the prefectural city of Suzhou on to Wujiang (which was also in Suzhou prefecture)—had suffered widespread upheavals.[3] During this time, in Hangzhou at least, urban workers, living from hand to mouth and renting their dwellings, resided in close proximity to wealthy households, a situation that gave rise to disagreements about labor duties and curfews and stimulated antigentry sentiment.[4] The benevolent societies of Gao Panlong's and Chen Longzheng's districts not only aimed to stabilize the population of nonagrarian laborers but also explicitly placed a high value on the lives of their beneficiaries.[5]

The materials on late Ming charity led to yet another unanticipated finding. With the exception of the Lu Shiyi of 1641 (in contrast to the Lu who would gain some recognition in the early Qing dynasty)—for whom no clear verdict may be reached as to whether it was personality, lack of talent, or lack of resources and social connections that kept him marginal—the charitable leaders in this study were exceptional, preeminent among their peers. Their personalities and specific life circumstances motivated them to reach for something high, a reach that resulted in a combination of outright competitiveness (most evident in Qi Biaojia) and an unwavering adherence to a high moral road (most evident in Gao Panlong). Their extraordinary examples in turn motivated fellow townsmen to join charitable causes.

Among the personal experiences that gave rise to charitable feelings was that of loss. Several of the men undertook charitable activities either while they had forebodings of a personal loss, during which time they did good explicitly to propitiate heaven to save a loved one, or while in mourning, when their own grief commingled with empathy for other creatures. In light of these coincidences, it would appear that among the many motivations for doing good was, not least of all, a genuine feeling of compassion.[6] This element of compassion elicited voluntary giving and distinguished charity from numerous other strategies (such as the collection of taxes) for enhancing the common good.

Materials regarding Chen Longzheng, and Qi Biaojia, in particular, reveal how circumstances over time socialized them to do good. Although fear of disorder was one incentive to be charitable, also powerful, in addition to

traumatic personal losses, were such pressures as the weight of a family reputation, keenly felt by Chen Longzheng, and moral arguments, loudly voiced
by men of integrity like Gao Panlong, Liu Zongzhou, and Wang Chaoshi.
Once elevated to a leadership position, Yang, Gao, Chen, and Qi each had
to authenticate his leadership role through hard work, financial contributions, and even martyrdom.

Their moral pronouncements testify to an expansive impulse among
some charitable leaders to give widely; benefactors often proved flexible in
defining the scope of their charity, occasionally giving, for example, to certain groups that they had labeled as undeserving. Some late Ming benefactors argued that territorial boundaries (whether they be the city walls,
urban wards, rural boroughs, or district borders) legitimately defined their
responsibility for fellow creatures, yet occasionally the news of suffering elsewhere moved them to transcend the boundaries they had mentally set. Reasons for their flexibility are several: the sight of suffering was often powerful; the competition to display one's merit occasionally propelled benefactors
to step beyond ordinary charitable routines; and far-flung social relationships often demanded that they extend charitable activities beyond kin and
district.

That benefactors in numerous instances wished to extend the scope of
their beneficence raises questions about the constraints on voluntary giving.
Qi Biaojia's charitable activities, and particularly his account of the official
tour of the soup kitchens in the rural areas of Shaoxing, show that even well-
intentioned charitable men had difficulty solving such problems as procuring grain during a food shortage, transporting grain to the rural areas, keeping records of the population of needy, eliminating corruption, allocating
handouts fairly, preventing the mobbing of soup kitchens, recruiting helpers
to run the dispensaries, and organizing manpower effectively so as to max-
imize outreach while maintaining accountability.

Yet, prior to those difficulties in executing plans for distributing resources
are other constraints on benefactors, best approached through the question of what determined the amount to be given by a person defined as charitable. As in the Western Judeo-Christian tradition, so too in the late Ming
did men occasionally mention the appropriateness of tithing. But, leaving
aside the question of precisely what was to be tithed (whether it was annual
income, disposable income, or net wealth), one might ask, given the in-
finitely expandable needs of the poor, by what standard was one tenth considered enough? Charitable activities involved more than aiding the needy.
They were a means by which one might reach for a higher good and an enhanced self-image—and those ends were most effectively achieved by making that reach in terms that members of the community comprehended and
appreciated. The vision of what constituted doing good was ultimately a communal vision; and charitable activities were ultimately social activities, af-

fecting relationships, not just between benefactors and recipients, but also between a benefactor and his peers. Those who made extraordinary grand gestures ran the risk of being attacked by jealous but greedy peers as trying to "buy fame" or being reckless. To mobilize cooperation in charitable activities, to make it a collective enterprise—and the distribution of grain and medicine, requiring substantial funds and a large organizations, had to be collective enterprises—one had to set goals for giving that would engage participation without threatening to deplete the wealth that backed the participants' social identity.

To ensure solidarity among benefactors, various guidelines placed ceilings on donations and credit for doing good. Examples are the parameters that Gao Panlong and Chen Longzheng set for individual donations at each benevolent-society meeting: from nine *fen* to ten times that amount, or nine *qian* (0.9 ounces of silver); or the limits set by Ni Yuanlu's and Qian Sule's guidelines for pagoda fund-raising campaigns, which instructed that any donor pledging to save more than one life should assign the credit for the additional lives to members of his family; and also made room for men without resources to participate by managing the registers.[7] Also to preserve the collective character of charitable activities, some leaders insisted that good deeds could be done at little or no cost and that recipients were sharing in the goodness.

Thus, even while exceptional leaders, in striving for something higher, passionately championed aid to the needy, their society was populated by men who wished to preserve their resources, whether to protect their families or to satisfy their own avarice. Self-interest and greed strained against the forces of generosity and justice. In itself this is an old story. New to the late Ming was that certain conditions—most notably but by no means exclusively the expansion of a literate but marginal social stratum—ensured that, out of this tug-of-war, highly visible charitable activities emerged.

CODA

How feelings of compassion and notions of justice are played out, and whether they take the form of collective acts of charity, depends on a raft of factors that change with time and place. The environment that spurred the five main subjects of this book to do good dissolved in the early Qing dynasty. Most briefly and broadly, the charity of the two periods differed in three respects: in the early Qing, the role of merchants and merchant wealth, barely perceptible in late Ming records, became more noticeable, with merchants who were clearly identified as merchants often assuming leadership roles; the routinization of charity, which late Ming men occasionally attempted by endowing estates, became far more developed with the sponsorship of the Qing state; and, as merchants and the state stepped in, members of the educated elite, finding that room for their leadership had shrunk, lost interest in using charitable activities as a vehicle for the moral transformation of society.[8] In institutionalizing benevolent societies and articulating the good that money could achieve, late Ming literati unwittingly made room for merchants to assume a legitimate and highly visible place in local affairs. Where Gao Panlong had seen the benevolent society as a vehicle for communicating moral lessons, early Qing merchants used philanthropy to advertise their own respectability.[9] Under such circumstances, the educated literatus may have lost interest in writing about charity. As a district gazetteer of 1751 noted, old gazetteers reported acts of filiality, righteousness, and good deeds—but had broadcast them "as loud as thunder, to the point of boring the reader."[10]

ABBREVIATIONS

Chen	Chen Longzheng, *Jiting quanshu*.
Diary	Qi Biaojia, *Qi Zhongmin gong riji*. The diary for each year bears a separate title and has independent pagination. I designate the titles by the closest corresponding year in the Western calendar, since the Western and Chinese calendars are not exactly matched. In parentheses I give the month and day from the Chinese lunar calendar by which Qi marked each diary entry.
Diary 1631	*Shebei cheng yan*.
Diary 1632	*Qibei rong yan*.
Diary 1635	*Guinan kuai lu*.
Diary 1636	*Zhulin shi bi*.
Diary 1637	*Shanju zhuo lu*.
Diary 1638	*Zijian lu*.
Diary 1639	*Qi lu*.
Diary 1640	*Ganmu lu*.
Diary 1641	*Xiaojiu lu*.
Diary 1642	*Renwu rili*.
DJL	Yan Maoyou, comp. and annot., *Diji lu*.
DMB	L. Carrington Goodrich and Chaoying Fang, eds., *Dictionary of Ming Biography*.
ECCP	Arthur Hummel, ed., *Eminent Chinese of the Ch'ing Period*.
Gao	Gao Panlong. *Gaozi yishu*.
Gao nianpu	Hua Yuncheng, *Gao Zhongxian gong nianpu*.
LHWJ	Zhang Dai, *Langhuan wenji*.
LZQS	Liu Zongzhou, *Liuzi quanshu*.
Qi nianpu	Wang Siren, *Qi Zhongmin gong nianpu*.
QBJJ	Qi Biaojia, *Qi Biaojia ji*.
Yang	Yang Dongming, *Shanju gongke*.
ZXL	Lu Shiyi, *Zhixue lu*.

NOTES

INTRODUCTION

1. Tsu, *The Spirit of Chinese Philanthropy*. For recent works in Japanese and Chinese, respectively, see Fuma, *Chūgoku zenkai;* Liang Qizi, *Shishan yu jiaohua*. Fuma examines late Ming benevolent societies in exhaustive detail, and Liang pays some heed to pre-Qing charity, but both authors focus mainly on the Qing dynasty. On nineteenth-century charity, see also Lum, "Philanthropy and Public Welfare in Late Imperial China"; Rowe, *Hankow: Commerce and Society,* 115, 248, 318; Ocko, *Bureaucratic Reform in Provincial China,* 53–55; Hsiao, *Rural China,* 194.

2. Early exceptions are Twitchett, "The Fan Clan's Charitable Estate," followed nearly two decades later by Liu, "Liu Tsai (1165–1238)"; Scogin, "Poor Relief in Northern Sung China."

3. Even Twitchett, "The Fan Clan's Charitable Estate," unintentionally reinforces the widespread Western view that Chinese benevolence mainly enhanced kinship ties.

4. On this drought famine, see Li, *Fighting Famine in North China,* 272–77.

5. Bohr, *Famine in China and the Missionary,* esp. 336.

6. Cited in ibid., 41.

7. Ibid., 113.

8. Ibid., 146, citing Richard, *Forty-five Years in China,* 158.

9. Cited in Bohr, *Famine in China and the Missionary,* 86.

10. Smith, *Chinese Characteristics,* 186–87.

11. Ibid., 190–92.

12. On Smith's confidence in Christianity as a cure for China's ills, see his *Village Life in China,* 341–52.

13. Palatre, *L'infanticide et l'oeuvre de la Sainte-Enfance en Chine,* 202; my translation. All translations are mine unless otherwise stated in the notes or in the bibliography.

14. Photograph of trackers by Dmitri Kessel, *Life Magazine,* 1956. Reproduced in Van Slyke, *Yangtze,* 122.

15. Salisbury, "In China, 'A Little Blood.'"
16. Morohashi, *Dai Kan-Wa jiten,* 9:9429, *s.v. yi,* item 8.
17. Handlin, *Action in Late Ming Thought,* 69, 71–72, 78, 83. For the nineteenth-century label, see B.B., "The Life Saving Association and Other Benevolent Societies at Wuhu."
18. See, for example, Scogin, "Poor Relief in Northern Sung China," 30–46.
19. Documentation of Buddhist philanthropy predating the twelfth century is actually scant. Early Chinese Buddhist donors made gifts to monasteries, both to support the institutions and to be redistributed as alms to the poor. Critics accused monasteries of impoverishing the people by draining their resources; and monasteries, probably in response to such attacks, subsequently expanded their philanthropic activities so as to appear socially useful. The imperial government increasingly relied on monasteries to administer welfare activities. See Michibata, *Chūgoku bukkyō to shakai fukushi jigyō;* Gernet, *Buddhism in Chinese Society,* esp. 217–23. On the misery that large Buddhist construction projects brought to the peasants, see Gernet, *Buddhism,* 17. On the paucity of information of early Buddhist charitable institutions see Gernet, *Buddhism,* 221. For one example of imperial co-optation—regarding Empress Wu (early eighth century), who had lay commissioners oversee all "fields of compassion" activities of the Buddhist monasteries, that is, care for orphans, indigents, the infirm, and the old—see Gernet, *Buddhism,* 331, citing *Tang huiyao,* 49.9b. Note also Gernet's comment that it was by penetrating existing cultural groupings or creating new ones based on these models that Buddhism spread rapidly in China—in urban and rural communities, which often used the gate of a monastery or some chapel for their reunion centers (*Buddhism,* 271). One might posit, as Brook does in *Praying for Power,* 106, Buddhist or "religious origins of gentry charity," but little textual evidence supports this claim; and, accustomed as Westerners are to the close association between charity and Christianity, one must guard against assuming such an association for China.
20. *The Works of Hsuntze,* 121–22, 125.
21. Wang Deyi, *Songdai zaihuang de jiuji zhengce,* esp. 86–131.
22. The exceptions would include Zhu Xi, Fan Zhongyan, and Su Shi.
23. On the official, see Liu, "Liu Tsai." References are also available on imperial sponsorship of welfare institutions (in particular, poorhouses) during the Song dynasty. See, for example, Scogin, "Poor Relief in Northern Sung China." For mention of a Song-dynasty orphanage (*ciyu ju*), see *Fushou quanshu,* 4.2a.
24. Rawski, *Education and Popular Literacy.*
25. The notion of *yinde* goes back at least to the *Shi ji* by Sima Qian (B.C. 145?–90?) and thus predates the first known reference to Buddhism in China (A.D. 65). See Morohashi, *Dai Kan-Wa jiten,* 11:12390, *s.v. yinde.*
26. On Su's philanthropy, see Egan, *Word, Image, and Deed in the Life of Su Shi,* chap. 5, esp. 130–31 (bridges); 128–30 (infanticide); 133 (secrecy).
27. Ibid., 132–33, citing Fei Gun.
28. On the "uncertainty" during the Song dynasty concerning the "ethical basis . . . of charity," see Hymes, *Statesmen and Gentlemen,* 162–63.
29. *Shanyin xian zhi* (1724), 33.8b, biography of Shen Maojian.
30. *Shanyin xian zhi* (1724), 33.5a, biography of Zhou Tingtan.

31. See Norberg, *Rich and Poor in Grenoble,* 116, 120 (wills); 21(confraternities); Fairchilds, *Poverty and Charity in Aix-en-Provence,* 19 (prostitutes). For mention of women donors in nineteenth-century China, see Rankin, *Elite Activism and Political Transformation in China,* 100.

32. *Oxford English Dictionary Online, s.v.* "charity"; "philanthropy."

33. This last term was introduced by Chan, *Religious Trends in Modern China,* 164.

34. See, respectively, Morohashi, *Dai Kan-Wa jiten, s.v. yi; yixue* (citing Hong Mai of the twelfth century).

35. *Xiaoshan xian zhi* (1672), 19.13a.

36. Hyde, *The Gift,* 16.

37. Weaver, *U.S. Philanthropic Foundations,* 6.

38. For a critique of "myths" about the nonprofit sector—especially that charity must be altogether voluntary, selfless, and independent of the state—see Salamon, "The Rise of the Nonprofit Sector," 109–22.

39. The term *Confucian* is problematical, since no term in Chinese exactly corresponds to it. It refers to a cluster of ideas found in ancient texts (the so-called Confucian classics) that Chinese scholars believed to have been written or transmitted by Confucius.

40. Dai Zhaozuo, *Yu gong Dezheng lu,* 7.18b.

41. *DJL,* "Tai ji," 51a.

42. On the many ramifications of the civil service examination system, see Elman, *A Cultural History of Civil Examinations,* esp. table 3.1 on p. 659. See also Miyazaki, *China's Examination Hell;* Ho, *The Ladder of Success in Imperial China.* To simplify matters, this study hereafter translates as "licentiate" the various names that Ming texts use for the *shengyuan* degree.

43. Himmelfarb, *Poverty and Compassion,* 73.

44. Hyde, *The Gift,* 137–38.

45. Dickens, *Bleak House,* chap. 30, 432.

46. Rothman ponders why "benevolence" should have acquired such a bad name in his introduction to *Doing Good,* x–xi.

47. On tracking merits and demerits, see Sakai, *Chūgoku zensho;* Brokaw, *Ledgers of Merit and Demerit.* See also Handlin, *Action in Late Ming Thought,* 186–212.

1. SOCIETIES FOR LIBERATING ANIMALS

1. On societies for liberating animals and the observation that that they anticipated benevolent societies, see Fuma, *Chūgoku zenkai,* esp. 151–64: this section first appeared in Fuma, "Zenkai, zendō no shuppatsu," 193–99, esp. 198–203. See also Kō Imai (Huang I-mei), "Kaisatsu hōjō to jin no shisō," esp. 31–38; Michibata, *Chūgoku bukkyō to shakai fukushi jigyō,* esp. 231–41; Ogasawara, *Chūgoku kinsei Jōdokyō shi no kenkyū,* 214–16; and Groot, "Miséricorde envers les animaux." On Zhuhong's promotion of these societies, see Yü, *The Renewal of Buddhism in China,* esp. 76–87; Araki, "Kaisatsu hōjō no hatten," in *Yōmeigaku no kaiten to Bukkyō,* 219–44; Standaert, *Yang Tingyun,* 38–41, 44.

2. In no passages before the fifth century is saving animals considered a meritorious act, according to Groot, "Miséricorde envers les animaux,"471. For a full translation of *Fanwang jing,* see Groot, *Le code du Māhayāna,* esp. 52–53. Although

most sources give the *Fanwang jing* as the locus classicus for *fangsheng*, in fact the term also appears in the *Liezi* (compiled ca. 300 A.D.), where the minister of Jin (511–474 B.C.), upon receiving a gift of doves on New Year's Day, stated: "We release living things on New Year's Day as a gesture of kindness," whereupon someone argued that, since the people vie to catch the doves, causing many of them to die, it would be best to forbid the practice; Graham, trans., *The Book of Lieh-tzu*, 178. Bodde argues that this anecdote was unconnected to the Buddhist practice of *fangsheng;* see his "*Lieh-tzu* and the Doves," 26n6, 30. Buddhism did not necessarily favor a vegetarian diet and the Pāli Vinaya permitted the consumption of fish and meat; see Mather, "The Bonze's Begging Bowl," 421.

3. Welch reported having observed in 1963 the release of sparrows and other types of animals to ward off a drought; *Practice of Chinese Buddhism*, 378–79. In personal communications Wai-yee Li and Chün-fang Yü have mentioned observing the practice of *fangsheng* in contemporary Hong Kong and Taiwan, respectively. On liberating animals in Burma, see Orwell, *Burmese Days*, 12–13. In the late nineteenth century, societies for liberating life were evident "in many parts of China," according to the commentary in Clarke, trans., "The Yü-li or Precious Records," 259. On releasing animals in honor of Sakyamuni's birthday in the early twentieth century, see Prip-Møller, *Chinese Buddhist Monasteries*, 163. On the releasing of goldfish and turtles by Buddhists in New York, see Debra West, "Good for Karma, Bad for Fish?" *New York Times*, 11 January 1997.

4. On bans imposed by Sui and Tang rulers against slaughtering animals and fish, see Weinstein, *Buddhism under the T'ang*, 43, 114, 123; and pieces in *Gujin tushu jicheng, juan* 212. For mention of Wang Qinruo's memorial, followed by Su Shi's comment that thousands of people attended the animal-releasing birthday celebration, see *Qiantang xian zhi*, "Jisheng," 44b–45a. On *fangsheng* in Tang and Song, see Zhao Yi, *Gaiyu congkao*, 699. See also Yu Zhi, *Deyi lu*, 7B.2a–2b. Societies formed in the Tang dynasty against the slaughter of animals did not specifically mention the term *fangsheng;* see Gernet, *Buddhism in Chinese Society*, 261.

5. See Bai Juyi, *Bai Juyi ji jianjiao*, 70, "Fangyu." I have been unable to find Bai's "Fangsheng yi," referred to in Yu Kai, "Xiao Yunqi fangsheng lu," 2b. Cf. also a comment by Ding Rui, whom I surmise to be of the Song dynasty, listing several reasons besides celebrating the Buddha's birthday why someone might wish to release animals: to pray for long life, to cure an illness, and out of pity for innocent animals; *Gujin tushu jicheng*, 212.2156.

6. See *Gujin tushu jicheng*, 212.2164, "Shen yi." Cited in Groot, "Miséricorde envers les animaux," 471. I have found no statement by Su Shi using the term *fangsheng hui*. One source for this assertion may be Su Shi, "Fangsheng he wei renzhu zhushou zhenfu," reproduced in Yu Zhi, *Deyi lu*, 7B.2a. Here Su Shi uses the term *huifang* (meeting for liberating animals), referring to an annual meeting at West Lake.

7. Zhang Dai (*ECCP*, 53–54) established a cockfighting society in 1622 but subsequently abandoned it after learning that he had the same birthday as a Tang emperor who was fond of cockfighting and then lost his empire; Zhang Dai, *Taoan mengyi*, 40–41; cited in Cutter, *The Brush and the Spur*, 28. On a pond for releasing animals that his maternal grandfather built in 1604 and where he subsequently released, over the course of thirty years, thousands of fish, see Zhang Dai, *Taoan mengyi*, 89–90; also Brook, *Praying for Power*, 42.

8. On Wang, see *DMB*, 1408–16; Wing-tsit Chan, introduction to *Instructions for Practical Living*, ix–xli. On Wang and his many followers, see Huang Tsung-hsi, *Records of Ming Scholars*, 100–201.

9. *Fayuan zhulin, juan* 87, *pian* 75.

10. On these two works, published in 668 and 981, respectively, see Nienhauser, Jr., ed., *The Indiana Companion*, 371–72, 744–45.

11. *Taiping guangji, juan* 118.

12. See, for example, the two collections, *DJL* and *Gujin tushu jicheng*.

13. *Diary* 1632/11/22. On Qi, see *ECCP,* 126, and chapters 6 through 8 of this book. On Yan, see Sakai, "Gan Moyu no shisō ni tsuite," 259–73.

14. *Diary* 1640/Intercalary 1/4.

15. *Diary* 1640/8/25.

16. See, for example, *Diary* 1635/12/8; 1636/1/8, 2/8, 3/8, 6/8, 7/8, 8/8, 9/8, 10/8; 1637/2/8, 4/6, 6/8, 9/8. Cf. Fuma, *Chūgoku zenkai,* 157–58, 198n43. Qi occasionally also met to liberate animals on days other than the eighth; cf. *Diary* 1637/10/15.

17. The meeting dates recorded by Feng Mengzhen in his diary follow no discernible pattern. Often meetings occurred toward the middle of the month (on the fourteenth, fifteenth, or sixteenth) or toward the end (on the twenty-ninth), but Feng also mentions meetings held on the fifth, eighth, and eleventh. See Feng Mengzhen, *juan* 58–62, passim. See also Standaert, *Yang Tingyun,* 38–40, esp. 40nn101, 103. Some writers cautioned against meeting at a fixed time or place, for fear that vendors would snap up the released animals; cf. Zhou Mengyan, *Yinzhi wen guangyi, xia.*9b.

18. Cf. Zhu Guozhen, 22.514. In the Song dynasty, Ouyang Xiu commented that during the Tang dynasty ponds for releasing life could be everywhere found; *Gujin tushu jicheng,* 212.2159.

19. Wang Siren, *Qi Zhongmin gong nianpu,* 10a, regarding the tenth month, 1635.

20. See, for example, *DJL,* "Ping ji," 1a–48a. See also Zhou Mengyan, *Yinzhi wen guangyi,* esp. *xia.*9a–15b; Yu Zhi, *Deyi lu, juan* 7. On the popular morality books in general, see Brokaw, *Ledgers of Merit and Demerit;* Sakai, *Chūgoku zenshō,* and "Confucianism and Popular Educational Works." See also Handlin, *Action in Late Ming Thought,* 186–212.

21. *DJL,* "Ping ji," 2b. See also Zhuhong, "Jiesha fangsheng wen," 14a.

22. On Feng, see *DMB*, 455–58.

23. Feng Shike, *Feng Yuancheng xuanji,* 19.39b, "An Qisheng jieniu ji."

24. The men referred to as Feng's brothers were actually half-brothers.

25. Feng Shike, *Feng Yuancheng xuanji,* 18.29b-30b, "Huo shu ji." The comparison between rats and ministers that follows would certainly have brought to readers' minds "Shi shu" (Big rat) from the *Shi jing,* Mao no. 113; Legge, *The She King, or, The Book of Poetry,* 171–72. See also Spring, *Animal Allegories,* 65. For an eighteenth-century exhortation against raising cats so as to spare the lives of rats, which are "basically harmless," see Zhou Mengyan, *Wanshan xian zi ji,* 1.7b–8a.

26. Feng Shike, *Feng Yuancheng xuanji,* 19.53a, "She yue ji."

27. Ibid., 18.13b, "Pudu an fangshengchi ji."

28. *Diary* 1638/5/8; 1639/12/20.

29. *Diary* 1635/10/15.

30. On his preface to *Diji lu*, see *Diary* 1631/12/20, 12/23.
31. *DJL*, "Ping ji," 1a.
32. On silk: Zhuhong, *Zhu chuang sui bi*, 28b, "Can si"; on meat: Zhuhong, "Jiesha fangsheng wen," 2b. The monk Hanshan Deqing also encouraged *fangsheng hui*; see Sung-peng Hsu, *A Buddhist Leader*, esp. 86–87.
33. Zhuhong, "Jiesha fangsheng wen," 3a–20b. See Yü, *Renewal of Buddhism*, 27n40, 76, 85–87. This essay is published as one piece with consecutive pagination throughout, though some commentators treat each of its parts as a separate essay. This piece is to be distinguished from another essay, "Jiesha," in Zhuhong, *Zhu chuang sui bi*, 25a–b.
34. On Wang, see *DMB*, 1408–16.
35. Zhuhong, "Jiesha fangsheng wen," 7a. Cf. Yü, *Renewal of Buddhism*, 86–87.
36. For example, excerpts from "Jiesha fangsheng wen" can be found in *DJL*, "Ping ji," 28b–29a, and Zhou Mengyan, *Wanshan xian zi ji*, 4.60b–69a.
37. Tu Long, *Qizhen quanji*, 10.24a–b, "Preface to 'Jiesha fangsheng wen.'" On Tu, see *DMB*, 1324.
38. *The Analects* (*Lun yü*), 6.20, trans. James Legge, 191. Translation modified.
39. Peng Shaosheng, *Jushi zhuan*, 42.5a–b. On Cai Chengzhi and other lay devotees, see Yü, *Renewal of Buddhism*, 90–93, esp. 93.
40. For the essay, "Fangsheng pian huo," see Tao Wangling, 13.58b–63b. On Tao, see Yü, *Renewal of Buddhism*, 85, 92–94; Peng Shaosheng, *Jushi zhuan*, 44.5b–9b (including the ten poems); and Huang Zongxi, *Mingru xuean*, 36.8a–b.
41. On Liu, see *ECCP*, 532–33.
42. Zhou Mengyan, *Yinzhi wen guangyi*, xia. 11a, citing *Guangci bian*.
43. For a biography of Huang, see *Ming shi*, 288.3238.
44. Peng Shaosheng, *Jushi zhuan*, 42.8a; Yü, *Renewal of Buddhism*, 93. In fact, Jiao Hong (*DMB*, 145–46) made distinctions between the Buddhist practice of nonkilling and the Confucian practice, which allowed the killing of animals for certain occasions and under certain conditions. See Jiao Hong, *Jiaoshi bicheng*, 2.33b–36a, "Jieshasheng lun."
45. Zhuhong, *Zhu chuang sui bi*, 25a–b, "Jiesha."
46. The only Ming item I have found that predates Zhuhong is a brief entry by Zhang Jin (1440–1501) in Meng Chaoran, *Guang'ai lu*, 17a. Texts postdating Zhuhong do, however, occasionally carry accounts of men who released animals before Zhuhong's day. Cf. the account of a mid-sixteenth-century man who failed the examinations seven times and lost numerous sons because he did good superficially, without genuine feeling, releasing animals while continuing to eat meat; see Carus and Suzuki, ed. and trans., *T'ai-Shang Kan-Ying P'ien*, 114. For essays by Qi's father on the avoidance of killing, see Qi Chenghan, *Dansheng tang ji*, 16.67b–72b, 76a–b. See also Zhou Rudeng's declaration that everyone, ignorant and wise, should bestir themselves to follow the lessons of Qi Chenghan's essay; *Dongyue zhengxue lu*, 10.42b.
47. The pertinent passage is translated in Yü, *Renewal of Buddhism*, p. 67. See also Groner, "The *Fan-wan ching*"; Groot, *Le code du Mahāyāna en chine*.
48. On the taboo against eating beef as a blend of Confucian, Daoist, and Buddhist beliefs serving a moral community from the Song dynasty on, see Goossaert, *L'interdit du boeuf en chine*, esp. 9–10; see also 66 (that even Zhuhong made exceptions);

and 178 (on the strict Confucian Liu Zongzhou endorsing the taboo on meat consumption). For Liu Zongzhou's statement, see his *Renpu, fu leiji*, 5.97–98.

49. Cf. Yü, *Renewal of Buddhisn*, 66.

50. On the relationship between the theme of *shengsheng* ("perpetual renewal of life"), developed by Luo Rufang (*DMB*, 975–78), and Zhuhong's ideas, see Fuma, *Chūgoku zenkai*, esp. 163. One of Zhuhong's admirers, the playwright Tang Xianzu (*ECCP*, 708–9), was a student of Luo's.

51. Wang Heng, 11.13a, "Fangsheng ting ji." On Wang, see *DMB*, 1378. On Tanyangzi (née Wang Daozhen), see *DMB*, 1427–30, and Waltner, "Visionary and Bureaucrat."

52. *The Analects* 7.26, trans. Legge, 203: "The master angled,—but did not use a net. He shot,—but not at birds perching." Many cite this passage to indicate a proscription against killing without paying due attention to its original implication that killing, if restrained, would be acceptable. See Gui Zhuang, *Gui Zhuang ji*, 6.371, "Fangsheng ji."

53. Legge, trans., *The Works of Mencius*, 141 (*Mencius* IA.8) (wording altered). Of course, Mencius and Zhuhong had entirely different messages. In *The Book of Mencius*, King Xuan of Qi simply substituted one animal for another, Mencius instructed that one should avoid the kitchen (without avoiding eating meats), and the main focus was on the topics of humaneness and profit, not abstention from meat (ibid., 140). Cf. Zhou Rudeng, who declared that keeping a distance from the kitchen and "not killing without reason" are "Confucian teachings that should not be neglected"; *Dongyue zhengxue lu*, 6.10a, "Chong jiansu."

54. Qian Qianyi, *Muzhai chuxue ji*, 26.825, "Fangsheng shuo." On Qian, see *ECCP*, 149–50. The Song statesman Wang Anshi instituted the New Policies, a radical program for reforming the economy and taxation, with the goals of strengthening the state and benefiting the people; in the end he managed to alienate and anger many landholding literati.

55. Gui Zhuang, *Gui Zhuang ji*, 6.371. On Gui Zhuang, see *ECCP*, 427. On Gui Youguang, see *DMB*, 759–61.

56. Xie Zhaozhe, *Wu zazu*, 15.23b. On Xie, see *DMB*, 546–50.

57. On Meng, see *ECCP*, 571–72.

58. Meng Chaoran, *Guang'ai lu*, 27a. On Chen Di, see *DMB*, 180–84.

59. Meng Chaoran, *Guang'ai lu*, 5b, 6b. That Chen Di and the Cheng brothers actually dabbled in Buddhism is irrelevant; in Meng Chaoran's eyes, they were quintessentially Confucian.

60. Ibid., 42b.

61. On Yang, see *DMB*, 1546–47; Handlin, *Action in Late Ming Thought*, 65–83; Des Forges, *Cultural Centrality*, 35–51.

62. Zhuhong, "Jiesha fangsheng wen," 6b–7a; Chün-fang Yü, *Renewal of Buddhism*, 86.

63. Zhuhong, *Shanfang zalu*, 2.15a, "Diaoyi shuo."

64. Araki, *Yōmeigaku no kaiten to Bukkyō*, 236–39.

65. Cited in Peng Shaosheng, *Jushi zhuan*, 47.1a ("ren shi yang, yang shi ren"). See also Meng Chaoran, *Guang'ai lu*, 1b. Cf. Zhou Mengyan, *Wanshan xian zi ji*, 1.14a–b. "The *Śūraṃgama sūtra* says: 'Because man eats ram, ram is killed by man'" (*yi ren shi yang, yang si wei ren*). Yan Maoyou similarly argues that by liberating animals

one can break away from an endless chain of successive killings; see *DJL,* "Ping ji," 1a.

66. Gernet, *China and the Christian Impact,* 44, 71.

67. Yü, *Renewal of Buddhism,* 87–90. On Yu Chunxi, see also Gernet, *China and the Christian Impact,* 44, 71, 256n110.

68. Zhuhong, "Jiesha fangsheng wen," 9b; Yang Dongming, *Shanju gongke,* 8.29b; cf. also Yan Maoyou, who criticized the view that animals are created to nourish people; *DJL,* "Ping ji," 10b.

69. Yü, *Renewal of Buddhism,* 87.

70. Legge, trans., *The Works of Mencius,* 139–40 (*Mencius* 1A.4–6). Translation modified. Commenting on King Hui's subsitution, Qiu Weibing argued that the practice of liberating lives in his day was, despite its strong Buddhist content, superior to that of ancient times; *Qiu Bangshi wenji,* 7b–8b, "Guang fangsheng hui yin."

71. Meng Chaoran, *Guang'ai lu,* 3b.

72. Zhou Rudeng, *Dongyue zhengxue lu,* 6.10a, "Chong jiansu."

73. Wang Heng, *Wang Goushan xiansheng ji,* 5.37a.

74. Feng Shike, *Feng Yuancheng xuanji,* 19.53a, "Sheyue ji."

75. *DMB,* 456.

76. Zhuhong, *Zhu chuang sui bi,* 25a–b, "Jiesha." Echoing this view, a writer of the Qianlong period asked: "Given that the foods and flavors available in the markets today are very bountiful, why need we for the purposes of food preparation slaughter even more than the ancients did?" See Meng Chaoran, *Guang'ai lu,* 27b, citing *Jiazheng xu zhi,* by Zhang Zhentao (1693–1780) of Fujian (Min).

77. Xie Zhaozhe, *Wu zazu,* 15.22a–23b.

78. On Qi's garden and the moral dilemmas posed by wealth, see chapter 6.

79. *Diary* 1640/6/16.

80. Yu Zhi, commenting on a piece by Peng Dingqiu exhorting people to establish *fangsheng* societies; see Yu Zhi, *Deyi lu,* 7A.1a. On Peng, see *ECCP,* 616–17.

81. Meng Chaoran, *Guang'ai lu,* 2b–3a, citing a Song text.

82. Zhou Mengyan, *Wanshan xian zi ji,* 1.15a–b.

83. Zhou Mengyan, *Yinzhi wen guangyi,* 1.4a. On the ancestor, Lin Cong, see *DMB,* 1582.

84. On Fan, see Twitchett, "The Fan Clan's Charitable Estate." On the notion that Fan died penniless, see chapter 4.

85. Wang Heng, *Wang Goushan xiansheng ji,* 21.5b–6a; "Jiesha wen."

86. Qian Sule, *Qian Zhongjie gong ji,* 4.13b–14a. On Qian, see *Ming shi,* 276.3106.

87. Feng Shike, *Feng Yuancheng xuanji,* 19.53a–54a, "Sheyue ji."

88. Wang Chongjian. *Qingxiang tang wenji,* 6.40a. On Wang, see *ECCP,* 815.

89. Feng Shike, *Feng Yuancheng xuanji,* 19.39b.

90. Qi Junjia, *Dunweng suibi, xia,* 18b.

91. Meng Chaoran, *Guang'ai lu,* 27b, citing *Jia zheng xu zhi,* by Zhang Zhentao.

92. See Zhuhong, *Zhu chuang er bi,* 22a–b, "Jie she hui" translation is from Yü, *Renewal of Buddhism,* 78. On Zhuhong stressing the importance of open ceremonies; see ibid., 84.

93. However, the Song account deals with the scholar alone; and although it may be read allegorically to refer to an unsated overlord, it does not explicitly involve collective activity.

94. *DJL,* "Ping ji," 6b–7a, citing Cai Xiang (fl. 1023). For another version, see Meng Chaoran, *Guang'ai lu,* 15b, citing Chen Yanxiao (Song dynasty), *Gengqi shihua.* In the *Guang'ai lu* version, one quail speaks on behalf of the thousands killed.

95. Cited in Meng Chaoran, *Guang'ai lu,* 8b; for "zi koufu zhi yu," see ibid., 7b; see also 4a, 9b, 37b. Far more parsimonious was the nineteenth-century Yu Zhi, who, though applauding the liberating of animals, maintained that, if dead, animals should be given to old people's homes and poorhouses; *Deyi lu,* 7A.4b, commenting on regulations by Peng Dingqiu.

96. Zhuhong, "Jiesha fangsheng wen," 10a.

97. Cited in Meng Chaoran, *Guang'ai lu,* 20a. On Gao, see *DMB,* 701–10 and chapter 2 of this book.

98. Tang Xianzu, *Tang Xianzu ji,* 30.1040, "Zhuhong xiansheng jiesha wen xu." On Tang, see *ECCP,* 708–9.

99. Meng Chaoran, *Guang'ai lu,* 37b.

100. On ancient textual sources, see Gernet, "Pitié pour les animaux," 293–94.

101. Eliasberg, "Practiques funéraires animales," 119–21.

102. Ibid., 140. The practice of burying at least some animals continued into later centuries. Qi and his brothers, accompanied by two Buddhist clerics, buried a turtle and chanted hymns in its honor; *Diary* 1640/5/4.

103. *Taiping guang ji,* 118.829, "Xiong Shen."

104. Her regard for the spider's intelligence was earnest. When she noticed upon reaching the end of the chapter that the spider had died, she gave it a burial and had a small stupa built over the grave; Peng Shaosheng, *Jushi zhuan,* 46.1a. Cf. a story about a centipede heeding Zhuhong's instruction, discussed in Yü, *Renewal of Buddhism,* 79.

105. *DJL,* "Ping ji," 10b and 3a, respectively. Cf. also ibid., 2b. Similarly, Zhuhong promoted nonkilling on the grounds that "all creatures with blood and breath have knowledge" (preface by Yan Na to Zhuhong, "Jiesha fangsheng wen"), 1a.

106. Zhuhong, *Zhu chuang sui bi,* 25a–b, "Jiesha."

107. Zhuhong, "Jiesha fangsheng wen," 8a.

108. Hu Zhi, *Henglu jingshe cang gao,* 14.4b.

109. Zhi Dalun, *Zhi Huaping xiansheng ji,* 22.10a, "Fangsheng he yue ji." In this piece, "An Agreement Concering a River for Saving Lives," Zhi was as concerned about water rights as he was about the lives of fish. For an illustration of one such waterway in Shandong guarded by a stele prohibiting fishermen, see *Zichuan xian zhi* (1743), 1.23b–24a. In some instances, designatng a pond for liberating fish was done to guard water bodies from fishermen or to resolve property disputes. On Zhi Dalun, see *Jiashan xian zhi* (1786), 13A.10b.

110. Zhou Mengyan, *Yinzhi wen guangyi, xia.*9a–b.

111. *Taiping guang ji,* 118.827, "Wei Dan."

112. Ibid., 118.824, 826.

113. Zhuhong, "Jiesha fangsheng wen," 5b. Elsewhere Zhuhong dwells on the cutting, scraping, and beheading of animals, and boiling and marinating them alive, see Zhuhong, *Yigao,* 30–31, 3.47a, "Pu quan jiesha fangsheng."

114. Zhuhong, "Jiesha fangsheng wen," 9a–b. The protagonist is from the Eastern Jin dynasty and is mentioned in *Wei shu, juan* 46, and *Taiping guang ji,* 14.98–100.

115. For pioneering comments on this theme, see Hsia, "Time and the Human Con-

dition," 250; and Pei-kai Cheng, "Reality and Imagination," 254–94, passim. Subsequently numerous scholars have explored this theme, mainly in reference to literary works. See, for example, Martin W. Huang, *Desire and Fictional Narrative,* esp. chap. 1 (regarding Tu Long and Tang Xianzu); and Chang, *The Late-Ming Poet Ch'en Tzu-lung.*

116. Zhuhong, "Jiesha fangsheng wen," 9b.

117. Tang Xianzu, *Tang Xianzu ji,* 30.1040.

118. Legge, trans., *The Works of Mencius,* 139–40 (*Mencius* 1A.4–6).

119. Zhuhong, "Jiesha fangsheng wen," 3a–b.

120. Tang Xianzu, *Tang Xianzu ji,* 30.1040.

121. Cf. Groot, *Le code du Mahāyāna,* 467; Yü, *Renewal of Buddhism,* 68.

122. Xie Zhaozhe, *Wu za zu,* 15.23a.

123. *Taiping guangji,* 118.824, "Mao Bao"; 829, "Wang Xingsi"; 826, "Yan Tai," respectively.

124. Zhi Dalun, *Zhi Huaping xiansheng ji,* "Fangsheng he yue shuo," in *Zhi Huaping xiansheng ji,* 10.10a–11a.

125. Deviating even further from putative Buddhist origins were the ceremonies for liberating animals in Japan, where the practice was amalgamated with Shinto in the Hachiman cult; Law, "Violence, Ritual, Reenactment, and Ideology."

126. Zhuhong, "Jiesha fangsheng wen," 8b.

127. Cowell, ed., *The Jātaka,* 1:34–36, no. 11 (stags); 1:91–92, no. 36 (birds); 1:256–67, no. 114 (fish).

128. An exception is a tale about interactions between a tortoise and monkey in *Fayuan zhulin,* 75.5b–6a, which, to my knowledge, was not retold in Ming-Qing materials on *fangsheng.* On the types of animals appearing in the Jātaka tales, see Chapple, "Animals and the Environment," esp. 134–36. On animals in *The Jātaka* committing wicked as well as good deeds, see McDermott, "Animals and Humans," 269.

129. Cowell, 1:114–15, no. 43 (viper); 1:95–98, no. 38 (crab).

130. Some early tales of kindness to rats can be found in *Taiping guangji* 118.825, "Cai Xifu"; and Spring, *Animal Allegories,* 73, citing *Taiping guangji,* 440.3591–92, "Li Jia." In both accounts, though, the rats in time used their powers to reward their benefactors.

131. On "the complex relationship between sympathetic concern for animals and manipulation of people" see Ritvo, *The Animal Estate,* 131.

132. Meng Chaoran, *Guang'ai lu,* 4a, citing Song Jingwen (fl. Song dynasty).

133. Zhuhong, *Zhu chuang er bi,* 35a–b, "Fangsheng ji." See also report by Tao Wangling, *Xie an ji,* 14.24b.

134. Zhuhong, "Jiesha fangsheng wen," 9b.

135. Gui Zhuang, *Gui Zhuang ji,* 6.372, "Fangsheng chi."

136. Feng Shike, *Feng Yuancheng xuanji,* 18.31a, "Shengying ji."

137. Ibid., 18.14b, "Pudu'an fangshengchi ji."

138. *DJL,* "Ping ji," 10b, 13a.

139. Lu Longqi, *Sanyutang wenji,* 10.10b–11a, "Dinghui hu fangsheng ji."

140. Meng Chaoran, *Guang'ai lu,* 13b.

141. Ibid., 41a. On Yao, see *ECCP,* 900.

142. See, for example, *DJL,* and Yu Zhi, *Deyi lu.*

143. *QBJJ*, 2.29, "Shiyao ji shi"; dated 6/8/1636.

144. *QBJJ*, 2.31, "Shiyao ji shi."

145. For a *fangsheng* society of the Kangxi period that used surplus funds "to do other good deeds," see Wu Chenyan, "Fangsheng hui yue," 3b.

146. For answers to six questions (including, "Is not saving animals like child's play?"), see Tao Wangling, *Xie an ji*, 13.59a, "Fangsheng pianhuo." For responses to twelve questions, see Yu Zhi, *Deyi lu*, 7A.6a–8a, "Fangsheng jueyi," author unknown. On obstructionists who oppose doing good on the grounds that aiding people is more important than releasing animals, see *Fushou quanshu*, 4.12b.

147. Standaert, *Yang Tingyun*, 40–41, 62–63.

148. Chen Longzheng, *Jiting quanshu*, 24.2a–b, "Tongshan hui jiangyu."

149. Lu Shiyi, *Sibian lu jiyao*, 16.22a–b.

150. Zhang Dafu, *Meihua cao tang bitan*, 34, "Fangsheng"; Tao Wangling, *Xie an ji*, 13.60b. See also Zhang Dai's account of the sorry state of fish crowded in ponds and animals caged on monastery grounds; *Xihu mengxun*, 63.

151. Wu Chenyan, "Fangsheng hui yue," 3a–b.

152. Tao Wangling, *Xie an ji*, 13.61a.

153. *Diary* 1640/2/10. Qiu Weibing makes a similar point: "Not only do the insects and fish get to survive, but the fishermen get money"; 10.8a–b, "Guang fangsheng hui yin."

154. *Diary* 1635/12/8.

155. *Diary* 1640 2/10. Qi uses the term *shi*. Wang Siren, *Qi Zhongmin gong nianpu*, gives the more modest measure *hu;* 11b. See also the entry on the distribution of a thousand taels for *fangsheng* (accompanied by inviting monks to read sutras) in *Diary* 1642/3/19; and, for comment that many lives were saved, *Diary* 1640/4/22.

156. *DJL*, "Ping ji," 10b.

157. Yu Zhi, *Deyi lu*, 471, citing *Yinzhi wen xinjie*, clearly one of the numerous variants of the "texts of secret acts" that circulated widely from the late Ming through the Qing. See Sakai, *Chūgoku zenshō*, chap. 6.

2. EARLY BENEVOLENT SOCIETIES AND THEIR VISIONARY LEADERS

1. On Yang, see *DMB*, 1546–47; Handlin, *Action in Late Ming Thought*, 65–83. See also Fuma, *Chūgoku zenkai*, esp. 92–97; Huang Zongxi, *Mingru xuean*, 29.8b–9a; Des Forges, *Cultural Centrality*, 35–51.

   For an exhaustive survey of benevolent societies from the late Ming through the nineteenth century, see Fuma, *Chūgoku zenkai*. This work grew out of and incorporated material from his articles "Dōzenkai shōshi" and "Zenkai zentō no suppatsu." See also Liang Qizi, *Shishan yu jiaohua*.

2. Yang, 1.7a, "Tongshan hui xu." For Lü Kun's declaration that the true gentleman ought to put surplus funds in a granary, see his *Quwei zhai wenji*, 3.24b–26a, "Tongshan cang xu." See also Fuma, *Chūgoku zenkai*, 73; and, for Lü Kun's thoughts on poorhouses (*yangji yuan*) and "the perpetual renewal of life" (*shengsheng*), 67–78.

3. Fuma, *Chūgoku zenkai*, 105.

4. See Chan, *Religious Trends in Modern China*, 174; see also 164–65.

5. Thompson, trans. and annot., *Mao Zedong*, 114–15, 249n53.
6. For a survey of poorhouses, whose history extends back to the Song dynasty (when they went by other names); promotion of poorhouses by Ming emperors; and material regarding examples of the gazetteers, see Hoshi, "Mindai no Yōsaiin ni tsuite," 131–50. For mention of *yangji yuan*, see also Chen, 26.19a–b; 23.16a; 20.17b–18a.
7. On the spread of cotton to the north during the sixteenth century, see Yan Zhongping, *Zhongguo mianfangzhi shi kao*, 19–20. By the late Ming and early Qing, roughly 80 percent of all counties in China were producing some cotton cloth, according to Dietrich, "Cotton Culture." See also Wiens, "Cotton Textile Production," 516.
8. Cf. Des Forges, *Cultural Centrality*, 140–42, which emphasizes the robustness of the late Ming Henan economy, but acknowledges that it was highly dependent on roads rather than the more efficient waterways.
9. Yang, 1.2b, "Cao xian shecang xu."
10. The phrase "Luo Society" might also allude to a poetry society formed by Ouyang Xiu or to a wine-drinking society formed by Sima Guang and others.
11. Yang, 1.7a.
12. Yang, 1.7a.
13. See, for example, *Jiashan xian zhi* (1800), 14.32b, 53b.
14. Yang, 1.8a–b.
15. Yang, 1.8a.
16. Yang, 1.8b.
17. Yang, 1.8b.
18. Yang, 1.8b.
19. Yang, 1.9a.
20. Yang, 1.9a.
21. Yang, 1.7a–b. For one such mutual aid sect, serving boatmen who worked the Grand Canal, which had its origins in the sixteenth century, see Kelley, "Temples and Tribute Fleets," 363.
22. Gernet, *Buddhism in Chinese Society*, 260.
23. Wang Zongpei, *Zhongguo zhi hehui*, 4.
24. Ibid., 87.
25. A small discrepancy: Yang's account specifies that thirty-one residents participated; the list appended to his account gives only twenty-nine names. Appended to the list are three nonresidents. See Yang, 1.9b.
26. Yang, 1.11a–b.
27. Yang, 1.9b.
28. Yang, 1.11b–12a.
29. Yang, 1.9b.
30. Yang, 1.11b.
31. Yang, 1.12a.
32. Yang, 1.8a.
33. Yang, 2.1a–2b.
34. Yang, 1.9b–10a.
35. Yang, 1.4b.
36. Yang, 1.10a.

37. Yang, 1.10a–b.

38. Yang, 1.9b.

39. Yang, 1.7b.

40. Yang, 1.7a–b. The second reference is to Song Jiao, who, though poor, showed reverence for life by providing thousands of ants with a bamboo bridge enabling them to escape downpouring rain; for a Qing version of this account, see Zhou Mengyan, *Yinzhi wen guangyi, shou.*10a ; see also *shang.*27a.

41. Yang, 1.2a–b.

42. Yang, 3.1a–2a.

43. Yang, 1.14a–15b. The donations listed actually add up to 180 ounces.

44. Yang, 1.15b–17b.

45. Yang, 1.25a–b.

46. *Zhuangzi*, "Pian mu," trans. Legge, *The Writings of Chuang Tzu*, 319.

47. Yang, 1.25a–b.

48. Yang, 1.26a.

49. The memorial is reprinted in *Yucheng xian zhi* (1895), 8.6b–11, but with the erroneous date of 1604 (Wanli 32). Tan Qian, *Guo que*, 4722 has 1594 (Wanli 22). Regarding the memorial and for reproductions of the illustrations (or later copies of them), see Des Forges, *Cultural Centrality*, 35–46. See also Yim, "Famine Relief Statistics," 4–5. Yim estimates that over twelve million Henan residents received aid, ibid., 13.

50. Fuma, *Chūgoku zenkai*, 92–93, 136n7, citing Zhong Hongdao, [Guangxu] *Tongxiang xian zhi, juan* 4, under "shan tang." See also Chen, 23.13a.

51. Gao, 9A.41b, "Tongshan hui xu"; Fuma, *Chūgoku zenkai*, 97, 138n14. On Qian Yiben, see Huang Zongxi, *Mingru xue'an*, 59.1a–b.

52. Gao, 9A.41b–42a; see also Chen, 7.5a; 23.13a–b. Gao visited Qian Yiben in Piling in 1593; see *Gao nianpu*, 7a. On Gao Panlong, see additional materials in appendix ("Fulu") to Gao; *DMB*, 701–10; Huang Tsung-hsi, *Records of Ming Scholars*, 234–43; Taylor, *The Cultivation of Sagehood*.

53. On Chen Youxue, see *Ming shi*, 281.3161; Busch, "The Tung-lin Shu-yüan," 136. Queshan is in Runing prefecture. See also *Qiantang xian zhi* (1718), 24.5b.

54. Gao, 9A.42a.

55. In addition to Gao and Chen there were Ye Maocai, An Xifan, and Liu Yuanzhen. See Fuma, *Chūgoku zenkai*, 98.

56. A set of regulations for the benevolent society has been attributed to Gao in Yu Zhi, *Deyi lu*, 1B.2a–3b, but authorship is ambiguous, for it does not appear in extant collections of Gao's works. The set, with some variations, appears in Chen, 23.14b–18b. On the uncertain authorship, see Fuma, *Chūgoku zenkai*, 141–42n58. Gao is also said to have written something entitled "Record of the Benevolent Society" (Tongshan hui lu); see *Gao nianpu*, 36a. To my knowledge, this work no longer survives. See also Fuma, *Chūgoku zenkai*, 109.

57. *Gao nianpu*, 2a.

58. This uncle was his grandfather's younger brother; see *Gao nianpu*, 1b; *DMB*, 701.

59. *Gao nianpu*, 11b.

60. *Gao nianpu*, 11b.

61. *Gao nianpu*, 31a.

62. Gao, 10B.24b.

63. *Gao nianpu,* 17b.
64. *Gao nianpu,* 31b.
65. This was in 1585; see *Gao nianpu,* 3b.
66. *Gao nianpu,* 4a–b, 1585.
67. *Gao nianpu,* 6b.
68. Twitchett, "The Fan Clan's Charitable Estate," 99–100.
69. *Gao nianpu,* 11b.
70. *Gao nianpu,* 14b, 31b. See also Ye Maocai's biographical narrative of Gao, in *Gao,* "Fulu," 45a–b; and Gao's biography of Gu Xiancheng, his fellow cofounder of the Donglin Academy, in Gao, 11B.26b: that Gu admired Fan Zhongyan, was himself charitable to the needy, and donated property to help the poor and of his lineage and draftees of his borough (*qu*).
71. "Kunxue ji"; see Taylor, *The Cultivation of Sagehood,* 125 ff.; Pei-yi Wu, *The Confucian's Progress,* 131–41.
72. *Gao nianpu,* 13a.
73. *DMB,* 704–8. On the Donglin Academy and the political tribulations of its associates, see Hucker, "The Tung-lin Movement," 132–62; Busch, "The Tung-lin Shuyüan": 1–163; Meskill, "Academies and Politics in the Ming Dynasty"; Dardess, *Blood and History in China.* Also see *The Cambridge History of China,* vol. 7, part 1, *The Ming Dynasty, 1368–1644,* 532–44.
74. An allusion to *The Analects;* see Legge, trans., *Confucian Analects,* 313. Legge, following Kong Anguo, insists that this is not to be understood as to "learn with painful effort"; ibid., 314. I follow Rodney Taylor, who in turn followed Arthur Waley in rendering the title as *Recollections on the Toils of Learning* (*The Cultivation of Sagehood,* 121).
75. Gao, 9A.41b–43a.
76. Gao, 9A.42a.
77. Gao, 9A.42a–b.
78. Gao, 9A.42b. See also. Brokaw, *Ledgers of Merit and Demerit,* 141–42. In a memorial on local governance that he drafted but did not submit, Gao similarly placed general moral integrity above charity in his ranking of three kinds of "good people": the best are those who are filial and brotherly; and "the next best are those who, having been stirred by a sense of righteousness/justice, like to be charitable (*haoshi*)"; see Gao, 7.35a.
79. Gao, 9A.42b–43a.
80. Gao, 9A.43a.
81. Gao, 11A.21a–25a.
82. Gao, 9B.15b–16a.
83. *Gao nianpu,* 28b. So Gao reported on the eve of his suicide.
84. See Hucker, "Su-chou and the Agents of Wei Chung-hsien."
85. An Xifan, Ye Maocai, Chen Youxue, and Liu Yuanzhen. See Fuma, *Chūgoku zenkai,* 98. For biographies of these four men, see *Donglin shuyuan zhi,* 8.7a–b (An), 8.8a–14b (Ye), 8.15a–16a (Chen), 8.22a–26a (Liu).
86. Gao, 11A.32b (on Liu Yuanzhen); see also *Donglin shuyuan zhi,* 8.23b–26a.
87. Gao, 11A.33a. An allusion to an anecdote from the *Zhanguo ze,* in which someone lost a snake-drawing contest; he finished first but then added legs, with the result that his drawing, no longer representing a snake, was disqualified. In

a marginal comment on this point, Gao's follower Chen Longzheng wryly remarked that simple-minded people would of course think joining to be superfluous.

88. On Chen, see *DMB*, 174; Mizoguchi, "Iwayuru Tōrinha jinshi no shisō," 111–341; Araki, "Chin Ryūsei no shisō," 1:1–16; and Fujita, "Minmatsu Kashan fu Kakyō hen ni okeru kyūkō ni tsuite," 23–44. Much information on Chen may also be gleaned from Fuma, *Chūgoku zenkai*.

89. Huang Tsung-hsi, *Records of Ming Scholars*, 240.

90. Chen, 21.18a, "Kunxue shuo." Chen later turned against Buddhism and cautioned that making contributions to Buddhist activities would ruin "the good name of charity" (Chen, 22.23b).

91. Chen, 21.18a–b. See also Chen Kui, "Chen Cibu," 1.1a–b.

92. Chen, 21.14a.

93. Chen, 21.14b.

94. Chen, 21.2b.

95. Chen, 21.1b.

96. Chen, 21.1a.

97. Chen, 21.1b.

98. Chen Kui, "Chen Cibu," 1.1a.

99. Ibid., 1.2a.

100. On Yuan, see *DMB*, 1632–35. See also Liu Ts'un-yan, "Yüan Huang," 108–32; Sakai, *Chūgoku zensho*, 318–55; Brokaw, *Ledgers of Merit and Demerit*.

101. Chen Kui, "Chen Zibu," 1b. The term "filial spirit" (*xiaosi*) comes from the *Shijing*, "Xia wu," trans. Legge, *The She King, or, The Book of Poetry*, 459. On Yuwang's receiving advice on accumulating merit, see Chen, 21.15b.

102. *DMB*, 1632–35; Sakai, "Confucianism and Popular Education Works," 344; Brokaw, *Ledgers of Merit and Demerit*, 64–95; Liu Ts'un-yan, "Yüan Huang."

103. Chen, 21.18a.

104. Chen Kui, "Chen Cibu," 1:1b; Okuzaki, *Chūgoku kyōshin jinushi no kenkyū*, 291–92.

105. Chen, 22.1b. See also Fuma, *Chūgoku zenkai*, 100, 138n27; Chen, 41.17a–b, letter in response to Qian Shisheng.

106. On Zhang, see *DMB*, 53–61.

107. *Jiashan xian zhi* (1800), 6.18a–b. On Qian see *DMB*, 237–39. See also the chronological biography *(nianpu)*, appended to his *Ciyu tang ji*.

108. *Jiashan xian zhi* (1800), 6.18b.

109. Ibid., 9A, "Xu zheng," 8a. See also Gu Qiyuan, *Lan zhen caotang ji*, 19.49a–52b.

110. Gao, 7.13a–14b.

111. Gao, 7.14b, Chen's marginal commentary. Chen's preface to Gao is dated 1631.

112. Chen Kui, "Chen Cibu," 1.5a–b. Zhou received the *juren* degree in 1621 and was recognized in the local gazetteer for his generosity, particularly for providing coffins to bring bodies home; *Jiashan xian zhi* (1800), 14.10a. Wei received the *juren* degree in 1642. See also Fuma, *Chūgoku zenkai*, 139n26.

113. Chen, 41.14a–b.

114. Chen, 14.17b, letter to Qian Shisheng. See also Fuma, *Chūgoku zenkai*, 100–103.

115. Chen, 23.13b.

116. See Yu Zhi, *Deyi lu*, 1.2a. See also Chen, 23.13a–19b. Comparing the two ver-

sions, Fuma deduces that the piece in *Deyi lu* ascribed to Gao was probably the original; see his *Chūgoku zenkai,* 141–42n58.

117. Chen, 23.13a–b, 7.5a.
118. Ding Bin, *Ding Qinghui gong yiji,* 8.3b–4a, letter to Yang Dongming.
119. Gui Zhuang, *Gui Zhuang ji,* 3.176–77, "Tongshan hui yue xu." On Gui, see *ECCP,* 427.
120. Peng Dingqiu, *Nanyun wengao,* 2.31a. On Peng, see *ECCP,* 616–17. Peng was introduced to *The Exalted One's Tract on Action and Response* (*Taishang gan-ying bian*) by his father and wrote several pieces on that work; *Nanyun wengao,* 2.1a–6b.
121. *Fengjing xiaozhi,* 2.6a–b. For identification of Huang Xuehai as Huang Yang, see *Jiashan xian zhi* (1800), 14.52a. For "Fengjing tongshan hui guitiao" (1744), see Yu Zhi, *Deyi lu,* 1B.3b–5b.
122. Chen, 24.1b.
123. Chen, 24.15b.
124. Fuma, *Chūgoku zenkai,* 99.
125. Chen, 24.15b. See also Fuma, *Chūgoku zenkai,* 102–3.

3. THE BENEVOLENT SOCIETY AMONG ITS ALTERNATIVES

1. Chen Kui, "Chen Cibu," 1.4a. See also Chen, 41.10b, where, in letter of 1630 to Tu Yuqian, on military matters, Chen asks, what is greater than *shengsheng?*
2. Gao, 3.26a.
3. Legge, trans., *The Works of Mencius,* 464 (*Mencius* 7.1).
4. Chen Kui, "Chen Cibu," 1.3b; see also 4a on *shengsheng.* On *shengsheng,* see Fuma, *Chūgoku zenkai,* pp. 100, 126. On the cock crowing and Gao Panlong, see Araki, "Chin Ryūsei no shisō," 10.
5. *Concordance to Yi Jing,* "Great Appendix" (Da Xici), *shang.*5.
6. On Luo, see *DMB,* 975–79. On his teachings as catalyst, see Hsia, "Time and the Human Condition in the Plays of T'ang Hsien-tsu," 249–50. Huang Zongxi, *Mingru xue'an,* 34.2b, 10a; See also Handlin, *Action in Late Ming Thought,* 41–54; Cheng Yu-yin, *Wan Ming bei yiwang de sixiangjia Luo Rufang.*
7. Yang, 5.21a; see also 1.2a, 5.30b–31a, 5.40b.
8. Chen, 16.13b.
9. Chen commentary, appended to Gao's "Zhi tian shuo," in Gao, 3.27b.
10. Chen, 24.2a. Chen's extant lectures (Tongshan hui jiangyu) are from meetings 1 (spring 1632), Chen, 24.1a–2b; 2 (summer 1632), Chen, 24.2b–5b; 3 (autumn 1632), Chen, 24.5b–7a; 5 (spring 1633), Chen, 24.7b–8b; 6 (summer 1633), Chen, 24.9a–10a; 7 (autumn 1633), Chen, 24.10a–12b; 14 (summer 1635), Chen, 24.13a–15a; 40 (winter 1641), Chen, 24.15a–18a; and 51 (autumn 1644), Chen, 24.20a–22b. Chen Longzheng received an official post in 1637, returned to Jiashan in 1640, and went back to the capital in 1642. Whether the extant lectures comprise all the lectures Chen gave is unclear.
11. Chen, 25.1a, "Gengwu ji jiuhuang shiyi."
12. Chen, 24.1a.
13. Wang Lanyin, "Mingdai zhi xiangyue," 107. On Wang Yangming's *xiangyue,* see his *Instructions for Practical Living,* 298–306; on the dating of Wang's *xiangyue,*

see ibid., 298n18. See also Hsiao, *Rural China*, 184–205; Sakai, *Chūgoku zensho*, 42–56; and Littrup, *Subbureaucratic Government in China in Ming Times*, esp. 162–73. On Song antecedents, see Übelhör, "The Community Compact (*Hsiang-yüeh*) of the Sung," 371–88. See also Hauf, "The Community Covenant." On the conscious use of a colloquial style by *xiangyue* organizers, see Wang Lanyin, "Mingdai zhi xiangyue," 116, citing "Shengyu jieshuo." Much may be gleaned about *xiangyue* sponsored by Wang Yangming's follower Luo Rufang in Cheng Yu-yin, *Wan Ming bei yiwang de sixiangjia Luo Rufang.*

14. On the *baojia* and *xiangyue,* see Brook, "The Spatial Structure of Ming Local Administration," esp. 37–43.
15. Gao, 7.29a–b, "Shenyan xianyue zecheng zhouxian shu."
16. Chen, 24.1b.
17. Chen, 45.20b–21b, letter of 1638; cited in Fuma, *Chūgoku zenkai*, 128, 145n86.
18. Chen, 23.15b.
19. Gao, 12.33a. The Six Maxims was but part of a program through which the Ming founder, who is best known as Zhu Yuanzhang or Ming Taizu, tried to reorganize village organization; see *The Cambridge History of China*, vol. 7, pt. 1, 178–79. On the Six Maxims, see also: Hsiao, *Rural China*, 186; Sakai, *Chūgoku zenshō*, 42–54; Wang Lanyin, "Mingdai zhi xiangyue," esp. 107 and (for Wang Qinnuo's lecture on the Six Maxims), 116–20; Chen, 24.1b, 22a. On the evolving relationship between the Six Imperial Maxims and the *xiangyue*, see Sakai, *Chūgoku zensho*, 39–54. According to Sakai, the Six Maxims were introduced to the community-compact system during the Jiajing period and had spread throughout China by the Wanli period.
20. Gao, 12.35b. The version of this lecture published in the Qing-dynasty anthology *Deyi lu* omits the words praising the Ming founder, probably because Qing rulers wished to delegitimize their Ming predecessors. In fact, Gao Huangdi had been a brutal and ruthless ruler.
21. Gao, 12.35a–b.
22. Gao, 12.35b.
23. Gao, 12.34b; cf. 12.33a; see also 12.35b–36a.
24. Gao, 12.33a.
25. Gao, 12.33a–b.
26. Wang Lanyin, "Mingdai zhi xiangyue," 117, citing Wang Qinruo as recorded in *Xiangcheng [Henan] xian zhi,* Wanli edition.
27. Although the term *Japanese pirates* was widely used, many pirates were Chinese. Even Portuguese pirates worked the coastal areas. See So, *Japanese Piracy in Ming China,* esp. 69–70.
28. Gao, 12.33b–34a.
29. Wang Lanyin, "Mingdai zhi xiangyue," 107.
30. Wang Yangming, *Instructions for Practical Living,* 300.
31. Chen, 23.14b.
32. Wang Lanyin, "Mingdai zhi Xiangyue," 113.
33. Gao, 7.29a–b.
34. Chen, 24.3b–4a.
35. Cited in Übelhör, "The Community Compact," 373; see also Wang Lanyin, "Mingdai zhi xiangyue," 106.

36. Wang Lanyin, "Mingdai zhi xiangyue," 117, citing Wang Qinruo.
37. Gao, 12.34b.
38. Gao, 7.28b.
39. Yang, 1.8a.
40. Gao, 12.34b.
41. Gao, 7.28b.
42. Gao, 12.34a–b.
43. Gao, 7.13a–14a. The memorial was drafted but not submitted. The two officials were Wang Zhong and Yao Gui.
44. Ding received the *jinshi* degree in 1571 and died in 1633, according to Qian Shisheng's biography of Ding in *Jiashan xian zhi* (1800), 6.18a. Other sources have 1631.
45. Gao, 7.14b. Ding sojourned in the Southern Capital for thirty years. Whenever there was a drought, he asked that there be food relief. Sometimes he used funds from his own household to provide aid. See *Ming shi*, 221.1557–58.
46. Gao, 7.13a.
47. Gao, 12.36a.
48. Gao, 9B.43a.
49. Gao, 12.34a. Calculating that Gao's benevolent society, like the society of Wu-jin (Piling) that had inspired him, met once each season—that is, four times a year—I guess that the fourteenth meeting was most likely held in the summer of 1618. None of Gao's three lectures is specifically dated.
50. Gao, 12.35a.
51. Comment by Chen appended to "Jia xun," in Gao, 10B.25a–b. "Jia xun" was written in 1607; *Gao nianpu*, 14b.
52. Gao, 10B.24b.
53. Ironically, in 1855, instructions for a community compact in Jiangsu advised that one follow the lecture method that Gao Panlong used for his benevolent society. See Yu Zhi, *Deyi lu*, 14A.21a.
54. Chen, 26.19b–20a.
55. Chen, 24.25a.
56. Chen, 26.2b–4b.
57. Chen, 23.16a–b.
58. Chen, 26.4b–6a. I surmise that this "Account of Burying Carcasses" (Maizi shu) was written in 1642 because the piece refers to the portable soup kitchen, which Chen supported that year. On the food dearth of 1642, see also Chen, 55.1a–b.
59. Chen, 26.6a–b. Appended to a piece dated 1642 and speaking of the previous year.
60. Chen, 24.4a.
61. Chen, 23.15a.
62. Qian, *Ciyu tang ji*, 10.17b. See also Xu Chongxi, *Ciyu tang nianpu*, 34b–35b.
63. *Gao nianpu*, 15b; see also 31b.
64. Ye Maocai, "Xing zhuang," appended to Gao, "Fulu," 45a–b. Cf. Fuma, *Chūgoku zenkai*, 98.
65. Gao, 12.32b.
66. Chen, 41.14a.
67. Chen, 41.17b, letter of 1632, cited in Fuma, *Chūgoku zenkai*, 100, 139n27.
68. Chen, 23.16a.

69. Chen, 23.16b.
70. Chen, 23.16b.
71. Gao, 12.34b.
72. Chen, 24.1b.
73. Chen, 24.1a.
74. Wang Lanyin, "Mingdai zhi xiangyue," 116, citing "Shengyu jieshuo."
75. Chen, 24.1b. Cf. the observation, in 1653, of Lu Shiyi's friend Chen Hu: "To-day, speaking and acting at the society meeting, where everyone sees and hears one another, there certainly is no one who is not good. But tomorrow, when you are sitting along, mulling over things, you should also examine your good and bad deeds"; Chen Zilong, *Chen Zhongyu gong quanji nianpu, shang.*32a.
76. Chen, 24.2b.
77. Chen, 24.3a.
78. Chen, 24.2b–3a.
79. Chen, 23.15b.
80. Chen, 23.14b.
81. Chen, 23.14b–15a.
82. Chen, 23.15b.
83. Yang, 1.8a.
84. Chen, 23.16a.
85. Chen, 23.16a.
86. Chen, 24.2a–b.
87. Chen, 24.1b.
88. Chen, 23.15a–b.
89. Chen, 23.17a.
90. Chen, 23.15a.
91. Chen, 23.15a–b.
92. Chen, 23.18a.
93. Chen, 23.15a.
94. Chen, 23.15a.
95. Chen, 23.19b–20a; see also 23.17b.
96. Chen, 23.17a.
97. See Will, *Bureaucracy and Famine,* 97–101. On appearance as an indication of poverty, see ibid., 99.
98. According to Chen, 25.2a, his district (*yi*) had twenty boroughs (*qu*), with a to-tal population of sixty thousand; see his note appended to a 1630 plan for famine relief, in Chen, 25.4b. The large boroughs had roughly thirty to forty wards (*fang*), and the small boroughs twenty to thirty wards; Chen, 25.20a. The word *yi,* which can also mean "city" was used most frequently by Chen to mean the entire *xian,* as when he stated, "Of the entire *yi,* only this *qu* is barren"; Chen, 26.17b–18a. In 1642, Chen would comment that in 1630 he had tested a famine relief technique in his home rural area (*xiang*); Chen, 55.1a.
99. Chen, 25.2a.
100. Chen, 23.15a.
101. Chen, 23.17b.
102. Chen, 24.25b.
103. Chen, 23.17b–18a.

104. Chen, 24.16a.
105. Legge, trans., *The Works of Mencius*, 249–50 (*Mencius* 3A).
106. Chen, 24.16a.
107. Chen, 23.16a–b.
108. Chen, 1.4a. On *shendu*, see *Daxue* 6.1, Legge, trans., *The Great Learning*, 366.
109. Chen, 23.16a–b.
110. Chen, 24.19a.
111. Chen, 26.19b–20a. On Cao Xun, see *Jiashan xian zhi* (1800), 13.11b–12a. Hanlin bachelors were metropolitan graduates with high promise; see Hucker, *A Dictionary of Official Titles in Imperial China*, no. 5419.
112. Chen, 26.20a.
113. Chen, 26.19b–20b.
114. Chen, 24.24b–25a.
115. Chen, 24.24b; 2.9a–b. See also Fujita, "Minmatsu Kashan fu Kakyō hen ni okeru kyūkō ni tsuite," 30–31, citing *Jiashan xian zuan xiu Qu Zhen tiaokuan*.
116. Chen, 24.25a.
117. Chen, 26.1a.
118. Chen, 26.2b–3a.
119. On Qian, also a native of Jiashan, see *DMB*, 237–39. For quotation, Chen, 26.3a–b; see also 26.8b–12a.
120. Chen, 26.4b.
121. Chen, 26.19a–b. Chen proceeds to draw an analogy to government officials.
122. Chen, 26.6a–b; see also Chen Kui, "Chen Cibu," 1.18a.
123. Chen, 26.4b; see also 26.8a.
124. Chen, 21.31a–36b. From regulations left by his father for a charitable estate.
125. Chen, 21.31a–b; Chen Kui, "Chen Cibu," 1.5b. Chen also cited as an inspiration the example of Fan Zhongyan; Chen, 21.35b–36a, 38a–b, also 25.7b–8a.
126. Chen, 21.31b–34a.
127. *Jiashan xian zhi* (1800), 4.9b–10a, 6.17b.
128. Chen, 21.39b, "Yizhuang cheng."
129. Chen, 26.18b.
130. Chen, 22.22a–b.
131. Chen, 21.35b.
132. Chen, 21.36a.
133. Chen, 21.34b.
134. Zhou Mengyan, *Yinzhi wen guangyi, shang*.37a. Gu's father Zhongli lived from 1495 to 1562 and served as an official in Guangxi.
135. On Wen Huang, see *Ming shi*, 277.3112; *Wucheng xian zhi*, 6.28a; and preface by an anonymous author to, and Chen Hongmou's comment on, the reprinting of this work in Chen's anthology, *Jiaonü yigui, xia*, 3b–4a.
136. Wen Huang, *Wenshi mu xun*, 6b.
137. *Yucheng xian zhi*, 6.16a–b.
138. Yang, 3.1a–b.
139. Yang, 9.5a–6a, "Record of a Charitable Estate" (Yitian ji), 1603.
140. In his "Record of a Charitable Estate," Yang writes roughly as follows of younger brother Yang Dongshu: "A state student (*guozisheng*), Dongshu was by nature

generous and truly took pleasure in being charitable (*haoshan leshi*). He managed the maintenance of our city roads and bridges whether they were near or far, and, as needs arose, he additionally made countless charitable contributions, to the point that he was praised as 'a benevolent literatus of the area.' He was unfortunately stricken by illness in his middle years, and his benevolence came to an end." Yang, 9.5b.

141. Gao, 12.34a–b.
142. The concern for lineage solidarity may have deepened in the late Ming; see Chow, *Rise of Confucian Ritualism,* 73–79.
143. Chen, 24.15a–b.
144. Chen, 24.19a.
145. Chen, 25.12b.
146. Chen, 24.19a.
147. Chen, 23.17a. Though focusing on the eighteenth century, Wong and Perdue note that relief efforts in China targeted rural as well as urban populations, whereas in Europe they focused on the populations of major urban centers. "Famine's Foes in Ch'ing China," 323.
148. Chen, 23.16b.
149. Chen, 24.19b.
150. Chen, 30.2b, "Youbei wuhuan yi."
151. Chen, 30.2b–3b.
152. Chen, 25.5b. "One or two" is ambiguous here and might be read as 10 to 20 percent.
153. *Jiashan xian zhi* (1800) notes that Chen Longzheng provided five hundred taels for schooling poor lads and five hundred piculs (*shi*) of grain to aid the poor of Xuwu qu; see *Jiashan xian zhi* (1800), 9.9a. On a charitable school (*yixue*) for poor lineage lads, see Chen, 22.33b.
154. Chen, 24.19a, "Proclamation to the Poor People," appended to lecture 40, of 1641.
155. Legge, trans. *The Great Learning,* 357.
156. Gao, 12.32b–33b.
157. Chen, 24.1b, 2b.
158. Chen, 21.20b.
159. For a brief discussion of Chen's famine relief, see Mori, "The Gentry in the Ming," 49–51.
160. Chen, 25.3a, "Shi Xuwu qu pinhu yu."
161. Chen, 25.4a.
162. Chen, 25.4b.
163. Chen, 25.3b–4a. This brings to mind the suggestion made by Leeuwen that poor relief was a means to regulate and maintain a reserve of unskilled laborers; see his *The Logic of Charity,* 74, 144.
164. Chen, 25.4a.
165. Chen, 24.5b; see also 24.4b.
166. Chen, 24.14a.
167. See, for example, Chen, 24.5a, 15b, 17a, 22b.

4. LECTURES FOR THE POOR—AND THE RICH

1. Chen, 24.23b.
2. Chen, 24.14a–b.
3. Chen, 24.15a.
4. Chen, 30.9b–10a.
5. Gao, 12.33b.
6. Chen, 24.2b.
7. Chen, 24.6a.
8. Chen, 24.14a.
9. Chen, 24.22a–b.
10. Chen, 24.5a.
11. Gao, 12.26a; 10B.23a.
12. Chen, 24.6a.
13. Chen, 24.6a.
14. Gao, 12.36a.
15. Chen, 26.8a–b.
16. Chen, 24.13a, 24.14a.
17. Chen, 24.14a.
18. Chen, 24.14a.
19. Gao, 12.35a.
20. Lin Xiyuan (ca. 1480–ca. 1560), for example, recommended that society be carved up into three rich and three poor categories. That Lin had been an overseas merchant as well as a scholar and official may have contributed to his economically based stratification of society. See Will, *Bureaucracy and Famine*, 98. On Lin, see *DMB*, 919–22.
21. Chen, 24.5b.
22. Chen, 24.5b.
23. Chen, 24.10a–b.
24. Chen, 24.12a.
25. Chen, 24.12a.
26. Chen, 24.11b.
27. Chen, 24.12a. On the didactic work *Weishan yin zhi*, see Brokaw, *Ledgers of Merit and Demerit*, 147n86.
28. Chen, 24.12a–b. For a translation of *Taishang ganying pian* (ca. 1164), see Carus and Suzuki, trans. and ed., *T'ai-Shang Kan-Ying P'ien*. See also, Legge, trans., *The Thai-Shang Tractate*.
29. Chen, 24.11a–b.
30. Chen, 24.5b–6a.
31. Chen, 24.6a.
32. Chen, 24.14a. Cf. Chen, 24.2b: "How can a district united not reap great benefits in the future?"
33. Chen, 46.12b. See Mizoguchi, "Iwayuru Tōrinha jinshi no shisō," 176. The editors of Chen placed this undated letter among letters of 1640.
34. Chen, 24.10b.
35. Chen, 14.5b.
36. Chen, 14.5b.

37. Chen, 14.5b.
38. Chen, 12.9a.
39. Chen, 22.23b–24a. See also Mizoguchi, "Iwayuru Tōrinha jinshi no shisō," 163–64. For a full translation of this passage, see Pei-yi Wu, "Childhood Remembered," 136–37.
40. *Fushou quanshu*, 4.10b–11a. The official is the Song-dynasty Sun Jue, who was on good terms with Wang Anshi; see *Song shi*, 344.10925–28. Regarding the false attribution of *Fushou quanshu* to Chen Jiru, see Qu Wanli, ed., *Pulinsidun daxue Geside dongfang tushuguan Zhongwen shanben shu zhi*, 302, which points out that *Fushou quanshu* has the same content as *Zuofei an ri zuan*, compiled by Zheng Xuan, who appears in part 2.
41. *Fushou quanshu*, 4.5b–6a. Ms. Luo was the wife of Yang Wanli (Yang Chengzhai), who studied with Hu Yuan and was on good terms with Wang Anshi; see *Song shi*, 433.12863–70.
42. *Fushou quanshu*, 4.4a.
43. Chen, 24.17a.
44. Chen, 24.17a.
45. On Zhang Dai, see *ECCP*, 53–54; Huang Guilan, *Zhang Dai shengping ji qi wenxue*, esp. 31–32 (correspondence with Qi Biaojia about naming garden scenes), and 37–38 (intermarriage between the Zhang and Qi lineages); Spence, *Return to Dragon Mountain*. See also Kafalas, *In Limpid Dreams*.
46. *LHWJ*, 101–29.
47. The great-great-grandfather was Zhang Tianfu; the great-grandfather was Zhang Yuanbian (*DMB*, 110), a renowned scholar and follower of Wang Yangming's disciple Wang Ji.
48. *LHWJ*, 113. The wasteful habits started with his great-(grand)-uncle, Zhu Shimen (brother of Zhu Geng), whom his father's generation imitated; *LHWJ*, 109.
49. *LHWJ*, 114 (carpentry); *LHWJ*, 106, 120–21 (drink); *LHWJ*, 116 (football and the like). The third uncle also entertained lavishly, often as many as fifty or sixty guests at a time (*LHWJ*, 116). Apparently Zhang Dai too liked to gamble in cock fights; Zhang Dai, *Taoan mengyi*, 3.40–41.
50. *LHWJ*, 125–27; Spence, *Return to Dragon Mountain*, 180–85.
51. The families of the two men were linked together in many ways. Zhang Dai appears often in Qi's diaries. He wrote a letter to Qi elaborating on how building a garden was more difficult than building a house (*LHWJ*, 90), and composed several poems celebrating Qi's garden, which are included in Qi Biaojia's *Yu shan zhu*, 1.5a, 1.8b, 1.10b, etc. Qi Biaojia visited and described the gardens of Zhang Dai, Zhang Dai's father, and Zhang Dai's uncle (*QBJJ*, 8.183, 195, 183, respectively). On Qi, see *ECCP*, 126; *DMB*, 216–20; Wang Siren, *Qi Zhongmin gong nianpu*. See also the two articles by Ying Yukang listed in the bibliography.
52. Qi's enthusiasm for various forms of opera eventually prompted him to compile an annotated catalog of 677 dramatic pieces, including several written by two of his brothers and a cousin; see Qi Biaojia, *Yuanshan tang Ming qupin, jupin jiao lu*, esp. 182–83 (brother Linjia); 199 (brother Junjia); and 11, 193 (cousin Zhaijia). For a list of all the comments Qi made in his diary about viewing or sponsoring performances, see the appendix in ibid., 298–303n24.
53. On the number of volumes, see *QBJJ*, 7.169.

54. *QBJJ*, 7.151. Qi later also mentions his "craving for construction" (*QBJJ*, 7.168). On the genesis of Yu Garden, see also *QBJJ*, 8.212. For another mention of forming garden plans in his dreams, see *Diary* 1636, 1a, preface.

55. *QBJJ*, 7.150. Zhang Dai also talks of "being unable to stop" his obsession; *LHWJ*, 109.

56. *LHWJ*, 112. See also, Zeitlin, "The Petrified Heart."

57. *LHWJ*, 118. Note also, Zhang Dai made a similar point about *pi* in reference to Qi Biaojia's cousin; Zhang Dai, *Taoan mengyi*, 58–59.

58. For brief biographies of Wang, see Qian Qianyi, *Youxue ji*, 32.4a; and fragmented bits of information (along with Qian's biography) in Wang Ruqian, *Chunxing tang shiji*. Hanan suspects that Wang may have patronized the famous fiction and drama writer Li Yu; see his *The Invention of Li Yu*, 217n41. Wang did consort with Chen Zilong and Qian Qianyi, both of whom consorted with Qi Biaojia.

59. "Xiao zhuan," 1a, in *Chunxing tang shiji*. Wang wrote about his "garden" in 1623 (ibid., 1.2b). On Wang's garden, see also Zhang Dai, *Taoan meng yi*, 4.45–46. Zhang describes taking a tour he took on this boat in the autumn of 1634, with a courtesan in tow. On the boat, he unexpectedly encountered eight other persons, among them an actress. Drinking and performances followed.

60. Wang Ruqian, *Chunxing tang shiji*, 1.1a.

61. Ibid., 1.1b.

62. Ibid., 1.2b.

63. Ibid., 1.12b.

64. On Dong, see *ECCP*, 787–89; Nelson Wu, "Tung Ch'i-ch'ang (1555–1636)"; and Riely, "Tung Ch'i-ch'ang's Life."

65. Chen Jiru, in Wang Ruqian, *Chunxing tang shiji*, 2.1b–2a. On Chen, see *ECCP*, 83–84.

66. *Diary* 1635/6/5.

67. *Diary* 1635/7/27, 8/22; 1636/9/25.

68. *QBJJ*, 3.53. Qi also asked Wang to write a poem on the garden; *Diary* 1637/5/30. For the poem, see Qi Biaojia, *Yu shan zhu*, 1.8a.

69. *Diary* 1638/3/30. On Wang's carousing, see also *Diary* 1638/3/30.

70. For a brief identification of Wang Ruqian as being a salt merchant, see *Liangzhe yanfa zhi*, 15.29a. Wang's own writings do not mention his source of income, only that his family came from She xian, Anhui, home to many salt merchants. On Wang Ruqian entertaining "the famous and talented" on West Lake, see "Xiaozhuan," 1a–b, and numerous pieces in Wang Ruqian, *Chunxing tang shiji*. According to Qian Qianyi, *Youxue ji*, 32.3b, Wang's father was a tribute student (*gongsheng*). This was a purchasable rank, however, and need not indicate a high level of education.

71. Cited in Twitchett, "The Fan Clan's Charitable Estate," 105.

72. *Diary* 1636, preface, 1a.

73. Wang is noted for his generous famine relief and the founding of Yaojiang Academy; *Shanyin xian zhi* (1803), 14.91b. Along with Qi Biaojia, he was listed among Liu Zongzhou's disciples in Liu, "Register of the Disciples of Ji Hill" (*Ji shan dizi ji*), 1.

74. *QBJJ*, 7.168–69. For a comment on the letter, see *Diary* 1637/2/20, 2/21.

75. *QBJJ*, 7.169. See also Wang Siren, *Qi Zhongmin gong nianpu*, 10b.
76. The extent of the prosperity is impossible to measure precisely but is intimated in numerous ways. Contrast, for example, Qi's catalog of roughly two hundred gardens with Li Gefei's Song-dynasty catalog of a mere nineteen gardens in Luoyang, *Luoyang ming yuan*, esp. 2b. Moreover, of the nineteen gardens described by Li, only Fu Bi's was established in Li's time (1a), whereas the vast majority of the gardens described by Qi were late Ming creations.
77. On this last point, see *QBJJ*, 7.150.
78. *Diary* 1637/3/5.
79. *Diary* 1637/4/13, 6/2, 6/24, 9/18.
80. For An Guo, see *DMB*, 9–10.
81. On Feng, see *ECCP*, 243. Similarly, as recounted somewhat cynically in a novelette of unknown authorship, the late nineteenth-century merchant Hu Xueyan simultaneously built an enormous garden for his concubines and sponsored a soup kitchen; see *Hu Xueyan wai zhuan*. Of the real-life Hu, the nineteenth-century Li Ziming (*ECCP*, 493) mentions no garden (only an enormous residence spanning several wards in Hangzhou) but does observe that Hu, by being charitable (by sponsoring a medicine clinic, a bureau for benevolence, and the distribution of coffins and food) gained the influence and trust necessary for establishing a network of banks throughout China; cited in *Hu Xueyan*, "Summary," 1.
82. *Liangzhe yanfa zhi*, 15.29a; see also, Qian Qianyi, *Youxue ji*, in *Muzhai quanji*, 32.3b.
83. *Diary* 1637, preface.
84. *Diary* 1635.1b, preface.
85. *Diary* 1639/1/1.1a–b.
86. See biography of Qi by Xie Jin in *QBJJ*, 252; translation by Campbell, "Qi Biaojia's 'Footnotes to Allegory Mountain,'" 244.
87. Chen Kui, "Chen Cibu," 2.3a.
88. On the brouhaha, see Zhang Dai, *LHWJ*, p. 125–26. For countless occasions when Qi dined with his father-in-law, see Qi's diary.
89. On Shang Zhouzuo, see Mao Qiling, *Xihe ji*, 63.3a–b.
90. *Diary* 1639/7/9 (garden); *Diary* 1637/Intercalary 4/4 (famine relief in 1637); *Diary* 1639/11/28 (lineage); *Diary* 1939/12/21 (village poor); *Diary* 1640/5/23, and 1641/10/25 (famine relief in 1640 and 1641).
91. Yang, 9.5a.
92. *Fushou quanshu*, 4.9a.
93. As Helen Dunstan, citing the *Li ji* and *Mencius,* notes: the "ideal agrarian taxation rate" was considered to be 10 percent; see *Conflicting Counsels to Confuse the Age*, 151n1.
94. For a discussion of the seventeenth-century work "Meritorious Deeds at No Cost" (*Bufei qian gongde li*), by Xiong Hongbei, see Sakai, "Confucianism and Popular Educational Works," esp. 250–62. The work itself was anthologized in Chen Hongmou, *Xunsu yigui*, 4.43a–51a.
95. Chen, 21.17b.
96. Gao, 10B.23b, "Jia xun."
97. Chen, 22.4a.
98. Chen, 24.13a.

99. Chen, 24.16a–b.
100. Twitchett, "The Fan Clan's Charitable Estate," 100.
101. Chen, 25.7b–8a. On the notion that Fan died so poor that his sons lacked the resources for a burial, see also Jin Zhijun, *Xizhai ji*, 4.16b. On Jin, see *ECCP*, 160–61.
102. According to Atwell, "Notes on Silver, Foreign Trade, and the Late Ming Economy," the influx of silver started soon after 1571 (1), slackened during the late 1620s, revived in the 1630s (10), and came to a "virtual standstill" in 1637 (12). The drop in silver exports into China in the 1630s and early 1640s, he suggests, may have contributed to widespread unrest (16–18). Von Glahn, moving away from the notion that China simply responded to the influx of silver, and finding holes in the argument that the cessation of silver exports to China precipitated a crisis, suggests that the Chinese demand for silver attracted foreign merchants; *Fountain of Fortune*, 6; see also 207 for his statement that in the 1640s and 1650s, Jiangnan had no "serious economic dislocation" but enjoyed "moderate prosperity." For the purposes of the discussion here it is unnecessary to choose between the two views. Suffice it to say that the subject of money and its dangers was much discussed in late Ming writings, as may be seen in the novel *Sanjiao kaimi guizheng yanyi*, which was published during the height of the silver influx—that is some time between 1612 and the 1620s; Berling, "Religion and Popular Culture," 188. As Berling shows, the novel explores the corrupting influences of money (201–5) and offered as a solution a view of religion as the "management of moral capital" (208–12), a view closely related to the development of Ming morality books (211). On the demonic and dangerous being embodied in the god of wealth, see also Von Glahn, "The Enchantment of Wealth."
103. Chen, 24.13a.
104. Chen, 24.13a.
105. Zhou Mengyan, *Yinzhi wen guangyi, shang.*12a.
106. Chen, 51.21a "Shengcai yi," dated 1642, according to Chen's son. See also Chen, 13.21b–22a, 22.17b. Arguments in favor of keeping money in circulation were rare. Around 1077, Shen Gua noted, "The utility of money derives from circulation and loan-making. . . . If the cash [in the amount of 100,000] is stored . . . even after a century, the sum remains 100,000. . . . If circulating continues without stop, the utility of the cash will be beyond enumeration." Cited in Liensheng Yang, "Economic Justification for Spending," 69. The fullest discussion of spending cited by Yang is by Lu Ji, who resided in Shanghai around 1540 and whose views are considered anomalous for China (ibid., 72–74).
107. Chen, 51.20b–21a; see also 14.5b. Chen's son dates this piece (changing *yi* to *lun*) to 1642; see Chen Kui, ed., "Chen Cibu," 1.18b–19a.
108. Chen, 12.8b. For a discussion of Chen Longzheng's fiscal views and translations of several key passages by Chen, see Von Glahn, *Fountain of Fortune*, 201–3.
109. *DJL*, "Tai ji," 16a.
110. Chen, 24.7a.
111. *DJL*, "Tai ji," 68b.
112. Chen, 57.8b–11a.
113. Legge, trans., *The Works of Mencius*, 139–41 (*Mencius* 1A.7).

114. Chen, 57.8b–11a. Alluding to *Mencius* 2A.6, in Legge, trans., *The Works of Mencius*, 202.

115. Zhou Mengyan, *Wanshan xian zi ji*, 1.9a.

116. DJL, "Tai ji," 13a–b.

117. Sakai, "Gan Moyu no shisō ni tsuite," 267.

118. *Jiashan xian zhi* (1800), 4/Gongshu.9b, citing Qian Shisheng. On Qian Shisheng, see *DMB*, 237–39. His second son had married Chen's daughter; see Hiroshi, *Chūgoku kyōshin jinushi no kenkyū*, 289.

119. Chen, 24.15b.

120. *Diary* 1640/5/16.

121. Chen, 25.12a, in a letter to Qian Shisheng. Chen was particularly taken by the method of having "each rural area (*xiang*) entrusted to one good literatus." On Qian, a native of Jiashan, see *DMB*, 237–39. In 1636, when someone proposed that the wealthy landholders of the Yangtze delta region be taxed, Qian opposed the idea so vociferously and persistently as to annoy the emperor, whereupon he was forced to resign. His argument that the gentry protected the common people's livelihood surely obligated him to make some benevolent gestures.

122. See, for example, Meskill, "Academies and Politics in the Ming Dynasty."

123. *ZXL*, 3/17.

124. Chen Kui, ed., "Chen Cibu," 1.4b.

125. Chen, 24.10b.

126. Chen, 25.1a–b; my italics.

127. Chen, 24.14b. The term *xiangguan* refers to all the subordinates and clerks in the bureau. *Hanyu da cidian*, 10:664.

128. See, for example, Mori, "The Gentry in the Ming."

129. Chen, 7.6a.

130. Chen, 14.4b. See also Will, *Bureaucracy and Famine*, 104. Chen advocated that "every *xiang* and *qu* set up a community granary," reasoning the granaries would not only feed the people but would bring an end to bandtry by distributing food widely; see Chen, 14.5a–b.

131. Chen, 23.1a.

5. A BENEVOLENT SOCIETY VIEWED FROM THE MARGINS

1. On Lu, see *ECCP*, 548, and the following biographies: Chen Hu, "Futing xiansheng xingzhuang"; Lu's son Lu Yunzheng, "Futing xiansheng xingshi"; and Ling Xiqi, *Zundao xiansheng nianpu*. See also Fuma, *Chūgoku zenkai*, 113–16.

2. Chen Hu, "Futing xiansheng xingzhuang," 3a–b. See also Wu Jinghang, *Chen Andao xiansheng nianpu*, shang.5a. This occurred in 1633, according to Ling Xiqi, *Zundao xiansheng nianpu*, 4b; and 1636, according to Wu Jinghang, *Chen Andao xiansheng nianpu*, 5a. See also Chen Hu, preface, 2a–b, in his *Shengxue rumen shu*. For a brief mention of Chen Hu, see *ECCP*, 549. On Chen, see Wang Yingsheng, "Chen Quean xiansheng zhuan," in *Shengxue rumen shu; Taicang zhou zhi* (1803), 27.20b; *Taicang zhou zhi* (1918), 19.41b. On *Gongguo ge*, see Sakai, *Chūgoku zenshō*, 356–400, "Confucianism and Popular Educational Works," 343; Brokaw, *Ledgers of Merit and Dismerit*, 26, 61. On late Ming diary

keeping and anxiety, especially as a prelude to early Qing diary keeping, see Wang Fan-sen, "Ripu yu Mingmo Qingchu sixiang jia—yi Yan-Li xuepai wei zhu de taolun."

3. Yang, 1.7a–b.
4. Lu is here using a phrase from *Zhuangzi*. "Letter on Gezhi pian" (here with *pian* instead of *bian*), in *Lunxue chouda*, 4.20b, cited in Brokaw, *Ledgers of Merit and Demerit*, 128.
5. Lu Shiyi, *Sibian lu jiyao*, 3.4a; Ling Xiqi, *Zundao xiansheng nianpu*, 5b, citing letter to nephew Xu Shunxian in *Lunxue chouda*, 4.20a. For the editor's note on the discrepancies in dating *Gezhi bian* (to either 1636 or 1637), see Ling Xiqi, *Zundao xiansheng nianpu*, 6a.
6. Ling Xiqi, *Zundao xiansheng nianpu*, 6a–b. Lu often abbreviated the title as *Kaode lu*.
7. Ibid., 6b; citing *Lunxue chouda*, 4.16b.
8. *Shengxue rumen*, preface, 2a–b. See also Ling Xiqi, *Zundao xiansheng nianpu*, 5b–6a; Wu Jinghang, *Chen Andao xiansheng nianpu*, shang.5a. On the four friends, see *Taicang zhou zhi* (1803), 27.19b–22b.
9. Lu uses the second and fourth characters in the phrase "shen si ming bian"; see *Zhongyong*, 20.19, Legge, trans., *The Doctrine of the Mean*, 413; Chen Hu, "Futing xiansheng xingzhuang," 4a.
10. Lu Yunzheng, "Futing xiansheng xingshi," 16b.
11. Qian Jingtang, preface (1830) to *ZXL*, 1b.
12. Ibid., 2b. The journals for the other years, to which the editor refers, are, to my knowledge, no longer extant.
13. See editor's note, *ZXL*, 34a.
14. Legge, trans., *The Great Learning*, 358–59.
15. *ZXL*, 3/4.
16. *ZXL*, 11/18.
17. *ZXL*, 12/8.
18. *ZXL*, 3/5.
19. See, for example, Chow, *The Rise of Confucian Ritualism*, 49; *ECCP*, 549.
20. *ZXL*, 3/5.
21. Cited in Qian Jingtan's preface to *ZXL*, 2a.
22. *ZXL*, 9/28.
23. *ZXL*, 7/8, 8/10; see also 8/9.
24. *ZXL*, 8/30.
25. *ZXL*, 4/1.
26. *ZXL*, 9/24, 5/9, 9/7.
27. On Wang, see *DMB*, 1382–85; De Bary, "Individualism and Humanitarianism in Late Ming Thought," 158.
28. *ZXL*, 4/22.
29. *ZXL*, 3/5.
30. *ZXL*, 4/1.
31. *ZXL*, 3/8.
32. *ZXL*, 4/7.
33. *ZXL*, 3/17.

34. This was in 1637, according to Chen Hu, "Futing xiansheng xingzhuang," 4a, and Ling Xiqi, *Zundao xiansheng nianpu*, 6b–7a.
35. *ZXL*, 3/8. Qian Fanhou had joined Chen Hu, Lu Shiyi, and one other resident of Taicang to form a literati society in 1627; see Chen Hu, "Futing xiansheng xingzhuang," 2a–b.
36. *ZXL*, 3/4, 3/14, 3/23, 4/5, 4/27, 5/4, 6/21, 6/26.
37. *ZXL*, 6/21.
38. *ZXL*, 3/4.
39. *ZXL*, 4/19.
40. Chen Hu, *Shengxue rumen shu*, preface, 2a–b. For Chen's explication of his methods, see *Shengxue rumen shu*, 24a–26b.
41. Legge, trans., *The She King, or, The Book of Poetry*, 503.
42. Chen Hu, "Futing xiansheng xingzhuang," 3b–4a. Legge, trans., *The Doctrine of the Mean*, 413.
43. Chen Hu, "Futing xiansheng xingzhuang," 5a.
44. Lu Yunzheng, "Futing xiansheng xingshi," 17a.
45. Chen Hu, "Futing xiansheng xingzhuang," 1b–2a.
46. Ibid., 2a.
47. Lu Yunzheng, "Futing xiansheng xingshi," 15b.
48. *ZXL*, 8/14.
49. *ZXL*, 9/21.
50. *ZXL*, 11/14.
51. *ZXL*, 10/29.
52. *ZXL*, 11/14.
53. *ZXL*, 6/30, 8/5, respectively.
54. Also known as "eight-legged examinations"; see Elman, *A Cultural History of Civil Examinations*, 526.
55. *ZXL*, 7/22.
56. *ZXL*, 11/2.
57. Lu Shiyi, *Fu she jilue*, in *Donglin shimo*, 2.207. Atwell, "From Education to Politics," 341. On Zhang Pu, with brief reference to Zhang Cai, see *ECCP*, 51–53. On Zhang Cai, among whose accomplishments was the compilation of *Taicang zhou zhi*, see also *Ming shi*, 288.3242, appended to biography of Zhang Pu.
58. Ling Xiqi, *Zundao xiansheng nianpu*, 3a; Chen Hu, "Futing xiansheng xingzhuang," 2b.
59. *ZXL*, 4/23.
60. *ZXL*, 7/3.
61. *ZXL*, 4/23. Lu may have had a premonition that he would be summoned to serve. Ten days earlier he had mentioned hearing "the hateful news" about the assistant headship (*yuefu*); see *ZXL*, 4/13; also 4/7. It is unclear why Lu later has shifted from the term "head" (*yuezheng*) to "assistant head" (*yuefu*) when discussing community-compact duties. The term *yuezheng* is variously translated as "compact director" and "*xiangyue* head." See Wang Yangming, *Instructions for Practical Living*, 299; Hsiao, *Rural China*, 616n9. Hucker renders the term *zhizhou* as "subprefectural magistrate" in his *Dictionary of Official Titles*, no. 965; for brevity's sake, I use the term subprefect.

62. *ZXL,* 4/24.
63. *ZXL,* 4/26.
64. *ZXL,* 4/28.
65. *ZXL,* 4/28.
66. *ZXL,* 4/28. Wang Han held a *juren* degree.
67. *ZXL,* 4/29.
68. *ZXL,* 4/29.
69. *ZXL,* 25b.
70. *ZXL,* 5/19. For Wang's essay, see *Wang Yangming quanshu,* 3:279–83. See also "The Community Compact for Southern Kan-chou [1518]," in *Instructions for Practical Living,* 298–306.
71. *ZXL,* 6/26.
72. *ZXL,* 6/27. Lu continued to take in interest in community compacts in the next dynasty. In 1654, he accompanied someone whom Chen Hu had invited to lecture at Wei Village; see Ling Xiqi, *Zundao xiansheng nianpu,* 28b.
73. "Zhixiang san yue" (preface 1640), 1b.
74. Ibid. On the immense unrest concerning labor services and attempts to reform them, see Fuma, "Late Ming Urban Reform and the Popular Uprising in Hangzhou."
75. *ZXL,* 3/1.
76. Feng Zhenqun, *Qian Zhongjie gong nianpu,* 6a.
77. Zhang Cai, "Song Qian hou ru xingcao xu," in Qian Sule, *Qian Zhongjie gong ji,* 23.4b–5b. "Gang" refers to a celestial constellation, probably the Big Dipper.
78. On several occasions after the fall of the Ming, Lu was offered official posts but declined. In 1657, he briefly read examination papers for a commissioner of education. Nonetheless, for the value of his writings, his name was placed in the Temple of Confucius in 1875; see *ECCP,* 548–49.
79. *ZXL,* 3/6.
80. *ZXL,* 3/27.
81. *ZXL,* 20b.
82. See, for example, his comment on worsening conditions, *ZXL,* 5/20.
83. Lu identifies Wang by his *zi* Wanwu; see *ZXL,* 19a.
84. In the passage cited, Confucius counseled a governor who was about to decline a present of grain, stating: "Do not decline them. May you not give them away in the neighbourhoods, hamlets, towns, and villages?" See *The Analects* 6.3; Legge, trans., *The Confucian Analects,* 186.
85. *ZXL,* 7/3.
86. Chen Hu, "Futing xiansheng xingzhuang," 11b.
87. Ling Xiqi, *Zundao xiansheng nianpu,* 3b.
88. Ibid., 3b–4a. The military manual is extant in his collected works.
89. Lu Shiyi, "Bidi san ce," 1a.
90. On the grain price, see Lu Shiyi, "Jiuhuang pingtiao yi," in *Lu Futing xiansheng wenji,* 5.4a.
91. Lu Shiyi, "Jiuhuang pingtiao yi," in *Lu Futing xiansheng wenji,* 5.4b.
92. Ling Xiqi, *Zundao xiansheng nianpu,* 8b–9a. To my knowledge, this work is no longer extant.
93. Lu Shiyi, "Bidi san ze," 1a.

94. *ZXL*, 3/3.

95. *ZXL*, 3/5. An allusion to *Zuo zhuan*, Duke He, 22nd year, trans. Legge, *Ch'un Ts'ew*, with *Tso Chuen*, 182; Lu modified the word order somewhat.

96. *ZXL*, 3/3.

97. Pierre-Étienne Will points out that dikes along the Han river had been destroyed by floods in 1636 and left in a state of disrepair because of hostilities there; see his "Un cycle hydraulique en Chine," 275–76, and, for location of Xiangyang on the Han River, see map on p. 287.

98. *ZXL*, 4/1.

99. *ZXL*, 4/1.

100. *ZXL*, 4/6. For friend Yunsan's surname, see *ZXL*, 51b.

101. *ZXL*, 5/20.

102. *ZXL*, 7/15, 8/3, 9/1, respectively.

103. *ZXL*, 9/1.

104. *ZXL*, 7/11, 8/7.

105. *ZXL*, 8/9 (pirates), 7/24 (crossbow).

106. *ZXL*, 8/24.

107. Lu Shiyi, "Bidi san ce," 1a.

108. *ZXL*, 4/13, 4/17.

109. *ZXL*, 5/2. On Gu, see *Taicang zhou zhi* (1803), 36.5a–b. During the early Qing dynasty Gu would play a role in a river project that took inspiration from Hai Rui, and would, along with Lu Shiyi and others, ask for a reduction in taxes for the prefecture. He lived into his eighty-fourth year.

110. *ZXL*, 5/2. On author, Mao Yuanyi, see *DMB*, 1053.

111. *ZXL*, 5/7.

112. Lu Shiyi, "Shui cun dushu sheyue xu," in *Lu Futing xiansheng wenji*, 3.7a; written seven or eight years after the group of friends had formed a study group in 1637 (ibid., 3.8a). The village mentioned in the essay was just to the northwest, between Piling and Taicang. Among the friends joining Lu was Chen Hu, who, with father in tow, retreated to Kunshan Wei Village, there to eke out a living by tilling fields. For brief mention of Chen's father see *Taicang zhou zhi* (1803), 35.13a–b.

113. Lu Yunzheng, "Futing xiansheng xingshi," 17a. I have been unable to find evidence for the claim made in *ECCP*, 548, that Lu Shiyi was the one responsible for organizing the benevolent society.

114. *ZXL*, 3/12.

115. *ZXL*, 3/12.

116. *ZXL*, 3/17. See also Fuma, *Chūgoku zenkai*, 103–4.

117. *ZXL*, 3/18.

118. *ZXL*, 9b.

119. *ZXL*, 16a–b.

120. *ZXL*, 3/17. See Wu Jinghang, *Chen Andao xiansheng nianpu, shang*.8b.

121. *ZXL*, 3/12.

122. *ZXL*, 3/22.

123. *ZXL*, 3/28. Lu often refers to working at the *guan*, referring to some official building, possibly a school (*xueguan*).

124. *ZXL*, 4/15. The city god, originally conceived as a protector of walls and moats

(*chenghuang*), was closely associated with bureaucratic presence. See C. K. Yang, *Religion in Chinese Society,* 155. Every district seat had a City God Temple, whose deity mirrored and was closely associated with the district magistrate.

125. *ZXL,* 4/15.
126. *ZXL,* 4/15.
127. *ZXL,* 4/15.
128. *ZXL,* 4/17.
129. *ZXL,* 3/17; see also 10/10.
130. *ZXL,* 10/15.
131. *ZXL,* 10/15.
132. *ZXL,* 5/5.
133. *ZXL,* 7/8.
134. *ZXL,* 7/11.
135. Wu Jinghang, *Chen Andao xiansheng nianpu, shang.*2a; this was in 1621, Chen's ninth year.
136. Chen Hu, "Lu xing zhuang," 2b.
137. *ZXL,* 12/18.
138. *Taicang zhou zhi* (1918), 19.39b; *Ren'gui zhi gao* (1880), 9.4a.
139. *ZXL,* 6/15.
140. *ZXL,* 11/8.
141. *ZXL,* 10/15.
142. *ZXL,* 12/1.
143. *ZXL,* 3/2.
144. *ZXL,* 3/6.
145. *ZXL,* 3/9.
146. *ZXL,* 3/9.
147. *ZXL,* 3/9.
148. *ZXL,* 3/10.
149. *ZXL,* 3/10.
150. *ZXL,* 4/17.
151. *ZXL,* 7/11.
152. *ZXL,* 12/18.
153. *ZXL,* 12/19.
154. Lu Shiyi, *Sibian lu jiyao,* 17.13b. For a reference to an eighteenth-century text that sets a standard adult ration for famine relief at half a *sheng* of husked grain per day, see Will, *Bureaucracy and Famine,* 130. Will points out that the term *mi,* which I generally translate as rice, meant any hulled grain; see ibid., 131.
155. *ZXL,* 12/23.
156. *ZXL,* 12/23.
157. *ZXL,* 10/15.
158. Lu Shiyi, *Lu Futing xiansheng wenji,* 4.22a.
159. *ZXL,* 12/28.
160. Lu Shiyi, "Bidi san ce," 3a–b.
161. *ZXL,* 12/29.
162. *ZXL,* 5/5.
163. *ZXL,* 7/8.

164. *ZXL*, 11/8.
165. *ZXL*, 11/14.
166. *ZXL*, 12/23.
167. Zhang Cai, *Zhiwei tang wen cun*, 10.2b–3a. Zhang here uses the name Loudong for Taicang.
168. Ibid., 10.2a–3a.
169. On Qian, see materials assembled in Qian Sule, *Qian Zhongjie gong ji, juan* 23: his biography from the *Ming shi* (*juan* 276), in prefatory *juan*, 1a–2b; and biographical essays by his contemporaries and descendants. Especially informative are the pieces by younger brother Qian Sutu (23.19a–23a) and Taicang resident Zhang Cai (23.3a–6b). See also a piece by Gu Xichou written upon the occasion of Qian's departure (23.1a–2b). Gu also wrote a preface to the edition of *DJI* held by the East Asian Library and the Gest Collection, Princeton University. See also Feng Zhenqun, *Qian Zhongjie gong nianpu*. My account is a composite of these materials, which overlap considerably and vary in details.
170. Feng Zhenqun, *Qian Zhongjie gong nianpu*, 6a.
171. At the time of writing the essay "Jie sha wen," Qian's household had already been following this regimen for a decade; Qian Sule, 4.13a–14b.
172. Feng Zhenqun, *Qian Zhongjie gong nianpu*, 6a.
173. "Liuyu shili," in Qian Sule, 8.14a and 8.16b, respectively. In contrast to Gao's and Chen's benevolent society lectures, Qian's are in the classical style.
174. Account by Qian Sutu, in Qian Sule, *Qian Zhongjie gong ji*, 23.20b.
175. Feng Zhenqun, *Qian Zhongjie gong nianpu*, 7a; see also Quan Zuwang's text for Qian's gravestone, in Qian Sule, *Qian Zhongjie gong ji*, prefatory *juan*, 14b–15a. Only Gu Xichou's biography mentions the attacks on merchants; ibid., 23.2a–b. Also in 1640, Qian introduced the ever-normal granary method (*changping fa*) to stabilize grain prices; Feng Zhenqun, *Qian Zhongjie gong nianpu*, 6a.
176. On the rain prayer, see *ZXL*, 5/13; and Feng Zhenqun, *Qian Zhongjie gong nianpu*, 7a. For Qian's rain prayer, see Qian Sule, 4.15b–17a. On the locusts, see Qian Sule, *Qian Zhongjie gong ji*, 23.21a; *ZXL*, 5/20, 8/14.
177. *ZXL*, 4/1.
178. *ZXL*, 4/1.
179. *ZXL*, 4/15.
180. Qian Sule, *Qian Zhongjie gong ji*, 8.17b.
181. *Taicang zhou zhi* (1678), 5.6a.
182. Zhang Cai's account in Qian Sule, *Qian Zhongjie gong ji*, 23.5b; see also Feng Zhenqun, *Qian Zhongjie gong nianpu*, 6b–7b.
183. *Rengui zhi gao* (1880), 1.13a–b.
184. *ZXL*, 11/12.
185. Earlier that year, Lu and a friend had discussed the issue of cannibalism in the north. The friend had declared, "There is nothing strange about this. People eating animals is no different from people eating people." Lu corrected his friend, arguing that one must make distinctions. The friend acquiesced (*ZXL*, 4/28).
186. *ZXL*, 12/26.

6. MOBILIZING FOOD RELIEF

1. On Chen, see *ECCP*, 102–3; Chang, *The Late-Ming Poet Ch'en Tzu-lung;* Atwell, "Ch'en Tzu-long (1608–1647)."

2. Chen Zilong, *Chen Zhongyu gong quanji nianpu, shang*.28b.

3. See ibid., *shang*.30a–31b. See also Ni Huiding, *Ni Wenzheng gong nianpu*, 3.4a.

4. Chen Zilong, *Chen Zhongyu gong quanji nianpu, shang*.30b.

5. Ibid., *shang*.31a. Qi uses the term *xiaolian* for *juren* (or "raised candidates"), and *zhusheng* for the licentiates, who are also called *xiucai* or *shengyuan*.

6. Chen Zilong, *Chen Wozi xiansheng anya tang gao*, 6.5a.

7. Cited by commentator Wang Chang in *Chen Zhongyu gong quanji nianpu, shang* .31a–b. For the same account, see also biography of prefect Wang Sunlan, in Mao Qiling, *Xihe ji*, 77.3b–4a. For the comment that the nineteen districts of the three prefectures Ning, Shao, and Tai all imitated Qi's relief method, see Mao's biography of Qi, in *Xihe ji*, 76.5a.

8. On Zhu, see *Shanyin xian zhi* (1724), 33.7a; (1803), 14.89a; on Ni, see *Shanyin xian zhi* (1724), 33.7b; (1803), 13.89a.

9. *Shanyin xian zhi* (1724), 33.8b; see also (1803), 14.76b.

10. *Shanyin xian zhi* (1724), 33.27a–b, regarding Hu Gongqu.

11. *Diary* 1641/1/16. On the official career of Qi's talented father-in-law, Shang Zhouzuo, see *Guiji xian zhi*, 23.12b.

12. *Diary* 1641/11/17, 2/25, 6/22, respectively.

13. *Diary* 1641/5/8.

14. On Liu, see *ECCP*, 532–33. On Ni, *ECCP*, 587; Ray Huang, "Ni Yüan-lu," 415–82. After coming out first in the *jinshi* examination of 1624, Yu Huang served in the Hanlin Academy.

15. Like Qi, Jin Lan and Ni owned gardens. On Jin's half-*mou* garden, see *QBJJ*, 8.187. On Jin Lan, see *Shanyin xian zhi* (1930), 14.43b–44a. On his grandfather Jin Lu, who was expert in pediatrics, and treated patients regardless of their means, see *Guiji xian zhi*. On Zhang Kunfang (*jinshi* 1628), see *Ming shi*, 291.3272; Zhang Dai, *LHWJ*, 122–24. Jiang Fengyuan earned a *jinshi* degree during the Wanli period and served in several posts; see his biography in Mao Qiling, *Xihe ji*, 75.26b–28a.

16. Reflecting this viewpoint is Huang, "1587, a Year of No Significance." On deterioration in late Ming social relations, see Wiens, "Socioeconomic Change during the Ming Dynasty"; Tanaka, "Popular Uprisings"; Kobayashi, "The Other Side of Rent and Tax Resistance Struggles." For a judicious overview of interpretations of late Ming social tensions, see Heijdra, "The Socio-Economic Development of Rural China during the Ming."

17. See, for example, *Diary* 1640/9/6; *Diary* 1641/1/28.

18. *Diary* 1641/4/10.

19. *Diary* 1641/5/5.

20. *Diary* 1640/1/17, 1/18, respectively. Cf. Lillian M. Li's statement that "the single most important variable" in determining harvests was the weather, in *Fighting Famine*, 37.

21. *Diary* 1641/1/14–15.

22. *Diary* 1641/1/23.

23. *Diary* 1641/2/17.
24. *Diary* 1641/2/28.
25. *Diary* 1641/5/5.
26. The book in question is Zheng Sixiu's *A History of My Mind* (*Xin shi*). On Yao Shilin as possibly the late Ming author, see *DMB*, 1559–60. Qi names a Zhang Yuzha as the publisher. Kang-i Sun Chang suggests that this book inspired Ming loyalists; *The Late-Ming Poet Ch'en Tzu-lung*, 7, 133n32. See Mote, "Confucian Eremitism in the Yüan Period," 234–35, on Zheng's declarations of loyalty; 352n50, for Mote's argument that *Xin shi* was not fabricated.
27. *Diary* 1641/1/23.
28. *QBJJ*, 6.116. In a section entitled "Miscellaneous Discussions of Famine Relief" (Jiuhuang zayi), *QBJJ*, 6.115–49, which covers numerous topics, such as registering inhabitants in *baojia*, capturing locusts, taking responsibility, and using merchants for grain transactions.
29. On food shortages stemming not from the availability of grain but from definitions of entitlement, see Sen, *Poverty and Famines*. For the role of politics and cultural assumptions in grain distribution, see, for one example of many, Woodham-Smith, *The Great Hunger*.
30. *Diary* 1631/2/12.
31. *Diary* 1631/2/10.
32. *Diary* 1631/12/28.
33. *Diary* 1637/Intercalary 4/4. See also *Diary* 1637/3/9 (brief mention of Wang Chaoshi's proposal for relief in neighboring Sheng xian); 3/15 (relief for Sheng xian); 4/2 (relief in Guiji [Shan xian]); 6/29 (Wang Chaoshi broaches subject of relief for Guiji [Shanzhong]).
34. *Diary* 1637/Intercalary 4/7.
35. *Diary* 1640/3/4.
36. *Qi nianpu*, 11b–12a; *Diary* 1640/8/15.
37. *Diary* 1640/Intercalary 1/26; *Qi nianpu*, 11b.
38. *Diary* 1640/Intercalary 1/28; see also 2/10. *Qi nianpu*, 11b.
39. *Qi nianpu*, 12a. See also *Diary* 1640/8/25.
40. Another charitable man, who, "without showing off his virtue," sold his property in order to provide food, medicine, and coffins during the dearth of 1641, had at the age of five "grieved like an adult" for his deceased mother; see *Shanyin xian zhi* (1724), 33.26a; (1803), 14.88b entry on Shen Mouyong. For Qi's mention of Han Lun, see, for example, *Diary* 1641/1/18, 5/22.
41. *Diary* 1640/3/27.
42. *Diary* 1640/3/29; Qi here refers to Yüyao by the name Yaojiang. See also 1640/4/21, 5/4.
43. *Diary* 1640/4/29.
44. *Diary* 1640/4/14.
45. *Diary* 1640/4/18.
46. Nelson I. Wu, "Tung Ch'i-ch'ang," 286–88. See also Riely, "Tung Ch'i-ch'ang's Life," 2:415–17, esp. 417 (the chant).
47. *Diary* 1640/5/1.
48. *Diary* 1640/5/7.
49. *Diary* 1640/5/7. Grain obtained through harmonious purchase would stock

"ever-normal granaries"; see *QBJJ*, 5.92. Qi often used the informal term *gongzu;* for the prefect *(tai gongzu),* subprefect *(fugongzu),* and other regional officials above the rank of magistrate. See Hucker, *A Dictionary of Official Titles,* no. 3492. Occasionally I translated the term as "official" or "local authority"; more often I have substituted the actual title the person held.

50. *Diary* 1640/5/18. Mr. Xing is Xing Xuan; see *Diary* 1641/4/28.

51. The map in *Shaoxing fu zhi* (1683) shows three such temples—for Shaoxing prefect, Shanyin xian, and Guiji xian—inside Shaoxing's city walls. The map is reproduced in Watt, "The Yamen and Urban Administration," 354–55; Cole, *Shaohsing,* xiv–xv.

52. The Bright Light Monastery was twenty *li* west of the city, at Ke Bridge, according to *Shaoxing fu zhi* (1683), 23.5.7a. An illustration of this monastery appears in *Shanyin xian zhi* (1724), 5.26b.

53. *Diary* 1641/1/11.

54. *Diary* 1641/3/24.

55. *Diary* 1641/4/13.

56. *Diary* 1641/7/20, 7/22.

57. *Diary* 1641/3/7–8.

58. *Diary* 1641/9/22.

59. *Diary* 1641/3/27.

60. Fines were, however, imposed on "friends" who failed to perform duties for which they had promised to take responsibility.

61. *Diary* 1641/9/13.

62. See, for example, *Diary* 1640/5/8. For an exception, see *Diary* 1641/3/27.

63. *Diary* 1641/1/18.

64. See, for example, *Diary* 1641/2/2.

65. See, for example, the meeting at the Prefectual City God Temple; *Diary* 1641/7/22.

66. *Diary* 1640/5/8. By "students," Qi has in mind candidates on the lower rungs of the civil service examinations: *shengyuan* (licentiates), *jiansheng* (state students), and *rushi* (scholars); see *QBJJ*, 6.148.

67. *Diary* 1640/5/10.

68. *Diary* 1640/5/11. This was Wang Siren, who will reappear.

69. *Diary* 1640/5/16.

70. *Diary* 1640/5/18.

71. *Diary* 1640/5/23.

72. *Diary* 1640/5/24. Ke Mountain was thirty-five *li* southwest of Shanyin, according to *Keshan xiaozhi,* 1a, in *Shaoxing xian zhi ziliao.*

73. *Diary* 1640/5/25.

74. *Diary* 1640/5/26. Judging from the contexts in which Chen Shengzhi appears, I surmise that he was Qi's secretary or clerk.

75. *Diary* 1640/5/27. On the signboard, *Diary* 1640/5/22. On Mituo Monastery, *QBJJ*, 4.64–67, esp. 66.

76. *Diary* 1641/3/23.

77. *Diary* 1641/3/23.

78. *Diary* 1641/3/24.

79. *Diary* 1641/3/27. One of the Zhangs was Zhang E.

80. *Diary* 1641/4/7.

81. *Diary* 1641/1/15.
82. *Diary* 1640/5/11.
83. *Qi Nianpu*, 11b. Qi mentions another piece, also in fifteen items but with a variant title, in *Diary* 1640/5/10.
84. *Diary* 1641/1/10.
85. *Diary* 1641/1/17.
86. On Xu, see *ECCP*, 316-19. Zhu Xiong, according to Chen Longzheng, was a commoner who "himself performed good deeds in famine relief" and who, "because medicines for distribution were limited but the prescriptions were limitless," had republished Dong Wei's *Huomin shu;* Chen, 55.1b, "Jiuhuang ce hui xu."
87. Chen Zilong, *Chen Zhongyu gong quanji nianpu*, shang.25a. Chen had his own noncommercial studio publish the work; see Chow, *Publishing, Culture, and Power in Early Modern China*, 77-78.
88. *Diary* 1635/7/5. For a catalog of his father's holdings, see Qi Chenghan, *Dansheng tang cang shumu*, in *Shaoxing xianzheng yishu*, 8.1a-2a. After his father's death, Qi commented that his own collection was not half the size of his father's; *Diary* 1635/9/8.
89. *Diary* 1637/4/2, 4/11, 4/15.
90. *Diary* 1639/6/17.
91. *Diary* 1641/3/17, 4/28. *Huang Ming jingshi wenbian* was published in 1638; see Franke, *An Introduction to the Sources of Ming History*, 5.1.8.
92. *Diary* 1641/2/23. See also *Diary* 1642/1/1 (on Qi reading Xu's work).
93. *QBJJ*, 5.93.
94. *QBJJ*, 5.79.
95. *Diary* 1641/1/13.
96. *Diary* 1641/3/12; see also 3/9, 3/12 (*dibao*); *Diary* 1641/3/13 (letters). On *dibao*, see Franke, *Introduction to the Sources of Ming History*, 8.
97. *Diary* 1641/3/17; see also 4/28, 5/21.
98. *Diary* 1641/3/22.
99. *Diary* 1641/8/16, 8/17, 8/18, 8/19.
100. Qi's diary notes many letters related to the food shortage. For mention of a letter regarding aid to vagrants, see *Diary* 1641/3/13. On Qi's reading famine-relief handbooks, see *Diary* 1641/2/23, 3/5, 4/8, 10/3.
101. *Diary* 1641/4/9.
102. *Diary* 1640/5/9, /5/10, 5/14.
103. *Diary* 1640/5/19, 5/22, 5/23.
104. The enormous quantity and range of these handbooks is made clear in Will, ed., "Official Handbooks."
105. See Zhang Bi, *Jiuhuang shiyi*, 3b, 4a.
106. *Diary* 1641/6/29.
107. *Diary* 1641/1/10.
108. *Diary* 1641/1/21.
109. *Diary* 1640/5/7.
110. *Diary* 1641/9/19.
111. *Diary* 1642/8/1. One draft manuscript of the unpublished *Jiuhuang quanshu* is in the National Library of China; another in Taiwan. See Will, ed. "Official

Handbooks," *s.v. Jiuhuang quanshu.* I have seen only copies of a few pages of this work, kindly provided to me by Fuma Susumu. Readily available is the published "Brief Prefaces to the *Complete Book on Famine Relief*" (*Jiuhuang quanshu* xiaoxu), *QBJJ*, 5.76–115, which I guess to be the essays introducing sections of *Jiuhuang quanshu.* The names of six sections of the eight "Brief Prefaces" correspond in name to the sections that, according to Qi's diary, constituted the completed work; see *Diary* 1642/2/27. Qi also mentioned working on "over twenty sections of *Jiuhuang xiaoji*"; see *Diary* 1641/10/16.

112. *Diary* 1641/1.15. For the letter, see *QBJJ*, 3.42.
113. *Diary* 1641/3/23, 9/22.
114. *Diary* 1641/3/23.
115. *Diary* 1641/2/20.
116. *Diary* 1641/3/3; cf. *Diary* 1641/4/16.
117. *Diary* 1641/3/24.
118. *Diary* 1641/3/3.
119. *Diary* 1641/3/25.
120. *Diary* 1641/1/20.
121. *Diary* 1641/3/18.
122. *QBJJ*, 3.51.
123. For example, Qi entrusted the job of burying the rural poor to monks and provided them with some funds; *Diary* 1641/5/5.
124. *Diary* 1641/3/29.
125. *QBJJ*, 5.109–10.
126. See, for example the letter to Circuit Intendant Zheng, preserved in *QBJJ*, 3.39–41, and noted in *Diary* 1641/3/28. See also letters from Yu Huang to various officials and Qi in *Yu Zhongjie gong yi wen.*
127. *Diary* 1640/5/22.
128. *Diary* 1641/2/19. Qi often mentioned Chen in 1638: planting (4/22), arranging rocks (5/13), managing construction (11/4), and helping with accounts (11/26). He also mentioned that Chen showed him an aria he composed (4/3).
129. *Diary* 1640/4/23.
130. Ni Huiding, *Ni Wenzheng gong nianpu*, 3.5b–6b.
131. In essence, the *baojia* organization made possible the parceling of responsibility for tax collecting and policing. In practice, *baojia* varied enormously. In theory, ten households (*hu*) formed a *pai* (not mentioned by Qi), and ten *pai*, or one hundred households, formed a *jia;* see Hsiao, *Rural China*, 44. Hsiao is speaking of the Qing dynasty. See also Hucker, *A Dictionary of Official Titles*, 90. See Brook, "The Spatial Structure of Ming Local Administration"; and, for a general survey of *baojia* from Song through Ming, see Wen Juntian, *Zhongguo baojia zhidu.*
132. *Diary* 1641/5/12, 5/22. On the use of "the *baojia* machinery," in particular the head counts, for famine relief going back at least to the fifteenth century, see Will, *Bureaucracy and Famine*, 108.
133. *Diary* 1641/1/17. On one "brother," Liu Shikun, see *Shanyin xian zhi* (1803), 14.92b–93a.
134. *Diary* 1641/1/18.
135. *Diary* 1641/1/18.

136. I read the term *tongdi* as a conflation of "letting grain through" and "purchasing at low prices." Qi invariably uses it to mean importing grain in, with merchant assistance, from other areas.
137. *Diary* 1641/1/19.
138. *Diary* 1641/1/19.
139. *Diary* 1641/1/21. On Qi's lodging at Jiuqu, see *Diary* 1641/5/2, 3/24.
140. Will, *Bureaucracy and Famine*, 130.
141. *Diary* 1641/1/21.
142. *Diary* 1641/1/25.
143. *Diary* 1641/1/25.
144. *Diary* 1641/1/28.
145. *Diary* 1640/5/11.
146. Ni Huiding, *Ni Wenzheng gong nianpu*, 3.6b.
147. *Diary* 1640/5/12.
148. *Diary* 1641/4/21.
149. *Diary* 1640/10/30.
150. *Diary* 1637/12/27. Qi's wife, Shang Jinglan, enjoyed much freedom of movement, was well educated, and, especially after the Ming fell, earned note as a talented poet; see Ko, *Teachers of the Inner Chambers*, 226–32.
151. *Diary* 1639/11/28.
152. *Diary* 1639/12/8 (school); *Diary* 1639/12/27, 12/28.
153. *Diary* 1641/1/15.
154. *LHWJ*, 122.
155. *Diary* 1641/3/4.
156. *Diary* 1641/8/15.
157. *Diary* 1641/12/8; see also 12/5.
158. *Diary* 1641/1/20.
159. On Zhang Bi, see *Shanyin xian zhi* (1724), 33.6a–b, 22b; (1803), 15.17b–18a. The two gazetteers differ on details. *Shanyin xian zhi* (1724), 33.6a, identifies Zhang Bi as Zhang Shaofang's son. *Shanyin xian zhi* (1803), 14.88b–89a, identifies him as Zhang Jinghua's son. On Zhang Yuanbian, see *DMB*, 110–11.
160. Zhang Bi, *Jiuhuang shiyi*, 1b–2a. On editions of this work and for a summary of its contents, see Will, "Official Handbooks."
161. *QBJJ*, 6.131–32.
162. "Over one thousand *shi*," according to *Shanyin xian zhi* (1803), 15.7b.
163. Zhang Bi, *Jiuhuang shiyi*, 2b.
164. Ibid., 2b–3a.
165. *Shanyin xian zhi* (1724) 33.7a.
166. Liu, preface, 1b, in Zhang Bi, *Jiuhuang shiyi*.
167. Chen Zilong, *Chen Zhongyu gong quanji nianpu*, shang.31a; Ni Yuanlu, *Hongbao yingben*, 27.24a. The date of the campaign was 1642, according to Ni Huiding, *Ni Wenzheng gong nianpu*, 3.8b. For a similar document, see Qian Sule, *Qian Zhongjie gong ji*, 4.17a–19b. For an illustration of a pagoda chart, see Yu Zhi, *Deyi lu*, 2.44a.
168. Ni states that the program should end on the fifteenth day of the seventh month; see Ni, *Hongbao*, 17.25b.

169. Zhang Bi, *Jiuhuang shiyi,* 8b.
170. *Shanyin xian zhi* (1724), 33.8b.
171. *Diary* 1641/5/9.
172. *Diary* 1641/4/15.
173. For the exception, see *Diary* 1641/4/24, regarding a discussion about "issuing the registers for the western *qu* in anticipation of official Chen tour." For casual references, to Zhang Bi, see *Diary* 1640/8/12, 7/20; 1641/5/2.
174. *Diary* 1640/5/11.
175. Wang Siren, preface, 1a, in Zhang Bi, *Jiuhuang shiyi.*
176. Lu Shiyi, "Jiuhuang ping tiaoyi," in *Lu Futing xiansheng wenji,* 5.8a.
177. Zhang Bi, *Jiuhuang shiyi,* 3b–4a.
178. Ibid., 4a.
179. On classifying the poor, see Will, *Bureaucracy and Famine,* 97–102.
180. *Diary* 1641/5/10.
181. In a letter to Magistrate Zhou, dated 1/18/1641, in Yu Huang, *Yu Zhongjie gong yi wen,* 10b.
182. *Diary* 1640/5/27.
183. Mao Qiling, *Xihe ji,* 76.5a.
184. *Diary* 1641/1/29; see also *Diary* 1641/2/4.
185. *Xiaoshan xian zhi* (1683), 9.5b–6a. During the dynasty's final years, conditions in Xiaoshan deteriorated: one man killed his son for food and was promptly executed; pestilence left many dead along the roads; the severe drought drove up the prices of rice and barley to 3.3 and 1.5 taels, respectively.
186. *Diary* 1641/5/4.
187. *Diary* 1641/1/13.
188. *Diary* 1641/5/7. For a sample form for recording a community granary's autumn intake and spring distribution, see *LZQS,* 24.35a–b.
189. *Diary* 1641/4/16.
190. *Diary* 1641/4/16. Qi Hongsun was Fengjia's son.
191. *Diary* 1641/5/16.
192. *Diary* 1641/2/10. West of Juzhong Hill; see *QBJJ,* 8.185.
193. *Diary* 1641/2/8, 2/15.
194. *Diary* 1641/ 2/21. On the monastery's location, see *Diary* 1641/6/23.
195. *Diary* 1641/5/2, 7/22.
196. *Diary* 1641/1/27. Zhonglie is the posthumous name for Sun Hui of the Yuan dynasty.
197. *Diary* 1641/3/5.
198. *QBJJ,* 3.51–52.
199. *Diary* 1640/5/27.
200. *Diary* 1640/6/1.
201. *Diary* 1641/2/30.
202. *Diary* 1641/3/1.
203. *Diary* 1641/1/18.
204. *Diary* 1641/5/4. On Pingshui, see *Shaoxing fu zhi* (Wanli edition), 1.26a.
205. *Diary* 1641/5/29.
206. *Diary* 1641/3/26.

207. Graham, trans., *Book of Lieh-tzu,* 55–56.
208. *Diary* 1641/4/7.
209. *Diary* 1641/1/25.
210. *Diary* 1641/3/28.
211. *Diary* 1641/5/2.
212. *Diary* 1641/5/23.
213. *Diary* 1641/2/2.
214. *Diary* 1641/2/8, 2/15, 3/5.
215. *Diary* 1641/2/18.
216. See *Diary* 1641/6/16 for report that locusts are arriving from the southwest.
217. *Diary* 1641/5/20, 7/1 (prayers), 6/29 (information), 7/2 (printing).
218. *Diary* 1641/7/2, 7/6.
219. *Diary* 1641/3/1.
220. *Diary* 1641/3/8.
221. *Diary* 1641/3/8.
222. *Diary* 1641/4/18.
223. *Diary* 1641/3/8.
224. *Diary* 1641/3/8. For the grand coordinator, who supervised provincial-level agencies, Qi uses the informal term *futai.* See Hucker, *Dictionary of Official Titles in Imperial China,* nos. 2103, 2731.
225. *Diary* 1641/3/10.
226. *Diary* 1641/3/10.
227. *Diary* 1641/3/15.
228. For identification of Zou as teacher, see *Diary* 1640/3/29.
229. *Diary* 1641/3/30.
230. *Diary* 1641/4/8–9.
231. *QBJJ,* 6.134. On Wu Qisheng's house having suffered an attack by bandits, see *QBJJ,* 3.47.
232. *QBJJ,* 6.134.
233. *Diary* 1641/6/13.
234. *Diary* 1641/6/24.
235. *Diary* 1641/7/1.
236. *Diary* 1641/7/22.
237. *Diary* 1641/3/18.
238. *Diary* 1641/5/8.

7. ALIGNING WITH OFFICIALS

1. *Diary* 1641/1/15; for the letter, *QBJJ,* 3.42. Using similar phrasing, the diary entry and the letter discuss three points that Qi made.
2. *Diary* 1641/1/16.
3. *Diary* 1641/1/16.
4. *Diary* 1641/1/16.
5. *Diary* 1641/1/17.
6. *Diary* 1641/1/17.
7. *QBJJ,* 3.47–48.

8. *Diary* 1641/1/19.
9. *Diary* 1641/1/19.
10. *Diary* 1641/1/20.
11. *Diary* 1641/2/2.
12. *Diary* 1641/1/22. Cf. *QBJJ*, 5.80. Qi's fellow townsman Wang Zhixue cited the ancient practice of exchanging labor for relief. After contributing one thousand *shi* to relief efforts, he provided residents with work opportunities to repair his decaying residence. Like Gao Panlong, Wang differentiated himself from his brothers by taking a high road; he treated his stepmother with utmost filiality and several times came to the rescue of his four younger brothers who, being lazy, wasted their resources; *Shangyin xian zhi* (1803), 14.89b–90a.
13. *Diary* 1641/2/7.
14. *Diary* 1641/2/15.
15. Ningfang, whom I have been unable to identify, was probably a cousin.
16. *Diary* 1641/3/1.
17. *Diary* 1641/3/2.
18. *Diary* 1641/3/5. Qi also mentions that men who had responded to an alarm on the twenty-ninth day of the second month were rewarded at the lineage shrine on three days later.
19. *Diary* 1641/4/1.
20. *Diary* 1641/1/22.
21. *Diary* 1641/4/9.
22. *Diary* 1640/5/18.
23. *Diary* 1641/1/19.
24. *Diary* 1641/3/1.
25. *Diary* 1641/4/9.
26. *Diary* 1641/6/6; reading *qu* (borough) for the character *wu* (shamen). Similarly Qi asked Bi for a placard forbidding rowdiness at the medical dispensary (*Diary* 1641/7/1).
27. *Diary* 1641/1/15. For the letter to prefect Wang, see *QBJJ*, 3.42.
28. *Diary* 1641/1/23.
29. *Diary* 1641/3/1.
30. *Diary* 1641/3/3.
31. *Diary* 1641/4/9.
32. *Diary* 1641/4/9.
33. *Qi nianpu*, 8b.
34. *Diary* 1641/7/23.
35. *Diary* 1641/7/25.
36. *Diary* 1641/1/15.
37. *Diary* 1641/4/10.
38. *Diary* 1641/4/27, 5/27.
39. *Diary* 1641/1/23.
40. *Diary* 1641/2/2.
41. *Diary* 1641/3/3.
42. *Diary* 1641/4/16.
43. *Diary* 1641/4/19.
44. *Diary* 1641/4/20.

45. *Diary* 1641/4/19.
46. *Diary* 1641/5/2.
47. *Diary* 1641/5/4.
48. *QBJJ*, 8.215.
49. *Diary* 1641/5/6.
50. For the location of the bridge, see *Shaoxing fu zhi* (Wanli edition), 1.25b.
51. *Diary* 1641/5/6.
52. A sign of resources in the hinterland being marshaled to facilitate transportation: in 1570 six residents of Linpu village had set up a charitable ferry service with four boats; *Xiaoshan xian zhi* (1751), 14.21b.
53. *Diary* 1641/5/7.
54. Ibid.
55. Shu Village was east of Jiuyan, according to *QBJJ*, 8.215.
56. *Diary* 1641/5/6.
57. *Diary* 1641/5/6.
58. *Diary* 1641/5/7. Earlier that day, at a stop opposite Xiaoshan's Taoyuan rural area, the various "friends" from Taoyuan came to visit, and magistrate Shi sent in registers for review.
59. *Diary* 1641/5/8.
60. *Diary* 1641/5/9.
61. *Diary* 1641/7/29. See also *Diary* 1641/8/3 regarding a feast for the physicians.
62. *Diary* 1641/5/6.
63. *Diary* 1641/5/6.
64. *Diary* 1641/5/7.
65. *Diary* 1641/5/9.
66. *Diary* 1641/5/7.
67. *Diary* 1641/5/9.
68. *QBJJ*, 8.211–12.
69. *Diary* 1641/4/1.
70. *Diary* 1641/4/28. Qi further notes another tour of soup kitchens, in the northern *qu; Diary* 1641/6/13. He mentions a visit from various friends who were managing each *qu*, and that brother Junjia came with the manager for the central *qu; Diary* 1641/6/24.
71. Cf. *Diary* 1641/4/19, 6/24.
72. *Diary* 1641/5/17, 5/23.
73. *QBJJ*, 6.137. Conceivably Qi's brother Junjia had special ties to Pingshui, for Qi once mentioned him supervising three soup kitchens there; see *Diary* 1641/5/29. Even so, this would simply underscore that social and familial ties extended Qi's interest to areas outside his own.
74. *Diary* 1641/5/27.
75. *Diary* 1641/5/28.
76. Zhang Bi, *Jiuhuang shiyi*, 2b.
77. *QBJJ*, 5.96–97.
78. *Diary* 1641/3/1.
79. *Diary* 1641/5/4.
80. *Diary* 1641/1/9.
81. *Diary* 1641/1/18.

82. *Diary* 1641/1/19.
83. Chen Zilong, *Chen Zhongyu gong quanji nianpu, shang.*31b.
84. *Diary* 1641/1/20.
85. *Diary* 1641/1/20.
86. *QBJI*, 3.40, letter to Zheng Xuan. who was circuit intendant of Ningbo and Shaoxing; this appears to be the letter in which Qi, according to his diary, summarized "the discussion of the previous day" at the Wang Yangming shrine (*Diary* 1641/3/27–28). For identification of Zheng, see Chen, *Chen Zhongyu gong quanji nianpu, shang.*31a.
87. *Diary* 1641/4/21. The habit of obtaining rice from outside Shaoxing was well established by 1640, when Qi mentioned that over one hundred people came from the lineage and village to buy at discounted prices and that he "helped somewhat" those who were unable to buy the grain. The transactions completed, Qi then handed the proceeds over to a Mr. Wang, commissioning him to go to Suzhou to buy more grain, for future use in relief; *Diary* 1640/4/23.
88. *Diary* 1641/4/24.
89. *Diary* 1641/5/15.
90. *Diary* 1641/5/18.
91. *Diary* 1641/5/18. "Garrison hall" is my expedient translation for *weiting*, which I have been unable to identify.
92. *Diary* 1641/5/22.
93. *Diary* 1641/3/1, 4/13.
94. *Diary* 1641/5/8. During the Qing dynasty, cavalrymen in Yunnan and Guizhou, were allocated .25 *shi* of husked rice (*mi*) per month. See Will, Wong, with Lee, *Nourish the People*, 439n9.
95. *Diary* 1641/6/12.
96. *Diary* 1641/1/19.
97. Zhang Bi, *Jiuhuang shiyi*, 1b–2a. For a succinct but excellent summary of price control mechanisms and granaries (though mostly of the eighteenth century), see Will, *Bureaucracy and Famine*, 177–91.
98. Ni Huiding, *Ni Wenzheng gong nianpu*, 3.5a.
99. See, for example, *Diary* 1631/8/2, 8/8, 8/29, 10/3.
100. Ni Huiding, *Ni Wenzheng gong nianpu*, 3.10a; Ray Huang, "Ni Yüan-lu," 442.
101. *Diary* 1641/1/19, 3/18.
102. *Diary* 1641/3/18.
103. Ni Huiding, *Ni Wenzheng gong nianpu*, 3.10a. See also Ni Yuanlu's reply to Magistrate Zhou Quan, in *Shangyu xian zhi* (1811), 13A.18a.
104. Ray Huang, "Ni Yuanlu," 429; and 430, citing Ni Huiding, *Ni Wenzheng gong nianpu*, 3.12b–13b.
105. Ni Huiding, *Ni Wenzheng gong nianpu*, 3.12a.
106. See his *Hongbao yingben*, 17.22a, "Yicang shiwen."
107. *QBJJ*, 6.135.
108. *Diary* 1641/5/8.
109. *Diary* 1641/5/8.
110. Chen Zilong, *Chen Zhongyu gong quanji nianpu, shang.*28a; see also Ni Huiding, *Ni Wenzheng gong nianpu*, 3.3b.

111. *Diary* 1641/5/8.
112. *Diary* 1641/5/9.
113. *Diary* 1641/5/9.
114. *Diary* 1641/5/10.
115. *Diary* 1641/5/10.
116. See "Register of the Disciples of Ji Hill," 1, in *LZQS*.
117. Rather Qi referred to Zou Rugong, Zhou Ruhui, and Zhou Aixuan as his teachers; see *Diary* 1641/2/2 and 2/20, respectively.
118. For the first letter to Wang, see *LZQS*, 20.26b–27a; see also Yao Mingda, *Liu Zongzhou nianpu*, 278. For information on the terms arranged, see "Chang'an shecang ji," in *LZQS*, 24.29a–30a, esp. 29a; "Shecang shiyi," in *LZQS*, 24.33a–35b, esp. 33a–b. For a sample of the form, see *LZQS*, 24.35a–b.
119. *Diary* 1640/10/29.
120. *Diary* 1640/10/30.
121. *LZQS*, 20.27a.
122. "Chang'an shecang ji," in *LZQS*, 24.29b (with two hundred *shi* as a rule). For Liu's detailed plan for community granaries in the thirty-nine wards, see *LZQS*, 24.31a–32b; on six benefits offered by community granaries—for example, avoiding transportation costs and circumventing corrupt clerks, see *LZQS*, 24.32a–b. For Liu's itemized proposal for community granaries, dated to the eleventh month of 1640 and signed by Liu Zongzhou and others of Chang'an ward, see *LZQS*, 24.33a–34b. For a sample chart for keeping track of the names and amounts of contributors to the community granary, disbursements through reduced price sales made the following year, and special relief to "good scholars, filial sons, and virtuous widows," see *LZQS*, 24.35a–b.
123. *QBJJ*, 3.41.
124. *QBJJ*, 5.85.
125. *QBJJ*, 6.117.
126. On grain preservation, see Will, Wong, with Lee, *Nourish the People*, 103–40.
127. *LZQS*, 24.30b.
128. On the lack of clarity about how Zhu Xi's granary actually operated , see Von Glahn, "Community and Welfare."
129. *QBJJ*, 5.77.
130. *QBJJ*, 5.77.
131. *QBJJ*, 5.83.
132. *QBJJ*, 5.100.
133. *LZQS*, 20.27b, dated 1641.
134. *LZQS*, 21.57b.
135. *Diary* 1641/3/5.
136. *QBJJ*, 8.187; Ni Huiding, *Ni Wenzheng gong nianpu*, 3.2b.
137. *QBJJ*, 8.187.
138. *QBJJ*, 8.191.
139. *QBJJ*, 8.187 (Jin), 8.189 (Zhang).
140. *Diary* 1641/1/15. For the letter to prefect Wang, see *QBJJ*, 3.42.
141. *Diary* 1641/1/29. Qi ended up working energetically on behalf of both urban and rural residents; one day, for example, he first went into the city to oversee

a soup kitchen and then made arrangements for touring the kitchens in the southern *qu;* see *Diary* 1641/5/23.

142. *Diary* 1641/4/19.

143. *Diary* 1641/2/3.

144. Atwell, "From Education to Politics," esp. 340, 343.

145. On Tao Shiling and Tao Wangling, see chapter 1.

146. The following is a composite account that draws from *LZQS,* 21.66b–67b; Yao Mingda, *Liu Zongzhou nianpu,* 242–43; and, with slightly different wording and details, Dong Yang, *Liuzi nianpu,* 40A.62b–63b. The latter version specifically dates this discussion to the third month. It thus meshes with Qi's diary entry that "Wang Chaoshi had a 'Proposal on Relief for the Starving People of Sheng district'"; *Diary* 1637/3/9. The White Horse Mountain Hut was located within the city walls, just northeast of Ji Hill, one of eight hills in Shaoxing; see *QBJJ,* 8.186.

147. Wang is noted for his generous famine relief and the founding of Yaojiang Academy; *Shanyin xian zhi* (1803), 14.91b. Along with Qi Biaojia, he was listed among Liu Zongzhou's disciples in *LZQS,* "Register of the Disciples of Ji Hill," 1.

148. *Diary* 1639/3/2.

149. Yao Mingda, *Liu Zongzhou nianpu,* 245; see also Dong Yang, *Liuzi nianpu,* 40A.63a, which provides slightly different figures: 3,330 ounces of silver and 42,130 people.

150. Yao Mingda, *Liu Zongzhou nianpu,* 275; *LZQS,* 21.67b–69a. Liu uses Yuyao and Yaojiang interchangeably. Qi registers his awareness of Yuyao's (Yaojiang's) crisis in *Diary* 1640/5/2, 5/4. During the crisis of 1588, Yang Dongming similarly supported mutual aid between districts. When joining the wealthy men of neighboring Cao district to establish a community granary (because his town, which abutted a river, had limited capability for producing grain), Yang observed, "We all valued virtue and liked to be charitable; moreover, they have long consorted with us"; Yang, 1.2a–b.

151. *LZQS,* 21.56a. Dated 5/13/1641.

152. The meeting took place in 1637, but here Liu, or the text, mistakenly dates it to 1636.

153. *LZQS,* 21.56a–b; see also 20.28a. The Outer Treasury (*waifu*) was used for the ruling family's gifts, clothing, and ritual expenses; see Hucker, *A Dictionary of Official Titles,* no. 7587.

154. *Diary* 1641/1/19.

155. *QBJJ,* 6.116. On the growing specialization in commercial crops and the increasing reliance on imports throughout late Ming China, see Will, *Bureaucracy and Famine,* 177–81.

156. *QBJJ,* 6.116; *Diary* 1641/2/25.

157. Letter from Liu to Qi, dated, 9/23/1641, in *LZQS,* 20.35b–36a.

158. *Diary* 1641/3/24; see also *Diary* 1641/3/3.

159. *QBJJ,* 7.82.

160. *QBJJ,* 8.214.

161. *QBJJ,* 8.213.

162. *QBJJ,* 5.78.

163. *QBJJ,* 5.81.

164. *Diary* 1641/1/27.

165. *LZQS,* 24.23b. Tianle was divided into four sections (*du*), two of which were barren.

166. *Diary* 1641/5/6. After reaching the Mao Hill Locks the next day, Qi proceeded to comment that he and the touring party considered whether water there could be used to irrigate Tianle *(Diary* 1641/5/7).

167. *Diary* 1641/4/24.

168. *Shanyin xian zhi* (1724), 33.8a; and, without specifying Tianle, (1803), 14.89a.

169. *Diary* 1641/4/9.

170. *Shanyin xian zhi* (1724), 33.6a–7a; see also 33.22b. The "charitable deeds" section of the 1803 gazetteer includes no biography of Zhang Bi but mentions him incidentally, and perhaps erroneously, as Zhang Jinghua's son; see *Shanyin xian zhi* (1803), 14.88b–89a. Shaofang's essays are now lost.

171. *Diary* 1641/10/13, 3/8. For a picture of Bright Light Monastery, see *Shanyin xian zhi* (1724), *juan* 1.

172. *Diary* 1641/4/18.

173. Chen Zilong, *Chen Zhongyu gong quanji nianpu, shang.*17a–18b. For Qi's mention of medical dispensaries (*yaoju*) and infirmaries (*bingfang*), see, for example, *Diary* 1641/5/26, 6/3, 6/6, 6/12, and chapter 8 of this book; on *baoying ju,* see *Diary* 1641/6/17.

174. *QBJJ,* 6.116.

175. *LZQS,* 21.57b–58a.

176. Zhang Lixiang, *Yanxing jianwen lu,* 31.6b.

177. *Diary* 1641/4/24.

178. *Shanyin xian zhi* (1724), 33.32a–b; (1803), 14.88a.

179. Zhang Bi, *Jiuhuang shiyi,* 10b.

180. *LZQS,* 20.27a, in a letter to Wang Sunlan.

181. Liu Zongzhou, preface to Zhang Bi, *Jiuhuang shiyi,* 2a.

182. One exemplar of generosity in the food shortage of 1588 was Gu Zhengxin, a native of Huating, Jiangsu, who provided twenty thousand *shi* of grain for relief. See *Huating xian zhi* (1878), 15.8b. For a comment that Gu was also active in famine relief in 1609, see Chen Jiru "Zhuzhou tiaoyi." Gu's father had been a provincial administration commissioner, a high official or rank 2b.

183. See Ye Shaoyuan et al., *Qi Zhen jiwen lu,* esp. 2.3a–11a. Cf. Will, *Bureaucracy and Famine,* 73–74. The preface (1638) to this work is by Ye; materials postdating Ye's death (1648) are clearly by others. On Ye, see *DMB,* 156–79.

184. Ye Shaoyuan, *Qi Zhen jiwen lu,* 2.7a–8a.

185. Ibid., 2.9b–10a.

186. Ye's account does mention one "beautiful deed," namely the commissioning of monks in three shrines to pray for the souls of the dead who had no one to care for their graves—this after reporting that, since the community had failed to bury the corpses of vagrants found along the streets, starving people, under the cover of night, hacked up the bodies for food; see ibid., 2.11b.

8. MEDICAL RELIEF AND OTHER GOOD DEEDS

1. On the epidemics in China in the 1580s, 1630s, and 1640s, the coincidence of the epidemics with food shortages, and the difficulties of identifying the dis-

eases involved, see Dunstan, "The Late Ming Epidemics." On the dispensary of Qi's town see Leung, "Organized Medicine." See also, Leung, "Medical Instruction and Popularization in Ming-Qing China."

I have translated as "dispensary" the term *yaoju* (literally, "medical bureau" or "medical office" (*QBJJ*, 2.30). Often Qi refers simply to *ju* (bureau), but the context clearly indicates that he has the *yaoju* in mind; see, for example, *QBJJ*, 2.29. Precisely what the bureaus looked like, and whether they were simply a space at the temples where the medicines were dispensed, is unclear. At least once Qi speaks of a *yaosuo* (*Diary* 1641/6/12), which I have translated as pharmacy. Whether this is simply another term for medical bureau is unclear.

2. See Gernet, *Buddhism in Chinese Society*, 221–22.
3. On Su Shi, see Leung, "Organized Medicine," 136. Predating Su Shi, Zhao Bian (1008–84) also founded a ward, according to *DJL*, "Du ji," 47b–19a; cited in Leung, "Organized Medicine," 136n10. On Su Shi, see also Egan, *Word, Image, and Deed in the Life of Su Shi*, 126–27: an infirmary funded by "personal and government funds." Cited in Wang Deyi, *Songdai zaihuang de jiuji zhengce*, 124–29. On dispensing medicine, see Egan, *Word, Image, and Deed*, 136. On putting a monk in charge of the infirmary, see ibid., 145.
4. Lü K'un, *Lü gong Shizheng lu*, 2.68a–72b. See Leung, "Organized Medicine," 140.
5. See Leung, "Organized Medicine," 140, citing Chen Longzheng, *Jiiting waishu* (Chongzhen edition), 3.21a.
6. Qi Chenghan, *Dansheng tang cang shumu*, 10.8b–13a.
7. *DMB*, 859–65.
8. In addition to Qi Biaojia's numerous diary entries pertaining to the dispensary, the following discussion draws heavily on essays in *QBJJ*: "An Account of Dispensing Medicine" (Shiyao ji shi), 2.29–31; "On the Origin of the Dispensary" (Shiyao yuanqi), 2.31–33; "Guidelines for Dispensing Medicine" (Shiyao tiaokuan), 2.33–34; "A Proposal for the Dispensary" (Yaoju yi), 6.144–46; and "A Second Proposal" (You yi), 6.146–47. Internal evidence (mention of 1636, mention of ten doctors enlisted, and mention of Wang Chaoshi, who died in 1640) suggests that the first three pieces were written concerning 1636. The dating of the two proposals is unclear. The "Second Proposal," was probably for 1641, because here the doctors are on three-day shifts; the dispensary of 1636 stipulated that the doctors serve six-day shifts. Moreover, it notes that women were to be treated at the Hall of Kings, which was not mentioned in reference to the dispensary of 1636. According to his diary, Qi wrote other pieces for the dispensary that apparently are no longer extant; see *Diary* 1641/6/13, 8/10. Qi's "Account" mentions "ten items" (*QBJJ*, 2.29), but only nine appear in the guidelines preserved in *QBJJ*, 2.33–34; see also mention of "nine items for collecting funds for medicines" in *Diary* 1636/6/9. See *Diary* 1636/8/20 for Qi's mention of having completed "Shiyao jishi."
9. In 1636 (sixth month), 1641 (fifth, sixth, and seventh months), and 1642 (sixth month).
10. *QBJJ*, 2.29.
11. *QBJJ*, 2.32.
12. *Diary* 1637/3/22; *Diary* 1637/10/10; see also 10/17.

13. *Diary* 1639/3/22, 3/24. In his diary, Qi refers to Xiangjia as his younger brother Wendai.
14. *QBJJ*, 6.144. One monk proposed that, in light of the high number of the dead to be buried, they should use cremation (*Diary* 1642/1/19).
15. *Diary* 1641/3/8.
16. *Diary* 1636/5/20–29. On Wang's taking Qi's pulse, see *Diary* 1635/10/9.
17. *Diary* 1632/4/3; *Diary* 1637/4/13, 4/24, 4/26, 5/24, 8/15.
18. See *Diary* 1637/2/10, 7/12, 7/25, respectively.
19. *QBJJ*, 2.30; *Diary* 1637/2/8.
20. *Diary* 1636/8/14; *QBJJ*, 2.31.
21. On the role of gentry residing at home, see Mori, "The Gentry in the Ming."
22. *Diary* 1636/6/8.
23. *QBJJ*, 2.29.
24. *QBJJ*, 2.31.
25. *QBJJ*, 2.29. On the Chan master, Mailang, see *QBJJ*, 4.64.
26. A set of nine regulations is preserved in *QBJJ*, 2.34–36. On composing a set of regulations concerning fund raising, see *Diary* 1636/6/9.
27. *QBJJ*, 2.29.
28. See *The Cambridge History of China*, vol. 7, *The Ming Dynasty, 1368–1644*, part 1, 622–25; and, on Abahai, who in 1636 declared himself emperor of the Qing dynasty, *ECCP*, 1–3.
29. Chen Zilong, *Chen Zhongyu gong quanji nianpu, shang*.32.
30. *QBJJ*, 2.29–30.
31. *QBJJ*, 2.33.
32. On palace physicians (*taiyi*) see Hucker, *A Dictionary of Official Titles in Imperial China*, no. 6171. Qi makes a distinction between palace physicians and the "famous doctors" (*mingyi*), but whether "palace physician" was for Qi anything more than a loose generic term for superior doctors is unclear. On the inflated use of the term, see Leung, "Organized Medicine," 150.
33. *QBJJ*, 6.145.
34. *QBJJ*, 2.33.
35. *Diary* 1636/6/18.
36. *Diary* 1636/6/20; see also 6/28.
37. *Diary* 1636/6/19, 6/28, 7/16, 8/13; *Diary* 1636/7/28.
38. *QBJJ*, 2.33–34, 2:33–34, 2.29–31; *Diary* 1636/8/20.
39. *QBJJ*, 2.30.
40. *QBJJ*, 2.34.
41. *Diary* 1637/2/8; *Diary* 1641/3/2.
42. *QBJJ*, 2.29.
43. *QBJJ*, 2.30.
44. *QBJJ*, 6.146. On dating this "Second Proposal" to 1641, see note 8.
45. *QBJJ*, 2.30. Fu Huiyu (with "yu" recorded differently in the diary and *QBJJ*) is one of the ten "famous doctors" of Shaoxing (Yue) whom Qi invited for a small meal to fix the agreement; *Diary* 1636/6/14.
46. *QBJJ*, 2.31.
47. *QBJJ*, 2.34.

48. Wang Siren, *Qi Zhongmin gong nianpu,* 10a, states: "When a pestilence struck in the sixth month, Qi and his brother contributed funds to set up a dispensary in the Guangxiang Shrine; over thousands of people were cured."

49. *QBJJ,* 2.30–31. The corresponding diary entry simply says that Qi went to the dispensary to thank the doctors; (*Diary* 1636/7/16). On Qi's completing this essay, "Shiyao jishi,"see *Diary* 1636/8/20.

50. *QBJJ,* 2.30–31.

51. *QBJJ,* 2.30–31.

52. *QBJJ,* 2.31.

53. *QBJJ,* 6.145.

54. *QBJJ,* 2.33.

55. On Wang, see *Diary* 1635/9/24, 9/26; 1636/2/13.

56. On Zhang, see *Diary* 1635/11/2, 11/8; Huang Zongxi, *Nanlei wenyue* 3.10a; or *Shanyin xian zhi* (1803).18.6b–7a (citing Huang's biography). Zhang accompanied his father to Peking, where he studied medicine with Jin Mengshi. He wrote *Leijing* (32 *juan*) as well as *Jingyue quanshu.* The death date of 1640 provided in *ECCP,* 26, is incorrect, since Zhang often appears in Qi's diary of 1642; see, for example, *Diary* 1642/6/7. The *ECCP* biography claims, without providing sources, that Zhang cured many theretofore incurable illnesses because he "paid more attention to the cause than to the symptoms of disease." In a private communication, Nathan Sivin questions whether there are grounds for ascribing such originality to Zhang.

57. For Wang, see, for example, *Diary* 1637/1/22; 1640/Intercalary 1/16; for Zhang Jiebin, see (on treating Qi's mother) *Diary* 1638/9/3, and (on treating Qi's wife) *Diary* 1642/1/13, 1/18, 2/3.

58. *Diary* 1636/6/14.

59. *Diary* 1636/7/16.

60. *Diary* 1636/8/13.

61. On seeking medical advice at the dispensary, see *Diary* 1641/7/8.

62. *Diary* 1636/8/13.

63. For Qi's commendation of Yuan, see *QBJJ,* 2.30. On Yuan's treating Qi's mother, see *Diary* 1637/1/24–25; on treating Qi, see *Diary* 1638/6/11.

64. *Diary* 1636/8/20, 9/18; 1639/3/16. Once he took his son Meier to Zhang's house to have pulse taken; *Diary* 1637/4/3. See also *Diary* 1642/1/9, 9/3.

65. *Diary* 1642/1/28.

66. Huang Zongxi, *Nanlei wenyue,* 3.9b–10b.

67. Ibid., 3.10a. Huang's father had denounced the eunuch Wei Zhongxian, only to end up in prison, where he died in 1626, the year when Gao Panlong committed suicide; *ECCP,* 351–54.

68. See, for example, *Diary* 1641/3/27.

69. On this last point, see his *Jingyue quanshu,* 3.45a–b; translated in Unschuld, *Medical Ethics in Imperial China,* 81–84.

70. Lu Shiyi, "Jiu huang pingtiao yi," in *Lu Futing xiansheng wenji,* 5.4b.

71. Zhang Jiebin, *Jingyue quanshu,* 48.926. See also Laufer, *Tobacco and Its Use in Asia,* 3.

72. *LHWJ,* 127–29, See also *Shanyin xian zhi jiaoji,* 18.5a, which notes Pei's generosity. Whether Pei was already practicing medicine at the time of the dispensaries is unclear. Zhang Dai probably wrote the account during the early Qing. Spence

notes that several members of the Zhang family had severe eye problems in *Return to Dragon Mountain,* 59. On Zhang Pei, see also ibid., 59–61, 215–16.

73. *QBJJ,* 2.30.
74. *Diary* 1636/6/14.
75. *Guiji xian zhi* (1683; typeset rpt.), 25.11a–b; see also 20.8a.
76. Cf. the late sixteenth-century local medical associations that held meetings where doctors discussed medical texts—discussed in Leung, "Medical Instruction," 148.
77. *DMB,* 1420–25.
78. On the father Jin Lu, see *Shanyin xian zhi* (1803), 18.6b.
79. *Guiji xian zhi,* 25.11a.
80. *Diary* 1635/9/24, 10/12.
81. *Diary* 1636/5/28.
82. See, for example, *Diary* 1637/2/20–21.
83. *Shanyin xian zhi* (1803), 14.91b. On Su Yuanpu, see *Yaojiang shuyuan zhi, shang.*54b–55a; on Zheng Xiyuan, see ibid., *shang.*55a–56b. On Wang Chaoshi, see ibid., *xia.*25.31b. On the importance of the academies to students seeking bureaucratic success, and why they were proscribed, see Meskill, "Academies and Politics in the Ming Dynasty"; Hucker, "The Tung-lin Movement of the Late Ming Period."
84. On the first three items, see *Yaojiang shuyuan zhi, xia.*31b; on the last, see *Diary* 1638/6/9, where Qi mentions having received a printed copy.
85. "Biography of Wang," in *Yaojiang shuyuan, xia.*26b. Wang Chaoshi is listed in the "Register of the Disciples of Ji Hill," 1a, in *LZQS.* See also Mao Qiling, *Xihe ji,* 104.1a–4b.
86. *Yaojiang shuyuan zhi, shang.*8a.
87. Yao Mingda, *Liu Zongzhou nianpu,* 175; this took place on the third day of the third month of 1631.
88. Liu Zongzhou, *Zhengren she yue,* 11a. The version in Yao Mingda, *Liu Zongzhou nianpu* omits these phrases.
89. *Yaojiang shu yuan zhi, xia.*1a.
90. *Yaojiang shu yuan, xia.*4b–10a; Qi identifies Guan by his *hao,* Xiabiao.
91. *Yaojiang shuyuan zhi, xia.*10a–15a. The Shis came from Yuyao. The father had served as assistant surveillance commissioner.
92. *QBJJ,* 2.30.
93. *Diary* 1641/7/19; see also *QBJJ,* 6.147.
94. *Diary* 1641/7/22, 7/24.
95. *QBJJ,* 2.31.
96. *QBJJ,* 2.31. The extant account of this dispensary provides neither names nor amounts. Qi mentions writing this piece in *Diary* 1636/8/20.
97. *Diary* 1641/5/26.
98. *Diary* 1641/6/6.
99. *Diary* 1641/6/11.
100. *Diary* 1641/6/12.
101. *Diary* 1641/6/12, 6/14.
102. *Diary* 1641/6/12.
103. I translate the term *jingli* as "marshal" because Qi explains that this person is in charge of ordering the queues into the dispensary; see *QBJJ,* 6.145.

104. *Diary* 1641/6/12.
105. *Diary* 1641/6/15. The diary and the essay use different terms for one of the managers. See *QBJJ*, 6.144–46; *Diary* 1641/6/12.
106. *QBJJ*, 6.144.
107. What follows is a quasi translation in which I have paraphrased and streamlined Qi's text while translating many portions literally.
108. The character used for "records" is incorrect in the first sentence in the typeset edition, but corrected further on in the text.
109. *QBJJ*, 6.144–45.
110. *Diary* 1641/6/22.
111. *QBJJ*, 6.147.
112. The elimination of the "manager" might account for a slight discrepancy between Qi's diary's list of managers and the list in the "Proposal," in *QBJJ*, 6.144–45.
113. *Diary* 1641/6/17.
114. *Diary* 1641/6/20.
115. *Diary* 1641/8/1.
116. *Diary* 1641/6/30.
117. *Diary* 1640/6/12.
118. *Diary* 1641/6/15, 6/17, 7/19.
119. Two physicians who served both dispensaries were Wang Peiyuan and Ling Jingquan; see *Diary* 1641/6/20.
120. *Diary* 1641/6/12.
121. *Diary* 1641/6/20.
122. See *Shanyin xian zhi* (1803), 18.7a–b. This text states that it was 1640, when Zheng Xuan, Jin Lan, and Qi Biaojia set up the dispensary; Qi's diary of 1640 does not mention the dispensary.
123. *Diary* 1641/6/20.
124. *Diary* 1641/7/5; *Diary* 1641/7/9.
125. *Diary* 1641/6/12.
126. *Diary* 1641/6/17. After this date, Qi continues to seek physicians and managers to help out in the dispensary. See *Diary* 1641/6/20 (where Qi asked Fu Yuliang, but Fu was unwilling).
127. *Diary* 1641/7/3.
128. *Diary* 1641/6/13–14, "Yaoju shiyi"; cf. "Yaoju yi," in *QBJJ*, 6.144–46.
129. *Diary* 1641/6/15, "Yaoju fenren shiyi."
130. *Diary* 1641/8/10–11, "Yaoju jishi"; cf. "Shiyao jishi," in *QBJJ*, 2.29–30.
131. *Diary* 1641/8/13.
132. *Diary* 1641/7/20–7/21.
133. *Diary* 1641/7/19.
134. *Diary* 1641/8/3–8/4.
135. *Diary* 1641/8/5.
136. *Diary* 1641/8/13.
137. *Diary* 1641/7/22.
138. *Diary* 1641/7/24.
139. *Diary* 1641/7/25.
140. *Diary* 1641/8/1.
141. *Diary* 1641/6/12.

142. *Diary* 1641/6/24, 7/19, 7/20.
143. *Diary* 1641/6/19.
144. *Diary* 1641/7/20.
145. *Diary* 1641/6/3.
146. *Diary* 1641/6/22.
147. *Diary* 1641/6/28.
148. *Diary* 1641/8/4.
149. *Diary* 1641/8/6.
150. *Diary* 1641/8/10–11. The piece had the title "An Account of the Dispensary" (Yaoju jishi) and appears to be no longer extant. It should not be confused with the extant "Shiyao jishi."
151. *Diary* 1641/8/30.
152. *Diary* 1642/6/19.
153. *Diary* 1642/6/29.
154. *Diary* 1642/7/1.
155. *Diary* 1642/9/3.
156. *Diary* 1642/5/24, 7/15, 5/29, 8/17 (distributing coins); 9/1 (visitor); 9/4, 9/7 (relief).
157. Cited in Zhang Lixiang, *Yanxing jianwen lu;* also in Leung, "Organized Medicine," 146. Qi mentions Zhao Gongjian as one of the persons responsible for famine relief for the western borough (*qu*); see *Diary* 1641/5/2.
158. *QBJJ*, 6.145–46. Zhao Gongjian may have been thinking of the rural infirmary.
159. *Diary* 1641/6/17; 1642/3/30.
160. Fuma, *Chūgoku zenkai*, 260n11, where Fuma has a meticulously transcribed passage from a manuscript copy of Qi Biaojia's *Complete Book of Famine Relief*, *juan* 17, held in the National Library of China.

    Tang Zhen of the next generation mentions that his servant was forced by circumstances to place his one-month-old daughter in a foundling home but occasionally visited her; *Qianshu, fu shiwen lu*, 148–49, "Compassion for Orphans" (Xugu). Cf. Tang Zhen, *Ecrits d'un sage encore inconnu*, 170–73. Placing children temporarily in orphanages was also done in France, according to Fairchilds, *Poverty and Charity in Aix-en-Provence*, 86.
161. Fuma, *Chūgoku zenkai*, 259–60n11, citing Qi Biaojia, *Complete Book of Famine Relief*.
162. Ibid., 260n12, citing Qi Biaojia, *Complete Book of Famine Relief*.
163. *Diary* 1642/3/30; see also Fuma, *Chūgoku zenkai*, 217–19; 260n12, citing Qi Biaojia, *Complete Book of Famine Relief*.
164. *Diary* 1641/3/8.
165. *Diary* 1641/3/11.
166. On Qi's interactions with clergy, much can be gleaned from the last two months of *Diary* 1639. Wuliang was among twelve monks Qi had invited to conduct Buddhist rituals; *Diary* 1639/12/20.
167. *QBJJ*, 4.61–64 (engraving for a stupa for monk Ermi), esp. 64. On Zhanran (Yuandeng), see also Qi's text for a stone engraving for a stupa for Mailang, in *QBJJ*, 4.64–67. *Guiji xian zhi*, 26.5a. Among other things, he collected funds for building a road. Tao Wangling greatly admired him.
168. *QBJJ*, 4.66.
169. *Guiiji ji xian zhi*, 26.5a. On Tao Wangling, with brief mention of Tao Shiling,

see Peng Shaosheng, *Jushi zhuan*, 44.5b–9b. See also Yü, *Renewal of Buddhism*, 85, 93. On Qi's friend Zhang Dai's involvement with Buddhism, see Brook, *Praying for Power*, 38–53; Wu, "An Ambivalent Pilgrim."

170. *Diary* 1638/11/6.
171. *Diary* 1638/7/14, 7/18.
172. *Diary* 1640/4/14.
173. *Diary* 1640/5/2.
174. *Diary* 1641/8/23.
175. Cf. *Diary* 1641/6/3.
176. *Diary* 1640/4/4.
177. *Diary* 1638/8/29.
178. One day Wuliang came with monk Benyuan, who discussed with Qi "the matter of buying wood" (*Diary* 1638/7/27). Another day, Qi sent a bondservant and Benyuan to go buy timber (*Diary* 1638/8/1). See also *Diary* 1638/8/21.
179. *Diary* 1641/3/11.
180. *Diary* 1641/6/3.
181. *Diary* 1641/4/9.
182. *Diary* 1641/3/8, 3/10.
183. *Diary* 1641/3/8.
184. On the initiative coming from Qian Huangzhong and subsequently being promoted by Circuit Intendant Zheng, see Fuma, *Chūgoku zenkai*, 217–19.
185. The precise date is not given, and much of Qi's diary for 1633 is no longer extant. On an uprising in 1633 and bondservant-landlord tensions, see Roberts, "Civil Disturbance in I-hsing in 1633," 58–72. Whether this was the incident to which Shen's biography refers is unclear. Qi was criticized for being too lenient in the Yixing incident (ibid., 64), which seems to contradict the gist of Shen's admonishment.
186. Legge, trans., *The Confucian Analects*, 345 (*Analects* 19.19).
187. *Yaojiang shuyuan*, xia.3a.
188. *Diary* 1641/3/11.
189. *Diary* 1641/3/15. Two days earlier, Qi had asked Wu to discuss methods of aiding vagrants; see *Diary* 1641/3/13. Qi wished to use a shrine as a temporary lodging for vagrants, but it was dilapidated (*Diary* 1641/3/25).
190. *Diary* 1641/6/19.
191. *Diary* 1641/6/21.
192. *Diary* 1641/7/19.
193. *Diary* 1640/5/16.
194. Chen Longzheng, *Jiting quanshu* 25.12a–b, in a letter to Magistrate Wu Binri (1641). Chen further states that the key to their success in famine relief was that they entrusted each *xiang* to one good "scholar" (*shi*).
195. *QBJJ*, 2.31.

9. BELIEFS IN CHARITY—AND THE RHETORIC OF BELIEFS

1. *DJL*, "Tai ji," 47a.
2. *Diary* 1631/11/27.
3. Huang Zongxi, *Sijiu lu*, 3b. For mention of Huang planning relief with Qi Biao-

jia, Ni Yuanlu, and a Wang Eyun in 1640, see Huang Binghou, *Huang Lizhou xiansheng nianpu*, 25b.

4. *Qi nianpu*, 6b—with no elaboration on why this concept so interested the group.

5. *Diary* 1637/3/4.

6. Tao Shiling's prose writings apparently are no longer extant. A brief note about him is appended to the entry on his brother Tao Wangling in Peng Shaosheng, *Jushi zhuan*, 44.9b.

7. See Huang Tsung-hsi, *Records of Ming Scholars*, 261.

8. This meeting occurred on 4/3/1631; see Yao Mingda, *Liu Zongzhou nianpu*, 177–78.

9. *Diary* 1635/12/4. On Shen and Guan, see chapter 8.

10. *Diary* 1636/9/4. The original guidelines stipulated that the meeting should take place on the third day of each month. Qi's diary mentions several meetings as taking place on the fourth. Another entry of 1636 mentions first that Qi went to his lodging in Jiuqu, and then that Tao Shiling and the various friends, sitting according to their rank, tackled the theme they had selected for discussion; *Diary* 1636/4/4.

11. *Diary* 1637/7/4; *QBJJ*, 8.186.

12. *Qi nianpu*, 11a.

13. Ni Huiding, *Ni Wenzheng gong nianpu*, 1.20a.

14. Ibid., 3.9a–b.

15. Ni Yuanlu, *Hongbao yingben*, 27.24a, "Yiming futu hui shu." Ni dates his piece the fifteenth day of the seventh month, and Ni Huiding, *Ni Wenzheng gong nianpu* dates it to 1642; see 3.8b–9b. On transfer of merit (*huixiang*), see Welch, *The Practice of Chinese Buddhism*, 97.

16. Zhang Bi, *Jiuhuang shiyi*, 2a–b.

17. Liu, preface to Zhang Bi, *Jiuhuang shiyi*, 2a.

18. *Diary* 1631/12/12. On his regard for two Chan Buddhist monks, see *QBJJ*, 4.61–62. See also chapter 8.

19. *Diary* 1635/9/1.

20. *Diary* 1638, passim; *Diary* 1640/10/8. On stopping reading the *Śūraṃgama sūtra* at midpoint, see *Diary* 1638, preface, 1a.

21. On this point, see Will, *Bureaucracy and Famine*, 138.

22. See the preface by Wang Zhongmin, in Xu Guangqi, *Xu Guangqi ji*, 10–11, citing Xu.

23. *QBJJ*, 5.79.

24. Chen Longzheng, *Jiting quanshu*, 20.22b–23a.

25. On Yan and a preface of 1637 Yan wrote to a tract against Christianity, see Gernet, *China and the Christian Impact*, 11, 142, respectively. See ibid., 166 (Lu), 142 (Gao). On Liu's opposition to the emperor's engagement of Jesuit Adam Schall, see *ECCP*, 532.

26. *ECCP*, 316–19.

27. Standaert, *Yang Tingyun*, 32.

28. Ibid., 66.

29. *QBJJ*, 5.90, under the subheading "Managing Crises" (Dang ji) in "Brief Prefaces." On exerting one's energies and combining the forces of many people, see Wang Zheng's *Introduction to the Humanitarian Society* (*Ren hui yue yin*), cited and trans-

lated in Zürcher, "Christian Social Action," 277–78. For exertion, Zheng uses the term *li*, not "shouldering responsibility"; see his *Introduction*, 2b.

30. Liang Qizi, *Shishan yu jiaohua*, 60.

31. On Wang, see *ECCP*, 807–9; Standaert, *Yang Tingyun*, 65–66. Zürcher has translated Wang's guidelines for the Humanitarian Society and analyzed the limits of Christian influence on Wang Zheng's agenda, in "Christian Social Action," 269–86.

32. Zürcher underscores this point in "Christian Social Action," 270.

33. Gernet, *China and the Christian Impact*, 141.

34. *Diary* 1640/5/8; on Qi reading Wang's *Chuanxi lu*, see *Diary* 1640/4/13, 4/15, 4/16. See also *Diary* 1632, preface, 1a; *Diary* 1637/5/21; *QBJJ*, 2.23. See also *Diary* 1638/1/28.

35. Yü, *The Renewal of Buddhism*, 11. In 1740 and 1741, a certain Xia Jing, not only saved thousands of lives by setting up a soup kitchen in a monastery; he also published, jointly with his elder brother, didactic works (*quanshan shu*) to be circulated throughout the world; see, *Jiashan xian zhi* (1800), 14.37a. See also Carus and Suzuki, ed. and trans., *T'ai-Shang Kan-Ying P'ien*, 86.

36. On these two works, see Brokaw, *Ledgers of Merit and Demerit*, 35. On *Gongguo ge*, see Sakai, "Confucianism and Popular Educational Works," 342–49. On *Taishang ganying pian*, see Yü, *The Renewal of Buddhism*, 102–18.

37. Brokaw, *Ledgers of Merit and Demerit*, 28–31, provides an excellent summary of these concepts. See also Lien-sheng Yang, "The Concept of *Pao*," 291–309. On the belief in cosmic retribution being common to all the major Chinese schools of thought, see Brokaw, *Ledgers of Merit and Demerit*, 31.

38. Brokaw persuasively shows that, although these concepts may be traced back to ancient texts, merit accumulation as a system that could be manipulated by human beings was new to the late Ming; see her *Ledgers of Merit*, chap. 2, esp. 31. See also Sakai, "Confucianism and Popular Educational Works," 331–66.

39. Gao, 9A.43a–45a.

40. Gao, 10B.20a, "Jia xun."

41. Chen, 26.24b.

42. Chen, 24.2b, 11b, 12b; Chen, 24.12a. On how Gao Panlong approaches Yuan Huang's view of "action and response" but subtly differs from it, see Brokaw, *Ledgers of Merit and Demerit*, 141–44; on Chen Longzheng, see ibid., 144–48. Both Gao and Chen regarded such ideas ambivalently, differing slightly. Brokaw effectively captures their ambivalence, but at times she also intimates that they occasionally use these ideas cynically, as when she states that "Gao and Chen approved the 'superstitious' variety of retribution in the *Tract on Action and Response* as a means of teaching the people to do good"; *Ledgers of Merit and Demerit*, 150–51. I find more evidence for their genuine belief in these ideas than for skepticism. In a preface he wrote for a reprinting of [*Taishang*] *ganying pian*, for example, Gao wrote: "Some people think that this approaches the Buddhist theory of 'cause and effect' (*yinguo*). They do not realize that the Buddhist theory of *yinguo* is precisely the 'principle of response and action' (*yinggan*) of we Confucians" (Gao, 9A.43b).

43. Concerning a Ge Fan of the Daguan period (1107–10). See *DJL*, "Tai ji," 1b–2b; and Li Changling, comp., *Leshan lu*, 1.1a. According to a nineteenth-century

morality book, Li Changling, while serving as a governor in Guangzhou, published and annotated *Ganying pian* to transform the people, stating; "To be a man or to serve as an official, one must follow this book every day"; *Taishang ganying pian tu shuo,* ed. Huang Zhengyuan, *ce* 3, 14b.

44. On Gu, see *Ming shi,* 216.2512–13. Gu also wrote a preface to the morality book *Fushou quanshu.* In the eighteenth century, Chen Hongmou would anthologize the *DJL* section "A Mirror for Officials" (Guan jian) in his *Congzhong yigui,* 2.14b–29b. See Rowe, *Saving the World,* 176, 184.

45. The Siku quanshu cunmu congshu edition of *DJL* makes it clear that the commentator was Gu.

46. *DJL,* "Ping ji," 64a.

47. Chen, 41.26b–27a.

48. *DJL,* "Yi ji"; section entitled. "Recompense for Memorials That Saved Lives."

49. *DJL,* "Du ji," 85a.

50. *DJL,* "Du ji," 51a–53a, 90b.

51. *DJL,* "Du ji," 88a–b. The allocation of merits signals Yan's priorities in charitable giving. He assigned two merit points for aiding an outsider but only one for aiding a resident of one's own district; see *DJL,* "Du ji," 87a.

52. *DJL,* "Tai ji," 14a. All coins were bronze, not copper; Von Glahn, *Fountain of Fortune.*

53. *DJL,* "Tai ji," 8b–9a.

54. *Qi nianpu,* 5a. This was two years before Yan completed *DJL;* see Sakai, *Chūgoku zensho,* 369.

55. *Diary* 1631/9/3.

56. *Diary* 1631/12/5.

57. *Diary* 1631/12/11.

58. *Diary* 1631/12/20, 12/23. The preface is reprinted in *QBJJ,* 2.23–24. See also *Qi nianpu,* 4a; Sakai, "Gan Moyu no shisō ni tsuite," 259–73, esp. 266–69 on an association for moral reform that Yan organized in 1624 and had as an entrance requirement the accumulation of good deeds. See also Terada, "Ki Hyōka to Gan Moyu," 471–88.

59. Sakai, "Gan Moyu no shisō ni tsuite," 261.

60. *DJL,* "Du ji," 37a–50b.

61. *DJL,* "Du ji," 51a–b, 52b–53a.

62. *DJL,* "Tai ji," 13a–14a.

63. *Diary* 1636/6/18.

64. *Diary* 1641/7/1. In reference to locusts, Qi did, however, note: "Today even people in the northwest are not deluded by prayer and sacrifice"; and he advocated methods, as explicated by Xu Guangqi, for overcoming this natural disaster. See *QBJJ,* 5.93, section "Emergency Measures" (Dang ji) in the "Brief Prefaces."

65. Chen, 25.1a. Cf. "I have heard that some threw their children into the river"; Chen, 21.21a.

66. Chen, 25.1a. Cf. "For one thousand *li,* the ghosts screamed out all day"; Chen, 21.21a.

67. Chen, 30.16a–b.

68. Chen, 30.2a.

69. *DJL,* "Du ji," 52b–53a.

70. Chen, 25.1b. On Yang Zhu, see Legge, trans., *The Works of Mencius*, 464 (*Mencius* 7A.26): "Though he might have benefited the whole kingdom by plucking out a single hair, he would not have done it." Cf. *Liezi* 7: Yang speaking of Pochang; trans. Graham, *The Book of Lieh-tzu*, 148: "Po-cheng Tzu-kao would not benefit others at the cost of one hair."

71. *DJL*,"Tai ji," 6a–7b.

72. For the point that members of small communities built up trust through good deeds, see Wang Zongpei, *Zhongguo zhi hehui*, 2.

73. Chen, 24.6b.

74. *DJL*,"Tai ji," 13a.

75. *Shanyin xian zhi* (1724), 33.7a, notes, for example, that Zhang Bi's father, Zhang Yaofang, lived to a ripe old age because of his good deeds.

76. Yu Zhi, *Deyi lu*, 7.3b; "Xiao Yunqi fangsheng yuan gui tiao."

77. Zhuhong, "Fangsheng wen," 13b. On Zhuhong's influential piece, see Yü, *The Renewal of Buddhism*, 76–87.

78. See Brokaw, *Ledgers of Merit and Demerit*, 128–38; Handlin, *Action in Late Ming Thought*, 200.

79. Chen, 23.14a.

80. Chen, 21.21a. Chen's family had for many generations resided in Xuwu, one of twenty boroughs of Jiashan, located southeast of the city. Here, Chen sounds defensive about helping only that borough, but, like Ni Yuanlu, he believed that the rich households of a ward (*fang*) should help the poor of that ward.

81. Chen, 21.21b.

82. Chen, 24.14b.

83. Chen, 21.20b, "A Sketch of the Conduct of Deceased Wife, Née Ding" (Ding ruren xinglue).

84. *Diary*, 1635/12/4; *Diary* 1636/10/8.

85. *Diary* 1640/5/2.

86. *QBJJ*, 2.32.

87. See Chu Wanli, ed., *Pulinsidun daxue*, 302. One preface to *Fushou quanshu* was by Gu Xizhou, who also wrote a preface to *Right Behavior and Good Fortune*.

88. See, for example, Brokaw, *Ledgers of Merit and Demerit*, 175–76.

89. *QBJJ*, 5.77.

90. Qi uses the abbreviated tags *gezhi* and *chengzheng* to refer to a passage in *Great Learning*: "Things being investigated [*ge*], knowledge becomes complete [*zhi*]. Their knowledge being complete, their thoughts were sincere [*cheng*]. Their thoughts being sincere, their hearts were then rectified [*zheng*]." See Legge, trans., *The Great Learning*, 358–59.

91. *Diary* 1641/9/25.

92. *Diary* 1641/10/4a.

93. *Qi nianpu*, 4b.

94. *Diary*, 1641/3/5.

95. *Diary* 1640/5/25.

96. *Diary* 1639/12/21.

97. *Diary* 1640/6/1.

98. *Diary* 1641/3/15.

99. *Diary* 1641/4/1; see also 4/22. Another community compact meeting, organ-

ized in the fifth month by "brother" Qin Fusi, left "villagers feeling encouraged";
Diary 1641/5/13. For other mentions of community compacts, see *Diary*
1641/5/27, 6/14.

100. *Diary* 1631/12/10, 12/28 (alms); *Diary* 1640/8/9 (prostitute); *Diary* 1637/4/22,
10/3, 10/5, 10/10; 1638/1/24, 6/6; 1639/9/22 (burials).
101. *LZQS*, 20.7b–8a; letter to governor Zhang, 1619.
102. On Meng (about whom little is known), see *DMB*, 1064–65.
103. *Diary* 1639/10/20.
104. *QBJJ*, 5.82. *Diary* 1640/Intercalary 1/19.
105. *Qi nianpu*, 10a.
106. *Qi nianpu*, 10a.
107. *Diary* 1635/12/23.30b.
108. *Diary* 1635/4/26.
109. *Diary* 1635/5/3.
110. *Diary* 1639/7/9 (construction costs); 1/1 (compassion for lineage).
111. *Diary* 1641/1/6.
112. *Diary* 1641/4/18.
113. *Diary* 1641/6/17.
114. Yang Yizhi, Zhao Gongjian, Liu Beisheng, and Lu Yongzhi. Beisheng's paternal uncle was Liu Zongzhou; *Shanyin xian zhi* (1724), 33.21a–b.
115. *Diary* 1641/4/16.
116. *Diary* 1641/5/3.
117. *Diary* 1641/5/7.
118. *Diary* 1641/5/14.
119. *Diary* 1641/5/15.
120. *Diary* 1641/6/6.
121. *Diary* 1642/8/25.
122. *Diary* 1641/4/6.
123. Ni Huiding, *Ni Wenzheng gong nianpu*, 3.9a–b.
124. *QBJJ*, 5.90, "Dang ji"; *Diary* 1640/5/18.
125. *QBJJ*, 5.90.
126. *QBJJ*, 5.90.
127. *QBJJ*, 5.90, 5.89.
128. *QBJJ*, 5.89.
129. *QBJJ*, 5.89.
130. *Diary* 1641/1/17.
131. *Diary* 1641/1/21.
132. *Diary* 1640/5/21.
133. *Diary* 1641/1/20.
134. *Diary* 1641/3/24.
135. *Diary* 1641/1/5. For other instances, see *Diary* 1641/3/13, 5/12, 8/3. See also:
"On my return, already by candlelight" (*Diary* 1641/4/19); "I had almost no
time to breathe. . . . Only in the middle of the night did I get to sleep" (*Diary*
1641/7/20); and "It was the second watch before I got home (*Diary* 1641/8/3);
and, after writing a proposal on soup kitchens by lamplight, "By the time I went
to bed, I was exhausted" (*Diary* 1641/3/25).
136. *Diary* 1641/1/19.

137. *Diary* 1641/5/24.
138. *Diary* 1641/12/29.
139. *Diary* 1641/5/10.
140. Legge, trans., *The Works of Mencius,* 249–50; with spelling Americanized. See, for example, discussion of this concept by Esherick and Rankin, introduction to *Chinese Local Elites and Patterns of Dominance,* 1; Ping-ti Ho, *The Ladder of Success in Imperial China,* 17.
141. *Diary* 1641/5/6.
142. *Diary* 1641/4/6.
143. Chen Zilong, *Chen Zhongyu gong quanji nianpu, shang.*32a.
144. Zhang Bi, *Jiuhuang shiyi,*" 3b–4a, citing a Song-dynasty official.
145. Zhang Bi, *Jiuhuang shiyi,* 9a.
146. Cf., for example, the account of Zhong Huamin riding on horseback (drawn from *Huangzheng congshu,* compiled by Yu Sen; 1690) in Will, *Bureaucracy and Famine,* 93.
147. *Diary* 1641/1/19.
148. See, for example, Hsiao, *Rural China,* in which seven chapter titles out of eleven have the word *control.* The theme of "control" also threads through Wakeman, Jr., and Grant, eds., *Conflict and Control in Late Imperial China.* See also (though they add much nuance to the issue) Esherick and Rankin, introduction to *Chinese Local Elites and Patterns of Dominance.*
149. *Diary* 1641/1/18.
150. *QBJJ,* 6.118, under the subheading "On Exalting Responsibility" (Longren yi) in "Brief Prefaces."
151. *Diary* 1641/1/20.
152. *Diary* 1641/5/28.
153. *Diary* 1641/1/10, 1/18.
154. *QBJJ,* 6.143, "Shizhu yi." Referring repeatedly to the "old guidelines," this piece on selling gruel is clearly a revision, perhaps written in 1642. The old guidelines may be the "Shezhu shiyi," mentioned in *Diary* 1641/3/25–26.
155. *Diary* 1641/3/5.
156. Zhang Lixiang reports hearing this from Zhao Gongjian in *Yanxing jianwen lu,* 31.5b.
157. Zhou Kongjiao, "Jiuhuang tiaoyu," appended to Chen Jiru, "Zhuzhou tiaoyi," 3b. Chen desisted from taking upper-level civil service examinations, instead pursuing a successful career in publishing; *ECCP,* 83–84.
158. Zhou Kongjiao, "Jiuhuang tiaoyu," 3b.
159. *QBJJ,* 6.138.
160. See, for example, *QBJJ,* 5.113–14, 6.147–49; *Diary* 1641/8/29. See also Qi's recommendation of various rewards, including letting students take the civil service examinations at the prefectural level; *QBJJ,* 6.147.
161. *Diary* 1641/5/9. The town of Qianqing was fifty *li* west of the city center and bordered on Xiaoshan, according to *Shanyin xian zhi* (1724), which adds: "Long ago there was a Qianqing river, which had a bund; it was an important river for going to Hangzhou. Now it is all silted up and boats cannot travel"; 1.8b. A map in the same gazetteer (toward the end of the first *ce,* unpaginated) locates Qianqing a bit beyond Ke Mountain.

162. *Diary* 1641/8/29.
163. *QBJJ,* 6.147–49, under the subheading "Tuishang yi." This proposal mentions one that Qi had written "the previous year," probably referring to the Qi mentions in *Diary* 1641.
164. *QBJJ,* 6.147–49.
165. Yu Huang, *Yu Zhongjie gong yi wen,* 10b, "Second Letter to Magistrate Zhou," dated 1/18/1641. Regarding a school teacher who first protested unfair conscription and eventually led a rampage against wealthy households of Hangzhou, see Von Glahn, "Municipal Reform and Urban Social Conflict," 291–93.
166. *Diary* 1641/2/21.
167. *Diary* 1641/4/9; see also 8/3.
168. *Diary* 1641/5/8.
169. *Diary* 1641/3/27.
170. *Diary* 1641/4/6.
171. *Diary* 1641/4/27.
172. *Diary* 1641/1/18.
173. Zhang Lixiang, *Yanxing jianwen lu,* 31.5a–b.
174. Chen Zilong, *Chen Zhongyu gong quanji nianpu, shang.*32a.
175. *Diary* 1641/5/7. Wu (whose given name was Daoxuan) of the Tang dynasty was renowned for Buddhist and Daoist wall paintings, which no longer survive, although a few rubbings are said to be of his compositions; see Lawton, *Chinese Figure Painting,* 6. In his *Jiuhuang shiyi,* 4a, Zhang Bi had also referred to Wu Daozi's painting.
176. *Diary* 1641/5/7, 5/8; on reading Chen's poems, *Diary* 1641/5/9.
177. *Diary* 1641/3/27.
178. *Diary* 1641/3/27.
179. Zhang Bi, *Jiuhuang shiyi,* 9a.
180. See Zhang Lixiang, *Yanxing jianwen lu,* 31.6b.
181. Ni Huiding, *Ni Wenzheng gong nianpu,* 3.8a–b.
182. Chen Zilong, *Chen Zhongyu gong quanji nianpu, shang.*32a.
183. *Diary* 1641/3/15.
184. *Diary* 1641/3/11.
185. *Diary* 1641/9/3.
186. *Diary* 1641/10/21.
187. Chen, 24.20a; Chen, 24.13b, also mentions Zou Yuanbiao and Wang Yangming.
188. On Zhu, see *ECCP,* 188–89.
189. For Yan, see Zhu Shi, *Guanghui bian,* 139–40; for Chen, ibid., 147–48; for Zhu Xi, ibid, 123.
190. *Taishang ganying pian tushuo,* 2.33a–b.
191. *DJL,* "Du ji," 54a, section entitled "Recompense for virtuous deeds done by gentry residing at home."
192. On Liu's audiences with the emperor, see Huang Tsung-hsi, *Records of Ming Scholars,* 256–57. For a list of 142 followers, see "Register of the Disciples of Ji Hill," in *LZQS.*
193. See, for example, "Liu Zongzhou very much agreed with what I said"; *Diary* 1641/1/20.

194. *Diary,* 1641/1/10.
195. *Qi nianpu,* 19a–20a.

CONCLUSION

1. Wakeman, "The Civil Society and Public Sphere Debate," esp. 111–13; In *Peking,* 639, Naquin reaches the conclusion that, because "government and local leaders both cooperated and competed," it is inappropriate to consider welfare activities as "an autonomous public sphere"; see also 248.
2. This hypothesis concerning the value of labor was suggested to me by Gouda, *Poverty and Political Culture.*
3. Chen, 25.23a.
4. On efforts to abolish urban labor duties, the effects on weavers, and associated urban riots, see Fuma, "Late Ming Urban Reform and the Popular Uprising in Hangzhou." For elaboration on these themes, in particular in reference to Nanjing and Ding Bin's involvement in the reforms, see Von Glahn, "Municipal Reform and Urban Social Conflict in Late Ming Jiangnan," 288–89.
5. In this connection it would be helpful to explore why, during the late Ming, the rich were setting up land endowments to free residents from the burdens of corvée services, and whether they wished to free labor for more lucrative work
6. Why American scholars with whom I have discussed this topic, should remain skeptical about late Ming expressions of compassion, while regarding with awe and admiration the outpouring of sympathy and relief for the victims of the tsunami of 2004 and of Hurricane Katrina, puzzles me.
7. See, respectively, Qian Sule, *Qian Zhongjie gong ji,* 4.18a, 4.19a; Ni Yuanlu, *Hongbao yingben,* 27.25a, 27.26b.
8. On the early Qing state's co-opting trends that were already underway, and officially sponsored welfare halls (*puji tang*), see Fuma, *Chūgoku zenkai,* 496, 499–506, respectively.
9. For a preliminary exploration of merchant philanthropy and clientalism in the early Qing, see Smith, "Social Hierarchy and Merchant Philanthropy."
10. *Xiaoshan xian zhi* (1751), 24.1a.

BIBLIOGRAPHY

Anfu xian zhi 安福縣志. 1872.

Araki Kengo 荒木見悟. "Chin Ryūsei no shisō—Tōringaku no ichi keishō keitai" 陳龍正の思想—東林学の一継承形態. In *Chūgoku tetsugaku ronshū* 中国哲学論集, edited by Kyūshū daigaku Chūgoku tetsugaku kenkyūkai 九州大学中国哲学研究会, 1:1–16. Fukuoka: 1975.

————. *Yōmeigaku no kaiten to Bukkyō* 陽明学の開展と仏教. Tokyo: Kenbun shuppan, 1984.

Atwell, William S. "Ch'en Tzu-lung (1608–1647): A Scholar-Official of the Late Ming Dynasty." Ph.D. diss., Princeton University, 1975.

————. "From Education to Politics: The Fu She." In *The Unfolding of Neo-Confucianism*, edited by Wm. Theodore de Bary and the Conference on Seventeenth-Century Chinese Thought, 333–67. New York: Columbia University Press. 1975.

————. "International Bullion Flows and the Chinese Economy *circa* 1530–1650. *Past and Present* 95 (May 1982): 68–90.

————. "Notes on Silver, Foreign Trade, and the Late Ming Economy." *Ch'ing-shih wen-t'i* 3.8 (1977): 1–33.

Bai Juyi 白居易. *Bai Juyi ji jianjiao* 白居易集箋校. Edited by Zhu Jincheng 朱金城. Shanghai: Guji chubanshe, 1988.

B.B. "The Live Saving Association and Other Benevolent Societies at Wuhu." *China Review* 6.4 (1878): 277–83.

Berling, Judith A. "Religion and Popular Culture: The Management of Moral Capital in *The Romance of the Three Teachings*." In *Popular Culture in Late Imperial China*, edited by David Johnson, Andrew J. Nathan, and Evelyn S. Rawski, 188–218. Berkeley: University of California Press, 1985.

Bodde, Derk. "*Lieh-tzu* and the Doves: A Problem of Dating," *Asia Major* 7.1–2 (1959): 25–31.

Bohr, Paul Richard. *Famine in China and the Missionary: Timothy Richard as Relief Administrator and Advocate of National Reform, 1876–1884*. Cambridge, MA: East Asian Research Center, Harvard University Press, 1972.

Brokaw, Cynthia. *The Ledgers of Merit and Demerit: Social Change and Moral Order in Late Imperial China*. Princeton, NJ: Princeton University Press, 1991.

Brook, Timothy. *Geographical Sources of Ming-Qing History*. Ann Arbor, MI: Center for Chinese Studies, 1988.

——. *Praying for Power: Buddhism and the Formation of Gentry Society in Late-Ming China*. Cambridge, MA: Harvard University Council on East Asian Studies, 1993.

——. "The Spatial Structure of Ming Local Administration." *Late Imperial China* 6.1 (1985): 1–49.

Busch, Heinrich. "The Tung-lin Shu-yüan and Its Political and Philosophical Significance," *Monumenta Serica* 14 (1949–55): 1–163.

Buswell, Robert E., Jr., ed. *Chinese Buddhist Apocrypha*. Honolulu: University of Hawaii Press, 1990.

The Cambridge History of China. Vol. 7, *The Ming Dynasty, 1368–1644*. Parts 1 and 2. Edited by Frederick W. Mote and Denis Twitchett. Cambridge: Cambridge University Press, 1988, 1998.

Campbell, Duncan. "Qi Biaojia's 'Footnotes to Allegory Mountain': Introduction and Translation." *Studies in the History of Gardens and Designed Landscapes* 19.3–4 (1999): 239–71.

Carus, Paul, ed., and Teitaro Suzuki, trans. *T'ai-Shang Kan-Ying P'ien: Treatise of the Exalted One on Response and Retribution*. Chicago: Open Court Publishing, 1906.

Chan, Wing-tsit. *Religious Trends in Modern China*. 1953. Rpt., New York: Octagon Books, 1969.

Chang, Kang-i Sun. *The Late-Ming Poet Ch'en Tzu-lung: Crises of Love and Loyalism*. New Haven, CT: Yale University Press, 1991.

Changsha fu zhi 長沙府志. 1747.

Chapple, Christopher Key. "Animals and the Environment in the Buddhist Birth Stories." In *Buddhism and Ecology: The Interconnection of Dharma and Deeds*, edited by Mary Evelyn Tucker and Duncan Ryūken Williams, 131–48. Cambridge, MA: Harvard University Center for the Study of World Religions Publications, 1997.

Chen. *See* Chen Longzheng.

Chen Hongmou 陳宏謀. *Congzheng yigui* 從政遺規. In *Wuzhong yigui*, by Chen Hongmou. In *Sibu beiyao*. Taibei: Zhonghua shuju, 1960.

——. *Jiaonü yigui* 教女遺規. In *Wuzhong yigui*, by Chen Hongmou. In *Sibu beiyao*. Taibei: Zhonghua shuju, 1960.

——. *Wuzhong yigui* 五種遺規. In *Sibu beiyao*. Taibei: Zhonghua shuju, 1960.

——. *Xunsu yigui* 訓俗遺規. In *Wuzhong yigui*, by Chen Hongmou. In *Sibu beiyao*. Taibei: Zhonghua shuju, 1960.

Chen Hu 陳瑚. "Futing xiansheng xingzhuang" 桴亭先生行狀. In *Lu Futing xiansheng yishu* 陸桴亭先生遺書, by Lu Shiyi 陸世儀. Beijing: 1889.

——. *Shengxue rumen shu* 聖學入門書. In *Jiguo zhai zongshu* 記過齋叢書, edited by Su Yuanshang 蘇源生. Tongzhi edition.

——. "Zundao xiansheng Lu jun xingzhuang" 尊道先生陸君行狀. In *Lu Futing xiansheng yishu* 陸桴亭先生遺書, by Lu Shiyi 陸世儀. Beijing: 1889.

Chen Jiru 陳繼儒. "Zhuzhou tiaoyi" 煮粥條議. In *Xuehai leibian* 學海類編. Shanghai: Hanfen lou, 1920.

Chen Kui 陳揆. "Chen Cibu gong jia zhuan" 陳祠部公家傳. Appended to *Jiting quanshu* 幾亭全書, by Chen Longzheng. 1665.

Chen Longzheng 陳龍正. *Jiting quanshu* 幾亭全書. 1665. Hishi copy held at the East

Asian Library and Gest Collection, Princeton University. Original held at the Naikaku bunko, Tokyo.

Chen Qiaoyi 陈桥驿. *Shaoxing difang wenxian kaolu* 绍兴地方文献考录. Hangzhou: Zhejiang renmin chubanshen, 1983.

Chen Zilong 陳子龍. *Chen Wozi xiansheng Anya tang gao.* 陳卧子先生安雅堂稿. Shanghai: Shizhong shuju, 1909.

———. *Chen Zhongyu gong quanji nianpu* 陳忠裕公全集年譜. In *Chen Zhongyu quanji* 陳忠裕全集, edited by Wang Zhang 王昶. 1803.

Ch'en, Kenneth. *Buddhism in China.* Princeton, NJ: Princeton University Press, 1964.

Cheng, Pei-kai. "Reality and Imagination: Li Chih and T'ang Hsien-tsu in Search of Authenticity." Ph.D. diss., Yale University, 1980.

Cheng Yu-yin 程玉瑛. *Wan Ming bei yiwang de sixiangjia Luo Rufang (Jinqi) shiwen shiji biannian* 晚明被遺忘的思想家羅汝芳(近溪)詩文事蹟編年. Taibei: Guangwen shuju, 1995.

Chow, Kai-wing. *Publishing, Culture, and Power in Early Modern China.* Stanford, CA: Stanford University Press, 2004.

———. *The Rise of Confucian Ritualism in Late Imperial China.* Stanford, CA: Stanford University Press, 1994.

Chu Wanli 屈萬里, ed. *Pulinsidun daxue Geside dongfang tushuguan zhongwen shanben shuzhi* 普林斯頓大學葛思德東方圖書舘中文善本書志. Taibei: Yiwen yinshu guan, 1975.

Clarke, George W., trans. "The Yü-li or Precious Records." *Journal of the Royal Asiatic Society, North China Branch,* n.s., 28 (1893–94): 233–400. Shanghai: Royal Asiatic Society, 1898.

Cole, James H. *Shaohsing: Competition and Cooperation in Nineteenth-Century China.* Association for Asian Studies Monograph no. 44. Tucson: University of Arizona Press, 1986.

Concordance to Yi Ching, Harvard-Yenching Institute Sinological Index Series, Supplement no. 10. 1935. Rpt., Taibei : Chengwen shuju : Chinese Materials and Research Aids Service Center, 1966.

Cowell, Edward Byles, ed. *The Jātaka, or, Stories of the Buddha's Former Births.* Translated from the Pāli by various hands. 6 vols. Cambridge: Cambridge University Press, 1895–1907.

Cutter, Joe. *The Brush and the Spur: Chinese Culture and the Cockfight.* Shatin, Hong Kong: Chinese University Press, 1989.

Dai Zhaozuo 戴兆祚. *Yu gong Dezheng lu* 于公德政錄. In *Ming Qing shiliao huipian* 明清史料彙編, 1st series. Facsimile rpt., Taibei: Wenhai chubanshe, 1967.

Dardess, John W. *Blood and History in China: The Donglin Faction and Its Repression, 1620–1627.* Honolulu: University of Hawaii Press, 2002.

De Bary, Wm. Theodore. "Individualism and Humanitarianism in Late Ming Thought." In *Self and Society in Ming Thought,* edited by Wm. Theodore de Bary, 145–247. New York: Columbia University Press, 1970.

De Bary, Wm. Theodore, and Conference on Ming Thought, eds. *Self and Society in Ming Thought.* New York: Columbia University Press, 1970.

Des Forges, Roger V. *Cultural Centrality and Political Change in Chinese History: Northeast Henan in the Fall of the Ming.* Stanford, CA: Stanford University Press, 2003.

Dickens, Charles. *Bleak House.* New York: New American Library, 1964.

Dietrich, Craig. "Cotton Culture and Manufacture in Early Modern China." In *Economic Organization in Chinese Society*, edited by W. E. Willmott, 109–35. Stanford, CA: Stanford University Press, 1972.

Ding Bin 丁賓. *Ding Qinghui gong yiji*. 丁淸惠公遺集. Preface 1638. Hishi copy held at the East Asian Library and Gest Collection, Princeton University. Original held at the Naikaku bunko, Tokyo..

Donglin shuyuan zhi 東林書院志. Edited by Xu Xian 許獻, Gao Tingzhen 高廷珍, et al. 1881.

Dong Yang 董煬. *Liuzi nianpu* 劉子年譜. In *Liuzi quanshu* 劉子全書, by Liu Zongzhou 劉宗周. Facsimile rpt. of Daoguang edition. Taibei: Huawan shuju, 1968.

Dunstan, Helen. *Conflicting Counsels to Confuse the Age: A Documentary Study of Political Economy in Qing China, 1644–1840*. Ann Arbor: University of Michigan Center for Chinese Studies, 1996.

———. "The Late Ming Epidemics: A Preliminary Survey." *Ch'ing-shih wen-t'i* 3.3 (November 1975): 1–59.

Egan, Ronald C. *Word, Image, and Deed in the Life of Su Shi*. Cambridge, MA: East Asian Council, Harvard University, 1994.

Eliasberg, Danielle. "Pratiques funéraires animales en chine ancienne et médiévale." *Journal Asiatique* 280.1–2 (1992): 115–44.

Elman, Benjamin A. *A Cultural History of Civil Examinations in Late Imperial China*. Berkeley: University of California Press, 2000.

Elvin, Mark. *The Pattern of the Chinese Past*. Stanford, CA: Stanford University Press, 1973.

Esherick, Joseph W., and Mary Backus Rankin. Introduction to *Chinese Local Elites and Patterns of Dominance*, edited by Joseph W. Esherick and Mary Backus Rankin. Berkeley: University of California Press, 1990.

Fairchilds, Cissie C. *Poverty and Charity in Aix-en-Provence, 1640–1789*. Baltimore: Johns Hopkins University Press, 1976.

Fayuan zhulin 法苑珠林. Edited by Dao Shi 道世. 668. Facsimile rpt. of Wanli edition, Shanghai: Shangwu yinshuguan, 1929.

Feng Mengzhen 馮夢禎. *Kuaixue tang ji* 快雪堂集. Wanli edition. Microfilm of copy held at National Library of China.

Feng Shike 馮時可. *Feng Yuancheng xuanji* 馮元成選集. 1611. Microfilm of copy held at National Library of China.

Feng Zhenqun 馮真羣. *Qian Zhongjie gong nianpu* 錢忠介公年譜. Appended to *Qian Zhongjie gong ji* 錢忠介公集, by Qian Sule 錢肅樂. In *Siming congshu* 四明叢書. 1934.

Fengjing xiaozhi 楓涇小志. 1911.

Franke, Wolfgang. *An Introduction to the Sources of Ming History*. Kuala Lumpur: University of Malaya Press, 1969.

Fujita Yoshimi 藤田佳. "Minmatsu Kashan fu Kakyō hen ni okeru kyūkō ni tsuite" 明末, 嘉興府嘉善縣における救荒について. *Machikaneyama ronsō* 待兼山論叢 18 (1984): 23–44.

Fuma Susumu 夫馬進. *Chūgoku zenkai, zendō shi kenkyū* 中国善会善堂史研究. Kyoto: Dōhōsha shuppan, 1997.

———. "Dōzenkai shōshi: Chūgoku shakai fukushi shijō ni okeru Minmatsu Shinshō no ichizuke no tame ni" 同善会小史: 中國社会福祉史上における明末清初の位置ずけのために. *Shirin* 史林 65.4 (1982): 37–76.

———. "Late Ming Urban Reform and the Popular Uprising in Hangzhou." Translated from Japanese by Michael Lewis. In *Cities of Jiangnan in Late Imperial China*, edited by Linda Cooke Johnson, 47–97, 204–14. Albany: State University of New York Press, 1993. A revised version of "Minmatsu no toshi kaikaku to Kōshū minpen, published in *Tōhō gakuhō* 49 (Feb. 1977): 215–62.

———. "Zenkai zendō no shuppatsu" 善会善堂の出発. In Ono Kazuko 小野和子, ed., *Min Shin jidai no keisei to shakai* 明清時代の政治と社会, 189–232. Kyoto: Jimbun kagaku kenkyū jo, 1983.

——— [Fuma Jin 夫马进]. *Zhongguo shanhui shantang shi yanjiu* 中国善会善堂史研究. Translated into Chinese by Wu Yue 伍跃, Yang Wenxin 杨文信, Zhang Xuefeng 张学锋. Beijing: Shangwu yinshuguan, 2005.

Fushou quanshu 福壽全書. Compiled by Zheng Xuan 鄭瑄; incorrectly attributed to Chen Jiru 陳繼儒. Chongzhen edition. East Asian Library and Gest Collection, Princeton University.

Fu Yiling 傅衣凌. *Mingdai Jiangnan shimin jingji shitan* 明代江南市民經济試探. Shanghai: Renmin chuban she, 1963.

Gao Panlong 高攀龍. *Gaozi yishu* 高子遺書. Edited by Chen Longzheng 陳龍正. 1876.

Gaylin, Willard. "In the Beginning: Helpless and Dependent." In *Doing Good: The Limits of Benevolence,* by Willard Gaylin, Ira Glasser, Steven Marcus, and David J. Rothman, 1–38. New York: Pantheon Books, 1978.

Gernet, Jacques. *Buddhism in Chinese Society: An Economic History from the Fifth to the Tenth Centuries.* Translated by Franciscus Verellen. New York: Columbia University Press, 1995. Originally published as *Les aspects économiques du Bouddhisme dans la société chinoise du Vᵉ au Xᵉ siècle.* Saigon: École Française d'Extrême-Orient, 1956.

———. *China and the Christian Impact: A Conflict of Cultures.* Translated by Janet Lloyd. Cambridge: Cambridge University Press, 1985.

———. "Pitié pour les animaux." In *Dunhuang au Japan: Études chinoises et boudhiques offertes à Michel Soymié,* edited by Jean-Pierre Drège, 293–300. Geneva: Droz, 1996.

Goodrich, L. Carrington, and Chaoying Fang, eds. *Dictionary of Ming Biography, 1368–1644.* 2 vols. New York: Columbia University Press, 1976.

Goossaert, Vincent. *L'interdit de boeuf en Chine: Agriculture, éthique et sacrifice.* Paris: Collège de France, Institute des Hautes Études Chinoies, 2005.

Gouda, Frances. *Poverty and Political Culture: The Rhetoric of Social Welfare in Netherlands and France, 1815–1854.* Lanham, MD: Rowman and Littlefield, 1995.

Graham, A. C., trans. *The Book of Lieh-tzu.* London: John Murray, 1960.

Groner, Paul. "The *Fan-wan ching* and Monastic Discipline in Japanese Tendai: A Study of Annen's Futsū jubosotsukai kōshaku." In *Chinese Buddhist Apocrypha,* edited by Robert E. Buswell, Jr., 251–90 Honolulu: University of Hawaii Press, 1990.

Groot, J. J. M. de. *Le code du Māhayāna en chine: Son influence sur la vie monacale et sur le monde laïque.* Amsterdam: Johannes Müller, 1893.

———. "Miséricorde envers les animaux dans le Bouddhisme chinois." *T'oung Pao* 3 (1892): 466–89.

Grove, Linda, and Christian Daniels, eds. *State and Society in China: Japanese Perspectives on Ming-Qing Social and Economic History.* Tokyo: University of Tokyo Press, 1989.

Gu Qiyuan 顧起元. *Lanzhen caotang ji* 嬾眞草堂集. In *Mingren wenji congkan* 明人文集叢刊, 1st series. Facsimile rpt. of 1614 edition. Taibei: Wenhai chubanshe, 1970.

Gui Zhuang 歸莊. *Gui Zhuang ji* 歸莊集. Beijing: Zhonghua shuju, 1962. Rpt., Shanghai: Guji chubanshe, 1984.

Guiji xian zhi 會稽縣志. 1683. Typeset rpt., Shaoxing xian xiuzhi weiyuan hui, 1936.

Gujin tushu jicheng 古今圖書集成. Edited by Chen Menglei 陳梦雷 et al. 1726. Rpt., Taibei: Dingwen shuju, 1977.

Hanan, Patrick. *The Invention of Li Yu.* Cambridge, MA: Harvard University Press, 1988.

Handlin, Joanna F. [*see also* Smith, Joanna F. Handlin]. *Action in Late Ming Thought: The Reorientation of Lü K'un and Other Scholar-Officials.* Berkeley: University of California Press.. 1983.

Hangzhou fu zhi 杭州府志. 1784.

Hanyu da cidian. 漢語大詞典. Edited by Luo Zhufeng 罗竹风. 10 vols. 1990. Rpt., Shanghai: Hanyu da cidian chuban she, 1991.

Hauf, Kandice. "The Community Covenant in Sixteenth-Century Ji'an Prefecture, Jiangxi." *Late Imperial China* 17.2 (1996): 1–50.

Heijdra, Martin. "The Socio-Economic Development of Rural China during the Ming." In *The Cambridge History of China,* vol. 7, *The Ming Dynasty, 1368–1644,* part 2, edited by Frederick W. Mote and Denis Twitchett, 417–578. Cambridge: Cambridge University Press, 1998.

Hightower, James Robert, trans. *The Poetry of T'ao Ch'ien.* Oxford: Clarendon Press, 1970.

Himmelfarb, Gertrude. *Poverty and Compassion: The Moral Imagination of the Late Victorians.* New York: Alfred A. Knopf, 1991.

Ho, Ping-ti. *The Ladder of Success in Imperial China.* 1962. Rpt., New York: John Wiley and Sons, 1964.

Hoshi Ayao 星斌夫. "Mindai no Yōsaiin ni tsuite" 明代の養済院について. In *Hoshi hakase taikan kinen Chūgoku shi ronshū* 星博士退官記念中國史論集, edited by Hoshi Ayao sensei taiken kinen jigyōkai 星斌夫先生退官記念事業会, 131–50. Yamagata: 1978.

Hsia, C. T. "Time and the Human Condition in the Plays of T'ang Hsien-tsu." In *Self and Society in Ming Thought,* edited by Wm. Theodore de Bary and the Conference on Ming Thought, 249–90. New York: Columbia University Press, 1970.

Hsiao, Kung-chuan. *Rural China: Imperial Control in the Nineteenth Century.* 1960. Rpt., Seattle: University of Washington Press, 1967.

Hsu, Sung-peng. *A Buddhist Leader in Ming China: The Life and Thought of Han-Shan Te-ch'ing.* University Park: Pennsylvania State University Press, 1979.

Hu Xueyan wai zhuan 胡雪岩[嚴]外传. In *Wan Qing xiaoshuo daxi* 晚清小說大系. Taibei: Guangya chuban youxian gongsi, 1984.

Hu Zhi 胡直. *Henglu jingshe cang gao* 衡盧精舍藏稿. In *Yingyin Wenyuange Siku quanshu.* Rpt., Taibei: Shangwu yinshu guan, 1983.

Hua Yunzheng 華允誠. *Gao Zhongxian gong nianpu* 高忠憲公年譜. In *Gaozi yishu* 高子遺書, by Gao Panlong, edited by Chen Longzheng. 1876.

Huang Binghou 黄炳垕. *Huang Lizhou xiansheng nianpu* 黃梨洲先生年譜. In *Lizhou yizhu huikan* 梨洲遺著彙刊, by Huang Zongxi 黃宗羲. Taibei: Yongji chubanshe, 1969.

Huang Guilan 黃桂蘭. *Zhang Dai shengping ji qi wenxue* 張岱生平及其文學. Taibei: Wen shi zhe chubanshe, 1977.

Huang, Martin W. *Desire and Fictional Narrative in Late Imperial China.* Cambridge, MA: Harvard University Asia Center, 2001.

Huang, Ray. *1587, a Year of No Significance: The Ming Dynasty in Decline.* New Haven, CT: Yale University Press, 1981.

———. "Ni Yüan-lu: 'Realism' in a Neo-Confucian Scholar-Statesman." In *Self and Society in Ming Thought,* edited by Wm. Theodore de Bary and the Conference on Ming Thought, 415–82. New York: Columbia University Press, 1970.

Huang Tsung-hsi. *The Records of Ming Scholars.* Edited by Julia Ching, with the collaboration of Chaoying Fang. Honolulu: University of Hawaii Press, 1987.

Huang Zongxi 黄宗羲. *Lizhou yizhu huikan* 梨洲遺著彙刊. 2 vols. Taibei: Yongji chubanshe 1969.

———. *Mingru xue'an* 明儒學案. *Sibu beiyao* edition. Rpt., Taibei: Zhonghua shuju, 1970.

———. *Nanlei wenyue* 南雷文約. In *Lizhou yizhu huikan* 梨洲遺著彙刊, vol. 1. Taibei: Yongji chubanshe 1969.

———. *Sijiu lu* 思舊錄. In *Lizhou yizhu huikan* 梨洲遺著彙刊, vol. 1. Taibei: Yongji chubanshe, 1969.

Huating xian zhi 華亭縣志. 1878.

Hucker, Charles O. *A Dictionary of Official Titles in Imperial China.* Stanford, CA: Stanford University Press, 1985.

———. "Su-chou and the Agents of Wei Chung-hsien." *Silver Jubilee Volume of the Zimbun kagaku kenkyūsyo.* Kyoto: Kyoto University, 1954. Rpt., *Two Studies on Ming History,* Michigan Papers in Chinese Studies 12, 41–83. Ann Arbor: University of Michigan, Center for Chinese Studies, 1971.

———. "The Tung-lin Movement of the Late Ming." In *Chinese Thought and Institutions,* edited by John K. Fairbank, 132–62. Chicago: University of Chicago Press, 1957.

Hummel, Arthur, ed. *Eminent Chinese of the Ch'ing Period.* Washington, DC: United States Government Printing Office, 1943–44.

Hyde, Lewis. *The Gift: Imagination and the Erotic Life of Property.* 1979. Rpt., New York: Vintage Books, 1983.

Hymes, Robert P. "Moral Duty and Self-Regulating Process in Southern Sung Views of Famine Relief." In *Ordering the World: Approaches to State and Society in Sung Dynasty China,* edited by Robert P. Hymes and Conrad Schirokauer, 280–309. Berkeley: University of California Press, 1993.

———. "Not Quite Gentlemen? Doctors in Sung and Yuan." *Chinese Science* 8 (1987): 9–76.

———. *Statesmen and Gentlemen: The Elite of Fu-Chou, Chiang-Hsi, in Northern and Southern Sung.* Cambridge: Cambridge University Press, 1986.

Hymes, Robert P., and Conrad Schirokauer, eds. *Ordering the World: Approaches to State and Society in Sung Dynasty China.* Berkeley: University of California Press, 1993.

Jiao Hong 焦竑. *Jiaoshi bicheng* 焦氏筆乘. In *Yueya tang congshu* 粵雅堂叢書. Facsimile rpt. of 1853 copy in National Central Library, Taiwan, 1965.

Jiashan xian zhi 嘉善縣志. 1786.

Jiashan xian zhi 嘉善縣志. 1800.

Jiashan xian zuan xiu Qi Zhen tiaokuan 嘉善縣纂修啓禎條款. 1650. Microfilm held at the Harvary-Yenching Library.

Jin Zhijun 金之俊. *Xizhai ji* 息齋集. Kangxi edition. Hishi copy held at the East Asian Library and Gest Collection, Princeton University. Original held at the Naikaku bunko, Tokyo.

Kafalas, Philip A. *In Limpid Dreams: Nostalgia and Zhang Dai's Reminiscences of the Ming.* Norwalk, CT: East Bridge, 2007.

Kang-i Sun Chang. *The Late-Ming Poet Ch'en Tzu-lung: Crises of Love and Loyalism.* New Haven, CT: Yale University Press, 1991.

Kelley, David E. "Temples and Tribute Fleets: The Luo Sect and Boatmen's Associations in the Eighteenth Century." *Modern China* 8.3 (1982): 261–91.

Ko, Dorothy. *Teachers of the Inner Chambers: Women and Culture in Seventeenth-Century China.* Stanford, CA: Stanford University Press, 1994.

Kō Imai (Huang I-mei) 黃依妹. "Kaisatsu hōjō to jin no shisō" 戒殺放生と仁の思想. *Ōryō shigaku* 鷹陵史学 13 (October 1987): 29–55.

Kobayashi Kazumi, "The Other Side of Rent and Tax Resistance Struggles: Ideology and the Road to Rebellion." In *State and Society in China: Japanese Perpectives on Ming-Qing Social and Economic History,* edited by Linda Grove and Christian Daniels, 215–43. Tokyo: University of Tokyo Press, 1989.

Laufer, Berthold. *Tobacco and Its Use in Asia.* Anthropology Leaflet 18. Chicago: Field Museum of Natural History, 1924.

Law, Jane Marie. "Violence, Ritual, Reenactment, and Ideology: The *Hōjō-e* (Rite for Release of Sentient Beings) of the Usa Hachiman shrine in Japan." *History of Religions* 33.4 (1994): 305–57.

Lawton, Thomas. *Chinese Figure Painting.* Boston: David R. Godine, in Association with Freer Gallery of Art, Smithsonian Institution, 1973.

Leeuwen, Marco H. D. van. *The Logic of Charity: Amsterdam, 1800–1850.* Translated by Arnold J. Pomerans. Basingstoke: Macmillan; New York: St. Martin's Press, 2000.

Legge, James, trans. *The Chinese Classics.* 5 vols. 1893–95. Rpt., 3rd ed., Hong Kong: Hong Kong University Press, 1960. See below for individual volumes within this multivolume edition.

———. *The Ch'un Ts'ew* with *The Tso Chuen.* In *The Chinese Classics,* vol. 5.

———. *Confucian Analects.* In *The Chinese Classics,* vol. 1.

———. *The Doctrine of the Mean.* In *The Chinese Classics,* vol. 1.

———. *The Great Learning.* In *The Chinese Classics,* vol. 1.

———. *The She King, or, The Book of Poetry.* In *The Chinese Classics,* vol. 4.

———. *The Thai-Shang Tractate of Actions and Their Retributions.* In *The Texts of Taoism,* with introduction by D. T. Suzuki. 673–86. New York: Julian Press, 1959.

———. *The Works of Mencius.* In *The Chinese Classics,* vol. 2.

———. *The Writings of Chuang Tzu.* In *The Texts of Taoism,* with introduction by D. T. Suzuki, 212–672. New York: Julian Press, 1959.

Leung, Angela Ki Che [*see also* Liang Qizi]. "L'accueil des enfants abandonnés dans la Chine du bas-Yangzi aux XVIIᵉ et VIIIᵉ siècles." *Études chinoises* 4.1 (1985): 15–54.

———. "Medical Instruction and Popularization in Ming-Qing China." *Late Imperial China* 24.1 (2003): 148.

———. "Organized Medicine in Ming-Qing China: State and Private Medical Institutions in the Lower Yangzi Region." *Late Imperial China* 8.1 (June 1987): 134–66.

Li Changling 李昌齡, comp. *Leshan lu* 樂善錄. Facsimile rpt. of Song edition. Shanghai: Shanghai yinshuguan Hanfen lou, 1935.

Li Gefei 李格非. *Luoyang ming yuanji* 洛陽名園記. Edited by Mao Jin 毛晉. Rpt., Tokyo: 1829.

Li, Lillian M. *Fighting Famine in North China: State, Market, and Environmental Decline, 1690s–1990s.* Stanford, CA: Stanford University Press, 2007.

Liang Qizi 梁其姿 [*see also* Angela Ki Che Leung]. *Shishan yu jiaohua: Ming Qing de cishan zuzhi* 施善與教化: 明清的慈善組織. Taibei: Lianjing chubanshiye gongsuo, 1997.

Liangzhe yanfa zhi 兩浙鹽法志. Facsimile rpt. of 1792 ed. Taibei: Taiwan xuesheng shuju, 1966.

Ling Xiqi 凌錫祺. *Zundao xiansheng nianpu* 尊道先生年譜. In *Lu Futing xiansheng yishu* 陸桴亭先生遺書, by Lu Shiyi 陸世儀. Beijing: 1889.

Littrup, Leif. *Subbureaucratic Government in China in Ming Times: A Study of Shandong Province in the Sixteenth Century.* Oslo: Universitetsforlaget, 1981.

Liu, Hui-chen Wang. *The Traditional Chinese Clan Rules.* Monographs of the Association for Asian Studies no. 7. Locust Valley, NY: J. J. Augustin, 1959.

Liu, James T. C. "Liu Tsai (1165–1238): His Philanthropy and Neo-Confucian Limitations." *Oriens Extremus* 25.1 (1978): 1–29.

Liu Ts'un-yan. "Yüan Huang and His 'Four Admonitions.'" *Journal of the Oriental Society of Australia* 5.1–2 (December 1967): 108–32.

Liu Zongzhou 劉宗周. *Liuzi quanshu* 劉子全書. Facsimile rpt. of Daoguang edition. Taibei: Huawen shuju, 1968.

———. *Renpu, fu leiji* 人譜, 附類記. Taibei: Taiwan shangwu yinshu guan, n.d.

———. *Zhengren she yue.* In *Baibu congshu jicheng.* Rpt. from *Xuehai leibian* edition, Shanghai: Hanfen lou, 1920. Taibei: Yiwen yinshuguan yinxing, 1965.

Lu Longqi 陸隴其. *Sanyutang wenji* 三魚堂文集. In *Yingyin Wenyuange Siku quanshu.* Rpt., Taibei: Shangwu yinshu guan, 1983.

Lu Shiyi 陸世儀. "Bidi san ce" 避地三策. In *Lu Futing xiansheng yishu*, by Lu Shiyi. Beijing: n.p., 1889.

———. *Fushe jilue* 復社紀略. In *Donglin shimo* 東林始末, 167–256. In *Zhongguo jindai neiluan waihuo lishi gushi congshu* 中國近代內亂外禍歷史故事叢書. Taibei: Guangwen shuju, 1966.

———. *Lu Futing xiansheng wenji* 陸桴亭先生文集. In *Lu Futing xiansheng yishu*, by Lu Shiyi. Beijing: n.p., 1889.

———. *Lu Futing xiansheng yishu* 陸桴亭先生遺書. Edited by Qian Jingtang 錢敬堂. Beijing: n.p., 1889.

———. "Lunxue chouda" 論學酬答. In *Lu Futing xiansheng yishu*, by Lu Shiyi. Beijing: n.p., 1889.

———. *Sibian lu jiyao* 思辨錄輯要. In *Yingyin Wenyuange Siku quanshu.* Rpt., Taibei: Taiwan shangwu yinshu guan, 1983.

———. *Sibian lu jiyao* 思辨錄輯要. In *Lu Futing xiansheng yishu*, by Lu Shiyi. Beijing: n.p., 1889.

———. "Zhixiang san yue" 治鄉三約. In *Lu Futing xiansheng yishu*, by Lu Shiyi. Beijing: n.p., 1889.

———. *Zhixue lu* 志學錄. In *Lu Futing xiansheng yishu*, by Lu Shiyi. Beijing: n.p., 1889.

Lu Yunzheng 陸允正. "Lu Futing xiansheng xingshi" 陸桴亭先生行事. In *Lu Futing xiansheng yishu*, by Lu Shiyi. Beijing: n.p., 1889.

Lü Kun 呂坤. *Lü gong Shizheng lu* 呂公實政錄. Facsimile rpt. of 1797 edition. Taibei: Wen shi zhe chuban she, 1971.

———. *Lüzi yishu* 呂子遺書. 1827.

———. *Quwei zhai wenji* 去偽齋文集. In *Lüzi yishu*, by Lü Kun. 1827.

Lum, Raymond David. "Philanthropy and Public Welfare in Late Imperial China." Ph.D. diss., Harvard University, 1985.

Mao Qiling 毛奇齡. *Xihe ji* 西河集. In *Yingyin Wenyuange Siku quanshu.* Rpt., Taibei: Shangwu yinshu guan, 1983.

Mather, Richard. "The Bonze's Begging Bowl: Eating Practices in Buddhist Monasteries of Medieval India and China." *Journal of the American Oriental Society* 101.4 (October–December 1981): 417–24.

Mauss, Marcel. *The Gift: Forms and Functions of Exchange in Archaic Societies.* Translated by Ian Cunnison, with introduction by E. E. Evans-Pritchard. Rpt., New York: W. W. Norton, 1967.

McDermott, James P. "Animals and Humans in Early Buddhism." *Indo-Iranian Journal* 32.4 (1989): 269–80.

Meng Chaoran 孟超然. *Guang'ai lu* 廣愛錄. In *Mengshi ba lu* 孟氏八錄, by Meng Chaoran. 1815.

———. *Meng shi ba lu* 孟氏八錄. Compiled by Chen Shouqi 陳壽祺 and Feng Jin 馮縉. 1815.

Meskill, John. "Academies and Politics in the Ming Dynasty." In *Chinese Government in Ming Times: Seven Studies,* edited by Charles O. Hucker, 149–74. New York: Columbia University Press, 1969.

Michibata Ryōshū 道端良秀. *Chūgoku bukkyō to shakai fukushi jigyō* 中国仏教と社会福祉事業. Kyoto: Hōsōkan, 1967.

Ming shi 明史. Compiled by Zhang Tingyu 張廷玉 and edited by Guofang yanjiuyuan Mingshi pianzuan weiyuanhui 國防研究院明史編纂委員會. Yangmingshan: Zhongguo meishu yinshua chang, 1962–63.

Miyazaki, Ichisada. *China's Examination Hell: The Civil Service Examinations of Imperial China.* Translated by Contrad Schirokauer. 1976. Rpt., New Haven, CT: Yale University Press, 1981.

Mizoguchi Yūzō 溝口雄三. "Iwayuru Tōrinha jinshi no shisō—zenkindaiki ni okeru Chūgoku shisō no tenkai" いわゆる東林派人士の思想—前近代期における中國思想の展開. *Tōyō bunka kenkyūjo kiyō* 東洋文化研究所紀要 75 (March 1978): 111–341.

Mori, Masao. "The Gentry in the Ming: An Outline of the Relations Between the *Shih-ta-fu* and Local Society." *Acta Asiatica* 38 (1980): 31–53.

Morohashi Tetsuji 諸橋轍次. *Dai Kan-Wa jiten* 大漢和辞典. 13 vols. Tokyo: Taishūkan Shoten, Shōwa 1955–60.

Mote, Frederick W. "Confucian Eremitism in the Yüan Period." In *The Confucian Persuasion,* edited by Arthur F. Wright, 202–40. Stanford, CA: Stanford University Press, 1960.

Naquin, Susan. *Peking: Temples and City Life, 1400–1900.* Berkeley: University of California Press, 2000.

Naquin, Susan, and Chün-fang Yü, eds. *Pilgrims and Sacred Sites in China.* Berkeley: University of California Press, 1992.

Ni Huiding 倪會鼎. *Ni Wenzheng gong nianpu* 倪文正公年譜. In *Yueya tang congshu* 粵雅堂叢書, 1853. Facsimile rpt., Taibei: Huawen shuju, 1965.

Ni Yuanlu 倪元璐. *Hongbao yingben* 鴻寶應本. 1642. Facsimile rpt., in *Lidai huajia shiwen ji* 歷代畫家詩文集. Taibei: Taiwan xuesheng shuju, 1970.

Nienhauser, William H., Jr., ed., *The Indiana Companion to Traditional Chinese Literature.* Bloomington: Indiana University Press, 1986.

Norberg, Kathryn. *Rich and Poor in Grenoble, 1600–1814.* Berkeley: University of California Press, 1985.

Ocko, Jonathan. *Bureaucratic Reform in Provincial China*. Cambridge, MA: Harvard University Press, 1983.

Ogasawara Senshū 小笠原宣秀. *Chūgoku kinsei Jōdokyō shi no kenkyu* 中國近世淨土教史の研究. Kyoto: Hyakken en, 1963.

Okuzaki Hiroshi 奧崎裕司. *Chūgoku kyōshin jinushi no kenkyū* 中國鄉紳地主の研究. Tokyo: Kyūko Shoin, 1978.

Orwell, George. *Burmese Days*. Vol. 2 of *The Complete Works of George Orwell*, edited by Peter Davison. London: Secker and Warburg, 1986.

Oxford English Dictionary Online, 2d edition. Oxford University Press, 2003.

Palatre, Gabriel. *L'infanticide et l'oeuvre de la Sainte-Enfance en Chine*. Shanghai: Autographie de la Mission Catholique à l'Orphelinat de Tou-sè-wè, 1878.

Peng Dingqiu 彭定求. *Nanyun wengao* 南畇文稿. In *Nanyun quanji* 南畇全集, by Peng Dingqiu. 1881.

Peng Shaosheng 彭紹升. *Jushi zhuan* 居士傳. Taibei: Liuli jing fang, 197–.

Prip-Møller, J. *Chinese Buddhist Monasteries*. 1937. Rpt., Hong Kong: Hong Kong University Press, 1967.

Qi Biaojia 祁彪佳. *Qi Biaojia ji* 祁彪佳集. Shanghai: Zhonghua shuju, 1960.

———. *Qi Zhongmin gong riji* 祁忠敏公日記. Shaoxing: Shaoxing xian xiu zhi weiyuan hui, 1937. Each year of Qi's diaries has a separate title and is independently paginated. References to the titles are to the closest corresponding year in the Western calendar, even though it is understood that the Chinese and Western calendars are not exactly matched: 1631: *Shebei cheng yan* 涉北程言; 1632: *Xibei rong yan* 棲北冗言; 1633: *Yinan suo ji* 役南瑣記; 1635: *Guinan kuai lu* 歸南快錄; 1636: *Julin shi bi* 居林適筆; 1637: *Shanju zhuo lu* 山居拙錄; 1638: *Zijian lu* 自鑒錄; 1639: *Qi lu* 棄錄; 1640: *Ganmu lu* 感暮錄; 1641: *Xiaojiu lu* 小捄錄; 1642: *Renwu rili* 壬午日歷.

———. *Yuanshan tang Ming qupin, jupin jiao lu* 遠山堂明曲品劇品校錄. Annotated by Huang Shang 黃裳. Shanghai: Chuban gongsi, 1955.

———. *Yu shan zhu* 寓山注. Chongzhen edition. Microfilm of copy held at National Library of China.

Qi Chenghan 祁承㸁. *Dansheng tang cang shumu* 澹生堂藏書目. In *Shaoxing xianzheng yishu* 紹興先正遺書. Guangxu edition.

———. *Dansheng tang ji* 澹生堂集. Chongzhen edition. Microfilm of copy held at National Library of China.

Qi Junjia 祁駿佳. *Dunweng suibi* 遯翁隨筆. In *Yangshi qian qibai ershijiu hezhai congshu* 仰視千七百二十九鶴齋叢書. Shaoxing: Morun tang shuyuan, 1929.

Qian Qianyi 錢謙益. *Muzhai chuxue ji* 牧齋初學集. Yonghe: Wenhai chubanshe. 1986.

———. *Youxue ji* 有學集. In *Muzhai quanji*. Rpt., n.p.: Suihan zhai jiaoyin, 1910.

Qian Shisheng 錢士升. *Ciyu tang ji* 賜餘堂集. In *Siku jinhui shu congkan*. Photo rpt. of 1739 ed., Beijing: Beijing chubanshe, 1997.

Qian Sule 錢肅樂. *Qian Zhongjie gong ji* 錢忠介公集. In *Siming congshu* 四明叢書. 1934.

Qiantang xian zhi 錢塘縣志. Wanli edition. Facsimile rpt. of *Wulin zhanggu cong bian* 武林掌故叢編 edition of 1883. Taibei: Tailian guofang chuban she, 1967.

Qiu Weibing 邱維屏. *Qiu Bangshi wenji* 邱邦士文集. 1875.

Qu Wanli 屈萬里, ed. *Pulinsidun daxue Geside dongfang tushuguan Zhongwen shanben shu zhi* 普林斯頓大學葛思德東方圖書館中文善本書志. Taibei: Yiwen yinshu guan, 1974. Rpt., Taibei: Lianjing chuban shiye gongsi, 1984.

Quan Zuwang 全祖望. *Qian Sule nianpu* 錢肅樂年譜. In *Qian Zhongjie gong ji* 錢忠介公集. Siming congshu ed. 1934.

Rankin, Mary Backus. *Elite Activism and Political Transformation in China: Zhejing Province, 1865–1911.* Stanford, CA: Stanford University Press, 1986.

Rawski, Evelyn Sakakida. *Education and Popular Literacy in Ch'ing China.* Michigan Studies in China. Ann Arbor: University of Michigan Press, 1979.

Rengui zhigao 壬癸志稿. Edited by Qian Baochen 錢寶琛. 1880.

"Report of the Foundling Hospital at Shanghai, translated from the original for the Chinese Repository." *Chinese Repository* 14.4 (1945): 177–95.

Rhoads, Edward J. M. "Merchant Associations in Canton, 1895–1911." In *The Chinese City between Two Worlds,* edited by Mark Elvin and G. William Skinner, 97–117. Stanford, CA: Stanford University Press, 1974.

Richard, Timothy. *Forty-five Years in China: Reminiscences.* New York: Frederick A. Stokes, 1916.

Riely, Celia Carrrington. "Tung Ch'i-ch'ang's Life." In *The Century of Tung Ch'i-ch'ang, 1555–1636,* edited by Wai-kam Ho, 2 vols., 2:387–457. Seattle: Nelson-Atkins Museum of Art, in association with the University of Washington Press, 1992.

Ritvo, Harriet. *The Animal Estate: The English and Other Creatures in the Victorian Age.* Cambridge, MA: Harvard University Press, 1987.

Roberts, A. D. S. "Civil Disturbance in I-hsing in 1633." *Ming Studies* 24 (Fall 1987): 58–64.

Rothman, David. Introduction to *Doing Good: The Limits of Benevolence,* by Willard Gaylin, Ira Glasser, Steven Marcus, and David J. Rothman. New York: Pantheon Books, 1978.

Rowe, William T. *Hankow: Commerce and Society in a Chinese City, 1796–1889.* Stanford, CA: Stanford University Press, 1984.

———. *Saving the World: Chen Hongmou and Elite Consciousness in Eighteenth-Century China.* Stanford, CA: Stanford University Press.

Sakai Tadao 酒井忠夫. *Chūgoku zensho no kenkyū* 中国善書の研究. Tokyo: Kokusho kankōkai. 1960.

———. "Confucianism and Popular Educational Works." In *Self and Society in Ming Thought,* edited by Wm. Theodore de Bary, 331–66. New York: Columbia University Press, 1970.

———. "Gan Moyu no shisō ni tsuite" 顔茂猷の思想について. In *Kamada Hakushi kanreiki kinen rekishigaku ronsō* 鎌田博士還暦記念歴史学論叢, 259–73. Tokyo: Kamada Sensei Kanreki Kinenkai, 1969.

Salamon, Lester M. Salamon. "The Rise of the Nonprofit Sector." *Foreign Affairs* 74.4 (July–August 1994): 109–22.

Salisbury, Harrison E. "In China, 'A Little Blood.'" Op-ed piece, *New York Times,* 13 June 1989.

Schafer, Edward H. *Tu Wan's Stone Catalogue of Cloudy Forest.* Berkeley: University of California Press, 1961.

Scogin, Hugh. "Poor Relief in Northern Sung China." *Oriens Extremus* 25.1 (1978): 30–46.

Sen, Amartya, *Poverty and Famines: An Essay on Entitlement and Deprivation.* 1981. Rpt., Oxford: Oxford University Press, 1991.

Shangyu xian (Zhejiang) zhi 上虞縣(浙江)志. 1811.

Shanyin xian zhi 山陰縣志. 1724.

Shanyin xian zhi 山陰縣志. 1803.

Shanyin xian zhi 山陰縣志. 1930.

Shanyin xian zhi jiaoji 山陰縣志校記. Edited by Li Ciming 李慈銘. Rpt., Shanghai: Shanghai shudian, 1993.

Shaoxing fu zhi 紹興府志. 1683.

Shaoxing fu zhi 紹興府志. Wanli edition. In *Siku quanshu cunmu congshu*. Jinan: Qi Lu shushe chubanshe, 1997.

Shaoxing xian zhi ziliao 紹興縣志資料. Edited by Shaoxing xian xiu zhi weiyuan hui 紹興縣修志委員會. N.p.: 1937–39.

Shek, Richard. "Testimony to the Reliance of the Mind: The Life and Thought of P'eng Shao-sheng (1740–1796)." In *Cosmology, Ontology, and Human Efficacy: Essays in Chinese Thought*, edited by Richard J. Smith and D. W. Y. Kwok, 81–111. Honolulu: University of Hawaii Press, 1993.

Smith, Arthur H. *Chinese Characteristics*. Rev. ed., New York: Fleming H. Revell, 1894.

———. *Village Life in China*. 1899. Rpt., New York: Greenwood Press, 1969.

Smith, Joanna F. Handlin [*see also* Handlin, Joanna F.]. "Gardens in Ch'i Piao-chia's Social World: Wealth and Values in Late-Ming Kiangnan." *Journal of Asian Studies* 51.1 (1992): 55–81.

———. "Social Hierarchy and Merchant Philanthropy as Perceived in Several Late-Ming and Early-Qing Texts." *Journal of the Economic and Social History of the Orient* 41.3 (1998): 417–51.

So, Kwan-wai. *Japanese Piracy in Ming China during the Sixteenth Century*. Ann Arbor: Michigan State University Press, 1975.

Song shi 宋史. Compiled by Tuotuo 脫脫 et al. Beijing: Zhonghua shuju; Shanghai: Xinhua shudian, 1977.

Spence, Jonathan D. *Return to Dragon Mountain: Memories of a Late Ming Man*. New York: Viking Press, 2007.

Spring, Madeline K. *Animal Allegories in T'ang China*. American Oriental Series no. 76. New Haven, CT: American Oriental Society, 1993.

Standaert, Nicolas. *Yang Tingyun, Confucian and Christian in Late Ming China: His Life and Thought*. Sinica Leidensia no. 19. Leiden: E. J. Brill, 1988.

Taicang zhou zhi 太倉州志. Edited by Zhang Cai 張采 et al. 1678. Microfilm of copy held at National Library of China.

Taicang zhou zhi 太倉州志. 1803.

Taicang zhou zhi 太倉州志. 1918.

Taiping guangji 太平廣記. Edited by Li Fang 李昉. 981. Rpt., Beijing: Renmin wenxue chubanshe, 1959.

Taishang ganying pian tu shuo 太上感應篇圖說. Edited by Huang Zhengyuan 黃正元. Rpt., Quzhou: Sanyu tang, 1880.

Tan Qian 談遷. *Guo que* 國榷. Edited by Zhang Zongxiang 張宗祥. Shanghai: Guji chubanshe, 1958.

Tanaka Masatoshi. "Popular Uprisings, Rent Resistance, and Bondservant Rebellions in the Late Ming." In *State and Society in China: Japanese Perpectives on Ming-Qing Social and Economic History*, edited by Linda Grove and Christian Daniels, 79–100. Tokyo: University of Tokyo Press, 1989.

Tang Xianzu 湯顯祖. *Tang Xianzu ji* 湯顯祖集. Edited by Xu Shuofang 徐朔方. Shanghai: Renmin chubanshe. 1973.

Tang Zhen. *Écrits d'un sage encore inconnu.* Translated and annotated by Jacques Gernet. Paris: Gillimard/UNESCO, 1991.

———. *Qianshu, fu shiwen lu* 潛書附詩文錄. Edited by Wu Zhemin 吳澤民. Beijing: Zhonghua hua shuju, 1955.

Tao Wangling 陶望齡. *Xie an ji* 歇庵集. Edited by Wang Yinglin 王應遴. Taibei: Weiwen tushu chubanshe, 1976.

Taylor, Rodney Leon. *The Cultivation of Sagehood as a Religious Goal in Neo-Confucianism: A Study of Selected Writings of Gao P'an-lung, 1562–1626.* Missoula, MT: Scholars Press, 1978.

Terada Takanobu 寺田隆信. "Ki Hyōka to Gan Moyu—*Tekikichiroku jo* no kakareta goro" 祁彪佳と顏茂猷—迪吉錄序の書かれた頃—. In *Dokyō to shūkyō bunka* 道教と宗教文化, edited by Akizuki Ken'ei 秋月觀暎, 471–88. Tokyo: Hirakawa shuppansha, 1987.

Tsu, Yu-Yue. *The Spirit of Chinese Philanthropy: A Study in Mutual Aid.* 1912. Rpt., New York: AMS Press, 1968.

Tu Long 屠隆. *Qizhen guan ji* 栖眞館集. 1590. Microfilm of copy held at National Library of China.

Twitchett, Denis. "The Fan Clan's Charitable Estate, 1050–1760." In *Confucianism in Action,* edited by David S. Nivison and Arthur F. Wright, 97–133. Stanford, CA: Stanford University Press, 1959.

Unschuld, Paul U. *Medical Ethics in Imperial China: A Study in Historical Anthropology.* Berkeley: University of California Press, 1979.

Übelhör, Monika. "The Community Compact (*Hsiang-yüeh*) of the Sung and Its Educational Significance." In *Neo-Confucian Education: The Formative Stage,* edited by Wm. Theodore de Bary and John W. Chaffee, 371–88. New York: Columbia University Press, 1989.

Van Slyke, Lyman P. *Yangtze: Nature, History, and the River.* Reading, MA: Addison-Wesley Publishing, 1988.

Von Glahn, Richard. "Community and Welfare: Chu Hsi's Community Granaries in Theory and Practice." In *Ordering the World: Approaches to State and Society in Sung Dynasty China,* edited by Robert P. Hymes and Conrad Schirokauer, 221–354. Berkeley: University of California Press, 1993.

———. "The Enchantment of Wealth: The God Wutong in the Social History of Jiangnan." *Harvard Journal of Asiatic Studies* 51.2 (1991): 651–714.

———. *Fountain of Fortune: Money and Monetary Policy in China, 1000–1700.* Berkeley: University of California, 1996.

———. "Municipal Reform and Urban social Conflict in Late Ming Jiangnan." *Journal of Asian Studies* 50.2 (1991): 280–307.

Wakeman, Frederic, Jr. "The Civil Society and Public Sphere Debate: Western Reflections on Political Culture." Symposium: "Public Sphere/Civil Society in China? Paradigmatic Issues in Chinese Studies," part 3. *Modern China* 19.2 (April 1993): 108–38.

Wakeman, Frederic, Jr., and Carolyn Grant, eds. *Conflict and Control in Late Imperial China.* Berkeley: University of California Press, 1975.

Waltner, Ann. "Visionary and Bureaucrat in the Late Ming." *Late Imperial China* 8.1 (1987): 105–33.

Wan Ming qujia nianpu 晚明曲家年谱. Edited by Xu Shuofang 徐朔方. 3 vols. Hangzhou: Zhejiang guji chubanshe, 1993.

Wang Chong jian 王崇簡. *Qingxiang tang wenji* 青箱堂詩文集. Preface. 1676. Hishi copy held at the East Asian Library and Gest Collection, Princeton University. Original held at the Naikaku bunko, Tokyo.

Wang Deyi 王德毅. *Songdai zaihuang de jiuji zhengce* 宋代災荒的救濟政策. Taibei: Taiwan Shangwu yinshuguan, 1960.

Wang Fan-sen 王汎森. "Ripu yu Mingmo Qingchu sixiang jia—yi Yan-Li xuepai wei zhu de taolun" 日譜與明末清初思想家—以顏李學派為主的討論 . *Zhongyang yanjiuyuan lishi yuyan yanjiusuo jikan* 中央研究院歷史語言研究所集刊 69.2 (1998): 245–94.

Wang Heng 王衡. *Wang Goushan xiansheng ji* 王緱山先生集. 1616. Rpt., Taibei: Wenhai chubanshe, 1970.

Wang Lanyin 王蘭蔭. "Mingdai zhi xiangyue yu minzhong jiaoyu" 明代之鄉約與民眾教育. *Shida yuekan* 師大月刊 21 (1935): 103–22.

Wang Mingsheng 王鳴盛. "Chen Quean xiansheng zhuan" 陳確安先生傳. In *Sheng xue rumen shu* 聖學入門書, by Chen Hu 陳瑚. In *Jiguozhai congshu* 記過齋叢書.

Wang Ruqian 汪汝謙. *Chunxing tang shiji* 春星堂詩集. In *Congmu Wang shi yishu* 叢睦汪氏遺書. 1886.

Wang Siren 王思任. *Qi Zhongmin gong nianpu* 祁忠敏公年譜. In *Qi Zhongmin gong riji* 祁忠敏公日記. Shaoxing: Shaoxing xian xiu zhi weiyuan hui, 1937.

Wang Yangming. *Instructions for Practical Living and Other Neo-Confucian Writings, by Wang Yang-ming*. Translated, introduced by, and with notes by Wing-tsit Chan. New York: Columbia University Press, 1963.

———. *Wang Yangming quanshu* 王陽明全書. 4 vols. 1953. Rpt., Taibei: Zhengzhong shuju, 1970.

Wang Zheng 王徵. *Renhui yue yin* 仁會約引. Photocopy of the copy held at the Bibliothèque nationale, Paris.

Wang Zongpei 王宗培. *Zhongguo zhi hehui* 中國之合會. 1931. Rpt., Nanjing: Zhongguo hezuo xuehui, 1935.

Watt, John B. "The Yamen and Urban Administration." In *The City in Late Imperial China*, edited by G. William Skinner, 353–90. Stanford, CA: Stanford University Press, 1977.

Weaver, Warren. *U.S. Philanthropic Foundations*. New York: Harper and Row, 1967.

Weinstein, Stanley. *Buddhism under the T'ang*. Cambridge: Cambridge University Press, 1987.

Welch, Holmes. *The Buddhist Revival in China*. Cambridge, MA: Harvard University Press, 1968.

———. *The Practice of Chinese Buddhism, 1900–1950*. Cambridge, MA: Harvard University Press, 1967.

Wen Huang 溫璜. *Wenshi mu xun* 溫氏母訓. In *Baibu congshu jicheng* 百部叢書集成. Taibei: Yiwen yinshuguan yinxing, 1965. Rpt. from *Xuehai leibian* edition, Shanghai: Hanfen lou, 1920.

Wen Juntian 聞鈞天. *Zhongguo baojia zhidu* 中國保甲制度. Shanghai: Shangwu yinshuguan, 1936.

Wiens, Mi Chü. "Cotton Textile Production and Rural Social Transformation in Early Modern China." *Journal of the Institute of Chinese Studies of the Chinese University of Hong Kong* 7.2 (1974): 515–34.

———. "Socioeconomic Change during the Ming Dynasty in the Kiangnan Area." Ph.D. diss., Harvard University, 1973.

Will, Pierre-Étienne. *Bureaucracy and Famine in Eighteenth-Century China.* Translated by Elborg Forster. Stanford, CA: Stanford University Press, 1990.

———, "Un cycle hydraulique en Chine: la province du Hubei du XVIᵉ au XIXᵉ siècles." *Bulletin de l'école française d'extrême-orient* 68 (1980): 261–87.

———, ed. "Official Handbooks and Anthologies of Imperial China: A Descriptive and Critical Bibliography." Ms. in progress.

Will, Pierre-Étienne, and R. Bin Wong, with James Lee. *Nourish the People: The State Civilian Granary System in China, 1650–1850.* Ann Arbor: Michigan Monographs in Chinese Studies no. 60, 1991.

Wong, R. Bin, and Peter C. Perdue. "Famine's Foes in Ch'ing China." *Harvard Journal of Asiatic Studies* 43.1 (1983): 291–332.

Woodham-Smith, Cecil. *The Great Hunger, Ireland, 1845–1849.* 1962. Rpt., London: Penguin Books, 1991.

The Works of Hsuntze. Translated and annotated by Homer H. Dubs. London: Arthur Probsthain, 1928.

Wu Chenyan 吳陳炎. "Fangsheng hui yue" 放生會約. In *Zhaodai congshu bieji* 昭代叢書別集. 1876.

Wu Jinghang 吳鏡沆. *Chen Andao xiansheng nianpu* 陳安道先生年譜. 1893. Library of Congress.

Wu, Nelson I. "Tung Ch'i-ch'ang (1555–1636): Apathy in Government and Fervor in Art." In *Confucian Personalities,* edited by Arthur F. Wright and Denis Twitchett, 260–93. Stanford, CA: Stanford University Press, 1962.

Wu, Pei-yi. "An Ambivalent Pilgrim to T'ai Shan in the Seventeenth Century." In *Pilgrims and Sacred Sites in China,* edited by Susan Naquin and Chün-fang Yü, 65–88. Berkeley: University of California Press, 1992.

———. "Childhood Remembered: Parents and Children in China, 800–1700." In *Chinese Views of Childhood,* edited by Anne Behnke Kinney, 129–56. Honolulu: University of Hawaii Press, 1995.

———. *The Confucian's Progress: Autobiographical Writings in Traditional China.* Princeton, NJ: Princeton University Press, 1990.

Wucheng xian zhi 烏程縣志. 1746.

Xiangcheng xian zhi 襄城縣志. 1746.

Xiaoshan xian zhi 蕭山縣志. 1683.

Xiaoshan xian zhi 蕭山縣志. 1751.

Xie Zhaozhe 謝肇淛. *Wu za zu* 五雜組. 1608. Rpt., Taibei: Xinxing shuju youxian gongsi, 1971.

Xu Chongxi 許重熙. *Ciyu tang ji nianpu* 賜餘堂集年譜. In *Ciyu tang ji* 賜餘堂集, by Qian Shisheng 錢士升. 1739. In *Siku jinhui shu congkan.* Beijing: Beijing chubanshe, 1997.

———. *Qian Shisheng nianpu* 錢士升年譜. In *Ciyu tang ji* 賜餘堂集. In *Siku quanshu jinhui shu congkan.* Beijing: Beijing chubanshe, 1997.

Xu Guangqi 徐光啓. *Nongzheng quanshu jiaozhu* 農政全書校注. Edited by Shi Shenghan 石聲漢. Shanghai: Shanghai guji chubanshe, 1979.

———. *Xu Guangqi ji* 徐光啓集. Edited by Wang Zhongmin 王重民. Shanghai: Zhonghua shuju, 1963.

Yan Maoyou 顏茂猷 [Guangzhong 光衷], comp. and annot. *Diji lu* 廸吉錄. N.d. Copy held at Harvard-Yenching Library. Another edition with a 1631 preface by Qi Biaojia at the East Asian Library and Gest Collection, Princeton University.

———. *Diji lu* 廸吉錄. In *Siku quanshu cunmu congshu.* Jinan: Qi Lu shushe chubanshe, 1997.

Yan Zhongping 嚴中平. *Zhongguo mianfangzhi shi gao* 中國棉紡織史稿. Beijing: Kexue chubanshe, 1963.

Yang. *See* Yang Dongming.

Yang, C. K. *Religion in Chinese Society.* Berkeley: University of California Press, 1967.

Yang Dongming 楊東明. *Shanju gongke* 山居功課. 1624. Hishi copy held at the East Asian Library and Gest Collection, Princeton University. Original held at the Naikaku bunko, Tokyo.

Yang, Lien-sheng. "The Concept of *Pao* as a Basis for Social Relations in China." In *Chinese Thought and Institutions,* edited by John K. Fairbank, 3–23. 1957. Rpt., Chicago: University of Chicago Press, 1967.

———. "Economic Justification for Spending: An Uncommon Idea in Traditional China." In *Studies in Chinese Institutional History,* by Lien-sheng Yang, 58–74. Rpt., Cambridge, MA: Harvard University Press. 1963.

Yao Mingda 姚名達. *Liu Zongzhou nianpu* 劉宗周年譜. Shanghai: Shangwu yinshuguan, 1934.

Yao Wenran 姚文然. *Yao Ruiyi gong wenji* 姚端恪公文集. Preface. 1685. Hishi copy held at the East Asian Library and Gest Collection, Princeton University. Original held at the Naikaku bunko, Tokyo.

Yaojiang shuyuan zhi 姚江書院志. In *Zhongguo lidai shuyuan zhi* 中國歷代書院志. 1794. Rpt., Nanjing: Jiangsu jiaoyu chubanshe, 1995.

Ye Shaoyuan 葉紹袁, et al. *Qi Zhen jiwen lu* 啓禎記聞錄. In *Tongshi* 痛史. Edited by Letian Jushi [Sun Yuxiu] 樂天居士 [孫毓修]. Shanghai: Shangwu yinshuguan, 1911–17.

Yim, Shui-yuen. "Famine Relief Statistics as a Guide to the Population of Sixteenth-Century China: A Case-Study of Honan Province," *Ch'ing-shih wen-t'i* 3.9 (1978): 1–30.

Ying Yukang 應裕康. "Qi Biaojia de shengping ji qi chuanji ziliao" 祁彪佳的生平及其傳記資料. *Gaoxiong shiyuan xuebao* 高雄師院學報 15 (March 1987): 94–86 (*sic*).

———. "Qi Biaojia zhuzuo kao" 祁彪佳著作考. *Muduo* 木鐸 11 (February 1987): 49–82.

Yu Chunxi 虞淳熙. *Yu Deyuan xiansheng ji* 虞德園先生集. N.d. Hishi copy held at the East Asian Library and Gest Collection, Princeton University. Original held at the Naikaku bunko, Tokyo.

Yu Huang 余煌. *Yu Zhongjie gong yi wen* 余忠節公遺文. In *Yue zhong wenxian ji cun shu* 越中文獻輯存書. N.d. Microfilm held at the Harvard-Yenching Library, Harvard University.

Yu Kai 與楷. "Xiao Yunqi fangsheng lu" 小雲棲放生錄. Facsimile reprint of *Wulin zhang-gu cong bian* 武林掌故叢編 edition, 1883. Taibei: Tailian guofang chuban shu, 1967.

Yu Zhi 余治, comp. *Deyi lu* 得一錄. 1869. Facsimile rpt., Taibei: Huawen shuju, 1969.

Yü, Chün-fang. *The Renewal of Buddhism in China: Chu-hung and the Late Ming Synthesis.* New York: Columbia University Press, 1981.

Yucheng xian zhi 虞城縣志. 1895.

Zeitlin, Judith T. "The Petrified Heart: Obsession in Chinese Literature, Art, and Medicine." *Late Imperial China* 12.1 (June 1991): 1–25.

Zhang Bi 張陛. *Jiuhuang shiyi* 救荒事宜. In *Xuehai lei bian* 學海類編. Shanghai: Hanfen lou, 1920.

Zhang Cai 張采. *Zhiwei tang wen cun* 知畏堂文存. In *Siku jinhui shu congkan.* Beijing: Beijing chubanshe, 1997.

Zhang Dafu 張大復. *Meihua cao tang bitan* 梅花草堂筆談. In *Zhongguo wenxue zhenben congshu* 中國文學珍本叢書, 1st series. Shanghai: Zazhi gongsi, 1935.

Zhang Dai 張岱. *Langhuan wenji* 琅嬛文集. In *Zhongguo wenxue zhenben congshu* 中國文學珍本叢書, 1st series. Shanghai: Zazhi gongsi, 1935.

———. *Shigui shu hou ji* 石匱書後集 In *Xuxiu Siku quanshu*. Shanghai: Shanghai shuji chubanshe, 1995–99.

———. *Taoan mengyi* 陶庵夢憶. Taibei: Kaiming shudian, 1957.

———. *Xihu mengxun* 西湖夢尋. In *Zhongguo wenxue zhenben congshu* 中國文學珍本叢書, 1st series. Shanghai: Shanghai zazhi gongsi, 1936.

Zhang Jiebin 張介賓. *Jingyue quanshu* 景岳全書. In *Yingyin Wenyuange Siku quanshu*. Taibei: Taiwan shangwu yinshuguan, 1985.

Zhang Lixiang [Lüxiang] 張履祥. *Yanxing jianwen lu* 言行見聞錄. In *Yangyuan xiansheng quanji* 楊園先生全集, by Zhang Lixiang, edited by Yao Lianyuan 姚璉原. Preface. 1644. Rpt., Suzhou: Jiangsu shuju, 1871.

Zhao Yi 趙翼. *Gaiyu congkao* 陔餘叢考. Shanghai: Shangwu yinshuguan, 1957.

Zhi Dalun 支大綸. *Zhi Huaping xiansheng ji* 支華平先生集. Wanli edition. Microfilm of copy held at National Library of China.

Zhou Kongjiao 周孔教. "Jiuhuang tiaoyu" 救荒條諭. Appended to "Zhuzhou tiaoyi" 煮粥條議, by Chen Jiru 陳繼儒. In *Xuehai leibian*. Shanghai: Hanfen lou, 1920.

Zhou Mengyan 周夢顏. *Wanshan xian zi ji* 萬善先資集. In *Anshi quanshu* 安士全書, by Zhou Mengyan. Rpt., Hangzhou: Foxue tuixing she, 1927.

———. *Yinzhi wen guangyi* 陰騭文廣義. In *Anshi quanshu* 安士全書. Rpt., Hangzhou: Foxue tuixing she. 1927.

Zhou Rudeng 周汝登. *Dongyue zhengxue lu* 東越證學錄. 1605. In *Mingren wenji congkan* 明人文集叢刊, 1st series. Facsimile rpt., Taibei Wenhai chubanshe, 1960.

Zhu Guozhen 朱國禎. *Yongchuang xiaopin* 湧幢小品. 1622. Rpt., Shanghai: Zhonghua shuju, 1959.

Zhu Shi 朱軾. *Guang hui bian* 廣惠編. Japanese reprint entitled *Kōkei hen zōkai, jō ge* 廣惠編像解, 上下. In *Nihon keizai taiten* 日本經濟大典. Explicated by Endō Kakushū 遠藤鶴洲, 119–90. 1833. Rpt., Tokyo: Keimeisha, 1930.

Zhuhong 袾宏. "Fangsheng wen" 放生文. In *Yunqi fahui*, by Zhuhong. Nanjing: Jingling kejing chu, 1897.

———. "Jiesha fangsheng wen" 戒殺放生文. In *Yunqi fahui*, by Zhuhong. Nanjing: Jingling kejing chu, 1897.

———. *Shanfang zalu* 山房雜錄. In *Yunqi fahui*, by Zhuhong. Nanjing: Jingling kejing chu, 1897.

———. *Yigao* 遺稿. In *Yunqi fahui*, by Zhuhong. Nanjing: Jingling kejing chu, 1897.

———. *Yunqi fahui* 雲棲法彙. Nanjing: Jingling kejing chu, 1897.

———. *Zhu chuang er bi* 竹窗二筆. In *Yunqi fahui*, by Zhuhong. Nanjing: Jingling kejing chu, 1897.

———. *Zhu chuang sui bi* 竹窗隨筆. In *Yunqi fahui*, by Zhuhong. Nanjing: Jingling kejing chu, 1897.

Zichuan xian zhi 淄川縣志. 1743.

Zürcher, Erik. "Christian Social Action in Late Ming Times: Wang Zheng and His 'Humanitarian Society.'" In *Linked Faiths: Essays on Chinese Religions and Traditional Culture in Honour of Kristofer Schipper,* edited by Jan A.M. De Meyer and Peter M. Engelfriet, 269–86. Leiden: E. J. Brill, 2000.

GLOSSARY

This list excludes the names of authors who appear in the bibliography, the names of persons who have biographies in *DMB* and *ECCP*, the names of such well-known figures as Mencius and Su Shi, and the names of incidental figures of little historical significance outside this study. It further omits the names of places that are represented by gazetteers in the bibliography. For little-known figures who play a significant role in this study, this list provides in parentheses the alternate name used in the diaries and other key documents consulted.

airen	愛人
aiwu	愛物
An Lushan	安祿山
An Xifan	安希范
anchashi	按察使
"An Qisheng jieniu ji"	安期生戒牛記
Ba chenfa ming	八陳發明
Baima shanfang	白馬山房
bao (reward)	報
bao (security unity)	保
baojia	保甲
baoying	報應
baoying ju	保嬰局
Bencao gangmu	本草綱目
Bi Jiuchen (Yutai)	畢九臣 (玉臺)
bian	編
bingfang	病坊

bushi	布施
Buxi yuan	不繫園
Cai Chengzhi (Huaiting)	菜承植 (槐庭)
Cai Xiang	菜襄
Cai Xifu	菜喜夫
"Can si"	蠶絲
Cao Xun	曹勳
"Cao xian shecang xu"	曹縣社倉序
ce	冊
Chan	禪
"Chang'an shecang ji"	昌安社倉記
changping fa	常平法
"Changping quanfa"	常平權法
changwu	長物
Changzhou	長洲
Chen Changyao	陳長耀
Chen Di (Yizhai)	陳第 (一齋)
Chen Huanzhou	成環洲
Chen Yanxiao	陳巖肖
Chen Youxue (Zhixing)	陳幼學 (志行)
Chen Yuwang	陳于王
cheng	城
Cheng Hao (Mingdao)	程顥 (明道)
Cheng Yi (Yichuan)	程頤 (伊川)
chenghuang	城隍
Chengshou quanshu	城守全書
chengzheng	誠正
chipi	癡癖
"Chong jiansu"	崇儉素
Chuanxi lu	傳習錄
cihui	茲[慈]會
cishan	慈善
cishan haoyi	慈善好義
Ci tuan	糍團
ciyou ju	慈幼局
"Dangguan gongguo ge"	當官功過格
"Dang ji"	當機

danran	擔任
da sikou	大司寇
dao	道
datong	大同
Daxue	大學
de (as a particle)	的
de (virtue)	德
de chan	德產
"Diaoyi shuo"	釣弋說
dibao	邸報
Ding Bin	丁賓
Ding Rui	丁銳
Ding Xuan	丁鉉
"Dinghui hu fangsheng ji"	丁滙湖放生記
ding kou	丁口
"Ding ruren xinglue"	丁孺人行略
dizi	弟子
Dong Wei	董煟
dou	斗
du	都
"Du ji"	度集
Dule yuan	獨樂園
Fan Zhongyan	范仲淹
fang (liberate, let go)	放
fang (ward)	坊
fangsheng	放生
fangsheng an	放生庵
"Fangsheng bian huo"	放生辨惑
fangsheng chi	放生池
"Fangsheng he wei renzhu zhushou zhenfu"	放生河爲人主祝壽禎福
"Fangsheng he yue ji"	放生河約記
fangsheng hui	放生會
"Fangsheng hui yue"	放生會約
"Fangsheng ji"	放生記
Fangsheng she	放生社
"Fangsheng shuo"	放生說
"Fangsheng yi"	放生儀

"Fangyu"	放漁
fang zhi	放之
Fanwang jing	梵網經
fen	分
fencai	分財
fengliu	風流
Feng she	楓社
fen yin er xing	分銀二星
foxing	佛性
fu	府
fugongzu	府公租
fugui	富貴
"Fulu"	附錄
fumu guan	父母官
Fu she	復社
futai	撫臺
gaifang	丐房
gaiguo bu	改過簿
Gang hui	罡會
ganying	感應
gao huangdi liu yan	高皇帝六言
ge	箇
ge de qi suo	各得其所
Gengqi shihua	庚溪詩話
"Gengwu ji jiuhuang shiyi"	庚午急救荒事宜
Gezhi bian/ pian	格至編/篇
gongdao	公道
gongfei	公費
gongguo	功過
Gongguo ge	功過格
Gongguo ge batiao	功過格八條
gonghan	公函
"Gong jian"	公鑑
gongju	公舉
gongsheng	貢生
gongsuo	公所
gongtong	公同

gongyong	公用
gongzu	公租
Gu Shilian (Yinzhong)	顧士璉 (殷重)
Gu Xichou	顧錫疇
Gu Zhengxin	顧正心
guan	館
Guan Zongsheng (Xiabiao)	管宗聖 (霞標)
"Guan jian"	官鑑
guangci	廣慈
Guangci bian	廣慈編
"Guang fangsheng hui yin"	廣放生會引
guangquan	廣勸
Guangren hui	廣仁會
guantou	關頭
Gui Youguang	歸有光
guiren	貴人
guo	國
guozisheng	國子生
Han Lun (Wuwan)	韓倫 (五完)
Hangzhou	杭州
Hanshan Deqing	憨山德清
hao	號
haoshan	好善
haoshan leshi	好善樂施
haoshan zhe	好善者
haoshi	好施
haoxian	好賢
haoxing shanshi	好行善施
haoyi	好義
hedi	和糴
hu	斛
Huang Hui (Pingqing)	黃輝 (平情)
Huang Yang (Xuehai)	黃泱 (學海)
huangdi liuyan	皇帝六言
Huang Ming jingji [jingshi] wenbian	皇明經濟 [經世] 文編
hui (kindness, charity)	惠
hui (association, society)	會

huifang	會放
huiguan	會館
"Huijiang ji shuo"	會講集說
huimin	惠民
huimin yaoju	惠民藥局
huixiang	廻向
huiyao	會要
"Huoshu ji"	活鼠記
jia	家
"Jian gaifang yi"	建丐房議
Jiang Fengyuan (Zhensheng)	姜逢元 (箴勝)
Jiang Shishao (Yuwan)	江士韶 (虞丸)
Jiangyou	江右
jiansheng	監生
jiantiao	減糶
jiaohua	教化
"Jia xun"	家訓
jiaren caizi	佳人才子
"Jiazheng xu zhi"	家政須知
"Jia zhuan"	家傳
jide	積德
"Jieshe hui"	結社會
jiesha	戒殺
"Jiesha fangsheng he lun bing wu jue"	戒殺放生合論并五覺
"Jiesha fangsheng wen"	戒殺放生文
"Jiesha lun"	戒殺論
"Jiesha sheng lun"	戒殺生論
jimi	給米
"Jimin tu shuo"	飢民圖說
Jin Lan (Chuwan)	金蘭 (楚畹)
jin	金
Jingang jing	金鋼經
jingbiao	旌表
jingji	經濟
jingshi	經世
jingtian	敬天
jinhui	金會

jinshen	紳紳
jinshi	進士
jishan	積善
"Ji shan dizi ji"	葄山弟子籍
"Jisheng"	紀勝
jishi lu	紀事錄
"Jihuang ce hui xu"	救荒策會序
Jiuhuang huomin shu	救荒活民書
"Jiuhuang pingtiao yi"	救荒平糶議
Jiuhuang quanshu	救荒全書
"*Jiuhuang quanshu* xiaoxu"	救荒全書小序
"Jiuhuang shiyi"	救荒事宜
"Jiuhuang xiaoji"	救荒小記
"Jiuhuang zayi"	救荒雜議
jiuji	救濟
jiumi	斜米
jiuming	救命
Jiuqu	九曲
ju	局
juan	卷
juntian	均田
junzi	君子
juren	舉人
Jurong	句容
Jusang riji	居喪日記
Kaode keye lu	考德課業錄
Ke (Bridge, Market)	柯橋, 市
koufu	口服
"Kunxue ji"	困學記
lao	勞
laoku	勞苦
laoku zhe	勞苦者
laoxin, laoli	勞心, 勞力
laoxin zhe	勞心者
le	了
Lengyan jing	楞嚴經
leshan	樂善

leshan haoshi	樂善好施
li (energies, exertion)	力
liangxin	良心
liangzhi	良知
Lianhua jing	蓮花經
lianling zhi hui	聯吟之會
lijia	里甲
liju yanyu	六句言語
Liming pian	立命篇
Lin Cong	林聰
Lin Jun	林俊
Liu Yuanzhen	劉元珍
Liu Zai	劉宰
liuju	六句
liuju yanyu	六句言語
liumin tu	流民圖
liuyu	六語
"Liu yu shili"	六諭釋理
"Longren yi"	隆任議
"Loudong tongshan hui yin"	婁東同善會
Lu Zhongyuan	陸重遠
Lunxue chouda	論學酬答
Luo she	洛社
"Lüshi xiangyue"	呂氏鄉約
Mailang	麥浪
"Maizi shu"	埋齒述
mantou	饅頭
Mao Yuanyi	茅元儀
"Mao Bao"	毛寶
menghui	蒙惠
min	民
minbian	民變
ming	名
ming yi	名醫
Mituo si	彌陀寺
mofa	末法
"Nan Gan xiangyue"	南贛鄉約

Ouyang Xiu	歐陽修
"Pengdang shuo"	朋黨說
pi	癖
pian	篇
Piling	毘陵
pingdi	平糴
"Ping ji"	平集
Pingshui	平水
pingtiao	平糴
pingtiao jimi	平糴給米
pinjian	貧賤
pu	舖
"Pudu an fangshengchi ji"	普渡庵放生池記
puji	普濟
puji tang	普濟堂
"Puquan jiesha fangsheng"	普勸戒殺放生
Qi Fengjia (Degong)	祁鳳佳 (德公)
Qi Ningfang	祁甯方
Qi Xiangjia	祁象佳
Qi Xiongjia (Wendai)	祁熊佳 (文戴)
qian	錢
Qian Sule (Xisheng)	錢肅樂 (希聲)
Qian Yiben (Qixin)	錢一本 (啟新)
qiancai	錢財
qiangdi	強糴
qianshan gaiguo	遷善改過
qigai	乞丐
qiming	乞命
qing	情
qingming	請命
Qiudao lu	求道錄
qiuming	求命
qu	區
Quan Zuwang	全租望
quanfen	勸分
quanshan shu	勸善書
quantiao	勸糴

Queshan	確山
ren (man)	人
ren (humaneness)	仁
Ren hui	仁會
"Renshen gongzhong"	壬申共塚
renshi	任事
ren shi yang, yang shi ren	人食羊,羊食人
renshi zhi you	任事之友
renshi zhu you	任事諸友
renxin	仁心
renxing	仁性
Renzong	仁宗
"Rijian pian"	日鑑篇
"Rixing bian ji"	日省編集
Rongguang si	融光寺
ru	儒
Runing, Runan	汝寧府, 汝南
rushi	儒士
ruxue	儒學
sangong	三公
sanjiao heyi	三教合一
"Sanqian yi"	散錢議
San Wu	三吳
shan	善
Shan Yiguan	單一貫
Shang Jinglan	商景蘭
Shang Zhouzuo	商周祚
shang ji	上饑
shanhui	善會
shanju	善舉
shanren	善人
shan tang	善堂
shanxin	善信
shanzhe bi fu	善者必福
Shanzhong	剡中
she	社
"Shecang shiyi"	社倉事宜

shen	紳
Shen Guomo (Qiuru)	沈國模 (求如)
shendu	慎獨
sheng	升
Sheng Jing (Shengzhuan)	聖敬 (聖傳)
"Shengcai lun/yi"	生財論/議
shengsheng	生生
shengsheng bu duan	生生不斷
shengsheng zhi xin	生生之心
shen si ming bian	慎思明辨
Sheng xian	嵊縣
"Shenyan xianyue zecheng zhouxian shu"	申嚴憲約責成州縣疏
"Shen yi"	神異
"Shengying ji"	生蠅記
shengyuan	生員
shenxian	紳賢
sheshi	捨施
"She yue ji"	社約記
"Shezhu shiyi"	設粥事宜
Shi Xiaofu (Zifu)	史孝復 (子復)
Shi Xiaoxian (Zixu)	史孝咸 (子虛)
shi (authority)	勢
shi (literatus)	士
shi (market)	市
shi (grain measurement)	石
shidafu	士大夫
shihui	實惠
shiji	施濟
Shilong	十龍
"Shi mianao ji"	施綿襖記
shimin	士民
"Shi pinmin yu"	示貧民諭
shishen	士紳
shishi	實事
"Shi shu"	碩鼠
"Shi Xuwu qu pinhu yu"	示胥五區貧戶論
"Shiyao jishi"	施藥紀事

"Shiyao tiaokuan"	施藥條款
"Shiyao yuanqi"	施藥緣起
shiyi (giving aid)	施義
"Shizhu yi"	市粥議
"Shuicun dushu sheyue xu"	水村讀書社約序
shuyuan	書院
Sibian lu	思辨錄
sihui	私會
siyi	私議
Song Jiao	宋郊
Song Jingwen	宋景文
"Song Qian hou ru xingcao xu"	送錢侯入形曹序
suhui	俗會
sui	歲
Su jun	蘇郡
Su Song	蘇松
Suzong	肅宗
Taicang (zhou)	太倉(州)
taigongzu	太公租
"Tai ji"	太集
Taishang ganying pian	太上感應篇
taiyi	太醫
Taizu gao huangdi	太組高皇帝
Tanshan	灘山
Tao Shiling (Shiliang)	陶奭齡 (石梁)
Tao Wangling (Shikui)	陶望齡 (石簣)
"Taohua yuan ji"	桃花源記
Tiangang hui	天罡會
Tianle	天樂
Tiaoxi	苕西
tiaoyue	條約
tiyong zhi xue	體用之學
tongle hui	同樂會
tongren hui	同仁會
tongren tang	同仁堂
tongshan	同善
"Tongshan cang xu"	同善倉序

tongshang gaodi	通商告糴
tongshan hui	同善會
"Tongshan hui gui"	同善會規
tongshan hui ji	同善會給
"Tongshan hui jiangyu"	同善會講語
"Tongshan hui lu"	同善會錄
"Tongshan hui tiaoyue"	同善會條約
"Tongshan hui xu"	同善會序
tongshan tang	同善堂
tongshan zhe	同善者
tongshan zhuang	同善莊
tongsu	通俗
Tongting	洞庭
tongxian	同縣
tongyi	通邑
tongzhi	同志
tu	圖
tuchan	土產
"Tuishang yi"	推賞議
waifu	外府
Wang Chaoshi (Jinru)	王朝式 (金如)
Wang Chengzhao (Jingxian)	王承昭 (景賢)
Wang Han	王瀚
Wang Qinruo	王欽若
Wang Ruqian	汪汝謙 (然明)
Wang Shangbin (Wanwu)	王尚賓 (完吾)
Wang Sunlan (Xuegan)	王孫蘭 (雪肝)
Wang Yuanzhao (Junyuan)	汪元兆 (濬源)
"Wang Xingsi"	王行思
Wei Dan	韋丹
Wei Dazhong	魏大中
Wei Xuelian	魏學濂
weishan	爲善
Wei shu	魏書
weiting	衞廳
wen	文
wenxue	文學

Wenzhou	溫州
wo	我
wokou	倭寇
wu	物
Wubei zhi	武備志
Wucheng	烏程
Wujiang	吳江
Wujin	武進
Wulong	烏龍
Wuxi	無錫
wuyi	吾邑
Xia Yunyi (Yizhong)	夏允彝 (彝仲)
xian	縣
xiang	鄉
xiangbang	鄉邦
xiangguan	鄉官
"Xiangguan lu"	相觀錄
"Xiangchou xu"	鄉籌序
xiang jia	鄉甲
xiang jin	鄉縉
xiangmin	鄉民
xiangshen	鄉紳
xiangshen fushi	鄉紳富室
Xiangyang cheng	襄陽城
xiangyi	行義
xiangyue	鄉約
"Xiangyue za shuo"	鄉約雜說
"Xianju gongke"	閑居功課
xiaolian	孝廉
xiaosi	孝思
xiao yi	孝義
"Xiao Yunqi fangsheng yuan gui tiao"	小雲棲放生園規條
"Xiaozhuan"	小傳
Xie Shi	謝室
xifu	惜福
Xinchang xian	新昌縣
xin fa	新法

xing gong	行宮
Xinghua fu	興化府
xingshan	行善
xingshi	行事
xingyi	行義
Xin shi	心史
Xinzhai yulu	心齋語錄
"Xiong Shen"	熊愼
Xishan	錫山
xiushen	修身
Xiyou ji	西遊記
Xu Shunxian	許舜先
Xu Yunsan	許允三
xueguan	學館
"Xugu"	恤孤
Xuwu qu	胥五區
xuzheng	卹政
Yan Na	嚴訥
Yang Dongshu	楊東曙
Yang Tingyun	揚庭筠
yange hui	掩骼會
yang ji yuan	養濟院
"Yan Tai"	嚴泰
yaoju	藥局
"Yaoju fenren shiyi"	藥局分任事宜
"Yaoju jishi"	藥局紀事
"Yaoju shiyi"	藥局事宜
"Yaoju yi"	藥局議
yaosuo	藥所
Ye Maocai	葉茂才
yi (charitable, justice)	義
yi (city, local community)	邑
yian	醫案
"Yicang shi wen"	義倉誓文
yidu	義渡
"Yi ji"	一集
yiju	義舉

yimeng	義蒙
"Yiming futu hui shu"	一名浮圖會疏
yinde	陰德
yinggan	應感
Ying she	應社
yinguo	因果
yinguo shu	因果書
yinqian	銀錢
yinwei zhi shan	陰微之善
Yinzhi wen xinjie	陰隲文新解
"yi ren shi yang, yang si wei ren"	以人食羊, 羊死為人
yitian	義田
"Yitian ji"	義田記
yixing	義行
yixue	義學
yiyi	義邑
yizhuang	義莊
"Yizhuang cheng"	義莊呈
Yongfu si	永福寺
"Youbei wuhuan yi"	有備無患議
youwu xiangji	有無相濟
"You yi"	又議
Yuan she	院社
Yucheng	虞城
Yue	越
yue	約
yuefu	約副
yuezheng	約正
Yu shan	寓山
Yuyao	餘姚
yuying tang	育嬰堂
Zhang Cai (Shouxian)	張采 (受先)
Zhang E (Jiezi)	張萼 (介子)
Zhang Jin (Shangjiong)	張錦 (商絅)
Zhang Juzheng	張居正
Zhang Kunfang (Jiushan)	張焜芳 (九山)
Zhang Shiyi (Mengze)	張師繹 (夢澤)

Zhang Tianfu	張天復
Zhang Yaofang	張耀芳
Zhang Yi (Pingzi)	張嶧 (平子)
Zhang Zhentao (Ti'an)	張甄陶 (悌庵)
zhang (measure)	丈
Zhanran	湛然
Zhao Guangsheng (Gongjian)	趙廣生 (公簡)
zhen	鎮
zhenju	賑局
Zheng Xuan	鄭瑄
Zhengren she	證人(仁)社
zhenshi	賑史
zhiguai	志怪
zhiping zhi xue	治平之學
"Zhi tian shuo"	知天說
zhixian	知縣
Zhiyi	知頤
Zhong Huamin	鍾化民
zhongren	中人
Zhongyong	中庸
Zhou Can	周燦
Zhou Jiaping (Yigong)	周家 屏 (扆工)
Zhou Pixian	周丕顯
Zhu Xi	朱熹
Zhu Xiong	朱熊
"Zhuhong xiansheng jiasha wen xu"	袾弘先生接殺文序
zhou	州
Zhuji	諸暨
zhuopi	拙癖
zhusheng	諸生
zhuren	主人
zi	字
zi koufu zhi yu	恣口之欲
zu	族
Zuofei an ri zuan	昨非菴日纂

INDEX

Bai Juyi (772–846), 16
bandits, 102, 103, 104, 196, 198, 260,
315n130; and famine, 157–58, 194–
95. *See also* pirates; social disorder
baoying, 17, 255. See also retribution and
response
Bearing Witness Society (Zhengren she),
211, 212, 223, 232–33, 236, 250, 251
beggars, 83, 84, 93–94, 163, 195, 245, 257
benefactors: and beneficiaries, 148–49, 150,
248; categories of, 181–84; childhoods
of, 10, 57–58; elite as, 5, 113–20; as
examplars, 263–64; filial piety of, 7, 57,
256, 323n40, 330n12; hard work (*laoku*)
of, 268–70, 273–74; independent, 72,
91–94, 181–84, 220, 241; moral authority of, 276–78; motivations of, 4, 9–11,
16–17, 67–68, 164, 181, 240, 267, 271–
76, 278, 279, 283–84; and personal loss,
164–65, 170, 171, 192, 222–23, 283–84;
poor, 232; records of, 5–6, 11, 43, 158–
59, 215, 267, 276; rewards for, 65, 66,
243, 247, 249, 267, 271–76, 348n160;
shared beliefs of, 248–78; and social
disorder, 11, 268, 269, 271, 278, 283;
women as, 5, 6
beneficiaries: beggars as, 83, 84, 93–94,
163, 195, 245, 257; and benefactors,
148–49, 150, 248; categories of, 179,
183–84; choice of, 88, 91, 139, 148;
deserving vs. undeserving, 84–85, 88,
91, 93–94, 97, 145–46, 147, 253, 284;
filial piety of, 83, 84, 88, 144; genteel
poor as, 84, 148, 184, 248; investigation
of, 88–89, 173, 176, 177, 178; marginal
elite as, 135–36, 148, 150; monks as,
84, 93, 96, 145–46, 165, 243, 262; prisoners as, 94, 96, 104, 108–9, 148, 159,
222, 249; records of, 86, 88–89, 100,
123, 183, 185, 208; rural vs. urban,
97–99, 283; of Taicang benevolent society, 142, 143–50; temporal distance
of, 148–49; vagrants as, 189–91, 193,
195, 197, 216, 242, 244, 245, 266, 276,
342n189; women as, 83, 84, 142, 178,
191, 234
benevolent societies: alternatives to, 72–101;
authority in, 62–70, 71, 72, 139, 140,
143, 154; behavior in, 47–48; buildings
of, 120, 141–42; and bureaucracy, 48–
49, 76; and burials of poor, 82, 83, 89;

221; of Chen Longzheng, 63–65, 66,
68–69, 70, 101, 107, 114, 115, 119, 121;
vs. community compacts, 72, 74–82,
139, 140; competition in, 52, 141–43;
cooperation in, 47, 79, 86, 139–43;
disputes within, 123–24, 130, 139–43;
donations to, 83, 87, 114, 262; early, 4,
43–71; elite view of, 150–53; and *fangsheng*, 39, 42, 43, 44, 54, 72, 74; first,
25, 43, 45–49, 69; and Gao Panlong,
59, 72, 75–82, 119, 121, 150, 154;
geographical scope of, 79, 97–101; vs.
individual charity, 82–86, 90, 148–50;
lectures to, 6, 69, 73, 75–82, 85, 102–
22, 140, 141, 142, 152, 256, 261, 264,
277; legitimacy of, 44, 50, 62–70, 76,
120–21; limited resources of, 91–94,
98, 100, 246; vs. lineage, 44, 71, 95–97;
as loan societies, 118–19; and local
community, 47, 72, 77, 99–101; and local
elites, 48–49, 70, 150–53; and Lu Shiyi,
121, 130, 136; and marginal elite, 114,
117, 123–54; moral leadership of, 51, 52,
68, 69, 94, 97; moral vision of, 83–86,
88, 101, 255, 258, 283; motivations for,
4, 9–11; and officials, 52, 63, 68, 76, 140;
and poetry groups, 46–48, 51, 53; proselytizing of, 79, 100, 101, 115; publicity
for, 48, 49, 90; in Qing dynasty, 43–44,
70, 286; records of, 48, 87–88, 123–24;
regulations for, 47–49, 69, 78, 86–91,
98, 140, 143, 285, 301n56; routinization
of, 47–48, 149; and social hierarchy, 48–
49, 51–52, 63, 70, 78, 79, 82, 83, 88,
140, 149–50, 280; socializing at, 47, 86;
spread of, 50–51, 52, 56, 71, 120; and
the state, 44, 46, 48–49, 52, 71, 72; and
temporal distance, 148–49; terms for, 7;
and transregional relations, 246; and
universal harmony, 43, 51, 99–101, 150,
154; and wealth, 50, 52, 56, 78, 79, 121–
22; and Yang Dongming, 43, 45, 46, 69,
86, 119, 121, 140, 150, 154, 167, 220,
223, 244, 246, 254, 279. *See also* Taicang
benevolent society
Benyuan (monk), 342n178
Bi Jiuchen (Yutai), 174, 193, 194, 197, 214,
271, 274; and dispensaries, 238, 239;
and granaries vs. imports, 207, 209; and
inspection tours, 199, 202; and Qi Biaojia,
198, 217

contract, 47–49, 86, 140–41, 176, 246
cooperation: in benevolent societies, 47, 79, 86, 139–43; and consensus, 170, 172, 174; and dispensaries, 224; of elite, 7, 181, 192; and *fangsheng*, 17; in food relief, 161, 168, 169, 170; vs. individual charity, 72, 82–86, 91–94, 148–150, 181–184, 241, 284–285; and leadership, 10–11, 192; and Legalism, 253; and official authority, 196, 197, 246; and shared beliefs, 248, 278, 282; between social strata, 120, 243–44, 246, 269, 274
corruption, 92, 116, 174, 200–201, 284, 314n102
critical juncture (crossroads; *guantou*), 73, 107, 120, 282

Daoism, 11, 63, 159, 249, 252, 255, 277. *See also* three teachings
Diamond Sutra (Jingang jing), 22, 251
diaries, 6, 123–54; and anxiety, 315n2; of Chen Hu, 125, 129, 130, 258; good deeds in, 129, 163, 267, 276; on labors *(laoku)*, 268–69; lacunae in, 174–76; of Lu Shiyi, 123–35, 258, 263, 281; of Qi Biaojia, 18, 21, 159–61, 258, 263, 264, 265–66, 276, 278; and social relations, 128–30
Diary of Mourning, A (Jusang riji; Lu Shiyi), 125
Dickens, Charles, 10
didactic tales, 25, 249, 277, 344n35; on *fangsheng*, 19–21, 22; on wealth, 116, 117. *See also* morality books
Ding Bin *(js. 1571)*, 66–69, 80, 94, 148, 277, 350n4; and Chen Longzheng, 84, 135
Ding Rui, 292n5
Ding Xuan, 66
"Directives for Famine Relief" (*Jiuhuang shiyi*; Zhang Bi), 181
"Distributing Money" (*Sanqian yi*; Qi Biaojia), 190
Doctrine of the Mean (Zhongyong), 125, 129, 249–50
Doing Good, Secretly Determined (Weishan yin zhi), 106
doing good *(weishan; xingshan)*, 72, 140; fondness for, 3, 87, 114, 141, 159, 232, 263–64, 271; rhetoric of, 281–82; terms for, 3. *See also* charity

donations, 113–20; amounts of, 146–47, 284; to benevolent societies, 83, 87, 114, 262; for dispensaries, 224–25, 234, 239; geographical scope of, 79, 97–101, 191, 284; and inspection tours, 199; to monasteries, 290n19; from officials, 203, 239; and self-image, 284; small, 114, 118; taking pleasure in, 87, 114
Dong Qichang (1555–1636), 111, 165
Dong Wei (fl. 1203), 171, 325n86
Dong Wulai, 224, 227, 228, 229, 230, 231, 243, 245
Donglin Academy, 59, 62–63, 120, 302n70
dynastic decline, 162, 218, 247, 279, 280, 328n185

economy, 17, 41, 218, 261; of Henan, 300n8; of Jiangnan, 45, 63, 111, 116, 314n102; Ming, 6; nonagrarian laborers in, 282–83; of Shanyin, 214–16; of Shaoxing, 163. *See also* commerce; merchants; wealth
"Eight Advantages of Setting Up Soup Kitchens" (Ni Yuanlu), 208
elite: anxiety of, 282, 315n2; as benefactors, 5, 113–20; on benevolent societies, 150–53; and Buddhism, 250–52, 275, 277, 303n90; and commerce, 45, 279, 283; cooperation of, 7, 181, 192; disputes among, 123–24, 130, 139–43, 168, 181, 183, 187–88, 192, 200–201, 207, 209–10, 217, 246, 281; exploitation by, 11, 269, 271; and *fangsheng*, 15, 18; and first benevolent societies, 50; and grain prices, 67–68; motivations of, 4, 9–11, 67–68; praise for and from, 274–75; in Qing dynasty, 285–86; and reputation, 67–68; self-serving, 1, 3; and social disorder, 165, 195–96
elite, local: and associations, 63, 223; and benevolent societies, 48–49, 70, 150–53; cooperation of, 167, 192; debates among, 179–81; and dispensaries, 221, 233–34, 236–40; and dynastic decline, 161, 162; and *fangsheng*, 19, 39; and food relief, 159–61, 162; leadership of, 198; and Lu Shiyi, 131–35; and monks, 242–44, 251–52; motivations of, 63, 181, 240; and officials, 9, 45, 121, 160, 170, 192, 198, 276, 280–81; and physicians, 228, 229–31, 244; power of, 277–78, 281;

176, 178, 181, 191; models of, 6–7, 184–
86, 216, 330n12; and officials, 157, 158,
176, 178, 194, 203, 217, 246; planning
ahead for, 160–61; and Qi Biaojia, 159–
61, 181, 183, 187–88, 192; records of,
177, 185–86, 216–17; recruitment of
volunteers for, 173–74; in rural areas,
169–70, 176; scope of, 100, 191, 284;
and shared beliefs, 258, 259; and social
disorder, 160, 176, 177–78, 184, 193–
96; and social hierarchy, 157–59, 180–
81; and social relations, 166, 180–81,
218; transregional, 193, 211–14
food shortages. *See* famine
foundling homes *(baoying ju)*, 159, 241–42,
244, 245, 266, 341n160
friends: acceptance of responsibility by,
267; and dispensaries, 224–25; fines
on, 324n60; and food relief, 167, 177,
185; and inspection tours, 200, 201;
inspiration from, 270; labors *(laoku)*
of, *269*, *273–74;* of Lu Shiyi, 128–30;
motivations of, 271–72, 275; of Qi Biaojia, 172–73; recruitment of, 173–74
frugality: and animals, 26–28, 42, 58, 119;
vs. charity, 114–16; and Chen Longzheng, 110, 111, 113, 115–16, 149; and
dispensaries, 236; vs. extravagance, 26–
28, 109–13, 149; and food shortages,
266–67; of Gao Panlong, 57–58, 115,
116; of Qi Biaojia, 269; in Six Maxims,
103; and vegetarianism, 26–30, 266–67
Fu Bi, 313n76
Fu Huiyu, 227, 337n45
Fu Yuliang, 237
fund-raising, 5, 224–25, 276; for burials,
221–22; for food relief, 164, 166, 170,
177, 178–79, 187, 189, 190, 191, 209,
212–13; independent vs. cooperative,
196; for medical relief, 228, 229, 230,
234. *See also* donations; Life-Saving
Pagoda Society

Gang Stars Society (Gang hui, Tian Gang
hui), 135, 152, 198
ganying, 255. *See also* retribution and response
Gao Panlong (1562–1626), 6, 107; on
accumulating merit, 255, 261, 344n42;
authority of, 63, 68, 69, 71, 283; and
benevolent societies, 44, 59, 72, 75–82,
119, 121, 139, 150, 154, 283; and Chen

Longzheng, 63, 73, 81, 82; and Christianity, 253; and community compacts,
74–75; and *fangsheng*, 15, 31; frugality
of, 57–58, 115, 116; and individual vs.
group charity, 97; leadership of, 56–62;
lectures by, 111, 263, 264; vs. Lu Shiyi,
128, 130; memorials of, 80; as model, 70,
278; moral message of, 43, 56–62, 83–
84, 272, 278, 284, 286; and politics, 62–
63; and Qi Biaojia, 275, 278; regulations
of, 86, 87, 285, 301n56; and shared
beliefs, 248, 249, 267; on social hierarchy, 100, 102, 103, 105, 280; status of,
63, 78, 251; suicide of, 63, 69, 71, 73;
and Yang Dongming, 57, 59
Gao Yuan (bandit), 194–95
gardens, 322n15; of Qi Biaojia, 202, 211,
212, 231, 264, 265, 278; and social
relations, 109, 110–13
gazetteers, local, 5, 7, 159, 183, 230–33,
237; on good deeds, 65, 66, 276; in
Qing, 286
gentleman *(junzi)*, 24, 121
Gold Star (bandit), 138
gong (official, public), 144, 146, 167, 170
good deeds *(yixing, shanju)*: and benevolent
societies, 43, 51, 78; and common
societies, 49; in diaries, 129, 163, 267,
276; and *fangsheng*, 16, 40, 41; and
frugality, 115; Gao Panlong on, 60–61;
gazetteers on, 65, 66, 276; and kinship,
8; and moral leadership, 53–55; public
vs. hidden, 5, 30, 41, 43, 51, 79, 90, 112–
13, 265–66, 276; records of, 43, 267,
276; rewards for, 60–61, 159, 255–62,
261; and shared beliefs, 249, 252, 258,
267–68; and social hierarchy, 105–7;
terms for, 3, 7; witnessing of, 30, 41, 74,
79, 86
grain: cooked, 175, 176, 191; fluctuations
in stocks of, 187; harmonious purchase
of *(hedi)*, 166, 170, 173; harmonious sale
of *(hetiao)*, 168; hoarding of, 116–17, 151,
172, 173; lending of, 206–7; mandatory
collection of, 211–12; procurement of,
177, 179, 203–5, 207, 208, 209, 284;
stealing of, 175; storage of, 45, 54, 55,
122, 199, 203, 205–11; and textiles, 101;
types of, 191
grain, distribution of, 136, 204; and merit,
43; procedures for, 82, 158–59; and social

113, 114, 119, 160, 267, 269, 276, 284; vs. hidden virtue, 5, 30, 41, 43, 51, 79, 90, 112–13, 265–66, 276; in Qing, 286

public place (*gongsuo*), 170

public recommendations (*gongju*), 144, 146

public sphere, 281, 350n1

public use (*gongyong*), 47

publishing, 5, 21–22, 23, 45

punishment, 198, 203, 213, 217, 253; in benevolent societies, 271–72, 273, 324n60

Qi Biaojia (1602–45), 6; acceptance of responsibility by, 264, 267–71, 276, 277; anxiety of, 282; and Bearing Witness Society, 233, 251; and Buddhism, 252; and burials for poor, 221–22; charity of, 113, 114, 120, 163–65, 180, 183, 241; and Chen Zilong, 195, 196, 197, 198, 217, 274, 275, 312n58; and community compacts, 74; compassion of, 265, 269; competitiveness of, 283; Confucianism of, 257, 262, 275, 277; diaries of, 18, 21, 159–61, 258, 263–66, 273, 276, 278, 281; and dispensaries, 220–41, 340n122; extravagance of, 27, 109, 110, 111–13, 264–65, 266, 267; and *fangsheng*, 15, 18–19, 21, 22, 23, 30, 38, 39, 40; and food relief, 159–61, 170–73, 176–79, 181, 183, 187–88, 192, 216; on foundling home, 241–42; friends of, 157, 172–73, 211; gardens of, 202, 211, 212, 231, 264, 265, 278; and grain procurement, 181, 205–11; and information, 170–73; and inspection tours, 199–203; labors (*laoku*) of, 268–70, 284; leadership of, 187–88, 192, 270–71; lineage of, 180, 186, 202, 211, 265; and Liu Zongzhou, 196, 199, 209–11, 251, 278; loyalties of, 180–81, 186; and marginal elite, 175, 197, 198, 231, 233, 279; and merchants, 197, 203–5, 283; and monks, 242–44, 257; and officials, 192, 193–219, 234, 281; and opera, 311n52; organizational strategies of, 165–70; personal losses of, 164–65, 170, 171, 192, 222–23; pragmatism of, 262–64, 268; and retribution and response, 257–58; and rewards for participation, 271–76; self-image of, 267, 269–70, 275; and shared beliefs, 250, 254, 277; socialization of, 282, 283–84; sui-

cide of, 278; transformation of, 264–67; and transregional relief, 211–14, 246–47; and vegetarianism, 266–67; and vertical relationships, 280; villages of, 180, 186, 188, 211, 333nn141; and Wang Chaoshi, 222, 231, 244, 257, 258, 278; writings of, 172–73; and Yan Maoyou, 257–58, 282; vs. Yang Dongming, 264; and Zhang Dai, 110, 311n51

Qi Chenghan (1565–1628), 171, 263

Qi Fengjia (Degong), 188, 190, 191, 201, 208, 211, 266

Qi Junjia (Jizhao), 208, 266, 311n52, 331nn70,73; and burials for poor, 221–22; and food relief, 187, 189, 190; and medical relief, 224, 225, 229, 234, 244

Qi Linjia, 311n52

Qi Ningfang, 198, 266, 330n15

Qi Tong, 222, 224, 226, 231

Qi Xiangjia (Weng'ai), 190, 222

Qi Xiongjia (Wendai), 202

Qian Fanhou, 129, 144, 317n35

Qian Huanzhong, 244

Qian Qianyi (1582–1664), 24, 312n58

Qian Qinzhi, 263, 266

Qian Shisheng (1575–1652), 66–67, 82, 83, 93, 98, 120, 306n44, 315n121

Qian Sule (Xisheng; 1606–48), 29, 285; and Lu Shiyi, 133, 142; as subprefect, 135, 150–53; and Taicang benevolent society, 139, 140, 141, 150, 152–53

Qian Sutu, 321n169

Qian Yiben (Qixin; 1544–1615), 56, 57, 62, 69, 70

Qian Yuandeng, 242

Qin Fusi, 347n99

Qin Hongyou, 237, 238

Qing dynasty, 112, 116, 184; benevolent societies in, 43–44, 70, 286; changes in, 285–86; Lu Shiyi in, 128, 318nn72,78, 319n109

Qiu Weibing, 296n70, 299n153

Recorded Conversations (*Xinzhai yulu;* Wang Gen), 128

"Record of Daily Self-Examination, A" (Rixing bian ji; Gao Panlong), 58

"Record of Dispensing Medicines, A" (Qi Biaojia), 225

"Record of Distributing Padded Jackets, A" (Shi mianao ji; Yang Dongming), 54–55

*Record of Examining One's Virtue and Studying toward a Career, A (Kaode keye lu; Lu Shiyi), 125, 129

"Record of Gazing upon Others" (Xiangguan lu; Lu Shiyi), 128

*Record of Military Preparedness (Wubei zhi; Lu Shiyi), 139

*Record of My Determination to Learn, A (Zhixue lu; diary; Lu Shiyi), 124, 125

*Record of the Yaojiang Academy (Yaojiang shu-yuan), 232, 233

*Records of Having Obtained What Is Good (Deyi lu; Yu Zhi), 70

*Records of Ming Scholars (Mingru xuean; Huang Zongxi), 250, 254

*Records of Right Behavior and Good Fortune (Diji lu; Yan Maoyou), 31, 255–58, 260–61, 277

*Records of Spreading Love (Guang'ai lu; Meng Chaoran), 24, 37

*Records of Taking Pleasure in Goodness (Leshan lu; Li Changling), 255–56

*Reflection and Discrimination (Sibian lu; Lu Shiyi), 125–26, 129, 130

regulations: for Bearing Witness Society, 232; of benevolent societies, 47–48, 69, 78, 86–91, 98, 140, 143, 285, 301n56; for cooperation, 285; defined, 47; for dispensaries, 224, 225, 235–36, 238; for distributing clothing, 55; and elite, 150; for food relief, 187, 198; and foundling home, 242; and inspection tours, 200–201; of Taicang benevolent society, 139–41; of Yunqi Society, 119

religion, 2, 11, 44, 46, 103, 105. See also Buddhism; Christianity; Daoism; monasteries; monks

Renzong (Song emperor), 26

Republican period, 44

reputation, 62, 69, 116, 270; family, 63–65; and merit, 260, 262; as motivation, 67–68, 272, 284; of physicians, 229; and shared beliefs, 276, 277, 282

responsibility, acceptance of: for food relief, 174, 177, 179, 183; and leadership, 281; by marginal elite, 177, 271; moral, 107, 122; as motivation, 278; by Qi Biaojia, 264, 267–71, 276, 277; rewards for, 273–74; and shared beliefs, 253, 255, 267, 271, 275; and status, 180

Restoration Society (Fu she), 132, 212, 223

retribution and response *(baoying; ganying)*: and animals, 17, 28, 32, 34, 35, 41; from heaven, 76, 77, 125, 163, 258–60, 267, 283; in morality books, 255–62; and shared beliefs, 252, 255–62, 277; and status, 255, 256, 257

rewards, 60–61, 159, 243, 247, 255–262; civil service examinations as, 23, 65–66, 273–274, 275, 348n160; for hard work, 273–74; for marginal elite, 273–74, 275; and shared beliefs, 249, 267, 271–276, 277, 278

Ricci, Matteo (1552–1610), 26, 253–54

Richard, Timothy (1845–1919), 1

Right Behavior and Good Fortune, 117

riots. See social disorder

rural areas, 122, 183, 309n147, 331n52; burials in, 326n123; common societies in, 49–50; community compacts in, 25, 134, 135; disorder in, 194, 212, 271; famine in, 98, 191–92; and *fangsheng,* 22; food relief in, 169–70, 176, 191; local vs. general relief in, 206; medical relief in, 220, 228, 241; and Ming Taizu, 305n19; official inspection tours in, 199–203; Qi Biaojia's ties to, 180, 186, 188, 211, 333n141; trade in, 215; and transregional aid, 193; vs. urban areas, 97–99, 211, 283

Salisbury, Harrison, 3, 290n15

Schall, Adam, 343n25

schools, charitable *(yixue),* 54, 67, 97, 180, 233, 309n153

secret societies, 44

self-cultivation, 99, 123–30, 253, 258, 262–63

self-image, 267, 269–70, 275, 284

"Set of Regulations for Taking Responsibility of the Soup Kitchens, A" (Qi Biaojia), 198

Shan Yiguan, 183

Shang Jinglan (1605–76+), 327n150

Shang Zhouzuo (js. 1601), 313

shanju. See good deeds

Shanyin district (Shaoxing), 110; economy of, 214–16; food relief in, 159–60, 168, 174, 176, 178, 181, 182, 185; officials of, 193; and transregional relief, 211, 213; and Wang Yangming, 254

Shaoxing prefecture, 157–59, 198, 218–19;

administrative divisions of, 176; disorder in, 193–94; and dynastic decline, 162; extravagance in, 265, 266; failures of relief in, 217–18; food relief in, 159–61, 166–70, 176–79, 185; and interregional trade, 203, 214, 332n87; literati in, 219, 232; medical care in, 221, 230; population of, 214; trade in, 214–16; and Wang Yangming, 254

sharing goodness *(tongshan)*, 43–44, 78–79, 80, 81; Society for (Tonghshan hui), 46–49

Shen Gua, 314n106

Shen Guomo (Qiuru), 190, 232–33; and dispensaries, 234, 236; lectures by, 263–64; as marginal elite, 244–45, 281; moral authority of, 244–45; and Qi Biaojia, 251

Shen Jingchu, 237

Shen Maojian, 159

Sheng Jing (Shengzhuan), 125, 144

shengsheng (perpetual renewal of life), 53, 72–73, 207

Shi Xiaofu (Zifu), 233, 236

Shi Xiaoxian (Zixu), 233

Shi ji, 290n25

Shijing (Book of Poetry), 36, 129

Shinto, 298n125

silkworms, 21, 25

Sima Guang, 300n10

Sima Qian, 290n25

Six Imperial Maxims, 75–82, 280; on accepting lot, 106, 257, 283; and community compacts, 135; on filial piety, 75, 76, 77, 79–80, 81, 103; lectures on, 203, 264; and Qian Sule, 151, 152

smallpox, 222

Smith, Arthur (1845–1932), 2, 3

social disorder: and benevolent societies, 71, 73, 84; and commerce, 9, 17, 283; and community compacts, 74; and dynastic decline, 162; and elite, 138–39, 160, 165, 194, 195–96, 197, 268, 281; and famine, 157–58, 218, 221; and food relief, 160, 176, 177–78, 184, 189, 190, 195–96; and grain distribution, 193–94; and grain prices, 203, 218, 221; in Jiangnan, 136–39; and Lu Shiyi, 126, 127; and medical relief, 221, 224, 233; as motivation, 9–10, 11, 268, 269, 271, 278, 283; and officials, 151, 152, 193–97; and opera, 265; preparations for,

136–39; and punishment, 193–94; in rural areas, 194, 212, 271; in Shaoxing, 193–94; and shared beliefs, 262, 266

social hierarchy: and associations, 119–20, 223, 232; and benevolent societies, 48–49, 51–52, 70, 78, 79, 82, 83, 88, 140, 149–50, 280; and charity, 10–11, 40, 60, 105–7; and community compacts, 77–78; and cooperation, 120, 243–44, 246, 269, 274; and dispensaries, 239–40, 245; and *fangsheng*, 17, 39–40, 41, 42; and food relief, 157–59, 180–81; and leadership, 10–11, 281; within lineages, 95; local, 70, 100, 120; and mental vs. physical labor, 89–90; and money, 117–19; and shared beliefs, 248; and social mobility, 66, 106, 282; and social relations, 9, 30, 42, 223, 232, 280–82; in urban areas, 98–99; and wealth, 41, 102–3, 121–22, 310n20. *See also* social status

social mobility, 66, 106, 282

social order, 107, 248; and community compacts, 79; and food relief, 158, 204; and official involvement, 193–97, 199, 205; and universal harmony, 43, 51–52, 77, 99–101, 104, 105, 106, 154

social relations: and benevolent societies, 71; and charity, 201, 266, 284–85; and civil service examinations, 61, 166, 206, 212; and diaries, 128–30; and *fangsheng*, 28–30, 39–40, 41, 280; and fictive kin, 147; and food relief, 166, 180–81, 218; and gardens, 109, 110–13; of marginal elite, 132, 149; and medical relief, 221, 239–40; and money, 117–19; and moral suasion, 113; of physicians, 228, 229–31; and social hierarchy, 9, 30, 42, 223, 232, 280–82; transregional, 206, 211–14, 246–47, 284; in urban areas, 98–99; vertical, 9, 280–82; and wealth, 114, 247, 285

social status: and authority, 10, 130, 245, 257; and behavior, 105–7; and benevolent societies, 63, 79; and charity, 52, 135–36, 201; of Chen Longzheng, 63, 71, 78; and consensus, 170; and dispensaries, 224; and food relief, 167, 180; of Gao Panlong, 63, 78, 251; and gardens, 110–13; and labors *(laoku)*, 269; and leadership, 281; of Lu Shiyi, 130–35; and retribution and response, 255, 256, 257;

Text: 10/12 Baskerville
Display: Baskerville
Compositor: Integrated Composition Systems
Printer and binder: IBT Global